CHILD BRIDE

Also by Suzanne Finstad

SLEEPING WITH THE DEVIL
ULTERIOR MOTIVES
HEIR NOT APPARENT

CHILD BRIDE

The Untold Story
of
PRISCILLA BEAULIEU
PRESLEY

SUZANNE FINSTAD

HARMONY BOOKS • NEW YORK

Published by Harmony Books, a division of Crown Publishers, Inc., 201 East 50th Street, New York, New York 10022. Member of the Crown Publishing Group.

Random House, Inc. New York, Toronto, London, Sydney, Auckland

http://www.randomhouse.com/

HARMONY and colophon are trademarks of Crown Publishers, Inc.

Printed in the United States of America

Design by Blond *on* Pond

Library of Congress Cataloging-in-Publication Data

Finstad, Suzanne
    Child bride: the untold story of Priscilla Beaulieu Presley / by Suzanne Finstad. — 1st ed.
    Includes index.
    1. Presley, Priscilla Beaulieu. 2. Motion pictures actors and actresses—United States—Biography. I. Title.
PN2287.P715F56 1997
791.45′028′092—dc21   97-8065
[b]

ISBN 0-517-70585-0

10 9 8 7 6 5 4 3 2 1

First Edition

For Natalie & Lisa & Paige
and for my grandmother, Edel

I think it is important to clarify that while Priscilla Beaulieu Presley agreed to be interviewed for this book, she in no way cooperated with or participated in the preparation of this book, and she has not endorsed *Child Bride*, nor does she authorize it.

—SUZANNE FINSTAD

CONTENTS

AUTHOR'S NOTE

I had no idea, when I conceived of writing a biography of Priscilla Beaulieu Presley in the summer of 1995, that I would be opening a Pandora's box.

In the then eighteen years since the death of Elvis Presley, a virtual cottage industry had arisen: a veritable library of Presley books, feature films, television movies, television series, documentaries, a university course, even a religion. Elvis Presley had transcended legend to become what one journalist I interviewed compared with popular culture's secular equivalent of a saint.

As his once notorious child bride, the woman with whom millions of Elvis fans have a love-hate relationship, Priscilla Presley seemed, to me, an important cultural icon in her own right, yet curiously little was known about her. Priscilla's life has always been veiled in mystery. As a teenager, she was cloistered at Graceland, trailed by whispers labeling her Elvis Presley's Lolita. Once married to Elvis, Priscilla retained her status as "Hollywood's best-kept secret," virtually unrecognized apart from Elvis. When Presley died, she was mentioned in passing in the Elvis biographies—often the first sections to which readers would turn, eager for more information about the King's mystery child bride. Of all the fascination surrounding Elvis, his bizarre courtship of fourteen-year-old Priscilla Beaulieu held the greatest intrigue. What was the *real* reason the parents of a ninth-grade girl permitted their daughter to date, then live with, a rock star? What spell did Priscilla cast over Elvis that drew him to her, and kept him attached? Those were the unanswered, burning questions of Elvis mythology. As proof, when Priscilla wrote her own memoir over a decade ago, it became an immediate publishing sensation.

Yet the story still had not been told. Priscilla's autobiography revealed next to nothing about her life before or after Elvis and contained no recollections from anyone but Priscilla. My intention was to research and write a definitive biography of Priscilla Presley, consort to arguably the greatest cultural icon of modern history, to fill a gap in the existing Elvis archives. I had no reason, at the time, to suspect that her book or the story she told were anything other than true, merely incomplete.

As I started on what would become two years of intensive research, clues began to surface suggesting that the story Priscilla told of her life was not as it was. Priscilla Presley, I discovered, was a woman of many and profound secrets, beginning when she was a child of three and continuing ever after. Deep in the attic of her past was a closet door, behind which were skeletons unimagined. Putting together the pieces of her hidden life was tantamount to solving a Rubik's cube.

What I uncovered, in part, was that the legend of Elvis-and-Priscilla rooted in Priscilla's memoirs and repeated as fact in countless Elvis biographies was an elaborate fiction created by Priscilla as a result of a series of byzantine, occasionally traumatic events leading up to her meeting with Elvis and continuing afterward. The real story is infinitely more powerful than the myth and, ultimately, tragic; the true Priscilla more complex. Priscilla Beaulieu Presley is not, and never was, the fragile, demure child-woman she has come to personify; she is, in a word, a *survivor,* a woman of indomitable will and almost frightening determination.

In reconstructing her life, I retraced Priscilla's footsteps from birth in Brooklyn, New York, to childhood in Connecticut, Texas, Maine, New Mexico, Germany, and Memphis, even sleeping in the bedroom where she first stayed at the Vernon Presley house adjacent to Graceland in March of 1963. I scoured virtually every book available on the Presleys, which number in the hundreds; haunted libraries and flea markets in search of the seemingly infinite magazine articles about Elvis, Priscilla, or Lisa; listened to Elvis Presley's music; watched his movies; screened documentaries; hunted for and scrutinized vintage photographs; rented Priscilla Presley pictures; pored through probate, divorce, and other civil court records and archives; immersed myself in Scientology literature; and interviewed close to three hundred people, each of whom held various pieces of the puzzle that were Elvis and Priscilla.

As my research deepened, I noticed a parallel between one of Elvis's signature songs, the hauntingly beautiful "Are You Lonesome Tonight?," and his ultimately doomed relationship with Priscilla. Elvis recorded the song in the spring of 1960, shortly after he returned from Germany, where he had just met Priscilla Beaulieu. Many who knew Elvis felt the song personified him, for he harbored, from birth, a deep, inexplicable loneliness, something Priscilla, as a child, shared with him, part of what bonded them initially. The spoken verse, which was inspired by Jacque's speech in Act Two of Shakespeare's *As You Like It,* was eerily prophetic of Elvis Presley's unfolding relationship with Priscilla Beaulieu and forms the structure of this biography. Elvis, who placed a mystical importance on such things, would have appreciated the symbolism.

What is personal integrity?
Personal integrity is knowing what you know—
What you know is what you know—
And to have the courage to know and say what you have observed.
And that is integrity
And there is no other integrity.

L. RON HUBBARD

The truth shall set you free, man.

ELVIS PRESLEY

I

CHILDHOOD: A HOUSE OF SECRETS

1

ANN'S STORY

In March of 1963, Priscilla Ann Beaulieu was at the crossroads of her life. Though just seventeen, a senior in high school, she was faced with a decision that she knew, with a child's wisdom, would forever alter the course of her destiny, and she had a strange foreboding.

She was desperately in love, as only a teenager can be—a forbidden love—locked in conflict with her parents, especially her mother, Ann Beaulieu. Elvis Presley—the twenty-eight-year-old rock-and-roll idol and movie star, the most famous sex symbol in the world—held the seventeen-year-old in thrall and wanted her to move into his compound in Memphis as his girlfriend-in-waiting while she finished high school and came of age.

But Elvis was not the object of Priscilla Beaulieu's teenage fancy that fateful spring. She was breathless over the handsome eighteen-year-old star of her high school football team. She did not want to leave her life in Germany for a dubious future with a rock star. It was *Ann* Beaulieu, her mother, who was obsessed with the idea of Priscilla moving to Graceland to become Elvis Presley's de facto child bride.

Both mother and daughter feared that Priscilla might be making the greatest mistake of her life: Priscilla, if she went to Graceland; *Ann,* if she stayed. In the end, Priscilla deferred to her mother, as she habitually did. She packed her bags for Graceland with barely a good-bye to the boy she left behind.

As this tale implies, it would be difficult to tell Priscilla's story without beginning with her mother's, for their lives and their destinies would always be linked in mysterious ways, ways understood only by Priscilla and Ann. They were bound together by secrets, secrets only Ann fully understood.

Ann, as would her famous daughter, began life with a different name: Anna. Anna Lillian Iversen. As a child, she was called Rooney, short for Annie Rooney. Where that nickname came from—possibly a 1920s cartoon character—the Iversens would not reveal to outsiders. They were Norwegians who considered the most trivial family detail "personal and private." Ann's family history, they still maintain, is nobody else's business. Outside the family, and even to Ann, it is a forbidden topic.

There was nothing of portent in her early life. Anna Iversen was the youngest of three children, all of whom were born in March, each two years apart: Albert Junior in 1922, James in 1924, Anna in 1926. Their father, Albert Iversen, was Nordic-handsome—big, strapping, and blond; their mother, Lorraine, was a petite mix of Scotch-Irish and English, "a pretty little peanut," in the words of Anna's maternal cousin Margaret. The year before Anna was born, Albert and Lorraine Iversen set up permanent residence in New London, Connecticut, a picturesque working-class town on the eastern seaboard known chiefly as a base for the U.S. Navy and Coast Guard. Albert, in keeping with his potent physical presence and ego, joined the police force.

As a child, Rooney sang and acted in skits with her favorite cousin, Margaret, joined a dance club, and discreetly followed the career of actress Priscilla Lane, the most famous of the five Lane sisters and a Warner Brothers contract player from 1937 to 1944 who costarred with Ronald Reagan, Dick Powell, and James Cagney. Like her movie-star role model, Rooney was fair and blue-eyed, with a wholesome girl-next-door prettiness. Her most impressive feature was a thick tumble of shoulder-length blond hair. If, as Oscar Wilde wrote, "We are all in the gutter, but some of us are looking at the stars," Rooney's eyes were fixed on the sky. She chafed under the thumb of her rigid policeman-father, waiting until she was out the door to apply forbidden lipstick, using Margaret or her best friend, Fay Heim, as cover for the nighttime adventures of adolescent girls.

Anna Iversen's turning point came when she sneaked out to attend a USO dance during her freshman year in high school. The dances, organized for the New London–based navy and coast guard fleets, were dangerous territory for any young girl; for Albert Iversen's daughter, they were taboo. Girls under sixteen were not admitted; Rooney was barely fifteen. There was a slight stigma attached to high school girls who attended USO functions; many of them "got in trouble," as Fay would remember.

None of this deterred Rooney. She was in single-minded pursuit of romance, the kind depicted in the movies, the kind that promised an escape from her stagnant lower-middle-class existence. One evening at the dawn of World War II, fate smiled on her. She was asked to dance by the handsomest soldier at the USO, a dark-haired dream of a boy named James Wagner—Jimmy to his friends, and he had a million of them, recalled his brother Gene. Jimmy was a storekeeper third class in the navy, stationed aboard the USS *Beaver*, a submarine tender in the Atlantic Fleet, berthed in New London. "It was certainly love right from the beginning," according to Rooney's best friend, Fay.

"He was *gorgeous*," remembered Anna's cousin Margaret, swooning. James

Wagner was slight—five feet six or seven—with an athlete's physique and a face that would melt a girl's heart: model-perfect features, dancing blue-green eyes, movie-star white teeth, and jet-black hair that formed a widow's peak. "Oh!" his mother once exclaimed. "If you see his picture it'll take your breath away!" He was a bit of a dandy, always immaculate and stylish, "but he was not conceited," according to his brother. "Jimmy wasn't like that. He didn't act like he knew he was handsome."

Anna Iversen concealed her romance from her parents, calling on Fay or Margaret to act as her accomplice when she wanted to rendezvous with Jimmy at the USO. "She'd use me as cover," Fay remarked, "and then she'd sneak into the background." Albert Iversen would never have permitted his adolescent daughter to date a twenty-year-old navy man; she wasn't even allowed to wear makeup. Desperate to appear older, Rooney smuggled a pair of her mother's high heels out of the house to wear at a dance with her soldier boy.

That April, James Wagner's ship set sail for Bermuda, returning to its berth at New London a few months later. As Americans held their breath, wondering whether the country would be drawn into war, the *Beaver* conducted its operations around Long Island Sound, docking at New London intermittently. For seven months, from May to December, Rooney continued her trysts with Jimmy. "We used to go up to the site where he was stationed, and we used to meet him on the state pier without her parents knowing it," Fay remembered. Rooney, her cousin Margaret stated, "was madly in love with Jimmy."

On December 6, with the scent of war in the air, the *Beaver* left New London under sealed orders to carry supplies to an unknown destination. The families and lovers of the ship's crew "stood on the dock and cried," recalled one wife. The next day the Japanese bombed Pearl Harbor.

Rooney took a part-time job after school at the Boston Candy Company, the local soda fountain, mixing milk shakes and dreaming of Jimmy. He materialized again in 1942, at the end of her sophomore year, for a few days' training in New London. That fall, the *Beaver* sailed to Roseneath, Scotland, with James Wagner aboard. The two exchanged love letters and became secretly engaged. After half a year, Jimmy wrote with news that he was one of a few men chosen to be trained as navy fighter pilots. A few months earlier, Rooney's screen idol, Priscilla Lane, had eloped with an army pilot and had revealed a secret first marriage and divorce. Anna Iversen's own forbidden romance must suddenly have seemed more enticing than ever.

James Wagner was sent back to the States to begin classes in March of 1943, and Rooney, who was then in her junior year, dropped out of high school about the same time. The family could use the extra money she would make working full-time, but more likely, she was angling to marry Jimmy. "She didn't seem too interested in school," recalled John Linkletter, a fellow student at Chapman Tech. "So it looked like she would rather get married."

Rooney took a job—most likely as a riveter—for Electric Boat, a dockside company that built submarines. Jimmy, meanwhile, progressed through a series of navy flight schools beginning in New Orleans and continuing in Natchitoches, Louisiana; Dallas, Texas; Athens, Georgia; Corpus Christi, Texas; and Pensacola, Florida.

While they were apart, a photographer took a few head shots of Anna, probably for Jimmy, though she told his brother, Gene, that she was "modeling, or at least had posed for something." The portraits are high glamour; in one, Rooney's hair is swept off her face in a partial pompadour and her head is tilted dreamily to one side. Her cupid's-bow lips are accentuated with deep scarlet, and her eyebrows are fashionably plucked. It is the image of a woman who cared greatly about beauty and allure and illusion.

The next chapter in Rooney's saga, like several that would follow, is slightly mysterious. On August 10, 1944, she and Jimmy Wagner eloped. She was several months past her eighteenth birthday; he was twenty-three. The wedding was in Pensacola, Florida, where Jimmy was completing advanced flight training. No one, including Jimmy's mother, with whom he was very close, seemed to anticipate this event. "It came as a shock right out of the blue!" Kathryn Wagner recalled. "We knew that he was going with the girl, and he seemed to think an awful lot of her, and she of him." Kathryn Wagner and her husband, Harold, were informed of the wedding by telegram. She remembered Jimmy saying, "Wish me luck. I just got married."

Jimmy had been back in the States for nearly a year and a half but had not seen Rooney Iversen in a long time. So why the sudden marriage in August of 1944?

This much is known: Rooney and her mother drove to Pensacola that August to visit friends and, one supposes, to see Jimmy. "When she went down there, they got married," Jim's mother recalled. "And then that was it!" Aside from the bride and groom, the only people present were Rooney's mother, Lorraine; a few navy pilots; a classmate of Jimmy's, Ralph Fielding; and Ralph's wife, Lorene, who acted as best man and maid of honor, respectively. According to the local paper, Rooney wore "a street-length dress in luggage brown and gold with forest green accessories."

Was Anna pregnant? That, of course, was the obvious speculation. "I know that she had a baby nine months later," said her friend Fay. But, she added, "I think it was something that happened on their honeymoon. I don't think they had to get married." If Rooney wasn't pregnant, why the sudden wedding after so long an engagement? Anna knew, but never told anyone, not even her best friend, Fay. "I feel that Rooney has probably kept some things private," Fay said years later, "and I think it should stay that way."

The air of mystery may have emanated from the Iversens' disapproval of James Wagner, though both of Rooney's brothers had joined the coast guard and her father was now in the merchant marine; they could hardly find fault with a serviceman. The age concern was less acute; Anna was eighteen when she eloped. Character was also not an issue; everyone who knew Jimmy Wagner adored him to the point of hero worship. What, then? Fay suggested that Rooney's parents might have been happier with someone more "social" than Jimmy. She also pointed out that "they didn't know anything about him or his background." Cousin Margaret laid the blame on Rooney's father, a "self-centered" man with high aspirations for his only daughter. "He probably wanted her to marry a millionaire!" she offered, half in jest. There is perhaps more to the story—missing subplots buried with those who have died, kept secret still by Ann.

Whatever objections her parents may have had, the new—and newly pregnant—Mrs. James Wagner was gloriously happy. Anna was radiant during her first visit back to New London after the wedding. Jimmy, recalled his mother, "seemed to be walking on cloud nine." Less than a month after the wedding, he got his wings at a ceremony in Pensacola; the next day he was promoted to ensign.

Jimmy and Anna spent their first Christmas together as husband and wife with the Wagners in Titusville, the small, Norman Rockwellesque town in western Pennsylvania where oil was first discovered. Jimmy's parents and his sixteen-year-old brother, Gene, embraced his bride. Gene found Anna "very neat, very pretty, and very nice. A lovely girl. Lovely, lovely, lovely." To Kathryn Wagner, the sort of small-town housewife who baked peach pies and left them on the front porch to cool, her daughter-in-law "was the picture of Ann Sheridan," the "Oomph Girl" of the forties, a comparison Rooney would have relished. Privately, Kathryn Wagner fretted slightly—worrying, with a mother's intuition, "that we might not be good enough for Ann," recalled Gene Wagner. "She was concerned that Ann was from the city. We were farmers."

Ironically, Anna Wagner spent the ensuing months in much the same fashion as did Priscilla Lane. She and the actress were both newly married to pilots and were following their husbands from base to base while awaiting the birth of their first child. Anna passed part of her pregnancy with her parents in Niantic, Connecticut; Jimmy flew up to see her "every opportunity he got," recalled his brother. "They were very much in love, very happy." The newlyweds also visited the Wagners "many times."

On May 24, 1945, Jimmy arrived in Titusville on leave. Rooney was spending the last days of her pregnancy at Sheepshead Bay, in Brooklyn, where her brother was stationed. Jimmy's plan was to spend a quick night with his family and friends en route to New York for their child's birth later that week. Shortly after midnight the Wagners returned home to a frantically ringing phone. "Jimmy got the call," remembered his mother, "and turned to us and said, 'Well, Grandma and Grandpa! We have a baby girl!'" Rooney gave birth to an eight-pound baby at 10:40 that night. Jimmy and Gene raced to the hospital in Brooklyn, driving all night. "Jim went right up to see Ann, and I went to see the baby," recalled Gene. "I said, 'I saw your daughter before you did!'"

Anna Wagner chose the name Priscilla Ann for her love child. The choice was a revealing testament to her dreams and aspirations.

This was the first secret of the little girl who would marry Elvis Presley. She was not, as the world believed for so long, Priscilla Beaulieu. Her real name was Priscilla Ann Wagner.

2

THE SECRETS BEGIN

Priscilla Wagner spent her first days shuttling between Niantic, Connecticut, where she and her mother stayed with her maternal grandparents, and Grosse Pointe, Michigan, where her father was taking his final pilot's course. The Wagners got their first glimpse of their only grandchild when she was less than a month old, during one of Jimmy and Anna's stopovers in Titusville. Even Jimmy's teenage brother, Gene, couldn't get over how *happy* his little niece was.

Jimmy and Ann (she had dropped "Anna") chose the Wagners' church, Saint Paul's Reformed, situated at the top of a hill up the street from the Titusville Library, for Priscilla's baptism in August. After the Sunday service, the family drove back to the Wagner place, an old-fashioned farmhouse, to gather on the front lawn for pictures. Gene did the honors, capturing his older brother and Ann standing side by side, holding Priscilla between them. Ann is smiling blissfully at Jimmy while he beams at the camera. There is a single, poignant photo of Jimmy, posing before a sprawling oak tree, tenderly cradling his infant daughter. He is dressed in full uniform, standing military-straight, flashing his matinee-idol smile as Priscilla bobs her head out of a white christening blanket.

Within weeks Jimmy received orders to report to the Fighting Seventy-fifth aboard the aircraft-carrier USS *Roosevelt,* stationed in Chincoteague, Virginia. He and Ann and Priscilla were reunited with the Wagners once more in Titusville circa September of 1945. Before he left his parents' home for Chincoteague, Jimmy pulled his parents aside. "Now, if anything should happen to me," he instructed, "I want Rooney to have my car." Kathryn Wagner didn't give it a second thought. The war was over; her darkest fears about her son's safety had not materialized. These were Jimmy's glory days.

Ann and Priscilla whiled away the autumn in New London with the Iversens while Jimmy stood by near Norfolk, waiting to report for duty aboard the *Roosevelt.* When his orders arrived in early November, he persuaded one of the other pilots to accompany him in a single-engine two-seater for a training flight to Groton. He wanted to spend a farewell weekend with Ann and Priscilla before shipping out for the South American coast near Rio, where he would make his first official flight as a navy fighter pilot. His copilot's reward was to be a blind date with Ann's friend Fay.

Ann expected Jimmy at her parents' house by ten that Saturday morning; he had not arrived by the time Fay knocked on the Iversens' door, dressed up and excited about her date. Excitement gave way to worry, then fear, finally panic, as the late afternoon wore into nighttime. "I think both of us . . . we really didn't say too much," recalled Fay. "Didn't talk about it." Around eight o'clock, Ann rang the Wagners, deeply worried, wondering if they had received any word about Jimmy. Her mother-in-law said no and reassured her that Jimmy would arrive any minute. "Rooney and I waited and waited until I don't know what time," said Fay. "We waited until it was obvious that they weren't going to be there. And I finally went home."

Ann and the Wagners spent a desperate Saturday night and all day Sunday hoping, praying, for word from Jimmy. At 5:30 P.M. on Sunday they received a curt telegram from the navy informing them that James Wagner had been killed in an airplane crash on Saturday, "further details being sent by telegraph and letter."

Jimmy and his copilot had flown into a heavy snowstorm as they approached the foothills of the Berkshire Mountains near Wingdale, New York, where they became lost in a fog. A hunter who lived in the area saw the two-seater crash upside down against East Mountain on Saturday morning, strewing fragments of the plane across the mountainside. It took New York State Police and local residents until Saturday night to make their way through the snow and underbrush to recover the bodies of Jimmy and his copilot, an ensign from Columbia, Tennessee, named S. R. Caulk. The plane had crashed just half a mile from the Connecticut state line.

"Anna was in a stupor," her cousin Margaret recalled. Lorraine Iversen called that Sunday, asking Margaret to come over and comfort her daughter. The house was like a tomb. "Nobody said too much. What can you say?"

The Iversens, who had softened toward Jimmy since the wedding, gathered in Titusville with the Wagners for the funeral. The local paper noted that Jimmy had attracted the largest number of mourners ever to call at the Flanders-Arnold Funeral Home. Priscilla's father's memorial service befitted a military hero. James Wagner was buried in a white uniform, encased in a metal casket sealed by the government and draped with the flag of his country, saluted by a firing squad. Kathryn Wagner was inconsolable. Jimmy was her heart, her soul—her favorite son. The sort of boy who held down three part-time jobs in high school and still found time to call on an elderly widow for whom his smiling face was "like the sun coming out," as she put it. "Jimmy was . . . well, he was just about perfect," his mother took to saying. "Too perfect for this earth." She took some solace in a letter she received after the funeral, informing her that the pilot who took Jimmy's place on the *Roosevelt* that week went down in his plane on takeoff near Rio de Janeiro and was lost at sea. It was, it seemed, Jimmy's time to die.

After the memorial, Ann and Priscilla stayed on in Titusville for almost three months, living with the Wagners past New Year's. "I think she wanted to give comfort to my mother," Gene said of Ann, "and I think she . . . realized that if she had left and taken the baby, my mother would have nothing." Having their daughter-in-law and granddaughter near them was a source of great consolation to Jimmy's parents. "Ann and the baby were here for Priscilla's first Christmas," Kathryn Wagner recalled. "We had a Christmas tree and made things as nice as possible. But there was a deep grief on both sides. Very, very bad."

As far as the Wagners were concerned, everyone in the household got along beautifully. "I dearly loved the girl," Kathryn Wagner remarked later. Gene and Ann grew particularly close. At nineteen, Ann was just two years older than Jimmy's brother, who was then a senior in high school. The two played cards together in the kitchen, often talking and laughing. "I couldn't have asked for a better sister-in-law," related Gene. Priscilla, at eight months, was the apple of everyone's eye—more so than usual, perhaps, because she was their lifeline to Jimmy.

By the middle of January 1946, it was time for Ann to return home. She had lived with the Wagners in a state of suspended emotion. "She was a bride, a mother, and a widow, within a year's time," as Fay pointed out. It was time to think about the future—hers and her child's.

She and the baby moved in with her parents, while Ann sleepwalked through a series of dead-end jobs. "She was lost for a long time," her cousin Margaret reflected. Ann often wrote to Kathryn Wagner, filling her in on Priscilla's progress, but also complaining of dizzy spells, weight loss, and deep depression. "Rooney was a very vibrant person," recalled her friend Fay, "and she had a terrible time accepting the fact that Jimmy had died." She would pull out photographs of him, according to Margaret, and play and replay a tape recording of his voice, "and she'd get real down and cry."

That year Ann took a secretarial course, realizing, as she wrote Mrs. Wagner, that she was responsible for supporting Priscilla. By the spring of 1947, the Iversens could no longer afford to maintain the run-down, rambling house they were occupying with Ann and their granddaughter, so the family moved to a small apartment in Niantic. By summer, Ann had recovered from the extremes of her depression, and she rallied when she found a clerical job in the business office of the University of Connecticut at Fort Trumbull.

It was a dismal denouement for the spirited Rooney, the girl who had once fancied herself a model.

Priscilla was her salvation. She had been blessed with a beautiful child, Jimmy's legacy to her. Ann channeled her grief into complete absorption with her daughter. She fussed over Priscilla's clothes and hair like a Parisian couturiere, dressing her in frilly frocks and Gibson girl blouses, arranging her baby-brown hair in a Kewpie curl. Priscilla seemed born to play the part. "Isn't she a little doll?" strangers would remark.

Ann's devotion gradually turned to ambition. She took Priscilla to a photographer for studio portraits, and avidly studied the results. Soon she was entering her daughter in baby contests, then children's beauty pageants. With her own glamorous dreams beyond her reach, Ann focused her ambition on Priscilla. The resulting mother-daughter relationship was intensely symbiotic, and both knew that the key to their success was Priscilla's appearance. The lesson for Priscilla was clear: looking pretty was her raison d'être.

By the spring of 1948, Ann was no longer working at the university. She wrote her mother-in-law that she was disgusted with drifting from job to dreary job and frustrated that two-and-a-half-year-old Priscilla had no yard to play in. She was longing to stay at home so she could devote herself full-time to her daughter.

Around this time she met a former marine who was taking a business course at New London Junior College. His name was Joseph Paul Beaulieu (pronounced "Bow-lee-eu") Jr. Paul, as he was usually called, came from a Catholic family in the neighboring town of Groton, where his father operated a floor resurfacing business. Ann, who had not dated much since Jimmy died, began keeping company with Paul Beaulieu.

She did not mention her new suitor to the Wagners when she visited them that May to celebrate Priscilla's third birthday. Ann and Priscilla were regular guests at Jimmy's parents' house—so much so that the neighbors across the street named *their* baby girl Priscilla. Jimmy's little daughter charmed everyone in sight. When her mother and grandmother took Priscilla downtown to buy her a pinafore for her birthday, Mrs. Wagner recalled that "right in the store there she did a little jig. This little beret that she had on would keep slipping down, and she would give it a push to get it out of her eyes. . . . She performed just like a little actress."

Perhaps Ann avoided talking to the Wagners about the new man in her life because Paul Beaulieu, according to her favorite cousin, "was jealous of Jimmy." Ann confided this piece of information to Margaret after she and

Paul began dating. Jimmy Wagner, by everyone's account, was the great love of Ann's life. Her relationship with Paul Beaulieu was different. "I *guess* she was in love with him," Margaret mused. "But, you know, after Jimmy, Paul just couldn't compete. Paul's *Paul.*" Physically, he was not in the same league with James Wagner, Ann's beau ideal. He was tall and dark but decidedly average-looking, with brown eyes and heavy brows that drooped slightly, giving him a basset-hound quality. What Paul Beaulieu did offer was security, stability, and an opportunity for Ann to quit her job and focus on Priscilla. He gave Margaret the impression "he wanted to be something important." Paul Beaulieu particularly enjoyed having Ann's little daughter by his side. "He liked the attention he got being with Priscilla," Margaret noted, "because she was so beautiful."

Ann wrote to Kathryn Wagner in August that she planned to remarry, but she did not say whom or when. Jimmy's mother responded immediately: "Be sure and bring your husband and come visit us, and bring Priscilla. . . ."

Ann Wagner married Paul Beaulieu on September 11, 1948, in a big Catholic wedding in Groton. Priscilla's paternal grandparents did not receive an invitation; in fact, unknown to them, the Wagners were being systematically eliminated from the lives of their granddaughter and Ann. There was an unwritten clause in Ann Beaulieu's marriage vows, a hidden condition. She had made a Faustian pact with her jealous fiancé in exchange for her newfound security: She agreed to obliterate all evidence of her first marriage. It was to be as if Jimmy Wagner had never existed. His family, by extension, would cease to exist as well.

Ann began lying to her daughter, telling Priscilla that Paul Beaulieu was her father. Paul basked in the association. Jimmy Wagner, her true love, became a dark secret that Ann had to keep from everyone, even his own daughter. Priscilla attended the bridal shower and was a guest at the wedding of her "parents" at Sacred Heart Church. Ann and Paul assumed that Priscilla, at three and a half, was too young to know the difference.

Shortly after marrying Ann, Paul Beaulieu enlisted in the air force and started advanced pilot training, just like Jimmy Wagner. That December, for Priscilla's fourth Christmas, Kathryn Wagner sent her granddaughter a bundle of gifts, though she hadn't heard from Ann since receiving a telegram over a year earlier notifying the Wagners of her remarriage.

Ann, perhaps regretful of her need to cut all ties with Priscilla's grandparents, sent Mrs. Wagner a thank-you note for the Christmas gifts and a card announcing the birth of her second child, Donald Paul Beaulieu, born December 30, 1949. "Priscilla is crazy about him," she wrote Kathryn Wagner, "and she is quite a little helper." It was in this letter that Ann told Jimmy's mother they were moving to Texas, where Paul would be stationed as a navigator-bombardier. In closing, she thanked Kathryn for the Christmas gifts and promised to write again soon.

Kathryn Wagner never heard from Ann again.

Ann Beaulieu was driven by fear. Fear of how Paul Beaulieu would react if she mentioned Jimmy or his family. The fear intensified when she and Paul had their first child; Ann was concerned, she would say later, that Priscilla might not be treated the same as the baby. Was that all there was to the story? *What* was Ann so afraid of? Whatever the real reasons were, Ann kept them to herself, but the fear was there and it was powerful—so powerful that Ann made a decision soon after Donald was born: She would never again contact the Wagners, depriving her daughter of her paternal grandparents and separating Jimmy's parents from their only grandchild. Priscilla's real father—Ann's true love—was a forbidden subject as long as Paul Beaulieu lived.

On April 17, 1950, a few months after Ann sent Donald's birth announcement to Jimmy's mother, Paul Beaulieu formally adopted Priscilla Ann Wagner. The perfect porcelain doll was now his. It had to torment him that her face, the face everyone commented upon, belonged to his dead rival.

The Wagners had no idea their son's only child was now Priscilla Beaulieu, or that they had been deliberately expunged from her life. They were simply confused by Ann's silence. Kathryn Wagner tried to send a baby gift to little Donald, but had no idea where in Texas Paul Beaulieu was stationed. Letters she wrote to Ann at her last known address were returned unanswered. Months passed with no word from Ann. "We were always in hopes that maybe she just was busy and didn't write. Every time the mail came, 'Well, maybe we'll get a letter today.' "

Jimmy's mother tried writing Ann in care of her parents in Connecticut, "to see if they would tell me where she was. We worried and worried and didn't know what to do. But I didn't receive any answers." Several years passed, and the Wagners grew desperate. "We didn't know for sure whether Priscilla was living or not," explained Kathryn Wagner. "They just seemed to disappear."

The Wagners decided, finally, to consider legal action to resume contact with their missing granddaughter. They made an appointment with an attorney, but the night before the consultation, he suffered a cerebral hemorrhage and died. The God-fearing Wagners took that as a sign. "Everything seemed to be against us," recalled Mrs. Wagner. "It seemed to me that we just were not to know. We thought, There's a reason for this. If we're supposed to meet her or hear from her, we will."

The Wagners, who considered Priscilla "kidnapped," carried on with their lives, heartbroken. They had already lost Jimmy; now their darling grandchild, the living link to their son, had been ripped from them. For Jimmy's mother, the hardest part of losing Priscilla was "the little things." She thought of her granddaughter happily running through the house on her third birthday, her sweet smile. "But I have those good memories," she would console herself. "I have those." And she had the other Priscilla, the little girl across the street named after her granddaughter.

Kathryn Wagner also had a premonition, "a feeling that some way, somehow, I would know where she was."

3

PRISCILLA:
LITTLE GIRL LOST

Outwardly, Priscilla Ann Beaulieu was a typical six-year-old. She started first grade in New London in September of 1951. Her father had advanced to the rank of captain in the air force. Her mother tended the family. She adored her little brother, Donny, almost two.

The inner Priscilla, however, the Priscilla no one knew, was in turmoil, haunted by flashbacks to an earlier childhood that seemed both familiar and strange: recurring visions of her mother in church, on a stage, wispy memories of a big party, intermittent recollections of time spent with her grandmother Iversen while her mother was working and her father was nowhere around. All of these were pieces of an hallucinatory puzzle that Priscilla couldn't put together, parts of a past denied. The flashbacks confused and tormented her, but she kept them to herself. Like her mother and the entire Iversen clan, Priscilla had learned, by the age of six, to suppress her emotions.

Her sanctuary was her mother. Priscilla and Ann had an almost mystical bond, distinct from her mother's love for Donny and the other children who would follow. "She was a love child," said Michael Edwards, Priscilla's boyfriend when she was in her thirties, who knew the story of her childhood. "And love children, if you look through history, are always different." Whether out of guilt or because Priscilla was her connection to her lost love, Ann Beaulieu doted on her daughter. "My mother has always been a best friend to me," Priscilla remarked later in life. "She was always there for me, and she always saw my side. Not that I was a perfect kid, but she was always very sensitive to all my feelings."

The dynamics of the family were established early. A childhood chum of Priscilla's recalled that Paul Beaulieu was often away on military exercises and that when he was home, he was a remote authoritative presence. Though Ann lived in fear of him and of disturbing the status quo, she was herself a formidable figure in the Beaulieu household. Now that she no longer needed to work, she lavished her attention on her home and her family, predominantly Priscilla. In matters involving her daughter, Ann ruled. "I think he was the man of the house," as Austin neighbor and friend Dora Keen put it, "but when it came to Priscilla, I think *she* would be the more dominant. She wanted the best and the most and all for Priscilla, and if it was to be done, that would be *her* challenge."

The family had little money. Priscilla would remember her mother using orange crates as end tables and concealing them with hand-sewn decorative cloths, a simple metaphor for the house of secrets and lies. However much the Beaulieus struggled financially, Ann spared no expense where her daughter's appearance was concerned. Priscilla as a child was more than pretty; she was exquisite. "She actually did look like a china doll," observed a grammar school beau, Bob Ellis. "You couldn't have *drawn* a prettier child." Ann recognized and exploited that beauty, fashioning for her daughter, at six and seven, coordinated cowgirl costumes and fancy dresses with matching hats and purses and gloves. Priscilla, an early friend remembered, hated to be called Prissy, but the name was perfect for her. In home movies, she waved at the camera, smiling and tilting her head like Shirley Temple, completely at ease in her role as little princess.

By the second grade, Priscilla had gotten a full dose of military life. She had been uprooted from school in the middle of first grade, when Paul Beaulieu was transferred to Walker Air Force Base in Roswell, New Mexico; the following year she was enrolled in three second-grade classes in three states, ending the year at Bergstrom Air Force Base in Austin, Texas. The moves were difficult for Priscilla, who later said, "It makes you grow up with a very insecure feeling. You begin to wonder who your friends are—and what are friends."

One would not have guessed that she felt insecure. Early teachers considered Priscilla extremely friendly, "pleasing," "cooperative," "dear." Pat Conroy, author of *The Great Santini,* identified this paradox—the ability to appear outgoing yet feel isolated—as a common characteristic of military children. They "can engage anyone in a conversation," he wrote, "become well-liked in a matter of seconds, yet there is a distance . . . a slight shiver of alienation, of not belonging." Katherine Patton, Priscilla's third second-grade teacher, got a glimpse of the lost little girl beneath the sweet, cheery facade. "She was kind of a little clinging vine, she stayed right along by my warm side!"

Ann was ever-present, offering her services as Mrs. Patton's room mother, volunteering herself and Priscilla for the class operetta. Priscilla's beauty exacerbated her growing sense of alienation. She was considered "the prettiest girl in school," she later wrote in her memoir, the one who was "always stared at." She had no girlfriends, even though people remember that she was nice to everyone. "She was living in her own private little world," recalled her later boyfriend Michael Edwards, who talked to Priscilla about her childhood. "I think she was always a little dreamer—back, away from everybody. You could see it in her eyes."

Priscilla, from her earliest childhood, was a boy's girl. She had the instincts of a born coquette. There were always boys around Priscilla, even when she was five and six. "I don't know how her parents could have missed that from the time she was a couple of days old, they were going to have to watch her very carefully," a school friend, Linda Williams, would say. With boys, Priscilla had an instant comfort level that was missing in other areas of her life.

She has said that she felt *different* as a child—beyond being a military kid or feeling prettier than the other girls in school. Her almost angelic demeanor concealed a conflicted and troubled psyche, and the rare beauty that defined Priscilla also confused her. She was aware, even as a small child, that she only slightly resembled her mother. "I had nothing of my *father*," she remarked later. "Nothing. You start thinking: Well, I'm different. There's something wrong with me. Why am I different? Why don't I *look* like them? Why am I different in *looks* than they are?" She had the odd, unsettling suspicion that she was from another family. It was more than a child's vivid imagination; Priscilla could *feel* it. She felt separate from her younger brother, Don, and the four siblings who would follow. "Because I knew that I carried— I knew there was something that was different about me."

"She felt different from her brothers and sisters because of the reality that they weren't truly her brothers and sisters," proclaimed Mike Edwards. "I think she sensed that. It's in the genes—you *know* when you're really connected. She doesn't look like her sister, and she doesn't look like her brothers."

Priscilla had to wonder why there were so few photographs of her as a young child, aside from the studio portraits Ann submitted to baby contests and a few snapshots of her with her grandmother Iversen. There were no pictures of her with Paul Beaulieu before the age of three. "It was explained to me that there were no photographs of myself taken with my father [because] he was in the military and he was away. And it made sense to me, and I never went any further than that." Still, Priscilla could not shake the feeling that she did not belong.

Priscilla's sense of separateness from her family gave rise to the same kind of longing that came with being a child of the military, traveling from post to post. Mary Edwards Wertsch, a captain's daughter who wrote *Military Brats*, about the effects of growing up inside the military, concluded there is "only one antidote": *belonging*. "It is not easy for a military brat to learn what that even means, much less to find it. Yet belonging is the single greatest quest of our lives." For Priscilla Beaulieu, who felt alienated from friends *and* family, the quest to belong, that "powerful unnamed yearning" that Wersch says is found in most military children, was even more profound.

There is no such thing as a secret in a family, according to John Bradshaw, the psychologist and author of *Family Secrets*; there is only denial. Priscilla was five or six when she first became aware of the unusual atmosphere around her house. She knew there was *a secret.* "When there is a secret in a family," she recalled later, "there's always this sense of wondering. Of 'Well, why are they avoiding me?' or 'Why hasn't this question been answered?' or 'Why are they being so secretive?' or 'Why are they whispering?' "

Bradshaw says that when a situation is confusing or a child does not get information, he or she will create fantasies. So it was with Priscilla. "When you're left with all these mysteries," she said later, "you start assuming things *yourself.*" Priscilla imagined she was born to different parents, that her real father was a faraway, unapproachable handsome prince. "My defense was to dream—to slide into a fantasy world, a world always teeming with animals." She took solace in stray birds and cats, bringing them home to nurse them to health. She found it easier to relate to animals than to people because "animals have no ulterior motives. And once they love you they're always there."

When she was five or so, Priscilla discovered a more romantic means of escape. "My father listened to opera. Mario Lanza, Caruso. We had all of their albums. Liberace, too." Listening to Mario Lanza, the darkly handsome, emotional tenor, sing "Be My Love" during the summer of 1950 touched a chord in the lonely, displaced little girl. "There was such strength in his voice and the songs that he sang. I used to sit down by the record player and listen to them." Enthralled by the magic of that powerful voice, Priscilla could imagine herself outside the house of whispers, comforted by the virile, masculine image of Mario Lanza. "And then someone said one day that he led a very lonely life, and I just became very fond of him. And had a lot of empathy for him also." The identification was complete. Not only did Lanza represent her savior, now Priscilla fantasized she could save *him.* "I used to play his records and talk to him and try to make him feel better." They were twin souls, lonely kindred spirits.

"She went into her own make-believe world," asserted Mike Edwards, who derived much from childhood photos of Priscilla. "They weren't pictures with great smiles—more kind of looking back, withdrawing into her little world. It was almost like she was waiting for someone like Elvis to come along."

No one outside of Tupelo and Memphis had ever heard of Elvis Presley in 1950. He was a fifteen-year-old boy attending Humes High in Tennessee, plucking at his guitar and singing gospel for his mama. Like Priscilla, Elvis was a lonely child, unusually attached to his mother, with a powerful affinity for Mario Lanza. Years later, during the filming of the 1972 documentary *Elvis on Tour,* he would tell the directors, Pierre Adidge and Bob Abel, that Lanza influenced his musical style more than any other singer.

For Priscilla, Mario Lanza represented a powerful, inchoate longing, a yearning for something she could not identify: the father she never really knew, yet psychically could feel.

There was something else that set Priscilla apart as a child, something more than the recurring flashbacks, the feeling of belonging to another family, the muffled conversations between her parents. Beginning when she was six or seven, an age when most little girls' imaginations extend no further than dolls and tea parties, Priscilla Ann Beaulieu was seized by an odd presentiment that something extraordinary was going to happen to her. She was not certain what or how or when, but "I just knew that there was something that was going to happen in my *life*. That was going to be very big. And it was going to create a big effect—on me *and* my family."

Except for her almost supernatural beauty, her birthright from her otherwise forgotten father, there was nothing unique or distinctive about Priscilla Beaulieu as a child that would have given her reason to entertain this premonition.

Time and events, of course, would prove her right.

4

FANTASIES OF ELVIS

By 1955, when she was ten, Priscilla had attended six schools from Connecticut to Maine to New Mexico to Texas and back. Despite her beauty—or perhaps because of it—she said that she "never fit in. It wasn't like people accepted me with open arms. I was always the *odd* one. Because, being in the military, you have to always find where you belong, who's the group that's going to take you in, where your little niche is."

She started fifth grade at I. W. Podham in Austin, where she had attended part of the second grade. It was in Austin that a sister, Michelle, was born. While Ann still indulged Priscilla, certain rules and chores were strictly enforced. Most of them were necessary because of the family's meager finances and Priscilla's unfortunate position as the eldest child. She was often called upon to baby-sit, "and her allowance would be docked for little things—for instance, if she didn't close the door right away, letting cool air out," recalled a Texas friend. "In some ways they were mean to her."

Still, Carol Ann Heine, a close friend of Priscilla's from the fifth through the eighth grade, said that in most other ways "Priscilla was pretty much in the bracket of spoiled child. She pretty much had her way; she was very pampered." Christine Laws, another classmate, remembered that during homemaking class "you could tell she hadn't been around the kitchen much."

Ann continued to dress her like a doll, in layers of petticoats and voluminous hoop skirts. If the other girls were wearing shorts, recalled classmate Frances Rhodes, Priscilla's would be made of gold lamé.

The cult of Priscilla's beauty also served to bond mother and daughter. Ann shared beauty secrets with Priscilla, tutoring her in the rituals of the toilette, showing her how to rinse her golden brown hair in beer to bring out the sheen. The other fifth-grade girls at the half-country, half-military Popham school looked upon Priscilla's "beautiful shining hair" in awe, finding her special rinse "exotic." Ann Beaulieu exaggerated her own glamour, telling her daughter she'd been a photographer's model in high school, posing for portraits and modeling for department stores. This modeling career, however, escaped the notice of Ann's best friend Fay, her cousin Margaret, and her other classmates in New London. "Maybe Priscilla meant her mom always *wanted* to [model]," offered Pam Rutherford, Priscilla's closest childhood friend, whom she met in the fifth grade. Ann, the once-frustrated secretary, was channeling her own thwarted ambitions into Priscilla.

For her part, Priscilla's interests clearly did not lie in school. She admitted later that she was more interested in having fun. "Grades were not Priscilla's strong suit," her classmate Christine said. "And there was not the emphasis at home either. Let's face facts. If your child is going to do well in school, Mother and Daddy have to be involved."

Priscilla had a few girlfriends at the start of fifth grade—including Donna Brooke and Linda Williams, both popular, outgoing girls—but still no close friend. Other girls saw her, she would later write in her memoir, as "a rival, afraid I'd take their boyfriends away." Yet she was not remembered that way. "No, she wasn't that type of person," suggested Christine. "You weren't *jealous* of Priscilla. She was just Priscilla. And she wasn't snobby; she was friendly and outgoing." She did gravitate toward boys, though. "And all the little ol' boys, they liked Priscilla a lot," said her fifth-grade teacher, Ann George, chuckling. "They really did!"

Though her Texas classmates regarded Priscilla as an extrovert—"bubbling with personality," in the words of older boy Bob Ellis—she would look back upon her entire childhood as detached. Priscilla was always discrete. "Even though I had friends," she would later explain, "there was always that sense of keeping a part of me *distant*. I never gave all. I always reserved a certain part that I just never shared, and wouldn't share." This was the key to Priscilla, and would remain so. "Not that I wasn't close to my friends, and we had great times and a lot of fun. But there's just a line. There's a line there that I wouldn't go across."

Her reserve was partly a by-product of her military upbringing, but because of all the secrecy in her family, Priscilla became *secretive*. This quality imbued her with a mystique she would carry into her Elvis years and beyond. There was something sphinxlike about Priscilla, a demureness that people remember as strangely seductive, especially in a child. "Priscilla had a quality about her," her childhood best friend's mother, Eddie Rutherford, later tried to explain. "As a child, in my presence, she was such a little lady." This ultrafeminine mystique in one so beautiful and so young cast a spell on people, bewitched them, intrigued them, fascinated them, compelled them to try to break through.

Priscilla's aloofness was reinforced by a reserve that could have been misconstrued as shyness. According to her classmate Christine, she "was anything *but*" shy. Christine considered her the class clown, witty and outgoing, "always the center of attention." Her excessive daintiness could also create the illusion that Priscilla was extremely modest, even prudish. On the contrary, she could be quite aggressive if she had a goal. "When she wanted something, she went after it," remarked a Texas beau, Calvert White. Another boyfriend, Chuck Burns, saw her the same way: "She knew what she wanted, and she didn't . . . let anything stand in her way. Once she set her mind, she'd go for it."

If there were two Priscillas—the "good" Priscilla, who was reserved and affectedly modest, and the "naughty" Priscilla, who was aggressive, determined, and overtly sexual—this dichotomy is consistent with her astrological sign. Gemini is, after all, the sign of the twins. One can never be certain with a Gemini, astrologers contend, which of the twins one is going to encounter. Certainly as an adult Priscilla was aware of her duality. She described herself as a "true Gemini," possessed of two seemingly inconsistent personas "that are both me." This split personality would be an underlying theme in her life and would make her exceedingly difficult to read.

The hidden Priscilla revealed herself around the time of her eleventh birthday, in the spring of 1956, when she watched a young Elvis Presley perform on Jimmy and Tommy Dorsey's *Stage Show* and found herself sexually aroused. Elvis triggered the same emotional responses in her as had Mario Lanza. Like Lanza, Elvis Presley communicated to Priscilla strength, virility, confidence, and a dark sensuality. The difference was that Elvis Presley projected raw sex and a hint of menace, and Priscilla responded. That March, Paul Beaulieu stood on line at the PX to buy his daughter a copy of Elvis's first album, *Elvis Presley*, which stayed at number one on the *Billboard* chart for ten weeks and featured "Blue Suede Shoes," "I Got a Woman," and "Tutti Frutti."

Elvis was a long way from Mario Lanza, and Priscilla never looked back.

Though it would later become part of the Priscilla Beaulieu myth and legend that she was not an Elvis Presley fan before she met him in Germany, the truth is that Priscilla was fixated on Elvis. A neighbor of the Beaulieus, Eddie Rutherford, whose husband was transferred to Bergstrom Air Force Base in 1956, remembered that after March of that year, "her record player was going *all* the time. She absolutely *loved* his records!"

Eddie Rutherford and Ann Beaulieu arranged that year for their daughters, Pam and Priscilla, to meet. "We immediately hit it off," Pam recalled. They shared a love of the outdoors, of horses, of fantasy, and of boys. "It seems like there was a horse on the base," recalled Pam, "and we'd either go ride or pretend like we could ride or wish we could ride. We had all these great schemes and dreams." "We were always playing horses," Priscilla remembered. "She was Fury, and I was the Black Stallion. We had a real bond."

Pam's dream was to own a horse ranch. "My dreams when I was small," Priscilla once told a British newspaper, "could be best described by reading *The Black Stallion*." Priscilla the romantic identified with the mystical children's books by Walter Farley about a boy named Alec, a loner who saves the life of a mythical black stallion. Once more, Priscilla was drawn to an image of dark strength and power—of savage grace. "The Black," as the boy calls the wild Arabian, in turn saves Alec's life and will allow no human to touch him but Alec. The Black Stallion remains an enigma, belonging to no one, except Alec, but worshiped by all who behold his refined black beauty. Though she didn't realize it at the time, Priscilla was reading a version of her future. Elvis Presley was the human embodiment of the Black Stallion, with his beautiful features and mythic status—admired by everyone and owned by no one, except, to a degree, Priscilla Beaulieu.

Priscilla was still living in a fantasy world, and Pam was her partner in illusion. "We talked so much," said Pam. "Make-believe and wishes." In the fifth grade, Priscilla and Pam began playing a new fantasy game called Let's Pretend, or Imagine If. The two girls would lie side by side on the bed in Priscilla's room for hours, telling each other about their fantasies. "Priscilla always pretended that she was gonna marry Elvis," Pam recalled. "And I was gonna marry Ricky Nelson. We'd pretend what their romance would be like and what mine would be like. We'd play Elvis records and make believe all kinds of glamorous things." The game varied only as to specific events. "Sometimes we played 'Imagine if you *met* Elvis,' " explained Pam. Other days it was Priscilla and Elvis's fantasy wedding, their romantic honeymoon, or their life together. "We didn't have a clue!" Pam laughed later. "Ride around in limousines, I guess. Wear shiny clothes."

The games of Let's Pretend were part of the glue that cemented the friendship between Priscilla and Pam. "We used to play Imagine If a lot. And she was always with Elvis and I was always with Ricky." It was the first, and probably the last, time Priscilla Beaulieu allowed another woman access to her fantasies.

That same year or early the next, Priscilla joined an Elvis Presley fan club, receiving Elvis buttons and black-and-white glossies in the mail. When her dream lover played Austin during the summer before she started the sixth grade, he was close to Priscilla yet far, far away.

5

STAGE MOTHER

Priscilla reached her golden pinnacle in Austin the fall of the sixth grade, when she was eleven-going-on-twelve. For the first time in her life she had a best girlfriend, an experience that was heightened when the Beaulieus moved across the street from the Rutherfords.

"Pam-and-Priscilla were one word," as Mrs. Rutherford put it. "They'd call every morning to see what the other girl was going to wear that day." They were the stars of the sixth grade, the two prettiest, most popular girls at Popham Elementary. It was a matter of debate who was prettier. Pam's supporters extolled her coltish figure and wavy blond hair. No one seemed *not* to like Pam Rutherford.

Priscilla, at nearly twelve, still had some baby fat, which gave her a lush, "Pretty Baby" look, set off by shoulder-length brown hair, which she wore curled under and fluffy about her face. Dora Keen, whose son Willie was a grade ahead, remembered a cameo moment of Priscilla at one of the Popham dances that year. "They were in the school auditorium, sitting on this long bench, a bunch of the kids. And she wouldn't know this, of course, she was just a child—but everybody's eyes would just sort of follow Priscilla."

Priscilla was beginning to explore her sexuality. She was part of a group of self-described "risqué" sixth-grade girls and older boys who met regularly by a trailer in classmate Linda Williams's side yard for spin-the-bottle sessions. "And we felt like we were getting away with murder," Linda recalled. At home, Priscilla "fantasized endlessly" about French-kissing. "Sometimes," confided Calvert White, a Popham beau of Priscilla's, "we would be on the school bus, and the kids used to hide down behind the seats and kiss her." When Paul Beaulieu would not allow her to wear tight skirts to school, Priscilla joined the Girl Scouts so she could wear the body-hugging uniform—a typical Priscilla maneuver. "She was like a little . . . well, I would say she was just a little ol' sexpot," remarked Drue Foradory, a sixth-grade football player Priscilla had a crush on.

She came of age in the fifties, an innocent era, when Popham girls, Priscilla among them, wore poodle skirts, bobby socks, and saddle oxfords, joining their secret crushes at sock hops, the "tween" club, and base dances, where entertainment was provided by a jukebox.

Puppy love was expressed by the exchange of signet rings. Priscilla wore sixth-grader Mike Hodnett's ring for a day, Pam wore Cal White's, and Patricia Heins wore Chuck Burns's; then they traded boys and rings in a round-robin that recurred throughout the sixth grade. By spring, however, Priscilla had caught the eye of an older boy, Jack Edwinson, who snatched glimpses of her in the yard between Del Valle Junior High and Popham. "I was kind of struck by how pretty she was even at that age," he recalled. "Sixth-grade girls are pretty gawky-looking, but she stood out." By summer, Priscilla and Jack were dating. "You know how things are at that age. You might think that it's something serious, and it's not. Of course, going on official dates with transportation, we didn't have the means. We were both too young."

Spin the bottle and car-less dates could not compete with Priscilla's growing fantasies of Elvis, though. She and Pam continued to play Imagine If all through the sixth grade; on Pam's twelfth birthday in October, Priscilla gave her two Elvis 45s: "Heartbreak Hotel" and "Hound Dog." She set her cap for the self-described tough guy of the sixth grade, Drue Foradory, a boxer with dark, slightly dangerous looks. To his surprise, Priscilla boldly walked up to him one day, told him he looked like Elvis Presley, and asked him on a date. "She was outspoken and flirty," Foradory said, recalling the encounter. "If she liked you, she'd just come up and *tell* you." It was clear why Priscilla pursued him. "She was just nuts about Elvis," said Foradory. "She began liking me in the sixth grade 'cause she always used to say I looked like Elvis. We all wore our hair greased back, and I had dark hair, and when I was young, I had . . . features like Elvis." Priscilla gave Drue signed pictures of herself, "and we held hands and kissed a few times and what have you in the movie theater." According to Drue, Priscilla was *"most definitely"* the aggressor. Mike Hodnett, another of Priscilla's sixth-grade beaux, also remembered Priscilla as "determined."

She came by her perseverance naturally. Ann Beaulieu was blossoming into a tamer version of the mother in *Gypsy*, promoting Priscilla at every turn. "When we'd spend the night," recalled Carol Ann, a friend of Priscilla and Pam's, "her mother would talk about Priscilla. She entered her in lots of baby contests, beauty contests, as a small child and baby, and made albums of Priscilla in these contests. And I remember, when I was over there, her mother would just love to go through the albums and look at pictures and just dwell on it. She seemed to be obsessed. At the time I probably didn't know what 'vicariously' meant, but I always felt that her mother had a plan for her. Her mother was really pushing her. I don't mean that in a derogatory way at all, but she was that type of mother."

"I remember the scrapbooks," Christine Laws agrees. Ann entered Priscilla in a "variety of things. At that particular time, officers' wives' clubs at various bases would have contests like this. And community photographers would have 'Pretty Baby' contests. Or newspapers would. Or maybe a civic organization. And you've got to realize that some of this may have come from being in the military. Her father was an officer, but he was not a *high-ranking* officer. There's a world of difference between a captain's family and a colonel's family."

Priscilla never boasted about the pageants or how she looked, according to her friends. Ann was the promoter. "There wasn't any question in my mind that she was always preparing Priscilla for an *event*," asserted Carol Ann. "It was just a matter of time. Priscilla was just one of the gang—we didn't feel she was any more special than anybody else. But her mom did." According to Pam, Ann Beaulieu "wanted Priscilla to be 'the one.' Whatever was going on, Priscilla was . . . the center of attention."

These dynamics began to foster competition between Priscilla and Pam. "We were best friends and rivals at the same time," Pam explained. "We were either very close or fighting." The instigator, according to members of the clique and Pam herself, was Priscilla's mother. "I think there never would have been a bit of rivalry between us if it hadn't been brought to the front by Ann," Pam once said.

Ann's competitive streak reached its height shortly after Pam's twelfth birthday in October, when the PTA sponsored a fund-raising contest for king and queen of the Popham Halloween Carnival, the big school event of the fall season. The nominees were chosen from the sixth-grade class, with the winners determined by which candidate accumulated the most votes, at a penny a vote, to be collected in a jar kept in the principal's office. After the contest, the money was to be put in a school fund.

The contest evolved into a cutthroat race between Pam and Priscilla. The rivalry agitated by Ann intensified during the campaign, with classmates drawing battle lines. The mothers worked for weeks on costumes for the Queen's Royal Reception, sewing elaborate floor-length satin robes with characters from Story Book Land stitched onto the fabric to promote National Book Week. The big event was to be held on October 29, when the queen and king were to be announced at the Halloween Carnival party in the school cafetorium. By the end of the campaign, the girls' friendship was severely strained. By their own recollection and that of friends, neither girl seemed driven to win; it was Priscilla's parents who had the emotional investment. "I considered quitting," Priscilla would later write, "but I felt I couldn't let my parents or supporters down." Priscilla's classmates, however, drew the line at that. "She wouldn't have quit on a bet!" claimed Christine.

Priscilla later insisted that she was certain she was going to lose, but her parents proceeded with confidence. Ann went shopping for a strapless evening gown for Priscilla to wear to the dance; her father, she recalled, "kept reminding me to practice an acceptance speech." Shortly before the coronation, a classmate warned the Rutherfords that Priscilla was going to win because her grandparents—Ann's parents—had sent a forty-dollar check to her campaign.

When the big night arrived, it was Priscilla Beaulieu who was crowned queen of the Popham Halloween Carnival. Pam Rutherford sat below her, as runner-up princess. "That was a funny deal, too," recalled Pam, who never spoke of it to Priscilla until years later, when Priscilla wrote about the contest in her autobiography. Priscilla claimed it was *she* who heard a rumor that *Pam's* grandparents "had put in a hundred-dollar bill for their vote. My parents were disappointed; there was no way that they could afford to match that much money and even if they could, they objected on principle."

"It's so silly now, because we're fifty years old and who cares!" Pam remarked after *Elvis and Me* came out. "She relates the same story, only in reverse. And I thought, 'Jeez! How could she get that so mixed up?' And I just assumed the way she told it is the way it was for her, and I'm not writing the book, so it doesn't make a bit of difference to me." Priscilla would later attribute the mix-up to "misinformation" from another girl, but there would always be lingering doubts.

The consensus, years after the fact, was that if there were any machinations to ensure the outcome of the contest, Ann Beaulieu was the more likely source. "This would have been very typical of Priscilla's mother," remarked Christine Laws, with an ironic laugh. "Honey, it was very important. What was important was looks, appearance. . . . Many mothers live vicariously through their daughters. And she did."

In 1956, the year of her greatest glory at school, Priscilla's sense of destiny returned, more powerful than before. "I would get this *feeling*," she later tried to explain. "Someone would ask me, 'What are you going to do in life?' You know, 'What are you going to be?' And I just remember that I had this incredible feeling that whatever it was going to be, it was chosen for *me*. And it was going to create a very big effect."

Just as Priscilla Beaulieu was being elected carnival queen, Elvis Presley was labeled the King of Rock and Roll. It was the end of 1956 and the beginning of his phenomenal trajectory to fame. By October he had earned five gold records in a single year, with two more to come; released his second album, *Elvis;* starred in a major feature film, the civil war drama *Love Me Tender;* and signed a ten-picture movie contract. He appeared in concert all over Texas that fall, fanning the flames of Priscilla's growing infatuation.

She and Pam went on a double-date to see her idol in *Love Me Tender* at the Base theater. Priscilla's date was her current beau, seventh-grader Larry Powell. Pam and Priscilla, he remembered, were hysterical over seeing Elvis on the screen. "She was definitely screaming," Larry recalled of Priscilla. "Standing up and hollering. You know those black-and-white reels of Elvis at some of his early concerts, with girls screaming and crying? She was just like you see in those old movies."

Both girls scrutinized Debra Paget, Elvis's costar. Pam idolized Paget, her "favorite movie star," while Priscilla was simply sizing up the competition. Earl Wilson quoted Elvis in *Photoplay* that January of 1957 describing Paget as "the most beautiful girl in the world," and fan magazines were reporting his unrequited love for her.

There was truth to the rumors, though the real story has never been told until now. The account repeated in most Presley biographies states that Elvis developed an intense infatuation with Debra Paget, who, at twenty-two, rejected the shy nineteen-year-old singer as unsophisticated. According to Debra Paget, however, she and Elvis Presley fell in love.

She "was a very young twenty-two," as she put it, and extremely shy, and "found Elvis to be a very sweet, unassuming, fun, and kind person." Their conversations, on and off the set, revolved around God. Debra's parents—particularly her mother, who dominated her life and her career—refused to allow Debra to date Elvis, because, she recalled, "there were stories going around about him," a side effect of his reputation as a rock-and-roll rebel. Willie Jane Nichols, Elvis's mother's best friend from Tennessee, would hear about Debra from Gladys Presley during the *Love Me Tender* shoot. "She talked to Elvis daily," recalled Nichols. "Gladys would say, 'I wish you could hear him talk about Debra Paget!' He was just overwhelmed with her."

Debra Paget was Elvis Presley's ideal in a woman. Like him, she had a close, intense relationship with her mother, a heavyset, formidable woman who physically resembled Elvis's own mother, Gladys, a fact that didn't escape either Elvis's or Debra's attention. Debra's mother noticed that her daughter bore a certain facial resemblance to Gladys Presley, a fact that could only further endear her to Elvis. These similarities may have marked the beginning of Elvis's obsession with physical resemblances between people close to him—an understandable preoccupation in a surviving twin, as he was.

Debra Paget was a stunning ingenue with a heart-shaped face, clear blue eyes, and cupid's-bow lips. Elvis the aesthete admired beauty in any woman. But Debra Paget offered more than a pretty face and a matching mother complex. She was also religious. And more importantly, she was a virgin. Her mother would not allow her to leave the house unchaperoned, so she had never been on a formal date. To Elvis, this combination was perfection. "He always said he'd marry a virgin," recalled Debra, "and maybe that's why he said he'd marry me. Because his mama always told him to marry a virgin."

Contrary to previously published accounts, Debra did not consider Elvis Presley an undesirable hayseed. "Had my parents not objected," she related, "I would have gone ahead. I thought a great deal of him." Because of her natural timidity and because her mother was so opposed to Elvis, Debra kept her feelings to herself, even from Elvis. "I was *very* shy then; I hardly talked."

Elvis continued to carry a torch for Debra. After *Love Me Tender* wrapped and before he went into the army, sometime in late 1956 or early 1957, he called Debra from El Paso, where he had stopped while driving home to Memphis from Los Angeles, and asked her to marry him. Debra told him it wasn't possible. "I know it's your mother and father," she remembered Elvis saying. "And if it takes twenty years, I'll get them to like me."

"I knew it was hopeless," Debra recalled. "My parents would never relent. It was an impossible situation. I'm not sure I ever told him how I felt, but he could feel it."

Elvis could not get Debra Paget out of his system. Willie Jane Nichols and her husband, Carl, accompanied Vernon and Gladys Presley to Hollywood in 1957 to watch Elvis shoot his second movie, *Loving You*. His sightseeing tours always included one stop in Beverly Hills. "Elvis carried us around and took us past Debra Paget's house," confirmed Nichols. "I think Debra saw us and remembers that."

Debra Paget's version of the tale is both romantic and sad. She and Elvis continued to have feelings for each other but were kept apart by circumstances (her mother). "I did *The Ten Commandments*," she recalled. "We had to see each other in passing on the Paramount lot, and we looked longingly at each other." Just before Debra's mother died, she confessed her regrets to her daughter. "She said she wouldn't have stopped me if she'd known I felt so strongly." By then it was too late; both Debra and Elvis had married other people. The actress kept the truth to herself, even after Elvis died. "There was no need to tell others," she explained. "I don't like to talk about Elvis; I've always felt it was private."

Priscilla Beaulieu did not know the intimacies of Elvis Presley's relationship with Debra Paget when she saw *Love Me Tender*. She only knew that Elvis was smitten with the actress, and if Elvis fancied her, Priscilla wanted to see more of her. She was learning how to actualize her fantasies, an endeavor that required homework and careful study. While she did not put that kind of effort into her schoolwork, if she had a goal, Priscilla could move mountains.

Priscilla was not the only female in the Beaulieu household who had a crush on Elvis Presley. As soon as *Love Me Tender* hit the marquee at the Majestic in downtown Austin, Ann Beaulieu was on the phone with Dora Keen, president of the Bergstrom Officers' Wives' Club, saying, "Let's go see Elvis!" They went to a matinee with two other air force wives.

"It was her idea!" recalled Dora Keen. "When we went to see it, she was crazy about Elvis. Ann was a big Elvis fan. She was following his career, you know, starting in movies. Ann was impressed with him. She could see something in him. We were all acting so stupid about the young man! And I know she was very fond of Elvis."

Who knows whether Priscilla was aware that her mother harbored a crush on her teenage idol? It was impossible to tell, since years later—for reasons that would soon become clear—Priscilla and all the Beaulieus would reconstruct history, claiming that Ann disapproved of Elvis Presley before Priscilla started seeing him.

More secrets, lies, and cover-ups in the house of hidden truths.

6

SECRETS REVEALED

The apparent existence of "two" Priscillas became more evident as Priscilla Beaulieu entered junior high in 1957. She was still outwardly demure, with the same catlike inscrutability—a facade her boyfriend Mike Edwards would later refer to as "the mask," because it so adeptly hid what was really going on. But just below the surface lurked the "naughty" Priscilla.

"She'd ask me to go to the movies with her," recalled Taylor Keen, "and then ditch me at the drive-in to meet the high school boys." It was Rooney all over again.

Priscilla and Pam, but especially Priscilla, attracted older boys. "Some of the freshman and sophomore boys thought she was the cutest little trick that ever walked and talked," recalled Christine Laws. Soldiers on the base—grown men—ogled Priscilla at twelve and a half. "We used to ride the bus," remembered Pam, "go to the root beer stand and to the PX. The soldiers all looked at her." The magnet was Priscilla's dainty doll-like features. "It was more her face than anything else," agreed Cal White, who dated Priscilla in Austin. "She had the prettiest features I have ever seen in my life." Even the boys' mothers marveled at Priscilla. "Her eyes were outstanding," Charlie Clements's mother, Mary, remembers. "[The irises] had a dark ring around them."

Though she didn't "put on airs," as her friend Evangeline put it, Priscilla was obsessed with her appearance. A seventh-grade teacher recalled Priscilla opening her mirrored compact in class more often than her textbook. She and Pam handled the attention of their older admirers with aplomb. "They acted like they were twenty," Taylor Keen remembered. "They were so much more sophisticated."

For the first time in Priscilla's childhood, the Beaulieus remained in the same city for three consecutive years, giving their daughter's life a semblance of permanence. Yet Priscilla herself was not stable. She was still intensely competitive with her best friend, had become quite aggressive around boys, and was developing a finely honed ability to get what she wanted by manipulating others. As one close Texas friend put it: "You like her, you can enjoy her company, but you can't feel one hundred percent sure of Priscilla. That's just part of knowing her. And you just have to accept it."

"She was kinda like a little honeypot," said Mary Clements, who lived across the street, describing Priscilla at thirteen, the birthday she celebrated on her last day of seventh grade. "She liked older boys and she'd sit in the yard and watch while they played football on our front lawn." Hoping to attract them, and succeeding. Overall, though, Priscilla was a popular girl in the popular crowd, a cheerleader who was great at the new dance craze, the twist, and friendly to all.

Until that summer, when everything changed.

It began like any other summer evening at the Beaulieus. Priscilla was baby-sitting for Don and Michelle, then six and three, while Paul and Ann attended a party. Bored, she wandered into her parents' bedroom while her little brother and sister were asleep and began snooping through the closet, "mulling through things." Her eyes fell on an old trunk buried in the back. Priscilla found herself drawn to it, strangely compelled to see what was inside. "And as I'm opening it," she recalled, "I had this *unbelievable feeling*." Inside, folded neatly on top, was an American flag, the type presented to widows of servicemen. Priscilla's heart raced. "And I kept thinking, I shouldn't be doing this. It was too private. But as I was exploring, I kept wanting to go on. But then something was saying, Don't go any further! And I kept going further and further."

Under the flag she found a cache of carefully preserved, yellowing love letters addressed to Rooney, her mother's nickname as a girl, from someone named Jimmy; beside them were her mother's passionate replies. Mesmerized, Priscilla reached inside the trunk for more. On the bottom was a sea of pictures—photographs she had never seen before of herself as a baby. Along with photos of herself alone and with her mother, she found a photograph of Ann beside a dark, handsome stranger as baby Priscilla lay in her arms. On the back, in her mother's handwriting, were the words, "Mommy, Daddy, Priscilla." A chill ran down Priscilla's spine as she studied the picture more closely. The face of the stranger in the photo was her own. She had stumbled onto her personal Pandora's box. "And I kept finding more pictures and finding more pictures, and finding certificates," she recalled, several decades later. A birth certificate. Baptismal records. "Finding my *life*, you know, in front of me! That was *different* from what I knew."

Priscilla sat in front of the trunk, unable to move, cognizant that in her hand was the solution to the riddle of her childhood, that she was face-to-face with the secret. She was not who she had thought she was: It was both her greatest fantasy and her deepest, darkest fear. "First you go into denial it's somebody *else*. And then you go into shock. That you've been betrayed. That someone has lied to you. You have so many different emotions that peak. *I* was in hysterics." Priscilla telephoned her mother at the party, "begging her to come home. Because I needed an explanation. I needed somebody to tell me the *truth*. What was this I was discovering?"

Ann Iversen Wagner Beaulieu raced home to her daughter, alone. She did not tell Paul Beaulieu she was leaving the party or where she was going. After years of denial, the call may have been almost a relief.

Ann arrived at the house to find Priscilla half crazed. She calmed her daughter, and then told her the truth about their past: She had been married to a handsome pilot named James Wagner who died in a plane crash, and he was Priscilla's real father. "And [she said] that he was wonderful," recalled Priscilla. "He loved me, he was coming home to see me. And that I was his *life,* and her *life*. And that she met my father [Paul Beaulieu] a few years later and married him. And that *he* was my father. He adopted me."

As her mother was talking, an image suddenly flashed in Priscilla's head—the vision of her mother on stage, one of the recurring images that had tormented her since she was five or six. "And I started realizing, Oh, my God! That was the *party* I went to! I remembered I was in my grandmother's lap, and I remembered seeing my mother—to me it was like on a stage—but it was in a church, it was at the Catholic church, a very big Catholic church. Everything was so *big*! My mind went right to the picture of that church. And all those flashbacks from when I was three started to make sense."

It was "very bizarre," Priscilla later acknowledged. The seeming delusions that had confused her since early childhood began to crystallize. "And it made sense to me why we had lived with my grandmother then, that there was no man in my life. That was why my grandmother took care of me. All the [pieces of the] puzzle were starting to fit now." She understood, finally, where her unearthly beauty had come from: "My *real* father. I look *exactly* like him!"

Priscilla would later say that discovering the truth about her identity from a hidden trunk at the age of thirteen was a devastating blow. In the hierarchy of family secrets devised by John Bradshaw, concealing a child's real parent is the second most dangerous, just below incest. For Priscilla, the *discovery* of the lie was almost worse than the lie itself. Her mother, the person she trusted most, had betrayed her, deceived her, was not who Priscilla had thought she was. Who did that make Priscilla?

Ann tried to console her daughter, telling her that she had been "haunted" by the secret all these years, that she had wanted to tell her beautiful daughter the truth, but that she'd been afraid. The critical word was "fear"—fear of upsetting the apple cart, fear of upsetting Paul.

"The big fear was my father," Priscilla admitted. "I don't think my father ever really *accepted* the fact–he really looked at me as his daughter. And now to have my real father come up . . . it was very important to my mother protecting *him* [Paul], protecting his feelings, his sensitivity." Ann Beaulieu still feared the consequences of revealing the secret. "The fear was that anything like this would maybe separate us. So let's just keep it the way it is."

Even after Jimmy's existence was out in the open, Ann barely dared to speak of her beloved first husband to his own daughter. Priscilla was provided with few details of the father Ann had hidden from her for ten years. Priscilla would later explain that Ann "doesn't want to really do anything that she thinks may sway me from my [adoptive] father."

Why was Ann so protective of Paul Beaulieu? The purpose of family secrets, according to John Bradshaw, is to preserve the status quo. Was Ann hiding something else, some more dangerous family secret? Her distraught reaction suggested that possibility. She pleaded with Priscilla, as they both cried beside the trunk, to keep Jimmy Wagner their secret, never to speak of her real father again, especially to Paul Beaulieu.

It was a side of her mother that Priscilla had never seen before. She sensed Ann's desperation, but still felt betrayed. Priscilla realized she had a crucial decision to make. She could either allow the truth to surface and accept the consequences, or protect her mother and herself by perpetuating the lie. "Any child who finds out that that's not your real *father* and that your mother was married to someone else–it's a very devastating impact that one has to deal with," she acknowledged years later. "And then how do you resolve that? How do you *resolve* that? Where do you fit in? And *do* you make something of it? Or do you just let it go? And I decided to let it go. Because my father–my stepfather, but I thought he was my father–I could never *hurt* him. So the decision was, 'Let's not ever discuss this. It will *never* come out.' "

The truth of Priscilla's identity became, as Priscilla put it, "a secret between my mother and myself." The subject–the very existence–of her real father became a forbidden topic.

It was the formative moment of Priscilla Beaulieu's young life. She had shifted from being the victim of secrets and lies to a coconspirator. At her mother's knee, she was learning that secrets and lies are acceptable, that the truth can be dangerous. Like her mother, her maternal grandparents, and her adoptive father, she was learning to act, to pretend, to keep secrets. That was a family tradition.

She put away the trunk that contained the mysteries of her childhood and she and her mother "never talked about it again."

Priscilla still had no idea she had paternal grandparents in Pennsylvania who were mourning her ten-year absence from their lives. She didn't know, couldn't know, that her grandfather Wagner would die a few months later, at fifty-six, "of a broken heart," his widow believed, at the loss of his son and his only grandchild. Kathryn Wagner had adopted a fatalistic attitude toward Ann and Priscilla's disappearance, "but Harold didn't look at it that way," she asserted. "He thought it was *meanness* or something." Through all of this, Jimmy's mother harbored "no animosity whatsoever" toward Ann. "I used to think, if I could only know where they are, I wouldn't hurt [them]. There's no anger in my heart. I just want to *know*."

For Priscilla, all that remained of the life-altering discovery of the trunk was a gold locket Jimmy had given Ann, which Ann presented to Priscilla as a memento. Priscilla wore it around her neck thereafter. Hidden inside the locket was a tiny photograph of her real father, dark and handsome in his pilot's uniform. Knowing nothing about him, Priscilla fantasized that her long-lost father died a great war hero. "In times of emotional pain and loneliness," she said, "he would become my guardian angel." For a brief time she wondered whether the discovery of her real father was the event she had been intuiting since she was five or six. But the premonition of "something big" coming into her life recurred. Priscilla decided there was something else awaiting her.

That July, according to Carol Ann Heine, she and Priscilla went to see *King Creole,* Elvis Presley's latest movie. As they were leaving the cinema, they caught a glimpse of the back of a dark-haired young man. According to the theater manager, it was Elvis Presley. "He was in the army then and was stationed in Fort Hood and hadn't seen the movie in a theater yet," recalled Carol Ann. "The manager told us [Elvis had] asked if he could come in after the lights were out and sit in the back so no one would see him." The story may or may not be apocryphal, but one thing is certain: Priscilla Beaulieu and Elvis Presley were circling ever closer to each other.

7
SEXPOT

Priscilla nearly collapsed under the strain of her sacred pact of silence with her mother. Ann Beaulieu had placed an enormous burden on a thirteen-year-old child by asking her daughter to keep her paternity a secret, even from her siblings and from the man she now knew was not her real father.

Other children might have cracked under the pressure or prattled the news to everyone at school; Priscilla was made in a different way. She assumed the responsibility with great seriousness. As she later explained: "If someone has entrusted me with something, I could never betray them." She told no one about the discovery of her true identity, not even Pam. As time passed, she became conflicted about wearing the locket containing the picture of her real father. "I felt *guilty,* because I felt now that I was betraying my *stepfather,* who was so good to me. Because now it's like I was hiding something from him." Ann Beaulieu had spun a tangled web of deceit and Priscilla was unwittingly ensnared.

The trauma of her mother's betrayal and her own suppression of the truth affected Priscilla's behavior. Her grades dropped, eliminating her from eighth-grade cheerleader tryouts, "and it was a big blow to her," recalled Carol Ann. Pam Rutherford moved to England just after school began, leaving Priscilla without, as she later wrote Pam, her "first real friend." Friends and neighbors, including Charlie Clements, noticed a "sudden shift" in Priscilla's behavior. "She went through a real change of personality," reflected Carol Ann.

Her friends had no idea what was going on with Priscilla. She had closed ranks with the rest of her family, locked into a drama of denial. Paul began doing extracurricular work for the CIA that year, which added to the secrecy and intrigue that prevailed at home. He would tell Priscilla of his covert work, but caution her not to say anything to anyone else. It was business as usual for the Beaulieu household.

Priscilla, instead of confronting the emotions aroused by her discovery of who she really was, simply shut down. It was not only the Iversen-Beaulieu way; it was the *military* way. "A 'good' military family," Mary Edwards Wertsch explained, "displays to the world what ought to be displayed—and conceals the rest." Mike Edwards, her adult beau, considered Priscilla's childhood "oppressed" and believed that Paul Beaulieu was an alcoholic, the secret problem of many military families. None of her childhood friends had a clear sense of Paul or of Priscilla's relationship with him. "I couldn't get a fix on it," Carol Ann admitted. "With Pam's parents it was a real comfortable setting. It wasn't the same at Priscilla's. I can't put my finger on anything."

"There were things that went on," Mike Edwards offered suggestively, mentioning "an oppressed family, the father is drinking." Priscilla, he maintained, was looking for an "escape."

Her twin sources of salvation were her fantasy father, Jimmy, who was her guardian angel, and her fantasy lover, Elvis Presley. She was unaware that destiny was about to intervene, causing her two worlds—real and fantasy—to collide. The first development was Elvis Presley's draft notice late in 1956; the second was Gladys Presley's death on August 14, 1958. Elvis's mother died just weeks after Priscilla's real father was reborn through her discovery of the hidden trunk.

A different Priscilla emerged after finding out her mother had lied to her. While she had long been a flirt, casually interested in the handsome boys two or three grades ahead of her, "Priscilla got to messing around with an older crowd," recalled Cal White. "She had the older boys going after her, and she started hanging around with them. And that kind of put her out of the 'in' crowd, you might say."

"She went for the big football stud," recalled Chuck Burns, who dated Priscilla intermittently. "Somebody who had a car." Sonny Washington and Henry Smith, two sophomore heartthrobs, hotly pursued Priscilla. "They would walk a mile on their knees just to hold her hand," recounted Mary Ann Holstrom, a classmate. "And everybody was just sort of gaga over her even when she was thirteen years old, because of the way she looked and the way she carried herself. And she had a lot of confidence. She knew what she had."

Unlike the fictionalized version of her life that Priscilla would later create, Paul Beaulieu was *not* a caricature of the strict military father, nor were her parents overprotective. "She could date more than the rest of us," recalled Carol Ann. "The rules and regulations at [her] home were fairly lenient, for air force parents. Most were *very* disciplined, and when we went to base movies with a boy, we were chaperoned, but Priscilla was not chaperoned that much."

That fall, with her mother's complicity, Priscilla became more daring. Henry Smith, the star of the high school football team, wanted to ask her to the homecoming dance, but "it was kind of frowned upon by the school administration for a junior high kid to go with a high school boy," recalled

Christine Laws. Henry mentioned his intention to Priscilla in passing, and Ann Beaulieu took it from there. Henry's mother worked at the day-care center where Ann dropped off Priscilla's younger brother and sister, "and my mother talked to [Ann]," Henry recalled. "And I think [the idea] excited her. I was the captain of the football team, and—not to be bragging—a lot of girls wanted to go with me." Henry felt it was Ann Beaulieu "who pushed for Priscilla to really go." Ann abetted Priscilla for two reasons: because she enjoyed the fact that her daughter was so sought after and, in the words of her cousin Margaret, "because Priscilla reminded Ann of Jim."

"I think all the guys were kinda figuring me to be a little crazy for being interested in a girl that young. But she could compete with the seniors! She was a little girl—but jeez, she just looked so mature!" recalled Henry. Priscilla wore a long formal low-cut dress to the dance.

The date that scandalized Del Valle High was actually very tame. Priscilla was not allowed to go on car dates, so Henry drove to her house and Paul Beaulieu chauffeured the couple to the dance. Henry was a perfect gentleman; at evening's end he and Priscilla did no more than kiss. "She was too young. She was just a kid. And I was really a nice guy. I didn't really mess around intimately with any woman until I was in college."

The relationship did not last much beyond the homecoming dance, though "I would just maybe kiss her in the halls," remembered Henry, who found Priscilla very receptive. "We liked each other, but she was so much younger. It was all a new experience to her. She was too young to really feel like she was going to be getting serious with anybody. I could tell that." He could also tell, Henry said later, that beneath her dutiful facade, Priscilla was chafing at the bit. "She was the type of girl I knew wouldn't be held back. If she wanted to do something, she was going to do it."

When the relationship with Henry cooled, Priscilla moved on to more notorious older boys. "She hung around with some guys who weren't in our crowd at all," recalled Carol Ann. "These were guys who were in school, but barely. It wasn't the kind of guy she should have been dating. They just sort of hung out around the corner of the school. They had cars and drank beer. She rode around with these guys."

Her close friends, Carol included, were baffled. "All of a sudden her personality just *changed* tremendously. She hung around the lockers with these really hoody boys. And you could tell that she didn't care about them, but . . . you really wondered about her. I guess if we had been less into ourselves and more into finding out what was wrong with our friends . . . but we didn't. I don't know if it was just a personal choice with her, or if something at home had caused her to rebel or what."

Something *had* happened at home. Priscilla had found her missing childhood, her true self, and had been pressured into denying that reality. She had been inducted into the society of secret-keepers. Keeping the pact with her mother, she found, was "a big responsibility," too big for a thirteen-year-old child.

She was also, classmates noticed, maturing faster physically than the other eighth-grade girls. Beyond the purely physical attributes, Priscilla had an ethereal quality that made her appear older: She was possessed of a poise that was worlds beyond her years and her family's social standing. It gave Priscilla the aura of the wellborn, an innate kind of class. Moreover, Priscilla was an instinctively sexual creature.

By the middle of eighth grade, Priscilla's reputation at school was suffering. "People didn't think much of her because she hung around with these guys who were not liked and were the kind who would be promiscuous," said Carol Ann, who stopped spending the night at the Beaulieus', "because it was really not a very good thing to hang around with her. She was beginning to get a poor reputation." What transpired between Priscilla and those older boys is not known, but it is clear from her class pictures that Priscilla had matured a sexual light-year between twelve and thirteen. For her eighth-grade picture, she assumed a sultry pose, looking worldly-wise, her lips a cherry-red pout.

Priscilla was still a sweet girl, but her "other" Gemini side now surfaced more often. She was bolder, more assertive. She attempted to dye her light brown hair coal-black, Elvis-style, that spring, "and it turned out more like blue-green," recalled Evangeline Segura, another friend. Priscilla wasn't fazed. "She had a lot of confidence," said Evangeline, "so things like that really didn't bother her." Mary Ann Holstrom, whose family moved to Austin that year, formed the impression that Priscilla Beaulieu "was a person who was used to getting what she wanted. A very exciting-looking person who got a reaction wherever she went. Here we were, all these gangly, adolescent types running around like idiots, and here she was. Obviously there was a big difference." Mary Ann considered Priscilla aloof, preoccupied with her looks. "One day I pushed her into the pool. She was fixing her hair, and it got wet. She never spoke to me again. Her hair was a big point with her."

Acclaim for Priscilla's beauty never wavered, even during her walk on the wild side that year. The Del Valle Junior High newspaper popularity poll voted her Most Beautiful, Prettiest Eyes, Best Dressed, Best All-Around, Prettiest Hair, and Class Couple (with Chuck Burns). Diane Edenbo, one of Priscilla's closer friends in eighth grade, claimed that strangers in downtown Austin would stop her on the street and ask if she was Priscilla Beaulieu. "I often wondered," pondered Mary Ann, "what it was like to be her parents and how they handled that, you know?"

The second great blow of Priscilla's adolescence came late that spring, when

Paul Beaulieu informed the family that he was being transferred to the U.S. Air Force base in Wiesbaden, Germany. "I was devastated," Priscilla recalled. The Beaulieus had lived in Austin for four years, a lifetime to a military brat; moving overseas seemed like the end of Priscilla's life.

She turned fourteen the day after graduating from junior high on May 23, 1959—a bittersweet experience for Priscilla, as she reluctantly prepared to move to Germany. At the same time, she later confided, "I felt this incredible *pull* to go there. Even though I wanted to stay, this *force* was pulling me to go. It's unexplainable. Sometimes when I talk about it, I can still feel the *pull* of wanting to go—but yet I was leaving all my friends and *didn't* want to go."

Fate was intervening once again, setting Priscilla Beaulieu's and Elvis Presley's lives on an unexpected course. Seven months before Captain Beaulieu received his orders to report to Wiesbaden, Private Presley was shipped to Friedberg, then Bad Nauheim, Germany, just an hour's drive from the air force base where Priscilla's father would soon be stationed.

Priscilla and her friend Evangeline, an Elvis fanatic, looked up the two cities on a map of Germany that May, calculating the distance between them. "My dad kidded her," recounted Diane Edenbo, "and said he didn't want her to go over there and meet Elvis!" Priscilla, she recalled, laughed.

"I think she was excited," said Evangeline, "but I don't think she ever dreamed she was going to meet him."

"We all kidded her that she was going to Germany and she was going to meet Elvis Presley," confirmed Charlie Clements, Priscilla's across-the-street chum. Chuck Burns, who was holding hands with Priscilla during Saturday matinees that fall, dismissed it all as "girl talk," just as Pam did not take seriously their childhood games of Imagine If. They had seriously underestimated Priscilla Ann Beaulieu.

Diane Edenbo gave Priscilla a farewell party in June. No one knew then that it would be Priscilla's farewell, at fourteen, to childhood. The Beaulieus, minus Paul, who had been sent to Nevada for a three-week survival course, flew to Connecticut to say good-bye to the Iversens and the Beaulieus. Priscilla palled around with her fifteen-year-old cousin Margaret Ann. The two girls went to dances at Ocean Beach Park and talked about rock and roll. Before the Beaulieus left for Wiesbaden in August, Priscilla told her cousin that she wanted to meet Elvis.

Priscilla had a goal that summer of 1959: to meet Elvis Presley in Germany. And once Priscilla Beaulieu had set a goal, nothing would stand in her way.

II

PRISCILLA MEETS ELVIS: LEGEND OR LIES?

8
THE MYTH UNRAVELS

When Priscilla arrived in Germany in the middle of August, she was "a lost kid, missing my friends." The Beaulieus temporarily checked into the Helene, a hotel in downtown Wiesbaden, far from the base, to await military housing. School had not begun yet, so Priscilla knew no one.

"I don't think she was real happy in Germany at first," recalled Christine Laws, who read Priscilla's letters to her friends back in Austin. Wiesbaden was a literal and figurative ocean away from Priscilla Beaulieu's glamour days at Del Valle. "She had to start all over again," as Christine put it. Ann Beaulieu had given birth to her fourth child, Jeff, a few months before the family left Texas, giving Priscilla three younger siblings under the age of ten to baby-sit. She was a teenager who was physically isolated from her peers and alone in a foreign country, except for her ever-present and demanding family.

Fate, however, had not forgotten Priscilla. The Helene Hotel was a ten-minute walk from the Eagle Club, a community center for American military personnel in Wiesbaden. The club had been converted from a majestic pre–World War II mansion built by a wealthy brewer for his daughter and modeled after the White House. It offered a travel service, a restaurant, a library, a record room, and, on Saturday nights, a live variety show called *Hit Parade*, featuring entertainment acts from around Europe. Priscilla quickly discovered the Eagle Club, and, as was the custom of her fourteen years, she did not go unnoticed.

One late summer afternoon—possibly her first at the club, though like so much Priscilla and Elvis lore, that is not certain—Priscilla strode through the castlelike entrance on Paulinenstrasse, perhaps with her younger brother Donny. The precise time—5:30 P.M.—was noted and engraved upon the brain of the attractive twenty-something man who spotted her, just as he would recall in minute detail each of his subsequent encounters with Priscilla Beaulieu. His name was Currie Grant and he was a Louisiana-born-and-bred airman first class who moonlighted evenings and weekends as assistant manager of the

Eagle Club. He was also something of a local celebrity as the host of the *Hit Parade* on Saturday nights, when up to a thousand people jammed into the auditorium adjacent to the Eagle Club. Although he was married with two small girls, Currie Grant was a notorious ladies' man, the self-described "club Casanova." On this late summer afternoon, his radar zeroed in on Priscilla Beaulieu.

"I was sitting in the foyer talking to Peggy Dotson, the director of the club. You had to walk up about six steps when you came in from the front door. And as she was walking up these steps, I looked up from talking to Peggy—and I saw Priscilla." Her Dresden-doll face and daintiness drew Currie like a magnet. Being a meticulous dresser, he was also impressed by Priscilla's immaculate grooming. She was wearing a cinched-waist 1950s-style dress with a full skirt that billowed over several petticoats, and her long dark hair was styled in sophisticated tendrils. "She was one of the most beautiful things that I had ever seen. She carried herself like a princess. She looked like a charming little princess, and that's the God's truth."

Priscilla Beaulieu could not have captured the attention of a more fortuitous person in Wiesbaden, for Currie Grant was a friend and occasional guest at the Bad Nauheim residence of Elvis Presley. In a way, *this* was the serendipitous encounter of her adolescence.

"Peggy was in mid-sentence. I jumped up and left her sitting there and went straight to Priscilla, threw out my hand, and said, 'Hi, my name is Currie Grant and I'm the manager of the club. Is there anything I can do for you?' " Priscilla, according to Currie, was reticent. In hot pursuit, he began questioning her, learning her name, that her family had just moved from Texas, and that she was waiting to meet her parents. After ten minutes of strained dialogue, mostly one-sided, Currie invited Priscilla to attend the *Hit Parade,* told her he was around most evenings if she needed anything, and rejoined his boss.

"When she walked away, down the hallway to the snack bar, I kind of watched her, and grown men—two of them—stopped and watched as she went past. That tells you a million things right there. They couldn't keep their eyes off her, her face was that beautiful. From then on, I felt the same way."

In reality, Currie Grant fell for Priscilla before Elvis Presley did. That was not surprising, for both men had the same taste in women—petite, extremely young brunettes. Their high sex drives were also similar. They even shared the same birthday, January 8—though Currie, at twenty-eight, was three years older than Elvis.

Currie Grant was not just attracted to Priscilla Beaulieu; he was *mesmerized* by her.

Over the next week or so, Priscilla visited the Eagle Club several more times. Currie tried to strike up a further conversation, eager to talk to her alone, but "every time I tried to stop her, she gave me a really sweet little smile, either looked down or looked forward, and just kept on walking. And I let it go at that. I didn't want to make a pest of myself with anybody. I wasn't demanding." But the playboy in Currie burned with the challenge, and his ego was bruised. He was entranced by Priscilla Beaulieu, and her cool, ice-princess mien aroused him further. "I was interested in her, period. Whatever it was for." Currie was not certain of her age, which added to Priscilla's sexual mystique. "She looked very young," he recalled, "but dressed like an older girl."

Priscilla started the ninth grade, her first year of high school, within days of meeting Currie Grant. Her arrival at H. H. Arnold, an American military high school adjacent to the base, caused a minor frisson. "Oh, darling!" recalled Mary Ann Barks, a classmate. "Everybody had been talking about 'Oh, God, you gotta see the new girl!' These military kids come and go, and over the summer there's always a buzz about who the new kids are. So it was like 'Who is this kid that everybody is talking about?' "

Priscilla had created a new look for herself upon arriving in Germany. She began wearing her hair in an unusual style: short and curly about the face and long in the back, with tendrils she would sometimes bring to one side or in a ponytail. Debbie Ross, a classmate who became friendly with her a few months later, got a firsthand glimpse into the styling ritual. "She used to pull it up. She had long hair, maybe halfway down her back, and then had the front cut short and curly, and she used to take it and pull it up on her head so it all became part of the same curl." To Debbie, at fourteen, the style seemed "very sophisticated."

To anyone who had seen *Love Me Tender,* the look was familiar: It was a replica of Debra Paget's hairstyle in the movie, the look that Elvis Presley fell in love with. Ann Beaulieu, who had seen *Love Me Tender* at the Majestic in Austin, used to help with Priscilla's hair and makeup in Wiesbaden, Debbie recalled.

The unique hairstyle, and Priscilla, captured the imaginations of the other teenage girls at H. H. Arnold. "Well, she was just exotic," Mary Ann Barks explained. The principal fascination, at first, was the hair. Priscilla's beauty habits even caught the eye of the faculty. Paul Büngener, one of the native German instructors, still remembered her makeup thirty-five years later. "She had special lipstick on: a bit of dark red, and with a purple touch!"

At H. H. Arnold, Priscilla quickly fell into the pattern of her troubled eighth-grade year at Del Valle, making poor grades and attaching herself to older guys. Linda Williams, Priscilla's friend from Austin, moved to Wiesbaden that same year and immediately tried out for the cheerleading squad, but Priscilla gravitated toward the black-leather-jacket clique, most of whom were members of the Teen Auto Club. She had no close friends and did not seek to rekindle her acquaintance with Linda. Part of the problem was physical isolation. No base housing was available to the Beaulieus that first year; after a month or so at the Helene Hotel, just as school was starting, they moved into a vintage apartment building in downtown Wiesbaden.

Priscilla's estrangement was more emotional than physical. She was oppressed by the burden of carrying the family secret. "As you get older," she said later, "all of a sudden you forget that you have to answer questions. Every day. And that's what happened." She wore the locket concealing her real father's picture less and less often, feeling she was betraying Paul Beaulieu. Priscilla was a confused teenager, riddled with guilt and overburdened with adult responsibilities. She was ripe for an escape, ready for her fantasy of Elvis.

As if on cue, Currie Grant emerged as the deus ex machina in her quest to meet her idol. How that happened is the source of a bitter dispute between Currie and Priscilla.

Contrary to the Elvis-and-Priscilla legend, Currie claims that Priscilla approached *him*, seeking entrée to Elvis Presley, after walking past him at the Eagle Club three or four times. His recollection of the day is vivid: "I got to the Eagle Club about five o'clock . . . and I was hungry. I went in the snack bar, got a hamburger, and went way back to the last table in the farthest corner so no one would bother me. I'd no more than taken a bite of that hamburger when I saw the swinging glass doors open and there's Priscilla. She looks around a minute, sees me sitting in the corner, and starts walking straight for me. She came directly to the table and stood there and said, 'Hi.' And I said, 'Hello.' First words out of her mouth: 'I understand you know Elvis.' At that split second, it was such a letdown—my ego just went straight to the floor. She's coming over only because she's found out that I go up and see Elvis all the time. And I said, 'I sure do.' She says, 'Well, I sure would like to meet him.' Her exact words. My exact words were, 'Well, so would a lot of other girls, but sit down and we'll talk about it.' "

Priscilla's version, as set forth in her 1985 autobiography, is that a stranger, Currie Grant, came up to her and her little brother Donny at the Eagle Club when she first arrived in Germany, introduced himself, told her he was a friend of Elvis Presley's, and invited her to accompany him and his wife to Elvis's house. This is the account that has been repeated as gospel in hundreds of Elvis biographies, documentaries, and movies, the Cinderella story of a young, innocent girl tapped by fate to meet Elvis Presley. But is it true, or is it a romantic fairy tale concocted by Priscilla?

Priscilla has her parents to support her version, and Currie has his former wife, Carol, to support his, but they were not present. The only other witness, according to Priscilla, was her brother Don, and he was a child.

Ever since he met Priscilla Beaulieu, Currie Grant has offered the same account of how she approached him and asked to meet Elvis. When she married Elvis Presley in 1967, Currie began to compile materials for a biography to be called *Elvis and Priscilla*, but the project was delayed several times and later put aside. When Priscilla published her own memoir in 1985 stating that Currie invited *her* to meet Elvis, "I really didn't pay that much attention to it," Currie stated, "because I had my own book coming out, and I'd think, 'Well, that's her story. I'll tell mine when my book comes out'—and mine was going to be the *truth*." Currie's reaction was similar to Pam Rutherford's when she read Priscilla's autobiography and saw that Priscilla had reversed the story about the carnival queen contest, claiming it was Pam's grandparents, not her own, who reportedly sent in money to fix the contest. "But people now are taking it for the Bible," Currie said of Priscilla's version of how she met Elvis. "And they are quoting lies. They don't bother to dig into things. They just pick up the book and think this is the way it happened, the way she's telling it, because she has a big name now."

On closer examination, Priscilla's rendition of how she met Elvis is seriously flawed. While Currie has related the same account for nearly forty years, Priscilla's story is inconsistent from telling to telling. Recently, in October of 1995, she claimed that Currie introduced himself to her and her brother as "Johnny Appleseed," which conflicts with her own book, where she said he introduced himself as Currie Grant. At times she contradicts herself *in the same conversation.* In her October 1995 version, she repeated her contention that Currie Grant was a stranger when he approached her with the invitation to meet Elvis Presley: "I never even knew this man. I never knew Currie Grant. . . . I never knew him, never saw him before." Then she contradicted herself, saying she "actually saw him a couple of times staring at me."

There is a witness who corroborates Currie's version. Peggy Dotson, the manager of the Eagle Club, with whom Currie claimed to be in conversation when Priscilla walked in, remembered the encounter exactly as Currie related it: "We were both there in that round lobby, and she came in and I said, 'Gosh, that sure is a pretty girl.' And Currie said, 'I'm gonna go check that out!,' being the young-man-about-town that he was. So he went over there, and she sat in one of those little chairs in the lobby. And he went over and talked to her . . . and then about an hour later we saw each other again, and Currie told me that she had just moved here and her father was a captain, I believe."

Peggy Dotson's confirmation of this exchange proves that Currie did not approach Priscilla as a stranger and invite her to meet Elvis the first time he spoke to her. Peggy Dotson's memory also verifies that Priscilla *had* to have known who Currie was when they had their eventual conversation about

Elvis—*whoever* instigated it—since she had met him in the foyer and talked to him.

After thirty years' estrangement, Currie Grant and Priscilla Presley agreed to meet in my home in May of 1996 to discuss their conflicting accounts of how she met Elvis Presley. Priscilla offered the "Johnny Appleseed" version of Currie's invitation to meet Elvis the first time he approached her at the Eagle Club. Currie repeated his usual, unwavering story: that he spotted Priscilla in the foyer and chatted, that he tried to engage her in conversation several times afterward, and that she later approached him in the snack bar asking to meet Elvis. Then the two bickered back and forth:

PRISCILLA: But you asked *me*. You asked me, "Would you like to meet Elvis?"
CURRIE: Well, that's the contention. That's the contention here.
PRISCILLA: You said, "Would you like to meet Elvis? I go to his house for parties."
CURRIE: Priscilla, I'm not going to argue about it. I *know* what happened. And I'm sure you think *you* know what happened, okay? We're at a standstill here. It *didn't* happen that way. In my opinion.
PRISCILLA: Okay. That's your opinion.

The exchange later grew more heated:

CURRIE: I'm going to tell you my version of it, which is the only true version that I know of. I've lived with it all these years, Priscilla.
PRISCILLA: So have I. I remember it very distinctly.
CURRIE: I've lived with it all these years, Priscilla. I think you've been reading your own publicity too much.
PRISCILLA: There hasn't been a— What do you mean, my own publicity?
CURRIE: Well, because that's what you put in your book.
PRISCILLA: That's how it— That's what *happened*, Currie.
CURRIE: That's *not* what happened. Had I known that my book wasn't going to come out for this long a period of time— I didn't care what you put in your book, because that's *your* story. I had *my* story, which is the true version. . . . Anyway, it's nothing to get upset about. It's just that your version and my version do not match. And they haven't matched for years. So that's *okay*.

As the debate continued, Priscilla modified several key details of her story. She admitted that she had "seen Currie around" the Eagle Club before he invited her to meet Elvis and that "he was known there, he worked there." She also admitted that she "vaguely recalled" Currie interrupting a conversation with

Peggy Dotson to introduce himself. *And* she changed her sequence as to when Currie invited her to meet Elvis, suddenly declaring that now she was "not saying" it happened the first time he spoke to her.

By her own admission in May of 1996, Priscilla's fairy-tale account of a complete stranger walking up to her to ask if she would like to meet Elvis Presley was untrue.

Since Priscilla admittedly knew, or knew of, Currie before they discussed meeting Elvis, it was conceivable she had learned that he was a friend of Elvis Presley's, thus she *could* have asked Currie to introduce her to Elvis. She also acknowledged, as she and Currie argued back and forth, that she "saw him rehearsing" for the *Hit Parade* and might have been to a show before he allegedly invited her to meet Elvis—indicating that she knew more about Currie than she had previously let on. Moreover, she confirmed that Currie was "looking at me and watching me for the few weeks that I was there" *before* the two of them discussed meeting Elvis—which was consistent with Currie's account of trying to say hello to Priscilla at the club three or so times after their initial encounter.

Since she had already revised so many points in her earlier accounts to conform with Currie's version, accepting Priscilla's word about the *key* element—who asked whom to meet Elvis—becomes problematic.

During her May 1996 confrontation with Currie, Priscilla offered yet *another* version of how he invited her to meet Elvis, which conflicted both with her book and with her subsequent "Johnny Appleseed" variation. This time she suggested that she and Currie were talking at the club and that Currie introduced her to a young Elvis impersonator named Peter Von Wechmar, whom he represented. "And that's how it all came about that Currie knew Elvis," she declared. "And he came to me and said, 'I know him. Would you like to meet him? My wife and I go there.' And I remember that *very* vividly."

She also challenged Currie's scenario by arguing that it was "*so* unlike" her, "*so* unlike" what she would do, to boldly walk up to someone, say she understood he knew Elvis, and state that she would like to meet him:

PRISCILLA: So if I'm this shy girl that you say I was, how would I ever get the guts to come to you and say— I don't even do that *today*, Currie. That's not even my *nature*.

CURRIE: You came in that snack bar like a rocket.

PRISCILLA: Never.

CURRIE: Came straight to that table, man.

PRISCILLA: People who know me know that's not the way I *am*.

CURRIE: Well, you were fourteen years old, Priscilla.

PRISCILLA: But I was so shy at fourteen, Currie, I mean—

CURRIE: You were shy when I met you—yes, that's absolutely true.
PRISCILLA: That's *so* unlike *anything*— It's so *uncharacteristic* of me.

Was it? It was virtually the same modus operandi Priscilla had employed at age eleven when she strode up to a startled Drue Foradory, told him he looked like Elvis, and asked him on a date. This dual aspect of Priscilla's personality, the good (shy and demure) Priscilla versus the naughty (brazen and sexual) Priscilla, would be recognizable to her classmates in Germany as well. The girls who didn't know her well at H. H. Arnold regarded Priscilla as "quiet and shy," but her closer male friends remembered a "ballsy" girl. In the words of one boy who recalled a history exam their sophomore year: "Priscilla got up, walked up the aisle, opened a finished test that was on somebody's desk, looked at the answers, turned around, walked back, and wrote on her own paper—and the teacher watched her and never said a word to her." Priscilla's male friends in Texas—Drue, Henry, and Mike—remembered her as aggressive when she had a goal. "When she wanted something, she went after it," to quote one boy. As an adult, Priscilla often referred to this same quality in herself. "When I get involved in something," she said when launching a new perfume in the fall of 1996, "I go crazy with it—all out." In the summer of 1959 she was going "all out" to meet Elvis Presley, and asking Currie to arrange an introduction was consistent with this "other" Priscilla.

Priscilla's second defense in her face-to-face encounter with Currie that day was that she wasn't even a *fan* of Elvis Presley's when she met Currie, therefore she would not have requested to meet him:

CURRIE: You're talking about Elvis Presley, the most famous entertainer in the world.
PRISCILLA: But I wasn't—but *I* wasn't— Wait a second, Currie. But I wasn't that— Currie, *Elvis Presley* wasn't the *item* for me! That wasn't, he wasn't, I wasn't—
CURRIE: That's not what you told *me*. "I have all his records, I've seen all his movies"—that's what you told me, sitting at that table.
PRISCILLA: Well, I may have said, in conversation, "Do you know him?" or "Do you like him?" I *may* have said, "I've seen his movies." I may very *well* have said that. I did *not* have all his records. My father got me *one* record. One album.

Priscilla had not counted on the memories of her Austin acquaintances, the ghosts from her past: Drue Foradory, the Presley look-alike she pursued because she told him she was "nuts" about Elvis; her neighbor in Del Valle, who heard her playing Elvis Presley records nonstop from the fifth grade on; girlfriends for whom she bought Elvis records as birthday gifts. And, most importantly, her onetime best friend, Pam Rutherford, with whom she played Imagine If for two solid years, pretending she was dating, honeymooning with, or married to Elvis Presley.

Priscilla was caught in a web of untruths and kept entangling herself further, insisting, during the confrontation with Currie, that she "didn't even know where Elvis *was*" in Germany, she "didn't even know the area," though *in her own book* she wrote that she had looked up Bad Nauheim and Wiesbaden on the map to calculate the distance between Elvis's house and her father's base. She insisted, to refute Currie, "It wasn't a big drive for me to meet—I mean, to hope to meet him. I wasn't *infatuated* with meeting Elvis Presley, you know?"

Priscilla had obviously forgotten—if she ever knew—that her cousin Margaret Ann Iversen had given a brief but telling interview to the New London, Connecticut, newspaper in March of 1960, shortly after the news broke that a young American girl named Priscilla Beaulieu was dating Elvis Presley in Germany. Margaret Ann recounted for the *New London Day* her cousin Priscilla's two-week stopover in Connecticut the previous summer and how, as she was leaving for Germany, Priscilla had said to her that she "would like to meet Elvis."

But there was more. Priscilla's final defense was that she *couldn't* have asked Currie for an introduction to Elvis Presley because she "didn't even know he knew Elvis." Currie was not certain how Priscilla discovered that he and Elvis were friends; it was common knowledge at the Eagle Club and he assumed she either picked it up there or heard it from one of her friends. Priscilla hotly disputed this, exclaiming, "I didn't *have* any girlfriends then! I didn't have any school girlfriends."

A half-American classmate of Priscilla's from Wiesbaden, Vera Von Cronthall, the adopted daughter of a German baron, remembered seeing Priscilla around the Eagle Club that late summer and early fall. Vera's best friend was a stunning German girl of fifteen named Stephie McCann, who lived next door to the Eagle Club and was friendly with Currie Grant. Stephie and Priscilla, Vera recalled, knew each other slightly from the Eagle Club and, later, at school. According to Vera, Priscilla was standing in line behind her and Stephie in the Eagle Club snack bar one day and mentioned to Stephie that she would like to meet Elvis Presley. "She asked to see Elvis. I remember that. My friend Stephie knew Currie, and Priscilla knew that was the way to meet Elvis . . . she was interested. She knew that Currie knew Elvis, and she was trying to get in there." Stephie McCann, years later, would not recall the specific conversation, but considered it "very possible that something like that was said because . . . we all knew each other. We hung around at the Eagle Club." And Priscilla knew that Stephie was a friend of Currie's and that Currie knew

Elvis. Vera, Stephie maintained, would "certainly not" have any reason to fabricate.

"I remember Stephie complaining about Priscilla," Vera insisted. " 'Oh, she's always bugging me, I guess I'll let her know. I'll get her to meet Elvis and get her off my back.' Just something like that."

It is not impossible to imagine that Currie Grant might have dangled an invitation to meet Elvis as a lure to Priscilla, since she had not responded to his attempts to talk to her alone. His story, however, stands up to scrutiny; Priscilla's does not. Priscilla and Currie clearly met and got acquainted in the foyer of the Eagle Club with no mention of Elvis Presley, just as Currie maintained. His boss, Peggy Dotson, confirmed this, and Priscilla eventually admitted it. He eyed her over the next few weeks while she ignored him—another element of Currie's account that Priscilla affirmed—and there is every reason to believe that Priscilla then approached *Currie* in the snack bar of the Eagle Club, hoping for an introduction to Elvis. She desperately wanted to meet Elvis Presley, despite her later protestations, and Vera Von Cronthall provided the missing link by confirming that Priscilla knew that Currie was a friend of Elvis's.

Why was Priscilla so desperate to establish such a seemingly trivial point—who asked whom to meet Elvis? And why would she deny that she was an Elvis fan who was determined to meet him? Those were the real questions. The explanation would not become clear until later in the unfolding Priscilla-Currie-Elvis triangle.

It involved more secrets harbored by the girl who was reared on hidden truths.

9

A FAUSTIAN BARGAIN

Currie Grant was toying with Priscilla Beaulieu, not certain whether he would bring her to meet Elvis Presley.

Her approach in the snack bar was the opening he had been hoping for. "In my mind I said, Now I've got her," he recalled, like a spider assessing a fly. "I thought, She wants something. She wants me to do a favor for her—but now I've got her. 'Cause she's coming to *me*."

Priscilla Beaulieu and Currie Grant had mutually compatible goals. Currie was Priscilla's ticket to Elvis, and Priscilla was Currie's passport to bliss. Currie studied his prey, making small talk and asking Priscilla a few "critical" questions, including her age. "When she said fourteen, I almost fell off my chair!" he remembered.

"I look older, don't I?" he recalled Priscilla responding, nonchalantly. Her tender age, however, did not deter either of them.

Currie began stringing Priscilla along, saying he *might* be able to take her to Elvis's house, making arrangements to meet her at the club several more times to talk about it. "If I said, 'Meet me at five o'clock,' she would be there at fifteen to five waiting for me." This went on, Currie estimated, for roughly a week.

Currie was playing a cat-and-mouse game with Priscilla. A few months earlier, he had brought a young girl with whom he was having an affair to Elvis's house. When they got to Bad Nauheim, Elvis took a fancy to Currie's date and took her to his bedroom. By the time she left, she had lost all interest in Currie. "Once she had been with him, you can forget about doing anything," he recalled. "She sat on the far side of the seat, almost glued to the right door." The experience burned into Currie's skin like a branding iron. If he hoped to get anywhere with Priscilla, he figured, it would have to occur before she met Elvis, *if* he took her to the house. When Priscilla informed him late in the week that she had already told her mother about the proposed visit, Currie was annoyed, but he softened when he saw the "sad look" in Priscilla's eyes.

Currie called Ann Beaulieu shortly thereafter. Priscilla's mother was delighted and suggested that Currie and his wife, Carol, stop by for coffee and dessert. Carol Grant, a petite dark-haired British beauty who sang occasionally at the Eagle Club, had heard from her husband about Priscilla Beaulieu and her obsession to meet Elvis, and she accompanied Currie to the Beaulieus'.

Contrary to legend, neither Ann nor Paul Beaulieu exhibited the slightest hesitation about sending their not-quite-ninth-grade daughter to meet Elvis Presley, according to both Carol and Currie Grant. "The father didn't say much," recalled Currie of that evening. "The mother wanted it real bad—because Priscilla wanted it real bad."

This, reduced to its essence, was the single element of the Elvis-and-Priscilla myth that mystified even Elvis's legion of fans: *Why* would the parents of a fourteen-year-old girl allow their daughter to meet a twenty-four-year-old sex symbol at his home? Priscilla later created the fiction, perpetuated in nearly all Elvis folklore, that her father and mother were extremely strict and opposed the meeting with Elvis—perhaps partly because she was embarrassed (what kind of parents *would* consent?) and partly because her parents' enthusiasm about the meeting and their consent were not consistent with the proper image she would present once her association with Elvis made her famous.

In reality, Ann Beaulieu was an accessory before the fact in her daughter's girlish quest to meet Elvis Presley. The reasons for this were psychologically complex. Priscilla was the center of Ann's universe, her love child, her remembrance of Jimmy. Ann permitted Priscilla to do things she would not have considered for her other children. Her daughter's infatuation with Elvis, moreover, must have struck an emotional chord in Ann. How could she not be reminded of herself at just past fourteen—sneaking out of the house to date a handsome, dark-haired older man in uniform? Ann would not deprive her daughter of the joy her own parents had denied her. "She had a lot of compassion for me," Priscilla said of her mother's attitude toward Elvis. "She understood."

Ann was also starstruck, for she had been drawn to Elvis Presley since the family's Del Valle days. During the Grants' get-acquainted conversation with the Beaulieus, "it was not a question of *if* Ann would let Priscilla go," recalled Currie, "it was rather a question of when I would take her."

Currie left the house without setting a date for the big night. He wished to perpetuate his amorous game with Priscilla Beaulieu awhile longer, capitalizing on his connection to the King. Priscilla had become for him the consummate challenge. He was a driven man who had to get past her look-but-don't-touch demureness. Currie Grant wanted, desperately, to *conquer* Priscilla Beaulieu.

During their next conversation at the club, he set the trap: "I told her we'd have to be alone." Priscilla at first demurred, Currie recalled. She told him her parents knew he was married. "Well, somehow we've got to be alone," he insisted. "I can't stand it." Priscilla then came up with a plan, according to Currie: Currie could ask her parents' permission to take her to a movie with him and Carol; then he could tell his wife he had to work late, pick Priscilla up alone, and tell her mother and father they would collect Carol on their way to the theater. "That was her idea, not mine," Currie said. "I thought, Man, that was pretty provocative. And if I get caught they will put me *under* the prison!"

Priscilla's and Currie's motives became clear the first night they were alone. "After we got in the hills, I tried to kiss her, tried to talk about things," he recalled. "All she wanted to do was talk about Elvis. Finally I just reached over and kissed her. She didn't really resist, but she didn't really want to do it. It was like kissing a table. I wasn't used to people being that way, stiff, and I let it go." Priscilla persisted in her questions about Elvis. "The girl would not give up. There was nothing I could do but talk to her about Elvis." Currie persisted in trying to kiss Priscilla "until she finally got used to it. After about half an hour there was nothing to it. We would talk in between."

As the evening progressed, he counseled her as to how to behave if he did decide to take her to meet Elvis. "I'd seen him meet about fifteen girls up to that point, and I saw him get turned off on three or four of those girls. If you started talking too much, asking too many questions, it bothered him. I advised her not to talk too much, to be very quiet and demure: 'Don't tell him how much you like his records, his movies. Just be quiet and let him ask the questions. You answer the questions. You'll get along with him a lot better.' "

That first evening ended on a note of frustration for both. "I was a little disappointed," declared Currie. "She probably saw this, because at the end I wouldn't even touch her. I knew she was too stiff and embarrassed and shy, and I didn't want to make a fool out of either one of us, so I just let it go—but she was ready to go out the next time."

Currie did not mention Priscilla to Elvis during those first days and weeks, when he was setting the stage for his own seduction. He *was* aware that the rock-and-roll star was attracted to younger women. Earlier that year Elvis had become involved with a sixteen-year-old Brigitte Bardot look-alike from Frankfurt named Margit Bürgin, and he began dating a young German girl named Heli Priemel in August. Margit Bürgin had aborted Elvis's child a few months before, unknown to Elvis—an experience that nearly traumatized Bürgin, who was a virgin when they met. Although Elvis was interested in younger women, Currie was not certain he would like Priscilla, "because she wasn't passionate, and I wasn't sure that E.P. would go for someone like that." He also had misgivings because of her age; sixteen was one thing, fourteen was quite another. And he still had designs on Priscilla himself.

In her desperate mission to meet Elvis Presley, Priscilla had fallen deeper into Currie Grant's web, a dangerous spot for any fourteen-year-old girl. By his own admission, Currie was taking advantage of his connection to Elvis, using himself as bait for Priscilla to fulfill her fantasy of meeting the rock star. "Oh, absolutely," Currie confessed. "I don't deny that at all. All the guys around Elvis would say the same thing. They get the leftovers that Elvis can't get to or doesn't want. I've done it many times myself. I'm not bragging. I'm just telling you what the facts are." He felt guilty "fooling" the Beaulieus, Currie later admitted. "I felt really bad, but I wanted Priscilla—to be with her—more."

Currie and Priscilla parked in the hills a second time, using the same movie subterfuge, sometime that late summer or early fall. These rendezvous were their secret, and secrecy was a concept with which Priscilla was intimate. In Currie's words, "I told her several times, 'Whatever we say or do, it always stays between you and me.' And she agreed."

Priscilla, according to Currie, would have done anything to meet Elvis Presley. By their fourth encounter in the hills, she had given herself sexually to Currie. "It actually started getting better on the third," he remembered, "but she did everything humanly possible to please me on that fourth time." It was then that Currie Grant made his decision to bring Priscilla Beaulieu to meet Elvis Presley: "I felt sorry for her, because she had tried so hard to please me, had done everything that we needed to do." By the end of their lovemaking, Currie told Priscilla he would take her to Elvis's house—"and she became a little aggressive herself."

As they were driving back to the Beaulieus', Currie became aroused again and pulled the car to a dark spot near the Wiesbaden Museum. "We just got into it, and this German police car with a big 'Polizei' on the side—a green Volkswagen, I'll never forget it—caught us a block from her house. It scared the living hell out of me! The windows were all steamed up, her blouse was loosened, and her skirt was up. I was getting ready to do it again, and we got caught before we got into the act itself. I thought they'd put me in prison. She was a minor, I was in the air force, her father was in the air force. But the German policeman was such a nice guy. . . . If it had been the American police I might have been dead. The cop said, 'You'd better be careful, and take her on home when you get ready.' "

Not only was Priscilla Beaulieu not a virgin on her wedding night, as she would later claim, but she was not a virgin when she *met* Elvis Presley, according to Currie Grant. She had entered into a Faustian pact to meet Elvis, and sex with Currie—the loss of her virginity—was the price he exacted.

According to Currie, Priscilla did not bleed during penetration, raising the question of whether she had already "gone all the way," perhaps with one of the faster older boys she associated with when she was in eighth grade. Currie doubted it, since she seemed so "green," but it might explain her willingness to have intercourse to further the Elvis dream, since she wouldn't have been a virgin anyway.

Priscilla vehemently denied Currie's account in May of 1996: "May God strike me dead if that ever happened to me. I am telling you on the life of my son and my daughter, that never happened. This man is a liar!" Priscilla maintained she did not go out with Currie even once on the guise of going to a movie.

Informed of Priscilla's denial, Currie stood his ground. "Her story was for her family and her good name. She wants to try to keep it clean. She knows about that, after being with Elvis all those years and through all the publicity people she's been around. She wants to control the things around her life. And Scientology. She can't do that with me. Did I have intercourse with Priscilla? Yes, I had intercourse with Priscilla. I had intercourse with Priscilla *more than once* that last night. But not after she started going with Elvis."

Priscilla and Currie fought over this point in their face-to-face encounter at my home on May 14, 1996:

CURRIE: You and I started going in the hills, once a week, together.
PRISCILLA: Oh, Currie. Currie, *please!*
CURRIE: No, I'm telling you. That's the way it *was.*
PRISCILLA: Currie, you *know* that's not true.
CURRIE: She's a great actress, isn't she?

. . .

PRISCILLA: You cannot look me in the eye and say we went somewhere in the hills.
CURRIE: I'm looking at you right in the *face.* We went somewhere. We not only went somewhere, honey, we made *love* somewhere, in the hills.
PRISCILLA: Oh, my God. Excuse me? Do you think for one minute I would make love to *you?*
CURRIE: You did it and you were glad to do it. Before I ever took you to meet Elvis, you did that.
PRISCILLA: You've got the wrong girl, Currie.
CURRIE: No, I've got the right girl. . . . I'm talking about this little girl, sitting right here. Right here. . . .
PRISCILLA: Don't give me this. You know darn well we never went up in the hills; you *never* made love to me, *ever.*
CURRIE: Four times [we went to the hills].
PRISCILLA: And now I'm sitting here and it's your word against *mine!*
CURRIE: The last one was the main one. That's the reason I took you to meet Elvis. Because we *did* make love.
PRISCILLA: Oh, my God. Oh, my God.

CURRIE: Think about it, Priscilla.
PRISCILLA: I don't *have* to think about it!
CURRIE: Think about what you're going to say to answer that one.
PRISCILLA: I don't have to think about it. It never happened!
CURRIE: It happened, honey.

No one but Priscilla and Currie could know what happened between them. Currie did not tell anyone he was trysting with Priscilla that summer (she *was* fourteen); just as predictably, Priscilla's parents denied that she left the house with Currie four times to see a movie. "Unfortunately, it's going to be her and her parents' word against mine, regarding the four times that I went to pick her up."

As before, with the who-asked-whom-to-meet-Elvis debate, there are gaps and inconsistencies in Priscilla's version. She generally claims that she was introduced to Elvis as soon as she got to Germany—"within two weeks," according to a 1996 interview. Yet more recently she said that Currie watched her for three weeks before he invited her to meet Elvis. In a third version, in her book, she recounted that Currie watched her for *several days,* invited her to meet Elvis, and then spent several weeks with her *parents* before the meeting occurred. All of these versions cannot be true, proving that Priscilla was either seriously confused or covering up the truth.

Perhaps Priscilla insisted that Currie took her to meet Elvis as soon as she got to Wiesbaden because she didn't want anyone to know she was fooling around with him for several weeks to persuade him to introduce her. According to two of her own versions of the story, there was unaccounted-for time. What were she and Currie doing during those undefined several weeks between their meeting and the introduction to Elvis?

There is, once again, convincing corroboration of Currie's account. Priscilla later discussed Currie Grant with Mike Edwards, her lover of seven years. She told Mike that she and Currie created a ruse for her parents of going to the movies, but instead drove into the Wiesbaden hills. "Currie met her, and he was kind of like pursuing her himself," Mike recalled Priscilla telling him. "And then that didn't go anywhere, and they had a little altercation in the backseat of his car, I think. And he said, 'Well, all right, I want to introduce you to somebody,' and that's what took her to Elvis."

By Priscilla's own account to Mike, she and Currie *did* sneak to the hills and engage in some kind of sexual activity, which led to an introduction to Elvis. The aspect that did not make sense to Mike was that Priscilla depicted herself as unwilling. "I'm a man and she's a woman," Mike said. "I know *her,* I know *me,* I know the *situation.* . . . I sensed—just circumstances—that it was, something wasn't—there was denial." Mike also thought that Priscilla did have intercourse with Currie. "*I* always believed it, and she always denied it. But the story that she laid out to me doesn't add up. Doesn't add up."

The other question begging to be asked is why Currie Grant would *lie* about having intercourse at twenty-seven with a minor of fourteen—an act that was against the law. As Mike Edwards noted, "I don't think he would *say* it—I don't think he would be so foolish as to say something like that—if it wasn't true."

In retrospect, Currie was not proud of his behavior. "I can't believe I risked my marriage and my career in the air force to fool around with a fourteen-year-old girl. It was crazy! My wife and my family were the most important things in the world to me. I was just in overdrive when it came to sex. I was crazy about it in those days; I craved it all the time. I was a sex addict. Anyway, that's the way it was."

10

"IMAGINE IF" . . . THE FANTASY COMES TRUE

The exact date of Priscilla Beaulieu's historic meeting with Elvis Presley is mired in mystery, mostly of her own making.

Since she obscured the sequence of events leading to the introduction, it is impossible to pinpoint the date by her accounts. In any event, she claimed not to know, or remember, the date on which she met Elvis Presley, a circumstance that seems odd in itself. What teenage girl would *not* record the day she met the most famous rock star in the world? Unless Priscilla did not *want* the date revealed—because it might refute her version of the story.

Priscilla asserted that she met Elvis a few weeks after she got to Germany, but sources other than Currie Grant claimed that the meeting was much later. "That's not what I recall," stated classmate Helen Delahunt, who remembered Priscilla dating a friend of Helen's brother before she met Elvis Presley. Another classmate, who lived down the street from Priscilla that fall, also remembered her dating a boy from school *before* she met Elvis. Since the first day of school was September 10, 1959, and Priscilla met Currie when the Beaulieus arrived in Germany in mid-August or so, she *had* to have been dallying with Currie for at least several weeks prior to the famous introduction.

Currie and Carol Grant placed the meeting sometime in September, probably on a Sunday, possibly the 13th; a few members of the entourage at Elvis's house in Bad Nauheim thought it might have been as late as October. These recollections fitted the surrounding circumstances.

Priscilla, true to her covert nature, did not tell a soul apart from her family that she was meeting Elvis Presley, the fantasy she had nurtured since she was ten years old. Then again, she had few friends to tell. Like Elvis, she was a loner, and lonely, in emotional exile in Germany; he, missing his mother who had just died, she mourning the father she had just discovered.

Carol and Currie Grant picked Priscilla up at the Beaulieu home around 7:00 P.M. The fourteen-year-old was chewing bubble gum, Carol remembered, and wearing an old-fashioned middy blouse and a wide skirt over a crinoline.

Currie's distinct recollection was that school had begun, for Paul Beaulieu made a point of mentioning that it was a school night. Like Cinderella, Priscilla had a twelve o'clock curfew. That was the only admonition given.

With that, the odd ménage à trois—Currie, Carol, and Priscilla—took off on the autobahn for the hour's drive from Wiesbaden to Bad Nauheim, where Private Presley had taken a house. Priscilla, Currie recalled, was delirious, "chattering like a little magpie: 'Do you think he'll like me? Does my hair look okay? Is my outfit all right?' Carol and I both told her she shouldn't talk like a little schoolgirl—he's not going to like it, and we'll be out of there in an hour. We both worked on her all the way up there."

When, around eight o'clock, they pulled up in front of 14 Goethestrasse, the ordinary-looking two-story German house Elvis was occupying, a miraculous transformation occurred. Priscilla stepped out of the car, removed her bubble gum, and became a different person. Carol Grant was mystified by her sudden composure. "My God, if it was James Dean and *I* was fourteen, I don't know how I would have handled it, but she was quite sure about it."

Priscilla was performing her first and most important acting role. She had successfully imitated the Debra Paget hairdo from *Love Me Tender* and taken direction from Currie; these she blended with learned behavior from her stage mother, Ann, and her own instinctive skill at manipulation. To a degree, Elvis Presley was set up for this legendary encounter, though no one dreamed anything serious would materialize.

"I was still a little leery of Elvis meeting her," Currie confessed. "And I didn't think anything would come of it. I thought maybe a one-shot meeting. He would say, 'Nice little kid, cute face,' and that would be it. Boy, was I wrong! *We* were wrong. My wife and I both thought nothing was going to come of it."

Priscilla and the Grants strode past the crowd of fans clustered outside the house and entered through the front door. A smaller than usual crowd was gathered inside: Elvis's grandmother; his father, Vernon; Elisabeth Stefaniak, his pretty blond German secretary and occasional girlfriend; another secretary, Vee Harris and her husband, Rod; Lamar Fike, Elvis's portly Memphis sidekick, who was a cutup; and an army buddy named Rex Mansfield. True to the *Rashomon* quality of this historic evening, two other people—Joe Esposito and Charlie Hodge, army mates of Elvis's—would claim to have been present, but Currie Grant swears unequivocally that they were nowhere around. "I just remember thinking, What am I gonna say?" Priscilla later remarked. "It was like a dream. What *does* one say to Elvis Presley? Or to a famous movie star?"

Currie introduced Priscilla to Rex in the hallway and walked toward the living room, where the object of all of Priscilla's childhood fantasies—Elvis

Presley himself—was sprawled in an armchair, dressed in a red sweater. Priscilla was partly hidden behind Currie, who took her by the hand and pulled her up next to him so his famous host could see his guest. Priscilla, true to her nature and upbringing, was preoccupied with her appearance, "wondering, Do I look okay?"

"Elvis, this is Priscilla—" Currie started to say, fulfilling his half of the Faustian bargain and releasing his moral obligation to the Beaulieus. In that split second, before Currie could even complete his introduction, the lives of Elvis Presley and Priscilla Beaulieu were forever changed and pop history was made. "If you could have seen his face!" Currie recollected. "He jumped out of that chair like he was sitting on a hot plate. I had *never* seen him react to any girl like that—and I'd seen him meet at least fifteen beautiful girls. He started bouncing off the walls!"

Priscilla's first impression was how "*extremely* good-looking" Elvis was, "I mean, he was even better looking than in *Love Me Tender.*" As she stood in the doorway to the living room, anxiously taking in the scene before her, Elvis got up and walked the few steps toward her. He smiled and shook her hand, his leg twitching, as it did when he was nervous. According to both Carol and Currie, who were standing right beside them, he stuttered, "H-hi! I-I-I-I'm Elvis Pretzel."

"He was kind of a joker, Elvis," Carol said.

"I don't know if he was doing it as a joke or it just slipped out like that," asserted Currie, who had heard Elvis stutter before when he was under stress or felt awkward. "He said 'Pretzel.' Then he grinned and said, 'What's your name?' He knew what her name was, but he got nervous. Carol and I looked at each other as he mumbled and stumbled there for about a minute, and said to each other, 'What in the hell is going on here?' " As one of Priscilla's schoolmates, Mary Ann Barks, would later say: "It was like this cosmic force. It was beyond everybody. A meteor lands and poof! I mean, the whole thing was just, like magical."

The moment would be remembered later by all who were present—and by some who were not—as they sought a clue, some hidden insight, into the profound impact of Priscilla's meeting with Elvis Presley. Priscilla's turn-of-the-century porcelain daintiness was powerfully erotic to Elvis Presley, an old-fashioned southern boy for whom innocence, purity, and beauty were the ultimate aphrodisiacs. Priscilla Beaulieu seemed to possess them all.

The deeper reason Elvis Presley was overcome when he first saw Priscilla would not surface for several months. "We were sitting around, about four of us, and we were talking about girls," recalled Currie. Currie told Elvis he had been wondering what possessed him the night he met Priscilla. "He gave me that funny one-sided grin," recalled Currie. "When you pulled her in here by the hand," Elvis responded, "what I saw was a young Debra Paget." *That* was the attraction so long searched for by biographers and other students of Elvis Presley. Priscilla's *Love Me Tender* hairstyle and eerie facial resemblance to Debra Paget triggered memories of Elvis's unrequited love for his former costar. "He was flipped over Debra," confirmed Joe Esposito. "From the stories I was told by him and some other people, he carried a torch for her all during the making of that movie and even after it. But it never happened." Perhaps, when he saw Priscilla Beaulieu, Debra's apparent reincarnation, Elvis felt he had been given a second chance.

He behaved that night as if a spell had been cast upon him, as in a way it had. Like the spoken words in "Are You Lonesome Tonight?"–his signature song–Elvis Presley loved Priscilla Beaulieu at first glance. What few people realize is that Priscilla did not have the same feelings for Elvis. She had yearned, in her teenage desperation, to meet her idol, but now that she was face-to-face with the man, she did not fall in love at first sight. "No," she acknowledged later. "No. There was definitely a *pull* there–the energy was very electric–but not in the sense that this is *it.*" What Priscilla did feel, upon meeting Elvis Presley, was that she had discovered, finally, the source of her strange premonition of destiny, the reason she had felt drawn to Germany. "You know," she reflected, when she was fifty, "I've gone through that night many many times. It was a setup that was meant to be. It was something that–again, that power, that drawing power–I felt that night."

Priscilla barely said a word as Elvis fell over himself trying to impress her; she was sweet, quiet, demure, and submissive, as directed. "She should get an Academy Award for what she did up there, because she was perfect," Currie said with admiration. Gone was the teenage-girl chattiness, worrying about whether her hair was right, if Elvis would think she was pretty. "She would talk only when he asked her questions–and very softly. Not 'I've got all your records, I've seen all your movies, I love you.' I said, 'Never ever say that to him,' and she learned from that first night how to be with him."

"I was very quiet," Priscilla agreed. "I was exceptionally quiet. I didn't say too much."

Priscilla's reserve weaved perfectly into Elvis's Debra Paget illusion, for Debra had barely spoken when they were together. Priscilla was a tabula rasa; because she uttered scarcely a word, Elvis could project whatever he wished upon her–and he did.

He chivalrously escorted her to a chair in the living room and went to the piano, frenziedly tinkling the keys as the others in the room looked on, bemused. Priscilla would later say that he sang "Rags to Riches" and "Are You Lonesome Tonight?" but others did not recall him singing–and Elvis had not yet heard or considered "Are You Lonesome Tonight?" The point on which they all agreed was that Elvis Presley was showing off like a schoolboy for Priscilla Beaulieu, who sat perfectly still, somewhere between a dream and a hallucination.

Elvis continued grandstanding, eventually lighting next to Priscilla. The other guests filtered into the kitchen, leaving them alone. The conversation was predictably mundane. Elvis asked her if she was in school, Priscilla said later, and when she told him she was starting the ninth grade, he grinned, exclaiming, "You're just a baby!"

Priscilla was not amused. "I didn't like that. He would tease me about that." Her self-possession, under the circumstances, was almost supernatural. "Well, I didn't know what to expect, first of all," Priscilla said later. "I didn't have a lot to talk about with them. I just remember being very nervous. It just was so out of my realm of being a teenager." Priscilla spent the evening, as she would much of her remaining adolescence and early adulthood, silently observing.

Elvis left Priscilla's side just long enough to bound into the kitchen, recalled Elisabeth Stefaniak, urging the rest of them to peek at her through the doorway. "She looks just like a beautiful little angel, doesn't she?" he exclaimed.

Less than ten minutes later, when Carol and Currie returned to the living room, "he had Priscilla backed up against the wall," recalled Currie, "kissing her." By eight-thirty or so, Elvis was taking her up the stairs to his bedroom. Priscilla would later claim, publicly, that she and Elvis were downstairs all evening, talking, but others who were in the house remember them disappearing to Elvis's upstairs room. Priscilla later admitted this to Mike Edwards. "He just took her by the hand, went up the stairs and said, 'We'll be down later,'" Currie recalled. "And she just went right with him. That's when I began to worry, because I know Elvis. There were many times when he'd taken girls up there. He's got no idea of timing. I had to get this girl back by midnight."

Thus Priscilla Beaulieu, who had just a few months earlier completed junior high in Del Valle, Texas, daydreaming of Elvis Presley, found herself in his bedroom in Germany their first evening together. The unlikelihood of this scenario captured perfectly the circumstances, for theirs was a match based entirely in unreality. He was literally her fantasy come true, the successor to Mario Lanza in Priscilla's childish fancy—*Elvis Presley!* Every teenage girl's paradise found. She was his dream girl, the perfect child-woman Elvis had created in his mind. He told Rex Mansfield the next day that he had "been looking for someone like that all of his life." Priscilla, he explained to Rex, had the physical look he was attracted to "and she was young enough [for him] to raise her up to suit himself." Mike Edwards characterized it as a "fantasy world, not a man and woman dying with love for each other."

On a deeper level, Elvis and Priscilla's union could only be construed as karmic. She represented the beloved mother he had just lost; he was the dead father she had just found—a beautiful, black-haired soldier who could remove her from reality, who would be her guardian angel and protector. Priscilla's resemblance to Debra Paget linked her with Elvis's mother in his mind, for as Joe Esposito would recall, Elvis considered Debra's face strongly similar to that of Gladys Presley. Of course, the person Priscilla Beaulieu really resembled was Elvis himself; they were mirror images of each other. This may have been the more mystical attraction, for Elvis still grieved over the death of his stillborn twin, Jesse Garon, and felt that he was missing his other half. He and his mother, recalled Gladys's best friend Willie Jane Nichols, would have "conversations" with Jesse in a special language; after Gladys Presley's death, Elvis became preoccupied with look-alikes. On a subconscious level, finding Priscilla may have symbolized a reunion with his dead twin.

There were clearly psychological and emotional undercurrents to the attraction within Elvis, for he felt instantly intimate with Priscilla in a manner that surprised even her. "He was very lonely over there," she said in the seventies. "And he wanted to talk to someone. And he *trusted* me. For some reason, he really trusted me. And he poured his heart out. I look back now and I go, 'My gosh. Yeah, I *was* so young. And I *was* only fourteen years old. How did that trust develop? I mean, how, *why* did he? But he did." Priscilla, at fourteen, was far more aware than Elvis of the surreal nature of their relationship—that she was a young girl, a stranger, sharing intimacies with a twenty-four-year-old international movie star. She was the practical one in the relationship, even then. Remembering that first night, she would recall in typical teenage-girl fashion only that "I just knew that we hit it off. He spent a lot of time with me, joking around." For Elvis, something deeper, more profound, was occurring. He spent much of their time in the bedroom talking to Priscilla, mostly about his career; and her natural inclination to shyness, the intimidating circumstances, and the advice she had gotten from Currie played into Elvis's needs beautifully, for Priscilla had been conditioned to listen, raptly, to his every word.

For all her poise and apparent maturity, the experience had to have been mind-bending for Priscilla Beaulieu. The previous October she had been the only eighth-grader to attend the high school homecoming dance, to which she was escorted by a sophomore who barely tried to kiss her. Apart from her secret dalliances with Currie and her liaisons with forbidden boys the year before, she had never been on an official car date. Now, at fourteen, she was being pursued by the most famous sex symbol in the world. Currie Grant would question her a few days later about what she and Elvis did that night up in his room. Elvis, Priscilla told Currie, was sweet and tender; they lay on the bed together while Elvis "kissed her very gently," then became more sexual.

"He just played with her. He was doing the hand thing: He was feeling her up, so to speak. He went under with his hand, very slowly, rubbing the skin, rubbing across her chest, stuff like that, and telling her to relax, that he wasn't going to hurt her, talking to her like she was a kid—which of course she was."

No one present at the house that night said a word about Priscilla Beaulieu being fourteen years old, either before or after Elvis disappeared with her into his bedroom. "It was not even discussed," Rex Mansfield confirmed. "Because she was there with her parents' approval." Such was the power of Elvis Presley. "It was just a whole different world," Rex said, "that world he was in." Conventional rules were not enforced, and no one questioned the propriety. "To me, to be honest, she looked like a little girl," Rex confessed years afterward. "A little young girl . . . I'm not even sure how I found out she was fourteen. Maybe it was mentioned later."

The only one who expressed concern that night was Currie, who expected to face the wrath of Priscilla's father, an air force captain and his superior, if he brought her home past her midnight curfew. "At eleven-thirty, I started pacing the floor." Lamar Fike, who was sitting nearby, merely laughed. "You might as well sit down," he said lazily. "You know once he gets up there he forgets all time."

"So I paced the floor for another hour and a half," declared Currie. "They came down a few minutes after one o'clock."

Priscilla and Elvis were holding hands, and Elvis was still reluctant to let her go, despite Currie's urgency. "He walked her out the front door," Currie remembered, "which he rarely did for anybody. He was still holding her fingers when we got to the steps outside. And when he let go of her hand he said, 'Bring her back, Currie.' " Currie hurried Priscilla into the car with Carol, clearly agitated, barely looking back. "I'll try," he responded.

Once inside the car, Priscilla seemed to be in a mild state of shock, Currie recalled. She questioned the Grants endlessly: "Do you think he likes me? Do you think he likes me?" "All the way back," Currie said later. "She was very unsure of herself." Stepping into his mentor role, he calmed Priscilla down, saying, "He wouldn't have taken you upstairs if he didn't like you, Priscilla." The performance had ended. "*Now* she started acting like a fourteen-year-old schoolgirl after her first date," noted Currie, which, in effect, she was.

What Priscilla did not know was that Elvis Presley was in a trance over her, talking about her to Charlie Hodge, just as he had to Rex Mansfield. "He called me over and said, 'Charlie, did you see the structure of her face? The bone structure? It's almost like everything I ever look for in a woman!' "

The first meeting had gone beyond Priscilla's wildest games of Imagine If. She had spent four hours alone with Elvis Presley in his bedroom. Though she was breathlessly agog at the fantasy she was living, there were hints of ambivalence on Priscilla's part that first night. She was bothered, she would say many years later, by Elvis's constant teasing. "I didn't know if I liked him or not. It was this energy that was there that I had never felt."

The Grants did not get Priscilla home until two o'clock that morning. Despite Currie's grave apprehensions, there were no repercussions from the Beaulieus. "I got kind of a funny look from the old man, so I talked ninety miles an hour: 'Elvis was real tired,' 'He was real happy to meet her.' I just kept it rolling. But [Paul] hardly said anything at all. He said, 'It is a little late.' That's about as grumpy as he got. Within five minutes I was out of there with Carol."

Currie seemed more concerned about the late hour than Ann Beaulieu did. Far from being disturbed by her fourteen-year-old daughter's midnight date with Elvis Presley, Priscilla's mother was thrilled. Her cousin Margaret later recalled, "She wrote me from Germany and said, 'Guess who Priscilla met? Elvis Presley!' She was all excited! Saying that Priscilla had met Elvis Presley and, you know, it was a big deal."

Ann seemed unfazed by the difference in Elvis's and Priscilla's ages or by the monumental chasm between them in life experiences. Priscilla Beaulieu may have looked older and *played* older than her fourteen years, but as Martha Smith, her eighth-grade English teacher from Texas said of her, "she was just a *little girl* to me. Back then little girls were little girls."

Priscilla told Currie, the next time they spoke, that she lay in bed wide awake after he dropped her off. "She couldn't even sleep, she was so excited."

"There are two tragedies in life," George Bernard Shaw wrote. "One is to lose your heart's desire. The other is to gain it." Priscilla Beaulieu was too young, at fourteen, to appreciate the irony of thanking God for *un*answered prayers.

11

PRISCILLA IN WONDERLAND

The sole person who seemed focused on the absurd difference in Priscilla Beaulieu's and Elvis Presley's ages was Priscilla. After their unlikely meeting and even more improbable bonding at the house on Goethestrasse, Priscilla continued her first days of ninth grade, dubious she would ever see the singer again. "Currie had introduced me to him and that's all I ever thought it was, so when I left I put it out of my mind."

The call to return came not from Elvis but from Currie. Elvis had not mentioned Priscilla to Currie since his request that first night to "bring her back." Whether she would see her idol a second time turned on Currie's caprice. Currie generally visited Elvis several times a week; two nights later, as he prepared to drive to Bad Nauheim, he invited Priscilla to come along. "I did it as a favor to E.P.; I didn't realize he was going to like her that much."

Priscilla's reaction was a mixture of adolescent giddiness and utter bewilderment. "I thought, 'It can't be. I'm only fourteen,' you know. 'He wants to see me?'"

"She said, 'I have to ask my mother,'" recalled Currie. Ann Beaulieu did not hesitate. "Ann got on the phone and said, 'It's okay, Currie. What time would you like me to have her ready?'" Currie, who knew Elvis was taking Priscilla to his bedroom, was stunned by Ann Beaulieu's nonchalance, despite having taken advantage of her daughter himself. "I thought, Lady, it's like giving your daughter to the wolves. I don't leave my fourteen-year-old daughter with some guy I don't know. She's doing it because he's famous. I would never do that to my kid. Never."

Priscilla's teen behavior and the sheer thrill of her fantasy took over once she was in Currie's car. She was skittish, insecure, asking a million questions. Currie, whose wife had stayed home, continued in his role as romantic coach. "I kept reminding her to keep a shy, quiet profile with Elvis. I told her, 'He flipped over your looks, but to keep him interested, you're going to have to keep playing the game of being everything he wants in a girl.'"

When Priscilla and Currie arrived, the regulars were milling about the house, listening to Elvis play the piano and sing. He stopped when he saw them and said hello. Once he began to sing again, Currie recalled, "he couldn't take his eyes off Priscilla." Geraldine Hopper, Priscilla's gym teacher in Wiesbaden, understood Elvis's infatuation. "Isn't he supposed to have admired virginity and purity? Innocence has a great appeal to a lot of men, especially in his business. I think she happened to come along in his life at a time when she must have been so different from the showgirls and the entertainers and the put-on sophisticates that he dealt with in his career, that I can see that appeal. And Priscilla projected that." Elvis's secret nickname for Priscilla, in fact, was "Pab," taken from her initials, but short for "Pablum"– baby food. Her angelic demeanor was Priscilla's secret weapon with men. Carol Grant saw this as a pose. "My mother recalls her being a prissy, assertive, you-think-she's-innocent-but-she's-not kind of girl," stated the Grants' daughter Karon. "And my mom is pretty perceptive."

Their second evening, Elvis and Priscilla again retreated to his bedroom, where they lingered for several hours. It was their private time together, setting a ritual for the visits to come. "We would listen to a radio show at night as we'd be talking," remembered Priscilla. It was the same program each time, often playing what Priscilla considered "sad" music, some of it country-western. Elvis poured his soul out to Priscilla, confiding in her intimacies the fourteen-year-old considered beyond her: his anxieties about his career, whether his fans would accept him when he returned from the army, his laments over the diminishing quality of the movies he was making, his unrealized ambition to play parts worthy of his role models, James Dean and Marlon Brando. "Sharing a lot of emotions, in a lot of areas. I was really a sounding board. He'd release a lot of his feelings to me." For Priscilla, finder of stray animals and keeper of secrets, the relationship felt familiar, if not natural. "I guess he *trusted* me. He trusted me a lot. And he was very close to me. The great thing about having Elvis at that time, before he came back from the army, was that he was *so* unaffected. I mean, he was still raw; he was still innocent. And I feel really fortunate that I got to see that part of him and be a part of that time in his life, or be a part of *him* at that time in his life." The true tragedy was that Priscilla had neither the experience nor the maturity to help him; all she could do, really, was listen.

Elvis scrutinized Priscilla's features with the meticulousness of a plastic surgeon–searching for validation that she possessed, for him, the perfect face. When he met the Beaulieus a few weeks later, Priscilla said, "his big thing was that I didn't look like anybody in my family. That was his big question: 'Why don't you? You don't look like your mother or your father. You look *different.*' " Elvis had stumbled onto the secret, and his suspicions left Priscilla conflicted, torn between her vow of silence with her mother and her growing intimacy with Elvis. For a short time she kept the truth about her identity from Elvis, but "the more I went to visit with him, the more we became closer and closer."

Elvis and Priscilla were discovering a common and extremely potent emotional and psychological bond. He talked about the devastating loss of his mother, who had died at age forty-five the summer before, and Priscilla could relate to his grief and longing for a missing parent. As Elvis probed deeper, finally asking her whether the Beaulieus were really her parents, Priscilla revealed the truth about Paul Beaulieu, showing Elvis the photograph of her real father. "It was one of those evenings we shared. We did a lot of talking at that time. We were sharing losses." Priscilla felt burdened with guilt afterward, so powerful was her apprehension at disclosing the family secret. "I told my mother that I had told Elvis because he asked me. Not knowing if that was the right thing to do. Because then it was a betrayal against her, you know. She was actually okay with it." It was Priscilla who was left carrying the emotional baggage.

The revelation stirred something within Elvis. He was by nature a tender, compassionate man; Priscilla's secret and the loss of her real father fostered in him a strong, almost primal desire to shield her. In a complicated way, Priscilla transferred her emotional dependence to Elvis, who assumed the mantle of Jimmy Wagner, Priscilla's fantasy father figure, guardian angel, and protector. "He had a lot of empathy for me," she said, when she told him about her traumatic discovery of the trunk and the stress of keeping her real father a secret. "He really did. And he protected me. Elvis was like that in a sense; if he saw you had a loss, he totally related to it." Mike Edwards romanticized Elvis as Priscilla's knight in shining armor, sent to rescue her, to fulfill the fantasies she had created to escape from a family—a father—to which she instinctively knew she did not belong. "And he came along," Mike said, referring to Elvis, "and it was perfect. It was meant to be."

Priscilla's lost father and Elvis's grief over his mother's death created an unbreakable bond between them. "He was drawn to me," Priscilla recalled. "I can't say it's *from* that, because our relationship had already started. But I felt more comfortable with him and had more trust in him, you know, and I felt that he was a trustworthy person that I could depend on."

In exchange, Priscilla filled an enormous void for Elvis, listening to him for hours as he reminisced about Gladys, talking with him in the private language he and his mother had invented. Priscilla's physical resemblance to Debra Paget reinforced their intimacy. It was an intricate, complicated psychosexual relationship, almost beyond fathoming to anyone but Priscilla and Elvis.

"I don't think he *saw* his mother," as Joe Esposito analyzed, "but he looked at Priscilla in that way because she had that look. I feel that had a lot to do with it. I feel he wanted her to be like his mother, to take really good care of him. No matter what he wanted, his mother would do that. Anything Elvis wanted, he got. And he wanted Priscilla to be the same way. As long as you take care of me, I'll take care of you."

Their evenings together always ended on the same bittersweet note, listening to "Good Night, My Love" on the radio. "That was a song that would always end off on the radio station at twelve o'clock at night in Germany," remembered Priscilla. "And his rule was, when that song would come on, it was twelve and I had to leave in a half hour or so."

Elvis and Priscilla were still intertwined as they walked down the stairs from the bedroom at 12:45 on their second night together, recalled Currie. "Bring her back, Currie," Elvis again entreated.

Currie was less apprehensive, considering the mild reaction from Priscilla's parents when he brought her home the first night two hours past her curfew. This time, with Carol at home, he could indulge his impulse for voyeurism and competition by pressing Priscilla for sexual details: "I was dying to know what had happened upstairs, but I wasn't going to ask her in front of my wife." Priscilla, being Priscilla, balked, saying she and Elvis "just talked a lot." Currie, being Currie, knew there was more. Though Priscilla would later claim she told Currie nothing, "I *made* her tell me what went on, exactly," Currie asserted. "I said, 'Wait a minute, Priscilla. I'm the guy who brought you up here, honey. Don't play coy with me. After what you and I have been through in the last three or four weeks? What did he do?' I made her tell me everything. I said, 'He's a friend of mine. You're a friend of mine. What's the big deal?' "

Priscilla was in a dilemma. Though her natural instinct was to reveal nothing, she was dependent upon Currie to see Elvis. Not only was Currie her transportation, he controlled her access; she visited Bad Nauheim at his discretion, for Elvis had not requested she return on a particular night, nor had he called Priscilla formally for a date. "He never called *me*," declared Currie. "He never even knew if I was going to come back. That's all fallacy." For Priscilla, Currie Grant occupied the unusual triad of sexual mentor, father confessor, and keys to the kingdom of Elvis.

"And then she changed her tune and started telling me what happened upstairs. I kind of coerced her into it the first time. She was afraid she might not ever see him again. In the beginning. And then she started telling me, little by little. She knew that I wasn't going to tell anybody. From then on, she had no qualms about telling me."

On the second visit, according to Currie, Elvis had Priscilla's blouse and bra off and she was lying half naked on his bed. "Not totally undressed—he knew how young she was. He was gentle with her the first couple of nights.

But by that time, she was a willing participant. His hands were going everywhere. He started to get under her dress."

Priscilla was loath to tell Currie her bedroom secrets with Elvis, yet she was in need of a sounding board herself. As a fourteen-year-old girl engaged in adult sexual activities with a superstar, she was desperately insecure and in need of counsel. To whom else could she confess such intimacies? She and Currie shared, as would be their history, a strange, symbiotic love-hate relationship.

When Currie returned Priscilla home at the end of that second visit, it was again close to 2:00 A.M. Paul and Ann Beaulieu greeted them with smiles. "I'm thinking, I can't believe these parents," observed Currie. "I used to say that to Carol."

In the coming weeks Priscilla must have felt as though she were in Wonderland. Like a small child collecting souvenirs of a favorite holiday, she stored the memories of her fairy-tale love affair with Elvis in a treasure box. "She had a piece of windshield glass in there," recalled a summer friend of Priscilla's named Robbie Jones. "He'd had an accident, and that was the glass from the windshield of the car."

Extraordinarily, Priscilla told almost no one about her dates with Elvis Presley. Her tendency to draw an imaginary line between herself and others, that aura of mystery she possessed even as a child, "got worse after I met Elvis," she said. "Where most girls would probably exploit it and would probably be giddy, I protected it passionately. And why, I do not know. I don't know why I was so protective of it—not that Elvis was so secretive." But of course Priscilla had been reared in a house of secrets amid a family that never talked about vital issues; she'd been trained by her mother to withhold the truth, to keep what was *real* a secret, sacred and untouchable.

"You really didn't become friends with Priscilla," Robbie Jones, who met her a summer later, declared. "She was very guarded, even then. . . . I did go to her house a couple of times and have a lot of respect for her in that she never brought up Elvis and never talked about him. And when she was asked a question, she would specifically answer that question and drop it."

In their way, Priscilla and Elvis were insulating each other. He embraced the little girl who had lost her real father and was confused by concealing it; she was honoring his trust in her by preserving his privacy, "which in retrospect," Robbie noted, "was a very mature and hard way to be at that age."

"I think that I was protecting *him*," Priscilla said. "Because I would never betray him. He confided a *lot* to me, that I would *never* share with a girlfriend that I might never see again."

Her relationship with Elvis was also kept under wraps because it was outside the bounds of conventional morality, especially in the military world the Beaulieus inhabited. It was an "unwritten rule," according to Priscilla's classmate Mary Ann Barks, that high school girls did not date GIs. "Any girl who dated a GI was considered trash."

"It was not considered proper to do that," agreed school chum Debbie Ross. "And particularly if you were an officer's daughter. That kind of mixing at the time was not approved, particularly since we were fourteen years old. That would have been a real problem." Debbie, whose family lived across the hall from the Beaulieus the next year, had to deal with her parents' concern about Priscilla's possible influence on their daughter. "I remember my mother didn't particularly like Priscilla. I think she was concerned about someone my age dating or seeing a man ten years older than we were. I think she thought there must be something more to it, or there must be something about it that I didn't need to be a part of."

Ann Beaulieu had no such compunction. As Priscilla's visits to Elvis's house became more frequent—two, three, sometimes four times a week—"her only question was, 'What time would you like us to have her ready?' " recalled Currie. He was still in control, to some extent, for it was he who decided how often he would go to Bad Nauheim and whether or not he would take Priscilla. "The first four to six weeks I was taking her up there, it was always my call."

Even in the army, Elvis was surrounded by a cadre of male followers, later labeled "the Memphis Mafia," who worked for him, played with him, and generally emulated him. The singular exception was Cliff Gleaves, a glib, highly intelligent, and original disc jockey and comedian whom Elvis met and became fascinated by early in his career. Cliff lived at Elvis's house in Memphis pre-Graceland and joined him in Germany at Elvis's request. Two points distinguished Cliff Gleaves from the others in Elvis Presley's entourage: He was strictly a friend, not on the payroll; and Elvis copied *him*. "Cliff was Elvis's alter ego," in the opinion of Currie, who became close to Cliff in Wiesbaden. "Cliff was the most charismatic human being I've ever met. He was something Elvis always wanted to be and wasn't. That's why Elvis wanted Cliff around all the time." In later years, after Elvis's death, some of the group would try to trivialize Cliff Gleaves's influence on Elvis's life in order to amplify their own, a common practice in Presley circles; Cliff, whose ego was not dependent upon his association with Elvis, did not bother to promote himself. "He was the closest thing to Elvis," confirmed Elvis's stepbrother, Rick Stanley, who witnessed Elvis's hero worship of Cliff. "Elvis seemed to sit at his feet. Cliff took the floor, he sucked up the air. He was like Robin Williams—everyone just sat while he went on a riff. Elvis sat in awe of him. Here's a guy that was better than Elvis! Cliff didn't have to sing to get people's attention. Anybody with any intuition who's being honest will tell you that Cliff Gleaves was *it*. Elvis'd fly him in from anywhere just to have him around. Cliff knew, 'I'm this guy's fix.' "

"Cliff was a dear friend," Charlie Hodge agreed. "An interesting character. There are actually some Hollywood stars who used to watch Cliff, and they admired his technique of talking and snapping his fingers, which they began to use in their acting."

Priscilla barely registered on Cliff and his girlfriend, a fetching young German woman named Gerta Heylmann. Gerta remembered that Priscilla was excited about being in the company of Elvis and that she was exceedingly quiet, "more eyes and ears."

"She just faded into the scenery more or less," Cliff confirmed in a conversation in 1978. "Almost unnoticeable. Looking back, if anything stood out—maybe it's because of what Currie told her to do—my impression would have been, for a girl her age, she held her own. . . . I can picture that scene in the living room—Priscilla sitting there, just kind of a little grin on her face."

Priscilla strove to appear older than her fourteen years, an assignment her mother helped her carry out. Ann, who had sneaked out of her parents' house in her mother's high heels, loaned her clothes to Priscilla to help create an illusion of sophistication far beyond that of a ninth-grader, and she assisted with her hair and makeup. Gerta, who was a model, recalled Priscilla as "older-thinking" and skillfully made-up. Her look, recalled a classmate, Donna Pollen, consisted of "foxy" skirts that billowed out over multiple petticoats, emphasizing her tiny waist.

12

A QUESTION OF VIRGINITY

Priscilla Beaulieu was not the only girl Elvis Presley was dating that fall in Germany. Heli Priemel, a fifteen-year-old German beauty nicknamed "Legs," recalled evenings when she would leave Elvis's bedroom as Priscilla was arriving. Heli eventually complained, something Priscilla never did. "Priscilla knew the rules," Currie explained. "She didn't make a fuss about . . . there being somebody else. Back then she was just happy to go see him."

"It wasn't only Priscilla coming to the house," confirmed Rex Mansfield, a member of Elvis's army entourage. "It was a lot of girls." Priscilla was a starry-eyed teenager in fantasy lust with a rock star; she dared not say or do anything that might give him an excuse to stop seeing her. The stress and insecurity for a ninth-grader in that position would have broken a girl who lacked Priscilla's iron will. Not only was Elvis romancing Heli in front of her, but he still enjoyed an occasional interlude with his young German secretary Elisabeth, who later married Rex, and he was known to have a steady girlfriend back in Memphis. The rivalry for Elvis Presley's affection was keen, and Priscilla had already demonstrated that she played to win.

She and Currie had developed a comfortable routine on the hour's drive back and forth. When Carol did not come along, Currie would question Priscilla for a few minutes about that night's bedroom activities with Elvis, "and after a while it would be boring, and then I'd let it drop and we would talk about other things or she'd take a little nap. She would tell me when I'd ask, whatever I'd ask: 'Oh, we did this and we did that. He put his hand between my legs. He played with my breasts. He took my clothes off and we just lay there, and his thing was sticking up like this. . . .' She would go into detail on what would happen, because she was still unsure of herself up there, especially with Heli up there and that competition going on."

During one of their early drives home, Currie found himself sexually excited by Priscilla's description of her foreplay with Elvis, and pulled the car off the autobahn for a quick tryst. "She was very cold," as he described it. "I was pushing her hair around, just to kiss her on the mouth. She was kissing, but not very enthusiastically. I tried to put my hand on her breast, and she kind of wriggled out of the way and turned to the side a little bit, and I stopped." Currie immediately recognized the "old syndrome," as he called it. "Now she's been with Elvis, up in the bedroom there, she didn't need me. And that's why she's acting this way."

Priscilla's version of this encounter is that Currie pulled her onto a dirt road and tried to rape her. "And I was terrified. I did everything in my power to keep him off me. He gave up because I made such a fuss. There was a house there, so if I had to crawl there, I could get there. There were lights there, I was going for that. I kicked doors open and blew horns. When the horn was going off, the lights came on at the house, and it scared him." Priscilla told no one, she says now, "because I thought I wouldn't see Elvis anymore. I thought Currie would never do it again."

Something had occurred, prior to this evening, that not only suggested a motive for Priscilla to allege that Currie tried to rape her, but that could also explain why they offered different versions of their entire relationship.

During one of the private talks in his bedroom, Elvis had recently revealed to Priscilla that he considered virginity sacred and that he would never date seriously or consider marrying a girl who had been with another man. "That was early on," she confirmed. "It was important to him that he was the first. *Very* important to him."

That conversation, by Priscilla's own account, was portentous. In reality, it must have been harrowing. Elvis naturally assumed, since she was barely fourteen, that Priscilla was a virgin, and she affirmed this while they were talking and making out in his bedroom. According to Currie, however, Priscilla had had intercourse with *him* a few weeks earlier in the hills above Wiesbaden. Elvis's old-fashioned southern insistence on a virgin bride was the quintessential Catch-22 for Priscilla Beaulieu. She had made the ultimate sacrifice—her virginity—in order to actualize her dream of meeting Elvis, only to discover that in doing so, she had effectively disqualified herself from ever becoming his wife. *If Elvis ever found out . . .*

It was at this moment that Currie Grant began to pose a threat to Priscilla Beaulieu, for he knew she was not a virgin. If he revealed their liaison, it would jeopardize her growing romance with Elvis.

Thus was born another secret in Priscilla's adolescent life. To ensure her chance for a lasting relationship with Elvis Presley, she would have to conceal the fact that she and Currie Grant had had intercourse before he took her to meet her idol. That is a secret Priscilla Presley guards to this day, for the key element in the Elvis-and-Priscilla myth—the single, powerful image with which she is most closely associated—is her assertion that she was a virgin bride on her wedding night with Elvis, seven years after they met.

Mike Edwards, in whom she confided that she and Currie had a sexual "altercation" in the hills *before* he took her to meet Elvis, suspected Priscilla was denying she and Currie were intimate for the same reason: to preserve her image as a virgin. "You know how, when you talk to someone . . . you hear stories, you kind of listen? *I* thought they did have intercourse, but I never pushed it. And I thought *other* things, that we talked about. I *always* thought they did. And I felt that she did not *want* that because she wanted to be a virgin for Elvis. I always sensed that."

This would explain why Priscilla was so desperate, years later, to conceal the otherwise harmless fact that she had been a huge Elvis Presley fan and that it was her fantasy to meet him. In admitting that, she would have felt exposed to speculation about how she made her dream come true. People might believe she was willing to do almost anything to make that fantasy happen. If, however, she *denied* that she was an Elvis fan—as she has done—who would believe Currie's account that she asked him to introduce her to Elvis and then slept with him to gain access?

"I think she is saying that, maybe, because she wants to appear like a different young lady," Karon Grant reasoned. "As far as I remember, and I'm going back many, many years, I was told many times, over and over again, that *she* walked up to my *dad* and said, 'I hear you know Elvis.' I don't see any other reason why there would be a dispute or another story of how it happened. It's kind of sad that she would be this way."

"She got lucky," declared Vera Von Cronthall, who recalled Priscilla asking around the Eagle Club that summer about meeting Elvis. "She probably would never have met Elvis if Currie hadn't taken a real liking to her."

Priscilla began writing to friends back in Austin, that November, that she had met Elvis Presley at a private party in Wiesbaden after he entertained at the officers' club. By Thanksgiving she had revealed that they were dating, with the fanciful explanation that Elvis had noticed her at the party and approached *her.* "It was so unreal to us," recalled Christine Laws, who had graduated from junior high with Priscilla only five months earlier. Priscilla told a teacher, Güdrun Von Heister, that Elvis was a "distant relative"—anything, apparently, to create a smoke screen, to divert attention away from Currie and the truth.

Currie was unaware of Priscilla's deception and her motivation for it. After the incident along the side of the autobahn, he continued to drive her back and forth to Bad Nauheim for nearly a month and, by his account, persisted in coaxing sexual information from her on those nights that Carol stayed home. Priscilla was trapped. Currie was still her entrée to Elvis.

According to Currie, Priscilla's legendary tale of Elvis withholding penetration until their honeymoon was another falsehood. "He didn't have intercourse with her the first night or two," Currie said. "He didn't get into the deeper stuff until the third or fourth time. Eventually he had intercourse with her. Not only once. She told me that. It was either the third or fourth time, I don't know which one."

Mike Stone, the karate champion with whom Priscilla had an affair at the end of her marriage to Elvis, always questioned whether she and Elvis had delayed intercourse until their honeymoon, and occasionally he asked her about it. She kept the secret, even from her lover. "Would you tell?" he asked. "I think a lot of things like that are best left unsaid, especially if you are involved with somebody, like we were at the time. There's some things you just don't want to bring up."

Elvis apparently told Joe Esposito he was "doing everything else" *but* intercourse with Priscilla in Germany. Priscilla did not express a concern about becoming pregnant, at least during her conversations with Currie; nor was Elvis bothered. "E.P. was like me," Currie noted. "He pulled out before anything. Because he and I talked about it." The withdrawal method of birth control may have been Elvis's interpretation of stopping short of penetration with Priscilla, for he told Joe that fall that what he and Priscilla were doing "was okay as long as you didn't finish the sex act. That was his thinking. In other words, 'I'm not doing anything wrong.' "

By five or six weeks into her relationship with Elvis, Currie noticed that Priscilla became more confident of her standing and balked at responding to Currie's routine sexual interrogation. One weekend when he called to arrange the hour he would be at her house, "she says, 'Oh, Currie, Elvis is sending Lamar down to pick me up.' " Currie felt he was doing Elvis a favor by taking Priscilla with him and wondered why Lamar would drive to the Beaulieus' and back. "I knew something was going on, because she'd clammed up on me a little bit on the last couple of nights." Currie did not perceive himself as a threat to Priscilla because he was not aware of Elvis's virginity fetish, nor did he plan to reveal he'd had sex with her, since she was a minor and it was against the law; he considered the episode in the hills "their secret."

Currie did suspect that Priscilla had asked Elvis to arrange for another driver because he was asking too many intimate questions, "because they had gotten really close now and she feels more secure around Elvis and doesn't need me anymore."

Priscilla claims today that Currie tried to rape her a *second* time, that she told Elvis about both attacks, and that he "went crazy" and banished Currie from his house and their lives. "I was afraid of him," she explained. "I had to tell Elvis. It was a very, very, very big decision to make, because I didn't know at that time, in the beginning, if Elvis would ever see me again. I didn't know . . . if he would say, 'This just isn't going to work.' I had to take that chance. Elvis was furious. He couldn't believe it. And that's why Currie never came to the house again."

Priscilla's rape scenario is fraught with improbabilities. The day she told Currie that Lamar Fike was going to drive her to Bad Nauheim, Currie spent the evening at Elvis's house *with Elvis and Priscilla.* If Elvis was irate and had replaced Currie as Priscilla's driver because she told him Currie tried to rape her, why would Elvis allow Currie into the house to socialize with them that night?

There were questionable aspects to Priscilla's description of the second rape attempt itself. During her face-off with Currie in May of 1996, she claimed that he had invited her to see a movie with his wife and him a few weeks after he attacked her by the side of the autobahn on the way home from Elvis's. "I asked my parents. My father said, 'Fine.' I went down, and Carol wasn't in the car. I said, 'Where is Carol?' He said, 'She isn't feeling well.' " According to Priscilla, she and Currie drove off, "and he took me by the river, the Rhine River. And he tried again." *Why,* if he tried to rape her once before and she was terrified of him, would Priscilla get in the car alone with Currie, especially on a ruse? She no longer needed him as a conduit to Elvis. Why even accept an invitation to the movies? "He said that Carol wasn't feeling well, so I went with him. I *trusted* this man!" Priscilla explained.

"No, it didn't happen, Priscilla," Currie argued in their head-to-head encounter in 1996. "Boy, you've made a lot of things up since I talked to you last. I mean *a lot.*"

During that same 1996 conversation, Currie also denied Priscilla's characterization of the earlier roadside incident as rape:

PRISCILLA: Did you pull off a dirt road and try to attack me?
CURRIE: You bet I pulled off the road.
PRISCILLA: And you tried to attack me?
CURRIE: No, I didn't try to attack you.
PRISCILLA: You never tried to?
CURRIE: No.
PRISCILLA: I didn't kick and blow the horn?
CURRIE: No, you did *not.* No, you did *not.*
PRISCILLA: . . . You tried to *rape* me, Currie.
CURRIE: Oh, you're a liar. You're a liar, Priscilla. And that's an outright lie.
PRISCILLA: . . . You didn't try to kiss me?
CURRIE: Yeah, I tried to kiss you, yes. Absolutely. I didn't try, I did. I did kiss you.
PRISCILLA: And did I not push you away?

CURRIE: No, you didn't push me away. You just weren't *into* it. Because you'd just left Elvis Presley's bedroom, and you were not into having anything to do with me at all. Which was fine. We took off within fifteen minutes, heading for Wiesbaden.

PRISCILLA: Excuse me, Currie. What do you think I just got finished saying? We drove out to a dirt road, you tried to kiss me.

CURRIE: We didn't go to a dirt road, Priscilla.

PRISCILLA: It was off a side of the road.

CURRIE: It was a rest area where other cars were sitting there just like mine. . . . If somebody was trying to rape somebody, you think somebody's going to try to rape somebody *there*?

PRISCILLA: Currie, did I not push the horn?

CURRIE: No, you didn't. No. No. No.

PRISCILLA: I did, Currie.

CURRIE: You were cold as ice. I said, "Let's go." I took you straight home. Because you just came down from Elvis's *bedroom*. Why would you want to have anything to do with *me* now?

PRISCILLA: Exactly. *Exactly!* Exactly. Why would I want to have anything to do with you?

CURRIE: . . . You've *now* been with Elvis. You've accomplished what you've tried to do with *me*.

PRISCILLA: And what did I try to do with you?

CURRIE: Get me to take you to Elvis, which I did. So now you don't need anything to do with Currie Grant at all. Well, that's fine. I didn't object. I took you straight home. The night you are talking about.

PRISCILLA: Yes, you did.

CURRIE: Yes, I sure did, straight home.

The timing of the alleged attacks was a weakness in Priscilla's account. She maintained that Currie did not make a sexual advance until *after* she had met Elvis. Since Currie had been rejected by a girlfriend who became involved with Elvis, it made no sense that he would wait until *after* Priscilla obtained what she needed from him—the introduction to Elvis—before making a romantic move. Priscilla's motivation for positioning the incidents *after* Currie introduced her to Elvis is clear, for she would not have wanted anyone to know she was in a compromising position with Currie *before* she met her idol, or people might believe she was desperate enough to have intercourse to make it happen. Mike Edwards, her 1970s beau, offered the most convincing proof, for Priscilla confided to him that she and Currie had an encounter in the hills *before* she met Elvis.

Priscilla's accounts of the attempted rapes are also inconsistent. In an interview just prior to her 1996 discussion with Currie, she stated that he tried to rape her "two or three" times, but when she met with Currie face-to-face, she said it happened twice. How could she have forgotten an attempted rape?

"I had at least ten girls that I could call any night and go have sex with them," countered Currie. "I'm not bragging—at least ten. I didn't need to rape anybody. Bringing up this rape thing, this is the most ridiculous thing I've ever heard. We were both young and foolish back then. I was older than her, but we were still young and foolish and this is what happened. And she can live the lie as long as she wants to, but in her mind she knows what the truth is."

Priscilla also offered different versions of when she told Elvis that Currie tried to rape her—whether it was after the first or the second attempt. The most glaring problem with Priscilla's account, however, was Elvis's friendliness toward Currie after she claimed to have told him. "Elvis would have wanted to *kill* him if that had happened," Joe Esposito insisted. Nor, seemingly, did Elvis ever mention Priscilla's accusations about Currie to his entourage. "He never told us," said Joe. Rex Mansfield and Elisabeth Stefaniak agreed, and believed Elvis would have mentioned it to them if Priscilla had accused Currie of rape. Lamar Fike, who took over Currie's role as Priscilla's driver, was offered no explanation by Elvis. "He didn't say anything," Currie recalled Lamar saying. "He just said, 'Go pick her up.' "

Priscilla further claimed that she told her parents Currie tried to rape her and they were "livid," but she offered a different version of when she told them each time she related the story. Yet neither Ann Beaulieu nor Priscilla's stepfather—who was Currie Grant's superior officer in the air force—said a word to Currie after supposedly learning that he attempted to rape their fourteen-year-old daughter. "She never told her parents *anything*," Currie disputed hotly. "If she had told her parents anything, Elvis and I would probably both be in prison today."

According to Priscilla, "After I told Elvis what had happened and how Currie made a play for me, Elvis kicked him out. He was not seen anymore there, he was out of the house." She and her parents, she maintained, did not see Currie the rest of the time Elvis was in Germany. "Once he was out, he was out. He was out of my life at that time. When I told Elvis what had happened, I did not see Currie. Currie did not come to the house again."

This, like much of Priscilla's "official" biography, is simply untrue. Rex Mansfield; Elvis's secretary, Elisabeth; and Cliff Gleaves's girlfriend, Gerta, all remembered Currie joining the nightly gatherings at Elvis's house regularly during the remaining five months Elvis was in Germany, and Elvis was always pleased to see him. It seems inconceivable that Elvis would continue to invite into his home a man he knew had tried to rape his fourteen-year-old girlfriend more than once.

In addition to the inconsistencies, inaccuracy, and implausibility of Priscilla's account, one has to consider who had the greater motivation to lie. What would Currie stand to gain by revealing that he lured a fourteen-year-old into sex? Why would Currie hurt his former wife and children and embarrass himself by saying this if it wasn't true? Priscilla attributed it to a "vendetta" against her or "like he wants to be known. . . . There's got to be a motive in there somewhere." Perhaps, she speculated, Currie wanted notoriety for claiming to take her virginity before Elvis.

Yet Currie has never offered or sold his story to tabloids, magazines, or newspapers in the thirty-seven years since he met Priscilla Beaulieu. When he recounted their history for this book, he was sixty-four years old, one of his sons had just died, and he was in need of a catharsis. He did not seek me out, nor did he ask for money. "I'm not trying to make up things against Priscilla," he explained. "I could care less. I had my fifteen minutes of fame years ago. I don't need any more. I don't want any more. But don't sit there and look in my face and tell me I'm lying and that never happened. Not when I know frigging well it did, and I was right there. I may not be Priscilla Presley, and I may not be a celebrity, but it's my life too, and my history too, and I want it to be the truth. If I really wanted to brag that I got her first, I'd have been telling people from the time it happened until now."

Priscilla, by contrast, had much to lose and much to protect. Her version of events was the foundation of the Elvis-and-Priscilla legend. As she put it after her heated encounter with Currie in 1996: "My life is on the line here. I mean all my credibility, everything. *Everything!* My life—my *image* that I worked so hard to create."

She was in a panic as the debate with Currie—over who asked whom to meet Elvis and whether they dallied in the hills—began to escalate. "May God strike me dead if I'm not telling the truth!" Priscilla exclaimed repeatedly. After an hour, she fled, agitated, and collided with another car on the fifteen-minute drive home.

Priscilla had been telling the myth for so many years and was so deep in denial that perhaps she had come to believe it herself. Dostoyevsky mentioned this phenomenon, saying, "There are secrets you'll even hide from yourself." Psychologists identify it as repressed memory. John Bradshaw, an expert on family secrets, believes that the harboring of secrets "sets up the autohypnotic ego defenses like repression, denial—how we set up ways *not* to remember." Bradshaw claims that denial "is largely unconscious. It's not the same as lying. Denial protects the person's options to keep the status quo."

Certainly that is what Priscilla wished to do; to preserve the Elvis-and-Priscilla story, to perpetuate the myth.

When Priscilla began writing her memoir in 1983, Mike Edwards urged her to be honest about her affair with Currie, to practice the Scientology principle of confronting one's past in order to release it. Priscilla chose instead to follow the path of denial, to continue the myth. "And I didn't push her," recalled Mike, " 'cause I guess, at that time, it was too late in our relationship."

The Currie affair was a trauma in Priscilla's life. Whether or not Priscilla had consensual sex with him, he committed statutory rape–as did Elvis–since she was only fourteen. As the adult in the situation, he was the responsible party, a fact that he acknowledges today: "She was only a young girl, inexperienced. Here I was in my twenties. It's true, I shouldn't have been doing those things."

The reality was that Priscilla and Currie used *each other;* a truth that Currie had accepted. Priscilla was still in denial. "I just felt sad for her," recalled Mike, speaking of his attempts to push Priscilla to confront the past. "She could have freed herself; she could have broken those chains. If she'd be honest, it sets you *free*. She wanted to do that book and set herself free, but she didn't do it."

In a way, Priscilla knew no other form of behavior. She had been indoctrinated by her mother in the art of deception and denial, often motivated by fear.

13

DARK FAIRY TALE

During Priscilla Beaulieu's five-month interlude with Elvis Presley in Germany, one thing was certain: She was a fourteen-year-old girl who was in far over her head.

Her "friendship" with Elvis, as her parents later characterized it to the media, was not the innocent fantasy they described; it was sex, drugs, and rock and roll, and Ann and Paul Beaulieu were too taken with Elvis's celebrity and their daughter's adolescent infatuation with a man of such importance to notice or intervene. When Lamar Fike pulled up to the Beaulieus' to fetch Priscilla in the early evening and then to drop her off at one or two in the morning, her parents did not communicate. He just picked her up and brought her home.

Priscilla had a succession of drivers from October on: Lamar, who joked with her and called her Ballou; Joe Esposito; Elvis's father, Vernon, sometimes with his new blond girlfriend, Dee Stanley, the estranged wife of an army sergeant; Priscilla's parents; and, on the rare occasion, Elvis himself. Joe, who got to know the Beaulieus slightly, also recalled that Ann "really liked Elvis a *lot.*"

Those in Elvis's inner circle, who saw Priscilla's parents rarely, regarded them as a nice ordinary couple. Paul Beaulieu, to them, was a figure in the background in a military uniform; Ann was friendly, though slightly reserved.

There were suggestions, when one peered more closely, of a darker, gothic side to Priscilla's home life. Sunhild Ernst, a sixteen-year-old Wiesbaden girl, baby-sat for the younger Beaulieu children a few times that fall. She stopped after an incident with Paul Beaulieu. "When he drove me home," she said years later, "he was drunk and hit on me, or tried anyway." Suni, as she was called, lived quite near the Beaulieus and was Currie and Carol's regular baby-sitter. She agreed to help out the Beaulieus when Carol called her one day saying that Paul and Ann could not find a sitter. "But after he tried to hit on me, that was it. I told her, 'Forget it. I don't need this.' "

Priscilla's stepfather, by Suni's observation, "was a drunk." On the last night she baby-sat for their children, Paul propositioned her as soon as they left the

Beaulieu house. "There was no physical [contact], because I would have gotten out of the car. I just said, 'Look, I'm not interested.' And then I kind of said, 'Forget it. No, uh-uh.' At the time, I wasn't allowed to go out or date or anything like that. And then to have some old captain coming on to you—that's kind of scary. I was glad to get out of the car." Suni stayed away from the Beaulieus after that.

Suni, who also baby-sat regularly for Currie and Carol's two small daughters, never had a problem with Currie. "He liked the ladies," she said, "but . . . he was always a gentleman. He *never* crossed the line."

Albert Corey Jr., a football player at H. H. Arnold who was a year older than Priscilla, spent the night in the maid's quarters of the Beaulieus' basement a few times after football games the next fall, a school practice for athletes who lived in the dormitories. He remembered his first extended encounter with Captain Beaulieu: "He came down to talk to me about the football game, and he had a drink in his hand and he was drunk and he wouldn't leave." Priscilla's father "always had [a drink] in his hand," Al recalled, "every time I stayed with them, from morning until night. Mother, too. Cognac all the time. Course over there it was like running water."

Suni also remembered Ann Beaulieu drinking heavily on the nights she baby-sat. Priscilla would be at Elvis's house, according to Suni, still not home by one or two in the morning when the Beaulieus returned. Paul and Ann never asked where Priscilla was. "When they came home they were both sloshed. She always went right to the bedroom. And you could tell, the way she was weaving."

Suni Ernst's and Al Corey's recollections were consistent with Mike Edwards's later impression of Paul Beaulieu as an alcoholic, the dark secret of military life.

"There is a lot of alcoholism in the military," observed Katie Neece, a classmate and acquaintance of Priscilla's. "I think it's a way of coping. And of course in Germany there wasn't a drinking age, and for the most part, people drank."

"In a military family," another Wiesbaden friend of Priscilla's, Joe Delahunt, stated, "what goes on and what people see on the outside—and how dysfunctional it is—is something else. But I would say, as a typical military family, [the Beaulieus] had problems. . . . [Priscilla's] dad was kind of a hard-ass."

When Suni baby-sat, she noticed how intimidated the rest of the family was by Paul Beaulieu. "They weren't happy," she said. "It was not a happy home life. The whole *behavior* of the children—you know, quiet when he was around. He was to a certain extent a male chauvinist, like he was head honcho and that was it." Robbie Jones, who attended summer school with Priscilla the next year and visited the Beaulieus' house several times, formed the same impression.

"I'm not sure Priscilla had a really joyful home life," she recalled. "I think she had a stepfather, and I don't *think* she was abused or anything, but I compare it to my life and I have wonderful parents."

"He was not a nice man," Al Corey concluded from his sleep overs at the Beaulieu home. "Everything was 'Yes, sir. No, sir.' I don't know that he ever physically *did* anything, but I do know that Priscilla had a lock on her bedroom door. And she used it." John Reddington, a reflective man who was principal of H. H. Arnold during Priscilla's sophomore and junior years, observed her with a concerned eye. He met with Captain Beaulieu for a parent-teacher conference, and formulated an opinion of the family dynamics. "And the lock on the bedroom door . . ." he later speculated. "If there was actual abuse there, it's doggone complicated, because at a certain stage of little girls' development, they can't even be seductive toward their fathers. So if you have a guy that, say, he's slipping over into drink, you don't know what kind of secrets there might be in the family."

Priscilla had been brought up in an atmosphere of illusion, and it extended to her intense, clandestine romance with Elvis, which continued throughout the fall, as she adjusted to high school. By day, she attended classes with other fourteen-year-olds, pretending to study world history and German, trying earnestly to blend in; when seven o'clock arrived, her chariot awaited, driven by Lamar or one of the others in Elvis's merry band, and off she would ride to her secret nightlife of sex, adult parties, and midnight celebrity confessions. It was a schizophrenic, extraordinary existence, and it was taking its toll on Priscilla. Cliff Gleaves perceived her as "overpowered. Every human being she was around was older. It was sort of another world for her, so that could stifle a younger person's personality."

Missing was the confident, effervescent Priscilla of Del Valle fame, queen of her domain. She had been replaced by an insecure adolescent under enormous pressure, striving desperately to fit into an unreal adult scene, to sustain the attention of a teen idol. "I know I didn't eat, I couldn't eat," she said years later. "I remember [Elvis's] grandmother always trying to get me to eat. I was always starved and feeling hungry but never wanted to look silly eating. I was always afraid I was going to have something on my mouth—you know, how when you first meet someone . . . ? And he always tried to get his grandmother to make me bacon sandwiches, things like that, but I never ate."

Linda Williams, Priscilla's classmate in Austin and Wiesbaden, noticed a personality change in her. Priscilla went from being a fun-loving, outgoing "bit of a clown" at Popham and Del Valle to being a more somber and serious person. "She had sort of withdrawn," Linda remembered. "We stayed friendly, but we really weren't friends."

Priscilla had been drawn into a complex, stressful adult situation. Her relationship with Elvis forced her to face issues and situations that were beyond the grasp of a teenager. "Now I had *another* burden that I was concerned about—him and his welfare," she said when she was fifty. "I was concerned about his career; I was concerned about his acceptance after being in the army for two years. My problems now were not my own problems. They were someone else's problems that I inherited."

She had no friends. Part of this, and an aspect of Priscilla's celebrated aloofness, may have been psychological in origin, for children who are taught to keep secrets often grow up to be observers. They may find it difficult to talk, fearful they may reveal what they have sworn to keep private. Priscilla's secrets now included a sexual relationship with Elvis Presley. How could other fourteen-year-olds possibly relate? "It might have contributed, in her own mind, to being far more sophisticated," as her high school principal, John Reddington, opined. "That she was in on secrets that other girls just giggled about, or talked about behind their hands. After all, the secrets of sex are great secrets."

What was mystifying about Elvis's sexual liaison with a fourteen-year-old was that no one questioned it. Everyone seems to have had a rationalization for looking the other way. Vernon Presley, Elvis's father, chose to ignore the Priscilla predicament, projected Lamar, because "he had his own deal goin'," dating someone else's estranged wife. Gerta, Cliff's fashion model girlfriend, would not comment later on how she felt about Elvis dating a ninth-grader. "Well, I'd rather not answer that. I did not know how old she was. When I met her, I could tell that she was young." Priscilla's principal at the time, Leslie Murray, "didn't think it was a concern at all, and certainly her parents would be the responsible party for that type of thing." Lamar Fike reportedly hooted and hollered at Elvis, "God Almighty damn! Eighteen is one thing, but fourteen? My God! There's a law called statutory rape, and it applies anywhere, I think." Elvis, so the story goes, said he had spoken to her parents and it was all right with them."

Priscilla's defense of her parents in her book, *Elvis and Me,* was weak and unconvincing. By her fourth date with Elvis, she wrote, "Dad had laid down the law: 'If you want to continue seeing Elvis, we're going to have to meet him.' My parents weren't so enthralled with his celebrity status that they were willing to compromise their principles." As long as they met Elvis, it was acceptable for their ninth-grade daughter to stay in his bed until two and three in the morning?

Currie and Carol Grant just shook their heads in wonderment. "Her parents used to take her there and drop her off after she got to know Elvis," Currie recalled. "And Carol and I both thought, Man, if they only knew what was going on in there. It's like leading a lamb to slaughter."

Dee Stanley, the soldier's wife who eventually married Elvis's father, accompanied Vernon when he drove Priscilla home. "It's almost like selling your child, when you really get down to it," she later remarked. "A child at the age of fourteen going home, in high school, at two o'clock in the morning."

Whispers of scandal were ever swirling, recalled H. H. Arnold schoolmate Donna Wells. There was "chatter around the school because apparently her parents were not discouraging the relationship." Though Priscilla was nothing if not discreet, her romance with Elvis Presley was too provocative to remain a secret. Before Christmas, Elvis fired an eccentric South African pseudo-dermatologist named Laurenz Griessel-Landau, who made a pass at him during a skin treatment. Landau later wrote several letters to Elvis, threatening to expose his teen lover and ruin him, a charge that made its way to FBI files before Landau dropped it.

Gerta Heylmann, who would later marry Elvis's close friend Cliff Gleaves, regarded Elvis as protective of Priscilla, mindful that she not be touched by scandal. Perhaps that was why, late that fall, Priscilla did something entirely out of character. Her school held a slave auction, with boys bidding for the services of a female student "slave" to carry their books and run errands for them for a day. Priscilla, because of her beauty and the Elvis mystique, generated the most money. She was pitted against a junior, Donna Wells. Though they barely interacted, "she came and asked me if I would like to go to a party at Elvis's place," Donna recalled. "Back then, Elvis wasn't the cultural icon that he is today. People either were into someone like him or they were not, and I was not. . . . I wasn't sure what her motive was in asking me, because I didn't know her very well, and I said no. Then she came back another time, about two weeks later, and asked would I care to come with some other American teenagers, and I agreed. My curiosity got the better of me."

Donna found the evening strange and discomfiting. She said that Elvis and Priscilla were there, as were "some people from Frankfurt High School whom I didn't know. [Elvis's] dad was there, I believe, and his grandmother. It was an uncomfortable situation. I was uncomfortable with the idea of meeting someone who was in his twenties. . . . GIs weren't supposed to be spending time with American girls. Here he was having parties, meeting some of the kids. . . . I remember I went into the kitchen with Grandma and made popcorn for everybody. And Elvis and Priscilla disappeared shortly after, and the rest of us who didn't know anybody from Adam were left standing around with a few GIs and Grandma and Dad. It was kind of odd."

To Donna, Elvis and Priscilla seemed "smitten" with each other, "shy, kind of," though the Lolita aspect disturbed her. "She was a little girl, really, in a lot of ways. She didn't act older than her age, except that she was kind of a self-possessed person; she wasn't giggly." What bothered Donna most was that she and the other teenagers who had been recruited for the evening "felt like we were kind of a shield of respectability."

Despite her unnatural circumstances, by many accounts Priscilla was cool, calm, and collected when she was at Bad Nauheim with Elvis. Whatever awkwardness she felt paled beside the sheer force of her ambition. Priscilla was almost inhumanly focused; she kept her eye always on the prize. "I did feel out of place," she admitted in a revealing conversation when she was fifty. "They were all older. But my main purpose was not to be with everybody; it was to be with *him*." Now that she was authentically dating Elvis Presley, Priscilla's competitive nature set in: She wanted him to herself.

Priscilla's key rival for Elvis's affection was someone she had never laid eyes on. Her name was Anita Wood, a sweet, bubbly blond from Memphis who had her own successful singing career. Elvis had been dating Anita since he filmed *Jailhouse Rock* in July of 1957; she was his first serious post–Debra Paget romance. Since he arrived in Germany, Anita had been writing to him faithfully from Memphis, and Elvis called her from time to time. Priscilla knew of Anita Wood before the Beaulieus moved to Wiesbaden; once she gained access to Elvis's bedroom, she became obsessed with her. "When he would be downstairs," she later confessed, "every letter that he got—he had a stack on the night table—and I would read them."

Priscilla had cause to be concerned, for Anita was no passing fancy. Elvis was charmed by her petite beauty and had affectionately nicknamed her "Little" for her size-four-and-a-half feet. Feet, which he and his mother called sooties, were one of Elvis's fetishes. Willie Jane Nichols, Gladys Presley's bosom friend, remembered how, on the day his mama was buried, Elvis had thrown himself on her casket, "wild to see her feet" one last time. There was nothing perverse about this, according to Willie; Elvis was simply "staggered" by grief. "Steady-talking all the time. It was breaking your heart. He'd just sit on the doorstep and cry." Anita was with Elvis the day of his mother's funeral, and as a southern girl, she understood their intimate connection, the deep ties of family. "He was just a real sweet, baby-talking guy," was how she remembered him.

She and Elvis, Anita declared, had talked marriage before he was drafted, but publicly downplayed their romance under the strict direction of Elvis's manager, Colonel Tom Parker. "I was supposed to go to Germany to visit him," Anita said. "I'd already had my shots, packed, and everything, but the Colonel put a stop to that. He's the reason I didn't get to go."

Ninth-grader Priscilla Beaulieu, stealing glances at Anita's love letters to Elvis while waiting to go to his bed, was sick to her stomach with jealousy. "I just remember thinking, Okay, I will cherish the time that I am with him, as long as I'm with him. And I can't control what happens after he leaves."

Anita, in the interim, had heard of Elvis's teenage playmate through the Presley grapevine, "and he assured me all the time he was over there—he was such a good persuader—that this poor girl . . . He just had a way of assuring me that this was nothing other than a friend, another army man's daughter. They were just friends. She was so young. There was nothing to it." Elvis wrote a few letters to Anita from Germany—a rarity for him. Anita recalled that "in one of the letters, he said when he got married, it would be to me."

Priscilla anguished over Elvis's complicated love life and the specter of Anita Wood. That she did so alone, unable and unwilling to confide in anyone, is a remarkable feat for a teenage girl. She felt, at times, she later told a magazine, "cheap and unloved." But for all her apparent fragility, Priscilla had a core of steel. "I don't know where I get—even now sometimes—the strength," she confided in 1996. "I certainly couldn't tell him what he could do and what he couldn't do. All I knew was that the time I spent with him was totally devoted to him. And that's all I could do. I couldn't change his mind; I couldn't do anything. So if it was meant to be, it was meant to be. I've done what I could do. And that's basically how I worked it out."

14

SEX AND
ROCK AND ROLL

Priscilla's claim to have left her future with Elvis in the hands of fate was not altogether true. She had a plan, a romantic strategy she had formulated in her enterprising teenage mind, to snare Elvis Presley. "In Anita's letters, I'd already spotted trouble," she recounted. "Doubts that were hitting her. She had heard about me through news or through someone. She definitely knew about me. She knew that there was someone else and 'Would you talk to me about it?' And he had told me that there were problems and that he didn't trust her anymore."

Priscilla began making mental notes from Anita's letters and Elvis's responses, silently assessing and categorizing what he liked and disdained in a woman, what might eliminate her from competition: "All those things that he would say, I internalized: you know, he didn't *trust* [Anita] anymore, that she was going out on him. So I knew what was important to him." Priscilla plotted how she would transform herself into Elvis's ideal woman, just as she had planned the strategy for their original meeting, right down to the Debra Paget hairstyle. It was an audacious plan for a ninth-grader, to contemplate competing with a sophisticated adult woman for the affections of a movie star. "You have to remember," she revealed years later, "it wasn't difficult to behave like that. I felt I was already like that. So I had a head start. I knew that he loved feminine girls. I knew that he loved small girls. . . . I knew his thoughts. I knew what he liked. I knew what he was attracted to. So what was I going to do? *Become* whatever it was."

In order to get what she most wanted, Priscilla had created a persona that she would find an increasingly uncomfortable fit. Elisabeth Stefaniak recalled that Priscilla would occasionally sneak a cigarette behind Elvis's back, even though she knew he did not approve of girls who smoke or drank. And she often felt out of place in Elvis's crowd, mostly GIs and good ol' southern boys in their twenties.

Priscilla was also discovering Elvis's sexual secret during their intimate evenings in his bedroom. It was a revelation that explained much about their unusual relationship and helped unlock the mystery of Elvis Presley's sexual psychology. Elvis confided in Priscilla that his reputation as an international sex symbol created performance anxiety when he had intercourse with a woman. Elvis Presley the consummate performer was so motivated to *please*, to gratify an audience of any size, that the expectation to deliver sexually was incapacitating to him. "And he mentioned that to me, even in Germany," Priscilla revealed.

Joe Esposito formed the same impression from his thirty years in close proximity to the star, though Elvis never expressed it to him in so many words. "Elvis knew very little about sex," Joe said. "He wasn't raised on it. He wouldn't talk to people about it 'cause he figured he knew everything. His ego wouldn't let him talk. Elvis never talked about his sexual affairs with women with us guys. Oh, once in a while [he'd say], 'She was great last night in bed,' but he never went into detail. . . . I don't think he had that much confidence in himself as far as sex goes."

From their exchanged confidences in the bedroom at Bad Nauheim, Priscilla concluded that Elvis did not derive much pleasure from intercourse, presumably because of his insecurity over his performance. "He had other preferences," she later said emphatically, "of making love. . . . And it's not abnormal." Elvis's preference, according to Priscilla, was extended foreplay as opposed to consummating the sex act by penetration. "And not just with *me*. That was just his preference."

That would explain Elvis's fascination with thirteen- and fourteen-year-old girls. He was drawn to them, both romantically and sexually, because that was their level of sexual development. They were innocents, just arriving at the make-out stage of sexuality, where Elvis felt most comfortable. They also had little or no sexual experience by which to judge—or criticize—his performance.

Willie Jane Nichols remembered nights at Elvis's house on Audubon Road in Memphis, his home before Graceland, where the up-and-coming singer, then in his early twenties, regularly invited a small group of fourteen-year-old girls for sleep overs in his bed. "A bunch of girls would come and stay up all night with him," she declared. "They were close little friends and talked and discussed things. Gladys was okay with that. And her home was well chaperoned—Gladys was there." Elvis felt comfortable with these adolescent girls. "He was so insecure," affirmed Willie. "That's why he needed younger girls. And they all wanted to be with him."

Elvis, at heart, was a shy, uneducated southern mama's boy, to a degree sexually ignorant, despite his fame and reputation for carnal knowledge. Alan Fortas, another member of the early Memphis Mafia, claimed Elvis was embarrassed to be seen naked because he was uncircumcised; others suggested he had an inferiority complex about the size of his penis, which according to his female partners, was on the slight side of normal. "Remember, Elvis's childhood was sheltered by his mom, and he wasn't around a lot of guys, so that's what it was more than anything," Joe Esposito surmised. "I saw him nude many times. But he wouldn't openly undress; he was shy about it."

Elvis was a victim of his sexually omnipotent image, knowing he was human, yet still desirous of fulfilling the fantasies of his female fans. His reaction, when it came to sex, was to "withdraw," as Priscilla learned that fall and analyzed thirty-five years later. "Because so much was expected from him. I heard that the same phenomenon happened with Marilyn Monroe. She was a sex symbol, a sex *goddess,* and anyone who was with her expected to be blown out the door with ecstasy. And because of that, she didn't date a lot and she was very insecure in that area. So it's something that I can honestly see how he . . . because women talk about it, you know? And I think he used other means of . . . ways of climaxing."

In a certain way, it begged the question whether Elvis and Priscilla had intercourse in Germany as Currie claims Priscilla told him, or if Elvis penetrated her prior to their honeymoon–the $64,000 question behind the legend–since intercourse, penetration, was not the sexual turn-on for Elvis.

For Priscilla, however, clearly it was. Priscilla Beaulieu, at fourteen, lacked the insight or understanding of Priscilla Presley at fifty vis-à-vis Elvis Presley's sexual pressures. She wrote in her autobiography of "begging" Elvis, during his last days in Germany, "to consummate our love." Elvis portrayed Priscilla to Joe Esposito as the sexual aggressor in Bad Nauheim, claiming she would even "sit on his face" to arouse him. Priscilla's sexual frustration in Germany would set the tone for her future relationship with Elvis and would lead to its eventual demise.

Priscilla was beginning to perceive that Elvis Presley, the person, was not what she had "imagined if" in her childhood fantasies back in Austin. He was a human being, a sex symbol with painful insecurities, a star of fragile complexity, not the demigod she had envisioned. Their relationship, though sexual and romantic, existed more firmly on another, largely symbolic, plane, for Elvis had truly succeeded Jimmy Wagner as Priscilla's fantasy father figure, and Elvis responded in kind. Suni, who saw them together at Goethestrasse that winter, "clowning around" with frozen Pepsis, perceived that Elvis treated Priscilla "like a little *sister.*"

Unbeknownst to Elvis, Priscilla had already found a surrogate for him in Wiesbaden, a punk rebel who embodied everything Elvis Presley the rock-and-roll renegade had seemed to be but was not. Tom Stewart, a sophomore at H. H. Arnold, resembled the boys Priscilla had been attracted to during her last year at Del Valle–dark, slicked-back hair, black leather jacket–a facsimile, in essence, of Elvis.

Former classmates spoke of Tommy in the hushed, reverential tones reserved for the near-mythic. Nouns and adjectives like "wild," "bad boy," "maverick," "James Dean" spilled out of their mouths. "That's poetic bullshit. He wasn't a moody James Dean," countered Tom Muldoon, who ran around with Tommy in Wiesbaden. "He smoke, he drank, he was a damn good athlete, Golden Glove champion, and not afraid to let people know that he was a sort of a dangerous guy. . . . He used to get into fights. Stewart was not a big guy, [but] he was a tough guy."

"He was a guy who was on the fringe," according to Steve Fox, a classmate. "Sociologically on the fringe. Not in the mainstream . . . and he certainly had the intimidation factor. People were careful around him."

In truth, Tom Stewart was an enigma. No one seemed to recall if he had any siblings, what his father did, which girls he dated other than Priscilla. He was a loner who disappeared after graduating, rumored to have been killed in a knife fight on a beach in New Jersey a year after he left Germany.

Above all, Tommy Stewart–Elvis's replacement in Priscilla's life–was *sexual.* Joe Delahunt, who was a member of the same gang, the Spartans, placed Tommy in the "sexually progressive" category. "He used to frequent a street in Wiesbaden where prostitution was legal," recalled Tom Muldoon, another Spartan. "Yeah, of course he had sex. Anytime he wanted he went down to Montestrasse and had sex."

The fact that sweet Priscilla Beaulieu would gravitate to Tom Stewart demonstrated the law that opposites attract. It was indicative, too, of the dark, dangerous side of Priscilla. "I'll tell you what," offered Al Corey, whose family arrived in Germany shortly after Elvis left. "She and Tommy Stewart would leave after school, and God knows where they went. She would wait for Tommy after soccer practice, and he wouldn't even get cleaned up. He'd go with *her* to get cleaned up." The relationship, according to several classmates, had begun even before Elvis returned to the States.

Tommy was virtually Priscilla's only nexus to school. Academic subjects held no interest for Priscilla. She got the answers to German exams from Dave Grant, the studious sophomore who sat next to her. She also drew a classmate, George Bennett, into service. "He did her homework," recalled his roommate, Bob Thomas. "He was awestruck." George's assessment of Priscilla's intellectual acumen was not high. "How can I say this kindly?" posed Bob. "She didn't even know how to *open* a book."

"The common thought about her was, frankly, that she wasn't very bright," Steve Fox explained, and Priscilla's grades bore this out. Jacqueline Momberg, dean of girls, described them as "below average. Whether that was her innate ability or lack of interest I have no idea." However, Steve, a sophomore whose father was a diplomat, sensed that people underestimated Priscilla, "and that's probably been a gift to her."

How could Priscilla Beaulieu be expected to focus on ninth-grade English when she was living a fairy tale? She spent Christmas with Elvis Presley at his private party, where he gave her a platinum watch inlaid with diamonds. She would later contend that a classmate betrayed her and leaked to the school that she was seeing Elvis, but Priscilla openly exhibited her watch that December—to the school secretary, to Stephie McCann, to Linda Williams. "She was really happy to show it off," recalled Barbara Sobelman, a bare acquaintance.

Currie Grant, sometimes with Carol, continued to appear at Elvis's parties, including Christmas. The Grants, in fact, spent New Year's Eve at the Von Steuben Hotel in Frankfurt with Cliff Gleaves and Gerta—and Paul and Ann Beaulieu. Currie had not been blacklisted by Elvis the previous October, as Priscilla claimed, nor had Priscilla or her parents ostracized him.

The Beaulieus, recalled Gerta, were cordial to Currie at dinner and the evening was pleasant, with one exception. "Priscilla's father," related Gerta, "put his hand on my knee or something—I don't know what they call it any-more—but it was very upsetting to Cliff." Captain Beaulieu, she recalled, was "tipsy." "She told Cliff," recalled Currie, "and he said, 'That old son-of-a-bitch! Girlie, are you sure you didn't cause that by sticking your leg up be-tween his?' Of course he jumped on her and they had one hell of a fight. She started crying, 'I had nothing to do with it! He stuck his hand under the table and was trying to feel me up!' " Gerta fled to the ladies room, with Cliff be-hind her, and was so distraught she lost her engagement ring. When she re-turned to the table, Paul Beaulieu "apologized," she recalled, "because Cliff said something to him. He was very upset about this."

Currie was also on the scene for Elvis's birthday party, held on their mutual birthday, January 8. He took the first photograph of Elvis and Priscilla that evening, a now famous shot of Elvis feeding Priscilla birthday cake. Priscilla was spending three and four nights a week with Elvis by then, but was still con-sumed by fear. When Elvis returned from a weeklong bacchanalia in Paris with a few soldier buddies at the end of January, Priscilla approached Currie at the Eagle Club "like a jealous fourteen-year-old, asking, 'What did you do? Did Elvis date a lot of girls? Did he like any of them?' "

Priscilla's reverie drew to a close at the end of February, as Elvis's tenure in the army ended and he prepared to return to the States and resume his inter-rupted career. She had been sprinkled with Elvis fairy-dust for just a little over five months, five months that would intrigue the world.

The public at large got its first inkling of Priscilla Beaulieu at 9:00 A.M. Ger-man time on Monday, March 1, 1960, from an unexpected source—Elvis him-self. The occasion was a farewell press conference the day before his departure, attended by seventy newsmen who had congregated in Friedberg to hear the singer-soldier wax eloquent on army life. They received an unexpected bonus when Elvis, clearly besotted, revealed that he had been seeing a young American girl named Priscilla Beaulieu, the daughter of an air force captain. Priscilla came by her later gilding of the truth naturally, for Elvis altered the facts that morning. Priscilla, he volunteered, was *sixteen,* and their meetings took place, he said, in her father's home.

That afternoon the Beaulieus' phone would not stop ringing. Paul Beaulieu, who had no idea Elvis had released Priscilla's name in a press conference, did his best to support the star's fabricated account, maintaining to reporters that his daughter's friendship with Elvis was "nothing serious." His only concern, he said later, was that he "not embarrass Elvis." Priscilla posed for pictures by a framed photo of Elvis and told journalists she was "very fond" of him. The press, according to May Mann, who often wrote about Elvis in American movie magazines, did not take the story seriously.

Priscilla was riding a rocket, holding on for dear life. She spent Elvis's last night in Germany in his bedroom, where they had spent most of their evenings together. It was, by her description, a desperate, passionate night, with Priscilla—a confused teenager saying good-bye to her boyfriend—making frenzied love to Elvis, pleading with him for intercourse. As they lay in bed, she later wrote in her memoir, he told her for the first time that he loved her.

Currie and Carol Grant were at the house that evening for the big farewell, and Elvis asked them to bring Priscilla to Bad Nauheim the next morning to say good-bye. This was another point in contention between Currie and Priscilla when they met in the spring of 1996:

AUTHOR: Did Currie ever see Elvis again after you told Elvis about—
PRISCILLA: He was not there after that. I never saw him at the house after that.
AUTHOR: Did he drive you to Elvis's house the day Elvis left?
PRISCILLA: No! To Bad Nauheim? No!
AUTHOR: Currie, don't you say that you and Carol drove Priscilla from her home to Elvis's home the day he left?
CURRIE: Uh-huh. At Elvis's request.
PRISCILLA: No. No.
CURRIE: Boy, she is revising the whole history book. . . . Carol and I picked her up at her house . . . because Elvis asked me the night before to bring her out to say good-bye. Then we drove from Elvis's house—after we were there for half an hour—to the base, so he could say good-bye to his friends. All four of us.
PRISCILLA: Wait. *Excuse* me? Excuse me? What is your recollection of this? Tell me again.

CURRIE: There's no recollection. It's exactly what happened. I just told you. We picked you up at your house, okay?

PRISCILLA: And you think my father would *let* you pick me up at the house?

CURRIE: Oh! He was glad to let me pick you up that day. He was *so* glad to let me pick you up that day.

PRISCILLA: I'm sorry, but you have *got* to talk to my father.

CURRIE: We just went up there, picked you up, and took you up there. Spent a half an hour in Elvis's house. Then we all got in my car. A *Life* cameraman took all the pictures around my car. I'm standing outside, holding the door, in fact, for Elvis and her to get in . . . so he could say good-bye to his friends. Priscilla, you don't remember that, huh? You've got something up here that's really blocking your memory. I think you've been in this town [Los Angeles] too long.

Priscilla left after this exchange, claiming Currie was "in a dream world." That night, Joe Esposito phoned me at Priscilla's request to cast doubt on Currie's story and to reinforce Priscilla's claim that Currie did not drive her to Elvis's house the day Elvis left Germany.

This conflict could be independently corroborated. An obscure German magazine, in the early 1960s, published a photo account of Elvis's last day in Germany. One of the photos showed Currie Grant opening the door of his 1955 Chevrolet Bel Air, just as he described, for Priscilla Beaulieu and Elvis Presley to go to the base.

Currie's veracity on this point did not prove conclusively that Priscilla was lying—or in denial—about all of their points of disagreement, but it went a long way toward establishing his legitimacy—and her desperation.

Ray Gunther, a scientist and expert witness with ten years' experience evaluating truthfulness by measuring the stress level of a person's voice via a special computer called a Personality Stress Evaluator, or PSE, analyzed the tape recording of Currie and Priscilla's May 1996 face-to-face confrontation. Of twenty-eight points in dispute between Currie and Priscilla, Gunther found Currie to be telling the truth *100 percent of the time.* He determined that Priscilla was "deceptive" in *all but one* of her statements: that she believed Currie introduced himself, jokingly, as Johnny Appleseed. Currie, however, was deemed truthful in saying he did not *remember* using the name Johnny Appleseed.

Gunther found Currie to be telling the truth:

- when he said Priscilla approached *him* in the snack bar and asked for an introduction to Elvis
- that he never told Priscilla he knew Elvis
- that *he* suggested he meet her parents first

- that it was *Priscilla's* idea they use the ruse of going to the movies to be alone
- that he and Priscilla *did* meet in the hills and make out on four different occasions prior to her meeting Elvis
- that he and Priscilla *did* have intercourse their last time in the hills before he took her to meet Elvis
- that he did *not* attempt to rape Priscilla
- that he *did* pick her up at her house on Elvis's last day in Germany
- that there *were* pictures taken of Elvis and Priscilla and him outside his car

The scientific evidence established that Priscilla was "deceptive," or lying, when she said:

- that she had no interest in meeting Elvis
- that it was *her* idea to have Currie meet her parents
- that Currie approached *her* and asked her if she wanted to meet Elvis
- that she did not know that Currie was a friend of Elvis's
- that she and Currie did not drive up to the hills to make out
- that Currie tried to rape her on their way home from Elvis's
- that she blew the horn
- that he pulled the car over onto a dirt road
- that Currie took her by the Rhine River and tried to rape her a second time
- that she told her parents and Elvis that Currie had tried to rape her
- that Currie did not pick her up to drive her to see Elvis on his last day in Germany

The computerized voice stress test is considered more accurate than a polygraph in determining whether a person is telling the truth—92 percent as opposed to 75 percent—and is used in nine hundred police departments in the United States. After conducting a voice analysis on Currie and Priscilla, Gunther concluded the two "definitely" had intercourse in the hills. Currie's 100 percent truthfulness in the test and Priscilla's deceptiveness were so conclusive, Gunther stated, that he would testify to the results in court.

Beyond the objective analysis provided by the PSE that Currie was telling the truth and Priscilla was lying about their history, the pictorial evidence that Currie picked up Priscilla at her parents' home to say good-bye to Elvis the day he left Germany demonstrated unequivocally that Elvis did not banish Currie, nor did the Beaulieus—*nor did Priscilla.* In fact, Elvis specifically requested that Currie be Priscilla's driver on his last day in Germany.

This would have been a bizarre request if he had been told Currie tried to rape her.

Carol Grant remembered that last morning clearly. "They [Elvis and Priscilla] sat in the back, and I sat in the front with Currie. She was wearing a scarf. Elvis, I remember, had put all this Tanfastic all over himself so he looked like he had a tan." Priscilla never mentioned, to either Currie or Carol, that she had spoken to reporters the afternoon before, nor did she tell her principal why she wanted to be excused from class, saying merely that she was seeing a "friend" off at the airport. She was ever the secret-keeper, a sphinx, her mother's daughter. Alone in the car with Currie and Carol that morning, however, she prattled like the teenager she was—until they drove up to Elvis's house, when the demure Priscilla stepped out of the car. "It was amazing," Currie marveled later, "to watch this transformation."

Priscilla and Elvis rode to the base that afternoon through a cold mist that was emblematic of their mood. As they approached Friedberg, Elvis gave her his army jacket, like a school football hero handing over his letter sweater, "to show you belong to me," he whispered romantically, adding, "I want you to promise me you'll stay the way you are—untouched, just as I left you."

Priscilla later said she felt a chill at Elvis's parting words, "Because he told me *he would know*. Scared the *daylights* out of me." Elvis kissed her and got out of the car to board a bus that would take him to his plane. Priscilla headed for the airport, "numb," as she later described herself, confused by her conflicting feelings for an adult celebrity whose bed she had been sharing for almost five unreal months, and whom she believed she would never see again.

A gaggle of Elvis's friends had gathered to watch his plane take off. Among them were the Grants and Cliff Gleaves. It was there that Currie first learned, from Cliff, that Priscilla had tried to "freeze him out" of Bad Nauheim the previous November. Cliff had waited to break this news until Elvis was en route home to avoid upsetting Currie. "Cliff told me that Priscilla told E.P. that I was asking too many questions," Currie recalled. "And E.P. just laughed about it. He wasn't going to ban Carol and me." Currie was irritated by Cliff's revelation. "We were flabbergasted. Carol and I were sitting in a booth at the airport, and we couldn't believe what we'd just heard. She had tried to slice us out. Cliff said, 'Currie, it's a common thing. Once somebody gets in with Elvis, that person tries to get the other person out.' In her childish way, she tried to get us barred from coming out there."

Priscilla, meanwhile, was in the midst of a mob scene of fans and mostly paparazzi on the tarmac, straining to see Elvis board the plane. She was dressed that day in a suede jacket and a poodle skirt, a demure scarf wrapped round her head with a halo of dark curls peeking through, looking far older than her fourteen years and heartbreakingly beautiful. When Currie heard Cliff's news, he raced to the airstrip, pulled aside the head of the press corps, and pointed out Priscilla as Elvis's teenage girlfriend. Elvis may have revealed Priscilla's name two days earlier, but Currie had let the genie out of the bottle. Within seconds, a cordon of paparazzi had formed about her and flashbulbs ignited. An enterprising photographer, looking for a dramatic shot, directed her to run toward the plane, and Priscilla, dazed and confused, dutifully complied.

The classic photograph of Priscilla Beaulieu, waving a wistful farewell to Elvis, was staged, as were several of the other airport shots of her that day. They all had a poignant, faraway quality—haunting, really—as if Priscilla could see into her future and was in a state of trepidation about what she saw. She described the experience, later, as "traumatic," saying, "I don't ever want to go through that again in my life."

Only two people present that day did not shed a tear as Elvis really left Germany a short time later: Cliff Gleaves and Priscilla Beaulieu. Priscilla had inherited, or acquired, the icy Iversen reserve; her later beau, Mike Edwards, was not certain that in their seven years together he ever saw her truly cry.

Carol Ann Heine, the oldest and wisest member of the Priscilla-Pam-Carol triumvirate, saw the mystical photo of Priscilla bidding good-bye to Elvis in the *Austin-American Statesman* the next day and was not surprised. "I always felt her mother had a plan for her. So it was like her mother got her wish."

In Titusville, Pennsylvania, someone else saw the photo of Priscilla, which was reprinted in *Life* that week. Kathryn Wagner, flipping through the Elvis-in-Germany pictorial, entitled "Farewell to Priscilla, Hello to U.S.A.," stopped when she came upon the portrait of Priscilla Beaulieu frozen in a half-wave. The age was wrong—the magazine said she was sixteen—and the surname was not her granddaughter's, but Kathryn Wagner recognized the face in the photo, for it was the same, she was certain, as her dead son, Jimmy.

15
TWO-TIMING ELVIS

Kathryn Wagner had been waiting eleven years for a sign, some glimmer of her granddaughter's whereabouts; her wildest dreams could not have foretold it would come through Elvis Presley.

The *Titusville Herald* picked up on the story a few days after *Life* hit the stands. "I'm almost positive it is my granddaughter," Mrs. Wagner told the local paper. "I want proof." By an odd twist of fate, the Wagners' surviving son, Gene, was the principal of an American school for children of U.S. Army personnel in Munich; Mrs. Wagner sent him the clipping from *Life* with a letter asking him to look up the Beaulieus in Wiesbaden to see if Elvis's girlfriend was their Priscilla. Then she did as she had for eleven years. She waited.

Waiting was also to be Priscilla's calling where Elvis was concerned for the next six years of her life, though she didn't know it yet. She would later write in her autobiography that she spent the two days after the pop star left locked in her bedroom, refusing to sleep or eat—high drama that seems unlikely. Though Priscilla, like Elvis, occasionally lived in a state of surreal romanticism, she was possessed of a more practical bent. For all her scheming, Priscilla perceived her romance with Elvis as a beautiful, impossible dream. She conceded, years later, that she was sure, as she stood on the tarmac and watched him fly off, that she would never see Elvis Presley again.

The picture Priscilla painted of herself in her memoir as devastated in the days following Elvis's departure was deeply romantic, but it did not comport with her actual behavior. When the press descended on her at school after Elvis left and asked about their relationship, "she herself laughed about it," recalled a teacher friend, Güdrun Von Heister, "because she said that she was not old enough." Nor did her acquaintances at H. H. Arnold observe that Priscilla seemed depressed or even despondent.

Elvis glided back into civilian life, his career, and his tangled love life seemingly effortlessly. Elisabeth Stefaniak followed him to Graceland, pondering an offer to continue as his secretary-companion. Anita Wood was in Memphis, ready to resume her active status as his girlfriend, encouraged by Elvis. Anita had seen the *Life* pictorial on Priscilla Beaulieu and pressed Elisabeth for the details, testing Elvis's dismissal of Priscilla as just a child. "I know she was asking Elisabeth a lot of questions," declared Rex Mansfield, who flew back from Germany with Elvis and was mulling over an offer to become his road manager. "Kind of put Elisabeth on the spot. And she had to be very careful about how she answered those questions." Anita accepted Elvis's explanation and Elisabeth's evasive responses about Priscilla, she said, "Because she was so young. And I just thought she was an ardent fan. I knew she was very pretty from the pictures of her, but . . . he always made me feel, even after I saw her picture, that I was it, I was his girl, and that we would have a future together."

Yet Elvis was telling Joe Esposito, on the set of *G.I. Blues* that spring, that he missed Priscilla and "was going to marry that girl someday." According to his cousin Earl Greenwood, Elvis had read a book on soul mates that deeply impressed him. Elvis felt that if he had a "twin soul," it must be Priscilla, because of her strong resemblance to him, to his mother, and to Debra. "Are You Lonesome Tonight?" was among the first songs he recorded when he got out of the army; not only would he be forever associated with it, but the bittersweet spoken verse, taken from *As You Like It,* would be an almost eerie parallel to his unfolding relationship with Priscilla Beaulieu.

Elvis was a confused man in matters of the heart that spring. After *G.I. Blues* wrapped, he gave Anita a diamond necklace, encouraging her belief that theirs was a potentially permanent relationship—though marriage, he made clear, was far off. "In his letter he talked about marriage, and when he came home he had to go right back to work and he couldn't have a serious relationship," Anita later explained. "We had to keep everything so quiet. Things we said, things we did, the way we felt about each other, could not be public because the Colonel said it would hurt his career." Whether that was true or whether Elvis was avoiding commitment was one of the mysteries of Elvis. Joe Esposito, who became Elvis's road manager when Rex Mansfield turned down the job to marry Elisabeth, saw Elvis as "young, wild, having a great time at the height of his career. I think marriage was the furthest thing from his mind." Elvis, judging by his frequent allusions to it, cherished the *concept* of marriage more than the practice itself.

Priscilla, in truth, was similarly conflicted about Elvis. She and Tom Stewart, the school bad boy, continued their hot-and-heavy relationship, which intensified that spring. "She didn't seem very heartbroken to me," remarked Donna Pollen, who became friendlier with Priscilla that semester. Yet Priscilla wasn't prepared to release the fantasy of Elvis. With her driven, goal-oriented personality, she continued to analyze and scrutinize the competition. When Nancy Sinatra met Elvis's plane in the United States to promote his appearance on a Frank Sinatra TV special, the press linked the two of them. "I used to wonder if he dated her," conceded Priscilla. "I used to envision him dating her, and I would talk myself out of it: 'I *know* she's not his type. It's not something that I know he's attracted to!' " She wrote him girlish letters on pink stationery, addressed to Joe, that amused Elvis's office staff–his cousin Patsy and his aunt Lillian.

Priscilla's parents emphatically had not let go of Elvis. Al Corey, who dated Priscilla during a brief breakup from Tom, stopped showing up at her house, he recalled, because the Beaulieus made him feel unwelcome. "The parents would say, 'Our daughter is with Elvis Presley; you need to find someone else.' Her mother was like a stage mother: 'You're seeing Elvis Presley' was said to her more than one time." Al got the impression that Paul and Ann were reserving Priscilla for Elvis.

For Priscilla, the Elvis side of her life was becoming increasingly surreal. Three weeks passed before Elvis called her from Hollywood, where he was beginning *G.I. Blues*–three weeks that must have seemed like three months in ninth-grade time. Her relationship with a movie star/rock-and-roll idol, though thrilling and exciting on one level, was torturous for Priscilla on another. She wondered if Elvis would ever call her again, she worried about how serious he was with Anita, and she bedeviled herself with images of him romancing his latest sexy costar. Her fears were not unfounded, for Elvis had begun an affair with Juliet Prowse, his leading lady in *G.I. Blues*.

The torture, for Priscilla, was that she had no control. Elvis determined whether he would call her and when, and whether he had any interest in pursuing the relationship. She was powerless to act and could only *react*, a position of submission that had to be especially galling to a girl who was accustomed to being the queen, not a member of the court. Her doubts and insecurities where Elvis was concerned led to a disturbingly schizoid existence. "It was very difficult to get back to being a teenager. . . . Even though I tried to carry on a normal life, it was constantly, Was I going to get a phone call tonight? When was he going to call me back? Is he going to call me back? What's he going through? Can he handle that? Will *she* still be there? My problems were now adult problems that I probably shouldn't have been concerned with at fourteen. Military outfits, combat caravans–I would see him in them; I would see him go along in the Jeeps. I would see him–everything reminded me of Elvis. 'Soldier Boy,' the song by the Shirelles. A different song related to everything."

While a part of Priscilla still clung to her Imagine If fantasies of Elvis, on a day-to-day basis she was embroiled in a real romance with Tom Stewart. "She wasn't pining at all," according to Al Corey, who became friends with her then. "Not at all. She wore Tom's class ring around her neck. Tommy was the only one she was hanging around with. Those two were *it*–every break, every recess, every lunch break. You couldn't put a piece of paper between them." Al recalled that Priscilla's parents tried to prevent her from seeing Tom, but she would sneak out of the house to meet him. "Her dad screamed about her seeing Tommy, and Priscilla just rebelled."

Contrary to her later portrayal of herself as completely involved with Elvis and unable even to *think* of anyone else, Priscilla was in a relationship with Tom that spring that those who knew them or saw them together in and out of school regarded as serious, intense, and powerfully sexual. "It was as intimate as it could be," declared Al, who was in the Spartan brotherhood with Tom and talked to him about his sex life with Priscilla. Did they have intercourse? "Had to be," Al averred. "Priscilla *told* me she and Tommy had sex."

"[Priscilla] and Tom Stewart had a hot relationship," confirmed another Spartan who was close to Tommy. "It wasn't across a milk shake at the snack bar. She was wilder than that, Stewart was wilder than that, and our group was wilder than that. Al Corey would . . . know. Three guys know, not including Tom Stewart, and I'm one of them. I do know the story firsthand." If so, Priscilla Beaulieu was certainly not a virgin on her wedding night; by the age of fifteen she had allegedly had intercourse with Currie, Tommy Stewart, and Elvis himself.

Priscilla not only had her insecurities about Elvis's other women to grapple with, but she was also haunted by his farewell warning to remain "untouched," or he would know. "That was enough to scare the heck out of me," she admitted later.

Priscilla's life in Germany, post-Elvis, was not the lonely endurance test she later depicted it as. Wiesbaden, at the time, was considered the Hollywood of Germany, a beautiful resort town with big-name entertainment. Classmates of Priscilla's described their time at H. H. Arnold as a charmed existence. "[We were] like little kings and queens living as teenagers in Europe after the war, skiing in the Alps and summering in Italy," by Mary Ann Barks's description. Both Mary Ann and Tom Muldoon, Tommy Stewart's close friend, remembered Priscilla drinking beer at the beer stübes, especially Grauerstein, a bar claimed by the Spartans as their hangout. "And then there was a place downtown that served pink champagne," offered Tom Muldoon. "She used to go to that place more than I did." From time to time Priscilla sneaked cigarettes—another item on Elvis's forbidden list—in the bathroom with some of the other girls.

"We were all just little model children, [but] we had this underground life," explained Mary Ann, speaking of the military kids at H. H. Arnold. Much of the mischief occurred when the school's mixed chorus, which included Priscilla, performed out-of-town concerts, staying in hotels. "We were allowed to get away from our parents," remembered Steve Fox. "And many of us, I remember, who were away from home were allowed to do things at fourteen—things like checking into hotels with our girlfriends. I mean, we led a fast-paced life." According to Al Corey, Priscilla was one of the girls who spent the night in a boy's hotel room.

She was also seeing a nineteen-year-old Elvis impersonator who performed at the Eagle Club, a Presley look-alike named Peter Von Wechmar, the self-described "hell-raiser" son of a German baron. Peter was a friend and something of a sexual protégé of Currie Grant's. He told Currie about his relationship with Priscilla. "[Peter and Priscilla] saw each other at the club and had something to drink at the snack bar, and it all started from that," according to Currie. "The club has beautiful grounds and they were walking around, and Peter started kissing her and she responded." Peter told Currie he met Priscilla several times over the coming weeks, primarily for sex. "Because he reminded her so much of Elvis," Currie speculated. "It kind of surprised me a little bit, but then it didn't. Because I knew she was so used to sex, she was really hot-blooded now." Both Peter Von Wechmar and the woman he married within a few years of the Priscilla affair died in the 1980s; Peter's uncle, who was in Wiesbaden when Elvis left Germany, remembered his nephew dating Priscilla. Peter also told his son Victor, now in his thirties, about the relationship. "I don't know if it was intimate," posited Victor Von Wechmar. "I just know they were dating." Peter's adult daughter, Michelle, said she "wouldn't doubt" that her father made love to Priscilla. "No, honestly. Not with my dad, no. He was a playboy back then. Especially looking like—he was almost a twin of Elvis."

"Peter told me they had sex several times after Elvis left and I believe him one hundred percent," Currie said.

As Priscilla carried on her active sex life with Tommy and Peter, occasionally dating Al, she maintained the illusion of purity for Elvis, who believed she was sitting at home waiting to hear from him. "He was assuming she wasn't dating in Germany," confirmed Joe Esposito. "He thought she was crazy about him, and I don't think he thought she'd be the type who'd try to [deceive him]. I'm sure he asked her on the phone if she did, and I'm sure she said no. I don't think she did. I'm pretty sure she was consumed with Elvis at that time." This was another of Priscilla's powerful self-created myths. She reinforced the illusion in her autobiography, declaring that after Elvis called her at the end of March, "I spent all my time writing and rewriting letters to him . . . living in a state of suspended animation, waiting for Elvis's infrequent calls."

"That's the manufactured truth of a celebrity or a quasi-celebrity," claimed Tom Muldoon, a classmate and eventual confidant of Priscilla's: "She is no longer who she was." This altering of reality fit with Priscilla's clash with

Currie; for if Priscilla "manufactured" the artificial reality of a lonely, celibate life after Elvis left Germany, what was to prevent her from creating her own whitewashed version of how she met Elvis and whether she slept with Currie?

Priscilla was so adept at projecting that seemingly innocent persona that the image is perpetuated by some who knew her even in Germany. Classmate Steve Fox, who never dated her, recollected, "My perception of Priscilla was that, in retrospect, she conducted herself with a lot of class. She might sit there and have a beer, but she would sit there and have one beer very slowly, while the rest of the people would get blotto. . . . She didn't. She conducted herself with class and dignity. That's how I would describe her." The Priscilla dichotomy—the Gemini double personality—rendered her alternately wild and refined. The demure Priscilla was the observer. "I hardly ever remember her verbalizing," conceded Steve. "She never was one to start a subject, change a subject, or interrupt a subject. She would just sit there and look pretty."

The daring, fun-loving Priscilla was always present, however, ready to surface when the circumstances were right. Some of her female classmates in Wiesbaden remembered Priscilla as closely chaperoned, unable to attend even girls' slumber parties. But this was another misperception. A month after Elvis flew out of Germany, Priscilla attended a sleep over at the home of Linda Plank, a classmate who worked in the school office with her. Several of the girls at the slumber party, including Priscilla, sneaked out of Linda's house around two-thirty in the morning, went to the school dorm, and pounded on the first-floor window of one of the boys' rooms. At this point the story became blurred depending upon whom one consulted. According to two eyewitnesses in a building across the street and a student in an adjoining dorm room, someone called the air police as the boys opened the window, unhooked the screen, and pulled three girls into the room. One of those girls apparently was Priscilla.

The students were questioned later by school counselors, and their parents met with the principal and vice principal. Donald Trull, the vice principal, confirmed afterward that Priscilla was a member of the slumber party "raising Cain . . . around the dorm. . . . It was a really wild night, apparently." The school's official report was that the girls knocked on a boy's window at about 2:30 A.M. and "one unidentified girl sat on the windowsill." Though they received accounts that a few of the girls, possibly including Priscilla, were inside boys' rooms, "we didn't catch any of them at the time," as Trull put it. "Even if they had," the principal, Leslie Murray, said then, "I would think the last thing that we'd want to do would be to publicize or sensationalize that type of activity."

Priscilla's lightning rod, Currie, heard about the "dorm scandal" from some of the teens who frequented the Eagle Club and took it upon himself to investigate, still somewhat piqued at Priscilla for trying to eliminate him and Carol from Elvis's parties. Posing as a reporter, he phoned the school and asked for details. The dorm incident eventually landed on the front page of the *Overseas Family,* an American newspaper for military families in Europe.

When Priscilla heard that Currie was asking questions, her parents had a friendly telephone conversation about it with him. Outraged to hear that Priscilla was being linked to the scandal, Ann told Currie it was "a big mix-up," claiming "somebody's trying to 'get' Cilla. I guess because she's been getting all this publicity." She denied that Priscilla even attended the controversial sleep over. "It kind of burns me up that anybody would think she was in one of those wild parties. What is going around amongst the kids is what's burning me up. They're trying to name *her* as one of the ones involved. There's very little I don't know as far as she's concerned, because I escort her to all these things. It's very rarely—in fact that's only the second occasion that she's been allowed to go. I mean, we just don't let her go anywhere at all." Former vice principal Donald Trull proclaimed that "Priscilla was definitely there."

Al Corey, who lived in the dorm, recalled recurring incidents where girls sneaked into the boys' rooms to spend the night. "Our windows were actually ground height. They were double windows that opened out, so you could step right into one room, walk down the hall, and go in somebody else's room." Donna Pollen remembered Priscilla meeting up with Tom Stewart at a party with the other girls from the sleep over that night *before* they sneaked out again at 2:30 A.M. By the account of one of the boys in the dorm room, Priscilla was supposed to be baby-sitting, not attending a slumber party. According to Al, this was how Priscilla maneuvered her secret rendezvous with Tommy. "Her mom and dad would go away for the weekend and Priscilla would stay home, or Priscilla would spend the night at a friend's house and Tommy would go over there."

Priscilla admitted, decades later, that she was part of the slumber party that raided the boys' dorm, but she called it "innocent stuff" and claimed that Currie was "stalking" her that night. "The whole time in Germany, I was being stalked by him." That night, she maintained, "all of a sudden I'd see a car creeping through and it was Currie, parked across the street, watching me. Then there was some article that I was in the dorm. You know, he reverses it."

Currie called this a "black lie." He was hosting the Saturday-night *Hit Parade* at the time Priscilla claimed he was "stalking" her in his car. How would he know she was at a slumber party or that she would sneak out at 2:30 A.M. and go to the dorm? The newspaper, moreover, did *not* mention Priscilla, as she claimed.

The whiff of scandal about Priscilla did annoy the Beaulieus, however, and they vented their anger on Currie for asking questions. "My father was going to have him court-martialed," declared Priscilla. "My father's commanding officer called him in the office and wanted to know what it was all about." Paul Beaulieu did report Currie to *Currie's* commanding officer for allegedly agitating the situation; Currie met with his superior, "who asked me what had happened. I told him, and that was the end of it." Priscilla's stepfather did not say a word to Currie's superior officer about Currie allegedly trying to rape his ninth-grade daughter, a strange omission if he was attempting to have him court-martialed. Currie continued in the air force without even a reprimand.

The great H. H. Arnold dorm scandal unfolded with no one in the cast of characters coming off too well: Priscilla, looking slightly soiled; Ann, lying to protect her daughter; and Currie, a bit fixated on Priscilla.

16

FAMILY SKELETONS

The weekend after the dormitory affair was Easter. Two weeks had passed since Gene Wagner received the letter from his mother bidding him to travel to Wiesbaden in search of their long-lost Priscilla. He had seen the pictures of Elvis's girlfriend in German newspapers, "but I didn't know that Priscilla was *that* Priscilla—that Priscilla Beaulieu was Priscilla Wagner."

Gene checked into the Von Steuben Hotel, looked up the Beaulieus' telephone number, and called their house. He eventually found Ann at home and confirmed that she was his former sister-in-law. "Ann said, 'Come on over,' " he recalled. She seemed pleased to hear from him. "I was excited about seeing Ann, 'cause she had been a big thing in my life. I couldn't imagine how Priscilla looked. I had no idea how tall, how big, what she looked like." The timing for Ann was fortuitous: Paul Beaulieu was out of town; only she and Priscilla were at home when their visitor arrived.

Gene Wagner, a shy, sensitive teacher, had no idea why his family had been kept from Priscilla for the past eleven years or why her name had been changed to Beaulieu, and he did not wish to make trouble for his late brother's wife. So he stood in front of his only niece, whom he had not seen since she was three, uncertain what to do. "I didn't know if Priscilla knew who I was. I didn't say anything because I didn't want to embarrass Ann. I didn't want to say, 'Hey, I'm your dad's brother!' I didn't know if Ann had even told her. . . . I just said, 'Hello. How are you?' "

The circumstances were made equally awkward for Priscilla. "My mother said that my uncle Gene was going to come by," she said later. It was the first time Priscilla had heard that her real father had a brother, that she had an uncle and grandmother she never knew about. "But I was very *contained*. There was only so much I felt comfortable with, because I knew my mother was uncomfortable. So I didn't really ask a lot of questions. . . . I didn't really go into anything. I mean, he was a stranger to me."

Ann and Gene had a "nice visit," by his description, laughing and reminiscing about Jimmy and old times. "In fact, she mentioned things that I had completely forgotten when she stayed with us for those couple months after my brother was killed." Ann also presented a considerably sanitized version of Priscilla's relationship with Elvis for the Wagners, reassuring Gene that the press accounts of a romance between Elvis and Jimmy's fourteen-year-old daughter "were not true. They were exaggerated. Elvis was not taking her out, they were not spending all night out and all that." Ann stressed that "school came first."

Gene had made hotel arrangements for the week, hoping he would find his niece and they would get reacquainted. When he returned to the Beaulieus' a day later, however, the atmosphere was tense. Paul was back in town, and Priscilla's two half brothers and her half sister were at home. Ann took him aside, Gene remembered, and asked him, sotto voce, if he would pretend he was just a "friend" and not Priscilla's uncle, because the other children did not know who her real father was "and [Ann] didn't want to have to explain to them that she was married before," though Priscilla knew. "So I visited as a friend of the family," recalled Gene.

"She was concerned because the other kids were going to be there," declared Priscilla. "And here was this *stranger.* I think my mother talked to Gene and asked him please not to say anything to my father."

Paul Beaulieu came home shortly after Gene arrived, making the situation even more tense. "When Ann introduced me to Beaulieu he left immediately," recalled Gene. "I sort of felt that he was a little uptight that I had shown up. He left the room, and I didn't see him again. In fact, I don't even [remember] if he shook my hand. He hardly acknowledged me. He was very cool and didn't say anything." Gene sensed the antagonism. "Well, there was something," as he put it later. "I sort of felt maybe I shouldn't have shown up unexpected. Maybe that was the problem."

Gene took photographs of Priscilla for Kathryn Wagner, who was waiting anxiously back in Pennsylvania. She posed prettily, first alone, then with her mother and siblings. Ann was no longer the Rooney whom Jimmy's mother had known. Her face had grown hard with the passing years. She still tried to project an aura of glamour, however; her figure was pencil-slim despite her four children, and she posed, model-style, with one high-heeled foot in front of the other. Priscilla's anxiety was nowhere apparent in the pictures. She was costumed neatly in a blue hoop skirt with a sweater draped over her shoulders, smiling like the girl who got Elvis—as she was.

Gene Wagner handed out gifts to all the children and left shortly afterward, without so much as a single conversation alone with his niece. "I think he brought me something," affirmed Priscilla. "I just know it was a very uncomfortable feeling and a very uncomfortable situation. And I know my mother was *extremely* uncomfortable. He didn't stay very long."

Gene wrote his mother in Titusville and broke the news that her missing granddaughter had been found, enclosing the snapshots he had taken. Kathryn Wagner was ecstatic. She wrote Ann a fourteen-page letter expressing how thrilled she was to have found her and Priscilla again, bringing her up to date. Not a word was mentioned about the eleven years she had missed of her only grandchild's life. She sent the letter in care of Paul Beaulieu at his military address in Wiesbaden and waited once more, this time with joy, for a letter or phone call from Ann and Priscilla. None ever came. Days passed, then weeks, finally months.

Kathryn Wagner concluded that Paul Beaulieu had gotten the letter and never passed it on to Ann or Priscilla. It was he, her woman's intuition told her, who had kept them apart all these years. "I know it as if . . . oh, as if I'd read it someplace or somebody had told me," she later remarked. "Everything was perfectly all right till she married this person. It was just through him that Ann wouldn't share Priscilla with us after she was married. He just didn't want that. I know Ann would listen. Whatever he would say, she would do." Mrs. Wagner could not figure out *why*. Perhaps, she conjectured, "Ballou," as she pronounced Paul's surname, bore a grudge against the Wagners because they were German Protestants and he was a French Catholic. She was grasping at straws. Gene Wagner would barely acknowledge, later, how hurt he was by the slight: "I keep it hidden, my feelings." He also was at a loss to understand why Ann excommunicated them. A female friend of his stumbled upon the reason Ann's cousin Margaret had revealed. "I had a close girlfriend, Connie," said Gene, "who told me she read someplace that the second husband can be very, very jealous of the first husband. And insecure. She said maybe he was very jealous of Jim."

"Maybe Ann was afraid of him," Kathryn Wagner speculated. "I can't fathom it. I can't solve it. So I just forget about it."

Mrs. Wagner decided to do nothing further. "I always look at it this way," she said in the 1970s. "It's the way God wanted it to be. My heart was broken for a long, long time. But I'd think, Well, if that's the way she wants it, that's the way it will be." At least she had the photographs of Priscilla, looking so like Jim, and she knew her granddaughter was alive and well—and dating Elvis Presley.

Priscilla never knew that her grandmother had sent her a letter that spring, expressing her constant love, anxious to reenter her life. She never saw it. Whether Ann did was another of Anna Iversen Wagner Beaulieu's closely held secrets.

Ann Beaulieu encountered a ghost from her past that April; in June, Priscilla nearly faced a ghost of her own. Pam Rutherford and her family, who were stationed in England, made plans to stop in Wiesbaden for a few days over the summer holiday. Pam wrote to Linda Williams in advance to arrange to spend time with both her and Priscilla, whom she hadn't seen in two years. The famed photograph of Priscilla waving good-bye to Elvis Presley had even made the British newspapers, and Pam had clipped it out in disbelief, stunned that her former best friend had realized her fantasy about Elvis from their games of Imagine If in Texas.

When the Rutherfords arrived in Germany, Pam met Linda as planned, but when she got to the Beaulieus' at the arranged time, Priscilla was nowhere around. Pam waited and waited for her childhood friend, but Priscilla never appeared. Pam left Wiesbaden feeling snubbed, and wrote Carol Ann how hurt she was. "I don't remember what the problem was," Linda said diplomatically.

In retrospect, Priscilla's motivation is clear. She *couldn't* see Pam Rutherford now, for Pam was the keeper of one of Priscilla's secrets: She knew that Priscilla was a longtime Elvis Presley fan and that she had hoped fervently, for three years, that she would one day meet Elvis, date Elvis, and marry Elvis.

The Beaulieus moved soon after Pam's visit, the summer between Priscilla's freshman and sophomore years. Base housing became available, enabling them to leave their flat in downtown Wiesbaden for more spacious officers' quarters in Aukamm, adjacent to the school. H. H. Arnold was situated picturesquely on one of the numerous hills above Wiesbaden, with military housing extending from its grounds like spokes on a wheel. After a brief stay in a smaller apartment, the Beaulieus took up residence on the third floor of a three-story building on Westfalenstrasse. Each floor contained two apartments, with maid's quarters in the basement.

Now that Priscilla was no longer physically isolated downtown and emotionally distanced by Elvis's presence, she spent more time with Al Corey and made her first real girlfriend, Debbie Ross, whose family lived across the hall from the Beaulieus. Debbie was Priscilla's physical and intellectual opposite—a cute, bookish blond cheerleader—which may have drawn Priscilla to her. "Because there was no competition. . . . I guess I was somewhat in awe of Priscilla, but I also knew that I had things she needed, in terms of just being a friend. I was one of the few girlfriends she had there." Debbie ate dinner with the Beaulieus, spent the night in their apartment, listened to records, and occasionally helped Priscilla with her homework.

The Elvis part of Priscilla's life, Debbie recalled, "was all sort of mysterious." Mary Ann Barks, who was in Debbie's clique, remembered spending the night at Priscilla's with Debbie when Elvis called. "I thought, Oh, my God, Elvis is on the phone! At that time calling the States was like calling the moon. You had to practically put a phone call in and wait a day to get the call back, and there would be crackling and God knows how much it cost. You'd only call back to the States if somebody was dying or you had to get some emergency information. And he was just calling her!" Mary Ann knew that Priscilla had gone to the airport to see Elvis off, and she'd heard the rumors, but still wasn't sure whether to believe them. "I just remember going into her room and seeing Elvis's combat jacket on her wall. That stands out. She nailed it up in her bedroom. I'm going, Oh, my God, this is for real!"

Priscilla was in a strange Twilight Zone, receiving sporadic but heart-stopping phone calls from Elvis, preserving a shrine to him in her bedroom; yet he was, to her, a chimera, a fantastical object of her youthful fancy. Interestingly, that was how her female classmates saw *Priscilla*, because of her contact with Elvis. "It was just like she was in an untouchable category," explained Debbie. "Not approachable. Too pretty, too unreal, not a part of us." Debbie was Priscilla's best friend at that time, but they were not what Debbie considered close.

"I didn't really get involved or ask a lot of questions about [her relationship with Elvis]," Debbie said years later. "I was interested in her as my friend, not as a way to get to anything, and maybe that's why we could be friends." Priscilla did show Debbie her treasure box, however, and lamented how difficult it was to get letters to Elvis, that she had to send them through Joe Esposito on special pink stationery—though Joe would not remember a color code. "She did show me some things [Elvis] had sent her or given her," Debbie recalled. "She used to bring her album that he had given her over to my house—I think I had a better stereo or something—and we'd sit there and listen to him." Debbie remembered that Priscilla became extremely upset when Debbie scratched one of her Elvis records.

Elvis shipped Priscilla other albums and .45s from the States, "songs that identified with our relationship," Priscilla recalled. " 'Sealed with a Kiss' was one. 'Hey, Hey, Paula, Will You Marry Me One Day?' " Elvis also sent Priscilla a copy of "Good Night, My Love," the song that signed off the broadcast they listened to in his bedroom. "So many reminders," as she put it. Debbie felt, from her conversations with Priscilla then, that she had a love for Elvis but, more significantly, that there "seemed to be some *security* there. Or something she knew there."

Priscilla began her sophomore year continuing her double life, deeply involved with Tommy, in a fantasy romance with Elvis—who still believed he was the only one. She made another girlfriend, an eighth-grade girl named Ronnie Garland, whose family lived in the apartment just below hers and whose parents socialized with Paul and Ann Beaulieu. Ronnie and Priscilla would keep each other company while they baby-sat for their siblings, and the two exchanged confidences, becoming as close as Priscilla allowed herself to be with another girl.

Ronnie described Priscilla's romance with Tom Stewart as "really serious," and noticed her tendency to be attracted to dangerous guys. "She was drawn . . . not to your clean-cut all-American . . . she was drawn to the bad ones. . . . I would have been scared to death with Tom." Like Al, she perceived Priscilla's relationship with Tommy as a "sneak-around thing," with Priscilla meeting him down the street or pretending to go to a girlfriend's house so that her parents would not find out, for "her father did not approve of this."

Priscilla's father, Ronnie and her parents observed, had a double standard. "I remember my dad kept saying, 'For him to be so strict and have so many rules, and then to let her go at such an early age and be alone with Elvis Presley . . .'" Paul Beaulieu's reputation for keeping a tight rein on Priscilla due to his behavior was *after* Elvis left Germany, when he tried very hard to prevent Priscilla from dating anyone *but* Elvis. "He was promoting this from the very beginning," declared Ronnie, who remembered Priscilla's father coming to the house for parties, showing off photographs of Priscilla with Elvis, which he said were taken the night they met—at a small reception the Beaulieus attended, in *his* version. "He was very proud of these pictures," said Ronnie. In these photos "Elvis had a crew-cut. I think he was sitting at a piano. But I know that Captain Beaulieu—Major Beaulieu, whatever he was—had pictures, and he showed them to my parents and the people they would get together with downstairs. And he'd talk about it a lot, too." Margaret Iversen Ramis, Ann's Connecticut cousin, had the same impression. Paul, she observed when she met him, always wanted to be somebody important; serving as Priscilla's connection to Elvis was his claim to fame.

Ronnie remained Priscilla's close friend and downstairs neighbor for the Beaulieus' three remaining years in Wiesbaden, and had abundant opportunity to observe the family dynamics, which she found strange. Paul Beaulieu especially disturbed her. "I was never comfortable around him," she admitted. Priscilla, Ronnie said, "was afraid of him. . . . That was real evident. She was absolutely panicked." Perhaps Suni Ernst had correctly surmised that Priscilla dated Elvis to escape from something at home, for Ronnie remembered that Priscilla seemed desperate to avoid her stepfather. "I just know what you sense as a person," Ronnie said. "She was definitely afraid of him. She'd have to baby-sit a lot, and that was usually when she would ask me up and we'd talk. She'd say little things." Ronnie's father had a similar foreboding about Paul, occasionally mentioning to Ronnie that he was a "strange man." Both the Beaulieus, by her recollection, "drank quite a bit." Ann, she commented, "was such a pretty lady. He was not a good-looking man."

Ronnie noticed the unusually tight bond between "Cilla" and her mother.

Priscilla's real father, James F. Wagner, when he secretly courted her fifteen-year-old mother.
Collection of Currie Grant.
Photograph courtesy of Kathryn Wagner.

Priscilla's mother, Anna Iversen ("Rooney"), in a glamour pose.
Collection of Currie Grant.
Photograph courtesy of Kathryn Wagner.

This is the photograph of Jimmy Wagner that his daughter secretly wore in a locket as her "guardian angel."

Collection of Currie Grant. Photograph courtesy of Kathryn Wagner.

The photo of "Mommy and Daddy and Priscilla" that Priscilla found in a trunk, revealing she was Priscilla Wagner, not Beaulieu.

Collection of Currie Grant. Photograph courtesy of Kathryn Wagner.

A picture of Priscilla with her real father, James F. Wagner. He would die tragically soon thereafter, on his way to see her. *Collection of Currie Grant. Photograph courtesy of Kathryn Wagner.*

Already a beauty—and beauty contestant—at three years of age. *Collection of Currie Grant. Photograph courtesy of Kathryn Wagner.*

Priscilla's school
photograph from
second grade.
*Photograph courtesy of
Katherine Patton.*

SCHOOL DAYS 1952-'53
I.W. Podham

Priscilla with friend
Donna Brooke in the
fifth grade at I.W.
Podham, 1955–56.
*Photograph courtesy of
Ann George.*

Priscilla is crowned Carnival Queen. Her best friend and rival Pam Rutherford
is second from right (in starred cape). *Photograph courtesy of Pam Gaines.*

A young Elvis backstage with fans, Barbra and Charlotte Dampier, after a 1955 concert in Conroe, Texas, a few hundred miles from an adoring Priscilla.

Photograph courtesy of Barbra Dampier LaCarter and Charlotte Dampier Spurlock.

With fans at New Orleans Municipal Auditorium, 1956.

Photograph courtesy of Beryl C. Quinton.

Priscilla, at thirteen (center), in Del Valle, Texas. Pam Rutherford, her best friend, is second from the right. *Photograph courtesy of Evangeline Anguiano.*

As a cheerleader, she was considered the prettiest girl at Del Valle Jr. High.
Photograph courtesy of Del Valle Jr./Sr. High.

A mature-looking eighth-grader at Del Valle, the year before she met Elvis.
Photograph courtesy of Del Valle Jr./Sr. High.

Elvis and friends at the Lido in Paris, January 1960. Currie Grant sits next to Elvis, two months after Elvis supposedly banished him. Joe Esposito is front left, beside Heli Priemel. Cliff Gleaves, Elvis's best friend, is at front right.
Collection of Currie Grant. Used by permission.

Currie Grant in 1977, standing in front of the house on Goethestrasse where he took Priscilla to meet Elvis in September 1959.

Collection of Currie Grant. Used by permission.

Elisabeth Stefaniak, Elvis's German secretary and sometime date, until Priscilla arrived.

Photograph copyright © 1997 by Currie Grant. Used by permission.

Elvis singing and playing for friends at Bad Nauheim in 1959.

Photograph copyright © 1997 by Currie Grant. Used by permission.

Priscilla "worshiped" Ann, and Ann, Ronnie felt, genuinely "wanted the best" for Priscilla. "Priscilla told me about her mother. She loved her mother. I liked Ann. But her mother was quiet. I really think she was afraid of [Paul Beaulieu] too." Ronnie's little sister and Priscilla's younger sister, Michelle, were also best friends and were the same age, so the two younger girls spent much time together, often spending the night at each other's houses. "Ann had a black eye one time," recalled Ronnie. "And Michelle told my little sister, 'My daddy hits my mommy.'" Ronnie didn't know whether to believe Michelle, since the girls were "just little twerps" of seven or so, but the child's story was consistent with Ronnie's intuitive discomfort around Priscilla's father.

Might this have been another dark secret that Ann and Priscilla shared—an unspoken element of their symbiotic bond? That Paul Beaulieu abused Ann, and possibly Priscilla too? If this was true, it would explain Ann's almost hysterical fear of revealing—to anyone—Jimmy Wagner's existence.

The Beaulieus were frozen in a web of fear and denial: Ann, forced to eradicate all traces of her first husband, the handsome, endearing father of her precious child; Priscilla, deprived of her identity and a relationship with her grandparents and uncle, pressured into harboring dark family secrets; her half siblings, kept in the dark about their sister's background and their mother's past. Paul Beaulieu had bullied them into enacting a charade to gratify his weak masculine ego, and they existed in an atmosphere of fear and repression. It was the irony of ironies that the fame and glory Priscilla's stepfather so coveted and finally achieved vicariously sprang from Jimmy Wagner, through the "daughter" Paul was so keen to call his own. Ann Beaulieu, like Paul, turned to alcohol as one way to numb her senses, as a buffer between herself and reality. Did that reality include abuse?

"At the time, all I knew was that [Paul Beaulieu] was creepy and I didn't like being around him," Ronnie remembered. "I really think that's what my daddy was trying to tell me about this man: 'There's something wrong with this guy, Ronnie.' But it was never said to me, I never saw it. Priscilla really held her emotions in check. . . . She was always in command of everything. If she was hurting or upset, you were never totally aware of it. Not by words, anyway."

If there was abuse in the Beaulieu house, confirmation of its existence would never come from Priscilla's lips. Yet her behavior did raise flags. Mike Stone found it odd that Priscilla "never really talked about her childhood. And it always was kind of a mystery. And I don't know why that is. Because we've talked about my childhood obviously, and there were a lot of things I wanted to share, that I didn't want to hide. But for whatever reasons *she* had, she rarely talked about her childhood at all." When Priscilla did speak of Paul Beaulieu, once she was famous, she lionized him, writing in her memoir of "my strong, handsome father, who was the center of our world," gushing to interviewers about how "wonderful" he was. Classic compensatory behavior for someone who has been abused. Or as Shakespeare wrote in *Hamlet*, "The lady doth protest too much, methinks."

"She was really afraid of him," Ronnie insisted. "And I don't know if it was just because he was strict or what." This fear of Paul Beaulieu may have forged an even tighter bond between Priscilla and her mother, explaining why Ann was so permissive with Priscilla. Out of mingled guilt, love, and remorse over exposing Priscilla to a harsh home life, and regret over her own lost love, Ann may have allowed her daughter to do things other mothers would never have sanctioned.

This may also have been why Priscilla viewed Elvis, in her friend Debbie's estimation, as a sort of haven, a sanctuary for her future. Mike Edwards saw the relationship with Elvis as something mystical that was placed in Priscilla's path as a means of escape from a troubled childhood.

Other clues also pointed in this direction. "I never considered her all that happy," Ronnie analyzed, "being as pretty as she was. You'd think, with the rest of us looking at her in envy–'Well, what more could she want?'–you know? But she never seemed all that happy to me."

17

BABY DOLL

Priscilla's relationship with Tom Stewart turned turbulent that fall. Friends gave different accounts of who broke up with whom, each claiming the other was devastated. Priscilla, true to what would become her romantic trademark, bounced back instantly.

While on the rebound from Tom, she dated Al Corey and then switched to a junior on the football team, Darrell Johnson. She and Darrell had a three-month fling consisting mostly of "passionate kissing" and sock hops, by his recollection. "She was a busy girl then," Al recalled. Priscilla painted this period with a different brush, describing herself as still pining for Elvis and declaring that "my head wasn't into dating." Classmates begged to differ, however. She was *always* dating, scoffed Donna Pollen. "There were so many it was kind of a joke." Elvis became almost a figment of Priscilla's imagination, a comet that passed through her life in the form of a phone call every few months.

By the middle of football season, Priscilla had bagged the star of the team, a good-looking senior quarterback named Ron Tapp. She was wearing his football jacket within days, going steady. This relationship demonstrated her democratic dating policy. "She did an about-face from dating the hood types," as Donna put it, to "a Joe College football player." Like a chameleon, Priscilla would adapt to the image of her latest beau. "She was very feminine, very refined, always very beautiful," Ron rhapsodized. "Maybe that was part of the overall aura of her."

Currie, who had been discharged from the air force and was living with his family in California, returned to Germany after Christmas for a short visit, and Elvis continued to socialize with him in Hollywood. When he heard that Currie was going to Wiesbaden, Elvis asked him to stop by the Beaulieus' and take some photographs of Priscilla. "Please, Currie," he entreated, "take some pictures and bring them back. I want to see what she looks like now." Priscilla, despite her claim that Currie tried to rape her, was thrilled to oblige, "desperate" for word from Elvis, through Currie. Outtakes from the photo session reveal an ebullient Priscilla and Ann, laughing and joking with Currie and Peter Von Wechmar, who was no longer dating Priscilla but tagged along. Currie recalled Priscilla as giddy at touching him, because *he* had touched Elvis.

Elvis was bobbing in and out with different women, his attention span lasting approximately as long as the six-week shoots of his increasingly formulaic films. Since leaving the army twelve months earlier, he had shot *G.I. Blues, Flaming Star, Wild in the Country,* and part of *Blue Hawaii,* enjoying serial romances with costars Juliet Prowse, Anne Helm, Tuesday Weld, and Hope Lange, as well as a brief affair with a script girl and his steady relationship with Anita Wood. His life was like an endless bachelor party, re-created nightly at a house he was renting on Perugia Way in Bel Air, cast with eager, comely starlets from his pictures and anyone else who was fortunate enough to meet him and catch his fancy. Elvis, in 1960, was the dashing prince in the kingdom of Hollywood who, with a wave of his magic wand, could transport some lucky girl into his fairy tale.

"When I was fifteen," remembered Patty Perry, "a girl I was working with at a beauty school decided that we were going to a frat party at L.A. City College. And we were driving this old Buick down Santa Monica Boulevard in November of 1960 and we see this black Rolls-Royce. We pull up and it's Elvis Presley! We pretend we don't know who it is. And he rolls down his window and says hi. I said, 'You look familiar. Do we know you from somewhere?' And he started laughing." Elvis, on his way to record the sound track for *Flaming Star,* gave the girls his phone number and invited them to come to one of his parties. Patty and her friend went to the fraternity house, behaving as if they had encountered a god. "He was gorgeous. Black hair, blue eyes. And he was wearing a sailor hat, always wore a sailor hat in those days. He did not like to wash his hair." When Patty called the house later and reminded Elvis's cousin who she and her friend were, he offered to send a limousine. Patty and Elvis became instant platonic friends when she visited him in Bel Air. Elvis, who was amused by her brash sense of humor, gave her a pet name (Patricia), hired her to cut his hair, and folded her into the entourage as its only female. "I don't call myself Elvis's hairdresser," Patty said. "I was his little sis." As such, she was privy to the revolving door of women in Elvis's life. "Every night there were parties at the house, and every night the girls would drive up. It was like an open party. . . . He was dating everyone that he was working with."

Priscilla was but a distant dream. Elvis, Joe declared, "never said to me, 'Hey, did we get a letter from her today?' He had Anita, his girlfriend at the time. He was busy with his movies. And Elvis—all his life he loved women. He always had affairs, no matter how much he loved somebody, he had to *be* with someone . . . but there were times he said, 'Hey, let's call her up.' So he did have [Priscilla] on his mind."

Priscilla, ever the competitor, fretted about Elvis's costars, poring over *Stars and Stripes* for any shred of Hollywood gossip, her imagination running rampant, fueled by rumors of on-set romances. A part of her was still driven to realize her childhood goal, but Currie, who answered her volley of questions about Elvis that spring, did not see her as in love with him. "She was starstruck. She didn't know what love was yet. It was just the name value and all the friends she had, all the oohs and ahs! 'You're dating Elvis Presley!' She was a schoolgirl, and it got to her, just like a proud peacock with her chest out: 'Yeah, I got Elvis!'"

Priscilla, ironically, was conducting her love life in the same manner as Elvis. "She had a life of her own *way* past anything . . . kind of in addition to her life with Elvis," as Al Corey put it. "Kind of like he did with her." Elvis had no clue. "He saw her as this young, innocent girl," posited Joe Esposito, "that he wanted to raise the way *he* wanted her to be. I could see that he knew she was innocent, and he had this thing about virgins and young girls. That's the reason he liked to date them, 'cause he didn't like the thought of other men having slept with them." When Currie presented his snapshots of Priscilla to Elvis that spring—holding daisies in a field behind her apartment, smiling and fresh-faced—it perpetuated his romantic illusion of the little girl he had left behind who was saving herself for his touch only. And that was just how Priscilla wanted it—and later falsely presented it in books and interviews.

In truth, she could have taught Elvis a trick or two about romantic manipulation and duplicity. Currie had given her proofs of the photos he took of her for Elvis, and Priscilla gave them to Ron Tapp, the football hero she was going steady with in Germany. Her good friend Ronnie Garland, a perceptive teenager, saw the Elvis relationship as a sort of fantasy to Priscilla: "You could look at her and see that this was like a fairyland. I'm sure she didn't relate this to life, to normal life—being a freshman in high school when she met him. It was like a princess story come true. She went back to her own boyfriend and her own group, everything. This has to have been very bizarre." Ron, who dated Priscilla exclusively all through his senior year, regarded their relationship as serious on both their parts.

The obstacle, in the opinion of Priscilla's closest friends, was her parents. "Apparently she was not welcome to allow her life to go on that way," Ronnie said, "[as] normal." Ron Tapp concurred, recalling that Paul Beaulieu was ultra-strict, even imposing a ten-thirty curfew on Ron's graduation night, causing them to miss the graduation party. "He wanted her back . . . right after graduation. We talked about that, but he won." Ron later found it difficult to believe that Captain Beaulieu had permitted Priscilla to stay at Elvis's house until two and three in the morning unchaperoned the year before. Debbie Ross, Priscilla's other close friend and neighbor, also found it incongruous: "As I grew older, I thought, Gee, that was really sort of strange that he was strict with her among teenagers and she was seeing a man who was ten years older than we were." Debbie—like Ronnie, Al, Suni, and others—recalled Priscilla's father "being strict and gruff about everything." Debbie concluded, as had the others, that the Beaulieus had a different policy where Elvis was concerned. "There were two sets of rules. Definitely. I recall discussing things like that with [Priscilla] and wondering, Well, how does that happen?" It happened, one could only conclude, because Paul and Ann Beaulieu were seduced by the glamour and glory of Elvis. Priscilla's teenage boyfriends didn't stand a chance.

The proof of Priscilla's feelings for Ron Tapp were in the pictures she gave him. The breezy photos Currie took of her for Elvis, romping in jeans and a sweater, showing off her Christmas watch, were innocent and youthful, as Elvis saw her. At the same time, however, Priscilla was giving Ron snapshots of herself posing in baby-doll pajamas, gazing into the camera with raw seductiveness. In one photo she is lying on her stomach on the Beaulieus' living room floor with her left leg bent at the knee suggestively, her baby-doll top pulled up above her waist to reveal her panties, a seductive look on her face. In another photograph she is standing in her baby dolls, looking straight at the camera with aggressive sexuality. Ron had no recollection of where the photos came from. "I don't know if I asked for a picture or what. She gave them to me. My memory is that her parents took them. I don't think I ever asked." It struck him as curious, though, that Priscilla's parents, who were so strict where he was concerned, would take cheesecake photos of their daughter in shorty pajamas—if they were the ones who shot the pictures. "I didn't really understand it, but they were nice pictures!" The fact that Priscilla, at fifteen, would present her high school boyfriend with provocative photos of herself in revealing lingerie, spoke volumes about her sexuality and the nature of their relationship, though Ron was too much of a gentleman to provide details.

She confided in Al Corey that she was concerned about Elvis's warning that he would know if she'd been with someone else, although the fear was more imaginary than real, since her only contact with the star was an occasional phone call and she had no idea whether or when she would see him again. In fact, to a bookmaker, the odds for survival of Priscilla and Elvis's relationship would have been slim. They lived on different continents, rarely talked, and were seriously involved with other people—not taking into consideration that one was a high school sophomore and the other a twenty-six-year-old rock legend in the making.

Priscilla was a mixed-up fifteen-year-old, a sex kitten masquerading as an innocent for a movie star with a virginity fetish. Her confusion and rebellion played itself out at school, where she was suspended twice, once for wearing a bare-midriff blouse, and another time by the gym teacher, Geraldine Hopper, with whom she had running "contests of will" over her refusal to take a shower, because, explained Miss Hopper, she "wouldn't have time for primping in front of the mirror."

"The P.E. teacher and Priscilla were always fighting," recalled the principal, "because Priscilla had this mass of gorgeous hair and didn't want to take showers." Priscilla's obsession with her appearance had, if anything, worsened since she met Elvis and started high school. "Even in class," recalled Güdrun Von Heister, who taught her remedial French that summer, "I would have to say to put her lipstick away. She . . . had her mirror out and her lipstick, and she's combing her hair and fixing her eyebrows and all that." Sex and vanity were Priscilla's two driving forces, the vestige of a childhood where her self-worth was connected to her physical beauty.

Ann Beaulieu, not surprisingly, supported and defended Priscilla in her battles with the school administration, dispatching Paul to take up Priscilla's cause with the principal, John Reddington. Reddington, who arrived the year after the Elvis frisson but knew of it, took measure of the situation. Captain Beaulieu, he recalled, was indignant "because he thought there were things at the high school that weren't being done properly; justice wasn't being done to Priscilla. . . . My perception of the encounter was that, for whatever reason, he had kind of come in to take us apart." Reddington concluded, after the fact, that Ann Beaulieu had pressed her husband into service, blindly accepting her daughter's explanation of her suspensions, "and little by little I unfolded to him some of the behaviors Priscilla had been engaging in, and I thought he gradually came to the conclusion that if there was correction to be done, then maybe he had to do it with his daughter." Nothing changed at home after Paul Beaulieu's conference with the principal. That was Ann's domain, and Priscilla could do no wrong where her mother was concerned.

John Reddington observed Priscilla Beaulieu over that year and the next with a certain unease. The principal interpreted her seductive outfits and her fixation on makeup and beauty as symptoms of a deeper problem. "My impression was that Priscilla . . . drew *attention* to herself by her physical appearance. . . . I perceived her as lonely, and I think maybe the term 'superficial' would come to mind . . . and I hoped for her that maybe with the celebrity life, she's gotten some therapy and gotten on better terms with herself. That's the way I felt about her as a high school kid." John Reddington sensed that Priscilla was suffering from an identity crisis, a perceptive observation considering her confusion at discovering, accidentally, her true father, a secret about which Reddington knew nothing.

Ronnie Garland, who probably knew Priscilla during her years in Wiesbaden better than anyone except Tom Stewart, "actually felt sorry for her. I think she was quite a bit screwed up. Too pretty for her own good."

Priscilla and Ron Tapp went steady the duration of her sophomore year, attended the senior prom together, and talked over his plans to enroll at Ole Miss after graduation. He was never aware that Priscilla even heard from Elvis. "I just didn't want to know. I didn't ask her. If I had, I don't know if she would have answered me or not. I just really didn't want to talk about it." At fifteen, Priscilla was successfully juggling the star of the football team and Elvis Presley, each believing his romance with her was exclusive.

Ron set aside an entire page in his senior yearbook marked "Reserved for Priscilla," and she filled it with high school endearments. Elvis was nowhere mentioned, nor did it appear to have been written by a girl who was carrying a torch for someone else:

> Dear Ronnie,
>   It's been really wonderful dating you Ron. I've never had so much fun since I've been over here. I can't really believe yet that your [*sic*] leaving soon, and that this will be all over. . . . I'll never forget you and will always remember the fun we've had. . . . You had better write to me (all the time).
>
>   Love you always,
>   Priscilla
>
> P.S. You just better not forget me.

This is not the letter of a girl who was madly in love with Ron Tapp, but neither is it a portrait of a girl pining by the phone as she waited for Elvis Presley to call.

Ron's father was transferred to Rapid City, South Dakota, in June. Ron left his football jacket with Priscilla, just as Elvis had left his army jacket, claiming her as his. Ron wrote his first letter to her while he was still on the plane, leaving Germany. When the Tapps landed at McGuire Air Force Base in New Jersey, Ron struck up a conversation with one of the sons in another military family, "a tall, good-looking guy. And he said he was going to Wiesbaden. He asked me who some of the girls were that he ought to know, so I gave him a bunch of names, but I didn't give him Priscilla's."

The young man was Barney Williams, who remembered the episode slightly differently. "My family was standing in line to get our baggage checked in, and this young man came up to me, and he dated Priscilla at the time. He was a big football hero at Wiesbaden High School. His name was Ron; I can't remember his last name. And he had a letter. And while we were getting our bags checked in, he heard Wiesbaden mentioned. He said, 'You're going to Wiesbaden?' and I said, 'Yeah.' Strange he came up to me. He said, 'Give this letter to Priscilla Beaulieu when you get there.' " Barney said that by an odd coincidence he ran into Priscilla at the American Arms Hotel a day or so after he arrived in Wiesbaden. "She was seeing some friend of hers off, and I heard them talking in the lobby and they said, 'Priscilla.' Really a small world, isn't it? And I said, 'I got a letter for you. It's from Ron.' And I gave it to her." (To borrow a phrase from *Life,* "Farewell to Ron, Hello to Barney.") "We struck it off then and there," Barney said. "I started going with her as soon as I got there."

Priscilla was instantly infatuated. She raced home, pounded on her friend Ronnie's door and gushed, "You're not going to believe what just came to town!" She told Ronnie there was a new family, the Williamses, with three children: Barney, Billy, and Liz. "The guys are fantastic-looking! The girl is gorgeous. The older [boy is] mine, and I'll get you a date with the [younger] one!" "Which she did," related Ronnie. "She set up a blind date for me with Billy." Barney and Priscilla were an immediate item, and Ronnie eventually married Billy. Liz Williams became Priscilla and Ronnie's friend, but she died several years later in a car accident.

Priscilla had not let forty-eight hours pass before replacing Ron Tapp with a steady boyfriend. Elvis Presley was not even a distant third.

After she married Elvis, Priscilla's characterization of this period was almost comical in its distortion and manipulation of the facts. In her autobiography and in media interviews, she created the illusion that she never dated anyone in Germany after Elvis left, that she was waiting for him exclusively. When *Elvis and Me* was published in 1984, Ron Tapp "rushed out to buy Priscilla's book," recalled his wife, Starr, "because we were sure Ron was mentioned in it. We were mystified that he wasn't, since Ron and Priscilla went together for a year." They thought of writing her, Starr related, "and asking, 'What happened to Ron?' " Recently, when a few of her beaux from Germany surfaced, forcing her to acknowledge that she had gone out with them, Priscilla downplayed the relationships, referring to them as "a kind of dating to kill time before I left. I knew I was leaving."

This was absurd. Her relationships with Tom Stewart, Ron Tapp, and Barney Williams were serious, sexual, two-sided romances, and Priscilla was not "killing time" because she "knew she was leaving." She had no idea in the ninth, tenth, and eleventh grades that she would move to Memphis to live with Elvis Presley. By her own admission, she wondered whether he would ever call her again.

Barney Williams, Ron Tapp's successor, fit all of Priscilla's requirements in a boyfriend: he was dark, he was gorgeous, and he was wild. He had dropped out of high school in the tenth grade, he was nineteen, and he worked at the Air Force exchange. Like Tom Stewart, and to a lesser extent Ron Tapp, Barney was persona non grata at the Beaulieu home. "I had to lie about my age," he recalled, "because she said her father wouldn't allow her to date someone who was nineteen years old. . . . I didn't have the money, and I wasn't a singer like Elvis." Barney remembered having dinner with the Beaulieus one night when Captain Beaulieu mentioned Elvis. "I remember him saying how much Elvis was worth. I can't remember exactly what he said, 'That young man's worth a lot of money,' blah, blah, blah, blah." Barney confirmed that Priscilla's father tried to prevent her from seeing anyone other than Elvis. Priscilla sneaked out to see Barney and invited him to her house on nights when she was baby-sitting. On one such evening, when Ronnie also stopped by, Priscilla thought she heard her father coming up the stairs and went into a paroxysm of terror. "She was laughing and talking with Barney," recalled Ronnie, "and she thought she heard the bottom stairwell door, and she absolutely panicked. We all hid in the closet. I don't know if Barney remembers that, but she was really afraid of [her father]."

"Her father was a jackass," pronounced Barney. "He was just a jackass. I didn't like him. I shouldn't talk about him like that, but I didn't like him at all. He was very strict, very hard." Barney sensed that Priscilla was afraid of Paul Beaulieu. "She was. Yes. She complained one time to me that he had slapped her or something like that. And I can't remember anything else. But I just remember her telling me one time, you know, her daddy'd slapped her."

Priscilla, in her later desperation to disguise her past in Germany, maintained that she "feigned" an interest in a few boys while she was in Wiesbaden to fool her parents into thinking she was adjusting to teenage life and that she was interested in someone other than Elvis: "I went through the motions of going to school, I went through the motions with my friends, I went through the motions of having fun. . . . My parents had to see that I was participating. But it was all a role." Priscilla was playing a role, but it was a role she wrote for herself—later, in her revisionist autobiography. To suggest that she dated other people after Elvis left Germany to assuage her parents was the reverse of the truth, for Paul Beaulieu objected to every boy she brought home. Priscilla was sneaking out, behind her parents' backs, to see Tom, Barney, and Ron.

"She was so excited about going out with Barney," declared her close friend Ronnie. "He was very, very wild . . . but that appealed to her the most, I think."

Barney admitted to being on the dangerous side back then. "I drank a little bit," he acknowledged, which kept him from driving. "I did pretty good, though, for the time we dated, without a car." He chuckled, referring to his sex life with Priscilla. "She liked me. Oh, yes! Kind of hit it off right from the get-go." He described Priscilla as sexually advanced. "Oh, yeah. She was very mature. She didn't act like a sixteen-year-old girl. Let me put it to you this way:

She didn't act that way at all. Not at all." He and Priscilla did not have intercourse. "We just didn't date that long, you know, and we just . . . I never did have sex with her."

While she and Barney dated exclusively that summer, Priscilla exchanged love letters with Ron in South Dakota, "writing how we missed each other, and would like to see each other," he remembered. The two wrote of meeting somewhere, "but I don't think we ever had any idea how we were going to see each other, unless she came back to the States, and I don't think that was in the cards for a while."

At the same time, Priscilla continued to send letters to Elvis on pink stationery, writing, as she put in her memoir: "I need you and want you in every way and, believe me, there's no one else. . . . I wish to God I were with you now. I need you and all your love more than anything in this world."

Elvis, a continent away in Nashville recording "Surrender" and "(Marie's the Name) His Latest Flame" and on location shooting *Follow That Dream*, clung to his mental image of Priscilla, the "beautiful little angel" of his memory, his personal Vestal Virgin, pure Priscilla, who so resembled Debra Paget, his dream girl, and who had materialized in his life after his mother died, just when he needed her.

"He always talked about this beautiful girl, this sweet girl, this nice girl," recalled Joan Esposito, a pretty blond who had just married Joe. "He just said how wonderful she was, how innocent and beautiful."

18
ILLUSIONS, DELUSIONS, AND HOLLYWOOD

Barney Williams was banished into romantic exile by Priscilla on Halloween, four months after they met, the approximate length of her German rhapsody with Elvis. The reason, he suspected, was that he didn't drive. As usual, Priscilla had a standby. Her new love interest was an old love, Tom Stewart.

The Tom-and-Priscilla relationship was an enigma to their classmates, who were never certain why they had stopped seeing each other the fall before. Thus they were not surprised when the two reconnected sometime after Halloween. "You never associate Tom with anybody but her," offered Ron Redd, another senior. "It was serious," confirmed Barney, who became close friends and "drinking buddies" with Tom after Barney's romance with Priscilla faded. "It was a serious thing. He said he loved her. When we would go out drinking, he would go into all kinds of stuff." Tom told Barney he had been intimate with Priscilla. "And I believe that's true. It's what *he* says, you know, but more than likely, what he said is probably true. . . . I remember he used to ask me all the time, 'Barney, did you ever have sex with Priscilla?' I said, 'No, I never did.' Course he didn't believe me, because he kept asking me. He was just jealous, and I guess he was in love with the girl, you know? He was *really* in love with her."

Priscilla, according to her friend Ronnie, felt the same way about Tom: "She really loved that guy." Al Corey, who was close to both Priscilla and Tom, said they spent the night together more than once, with Priscilla using the familiar ruse that she was at a sleep over. This was plausible, for Ronnie remembered a slumber party at her house that Priscilla and Liz Williams attended, "and they both snuck out the window, and they came back the next morning about the time that my daddy was getting up to go golfing." Al added that "The old man [Paul Beaulieu] would call the air police to pull Priscilla away from Tommy."

Priscilla and Tom were in their own world that fall, the first semester of her junior year, his last year of high school, just as they had been during Priscilla's freshman year and part of tenth grade. Sometime after Christmas, however, the relationship fell apart again. Another Spartan gang member, Tom Muldoon, insisted that Tommy ended the relationship and that Priscilla was crushed. Barney thought otherwise: "[Tom] was really, really torn up about her. I think he'd gone out with her, all total, two and a half years at least. Broke his heart. Poor guy."

Something unexpected and extraordinary happened around this time that precipitated the breakup. Elvis, who had called Priscilla less than ten times since he left Germany in the middle of her freshman year, suddenly telephoned one afternoon in February or March, saying he wanted Priscilla to visit him in Los Angeles, where he was shooting a film. Priscilla had not seen Elvis Presley in two years, had not expected ever to see him again. "It had been months," she stated later, "since we last spoke." Elvis, up to then, was a black-and-white glossy taped to her mirror; she would sit in class sometimes, Priscilla told Barney, and think about Elvis and say to herself, "It's just a dream. A dream." By her own description, she was unprepared for and flustered by his sudden invitation.

According to her memoir, Priscilla did not give Elvis an immediate answer. It was Paul Beaulieu who got on the telephone and began negotiating with the star. This coming-to-terms lasted over several conversations and was conducted in a manner more befitting a talent agent hammering out the fine points of a performer's contract than a strict father worried about his daughter's honor. Captain Beaulieu's "demands," as Priscilla later described them, could hardly be called demanding: a first-class round-trip plane ticket for Priscilla, a two-week stay in L.A. once school was out for the summer, an itinerary, and unspecified chaperons. Barney laid the blame for Priscilla's breakup with Tom on the Elvis factor. His unexpected reemergence in her life that spring coincided with the end of their relationship.

Paul Beaulieu accepted Elvis's offer in March; yet interestingly, Anita Wood remembered finding a letter from Priscilla in Elvis's study in May, while he was on location filming *Blue Hawaii,* referring to a future visit to L.A. as merely a possibility. Anita, who read it top to bottom, did not consider it a love letter. Both facts hinted at possible doubts on Priscilla's part.

There were other indications that Priscilla may have had mixed feelings about seeing Elvis. That fall she bonded in a platonic way with Tom Muldoon, who was considered the class character. Priscilla and Tom Muldoon pretended to go to Catholic catechism together, but ducked out to the Teen Club or some other forbidden venue to talk. Tom, who became her confidant, described her later as despondent over her breakup with Tommy, which *he* insisted was Tommy's doing, presumably because he was jealous and angry over Priscilla's planned trip to California. "He was upset," Barney affirmed. "But who can compete with Elvis Presley? I told him he should just forget about her. Course he didn't. He really loved her a lot."

Priscilla reacted by spinning into a dating frenzy from March to May, when her trip to see Elvis was scheduled. The mythic version was that she did this for her "parents' sake." She later said, "I had to be very careful. I withdrew a bit, and they were concerned about me. Even though I had no desire to date, I had to become normal again, get back to reality, because my parents would see this change in me and they would be concerned, and I was afraid that would be a deciding factor of whether I would be able to visit Elvis or not. So . . . I had to . . . start calculating or manipulating my own feelings so that I could participate as a typical teenager." The reality was that Priscilla had been dating nonstop in the two years since Elvis left Germany; if she "withdrew" after he invited her to California, it was over her breakup with Tom Stewart. Her dating marathon that spring was the behavior of a teenage girl on the rebound. What was interesting about her fictional version, however, was Priscilla's choice of words—"calculating or manipulating my own feelings"—for that was what she would soon do, except that, ironically, it would be with respect to Elvis.

Priscilla selected, as her first candidate to make Tom Stewart jealous, a conservative BMOC named Mike Kimball, an all-around jock later voted Best-Looking Senior, the type that normally produced yawns in Priscilla but was certain to ignite Tom. The Spartans, Tommy's fellow gang members, "were not real pleased with me taking her out, to be honest," Mike admitted. Priscilla, he recounted, consorted with a different crowd, Tom Stewart's crowd. "The girls puffed their hair up like the Germans; they wore their hair in, I would say, like a beehive. And she ran around with some of the kids who wore leather jackets and sort of dark clothing, and they weren't really involved in a lot of school activities. . . . I played football and ran track and wrestled."

Priscilla, Mike confirmed, did *not* go out with him to please or appease her parents. The Beaulieus, he recalled, treated him with veiled disdain when he arrived to pick up Priscilla, just as they had all her suitors, with the exception of Elvis. "I wasn't welcome. Her father didn't sit in the living room and talk. I just wanted to get out of there." Mike shared the impression that Priscilla's parents actually discouraged her from dating high school boys. "I think they found excuses for her to be involved in the home, things like baby-sitting, which would be a logical excuse why you couldn't go out."

The dates with Mike Kimball were not solicited for Priscilla's amusement, for she was bored senseless, according to Ronnie, who double-dated with them. "Mike was an absolute all-American apple-pie kind of guy—just precious. But that just did not turn her on. I remember the double date. She would look at me and make these little eyebrow lifts." Despite her lack of interest, Priscilla was characteristically responsive to Mike's sexual advances. "If you went out with her, you made out. I mean we didn't have intercourse. And I'm not sure, at that age, that I was initiating anything like that." That may have contributed to Priscilla's boredom, for the boys Priscilla Beaulieu had dated—Tom, Peter von Wechmar, and their ilk—were known for exploring deeper sexual waters, and Priscilla was their companion in danger. "My father's dead," remarked Mike, "but my mother still jokes about the fact that my dad enjoyed my bringing Priscilla over because her dresses were so tight."

Priscilla endured only so many dates with Mike before she flitted from Spartans Joe Delahunt to Danny Mason to "Spider" Murphy, also accepting a date or two with boys outside the gang, such as Daniel Dodd. "Spider! Ooh!" Ronnie recalled gleefully. "He was sort of the leader of the outlaws." Most of the Spartans, Tom Stewart among them, were also members of the Teen Auto Club, or T.A.C. Both groups wore special jackets with secret insignias, the self-proclaimed Wild Bunch of Wiesbaden, racing cars, smoking cigarettes, quaffing cognac, and having sex. Priscilla and Spider doubled one night with Ronnie and another T.A.C. member, Bruce McKay. "He took us around . . . the Nürnberg Ring. Nürnberg was the racetrack over there that Steve McQueen raced at several times. They had a course mapped out there in Wiesbaden that was dangerous. I still cannot believe . . . drinking beer and riding with those guys around that course." Priscilla had to slip out of the house for these adventures, sometimes borrowing clothes from Ronnie, but she was fearless. She took Ronnie to a few parties given by the brother of another friend, Becky Lippett, "and they were wild!" Ronnie recalled.

Yet she also still managed to project the tender innocence Elvis found so beguiling. Ron Redd was a football player who'd had his eye on Priscilla since her freshman year and could not believe anyone so refined would date Tom Stewart. "That was a perplexing question—why was she attracted to him?" Ron made a play for Priscilla that spring, as soon as he saw his opening. He saw Priscilla Beaulieu in the same idealized light as Elvis, and she played the role to perfection. "There was a sweetness about her. Almost innocence. Her face was so chiseled; it's like she didn't even put soap on her face, her skin was so incredible." Ron spent a good deal of his time with Priscilla in the backseat of his car, "making out and trying to get really heavy into the petting [but] she wouldn't have any of it." Like Mike, Ron did not attempt intercourse; he was "too scared. We didn't have the Pill, so we didn't do any of that stuff." Priscilla nonetheless stood out. "Damn, she could kiss! Oh, man. She was just a very passionate kisser." The relationship did not last more than a few weeks, with Priscilla as Ron's trophy date at the Senior Graduation Ball.

Priscilla charmed men of all stripes. John Love, who taught her history that year, was so overcome by her perfect manners and dress that he extended liberties to Priscilla not afforded lesser beauties. He asked her in class one day what Grant said to Lee at Appomattox Courthouse, "and she kind of smiled and looked up at me and said, 'I don't know, Mr. Love.' And I just remember saying, 'Ahhh, that's all right, Priscilla,' and asked someone else. She was so pleasant and courteous and polite you kind of let her off the hook."

So it was and ever would be with Priscilla Beaulieu. She beguiled her way through childhood and adolescence. Even girls were not immune. Katie Neece, another junior who knew her only slightly, still believed years later that Priscilla was "completely unaware of how beautiful she was." Almost everyone who attended school with Priscilla commented upon her sweet disposition, which had remained unchanged since her second-grade teacher remarked on her "pleasing personality." Students at H. H. Arnold in general found Priscilla pleasant and nice and did not consider her conceited, despite the attention she received when Elvis left.

Al Corey remembers that as May approached, Priscilla grew increasingly nervous about seeing Elvis. She cornered Al in the school library, frantic with fear that Elvis would be able to tell she'd had sex with Tom Stewart. "She was concerned Elvis would find out. *Desperate*." Priscilla still registered alarm thirty-five years later, when she recounted Elvis's warning that she remain "untouched." Now that she had plans to actually see him, Priscilla felt vulnerable and panicked. "She showed me some letter [he had sent] where he was gonna send her to a doctor when she got there, to make sure she was capable of having children," Al recounted. "She came up to me in the library *all the time* to talk about it. She'd ask me time and again about going to this doctor, because she was worried Elvis was gonna find out she'd been intimate with Tommy. I finally told her, 'Just tell him you rode a horse.' "

Another confidant of Priscilla's from that spring, who was not in touch with Al, remembered Priscilla expressing similar fears that she would be checked by Elvis's doctors. Priscilla was evidently concerned that Elvis, or his doctor, would be able to observe that her vaginal area had stretched from sexual activity.

While Priscilla wrestled with her private demons in Wiesbaden, Elvis was reaching a crisis in his relationship with Anita Wood. Just as Priscilla had once agonized over Anita's correspondence, Anita had by now stumbled upon the letter from Priscilla in Elvis's study in Bel Air, referring to her anticipated trip to Hollywood to see him. The "child" Elvis had befriended in Bad Nauheim took on a different and dangerous connotation to Anita Wood. She confronted Elvis with the letter. "It was the beginning of the end," by Anita's later description, "because I was furious. *He* was furious. I don't know if he was mad that I found the letter or that I said something about it."

Elvis had no desire to end his courtship of Anita simply because Priscilla was coming to see him. Despite his extracurricular activity with starlets and his fixation on Priscilla, he and Anita had a close relationship, which she believed was leading to marriage, and there is reason to assume Elvis felt the same way. Gladys Presley, according to her good friend Willie Jane, had already sanctioned Anita as her son's future bride. "She loved Anita Wood," Willie said. "Gladys wanted Elvis to marry Anita, but Colonel Parker didn't think it was good for his career. Anita and Elvis had more in common; she was a good southern girl." It is not altogether clear *why* Elvis Presley summoned Priscilla that spring: perhaps he and Anita were having difficulties, as some—though not Anita—have suggested; or perhaps he and Priscilla had discussed such a visit in the abstract, and in a moment of impulse or boredom, he phoned.

Priscilla responded to her imminent reunion with Elvis by having a last fling, this time with a Lancer, a member of the Spartans' rival male club. Lee Rushing was considered by some to be the handsomest boy in Priscilla's class, though he would turn out to be but a dalliance. She scored her second prom date of the season as Lee's consort at the Junior Class Ball, making him Priscilla's eighth official beau in the last half of the eleventh grade alone, more than some girls date in a lifetime.

Even if she was not intimate with any of her boyfriends in Germany, Priscilla was not leading the cloistered life Elvis envisioned. She knew she was playing with fire. Priscilla had already made a mental note of Elvis's displeasure with Anita when he suspected she was seeing someone while he was in Germany. "He told me on a couple of occasions that if a nice girl turned out *not* to be so nice, he wanted nothing to do with her," Alan Fortas, who traveled with Elvis in his post-army days, later wrote. The mere fact that Priscilla *had* these relationships suggests she was either ambivalent about Elvis or did not seriously expect her Elvis fantasy to materialize—or both.

Priscilla had felt twinges of apprehension about Elvis while he was still in Germany: the difference in their ages, her discomfort around his much older friends, the teasing, her frustration over his sexual restraint. Priscilla's five months in Germany with Elvis were like the romance of the characters in the movie *Roman Holiday,* in which a reporter and a princess have an unexpected encounter. Their interlude together was magical and bittersweet, for they knew it had to end and they would resume their normal lives. Priscilla the realist had accepted that.

There were glimmerings that Elvis, ever the impossible romantic, saw their relationship as something more. As Priscilla panicked over the loss of her virginity, Elvis was telling his friend George Barris that "this is a different type of girl, not very forward," and purging the house he was renting in Bel Air of unsavory elements in anticipation of his virgin goddess's visit. "One night we are sitting there," Patty Perry recollected, "and he takes all of the girls into a room—all of the groupies—and says, 'Sit down. I want to tell you something. There is this little girl, Priscilla, that I met in Germany that I have a relationship with, and she's coming to L.A. So I want to tell you girls, no more parties. It's going to end now, because I am into her and I want her and I have a relationship with her.' And I was the only girl who was allowed to stay."

Patty knew that, coming from Elvis, this was tantamount to a commitment. "Which was very special and she should be proud of that." Patty saw Elvis often and at his most vulnerable and regarded him as "the sweetest, gentlest, most insecure man you would ever want to meet in your life." Patty sometimes slept in the same bed with Elvis, though they did not have sex. "Elvis sleepwalked," as Priscilla would later explain, "and so he had people sleep with him. His mother was fearful for him because he nearly jumped out of a window on a couple of occasions, and so, because of that, she had asked for someone to sleep with him, if *she* did not, just to watch his back. Stories and rumors flew and grew from these kinds of stories." For all his womanizing, Elvis craved mothering; Patty understood this and happily met that need. "He was like my little baby. He would say, 'Patty, rub my back. Cut my toenails.' I was so fortunate, because I became the sister he never had."

Elvis cleared his latest rental house, on Bellagio Road, of one other significant female before Priscilla's arrival in May of 1962: Anita. According to Joe Esposito, Elvis made arrangements for Joe's wife to keep Anita occupied at Graceland while Priscilla was in L.A. This would not be the first or last game of musical chairs Elvis would play with women, using members of his entourage as accessories before the fact. "I was in Saint Louis at the time," recalled Joan Esposito. "I got a phone call from Joe saying, 'I want you to go to Memphis and stay with Anita, to keep her busy because we are going to be out here.' They were making a movie. He said, 'Go on back and keep Anita company. Anita's getting angry, so you go take care of it.' "

"I was furious," Anita confirmed. "We had a really terrible row about it when I found [Priscilla's] letter. I went home the next day on the airplane. I thought he was lying all the time, anyway. I went straight home to Graceland and I stayed with Grandma [Presley]. I stayed with Grandma a lot when he was away."

Priscilla, who was unaware of Elvis's machinations with Anita, later wrote of her own anxieties over the visit, fearful that she might be "hurt," though Judy Comstock, a new friend from school, "never saw any doubt." A part of Priscilla was giddy and excited at the thought of seeing Elvis again, for she wrote in a senior's yearbook that April, "I'll be leaving about the same time, but I will return, darn it." Judy perceived Priscilla as a projectile headed straight for its target, Elvis Presley. But whose target was he—Priscilla's or her parents'? It would be ludicrous to accept the Beaulieus' self-portrait as over-protective parents opposed to Priscilla's trip to L.A. to see Elvis. How many parents—*military* parents especially—would allow their just-turned-seventeen-year-old daughter to spend two weeks in another country with a movie star famous for bedding starlets and introducing sex into rock and roll? The myth once again crumbles beside the facts. "Her father thought this thing was wonderful!" proclaimed Ronnie Garland, who observed the Beaulieus' Elvis frenzy from the apartment below. Judy Comstock remembered Priscilla's mother as being "in charge" of the family, and Ann supported the trip to Hollywood to see Elvis.

When Tom Stewart dropped out of the picture, Ron Redd became Priscilla's date to the Senior Ball. He began going out with her shortly after Paul Beaulieu negotiated the arrangements for his daughter's L.A. trip. He felt the die had already been cast for Priscilla's future. "I knew shortly after really starting to spend time with her . . . that it was a done deal," Ron Redd admitted. "And I told people for years, I said, 'You watch. When Elvis gets married, he's going to marry a girl named Priscilla Beaulieu.'"

H. H. Arnold closed its doors for the summer in May of 1962; within hours, Paul and Ann Beaulieu put their eleventh-grade daughter on an airplane, alone, to stay with Elvis Presley in Bel Air for two weeks. Tommy Stewart, who graduated in May, took off for the States, never to be heard from again by any of his classmates until the report surfaced that he had been killed in a knife fight on a beach in New Jersey within months after leaving Wiesbaden. Years later, when Priscilla was forced to amend her fictitious history to include a few "kind-of dates" she had in Germany after Elvis left, Tom Stewart was conspicuously missing from her short list.

When Priscilla Beaulieu's plane landed at Los Angeles International Airport, Elvis Presley had just finished filming *Blue Hawaii.* He was still in bed when her plane landed in the early afternoon; Joe Esposito, whom Priscilla knew and liked from Germany, was assigned to pick her up. "Elvis didn't do those things," he explained. "I think maybe he thought it was more dramatic or something. Elvis had to do everything in dramatics: 'She'd walk in the room and there I am standing waiting for her.'"

Joe and Priscilla fell back into their comfortable friendship, with Joe playing the familiar role of driver-to-the-ingenue. "We hit it off pretty good. . . . I think she trusted me." Joe played tour guide en route to Elvis's rented house on Bellagio Road, driving Priscilla past MGM, where Elvis had an office, and through the streets of Bel Air. Priscilla, who was "very nervous" when Joe met her at the airport gate, suddenly came alive. "She was excited," he recalled. "It was a big adventure for her. She would ask questions: 'What do you guys do all day?' 'Is it fun to make movies?' And I told her it's not as much fun as people think it is—you sit around the set all day. But she was anxious to experience some of that stuff."

When Priscilla and Joe arrived, Elvis was downstairs watching television and playing pool with Patty Perry and a gaggle of his male friends, who were "pissed," declared Patty, "because they couldn't have their girlfriends over." Patty, who witnessed the fabled reunion of Priscilla and Elvis after two years apart, did not see eyes locked in shared passion or Priscilla frozen in a movie moment of pure ecstasy when Elvis looked up. "I saw *fear.* I think she was scared to death when she walked in and there were eight guys and Elvis."

The first thing Elvis focused on was Priscilla's appearance. Her spiral-curl ponytail, worn with a white blouse and skirt, while appropriate for a schoolgirl in Germany, seemed out of place amid Elvis's Hollywood set. Before they had a chance to get reacquainted, Elvis sent Priscilla upstairs with Patty for a quick makeover. Others would point to this as Svengaliism on Elvis's part, but Patty took it as an act of consideration: "He wanted her to feel comfortable." It was likely both. Elvis had a physical standard with respect to his ideal of feminine beauty: He loved long hair, dark hair, and smoldering eyes, and it was his desire that Priscilla emulate that ideal. The moment had elements of trauma, however, for Priscilla, whose identity since early childhood had been centered on her physical appeal, and her anxiety must have been compounded by her understandable insecurity as a seventeen-year-old attempting to compete with starlets. She found Elvis Presley's scrutiny of her clothes and makeup unbearable. "He might find flaws," as she put it later.

Patty took Priscilla upstairs to the bathroom, undid her girlish ponytail, and started to tease, pluck, and pencil. "Make it higher," Priscilla beseeched, desperate to undo whatever damage had been done by her high school hairdo and to appear more actressy in Elvis's almighty gaze. Patty recalled her as "nervous as hell."

The evening did not unfold as Priscilla's dream date. Elvis, she wrote in her memoir, continued to play pool and joke with his other guests, occasionally pecking her on the cheek as if she were a favorite child. She claimed there were groupies around that night, despite Patty's vivid recollection of Elvis temporarily banishing them. Priscilla noted his new, darker hair color disapprovingly and felt he had metamorphosed from the "gentle, sensitive and insecure boy" she had known in Germany into someone "mischievous and self-confident to the point of cockiness" and "quick to anger." Apparently Priscilla did not take kindly to sitting invisibly on the sidelines, gazing adoringly at a man whose full attention was not directed at her.

The foreshadowing of sexual incompatibility between Elvis and Priscilla in Germany became clear during their reunion in L.A. Priscilla had been barely fourteen when she and Elvis retreated to his bedroom in Bad Nauheim for their late-night sexual games of extended foreplay and, according to what she told Currie, occasional intercourse. Priscilla had physically, emotionally, and sexually matured in the two-plus years since then. She had also acquired a considerable amount of experience: a short-term sexual relationship with Peter Von Wechmar, a long-standing and active sex life with Tom Stewart, an eight-month relationship with Ron Tapp that was sexual enough for Priscilla to give him pictures of herself in provocative lingerie, a three-month exclusive relationship with a nineteen-year-old hell-raiser who considered her sexually advanced, and frequent dates with at least seven or eight popular high school juniors and seniors. The Priscilla who waited impatiently for Elvis to break away from his buddies and take her to his bedroom on Bellagio Road was a different girl from the young fan he had encountered in his living room on Goethestrasse.

She would later re-create the experience with unconcealed frustration in *Elvis and Me,* complaining of Elvis ignoring her until twelve-thirty in the morning, when he whispered a request that she quietly make her way to his bedroom. Priscilla, who had been starstruck and inexperienced enough at fourteen to go along with Elvis's routine, was no longer so puppy-eager to play his celebrity games. "I'd waited too long to be discreet," as she put it. She made a production of exiting the den for Elvis's upstairs bedroom, "making sure everyone knew he was mine—at least for as long as I was here."

Freshly powdered and perfumed, she waited for Elvis and dutifully crawled into bed beside him when he finally arrived ten minutes later. It had to be strange for Priscilla to be *expected* to fall into bed with a man she hadn't seen in two years, someone she thought she might never encounter again, someone she had replaced with other lovers. "This new Elvis," she later spoke of, "I hardly knew at all."

In her memoir, Priscilla described her first few minutes alone with Elvis almost gynecologically, confirming, unwittingly, her phobia that Elvis might find out she had been with other men. "As we lay in the dim light," she wrote, "he soon discovered that I was still as untouched as he'd left me two years before. Relieved and pleased, he told me how much this meant to him." How, short of a complete physical examination in his bedroom to confirm that her hymen was intact, or bleeding from first-time intercourse (and Priscilla claimed they did not have intercourse that night), could Elvis possibly have discovered she was "untouched"? Priscilla was in a panic, at the time, anxious to convince Elvis that she had "saved" herself for him, and she was desperate, years later, to perpetuate the illusion she was a virgin when in truth she had dallied with a dozen boys or men and had intercourse, by their accounts, with three, not counting Elvis.

The ensuing hour or so in the bedroom with her childhood idol was bizarrely unfulfilling to the "new" Priscilla. Though she may have felt awkward being reunited with a man she considered a comparative stranger, Priscilla was above all a sexual creature; once in bed with Elvis, she wanted satisfaction. She described their sexual encounter as a battle, with the two of them engaged in heavy foreplay, fully aroused, when Elvis withdrew, leaving Priscilla alternately demanding and begging for intercourse. The mythical version, in Priscilla's book and movie, was that Elvis told her he was reserving the moment of penetration for "a right time and place," but this did not make sense in light of her confession to Currie that she and Elvis had already consummated their relationship in Germany. If Elvis did stop short of penetration in his bedroom in California, the more logical explanation was that it was because he *preferred* foreplay to intercourse, a preference he had already revealed to Priscilla.

By either scenario, the evening ended on a note of intense disappointment for Priscilla, made more so by Elvis's insistence that she leave immediately afterward to spend the remaining few hours of the night at the house of his friend George Barris, who designed custom cars for motion pictures. This was not for propriety's sake, nor was it for the Beaulieus, who had placed no restrictions on where Priscilla spent the night. Elvis wanted Priscilla out of the house so he could telephone Anita, concerned that she might cause a scandal by revealing that he was entertaining a teenage girl.

"The minute I walked in, the phone rang," said Anita. "I was so mad, I think he was afraid I was going to do something and get him in serious trouble. But I didn't."

If George Barris and his wife, Shirley, were surprised by Elvis's request to have them act as beards for his affair with a visiting seventeen-year-old, they kept it to themselves. They recalled that Priscilla seemed "overwhelmed" when one of the group dropped her off that night, "moving into a world where she didn't know what to expect or where she was going to go."

The first place she went was Las Vegas, the archetype of all that is surreal, as Priscilla's life from then on would be. The Presley entourage checked into the Sahara Hotel, where Elvis smuggled Priscilla into bars and casinos and taught her to play twenty-one, though she had to count the numbers on her fingers underneath the table. When she couldn't keep up with the Vegas hours, Elvis gave Priscilla amphetamines and sleeping pills to help her sustain the pace, a practice he had been introduced to during night drills in the army in Germany. As George Barris observed, "She was coming from a simple, quiet environment, going into this dramatic world, which was a make-believe world for a girl."

Priscilla lived the *Pretty Woman* script in Vegas. Elvis sent her on a shopping spree to the most expensive boutiques on the Strip—but Priscilla bought Julia

Roberts's hooker character's "before" dresses—sexy, flashy clothes from Suzy Creamcheese, a trendy designer who embodied the glamorous excess of the sixties. Elvis preferred to see women in tight, sexy clothing, and Priscilla, eager to please, followed his lead. Her Pygmalion-type transformation that May included a session with Armand, the Sahara Hotel hairdresser, who piled Priscilla's long hair on top of her head, teasing and spraying and twisting it around until it resembled two birds' nests atop each other. Then he rimmed her blue eyes with black liner and false eyelashes, creating the Cleopatra look that later became a caricature. Eventually Elvis was blamed for pressuring Priscilla into this extreme, supposedly to match his own dyed-black hair and mascaraed eyes. Elvis had taken to blackening his hair after seeing and admiring Tony Curtis's look in an early picture, and he sometimes used mascara, according to Joe, to emulate Rudolph Valentino and to emphasize the blue in his eyes.

Kohl-darkened eyes and back-combed hair were also hallmarks of the 1960s. Elvis Presley did not invent the style; he merely followed and perhaps exaggerated it. The Barrises, in fact, recalled that Priscilla was the one who went overboard in her childlike attempts to appear older and more glamorous. Elvis, according to the Barrises, preferred to see her with a more natural look. "He walks in the door, and she's coming down [the stairs]," Shirley Barris related, "this elegant, beautiful young child, but all of a sudden she looks sophisticated. And he walks in and looks at her and he doesn't say hello . . . or anything. He looks at her and says, 'Go back upstairs and get rid of that hairdo.' You could see her anxiousness. And not that she was waiting to hear a compliment. I'm sure in her heart it was all to please him . . . and you see the expression on this angelic face. It was as if her whole world stopped and ended and she was so overwhelmed by it all. And little tears started coming. And she starts running up the stairs, and of course I run after her. And then she let her hair down. And when he saw that, he said, '*This* is how I love you.' Then you see the glow in her face come back." Priscilla was overcompensating by using too much mascara and teasing her hair in a relentless bid to impress Elvis. How else could an eleventh-grader compete with Tuesday Weld and Natalie Wood?

Her two weeks in Los Angeles and Las Vegas were an emotional roller coaster for Priscilla, a seventeen-year-old thrust into an adult Disneyland, on a mission to captivate the star she had fantasized about since childhood, yet finding herself increasingly ambivalent about him and his lifestyle. She told her friend Judy, when she returned to Germany, about "taking off" in his limousine and driving around the field to amuse herself when she became "bored" with watching Elvis play football.

Priscilla was rediscovering, as she spent more time with him, that Elvis

Presley and the *image* of Elvis Presley were two discrete entities; Elvis was not the smoldering, oversexed bad boy of rock who had attracted her as a fan; it was *she*, ironically, who was pleading with him to make love to her. Priscilla was magnetically drawn to dangerous, overtly sexual men; Elvis, to her growing disappointment, was a sensitive artist with complex notions about virginity and intercourse. Her confusion between fantasy and reality with respect to Elvis became obvious in a passage from her autobiography about her trip to L.A. In it, she wrote of being disillusioned by Elvis's criticism of her hair, until he put on one of his records, sat beside her, and sang along with his own recorded voice. "In that moment, I fell in love all over again," Priscilla wrote. The passage is profoundly self-revelatory. It was "Elvis Presley," not Elvis Presley, with whom Priscilla Beaulieu was in love.

Elvis, who had established the rules of their courtship and found Priscilla a willing participant, considered the visit, and Priscilla, a romantic triumph. Before she left, he gave her the jade, gold, and onyx ring he had worn in *Blue Hawaii,* telling her he wanted his "little girl" to visit him at Graceland for Christmas. Elvis Presley was falling deeper and deeper under the spell of Priscilla Beaulieu. The tragedy, for them both, was that the girl he was falling in love with was not really Priscilla but the submissive persona Currie had created for her in Germany to impress Elvis.

Sooner or later, however, the real Priscilla would emerge.

19

MERRY, MERRY
CHRISTMAS, BABY

Priscilla Presley, in her mythical retelling of her life, described herself as possessed to rejoin Elvis at Christmastime, but by intimates' accounts, she was a frightened and confused teenager swimming in deep and treacherous waters when she returned to Germany in June of 1962.

Her own account of Elvis's Los Angeles farewell echoed the apprehension her close friends in Wiesbaden described. "I want you back the way you are now," Elvis whispered to her. "And remember I'll always know."

"I smiled and nodded," Priscilla later wrote. "I couldn't conceive of wanting anyone but him."

Priscilla was actually panic-stricken, according to Al Corey, terrified of the looming threat that Elvis might learn that she'd led an active sex life during the two years they were apart. Her entire relationship with Elvis Presley was based upon a lie—that she was a virgin when they met—and the lie gradually acquired another dimension as she continued to maintain that she was "saving" herself for him. There was nothing wrong with Priscilla going steady with Tom Stewart, Ron Tapp, and Barney Williams, or dating the other boys; she was a teenage girl with a powerful sex drive who had spent five months with Elvis Presley and thought she would never see him again. The problem arose when Elvis *did* resurface and Priscilla found herself tangled in a tissue of lies all predicated upon the myth that she was a virgin who desired only Elvis.

After she flew back to Wiesbaden from Los Angeles in June, the Beaulieus took a family holiday in Spain. When they returned in July, Priscilla's school chum Donna Pollen recalled, "their apartment had been done over. It was all done in teakwood furniture, which was, even then, quite expensive. And we were all wondering how—with all the children and everything and her father's salary—they were able to afford this." Donna and a few of the other girls gradually gleaned from their visits that Priscilla was seeing Elvis Presley again and he was sending the Beaulieus gifts and buying presents for Priscilla. "When she came back she had a new suede coat. It seemed like she was getting more and more and more neat new things . . . so then all this began to fall into place about Elvis."

Priscilla's childhood game of Imagine If was unfolding before her eyes, but the fantasy was spinning out of control and the real Priscilla was getting lost. She had played a role to get Elvis Presley, and now—to her surprise as much as anyone else's—it was coming true. She described herself later as "dumb-founded" by Elvis's invitation to fly to Graceland for Christmas. "Priscilla didn't know what to do about Elvis," confirmed Al Corey, to whom she confided her misgivings that summer. "She was confused. Her parents were telling her what to do. She felt that she was in *way* over her head with [Elvis]." Priscilla Beaulieu's childhood imaginings of a fairy-tale romance with Elvis Presley did not match the reality of a complicated relationship with a conflicted man, but events and circumstances were moving so quickly, fueled by Elvis and her parents, that Priscilla had become an almost incidental member of the cast.

She was uncertain about spending Christmas at Graceland, filled with trepidation about Elvis yet still addicted to the fantasy, propelled along by her own and, more powerfully, her parents' overriding ambition. "She wasn't thrilled," confessed a close friend from that period. "She'd make comments about it."

Priscilla's mixed emotions were apparent that summer. On July 20, barely a month after she left Elvis's arms, she attended a tea dance at the Von Steuben Hotel for the arriving members of the Air Force Academy class of 1964. Jane Breighner, a classmate and new friend, was at the same party that Friday night and immediately spotted Priscilla. "I just remember her standing and talking to probably the best-looking guy in the whole room," Jane said.

Priscilla had come back from the West Coast that June with a dramatic new look, courtesy of Armand at the Sahara. Though she later claimed her parents made her remove every trace of her Vegas makeup, Priscilla's schoolmates recalled a "radical" change in her appearance from ingenue to sophisticate. Her school picture that fall bears them out, showing Priscilla with heavy eye makeup and a beehive hairstyle. She told her pal Judy that she "loved the way she got her hair fixed over there." It was thus all the more surprising when Priscilla turned up at school one day that fall with her trademark long hair—her crowning glory—shorn to ear-length. "She had like one ringlet down the middle of her back," recalled Jane Breighner. "*One* day it was just *gone*. It was like the front of her hair was the same but the back was gone! She cut it off." Dee Dee Saunders, a sophomore friend, called it a "shocking development."

Elvis emphatically preferred long hair and told Priscilla so. If she was desperate to please him, why would Priscilla cut the long hair Elvis adored just before her Christmas trip to Graceland? It made no sense, considering she had meticulously studied Elvis's every desire so that she could become his female ideal—unless Priscilla really was having doubts. By her own admission, she was humiliated by Elvis's criticism of her hairstyle and makeup; what better way to declare her independence from him than to lop her hair off? It was a subtle act of defiance—or at the least a test of Elvis's devotion.

Though Elvis was obsessed with Priscilla in his way and looked forward to her Christmas visit, he too was in conflict. He was still involved with Anita, and she understood the implied contract that existed between Elvis and any woman he was seeing: The woman had to be monogamous, but he could date other women *because he was Elvis Presley;* to assume otherwise would have been unrealistic and naive. "I didn't expect him not to date anyone but me," Anita said. "Of course, when he was in Memphis, I expected that." When Priscilla left L.A. for Germany in June, Anita chose to overlook Elvis's indiscretion. "We dated a little bit longer after that, but then I think he began to get confused."

Late in the summer, as Anita was coming down to breakfast at Graceland, she overheard Elvis in the kitchen talking to his father and a few of the guys about Priscilla's Christmas visit and how he couldn't make up his mind between her and Anita. "And I told him I'd heard him," Anita recalled, "and that he wouldn't have to make that choice. I'd make that choice for him." Elvis had crossed an imaginary line with Anita. Inviting Priscilla to Graceland violated Anita's sense of southern propriety; Memphis, Elvis's *home,* was her turf. "I was a very prideful young lady. I couldn't stand the thought of him making a choice between us. I said, 'It's just not going to work.' "

Ricky Stanley, Vernon Presley's then six-year-old stepson by his army bride, Dee, was in the kitchen that morning and witnessed the fireworks. "Oh, wow! . . . Elvis wanted to continue to date Anita. She was a southern girl who was pretty popular there in Memphis, had her own kind of talk show thing; she was a dancer and a singer. And Elvis wanted to date her *and* he wanted to bring Priscilla over for Christmas, *and* he wanted Anita to go along with it. And Anita said, 'Sorry buddy, forget it.' And he threw a fit. He started tearing the kitchen apart, throwing dishes—there was language. There was a big hassle with yelling and everything. And . . . she was not gonna give in, and she hooked it. She just walked out. And that was it . . . and I thought, 'Welcome to Graceland!' "

"I called my brother and he came out, and I left," Anita remembered. "It was a very tearful departure. It was a sad situation." The decision to leave Elvis was "very difficult" for her. "We did have a special relationship for a number of years. It was wonderful. I wouldn't take anything for it. I wouldn't change any of it. But I did have to make that decision to leave. . . . The other girls he had dated, that was fine. That's what was supposed to happen . . . but he didn't want me dating anybody. I thought that was not fair."

Family friend and Memphian Willie Jane Nichols, who had known Elvis for years and spent considerable time with him and Anita, considered *Elvis* the one who was spurned. "[Anita] got fed up with it. She could have stayed longer. *She* walked out. Lotta people think he dumped her. But she walked out of Graceland. And he said, 'You'll be back.' But she didn't go back."

Wes Bryan, a young singer-actor touted by United Artists in the late fifties as the next James Dean, had caught Elvis's fancy and occasionally dropped by Graceland at his invitation, so Wes had seen Elvis with Anita quite often. Like Willie Jane and several others in the circle, he considered Anita a more suitable match for Elvis than Priscilla, whom Wes found "cocky and cold." Anita, to his mind, was "a beautiful girl with a beautiful personality. I was highly impressed. That's the girl Elvis Presley should have married. She waited for him for seven years. It was unfortunate that he didn't marry her."

Elvis's argument with Anita that August morning in the kitchen at Graceland was a turning point in Priscilla's life, though she didn't know it; for by leaving, Anita Wood had unwittingly helped seal Priscilla Beaulieu's fate. With Anita no longer present in his life, Elvis focused his romantic attention obsessively on Priscilla, his teenage dream girl. He began making plans in earnest for her Christmas visit, entreating Joan Esposito, in November, to begin weaning her new baby so she could fly to Germany the next month to escort Priscilla to Graceland. "I didn't even have a passport," Joan would later recollect. "So I had about four weeks' notice. I started slowing down so that I could go there. I was to fly over, pick her up, turn around, and fly back."

Elvis, recalled stepbrother Ricky Stanley, "was like a fifteen-year-old kid with his first crush. . . . I was real little and he was talking about a beautiful girl he called Cilla. Oh, he just went on and on: 'She's so pretty, you're gonna like her. Just thinking about her I'm so excited that she's coming. Everybody is gonna like her.' It was like prom night. Because, see, that's the way he was. He was like a little kid." Elvis could barely contain his enthusiasm around his close Memphis friends, one of whom was disc jockey George Klein, a schoolmate. Elvis told Barbara Little, George's girlfriend and eventual wife, "that he met this little girl, and he said, 'I think that I love her.' " According to Barbara, Elvis told George that Priscilla was "waiting for him" in Germany, saving herself for him.

Elvis and Priscilla were both in love with illusions. Elvis, with an idealized child-woman with the combined qualities of his mother and Debra Paget, a woman who subscribed to his southern mores concerning purity and fidelity. This fictional virgin goddess bore little more than a physical resemblance to Priscilla Beaulieu, whom he barely knew. The fact that Priscilla lived in another country reinforced Elvis's grand passion, for he could ascribe to her all the qualities he wished her to possess—and in his mind, she did possess them.

Priscilla still clung to the image of Elvis Presley that had magnetized her as a child—the darkly erotic, powerful star who had supplanted Mario Lanza in her imagination. Each had romanticized the other out of all proportion to reality. The difference was that Priscilla had peered at the real Elvis, and she was not certain she liked what she saw.

In September or October of her senior year, Priscilla accepted a date with Jamie Lindberg, a senior whose family had just been transferred to Wiesbaden and who had telephoned her on a bet. By Homecoming, they were going steady. Like Ron Tapp, Jamie was a football player and part of the school's social clique, not Priscilla's typical boyfriend; he was, however, exceptionally good-looking and popular, with wavy brown hair and a *GQ* face. Both Priscilla and Jamie fell hard and fell fast, to hear classmates tell it. Mike Kimball, Jamie's best friend, remembered them as "off in their own thing" from their first date.

Priscilla Beaulieu found herself in the center of a risky triangle that fall—infatuated with Jamie Lindberg but promised to Elvis Presley, who, according to several of her confidants, had already effectively negotiated for her hand with Paul and Ann Beaulieu. "There was a secret there," as one of them confided.

Jamie was another skeleton in Priscilla's increasingly crowded closet, an unknown rival to Elvis Presley, who believed his teen dream was counting the days until Christmas, just as he was. Priscilla had in fact been living a lie with Elvis since their earliest dates in Bad Nauheim, and she perpetuated that lie over the next three years with her false assurances to Elvis that she was "untouched." As the deceit deepened, so did the elaborate cover-up, prompting Priscilla, once she married Elvis, to reinvent her past.

She fostered this illusion in interviews, creating the fiction that when she returned to Germany from her California trip, she was so consumed with Elvis that "this time," she told the *Memphis Commercial Appeal* in 1974, "I could not bring myself to date anybody." The truth was one of her closely guarded secrets. Priscilla was actually in love with Jamie Lindberg that autumn, but later on, she was desperate to conceal that fact from the public, for it would have undermined the romanticized image she had so carefully constructed of her perfect love affair with Elvis Presley. Asked recently about her senior year, she confirmed her earlier statement that she did not date anyone. When presented with the fact that she went out with Jamie, Priscilla claimed it was to placate her parents so they would not think she was obsessed with Elvis and would permit her to go to Memphis at Christmas. "My heart and soul [were] not in Germany at that time," she insisted. "[I] was *consumed* by Elvis. My every *move* was him. My every *thought* was on *him*. I *lived* and *breathed* him."

Like Priscilla's earlier attempts to revise the past by asserting that she dated her previous boyfriends in Wiesbaden "for her parents' sake," this was a complete reversal of reality. Jamie—like Tom Stewart, Ron Tapp, Mike Kimball, and

Barney Williams—vividly recalled Priscilla's parents, her mother especially, *obstructing* his senior-year romance with Priscilla. "I could just basically see it. I know her mom had a real strong influence over her, and does to this day. And she's a very powerful woman. But her mom definitely picked up on the fact that Priscilla and I were really getting close."

Priscilla, anticipating seeing Elvis at Christmas, was again tormented by his stern warning that he would somehow know if she had been unfaithful. Al Corey had graduated and moved away, but she confided her fears in another classmate, expressing her concern about being examined by Elvis's doctors for evidence of sexual activity. Jamie would not say, later, whether he and Priscilla had intercourse that year, calling it "a privacy-type thing," but a classmate, Pat Mayo, claimed to have tutored Jamie that spring in exchange for information about Priscilla, "and as high school chums would talk," said Pat, "to the best of my knowledge, she was not chaste when she married Elvis." Jamie told Pat that he and Priscilla had intimate relations. "If you can believe one good buddy to another, sitting around talking as boys talk . . . I think he was being truthful." Priscilla, Jamie would say of their sexual relationship years after the fact, "was much more sophisticated than I was, I'll tell you that. I went, 'Wow!' " Jamie also admitted that "when her parents would go out, that's where I would go."

Mike Sinclair, who double-dated with Priscilla and Jamie that year, confirmed this. "I know that Priscilla generally wasn't allowed to have boyfriends over. And I know that there were times when Priscilla's parents were gone that Jamie came over. . . . He climbed up the window."

Priscilla confided in Jamie her anxieties about Elvis, her grave doubts, her discomfort around his older crowd, her feeling "that it was not her place in time right then. And I think that she was a little afraid of the whole relationship," Jamie said. "And she was comfortable in the one we had, because it was the right relationship for a girl that age. . . . We did fun things, and she had a blast. We were just two people—you know how it is—we just sort of clicked. We never had a fight or an argument or anything. Had a lot of laughs and some really good times."

According to her confidants, Priscilla was being steered by her parents toward the relationship with Elvis. Throughout the fall she got phone calls from the star, who was excited about her Christmas visit. These calls caused the seventeen-year-old Priscilla great confusion and anxiety. "I'm sure the Elvis thing was kind of a pressure cooker," as Jamie put it. "And I was just a kid, just having fun. And I think at the time, that was her maturity level, too. And probably . . . Priscilla would have been better off in the whole relationship with Elvis if her mom had let her do her little high school thing and let her grow up and press on."

Ronnie Garland recalled Paul Beaulieu promoting Elvis to Priscilla "excitedly" and the family receiving more gifts from the singer.

Jamie perceived Priscilla as "bewildered by the entire *complexity* of the situation." Her behavior in school corroborated Jamie's account. Priscilla failed English and German that fall and did not show up for meetings on class projects.

Priscilla Presley's reconstructed account of her senior-year relationship with Jamie as "marking time" until she saw Elvis at Christmas was "definitely not the case," according to Jamie. Those who were closest to Priscilla that fall believed that she was in love with Jamie Lindberg, not Elvis Presley. Certainly Jamie considered them in love. "We'd talk for hours. It was never boring; we were never looking for the next sentence."

"It was more than a casual affair that they were having," as his senior class tutor Pat Mayo defined it.

When Priscilla left for Memphis in December, "she told me she was just going for Christmas," Jamie recalled, "and I said, 'God! You really are?' and she said, 'Yeah.' I said, 'Do you really want to go?' and she said, 'I'm just going for Christmas. I'm coming back.' " Jamie was upset that Priscilla was seeing Elvis, and Priscilla appeared to feel the same way. Jamie was under the impression Priscilla wanted out of the Elvis relationship, that she would have preferred to stay with him in Germany. "That song 'Return to Sender' came out when I was seeing her. . . . Listening to the words . . . I think during that time she was trying to say [to Elvis], 'Hold off.' And I don't think she was not returning [his] *letters*—I think she was not returning [his] *sentiment*. I always thought that was what the song was about. It might have been an egotistical outlook, but it seemed [valid] at the time."

Elvis's plan to have Joan Esposito go to Germany fell through and Priscilla flew alone from Frankfurt to New York in late December and was met at La Guardia by Vernon and Dee Presley, who drove her to Memphis. "[Elvis] asked me would I do him a favor," recalled Dee. "When he told me who was coming over . . . for Christmas, I guess I was a little bit surprised. I really liked Anita." Dee Presley found Priscilla wide-eyed at her "first time coming to Graceland, wondering what it was going to be like."

Elvis had arranged for a gathering of friends to be at the house when Priscilla arrived, "and he carried her around and introduced her to each and every person there, one by one," remembered Willie Jane Nichols, who was one of the guests, "saying, 'This is Priscilla.' Elvis was very attentive to her and took care of her like she was a little girl." The dynamics of the Elvis-and-Priscilla relationship crystallized in that moment, with Priscilla responding, in Ricky Stanley's observation, "like a scared kid: just big-eyed and excited and reluctant, timid."

The guests who were there would forever remember Priscilla, dressed in a deep pink sweater–"the most beautiful girl I had ever seen!" exclaimed Willie Jane, whose breath was taken away by Priscilla Beaulieu. "She had such a quiet, gentle type of beauty." The Priscilla of Elvis's imagination–the demure Priscilla from Bad Nauheim, the porcelain figurine who had captivated Currie–was very much in evidence at Graceland and his houseguests were as bedazzled as Elvis. "She was different from any girl we'd ever seen Elvis with," Willie explained. "She was very tiny, she was very sweet and sensitive, and she had *such* manners! She had a lot of class. Everyone adored her . . . because she had a sweet way about her." Elvis, recollected Gladys's friend, "treated her as if she might break if you dropped her, like a China doll. She was very shy and reserved."

By the end of the evening Priscilla and Elvis were upstairs in his bedroom and did not emerge for five days, according to Alan Fortas. Once again the Beaulieus had imposed no restrictions on Priscilla's sleeping arrangements. Their seventeen-year-old daughter spent her second and third days at Graceland in Elvis's bed, in a coma, overdosed on Placidyl, which he had given her so she could keep up with his nighttime schedule.

The master bedroom bore eerie testimony to the rock star's complicated psyche. The ceiling was upholstered in black patent leather, and two televisions were mounted above the bed so that Elvis, a compulsive in all things he loved, could watch them simultaneously. The art reflected his two great loves: his mother and Jesus Christ. From Elvis's bed, Priscilla could see a framed picture of Gladys Presley and various renderings of Jesus. "The image of that seventeen-year-old child going upstairs into that jet-black bedroom–my God!" remarked Larry Peerce, who directed the miniseries based upon Priscilla's memoir and who visited the off-limits second floor of Graceland. "My God. And the televisions in the ceiling and the religious icons around the room, Christ pictures. It must have been very bizarre for a fifteen- or sixteen-year-old kid. The whole thing looked like the Marquis de Sade or something."

The strange schizophrenic nature of their relationship, older lover–Lolita and father-daughter–revealed itself vividly at Christmas, when Elvis gave Priscilla a diamond ring–and a puppy. "He *patted* her all the time," recalled Barbara Little. "He called her Nungin, which I understood his mom always called him. That was his pet name for her. They called each other that." Barbara's first thought, when she met Priscilla in the kitchen at Graceland, "was that she reminded me of Debra Paget."

Ricky Stanley, who was there all through Christmas, compared Elvis and Priscilla to a high school couple: "They sat and held hands, he kept his arm around her all the time, and he really, really flipped over her."

Elvis had but one disappointment in Priscilla that Christmas: She had cut off her long hair. He failed to recognize this as a sign of her withdrawal, however. For Priscilla Beaulieu, the Memphis visit was at once intensely romantic and harrowing. Barbara Little remembered Priscilla standing in the kitchen that first night, nervously filing her fingernails, trying to disguise her awkwardness as a teenager in bobby socks and a cardigan sweater mixing with a circle of adults she did not know. Joan Esposito, who met Priscilla that Christmas, was struck by "how young she was" and how "very, very quiet." She struggled valiantly to adjust to Elvis's schedule of partying at night and sleeping by day, resorting to the uppers and downers he offered her in a naive but misguided effort to be awake and asleep when he wanted her to be. A picture of Elvis and Priscilla at the Memphian Theatre that December captures the surreal glamour of Priscilla's Christmas trip; Elvis stands defiantly in front of the billboard of coming attractions, looking movie star–stunning in a blue velvet blazer and admiral's cap, his black hair gleaming, a pistol protruding slightly from his pants pocket. Behind him, barely seen in profile, hides a teenage Priscilla, all black hair and legs.

Elvis increasingly saw Priscilla Beaulieu as "the one," a function of his flair for the melodramatic and the mystical; but he was also drawn to her due to the sexual proclivities he had confided to Priscilla on Goethestrasse. Priscilla Beaulieu, at seventeen, was Elvis's romantic ideal, a teenager who could be satisfied–or so he believed–with making out. "Think about it," suggested Patty Perry, who discussed the subject with Elvis, something he would never do with his male friends: "[He was] a nineteen-year-old truck driver who had no sophistication and became [famous as] a superstud–though he was not a stud– and all of a sudden . . . *everything*. He was so scared and so shy." Elvis's fatal error in judgment was his underestimation of Priscilla Beaulieu's sexuality.

On New Year's Eve, Priscilla's last night in Memphis, Elvis arranged for a private party at the Manhattan Club, since she was under age. While they were at the club, Priscilla recalled, Elvis suddenly declared that "he wanted me to stay. He didn't want me to go back to Germany." Priscilla's reaction to this declaration was telling: She drank four double screwdrivers, became ill, and was driven back to Graceland by George Klein and Barbara Little. When Elvis, who seldom drank alcohol, came home slightly drunk in the early hours of the morning, Priscilla was passed out on his bed wearing only her bra and panties. He undressed her and then himself, arousing them both. Priscilla's parting memory of Elvis, that Christmas, was one of sexual dissatisfaction. "My passion had gotten to him," she later wrote, "and under the influence of alcohol, he weakened. Then, before I knew what happened, he withdrew. . . . I have to admit that, at that moment, I didn't care if it was special and I didn't care what he'd vowed. I didn't care, in fact, what *he* wanted at all. I only knew I wanted him."

Priscilla's feelings for Elvis were a complicated cocktail of star lust, fantasy love, and filial affection for a father figure. As one of her friends had described it, she felt *a* love for Elvis more so than actually being *in* love with him, and sexual incompatibility was but one of her concerns. She still regarded him possessively, however, demanding, Alan Fortas would later write, that "Anita Wood be cut out of his life forever."

On New Year's morning, as Priscilla prepared to fly home, Elvis, acting on his impulse from the night before, telephoned Paul Beaulieu in Wiesbaden to negotiate for a few extra days of Priscilla's time. Captain Beaulieu, in his self-appointed role as agent, took a tough stance, telling Elvis their "deal" extended only through January first. "He said it was out of the question that I stay any longer than I was supposed to," Priscilla said. "My father was quite firm." Elvis, by now possessed by Priscilla and accustomed to getting his way, began brainstorming, coming up with different ruses, suggesting, Priscilla explained, that "I could get sick, maybe—something would happen where I would have to stay. 'Cause he didn't want me to go."

It was then, according to Priscilla, that the fantastic idea was born to Elvis that Priscilla live at Graceland with him on a permanent basis. Priscilla's own account of her reaction to this proposal was extremely revealing: "I was dumbfounded," she said later, indicating that Jamie Lindberg and Priscilla's other intimates in Germany were correct in describing her as confused vis-à-vis Elvis that Christmas.

Another phone conversation ensued between Elvis and Captain Beaulieu, with Elvis proposing his outrageous scheme, according to a recent admission by Priscilla, who omitted this incident from her own book. Astoundingly, Paul Beaulieu—who, minutes earlier, had refused to extend Priscilla's visit by even two days—*did not say no* to Elvis Presley's proposition that his seventeen-year-old daughter move to Memphis to live with the movie star. "My father didn't want to make any commitments at that time," Priscilla said of this extraordinary conversation. "He just said, 'She needs to come home, and we'll talk about it after she gets home.' That we would talk about it at the right time."

Priscilla and *her* feelings, once again, seemed to be no more than an afterthought to the three people who controlled her destiny: Elvis Presley and Paul and Ann Beaulieu.

20

MAIL-ORDER BRIDE

Priscilla Beaulieu flew back to Germany in January 1963 much as she had the previous June: in a state of utter panic and bewilderment, a puppet in the hands of her overly ambitious parents. She told a close friend "she was afraid that they were going to make her go back and stay all the time."

This was the contrapuntal opposite of the Priscilla-and-Elvis legend, where Priscilla described herself as obsessively driven to move into Graceland that January. The myth was that Priscilla confided first in her mother and gradually revealed Elvis's invitation to her father—supposedly starving herself, withdrawing, cutting class, failing in school, and threatening to run away in order to coerce her parents into allowing her to rejoin Elvis. Yet the dean of girls at H. H. Arnold, Jackie Momberg, had no record of absences for Priscilla during that spring semester, and her classmates did not recall her missing anything. She was always with Jamie, by their recollection, and for the first time in her high school life Priscilla was actually participating in school activities—because Jamie did. "She was never rebellious," insisted her friend from that year, Judy Comstock. "I don't remember it." Another confidant reported that "There was never any 'convincing.' That isn't true. That is part of the manufactured [story]."

The truth, according to Jamie and the few others who knew Priscilla well, was that Priscilla's parents were concerned that she was getting too close to Jamie and they were pressuring Priscilla to move to Graceland to sustain the romance with Elvis Presley. "I'm sure—positive—in retrospect that was the case," Jamie affirmed. "She kind of got caught up in a very enthusiastic mom who had great plans for her, and that's how she ended up there." Priscilla told Jamie that she did not want to go to Memphis and feared she might be making the worst mistake of her life. "We were real serious," he asserted, "and she's saying, 'I can't believe it. I'm going to maybe be giving up all this for a *buffoon*.' "

Another friend, who knew the situation between Priscilla and Jamie, described her as anxious that winter, concerned that she would be unhappy and unfulfilled at Graceland: "She didn't want to be forced into it. I knew that. She knew she would be stuck someplace where she wouldn't get to do anything."

But Priscilla Beaulieu was in too deep; her relationship with Elvis was like a runaway train, and she was powerless to stop its momentum. "My impression has always been that she was like a little high school girl, and I don't think she wanted to step out of that environment at all," recounted Jamie. "But I think her mom more or less said, 'You are going.'" Jamie's recollection was seconded by a confidant of Priscilla's from that year and the year before: "The real reason for her coming back to Memphis [has] never been published. The reason that has been given is not the true reason. And Jamie does have something to do with . . . the true reason. She did not *go* back; she was *sent* back. There was a very great danger that she was not going to marry Elvis. And Jamie had a lot to do with that. . . . And her parents thought it best to get her out of Wiesbaden. In fact, she did not want to go." According to Priscilla's friend, Ann Beaulieu was orchestrating the impending move to Memphis. "Priscilla did not leave on her own. She was forced. [She and Jamie] were growing too close, and her mother was afraid she was going to throw Elvis over for Jamie. . . . That is the truth. I am absolutely certain." The legend of ever-faithful Priscilla, living for the moment she could join Elvis at Graceland, was just that: a legend, the romantic invention of a young woman desperate to disguise her real history, or as her friend described it, the "manufactured past of a celebrity." Priscilla and her parents were experts in maintaining a fiction; they had been doing it since Priscilla was three, concealing her real identity. But it's also likely that Priscilla was highly flattered by Elvis's affections and unable to say no to his invitation. After all, he was one of the most desirable men in the world, and she was a high school senior, dazzled by that sort of fame and fortune. More important, it was part of the plan she had had since childhood.

Sometime in mid-March a special "arrangement" was made between the Beaulieus and Elvis Presley. The exact terms may never be known, but they included Priscilla completing the remaining few weeks of her senior year at a Catholic girls' school and ostensibly moving in with Elvis's father, Vernon, and his wife, Dee, who lived in a smaller house on the Graceland compound with Dee's three young sons by her first husband. According to Priscilla's most recent account, "the deciding factor, I think, was the fact that I would stay with Vernon and Dee. And that it was a Catholic school, and that it was a girls' school. Elvis had found the school. He enrolled me in the school. I would be staying with Dee and Vernon. And they had their three children there. And, you know, he would like—he lived close to them. And that he did plan on marrying me. And he didn't give them a time. He just said, 'I want her here.'"

The Beaulieus had, in effect, made an arranged marriage for their teenage daughter. Priscilla, recalled her friend Judy, was "certain" she would marry Elvis sometime after she moved to Memphis, and the singer told his stepmother, Dee, at the time that he had "promised Priscilla's father" he would marry her. Al Corey, who had shared confidences with Priscilla for two years, did not feel she was in love with Elvis Presley. "She got sold," he said.

Few people in Wiesbaden knew that Priscilla was even thinking of leaving that winter. She attended school in Germany throughout January, February, and early March and was seen everywhere with Jamie Lindberg. As the situation with Elvis became clear to Jamie in the middle of March, he invited Priscilla on a "last date" to a beer festival, telling her he would practice his German so he could make an announcement at the festival "to the whole state of Germany" that she was leaving. "And she laughed. She says, 'All right, we'll go.' I said, 'Great.' A few hours later she calls back. She was crying a little bit, and she says, 'My mom won't let me go.' She was really out of sorts. So that was it." That was the last time Jamie Lindberg talked to Priscilla in Germany.

Ronnie Garland and Barney Williams's sister, Liz, were two of the few friends Priscilla Beaulieu entrusted with the information that she was leaving that March. Liza's mother gave a small going-away party for Priscilla. "She told everyone she was going back [to the States] to finish high school with friends of her parents," said Ronnie. "That's what we were told. There was a great deal of speculation." Ronnie thought Priscilla seemed distressed. "I'm sure she said something. I remember one day she wanted to come to my house to listen to records, and I said sure. She said, 'I need to get out of here, but I can't get past my daddy unless we go out the window.' And she said, 'Let's just tell him we are going to take a walk.' She put a scarf on, and we walked out. She said she was going away to finish high school with friends of her parents. She was just not real overjoyed, you know?" Paul Beaulieu, by contrast, appeared thrilled, to Ronnie. "He—let's put it this way—was a very strange man."

Priscilla Beaulieu was spirited out of her parents' home in Wiesbaden in March. There was a sense of urgency to the departure. "It was kind of like she was *gone*," remembered Jane Breighner. "It wasn't like 'She's going.' It was kind of like: 'She's gone.' " Priscilla did not even inform her classmates that she would not be completing a group project. "She disappeared one weekend," said a close friend. "I remember what she was doing, and suddenly she was gone. And she was aware that could happen. No one heard from Priscilla. She was just bundled up, and she didn't come back." Judy Comstock, who considered Priscilla a good friend, felt betrayed. "That really hurt me. It hurt me that she didn't say good-bye."

The timing of the move, in addition to its suddenness, was curious. Spring break was a few weeks away, a logical time to transfer in midsemester. School would be out for the summer in less than two months. Why, after Elvis and Priscilla had been apart for four years, the sudden pressure to transfer Priscilla to another high school with less than six weeks left in her senior year? What was the urgency? Priscilla seemed not to know, years later, how that weekend was selected.

There are those who contend that Priscilla Beaulieu's parents sold her into marriage, or at the least the *promise* of marriage, to Elvis Presley, the most popular rock-and-roll singer in the world. "I really believe that there was money involved in having Priscilla sent to Tennessee," Al Corey posited. "I mean I never saw anybody go to the bank, but I suspect that."

Mike Stone, Priscilla's lover following her divorce from Elvis, was among those who wondered. "There are a lot of things that are a mystery to *me* still." In the entire five years they were together, Priscilla never told him how or why it was arranged that she should go to Memphis. She was, still and ever, the secret-keeper. "But I think . . . she wasn't aware of some of the things that may have taken place. And if she was, she probably did not want to talk about it." She and her parents, Mike observed, had "kind of a strange relationship." Mike believed Priscilla was "a pawn in some kind of game she didn't understand" where Elvis was concerned.

"I was surprised when she was permitted to go to Graceland," commented Priscilla's principal of the previous two years, John Reddington, who had met with Captain Beaulieu about Priscilla, "and this is only my reaction. Seems to me to be a crass, shallow reaction in allowing the daughter to cue herself into fame and riches at a tender age."

There was another oddity concerning Priscilla's departure date. Paul Beaulieu had already received notice from the air force that he and his family would be transferred to California in June, only nine weeks away. Priscilla could have completed her last six weeks of high school in Wiesbaden and then flown to the States with her family. Were the Beaulieus concerned that Priscilla might reject Elvis for Jamie? Were they concerned that Elvis's attention might wander if he didn't get what he wanted right away? Why would Paul Beaulieu have agreed to withdraw Priscilla from high school and obtain special military leave to fly her to the United States in mid-March when he would have been taking her there anyway in June? "We always wondered about that, too," conceded classmate Donna Pollen. "It seemed very odd." Elvis's circumstances that March made the timing even more suspicious, for he was in Los Angeles filming a movie, *Fun in Acapulco,* and would not return to Graceland until June—*after* Priscilla would have graduated with her class from H. H. Arnold.

All of Wiesbaden was gossiping about Priscilla's mysterious departure, with Americans and Germans alike eyeing the Beaulieus disapprovingly for sending their seventeen-year-old daughter to live with a twenty-eight-year-old movie star/rock star–sex symbol. "People talked," as Donna Pollen put it. "It wasn't something that was done at the time." Priscilla herself was not seen as the transgressor; Paul and Ann Beaulieu were held to blame. As adults they understood the consequences, and as her parents, they should have protected her. The Rosses, the Beaulieus' former across-the-hall neighbors and parents of Priscilla's good friend Debbie, were aghast. "All I recall," said Debbie, "is my mother's comment: 'Well, we can figure out what that's all about. . . . My friend Laurie wrote me about it. . . . 'This is the latest scandal. This is the gossip. Can you believe this is happening?' "

"I know there was lots of gossip," confirmed Donna Wells, who had accompanied Priscilla to Elvis's house in Bad Nauheim four years earlier. "Talk about Priscilla and her dad. Everybody was shocked that she did this because of her age and the way it was presented—that she was living with [Elvis], that he was sending her to school, that she was being chaperoned."

The disapproval extended to Ann Beaulieu's family back in Connecticut. "We all thought it was terrible," recalled Ann's cousin Margaret, who was surprised that Ann sanctioned the arrangement. "I have my opinion. I think it might be more Paul. He liked to be something important."

Priscilla Presley, years later, at fifty-one, had a difficult time answering whether she would have allowed her own daughter, at seventeen, to move in with a rock star eleven years older. "I don't *know*," she responded carefully, measuring her words. "I can't say no. You know, my daughter has gone through things, too, that as a parent I have to kind of get into her head and see where she is. If she was truly in love with someone and wanted to be with him and that was the priority—and even though I *knew* she was going to make a mistake? You know, do I let her make her own mistakes and let her see? Or do I fight it and have her hate me?" Priscilla Presley let the question dangle.

Even if Priscilla *had* been desperate to move in with Elvis, how could her parents have approved the romantic folly of a seventeen-year-old girl? One of Priscilla's closer friends in Wiesbaden, who knew of her apprehension, considered her "in fantasy" with Elvis, not in love: "We are talking about a seventeen-year-old girl dating the guy that every woman in the world wanted. I wouldn't say she wasn't excited. She talked about Elvis plenty, but I never heard her say she was in love with him . . . but I'll tell you, if you ask whether a seventeen-year-old girl is enamored with the guy because he was a superstar . . . I'd say, 'Yeah, that's true!' "

Elvis, to Priscilla, may have also represented an escape, a sanctuary, from a home life that was rumored to be unhappy, which would explain her eagerness, at fourteen, to spend countless nights in the bed of a twenty-five-year-old man. Priscilla Presley revealed this in so many words to Barbara Walters in

1985, when she was asked if she was "mad" about Elvis. "I was," she answered, then immediately added, "but our relationship was very different. It was a very protective relationship from the very beginning. I don't know what it was about him, but he kind of took me under his arm and nourished me in many ways." *If* there was abuse in the Beaulieu house and Elvis sensed it, he might have invited her to live at Graceland to protect her; and Priscilla may have seen it as a safer haven, for ultimately she did consent to go. There was a connection there; a soul contact between Elvis and Priscilla that bordered on the mystical and involved their own complicated spiritual-psychic connections to their dead parents.

And what of Elvis? He was, it seemed, in love—but with what? Or whom? He was in love with ghosts—the ghost of Debra Paget, the ghost of his dead twin, the ghost of his late mother—and they all coexisted, at least in his mind, in the person of Priscilla Ann Beaulieu. His promise of marriage must have appeared, to him, a long way off in an uncertain future, since Priscilla was but seventeen and would not begin to pressure him about it for several years—another benefit of her tender age. And Elvis, by everyone's account, was not the marrying kind. Colonel Tom Parker had convinced him that marriage could damage his career and put a crimp in his dating pattern, neither of which Elvis Presley was keen to sacrifice for any woman, including Priscilla Beaulieu.

"Destiny is a funny thing," Jamie Lindberg remarked, thirty-four years after his aborted love affair with Priscilla Beaulieu. "You really are not in control. You're along for the ride, so you might as well enjoy it."

III

MARRIAGE AND DIVORCE: THE DREAM BECOMES A NIGHTMARE

21

LOST IN GRACELAND

Priscilla's life was unfolding just as her childhood friend Carol Ann had prophesied, when she said that Priscilla's mother would one day push her into an "event" that would bring Priscilla fame and fortune. Even Carol Ann, however, had not imagined an event of such epic proportions as Priscilla was drawn into in March of 1963–leaving her family, at seventeen, to move to another country to live with Elvis Presley.

Unlike Priscilla's two previous trips to visit Elvis, this time she had an escort. The family's official explanation was that Paul Beaulieu wanted to talk to Elvis in person before releasing Priscilla to him; but one had to wonder whether her father wasn't taking Priscilla there to be sure his deal with Elvis Presley was sealed with at least a handshake.

Elvis was not at Graceland to welcome Priscilla and Paul because he was filming *Fun in Acapulco* in Los Angeles. So the mountain went to Mohammed or, in this case, Paul Beaulieu and Priscilla flew to Los Angeles to see Elvis.

If Paul Beaulieu was striving to be important, he had arrived in the right place. Elvis, correctly assessing his teenage girlfriend's father, shrewdly provided the military man with a personal grand tour of Hollywood, conducted by its reigning star, as they finalized the terms of their "arrangement" for custody of Priscilla.

After a few days of sightseeing, Paul Beaulieu flew to Graceland with his daughter to deliver her to Vernon and Dee Presley's comparatively modest two-story Colonial on Dolan Street, at the end of the pasture from Elvis's *Gone With the Wind*–inspired estate. "My father went with me to check out the house where I was staying and to talk to Vernon," Priscilla explained after the fact. Two days later Paul Beaulieu flew back to Germany, leaving his daughter alone to face her destiny.

Priscilla Beaulieu's first days at Graceland were not the fairy tale that Elvis Presley's female fans later imagined. Cinderella had arrived to an empty castle with no Prince Charming, feeling very lost and very alone. "It was awkward and a bit intimidating," Priscilla later admitted, reinforcing Jamie's parting memory of her as anxious and confused about Elvis. "Because these were *his* grounds, his place," Priscilla said. "And I really didn't know anyone. I hadn't seen Vernon in a while. I had seen Elvis, but I hadn't seen Vernon or Dee." The fact that Elvis was not there to help her settle in revealed an ambivalence on his part that added to Priscilla's torment.

If, as Priscilla Presley maintained, the "deciding factor" in her parents' decision to permit her move to Graceland was the selection of a good Catholic girls' school, it seemed strange that Paul Beaulieu did not take the time to register her or to inspect Immaculate Conception High School while he was in Memphis. Priscilla claimed her father "saw" the school, but it must have been from a distance, for the nuns on the faculty did not meet either of Priscilla Beaulieu's parents during her tenure at Immaculate Conception. Sister Mary Adrian, the principal, had first heard of Priscilla Beaulieu through a letter from a Memphis attorney earlier that March, "saying that this girl would be coming to our school from Germany, and she was a senior." Sister Mary Adrian did not know of the Presley connection until the day Priscilla was registered, when Vernon Presley arrived in her office with Priscilla around six-thirty or seven o'clock at night. "I was expecting an attorney and a German girl," recalled Sister Mary Adrian, "and I wondered what Vernon Presley would want. He said that the attorney couldn't come, so he was bringing Priscilla. And then it clicked—'Ah, the girl in Germany!'—and I realized who she was, because I'd read in the paper that Elvis was dating a girl in Germany."

Sister Adrian admitted she "really didn't question the arrangement" when Vernon Presley told her Priscilla would be living with him and his wife, even though she knew Priscilla was Elvis's girlfriend. "Well, back then, I probably . . . thought she was living with his mother. They told me that, and I trusted them. I'd do that until I'd found something out for sure."

One of the other teachers, Sister Rose Marie Barrasso, Priscilla's English, homeroom, and Problems of Democracy instructor, acknowledged that she and the rest of the faculty knew that Priscilla was living at Graceland, not with Vernon and Dee: "We were told that she was living at the Presley mansion as a houseguest, and that Elvis and she were going together and that he had brought her over from Germany. . . . A great deal was made of the fact that Elvis's grandmother was more or less there and everything was on the up-and-up. It was all put up in a pretty package. And in those days, Catholic schools were very strict and did not stand for anything out of line." She felt Sister Mary Adrian and the rest of the administration "probably knew what was going on, but they kept it quiet. [Priscilla] only had a few months there at school. I think they just wanted things to go smoothly. That always kind of amazed me—you know, a nun, the principal of the school—and she didn't make any comment on the fact that here was this young girl, unchaperoned, living in a man's house!

Course his grandmother was there, which supposedly made everything all right."

So beloved was Elvis Presley in Memphis, Tennessee, and so powerful and far-reaching his star power in 1963, that even the nuns at Immaculate Conception High School looked the other way.

Other privileges were granted as well. Priscilla, according to her guidance counselor in Germany, transferred that March without enough credits to graduate from H. H. Arnold due to three F's her senior year, yet Sister Mary Adrian permitted her to qualify for graduation from Immaculate Conception taking only three classes and attending half-days. "We thought she got special treatment," recalled classmate Sherry Adler. "She only had to come for a half-day. For the rest of us it was eight-thirty to three."

Priscilla also missed morning mass at eight, customarily arriving, during her first few weeks, around eight-thirty, just as mass ended and first period began. She would arrive in a Cadillac driven by Vernon Presley, whom the other girls mistakenly assumed was her chauffeur. Sister Rose Marie, her religion instructor, regarded Priscilla as a "nonpracticing Catholic" who knew little about the religion. This seemed odd, considering Paul Beaulieu's supposed insistence on a Catholic school as a condition of the move—another "manufactured truth," according to a close friend of Priscilla's in Germany. The selection of Immaculate Conception turned on the fact that it was a *girls'* school, not that it was Catholic. Priscilla's parents, like Elvis, wanted to keep her away from boys.

Priscilla arrived for her first day at I.C. dressed in a pink linen suit, looking "like a showgirl," according to one of her teachers. "She had on makeup enough for three people," stated Sister Rose Marie, who was considered the sophisticate of the faculty. "Very heavily made-up eyes and dark lipstick. This took away from her beauty, I thought. I don't know whether she was trying to be Elizabeth Taylor or what. That's one thing we frowned upon. We didn't object to makeup, but such a heavy display of it we felt did not enhance a young girl's looks." Sister Rose Marie or one of the other nuns would have said something to Priscilla about it, "if she had not been Elvis Presley's girlfriend." The principal did insist that Priscilla wear the school uniform, compelling her to replace the tight sweaters and skirts she had taken to wearing in Wiesbaden with a schoolgirl plaid skirt, a light blue I.C.-monogrammed vest, and a white blouse, a bizarre contrast to her theatrical makeup and teased black hair. "Priscilla didn't look like we did in a uniform anyway," remembered a classmate. "We looked like children, and Priscilla looked sophisticated."

Nonetheless, she tried to fit in despite the unnatural circumstances of her enrollment and her Vegas glamour. Theresa Giannini, a senior and the president of the Student Council, was asked to take Priscilla to class and show her around during her first few days. Theresa remembered her as "real nice, and quiet. She seemed pretty normal to me. She was very cooperative, didn't put on airs or anything."

By Priscilla's second day at Immaculate Conception, word had reached the Memphis papers that Elvis Presley's "houseguest" was enrolled at the school, and reporters and photographers from the *Press-Scimitar* and *Commercial Appeal* descended upon the genteel campus en masse. Sister Mary Adrian allowed Priscilla to decide whether to talk to them or not, and Priscilla decided to meet the press. The result was an astonishingly polite account of Elvis's illegal domestic arrangement, with the Memphis papers repeating Priscilla's story that Vernon and Dee Presley were "friends of the family, and it was lucky it worked out so I could come and visit them and finish my last semester." With that and a photograph of Priscilla in her school uniform, the story, extraordinarily, faded out of sight in the press, though according to Anita Wood, "there was something of a scandal in Memphis. There was much talk there. Much talk. People in our hometown would never, ever [understand why] the parents of a girl that age would let her come across the ocean, to another town, and live there. It was unbelievable. It was unheard of back then."

By Priscilla's own accounts, she stayed with Vernon and Dee less than a week before moving into Grandma Presley's room in Graceland until Elvis returned and she could share his bed. "Everyone has always wondered how that happened," remarked Joe Esposito's then-wife, Joan. "Maybe her parents trusted Dee and Mr. Presley."

According to Dee, Priscilla left her house and moved in with Elvis with the Beaulieus' knowledge and consent: "I made sure. I said, 'Vernon, make sure that the Beaulieus know.' I know that I did inform them and get their permission. It was with their permission that she left my house and moved into Graceland. They knew she was there."

No one close to Elvis questioned his arrangement with Priscilla, or the propriety of a girl of seventeen living with an adult star, for they were all on his payroll, and who would question the boss? As Geraldine Kyle, Dee's best friend and a visitor to the Presley house, put it, "That was the way Elvis wanted it, and what Elvis wanted, Elvis got. You didn't question Elvis. That was it. Dee never had first or second thoughts about it; I am sure that she would have been looked on as a troublemaker and that was the last thing she wanted."

The assumption was that Elvis planned to marry Priscilla at some point. Joan Esposito's attitude was typical. "I assumed he did," she said later. "I don't know whether she said it or I picked it up."

Everyone assumed that Priscilla believed she and Elvis would marry. "It was obvious," said Willie Jane Nichols. "That's why she came."

Remarkably, no special precautions were taken by Elvis or his family or staff to shield the fact that he was sheltering a teenage schoolgirl-lover under his roof, but certain "house rules" were laid down for Priscilla: she could invite only a few friends to Graceland, and she would have to stay close to home and not call attention to herself. Priscilla, so adept at keeping secrets, complied dutifully as she began to play the role for which her entire life had been an almost eerie preparation. Just as she had maintained the illusion since childhood that Paul Beaulieu was her real father, so she repeated convincingly the public relations invention that the Beaulieus were "friends" of the Presleys. She told this story to the Memphis newspapers and to show business reporter May Mann that spring, to throw them off the criminal cohabitation that was really happening at Graceland. The line between reality and fiction had become so blurred in Priscilla's young life that it was small wonder she would later confuse the truth with her own fabrications during her confrontation with Currie Grant. She had passed from one household of illusion directly into another; living this way was all she knew.

Priscilla spent her first several weeks at Graceland utterly alone, waiting for Elvis. Mornings, she went through the motions at Immaculate Conception, plainly miserable, apprehensive of making friends, physically, socially, and emotionally isolated. "She went to school, and she went home," as former student Theresa Giannini put it. "She would leave [school] at lunchtime. She didn't eat lunch or socialize with us." Priscilla was as silent as a sphinx at I.C., continuing the ruse—even with her classmates—that she was not Elvis Presley's live-in girlfriend. "In fact," said another senior, "she told people that she lived with 'a family in Whitehaven,' " the neighborhood in Memphis where Graceland was located. Priscilla's discretion impressed the principal, Sister Mary Adrian, who "really admired her for the way she just did not capitalize on Elvis's popularity. And her loyalty to him. I *really* admired that." Priscilla did have an identifying symbol that marked her as "Elvis's girl," however, remembered a classmate; she wore his *Blue Hawaii* star sapphire ring, "so we all knew exactly who she was." The ring, according to Willie Jane Nichols, was a trophy for Priscilla, visible proof that Elvis was hers. "She put tape inside and wrapped it and wrapped it and [wore] it on her little finger."

Surprisingly, the other girls at I.C. didn't gawk at Priscilla; in fact, remarked Sherry Riggins, another senior, "no big to-do was made of her." It was beyond the realm of her conservative Catholic classmates even to contemplate the lifestyle Priscilla was leading; in their innocence, insisted Sherry, they assumed Priscilla and Elvis were innocent, too. Having sex, to the girls at Immaculate Conception High School in 1963, was not even a consideration. Priscilla's primary distinction, according to Sherry, was her hair and makeup. "Hardly any of us wore makeup to any extent, and she was like ready for the stage." Priscilla had conformed to Elvis's wishes by letting her hair grow and she wore it in an enormous black beehive.

When she got home from school those first days, recalled Dee, Priscilla spent much of her time "locked up in her room," a stranger in a strange land, living under a set of rules she had not yet decoded, uncertain whom to trust. Her years as a silent observer stood her in great stead, for Priscilla watched, listened, and learned. "I think the first phase she went through was awe," said Ricky Stanley, Dee's middle son, who observed Priscilla. "She was trying to get the big picture here: Who were the players? I'm not saying she is calculating, but she is not stupid. She's a smart girl. And when she found out how things worked, then she felt comfortable." The days of comfort would not arrive for several years, however. Priscilla's best friend during those first months was her toy poodle, Honey, her Christmas gift from Elvis.

The two hundred dollars Paul Beaulieu had given her quickly dwindled, leaving Priscilla in the awkward and humiliating circumstance of having to ask Elvis's father, who controlled the finances, for money to live on. Though Priscilla, by everyone's account, was extremely conservative about spending, Vernon Presley, in Joan Esposito's description, "was tight. *I* would not want to have to ask him [for money]. 'What did you do?' [he would demand.] 'I had three milk shakes.' " Neither Paul Beaulieu nor Elvis had provided an allowance for Priscilla. Captain Beaulieu likely assumed that money would not be an issue, since Elvis Presley was a millionaire, and "Elvis didn't think about those things," Joe Esposito explained. "Elvis never thought about money. I'm sure that Priscilla had a hard time being young, like 'I need money, what do I do?' So she had to go to Vernon. He didn't make it easy for you to ask him for money; he made it seem like you were taking his last dollar. . . . Elvis wasn't thinking that she should have a credit card in her wallet, she should have an allowance every week."

"His father could be brutal," Priscilla admitted later. "But he was good to me." Vernon's second wife, Dee, on the other hand, vexed Priscilla considerably: "If I wore . . . an extravagant dress, I was criticized on how much I had spent for that dress—you know, was I going to be like another girlfriend, who was extravagant?"

Priscilla was feeling constricted her first days at Graceland. Joe Esposito did not recall that anyone actually forbade her to bring friends to the house, as long as the "timing" was right, but he admitted that "she was a prisoner as far as leaving and [the family] not knowing where she was. That wasn't good. We didn't have cell phones in those days." Anyway, the reality was that Priscilla had no friends in Memphis, and she was not permitted to leave the grounds of Graceland without one of the entourage. There was a rationale behind this. Elvis, who had played the celebrity game for seven years, was wary of opportunists seeking access to him by pretending to befriend Priscilla. He wanted to protect her *and* to keep her under surveillance whenever she left the house.

The resulting lifestyle, for Priscilla, was akin to being the daughter of a Saudi sheikh, pampered and sequestered, living behind a metaphorical veil. "My friends were chosen for me," she recalled. "They . . . were the wives of the husbands in Elvis's group. Never could I bring in an outsider. I didn't bring anyone in. It was made very clear to me that I [was not to] encourage outsiders to come in, when I first got there."

Her sharpest critic, according to Priscilla, was not Elvis but Dee, Vernon's second wife. "I was so young," Priscilla later reflected, "so naive. I had a picnic out in the front of Graceland. There was a big oak tree, a beautiful oak tree, and I took my dog up there. I had a *picnic.* An innocent picnic. I was criticized [for] trying to make a spectacle of myself and show people on the streets that I was there at Graceland, [for] calling attention to myself. I couldn't believe this! I was having a picnic with my dog, never, ever thinking that I wanted to be seen from the street!" The incident left emotional scars on Priscilla, who had been reared to be dutiful—to *please*—and who was doing everything in her power to blend into her strange new world. "I was *picked apart.* So what did I do? I chose a tree way in the back part of Graceland, and I stayed there. Because I didn't want people to criticize [me]. . . . So I came down to their level. And I have some anger for that, because I fell into that *trap,* not being prepared. Those were the kinds of things that I was approached on, and Dee would do that to me, you know: 'You shouldn't do this. You shouldn't do that.' " Priscilla felt increasingly persecuted, and her reaction was to become invisible. "I was so criticized for every little thing that I did that I withdrew, thinking that everything I did was wrong."

Dee Presley characterized Elvis's household as cautious, determined to contain a potentially explosive situation. "Vernon lived in fear [because] there was a child living in Graceland," she declared. "She could surely get pregnant, or the news would pick it up, and it looked like Jerry Lee Lewis. Actually, [Priscilla] was hidden inside Graceland for a lot of years."

Ignorance and romanticism later painted over the reality, creating the fable that the teenage Priscilla Beaulieu was living at Graceland in a grand love affair with Elvis Presley, when the more bittersweet truth was that she was a confused child driven by her parents' ambition and her own fading fantasy.

Elvis returned home from the set of *Fun in Acapulco* a few weeks after Priscilla arrived at Graceland, and the fairy-tale patina of her seemingly charmed life reemerged, albeit briefly. "I remember he took her shopping in Memphis, and he bought her hundred-dollar blouses—ten of them," said Joan Esposito. "This was like, 'Gosh!' Her eyes got *this* big." Priscilla had entered a different world that spring, the world of the nouveaux riches. Elvis, in contrast to Dee, never criticized Priscilla's spending. *"Never,"* she emphasized. "He wanted me to look great."

On April Fool's Day, Elvis surprised Priscilla with a Revlon-red Corvair wrapped in a giant satin ribbon and tied with a bow. "She was all excited about it," recalled classmate Ann Dickey, who watched in amazement with the other I.C. girls as Priscilla drove up to campus in her new Chevrolet. The car was a particular thrill for Priscilla, who was embarrassed at being driven to school by Vernon or Dee and longed for the independence and relative anonymity of her own transportation. Her classmates all knew the Chevrolet was a gift from Elvis, but Priscilla kept up the pretense of her fabricated lifestyle with reporters from the *Memphis Press-Scimitar,* who turned up in the school parking lot that morning. When they asked who bought her the Corvair, Priscilla responded with a publicist's skill of evasion, saying, "It's my car." The resulting puff piece in the paper–"Priscilla Arrives in Her Bright, New Red Auto"–put a wholesome spin on a story that for any star other than Elvis Presley would have meant certain scandal. The national wire services picked up the *Scimitar* piece– and its innocent nuance–reporting that *Vernon* Presley had flown "nineteen"- year-old Priscilla Beaulieu from Germany to complete her schooling as a guest of Vernon and his wife. As before, the story died there.

Rona Barrett, one of the more famous gossip columnists, acknowledged they "all knew" Elvis was hiding a teenage girl at Graceland, but she went no further with the story because "it was beyond anybody's comprehension" that the singer was actually keeping Priscilla Beaulieu as his sexual plaything. "At that time, there were too many writers who were from the old world who would never even think twice [that] Elvis would have an affair with a thirteen-year-old [*sic*]!" The reason there was never a Jerry Lee Lewis–type scandal, the columnist suggested, was that Jerry Lee and Elvis were "very different people. Jerry Lee Lewis always had a public persona of being a very wild, crazy, nutty, fruitcakey kind of guy. Elvis never had that image. They protected that image: He was the sweet, southern gentle fellow." Elvis and his image makers invented the fable that Vernon and Dee were old friends of the Beaulieus, the press accepted it, and Priscilla learned from that experience how to manipulate the media and the public–a lesson that would serve her well when she began her own reconfiguration of the truth.

Dee Presley remembers that Priscilla seemed detached from the Beaulieus, who, she says, "very seldom" called. This was odd behavior in parents who claimed to have sent Priscilla to Graceland under duress. "I don't think Elvis felt comfortable around [Priscilla's parents]," remarked Dee. None of the teachers or students at Immaculate Conception remembered Priscilla talking about her family or saying that she missed them. Sister Mary Adrian, the principal, admitted later that it "surprised" her that the Beaulieus never inquired about their daughter's progress or her adjustment to Immaculate Conception. Their apathy cast even more doubt on Priscilla's later claim that it was the selection of a "good Catholic girls' school" that convinced her parents to send her to live with Elvis.

Jamie Lindberg was convinced, then and years later, that Priscilla was the innocent victim of a well-intended mother with delusions of grandeur for her beautiful daughter. "And I'm sure [Priscilla] ended up there out of her element," he asserted. "I'm sure that was the main difficulty. I'm sure she never had a chance to really grow up." Donna Pollen, Priscilla's classmate in Germany, flew back to the States on the same plane as the Beaulieus that June. When she saw Priscilla greeting her family at McGuire Air Force Base, Donna beheld a changed person. "She looked totally, totally different. Black hair, the beehive, Cleopatra eyes." Donna felt that Priscilla's entire manner had been altered. "She was a little distant. Not as friendly and lovely as I remembered her."

Priscilla Beaulieu had transformed herself into the child-woman she knew Elvis Presley desired. The H. H. Arnold 1963 class yearbook contained a picture of Priscilla taken earlier that year, sitting at a desk idly writing, her hair still cropped rebelliously short. Beneath it was the caption, "Dear John, err, aaa . . . Jamie," a parody of a "Dear John" letter. "They put that in there to poke a little fun at me," Jamie said later. " 'Cause I was pretty upset, kind of." Pat Mayo confirmed that "We on the yearbook staff put [in] something comical. It was reasonably common knowledge that there was something going on between Priscilla and Jamie."

There were hints of regret for her lost youth on Priscilla's part. She entreated Patsy Lacker, the wife of Marty Lacker, an Elvis aide, to accompany her to gospel-music concerts in the Memphis auditorium that spring, because according to Patsy, Priscilla was infatuated with a seventeen-year-old singer in the Southern Gospel Quartet. The young man, Mylon LeFevre, now a minister, downplayed any romantic interest on Priscilla's part, though he acknowledged that she "would come to the concerts" and she "spent a lot of time talking" to him backstage. Mylon was drawn to Priscilla for her "peaceful attitude," a kindness and gentleness that stood out from the "groupie mentality" at concerts; Priscilla gravitated to Mylon in part because they were the same age.

The attraction remained at the flirtation level once Mylon learned who Priscilla's boyfriend was. "I would have dated her if I could," he admitted. "But I was so amazed at Elvis, you know. I was a poor white guy that liked that kind of music, and I was living my own dreams, and the code that I grew up under in the South is that you don't try to date somebody else's girlfriend. . . . When I heard that she was Elvis's girlfriend, I was just friendly, you know. That changed the way I viewed her. Had she not been, things might have been different."

The triangle had a happy ending for Mylon. Priscilla went so far as to promote to Elvis a song Mylon wrote called "Without You," and Elvis recorded it on his gospel album, *How Great Thou Art.* Mylon's respect for Elvis Presley did not go unrewarded. When Elvis chose the song, he allowed Mylon to keep the publishing as well as author's rights, an almost unheard-of act of generosity from a major star to an unknown writer. "Elvis told the Colonel and his businesspeople, 'Don't take the kid's publishing. Let him keep it.' And that song made me about a half-million dollars that *he* would have made—he just *gave* it to me. He knew I was seventeen, that I knew nothing about publishing, that I knew nothing about the business. They could have easily taken it, but he didn't let them. . . . [Elvis] did for me what no one else did. He had a heart for God, even though, in that running-and-gunning lifestyle, he wasn't surrounded by people who wanted to help him with that pursuit."

Priscilla's interaction with Mylon that spring may have signified her divided feelings about her relationship with Elvis, but Mylon remembers Priscilla being as "excited as any young girl would be if the guy that was giving her a lot of attention was the biggest musician in the world." She was also still faithful to the vision she had spun for herself since childhood. And Priscilla was, still and ever, an intensely goal-oriented girl, just as she had been at eleven, when the boys in Del Valle, Texas, considered her relentless once she knew she wanted something. Elvis Presley was her "Imagine If" fantasy, and now that she was ensconced in Graceland, set up by her parents to marry him, Priscilla determined to actualize the fantasy. "I had a *dream,*" as she put it later. "I had a goal. It was all moving toward that."

The goal of getting Elvis actually to marry her seemed at times as fragile and elusive as a real dream, capable of disintegrating in an instant, despite her physical presence at Graceland. Elvis had scarcely arrived home from filming *Fun in Acapulco* when his costar, Ursula Andress, the sexy Swiss film goddess made famous as a Bond girl in *Dr. No,* began calling. Priscilla found herself once again a desperately insecure teenager amid starlets. Elvis assured her that he was not having an affair with Ursula Andress, but Priscilla, who had no way of knowing if he was telling the truth, imagined the worst.

She was also deeply jealous of Anita Wood, according to Willie Jane Nichols, who spent some time with Priscilla. Elvis had been in love with Anita. Priscilla knew this from her time with Elvis in Germany, and she feared they could get back together. "Anita was the only girl Priscilla was ever *really* jealous of," according to Willie Jane. "If Anita called, Priscilla went to pieces— and Anita did call Elvis from time to time." Priscilla admitted, years later, that she considered Anita a threat to her relationship with Elvis. She was even suspicious of Becky Yancey, a former fan who worked in Elvis's office at Graceland, saying, over thirty years later, that Becky "may or may not have had an affair with him. I don't know."

Priscilla was on a treacherous emotional merry-go-round, ambivalent about

Elvis yet ferociously possessive of him, terrified he might leave her for some-one else. Driven by the fear that she might be replaced, she played the role of the perfect girlfriend to an obsessive degree, continuing to defer to Elvis, im-mersing herself in his interests, seeking to fulfill his every desire, to become the personification of all he wanted in a female. "I knew that to be with him, you had to be *with* him—not just physically but you had to have something in common with him. That's why I would always *devour* whatever he put out there [his interests, his pursuits]. I would devour it . . . something women don't do today."

Both Elvis and Priscilla were compulsive in their passions. As Joan Esposito described it, "They both had this need. Whenever they got involved in some-thing, they really went the distance. They wanted to know everything about it, whatever it was." Priscilla could focus with a ferocity that was almost frighten-ing, and in 1963 she was focused on Elvis—twenty-four hours a day, seven days a week.

This ability to fixate on one thing, combined with a fierce competitive streak, was at the core of Priscilla's character and defined her. "I'm not about to fail at anything I do," she recently declared. "I will not. I have so much pas-sion for everything that I do." Priscilla herself did not know where this trait came from and had never tried to analyze it—but it was not from her parents, she maintained. "I just don't want to fail. . . . Once I make a commitment to something, I have to make it work. . . . If *I* can't make it work, trust me, it can't work."

Whatever Elvis required Priscilla to be in those early months at Graceland, she became. When he wanted her to improve her posture, Priscilla walked with a book on her head; if the polish on one of her nails had a tiny flaw, she painted them all again. If she made the mistake of frowning, creating potential wrinkles, Elvis would tap her between the eyes and Priscilla would stop imme-diately. Before joining him in bed, she bathed, powdered, perfumed, and made herself up the way he preferred. Priscilla was taught how a woman should pre-sent herself to Elvis in order to make love. She was an excellent student.

As with his music, Elvis Presley aspired to perfection in physical beauty. He was by nature a fantasist, and occasionally dreamed up outrageous schemes to improve upon the human form. When Priscilla, who was five feet two at four-teen when he met her, failed to grow any taller, recalled Joe Esposito, "he was kidding around about having implants put into her legs. Extensions—some kind of bone thing that would make [her] legs longer." According to Sheila Ryan Caan, a tiny blond who dated Elvis in his last years and discussed this subject with him, Elvis was not joking. "He wanted to have Priscilla's legs lengthened and talked about wanting to put her on some kind of a machine to stretch them." The idea came from a rich, eccentric friend of Howard Hughes and Mario Lanza named Georgie Stoll, whom Elvis worked with and became intrigued by on one of his movies. Charlie Hodge, an army buddy and musician who had joined the Elvis entourage, visited Stoll at his castle in northern California with Elvis. "Georgie was about my height, I'm five-three," said Charlie, "and he had a rack in the basement of the castle. He used the rack—the rack that they used to torture people on in the old days—and he'd stretch himself until he was four or five inches taller. And he told us this was truth." Elvis's plan was to construct such a rack for Priscilla.

"He never did that to me," declared Anita Wood. "He never once told me what to wear, how to wear my hair. Once, soon after we met, we went swimming in his pool and he had me stand up and turn around, and he said one of my hips was a little larger than the other, but other than that, I had a perfect figure. I had a little gap between my two front teeth, which I got capped, but except for that once, he never told me what to do, never. Ever. It wouldn't have mattered; I wouldn't have done it anyway. He didn't ever try."

Elvis's and Priscilla's corresponding obsessions and insecurities fitted into each other like interlocking pieces of a puzzle: Elvis had an artist's sincere appreciation for beauty, and Priscilla had been brought up, by Ann, to be the beautiful princess; she'd been trained to please. She was also a malleable, impressionable child of seventeen to Anita Wood's twenty-something. "[Priscilla] would do anything for Elvis at that time," asserted Joe Esposito. "She was a little doll that he took and moved around, dressed her up the way he wanted to." According to Joe and others, Priscilla eventually developed a complex about her height. "She never told anybody," said Joe, "but I knew that she did. She made little comments about being short, comments that [let me] know [she had] a complex. I make jokes now about not having hair; I know it bothers me." The insecurity lingered even after Priscilla and Elvis were divorced, when she would still exaggerate her height in interviews, claiming to be "almost five-four."

"When I met her," said Joan Esposito, "I was surprised at how tiny she was." Mike Edwards visited Georgie Stoll's medieval castle with Priscilla in the late seventies and watched Stoll elongate himself on the rack. "She was so intrigued with that," Mike recalled. "In the morning, he'd stretch and he'd be five-seven, but by the time he went to bed at night he'd be five-five!"

Priscilla spent that first spring at Graceland as she had her freshman year in Germany: schoolgirl by day and Elvis's femme fatale once she pulled her little red Corvair into the driveway. She would sneak in at noon, Alan Fortas remembered, because she was embarrassed to have the guys see her in her school uniform, and she'd disappear upstairs to change into something suitably sultry for Elvis, who was often still asleep. Priscilla kept up a grueling pace the last seven weeks of her senior year, staying up until five or six in the morning with

Elvis and the entourage at the Memphian Theatre or the Rainbow Roller Skating Rink or the fairgrounds, then getting up at eight to drive to high school and face the nuns at Immaculate Conception, fortified by diet pills and Dexedrine furnished by her rock-star lover. Hidden inside her purse, recalled Joe Esposito, was "a little twenty-five-caliber automatic. Elvis told her to carry it."

"She was living the kind of life we *thought* was neat," recalled a classmate. "We didn't have a clue that drugs were involved, and sex. You have to realize, drugs did not exist for anyone other than indigent people at that time." In retrospect, Sister Rose Marie wished she had looked into the situation more closely. "I regret it now, to tell you the truth," she admitted. "But things were different in those days and . . . what transpired after school hours I felt wasn't my business." Dee Presley, who later became outspoken and at times outrageous in her comments on the Presleys and the Beaulieus, called Priscilla "a victim of circumstances—really, child abuse."

Ann Dickey, a cheerleader who considered herself "as close to a friend as anybody she had there," regarded Priscilla as "kind of overwhelmed. We knew she was [Elvis's] girlfriend. And we knew she was living with him, and we knew she stayed out all night. She would come to school, having been awake all night long. Course, as a child, you aren't in control of your life anyway. She didn't have an option about going out and staying out all night. . . . That was her job." Priscilla told Ann she wanted to become a model. "I'm five-five," Ann said, "and she's shorter than I am, and I was thinking, 'And she wants to model?' "

Ann saw Priscilla as "a really sweet girl," trying gamely to fit in. "I always felt kind of sorry for her, because most of us had gone to school together since grade school." Priscilla, Ann noticed, "was very careful" about what she revealed about Elvis, even to Ann, which added to her isolation. "She gave the impression that he wanted her to be very private about what they did together. . . . She just had a very strange life. She dealt with it very well."

Joan Esposito recollected that Elvis was concerned that people might misconstrue his relationship with Priscilla, which he regarded as sacred and special, if they knew she was living with him. "Elvis was a God-fearing southern gentleman. . . . He served in the army. He knew that he had an image to protect—like the sports figures today. If people are following you, you should be [discreet]. People loved him and he was a genuinely nice person, so he didn't want to destroy that."

The truth that was being denied was that Priscilla was in fact still a child, despite her sexual precocity and adult beauty. When Elvis was away, she often spent the afternoon with Dee's three young sons—David, Billy, and Ricky Stanley—playing tag or hide-and-seek. The Stanley brothers were living their own fairy tale at Graceland. While Dee and their natural father were having marital problems, the three boys had been placed in a foster home. Dee reclaimed them when she married Vernon Presley. David, Billy, and Ricky Stanley were removed from foster care and driven to the gates of Graceland, where they were introduced to their new half brother, rock star Elvis Presley. Though Elvis had little affection for Dee and resented his father for remarrying so soon after Gladys Presley's death, he filled the backyard at Graceland with toys and bikes for the boys. "I had pretty much made up my mind I'm not letting him [Elvis] in my life, 'cause I hadn't got over my parents' divorce," recalled Ricky, "and he looks at me and says, 'I've always wanted a little brother, so now I have three.' And I thought to myself this was without question the most hip human being I had ever met." For Dee's three young sons, it was instant hero worship. "Elvis was kind of a hip dad to me," Ricky explained. "Not like a brother—he's nineteen years older—so it's like I've got the coolest father figure in the world here." The Stanley brothers, who were between seven and eleven years old, considered Priscilla their peer and taunted her mercilessly about her heavy eye makeup and teased black hair, calling her Lady Dracula. Once Elvis was home, however, she became Lolita again.

One aspect of her bizarre double life came to a close on Wednesday, May 29, 1963, when Priscilla Beaulieu finally graduated from high school five days after her birthday. She was only eighteen years old, but she had experienced more, in her compressed four-year adolescence, than some adults do in a lifetime. Priscilla and Elvis earned the respect of the Catholic faculty by deciding that Elvis remain outside the Church of the Immaculate Conception during the 8:00 P.M. graduation ceremony to avoid turning the graduation into a spectacle. "I really appreciated his sensitivity," acknowledged Sister Mary Adrian. "Not taking from the presence of the girls who were graduating. But I think the girls were a little disappointed!"

Apart from a summer electrical storm that blacked out the city, delaying the ceremony an hour, Priscilla's commencement proceeded with solemn dignity. She was dressed, like the angel Elvis first compared her to, in a flowing white silk graduation gown, "and she was beautiful, of course," said Sister Rose Marie. "With her dark hair and all, against the white cap and gown, she was just exquisite." Priscilla walked down the aisle of the church as her name was announced, "and everybody was whispering, 'That's her,'" recalled fellow graduate Theresa Giannini. "You could hear the whispers of 'She's the one.'" When Priscilla reached the altar, she performed the graduation ritual, kneeling to kiss the ring of Monsignor Merlin Kearney, who handed Priscilla her diploma, then moved the tassel to the other side of her cap to signify that she had graduated from high school.

The instant the last girl's name was called, students, parents, and nuns raced out of the church and across the street, where Elvis Presley was leaning against a black limousine waiting for Priscilla. He patiently signed autographs, recalled Sister Rose Marie, who found the rock-and-roll star "cordial and courteous and a gentleman."

Missing from the crowd of well-wishers were Paul and Ann Beaulieu, who would fly from Germany to the United States just two weeks later to transfer to Travis Air Force Base outside Sacramento. Their absence surprised Sister Mary Adrian, who found it odd that Priscilla's parents had never contacted her about their daughter's schooling. Elvis was in fact more like the proud father, beaming at his daughter on her graduation from high school, giving Priscilla a congratulatory party afterward at Graceland.

At H. H. Arnold, Priscilla Beaulieu was named, in absentia, the Best Looking Senior in the class she was a part of for all but nine weeks of her four years of high school. The graduation ceremony was held in the same Wiesbaden theater where *Love Me Tender,* Elvis's first movie, was shown.

Priscilla's goal, now that she had been released from the bondage of high school, was to acquire a "Mrs." next to the name Elvis Presley. She was both driven and desperate, willing to do anything Elvis bid of her to make it happen. "A young girl fearing that if I didn't do it," she said later, "maybe someone would take my place . . . and I wanted to be the one."

22

ANN-MARGRET AND
MIRROR IMAGES

Immediately following her graduation from Immaculate Conception, Priscilla shared a golden interlude with Elvis. For thirty brief but glorious days, she enjoyed the undivided attention of her sex-symbol boyfriend without the distraction of a movie, an album, or his entourage.

They spent much of their time in Elvis's blackened bedroom on the second floor of Graceland, sequestered for days at a time. Elvis loved the intimacy and privacy of these long intervals, which Priscilla referred to as "cocooning." He kept the master bedroom suite frigid and the draperies closed day and night, for he preferred the darkness, opening the door only to receive meals. Inside this private sanctuary, Priscilla and Elvis played like children, listening to music, having pillow fights. When they emerged for brief spells, Elvis organized shooting contests in the back pasture or go-cart races down the winding driveway from the street to the mansion, as if Graceland were his private amusement park. Priscilla, by all accounts, played as hard as Elvis, throwing herself into his childlike diversions.

This idyll ended on July 1, 1963, when Elvis left for the West Coast to begin his next film, *Viva Las Vegas*. Priscilla was expected to remain at Graceland while Elvis was shooting a picture—another of the rules, ostensibly devised to prevent Elvis from becoming "distracted" but in practice designed to give him latitude to commingle with his costars. He was notorious for having flings with female members of the cast or crew of his movies and had even confessed a number of them to Priscilla while they were secreted in his bedroom at Graceland. In *Viva*, Elvis was cast opposite singer-dancer Ann-Margret, who was, in the words of a friend of Elvis's, "sex personified." Priscilla had a premonition that Elvis and Ann-Margret would have an affair, and she was skittish and unsettled about staying behind in Memphis.

She occupied some of her time at the house of Willie Jane Nichols, who raised poodles and had sold Elvis the apricot toy he gave Priscilla for Christmas. Gladys Presley had coaxed her best friend into the poodle business, because it seemed glamorous, proclaimed Willie. "Gladys dreamed of being a movie star when she was young. She learned to dance the Charleston, and she read books about it. And she said, 'We're going to get us a French poodle.' "

Priscilla took her dog, Honey, to Willie to be groomed, "and she got to coming over to the house because she loved the poodles. She loved little animals." In her loneliness, Priscilla regarded Willie Jane as a mother confessor of a sort, even sneaking cigarettes at her house. "She always invited me to everything—the midnight shows at the Memphian and all. In fact, Priscilla would always say, 'I consider you family.' "

Priscilla questioned Willie endlessly about Gladys Presley during their long afternoons together, picking her brain for clues that might help her understand what endeared his mother to Elvis so that she might appropriate them for herself. "I told her what high morals Gladys had, and she was eager to know. She was sincere in it, too."

When she was home alone, recalled Dee, Priscilla "would go up in the attic at Graceland," where Elvis had preserved his mother's belongings, and try on Gladys's dresses, as if wearing her clothes, absorbing her smell, might somehow merge Priscilla's spirit with the mother Elvis so adored. She was experiencing a variation of the *Rebecca* theme: living in a house built for another woman, surrounded by her taste and influence, trying vainly to win the affection of a man who was in love with a memory, except that in Priscilla's case it was Elvis's mother, not a former wife. The image of Priscilla in the attic at Graceland wearing Gladys's clothes was poignant, almost tragic, but at the same time very revealing.

"There was some intimidation," Joan Esposito said, speaking about Priscilla's adjustment to life at Graceland, "but she has real inner strength and she is very determined. And she knew what it was going to take to stay there. She had the right intuition, she knew how to make him happy, and that was it. And I don't mean this in a negative way: *She knew what her primary purpose was.* And as long as she was focused on how much it meant to her—what she had to do with her family, what she had to do to get there, what she had to give up—and she was gonna stay in this."

Priscilla's feminine intuition about Ann-Margret had, of course, been correct. Elvis and Ann, according to members of their retinues, had an immediate sexual electricity that crackled on the set and quickly developed into what was obviously a serious love affair. Priscilla had not been in Memphis for four months when she was put to her first and most acid test.

Ann began showing up at football games Elvis organized with actor Robert Conrad and other Hollywood stars at Beverly Glen Park. Visitors and Memphis Mafia members attested to her spending nights at Elvis's rented house on Perugia, where he had returned after staying on Bellagio Road. "He loved Ann," declared Patty Perry, who had a small part in *Viva* and was on the set throughout the shoot, "and when Ann came, the parties stopped again and I was the only girl again. He had the best time with Ann-Margret that I have ever seen with any woman. They were like two kids. They partied, they had a good time." Like Elvis, the red-haired actress and dancer loved motorcycles, and the two took off on their bikes for long rides together in the canyons—just Elvis and Ann, no entourage. This was an increasingly rare occurrence for Elvis, who liked the camaraderie of his salaried band of good ol' boys and felt more comfortable with them around. Even more unusual, he often picked Ann up himself rather than sending one of the guys. Patty considered them "soul mates."

That concept was endlessly absorbing to Elvis, who was convinced that everyone had a twin soul, that those two souls were one on the "other side," then were separated and later reunited on earth. One could tell if two people were soul mates, so the theory went, if they looked like each other. The idea of a twin soul had particular resonance for Elvis, who mourned his stillborn twin, Jesse Garon, and may have clung to the concept of a soul mate as a means of making himself somehow spiritually whole.

Ann-Margret fit almost spookily into Elvis's metaphysical belief system and his growing intrigue with mirror images. In fact, she was known at the time—just after her breakthrough in *Bye Bye Birdie*—as the "female Elvis," a high-voltage sex symbol who could sing, dance, and act. She described herself and Elvis, later, as "eerily similar." In fact, Ann-Margret and Elvis actually physically resembled each other; their faces and bone structures were strikingly alike, down to the crooked half-smile. Ann was taken aback by this duality, later writing in her autobiography that "it was like discovering a long-lost relative." Just as intriguingly, Ann bore a likeness to Priscilla. The Swedish star and the part-Norwegian eighteen-year-old both had pouty lips, pert noses, wide-set eyes, and heart-shaped faces; as Priscilla grew older, it often became difficult to distinguish her from Ann in certain photographs. They even sounded alike; Ann spoke in a breathy, sexy, baby voice that Priscilla was either born with or affected to emulate the actress, whose kittenish growl was her trademark. To complete the bizarre circle, "when Elvis first met Ann-Margret," Debra Paget would later recount, "we had the same makeup person at the studio, and he used to tell me that my face and Ann-Margret's face—our bone structure was exactly the same." Debra also told of how, in a Vegas hotel in the seventies, her own parents once mistook her for Priscilla. The "twinning" theme seemed to dominate Elvis's love life: Debra Paget's mother and Elvis's mother; Gladys Presley and Debra; Debra and Priscilla; Priscilla and Elvis; Elvis and Ann-Margret; Ann-Margret and Priscilla; Debra and Ann-Margret. These were the sorts of parallelisms Elvis found fascinating and could spend hours pondering.

Elvis and Ann-Margret had a relationship that was both intimate and hot. His nicknames for her suggested as much: He called her either Rusty Ammo, after her character in the movie, or Scoobie. "They had a great time and were madly in love," in the opinion of Joe Esposito, who knew Elvis's thoughts probably as well as any of those around him. "Ann and Elvis . . . liked a lot of the same things. They had a good time together. They were always happy." Even Joe's wife, Joanie, whose loyalties would lie with Priscilla, considered Elvis and Ann "terrific" together. "Ann has a great sense of humor, and [their romance] was fun and light."

Priscilla meanwhile was mad with worry, cloistered at Graceland, hearing rumors about Elvis and Ann, reduced to scouring newspapers for bits of gossip. During the first week of August her worst fears were confirmed in Hedda Hopper's column, which appeared in the *Memphis Press-Scimitar.* Hopper reported that Elvis and Ann-Margret were dating, and she quoted Ann as saying he was "wonderful." Priscilla was already despondent over love letters she had found in the office at Graceland from Anita to Elvis, confirming that Elvis had pursued Anita after he left Germany. The fact that Priscilla was herself in love with several other people during that time period did little to assuage her battered feminine pride and not insignificant ego. The problem was that Priscilla and Elvis were essentially the same in matters of sex and romance: Each was accustomed to being the object of others' intense desire. Priscilla's dilemma was accepting that she had undertaken to become the girlfriend of a star who would forever relegate her to the background and into a double standard her ego found untenable.

"We already had been talking about *marriage,*" she said later of her reaction to the gossip from the set of *Viva.* What was Elvis doing with Ann-Margret? Priscilla wondered as she waited, anguished and alone at Graceland. "I knew he was dating her. So there was like 'Wait a minute. What is this?' And that was where the insecurities were coming in." Priscilla, as she had with Anita in Germany, methodically studied and ruthlessly critiqued both herself and her latest competition to assess where they stood with Elvis. Ann-Margret, she rationalized, "wasn't his type." Or so she tried to convince herself. "As far as a woman to marry, to have children with, it wasn't there. And I knew how important that was to him, to have kids."

Elvis Presley was at a turning point in his personal life, faced with a choice between two women, Ann-Margret and Priscilla, that would determine the direction of his future. Several of the Presley aides, later in life—Marty Lacker, Lamar Fike, Billy Smith—would contend that Priscilla was Elvis's second choice, but it was impossible to know whether their opinions were valid, for they were by then disenchanted with Priscilla Presley and embroiled in power struggles with her in her role as executrix of Elvis's estate. Patty Perry, who had no ulterior motives and spent time observing Elvis with both Ann and Priscilla, considered Ann "the love of his life," and it was clear, both then and later, that Ann-Margret felt the same way about Elvis. Although she refused, out of respect for Elvis, to discuss their love affair publicly, she referred to him in her 1994 memoir as her "soul mate."

Priscilla distracted herself that August with a visit to her family, then living at Travis Air Force Base in northern California and celebrating Paul's promotion to major. When the filming of *Viva* wrapped at the end of the summer, she and Elvis were reunited at Graceland, where Priscilla spent a gloomy September, morose and anxious about Ann-Margret, whose calls Elvis was not so secretly taking at the house. According to Dee, Ann began phoning her house on Dolan Street, which Elvis took to using for clandestine conversations with the actress. "He was stuck on Ann-Margret, I think," Willie Jane Nichols contends. "At that time, that's all he'd talk about." Priscilla would mention to Willie how "bothered" she was by Elvis's affair with Ann-Margret, and she also turned to Dee for occasional consolation.

"She did a lot of crying, and she was angry," Geraldine Kyle remembers. "She was extremely jealous, as I would have been, very unhappy."

According to Willie Jane, Elvis invited Ann to Graceland. "I'm not coming there with that woman there," she reportedly responded.

When Priscilla brought up the subject of Ann to Elvis, "he would keep telling her that it wasn't happening," recalled Joan Esposito, who found herself in the uncomfortable middle, friend to Ann, Priscilla, and Elvis, uncertain what to say to whom: "Elvis just denied everything." Priscilla had little choice but to reluctantly accept his denials. "But you know," said Priscilla later, "what he would say to *her* and what he would tell me were two different things."

Elvis was playing a cagey romantic game with two strong-willed, jealous females, just as he had juggled *Anita* and Priscilla the year before. Sooner or later something had to give.

The situation reached a flash point in October, when Elvis went back to Los Angeles to film his next movie, *Kissin' Cousins.* Ann-Margret was in London promoting the British release of *Bye Bye Birdie,* so Elvis took Priscilla to Hollywood, which temporarily cheered her. Priscilla found both the movie business and L.A. stimulating, in contrast to Memphis, where she had nothing to do and which she considered dull. Yvonne Craig, Elvis's female lead in *Kissin' Cousins,* had met Priscilla briefly during her spring visit to L.A. the year before and noticed a tremendous difference in her bearing and confidence. She had successfully transformed herself into something of a Hollywood sophisticate already, and Yvonne, a starlet of the first order, considered Priscilla stunning and "would never have guessed her to be seventeen [*sic*]." She thought Priscilla seemed proprietary toward Elvis, as if "she had a sense of her place in his life now." Elvis's five-star sapphire had moved from Priscilla's pinkie to "the correct finger," as Yvonne put it, a not so subtle suggestion of an engagement ring. Yvonne, in fact, thought Elvis had secretly married Priscilla, which was no doubt the teenager's intent.

During the *Kissin' Cousins* shoot, quotes attributed to Ann-Margret, taken from London newspapers, began filtering back to the States. It was reported that Ann told the British press that Elvis had given her a round pink bed and that they were going to be married. Elvis, by a number of accounts, was furious. This publicity, according to Priscilla, led to a much-written-about fight between Priscilla and Elvis at the Bel Air house. "He was angry," Priscilla explained. "He was infuriated, and it [the marriage gossip] caused friction between the two of us. So I asked him what was wrong, and he said I had to leave because [Ann-Margret] was coming back and he had to settle things."

Priscilla claimed that she used Elvis's response as an opening to confront him about his affair with Ann, "and then he got *really* angry with *me* because now I *knew*. And he told me that that was *it*. He confided—not confided, it was an argument—that he [had been] seeing her [but] that he was not seeing her anymore. And he told me that he got this bed for her. I mean, he just *told* me *everything*. And then I said, 'Well, what attracted you to her?' And he told me he was attracted to her because she was the ultimate complement to *any* man. To his ego, more or less. She imitated *him*. And he was attracted to that. But he knew that [she] wasn't what he was looking for . . . that she was very . . . nice, but that she would always be competitive with him. And that she was very career-minded, and that he was looking for someone to marry. And that she was a novelty for him. Not long after that, I went back to Memphis."

Others, including Priscilla's soon-to-be best friend Joan Esposito, offered a different account. "What happened," said Joan, "was that [Elvis] called Priscilla's bluff." Priscilla, according to Joan and others in the Perugia house, confronted Elvis about Ann-Margret, and he pulled Priscilla's clothes out of the closet and tossed them out onto the driveway, threatening to send her back to her parents—Elvis's typical reaction when charged with infidelity. "The best defense is offense," as Joan interpreted his pattern. "He would say, 'Well then, we're finished.' She wasn't ready for that, so she would get back into line."

The fight about Ann "hurt deeply at that time," Priscilla acknowledged later. She retreated to Graceland as commanded, while Elvis remained in L.A. another two weeks or so, the duration of his *Kissin' Cousins* shoot. Exactly what transpired between Elvis and Ann-Margret in the weeks that followed is still something of a mystery and is likely to remain that way, for Ann will not discuss it, or Elvis—"even with me," remarked comedienne Mitzi McCall, "and I'm her closest friend!" Ann-Margret considers Elvis and his memory too special. She insisted, then and later, that she never told British reporters she was going to marry Elvis, only that they were dating, and she wrote in her book that she cleared this up with Elvis that fall. Yet from that point on, Elvis did a mysterious slow fade from her life, despite the fact that he was in love with her. "I think that [the marriage publicity] was sort of an excuse for him," was Joe Esposito's theory on the breakup. "How to end [the romance]. He knew it wasn't going to go any further. I think that was his reasoning how to break off [with Ann]."

Ann-Margret later referred cryptically to a "promise" Elvis had made that prevented them from being together, though in her words they had "talked about" marriage. "His wish was that we could stay together," she wrote in her 1994 memoir. "But of course we both knew that was impossible, and that's what was so very difficult about our relationship. Elvis and I knew he had commitments, promises to keep, and he vowed to keep his word." Though she has never said so directly, Ann-Margret was obviously referring to the Beaulieus' arrangement with Elvis for Priscilla. "I really believe Elvis told [Priscilla's parents that] he was going to marry her . . . and that was the deal," Joe explained.

Elvis returned to Memphis, and to Priscilla, early in November. What happened next at Graceland indicated that he might have communicated his decision to Ann-Margret, who sent him a telegram that read, "I just don't understand." It was signed "Scoobie," Elvis's pet name for her. "And then I found the telegram," related Priscilla, "and in that telegram was what happened. [There were] *two* telegrams. One said, 'I just don't understand,' and I believe there was another one with a song title on it, and I don't recollect what it was. But it indicated that [the affair had] ended. It was over." Ann-Margret, according to Joe, who kept in touch with her, "was devastated [by] the way it ended."

Elvis's choice of Priscilla over Ann-Margret was persuasive proof that the die had been cast for Priscilla Beaulieu's future; that in fact Elvis had committed himself to an eventual marriage.

"Elvis did tell me," affirmed Charlie Hodge. "Annie used to come up to the house, and he said, 'Charlie, I stopped going with Annie on purpose, because I was beginning to feel too much for her, and I knew I was going to marry Priscilla.' "

There were, in the collective judgment of Elvis's friends, supporting arguments for the decision to eliminate Ann, most of them turning upon Elvis's perception that he could more readily subjugate Priscilla. "She represented something that he could bring up," suggested Patty. "He brought her in at fourteen, and he was going to bring her up. He liked to control her."

"It was a different kind of love," according to Joan. "Priscilla was still the home and strength. Ann was making him stretch. I think that Ann made him get outside his comfort zone; in many ways he liked that, but was also afraid of that. And Priscilla was malleable."

By casting aside Ann for Priscilla, Elvis had rejected an adult relationship with a woman, an opportunity for a mature love. He was threatened, in the judgment of virtually everyone who knew him, by Ann-Margret's fame and independence. "Priscilla was like me," Patty said. "I was in awe, but Ann-Margret—she and Elvis were equals. She was the best girl, the most fun. They would have been the perfect pair. But she wouldn't give up her career, she wouldn't be with him twenty-four hours a day, and he wanted someone who would be there twenty-four hours a day."

Many of Elvis's intimates shared this opinion. "Ann-Margret was a great time," Joe reported, "but Elvis knew Ann had a career and wasn't going to give it up for him. He wouldn't expect her to. And he knew he could never be with someone who was in the limelight; when he wanted them there, he wanted them. Not like 'I'm on location, I can't do it.' Priscilla he knew would be there whenever he wanted her; he raised Priscilla that way. And that's why he would take her, knowing he could still fool around. Ann-Margret wouldn't have let that happen." Elvis apparently told Charlie Hodge, "Charlie, it wouldn't work, anyway, with both of us in show business. She'd have her managers and I'd have my managers. There'd be conflicts all the time."

There was also the ever-present issue of Priscilla's alleged purity, the importance of which never diminished for Elvis. Geraldine Kyle overheard Vernon's side of a telephone conversation at Graceland shortly before Elvis and Priscilla finally married in 1967. "I was leaving to go out the front door through what they would now call the Jungle Room," Geraldine recalled, "and . . . Vernon was talking on the phone. I don't know who he was talking to, but I heard him say, 'Well, Elvis told me that he knew for sure and certain Priscilla had never been with a man, and that is what Elvis saw in her.'" Priscilla's original pose as a vestal virgin, untouched by anyone but Elvis, had become not only her image but also part of her hold on Elvis, her raison d'être. How could she look back now?

Though she had seemingly prevailed in the triangle with Ann-Margret, Priscilla was anything but confident of her footing with Elvis. He remained romantically involved with Ann for another seven or eight months after the London publicity incident, making her a continuing threat to Priscilla's emotional, financial, and domestic security. Her reaction, true to her conditioning, was to focus obsessively on her appearance, to make herself so alluring, so sophisticated, so glamorous, so *Hollywood*, that Elvis would not think of looking at another woman. Priscilla already felt inferior to the starlets who passed through her movie-star boyfriend's working milieu; she, by comparison, was an eighteen-year-old girl, several months out of high school, determined to level the playing field.

Thus was born the outrageous makeover with which the name Priscilla Beaulieu would be forever synonymous. If the students and nuns at Immaculate Conception thought she resembled a showgirl that spring, they would have presumed she'd turned to prostitution by Christmas. Her back-combed coiffure, which had been a spectacle at the school, now grew in height until it resembled a wedding cake. In retrospect, Priscilla's hairstyle seemed as ludicrous as the powdered wigs worn by the French aristocracy during the reign of Louis XVI. Patty Perry had started styling Priscilla's hair, and reluctantly created "the big boomba," as she called the beehive for which Priscilla would later be lampooned. "I used to comb her hair in this boomba, and she would say, 'Make it bigger, bigger,' and then we would go into the den and Elvis would say, 'It's too big,' and she would blame it on me. And then she dyed it black." Patty eventually tired of the battle, and of being kept waiting by Priscilla, with whom she did not always get along, "so I said, 'I am not doing this anymore.' "

Priscilla—not Elvis, as she would later claim—was clearly the architect of her famed Elvira look, though she doubtless exaggerated it in a teenager's attempt to impress him. Elsie Boaz, the owner of a Patricia Stevens charm school in Memphis where Priscilla had enrolled to further her modeling ambitions and occupy her time, remembered the eighteen-year-old as obsessive about cosmetics. "She liked the heavy makeup, the Cleopatra eyes, and the black hair. We would tone it down, and as soon as class was over, she'd go to the bathroom and put more makeup on." At the height of her mania, Priscilla was wearing five pairs of black false eyelashes simultaneously in addition to jet-black eyeliner extended outward, Catwoman-style, and heavily penciled black eyebrows.

She had become a parody of the painted china doll she was so often compared to. "Well," commiserated Willie Jane, "you know how a young girl would feel. Elvis was in the movies. He was with all these . . . like Ann-Margret. . . . And she was competing with them, she thought. That was my own opinion of why she took on the theatrical look." In Willie's opinion, "Elvis didn't like it. He'd begged her not to do it. But she thought she had to."

"I was definitely under a spell of what I thought was love," Priscilla said later to Barbara Walters, in a revealing choice of words. In reality, it was competition, ego, and Priscilla's goal-driven personality.

The truth of this became almost pathetically obvious when Priscilla suddenly enrolled in a dance class in Whitehaven, the Memphis suburb where Graceland was located, then tinted her long hair Titian and pulled it back from her face in a mod-style bouffant, the way Ann-Margret wore hers in *Viva*

Las Vegas. "The one person Priscilla wanted to look like, when she did her hair, was Ann-Margret," confirmed Dee, who was fashion-conscious herself and noticed the transformation. "Everything like Ann-Margret she wanted to become." "That's because [Ann-Margret] was the love of his life, and Priscilla knew it," commented Patty.

Even Joe, who was less inclined to notice such things, agreed that Priscilla was emulating Ann: "She would never admit it, but I think so." Joe's opinion was valid, for Priscilla Presley, at fifty, would belittle the threat Ann had once posed to her love affair with Elvis. "I wouldn't say Ann was the most difficult [challenge]," she commented, speaking from the comfort zone of a woman who had married, divorced, and buried Elvis. Joe knew better, for after Elvis died, Priscilla asked him to tell interviewers "that he didn't love Ann-Margret, that he was [just] going out with her, that it was no big deal." Ann-Margret, despite the protests, struck a jealous nerve in Priscilla. "Still does today," declared Joe. Elvis's feelings for the actress remained constant throughout his life; from 1964, when they broke off their relationship, until August 16, 1977, the date of his death, he sent her roses before every one of her performances.

Priscilla's imitation of Ann revealed yet again how methodically she analyzed her rivals and the lengths to which she would go to accomplish her objectives. "I had an older dance class," recalled Jo Haynes, Priscilla's instructor that year. "I would say that maybe they were like seventeen to twenty . . . and they were quite experienced in ballet, tap, and jazz. . . . It was very hard for Priscilla to dance with them at that level," but Priscilla impressed Jo Haynes with both her talent and her tenacity. "I was very proud of her. I really couldn't believe it, coming into a class with girls who had at least eight to ten years of dance training." That was vintage Priscilla; when she put her mind to something, as Joan observed of her, "she makes every point to *delve* into it."

Priscilla's eagerness to please, to get her man, was nowhere more evident than in her sex life with Elvis. She was willing to do virtually anything he asked to gratify Elvis, whose sexual tastes still occasionally ran to the unorthodox. "I knew what he liked," as she said recently, "and where his head was. And I wouldn't say that he was different; I wouldn't say that he was abnormal. He was very healthy—very healthy in a sexual way too—but, as with many men, they have their preferences." Heavy make-out sessions, rather than penetration, continued to be Elvis's sex of choice with Priscilla; he got more pleasure, other sexual partners would attest, from dry-humping than from intercourse, due at least in part to his performance anxiety.

"Yeah, he had hang-ups," confirmed Sheila Ryan Caan, Elvis's girlfriend in the seventies. "He had a hang-up about having an ejaculation inside of a woman." This was in some measure, Sheila believed, a residual fear of getting a woman pregnant and being sued for paternity. "Plus, he was a southern small-town guy. I mean, he kind of never grew up and dry-humping was kind of a thing, you know? Actually, I kind of liked it, because it was high school. At the time I thought, Oh, my God!—but that's not bad after what I've been through with other men. He was not perverse at all. He liked the *playing* part."

Elvis's reluctance to complete the sex act with Priscilla left her frustrated, but as an impressionable young girl, her ego must have been shattered. Sheila Caan, who was a teenager herself when she met Elvis, had a similar experience. "I remember the first time that we had sex and he masturbated instead of having completed intercourse," Sheila reported. "And I thought, This is gonna be like all of Hollywood! 'Cause your dreams just shatter one by one by one by one by one. And this was only like the second man I'd been with! So I just thought this is what men were like. Instead of having orgasm inside, when we were about finished, Elvis finished off the job himself. I was devastated. I thought, Oh my God! I'm not enough. What's the matter with me?"

Priscilla suffered her insecurities silently, keeping her own needs to herself, focused solely on pleasuring Elvis, motivated by the fear that she might lose him to a rival. While she was still at Immaculate Conception, she acted out his favorite sexual fantasies, dressing up as a nurse or secretary or schoolgirl while Elvis took photographs of their sex games. She became a regular at the Whitehaven all-night pharmacy, picking up developed film of her sexual role-playing with Elvis Presley before getting into her Catholic school uniform to study religion with Sister Rose Marie.

To keep Elvis happy, Priscilla later admitted, she consented to have sex with other teenage girls while he watched. Elvis sometimes videotaped these encounters, which occurred in his bedroom at Graceland, and occasionally he would join Priscilla and her female partner afterward for a ménage à trois. "They were all handpicked," she made clear later, uncomfortable at recounting her private sex life with Elvis, "so there was a trust level there."

"Elvis loved watching two women together," affirmed Joe, who was aware of his boss's ultimate fantasy, seeing two girls wrestle in white panties: "Not naked. White underwear, cotton. I guess the virgin thing." Alan Fortas, a Presley aide, claimed the singer once explained that this stemmed from a time when, as a boy, he saw two girls fall down, exposing their white underpants.

According to Priscilla, Elvis would later watch with her the videotapes of her lesbian encounters instead of having intercourse with her, "and that gave him a lot of sexual gratification." She characterized Elvis's sexual preferences, to a degree, as part of his need to be "different. And I think that's what he resorted to, something different. Because that was expected from him. . . . You know, he was always so identified with being different, being an innovator."

There was about Priscilla's acquiescence to lesbian sex and video voyeurism an air of pathos and quiet desperation, so tragically fixated was she on acquiring this flawed fantasy man as her husband at any cost. And still the Beaulieus allowed their little girl to cohabit with the singer-superstar, unaware, presumably, of the dark side of the fairy tale that Ann, who was ostensibly ignorant of the emotional torment Priscilla was enduring, so desired for her daughter.

That Elvis Presley was keeping a teenage lover hidden at Graceland became an unspoken scandal, an open secret in the corridors of the music industry in Nashville, common but hushed gossip in Hollywood. Columnists either ignored the rumor, pretended not to believe it, or blindly accepted Elvis's transparent ruses. May Mann, a former actress who interviewed the star for movie magazines and questioned him about his love life, admitted she "hadn't met or given Priscilla a thought" from the time she moved into Graceland in 1963 until Elvis married her in 1967. May professed to be under the impression that Priscilla had moved back in with her parents in Sacramento once she graduated from high school and that she occasionally visited "all of the Presleys" or "reportedly" stopped by the set to see Elvis. "It was considered a very private personal matter," May later wrote. "Even Elvis's studio press agent admitted to me that while he had worked on three pictures with Elvis, he'd talked to him only twice, very briefly. He had never asked Elvis a question, not even one." The press of the sixties subscribed to a gentleman's agreement that veiled the sex lives of certain celebrities, and Elvis Presley's secret child-lover fell into the same exalted category as Jack Kennedy's White House mistresses and Rock Hudson's homosexuality. The divine right of kings.

Elvis and Priscilla were "outed" late in 1963, when *Photoplay* magazine ran the first of two articles with the cover headline "Elvis Secretly Engaged! Love Began When Priscilla was 15." The source of this information was Currie Grant, Priscilla's future nemesis and former entrée to Elvis, the "only person," *Photoplay* hyperbolized, who "could write this story—the man who introduced Elvis to Priscilla Beaulieu!" Currie decided to sell one of his photographs of Priscilla to *Photoplay*. "They wanted the picture, but they wanted the story to go with it," he explained, so he agreed to provide the magazine with a superficial account of Priscilla's first dates with Elvis, to be written by a *Photoplay* writer but published under Currie's byline. When the article and several of his photographs of Priscilla came out, Currie was annoyed by *Photoplay*'s reworking of the story, which stated inaccurately that it was Currie who had asked Priscilla if she wanted to meet Elvis—a point that would become their future bone of contention. "This guy who took the story from me changed it around, so I got mad and called them up," Currie said. Nancy Anderson, then West Coast editor of *Photoplay*, took Currie's call. "She tried to gloss it over," Currie explained, "saying movie magazines had to be very careful and really nice, that it was a family magazine and it wouldn't look good to publish a story about a young girl asking to meet Elvis, and I let it go." Nancy Anderson recently confirmed that Currie was upset when the piece came out and that his story had been reversed. "That's where Priscilla got the idea, I guess," proposed Currie.

The *Photoplay* piece was actually relatively harmless, repeating the Presley propaganda that Priscilla was living with Vernon and Dee, omitting any reference to Priscilla's sexual relationship with either Currie or Elvis. What it *did* do, however, was put the spotlight squarely on Priscilla Beaulieu, Elvis's teen lover, which no publication had done before. *Photoplay* printed photographs of her and even suggested that Elvis planned to marry her. This claim was based on a statement the singer had made the year before when, after a phone conversation with Priscilla, he said to Currie, "You introduced me to the girl I'm gonna marry."

The *Photoplay* piece, according to Charlie Hodge, annoyed both Elvis Presley and Paul Beaulieu, "because Currie had taken pictures of her and [had sold] them to magazines. . . . If we wanted a story leaked, we had our sources that we used." At that point, according to Charlie, Elvis's group began freezing Currie out.

They needn't have worried, for the exposure did no damage to Elvis's immense popularity or public image. The press, which easily could have made a scandal of the Priscilla affair, instead perpetuated the sweet romance depicted in *Photoplay*. "It was like Rock Hudson," confirmed Rona Barrett, the premier gossip of the era. "Why didn't anybody ever talk about his sexuality? One of the reasons was that [Rock] was always one of the most considerate movie stars. . . . He always went out of his way to be accommodating. He was always kind to the press, and . . . the Hollywood press, at that time, were not about to go out of their way to destroy somebody like Rock. I'm only using Rock as an example because that's the way Elvis was treated. He was so polite, so deferential—that was really it. And his people always knew how to couch it, so you really didn't know for sure." Elvis Presley, moreover, occupied a status in show business that Rona Barrett considered unparalleled: "Nothing destroyed Elvis Presley, and nothing ever will."

A few weeks before the first *Photoplay* story hit newsstands, Nancy Anderson asked Currie to telephone Priscilla at Graceland to find out whether she and Elvis were already married, so she could use the information in the follow-up. It was this phone conversation with Priscilla, Currie believed, that led to his eventual estrangement from Elvis. Currie and Priscilla, who had not seen each other since the photo session in Germany two years earlier, chatted for a long time on the phone, with Priscilla asking "very subtle" questions about Ann-Margret, "pumping me about what goes on at the house at Bel Air, but in a very vague, childish, schoolgirl-type way." The conversation meandered agreeably until Currie asked Priscilla whether she and Elvis were married and Priscilla refused to answer. "She was," he perceived, "like a caged animal. She became very, very aware of what she said to people, didn't want it to come back to the wrong person. She was very, very afraid that she might lose her position or be sent back to her parents." Currie "got a little huffy" with her. "I said, 'How do you think you got where you're at?' I told her, 'I just want to know . . . if you guys got married.' " When Priscilla still refused to tell him, "I probably made a few remarks I shouldn't have," said Currie, who was having marital problems and had reduced his visits to the Bel Air house because he disapproved of Elvis's developing lifestyle. "I made the mistake of saying, 'Well, I'll tell you one thing: I have a family. I would never—with all the booze and the pep pills and the things going on—I'd never bring my two young kids over there around Elvis.' I wasn't even thinking it would get back to Elvis."

Currie later surmised that when the *Photoplay* piece came out and Elvis became angry with him, Priscilla used the opportunity to tell Elvis what he had said, possibly because Elvis thought she had played a part in the article but, more likely, "it was her chance to get rid of me," something Priscilla had been attempting to do since Bad Nauheim, once she discovered Elvis's preoccupation with virgins and the threat Currie posed, since she had been intimate with him. The Beaulieus, according to Currie, did not have a problem with the *Photoplay* piece about Priscilla. "I kept in touch with them after that," Currie said. "I think they wanted the publicity at that time. Really, there wasn't any animosity. It's a nice little story. . . . My God, it's a fairy tale; they made up a lot of things in there."

The *Photoplay* two-part series, as the first extended publicity about Priscilla Beaulieu, may have helped shape the public's image of her as a modern-day Cinderella, as opposed to the rather tragic figure she really was. From the outside, Priscilla's life appeared to be a dream come true. Even Nancy Sinatra, who was a friend of Elvis's and knew Priscilla slightly around this time, was swept up by the illusion of romanticism that swirled about Elvis and Priscilla. She told biographer Albert Goldman in the late 1970s, when he was researching his acid account of the singer's life, "Someday somebody should do a love story based on these two people, because it's an incredible story. It's like *Snow White* or *Sleeping Beauty*. Elvis asked her father if he could . . . marry her and . . . take care of her schooling and take care of her. And [Elvis] put her in a convent, and he saved her, kept her for himself. He didn't want anyone to touch her, except him." Nancy Sinatra's idealized perception of Priscilla as the heroine of a storybook romance fitted perfectly into her childhood role as a fairy-tale princess, the part her mother had created for her and groomed her to play. This fantasy was eagerly embraced by Elvis fans, who saw their hero as the archetypal White Knight. It was then perpetuated by Priscilla herself, struggling to match her life to the myth of a relationship that never existed, except in Elvis's imagination.

The Priscilla-and-Elvis story, like most legends, contains an element of truth, for if soul mates exist, Elvis and Priscilla had a karmic connection that seemingly predestined them to come together—perhaps, as Mike Edwards suggested, for Elvis to "save" Priscilla from an unhappy childhood and for her to replace, in Elvis's mind, the mother and girlfriend he loved and lost.

If Priscilla fit the part of a fairy-tale's heroine, it was the dark tale of Rapunzel, locked in a tower, lonely and bereft and untouched. She was a virtual prisoner at Graceland, leading a controlled life that, for all its poetry, was emotionally harrowing for her. Elvis was very often away, either making one of his three or so films a year or recording music, leaving Priscilla alone and bored in Memphis, restricted in whom she could befriend and unable to leave the grounds without an escort. "Priscilla couldn't have made it without Grandma," Willie Jane noted sympathetically. "She spent the night with her when Elvis was away." Graceland in certain ways resembled the Clampett mansion in *The Beverly Hillbillies*. The Presleys, like the Clampetts, were dirt-poor southerners who, with Elvis's meteoric success, found themselves suddenly rich. Vernon was a latter-day Jed; Elvis was a well-intended, oversexed Jethro; and Grandma Presley assumed the role of Granny, whom she favored slightly. Elvis's grandmother, according to Willie Jane, used to say to Priscilla, "You little girls shouldn't leave home and come here."

Priscilla hadn't many girlfriends, her lifelong pattern, and "didn't associate with many people," according to Willie, who spent many an afternoon with Elvis's young, beautiful, and trapped girlfriend. Priscilla's one attempt to bring in an outsider—an acquaintance from her ballet class whom she invited to the house for dinner—was disastrous. Grandma Presley happened to mention the incident to Dee, who castigated Priscilla. "I never heard the end of it," Priscilla recalled. "How could I bring somebody into Graceland? They might steal something. Well, what did I do? I again withdrew, didn't have any friends over, because I didn't want anything stolen from the house."

Her two closest companions, outside the Memphis Mafia wives—Marty's wife, Patsy; Richard Davis's wife, Peggy; Gene Smith's wife, Jo; and Joe's wife, Joan—were Memphians Carolyn Jones and Jean Boyd. Jean was the cousin of Pat Boyd, who worked in the office at Graceland and later married Elvis's school friend Red West, the unappointed ringleader of the entourage. Priscilla and her girlfriends played cards, a favorite pastime of Priscilla's, or went horseback riding, her childhood passion. "She didn't go out a lot," said Willie. "She liked to eat Mexican food. She'd go down to Pancho's a lot." Priscilla was possibly closest to Patsy Presley, Elvis's double cousin, who was another Graceland employee. Becky Yancey worked in the office with Patsy and remembered Priscilla scampering in nearly every day, wearing little black Capri pants and Capezios, reading Elvis's fan mail or finding and weeding out her own letters to him from Germany. Or she passed the time with the Stanleys, mostly Ricky, who had a huge crush on her that he would carry to adulthood. With Patsy or Ricky, Priscilla went bowling, to the movies, or to Leonard's Drive-in, a local hangout. She was desperate for something to *do.*

When Elvis was around, Priscilla had to vie for his attention against the stiff competition of his male disciples, who included his cousins Gene and Billy Smith; Lamar Fike; former classmates Red and Sonny West, who were cousins; Richard Davis; Charlie Hodge; and Marty Lacker, all of whom did his bidding and received a salary. Joe Esposito was ever about, and others would come and go as it suited Elvis's mood. The atmosphere within the retinue was one of extreme competition, with everyone jockeying for Elvis's approval, for the position of Most Favored, but more meaningfully for his *time,* the rarest commodity in Elvis's harried life. "There was always the one-upmanship," Priscilla recalled. "Who was going to sit next to him? Who was going to be next in line? Who was going to be invited to the movies? Where were they going to be sitting? Everybody in the theater had their positions, and *no* one dared touch that position if it was close to [Elvis]. There was a definite pecking order. So thank God I didn't have to worry about that, because I sat next to him! But what went on behind that seat, I didn't even want to know." Priscilla and the members of Elvis's male entourage eyed one another with mutual wariness; everyone was a threat in Elvis's rarefied world. Willie Jane thought that "The guys wanted to break Elvis and Priscilla up, because Priscilla didn't want him to do some of the things they wanted to do. *They* wanted him for themselves, let's face it."

Priscilla was never quite sure where she stood, despite her father's arrangement with Elvis. She told Barbara Walters, years later, that Elvis "was reluctant in mentioning marriage." Naturally this added to Priscilla's uncertainty over her standing with Elvis, and the situation was exacerbated by his chronic womanizing. Nancy Sinatra, who had proclaimed Elvis and Priscilla the ultimate romantic couple, told Albert Goldman later that she herself was "dry-humping" him during the filming of *Speedway* in 1965.

The seeds of a deeper discontent were being sown in Priscilla's early Memphis years. Joan Esposito remembered that Elvis "did not want Priscilla in the public light or spotlight at all. He did not want her acting or modeling. He squelched anything of that nature, anything public that she wanted to do. And she was always trying to improve herself and keep up." Priscilla had modeled on a very minor level while she was taking classes at the Patricia Stevens charm school. The context was almost comical for the girlfriend of Elvis

Presley: Priscilla modeled fashions from a local Memphis boutique during lunch hour at the Piccadilly Cafeteria in a strip mall close to Graceland. That she would do this demonstrated her unquenchable interest in fashion and glamour and show business of a sort. Though she spoke of her desire to give Elvis children, Priscilla confided to Becky Yancey that year that she did not want to get pregnant "because it would ruin her figure."

Priscilla was drawn to the performing arts. She might have enrolled in Jo Haynes's class to compete with Ann-Margret, but she soon found that dancing was an outlet for her unused energy and drive. Dance freed her, gave her a means of expression, provided an arena where she was able to be herself. Jo Haynes observed that Priscilla seemed truly happy when she was dancing.

She went dance-crazy in Memphis, transferring from Jo Haynes's school to one run by Maylee Kaplan. Then, when she heard that Willie Jane had a military friend who taught ballroom dancing as a hobby, Priscilla scheduled private lessons at his home each Tuesday afternoon at two o'clock. She was accompanied to her lessons by Patsy Lacker, who sat and watched. "She danced the cha-cha, the waltz, the tango, the fox trot, the jitterbug, a little rock and roll, even folk dancing and the polka," recalled Willie's instructor friend, Jack Kenner. "Anything you could do to music. She was quick to catch on. She responded beautifully to a leader, a leader who knew dancing would make her look like a professional, because she was good at following."

Priscilla coaxed Elvis into dancing with her at the house. "I never had seen Elvis do ballroom dancing before, but he did with Priscilla," Willie remembers. Jack Kenner and Priscilla put on a demonstration for one of his children's classes at the Millington Naval Airbase one rainy night in 1965, "and the word got around who she was and some of the kids kind of whispered, 'That's Priscilla Beaulieu!' and . . . they wanted her signatures. She excited them, 'cause they knew she was Elvis's girlfriend." That year, the year Priscilla turned twenty, she and Jack Kenner discussed the possibility of opening a dance studio. "We were gonna teach here in Memphis," Jack said.

Those plans, like so many others of Priscilla's, never materialized, because Elvis's life was an unrelenting barrage of show business commitments, and he wanted a girlfriend who would be there for him at a moment's notice. Dee Presley thought Priscilla had aspirations to perform—and possibly a touch of envy of the idol who now effectively held her captive.

With the frustration Priscilla was experiencing, one might wonder why she chose to stay with Elvis Presley, for she was, after all, a willing participant in his domestic arrangement. The answer to that riddle was the same as the underlying problem: Elvis. For all his control issues, his sexual double standard, and his occasional egomania, when Elvis focused his attention on someone, he was *magic:* hysterically funny, with a sharp, incisive wit and flashes of brilliance. He was the most charismatic human being that Patty Perry, Rick Stanley, and countless others had ever met. His endearing traits, in many instances, were the mirror images of the characteristics that made him so difficult to bear at times. His need to control, for example, manifested itself positively in his tenderly protective and nurturing side; the exaggerated self-gratification brought on by his stardom and power was equaled, and possibly surpassed, by his legendary generosity; his double standard reflected the southern tendency to place a woman on a pedestal as a creature to be revered, almost worshiped; his egocentricity, when reversed, gave Elvis an almost supernatural ability to empathize. Elvis Presley was a man of many paradoxes—alternately megalomaniacal and humble, oversexed yet strangely prudish.

Loneliness hung about Elvis like a shroud. "For some reason," Priscilla was later to say, "the Presley family . . . always [had] that quality of loneliness. . . . His grandmother was that way, his father was that way, and he would have times of loneliness, of just *feeling lonely,* and there was nothing anyone could do." These times made women want to take care of him, to mother him, and it was powerfully compelling. Cybill Shepherd, who dated Elvis at the end of his marriage to Priscilla, felt that the song "Are You Lonesome Tonight?" "said a lot about Elvis," whom Cybill found "fragile." Priscilla was no exception; she cut Elvis's meat for him, even in restaurants, for he had never learned proper table manners and was embarrassed by his ignorance; she spoke baby talk to him. Elvis projected a vulnerability that was irresistible in one so brilliant, so famous, and so beautiful; this same tenderness registered when he sang a ballad. Elvis did not merely sing the words; he *lived* his songs as if each one had been written from personal experience, and he communicated that intimacy to his fans. His tremulous, emotional voice could move a person to tears; it seemed to touch one's very soul. To listen to Elvis Presley sing was to experience the divine.

With that genius came privileges and concessions that ordinary humans would never have been granted. Priscilla stayed with Elvis for all those reasons and more—out of faithfulness to her childhood dream, to honor her parents' arrangement, and because she and Elvis loved each other in a mystical way that even Priscilla found difficult either to describe or to fully understand.

23

I DO, I DON'T

In a way, Priscilla's heartbreaking beauty had been as much a curse as a blessing to her. It had transformed her, from birth, into the object of her mother's frustrated ambition; when she was only three, it had drawn Paul Beaulieu, who wanted her for himself, leading to the family secret that would tarnish her childhood and forever blur her identity; it had isolated her, in school, as a creature too rarefied to be friends with normal girls; and at fourteen, her exquisite face had attracted superstar Elvis Presley and initiated a fantasy with dark, sometimes dangerous undertones.

Through it all, Priscilla Beaulieu demonstrated a remarkable ability to adapt, a consequence, in part, of her military upbringing. Beneath her porcelain facade, she was a survivor. "You'd think she was made of iron," pronounced Willie Jane Nichols, the Tennessee sage who watched Priscilla go through adolescence competing with fame, Ann-Margret, drugs, Elvis's cohorts, rock and roll, and movies. Patty Perry, who observed Priscilla on the West Coast, regarded her as supremely self-possessed: "She always carried herself. She dealt with it and dealt with it well. I think inside she was a mess . . . but she also knew that she had Elvis Presley."

Priscilla's real life as the girlfriend of Elvis Presley was far and away from what she must have pictured when she was twelve, listening to "Hound Dog" while curled up on the bed in her pajamas with Pam. The celebrity whom Priscilla had taken up with was now a movie star, not a rocker. By the mid-sixties, five years into the relationship, Priscilla still had not seen Elvis perform live; he had given his last concert in the spring of 1961, while she was in Germany. The Elvis who mugged his way through bad but entertaining B pictures was not the electrifying, slightly menacing rock rebel of Priscilla's earlier years, and this may have been a subtle factor in their growing estrangement.

Elvis the movie star had settled into a routine of three or so pictures a year, which brought Priscilla back to Los Angeles once Ann-Margret had receded into the background. She was, to Joe Esposito's watching eyes, still enamored of Hollywood and moviemaking, in contrast to Elvis's deepening disillusionment. In a span of nine months in 1964, he shot *Girl Happy,* *Tickle Me,* and *Roustabout,* fluff films that Elvis, who had aspired to follow in the tradition of Dean and Brando, found increasingly embarrassing and stultifying to his singing and acting ability. He was hindered, ironically, by success, for the formula films were so profitable that Colonel Parker, Elvis's money-minded manager, kept him contractually enslaved to the genre. "Elvis could have changed that probably," Priscilla proclaimed to Barbara Walters years later, "if he had had more of a confront"—a Scientology term meaning "to confront"—"with Colonel Parker." Elvis, to his occasional detriment, left the negotiating to the Colonel and concentrated on the creative. Priscilla, for all her postmortem bravado, would not have presumed to make a business suggestion to Elvis; she knew her place. Elvis, by the later observations of those who were around him, seemed not to give much thought to Priscilla's intelligence. "I don't think he thought she was a rocket scientist," Joe ruminated, "but I don't think he thought she was stupid, either." Her intellect simply was not an issue.

Even then Priscilla's interests seemed to drift in the direction of film; she read movie magazines, recalled Barbara Little, took a drama class in Memphis, and projected the frustrated air of someone weary of remaining in the shadows. Elvis's stepmother, Dee, whose later clashes with Priscilla occasionally colored her accuracy, considered Priscilla envious of Elvis and a simmering pot waiting to boil over. This observation made good sense. Priscilla was accustomed to a degree of adoration and interest that she would never attain in the presence of Elvis Presley. "She went . . . to Universal once, on a tour," remembered George Klein. "From what I understand, one of the producers on the lot saw her and offered her a screen test, not knowing who she was." The screen test, or any career in show business, would never happen as long as she was Elvis's girlfriend or wife, a limitation Priscilla accepted, reluctantly.

Her life was carefully circumscribed to fit Elvis's needs. She avoided his movie sets, tolerated his ever-present circle of aides, and adjusted to life inside a glass cage, where fans congregated outside the gates of whichever house Elvis was occupying. "I know she didn't care for the fans," commented Sandi Miller, one of the girls who spent weekends at Elvis's later houses in Palm Springs. "You can't blame her. She couldn't go outside her house without having thirty to forty kids outside her gate, and guys who worked for Elvis would bring their girlfriends to the house. I might get a little tired of that." Priscilla bore this with varying degrees of patience, alternating between a detached friendliness, occasional warmth, and thinly veiled scorn. "She went out and told the fans to 'all go home and leave us alone' on several occasions," said Sandi. "She went to the point of calling the police. I know that at the Hillcrest house, she called the police and had barriers put up. . . . Elvis basically reversed that. He called the police and told them, 'They are allowed to stay; they are welcome!' " Priscilla was treading on sacred ground when it came to Elvis Presley's fans. Elvis and his fans loved each other unconditionally, and Elvis embraced them, both literally and figuratively, stopping by the gate no matter how tired he might be to sign autographs, take pictures, swap stories. He was a warm and open-hearted man who truly loved people, and he understood that his fans were the reason for his success. Priscilla, who was aloof by nature, kept them at arm's length; she also recognized herself as their rival, for she occupied the position Elvis's female fans only dreamed of: She was the King's girlfriend.

Being banished to Memphis while Elvis was shooting in L.A. or recording in Nashville was tantamount to solitary confinement to Priscilla. "Because I didn't have anything to *do*!" she told a documentarian. "He didn't want me to work. I remember shopping every single day! There must have been about three or four stores that I would faithfully return to each day. And I got to where I knew the stock more than I'm sure the people that worked there did. And one day I said, 'This is ridiculous! *No one* can shop this much!' . . . It was just something to do, to kill time."

Her sex life with Elvis still consisted largely of foreplay or videotaped sex games between herself and another girl. It was not Priscilla's ideal. "At first I took this personally, but even the relationships he had *after* me . . . were not consummated. Long-term relationships. Like the relationship with Ginger . . . there really wasn't sex involved." Hollywood reporter Rona Barrett, who was a close friend of Juliet Prowse while Juliet was dating Elvis, recalled Juliet telling her "that the minute that relationship had its first, second, third night, it was over." Elvis, according to Juliet and others, had intercourse with them only a few times. "Like he could do it once, but not again," said Rona. Currie Grant, who was as much of a playboy as Elvis during their years in Germany, felt that Elvis loved the thrill of the chase, the need for conquest, but once he had a woman where he wanted her, he grew bored and wanted to move on to the next one.

Priscilla by now had become more confident of her standing in Elvis's life, even instituting changes here and there at Graceland. She never had to look at a checkbook, much less balance one, and had an unlimited clothes budget. She started designing some of her own outfits and presenting her ideas to a Memphis dressmaker to sew. To a different young woman, a life of leisure with Elvis Presley might have been a fabulous fantasy, but for Priscilla, who craved variety and action and a full-throttle sexual relationship, it was a form of exile. Elvis had not changed fundamentally since she first met him, nor did he pretend to be anything other than what he was. He was seeing other women while they were still in Germany, and it was there that he revealed his sexual preferences and insecurities; Priscilla had experienced his nocturnal lifestyle, seen his male circle of friends. "She knew all of that, she accepted that," a later girl-friend of Elvis's remarked. "He was just going on with his life."

It was *Priscilla* who was the poseur; she had assumed a false persona in Wiesbaden to get close to Elvis, beginning with the first visit to Goethestrasse, when Currie coached her on how to behave. Mike Edwards later described her as "this little enigma, who projected being demure." A lot of people hide who they are, and I think she created that aura when she first met him way back in Germany when she first went to [his] house."

In the process of pretending to be something she wasn't, the *real* Priscilla was disappearing. Yet she was driven, still, to achieve her ultimate goal, the one she had set for herself as a child, the life her parents had determined for her: to marry Elvis Presley. The deeper problem was Priscilla's ambivalence toward Elvis, and by sustaining this act, she only brought herself greater unhappiness.

The Beaulieus visited the Bel Air house during the filming of *Girl Happy*, Priscilla was later to write, and they questioned Elvis about marriage while Priscilla pretended to occupy a separate bedroom for their benefit. The movie magazines had basically accepted her role as Elvis's "hidden lover" without creating a scandal. A sense of complacency had set in, leaving Priscilla, and her parents, increasingly edgy. Elvis, Priscilla admitted, balked at the subject of marriage, but she felt she had no choice but to continue her campaign in full force.

In her way, she loved Elvis, whether or not she was *in* love with him. He had become a father figure to her. She would tell a later beau how Elvis used to call himself Daddy when they were alone. "Elvis had this hard time dealing with 'Mother' and 'the little girl' that I was to him. I didn't know it then but . . . I finally realized in later years that he was a father to me. He was my mentor."

In the spring of 1964, Elvis met someone who would have a profound influence on his life. Larry Geller entered Elvis's world as his personal barber. Jay Sebring, who was later killed along with Sharon Tate in the Manson murders, had arranged the introduction. In the post-Elvis literature, Larry occasionally would be hyperbolized as a wild-eyed, bearded swami who cast a spell over Elvis, but in fact he was a clean-shaven, soft-spoken, easygoing man who, though raised Jewish, had embraced New Age spirituality. Larry, like Elvis, was attracted to the metaphysical and pondered the deeper philosophical questions the Memphis Mafia did not begin to fathom and thus ridiculed.

Elvis, and Larry, *lived* for philosophy, spirituality, unanswerable questions on the meaning of life. Elvis's interest was nascent, while Larry had done an extensive amount of reading and shared that knowledge, and his books, with Elvis, who consumed them, as he did all things he loved, with the appetite of a longshoreman. Larry became, in the Elvis vernacular, "Lawrence of Israel," assuming the role of spiritual adviser and becoming a trusted confidant. He did not arrive, as has been written, a full-blown guru to Elvis, according to Jerry Schilling, who had met Elvis as a youngster when he participated in Memphis Mafia football games. After Jerry graduated from college and was about to start teaching history, Elvis asked him to go on the road with him. He joined the entourage as Elvis was boarding his bus to drive to L.A. to start filming *Tickle Me*. "God, we had these major hours of conversation!" Jerry recalled of that first bus trip with Elvis. Unlike the other guys—"we were all these macho, ex–football players"—Jerry felt that Larry Geller "brought another dimension to Elvis" that Jerry, who was more open to philosophical debate, considered fascinating. Elvis was having a difficult time coping with his enormous fame, and yearned to understand why he, a simple truck driver from the South, had been chosen for such adulation. He looked to Larry and Larry's library—which included books about everything from Buddhism to Christianity to numerology—to help guide him on his spiritual journey.

Elvis entered a period of intense seeking and discovery, most of which made the Colonel, the entourage, and Priscilla—all of whom were vying for control of Elvis—exceedingly nervous. Priscilla was wary of Larry Geller from the outset. She was jealous, like the rest of the household, of the time Elvis spent with him, but she was also uncertain enough to feign an interest in Elvis's passion.

As an experiment, Elvis, who was strongly opposed to recreational drugs, decided, in the mid-sixties, to try LSD under Larry's guidance to find out whether there was indeed another level of consciousness, and he persuaded Priscilla and Jerry Schilling to join them on an LSD trip at Graceland. "Elvis was very serious about it," recalled Jerry. "He said, 'We are going to experiment with this, but do it the right way.' Sonny West was . . . the designated driver. I was a health fanatic, Mr. Milk, and not into drugs, but still, being young and the baby of the group, anything Elvis wanted me to do within reason, I felt very safe. I was surprised Priscilla was going to do it. I don't think she was curious. For some reason she took it; it was one of those uncharacteristic things. We were in the upstairs part of Graceland, a conference room, which I think now is Lisa's room, and we sat down at a long table." The group, recalled Jerry, was "cautious. I don't know what the normal amount was, but I think Elvis didn't take all of his. The first thing I remember is noticing that something was changing. Elvis was sitting on a chair, and I just saw his legs get smaller and smaller until he became this little fat boy, and I started laughing. He got caught up in the laughing, so we had this laughing thing going on."

Priscilla's response to dropping acid was illuminating. She freaked out, according to Larry Geller, and ran from mirror to mirror screaming that she was ugly, sobbing at Elvis's feet that he "didn't really love her," her two greatest insecurities in her conscious state. "I had left the room and was on the floor inside a walk-in closet in the master bedroom," recalled Jerry, "and Priscilla came into the room. She didn't see me. She was looking in the mirror and brushing up against the walls, just like a cat." When the effects of the LSD wore off, Priscilla found herself in the same closet, purring. That was the first and last LSD trip for Elvis and Priscilla. "I think that it was . . . pretty scary for all of us that we even attempted it," said Jerry. For Priscilla, drugs were never a serious option; she was too intent on maintaining control.

Priscilla, who longed for greater intimacy with Elvis, soon had another reason to resent Larry's entrance into their lives, although Larry was not responsible for this development. Elvis told Larry that when he first became famous, he was with so many women he was placed in the hospital for exhaustion, teaching him that he was not a sex machine and that sex for its own sake, without love, was meaningless. As part of his spiritual cleansing in the sixties, Elvis determined to abstain from sex altogether for a time to demonstrate that he had control over the weaknesses of the flesh, like Christ and other great religious teachers. "You understand this southern mentality," explained Larry. "You understand fundamentalism, and [with] people who grow up in that soil, sex is probably one of the most important subjects. . . . Elvis felt that sex could either uplift you or destroy you. Simple as that. It's a power that is so important that if you misuse it, you are going to pay the consequences. And he did not want to, for his own self-image, feel that he was a promiscuous person, and most importantly, he didn't want to misuse what 'Elvis' was. He respected the Elvis persona." He also confided in Larry the same sexual insecurity he had confessed to Priscilla in Bad Nauheim: his powerful need to please, which came from being a performer, and his fear that he might not meet a woman's sexual expectations during intercourse, another reason he withdrew from sex. "Elvis–the image of Elvis–was godlike," said Larry. "It was powerful, it was Superman; therefore he had to be the great lover. Therefore he didn't want anyone talking; he didn't want any secrets leaked. Therefore he was very [careful] about who he fooled around with, because he didn't want someone to say, 'Well, this is not the world's greatest lover.' And I think that he felt a certain inadequacy about his own prowess."

Priscilla's sex life with Elvis, which had been a problem since they met, now blossomed into a crisis in their relationship. Priscilla had been driven by her sexual impulses since childhood; she was also a ripe twenty to Elvis's world-weary thirty-one. She had no interest in his spiritual journey or the books he pleaded with her to read. She wanted to have sex with him; he wanted to see inside her soul. During his moratorium on sex, Priscilla literally dropped to her knees one night as Elvis was reading to her from one of his philosophy books, begging him to make love to her. He fell asleep holding his book. The moment encapsulated the problems and basic incompatibilities in their relationship.

Elvis's self-questioning reached a peak during the long bus ride from Tennessee to California to begin shooting *Frankie and Johnnie* in May of 1965. He believed he experienced a vision of Jesus in the desert, and interpreted it to mean that he should join a monastery, that his epic popularity had been given to him so that he could teach the masses about the divine. That "changed his life," said Larry. "When we got to L.A., Elvis was totally different. We go into the den, he closes the doors; there on the other side are Joe, Red, Alan–they're listening."

"That's it," Elvis told Larry. "I quit. I've had it. I'm through with show business, Larry."

"I said, 'What? What do you mean?' "

"Larry, after what I've seen, I'm not going to go out and make another teenybopper movie," responded Elvis. "You've got me on the spiritual path, and that's good. I want you to find me a monastery. I want to become a monk."

Elvis was pilloried, after his death, for this detour from the path of fame, but he was, in the opinions of those closest to him, completely sincere. "He was trying to get out of making a movie that he wasn't happy making," said his later Vegas backup singer Kathy Westmoreland. "And he wanted to stop making movies, and he wanted to know what to do with his life and yearned for the public again, for live performances. And he was questioning everything and wanted to go to a monastery, and checked one out." The spiritual leader whom Elvis met at the monastery convinced him that he was on the right path, according to Kathy, "that God had him where he was supposed to be. It helped to establish in his mind that he was doing what he was supposed to do, he was just being used in a different way; not everyone had to be a priest." To sing was Elvis's calling, his pulpit; that was how he touched people's souls.

Elvis's forays into the metaphysical ranged from the sublime to the ridiculous. One time, for example, Priscilla and several of the wives attempted to communicate telepathically with Elvis and their husbands, and were convinced they had reached each other through ESP. Despite Priscilla's occasional efforts to humor Elvis, the chasm between them was growing ever more immense. Elvis's fondest wish was that Priscilla would accompany him on his spiritual quest; if they were true soul mates, he would say to her, she would join him. He had Larry prepare her astrological chart and study her numerology to see if they were compatible. Larry also created lexicons from the letters in her name, part of Elvis's concentrated effort to see whether they belonged together, if he could *trust* her. "That was an issue with Elvis," recalled Larry. "Elvis was not into astrology or tarot cards or telling the future. That bordered on the occult, and he was not into anything occult. However, Elvis was *very* much into numerology." One of his favorite books was Cheiro's *Book of Numbers*. He also spent time with

Daya Mata, the leader of the Self-Realization Center on Mount Washington in Los Angeles, and entreated Priscilla to attend lectures by Manly Hall, a multilingual intellectual spiritualist whose talks bored her. In Larry's opinion, she lacked intellectual depth. Elvis and Priscilla were on two separate paths with different interests; what kept them together was his intense belief, or hope, that they were twin souls and her determination to get married.

Elvis's metaphysical pursuits did not cause him to abandon his love for or belief in Jesus, and though he sometimes saw himself as a modern quasi-prophet, he disliked his nickname, "the King." "He would never let one time go by when someone hollered out in the crowd that he's the King," recalled Kathy Westmoreland. "He said that there was only one King, Jesus Christ." Willie Jane Nichols recalled Priscilla reading the Bible to Elvis once when he was sick. "He liked to hear her read the Bible. And I imagine he was explaining things to her." Elvis would watch *The Ten Commandments* again and again, describing the biblical events on screen to whoever was with him; one of the stars of that movie, unsurprisingly, was Debra Paget.

The rented house on Perugia Way in Bel Air became the setting for an almost nightly ritual of Elvis holding court in the manner of a sultan, seated in the center of a circle of nubile young women who hung on his every word as he recited the Gospel or pontificated on his latest interest or theory—adoration and interest he was not getting from Priscilla, who had lost all patience with his spiritual quest. "Oh, he'd go off on many different subjects, whether it be metaphysical or religion—could be history or politics, television, movies, movie stars," said Sandi Miller, one of the girls in attendance. "If something came on the TV that triggered something, maybe somebody would bring up a subject, or if somebody had an unusual name, he'd go into, 'How did you get that name?' Medical stuff. He loved medical stuff." Priscilla grew to detest the Perugia house and Elvis's Bible readings, which went on "into the wee hours of the morning. I'd walk in, and I'd walk out. And he'd want me there next to him, but I mean there's only so much you can *take*. Especially when the other women have other ideas, too. And they were all listening, you know: 'He's so *wonderful!*' [Asking me jealously,] 'What do you mean you're going to get water for him?' And this is someone I'm, you know, ready to *marry*! They were like little birds, with their little feeding mouths, on the floor, and he's feeding them. I look back, and it's such a decadent kind of *bizarre* picture, when he held his court." Priscilla saw each quivering starlet in the living room as a rival or potential replacement. "I was also a threat to these girls. I mean, I was *hated*. I was not someone they were happy to see. They *coped* with me. I was just as much of a threat to them as they were to me. You had this conglomeration of people who were constant intruders—for *me*."

Priscilla, one of the aides would recount, "tolerated Elvis's fucking around because she knew she was gonna marry him." The soirees at Perugia were not entirely bacchanalian; Elvis, according to later girlfriend Barbara Leigh, "was happy when he was sharing and teaching. He liked to do that with women or men, or whatever. There was something endearing about being with a young girl or a woman who is listening to you and you can teach them something. That was one of his greatest pleasures." The misfortune was that Priscilla had no interest in or curiosity about Elvis's religious pursuits, any more than did the majority of his mostly redneck retinue, who saw them, and Larry Geller, as dangerous distractions from his life and career. "Him and Larry would sit there and talk about what he was on earth for, to teach people," Joe Esposito complained. "Trying to make Elvis a philosopher. It was twenty-four hours a day. While things were going by, time and music was going by, and they were just talking about this philosophy, and nothing was happening. So it offended a lot of people around Elvis. And Priscilla, too."

Priscilla took to playing Hollywood gin with the other girlfriends and wives while the court was assembled in the living room. Patty Perry saw her as "very secure. She was a toughie, but she didn't know what was going on." Priscilla knew enough to be embarrassed by the recurring harem in the living room, and to question whether she and Elvis would ever marry.

"The guys were all handpicking who could come in, you know. They were choice girls," Priscilla said. "Every time I'd come by, there'd be some new girls at the gate, and Sonny and Red would bring them in and they'd be on the floor. I mean, it was just—it was so unhealthy, so bizarre, that you become— you just don't feel good; you just don't care. You wonder, 'What's all this *about*? This is, you know, my future *husband*.' This was someone that we'd been talking *marriage* about."

According to Dee, Elvis would hear from the Beaulieus "every day, 'When are you going to marry my daughter?'" Elvis would tell Priscilla, she would later say, "Okay, we're not going to do it *this* year, but in two years, *sure*." "And you go, 'But in the meantime, what's going to happen in two years?'" said Priscilla. "Someone downstairs is going to be—you know, with their mouths open—could be the right one!" Elvis was full of rationales for the delay. "Career had a lot to do with it," was Priscilla's explanation. "He was just starting out again. I was still in the background. . . . It meant a lot to the Colonel that [Elvis] still be number one. Meant a lot to Elvis, too—still be a bachelor. That was the thing, that he had to be a bachelor. They had pretty well come to terms on that."

Elvis spoke publicly as if Priscilla existed not at all. He told columnist Hedda Hopper, as part of the press surrounding *Tickle Me* in 1964, that he was "really looking now" for the right girl to marry. "When I do, it will be for just that once. I know that means I'll have to follow the rules. Maybe I'm not ready for that yet. Or I haven't met the right one." Hopper repeated rumors that Elvis had been "rushing" his costar, Jocelyn Lane, words that scarcely added to Priscilla's sense of security.

Elvis was also jealous where Priscilla was concerned. He reportedly warned a few of the entourage to keep their distance, and he lashed out once at Jerry Schilling in Graceland. "Priscilla came down the stairs one day," Jerry recalled, "and she didn't really look good and she said she wasn't feeling well. I said 'How are you? Is there anything I can get for you?' That was the essence of it. I didn't know that she and Elvis had been in a major fight. She goes back upstairs and she said, 'At least Jerry Schilling cares.' So I'm sitting down there—I hadn't been working for Elvis that long—and he comes down and you could tell his attitude, the way he came down the stairs. And he goes, 'Goddammit! I don't need anyone asking Priscilla how she feels. I'll take care of that!' He never looked at me, but I knew where he was coming from. It was the hardest thing he'd ever said to me."

Rumors flew, after Priscilla's memoir came out and she repeated the incident, that she and Jerry, who was an extremely polite and attractive man, had an affair. "Contrary to all beliefs and speculation, no, we never did," he said. His wife in later years, Myrna Smith, said Jerry told her he and Priscilla were never romantically involved, and this was likely the truth, despite Elvis's fans' suspicions, for Jerry was not known to lie and idolized Elvis too much to betray him with his girlfriend or wife.

By 1964–1965, Priscilla was completely lost in the relationship with Elvis, unhappy with the lifestyle, uncertain whether they would ever wed. The ritualistic parties on Perugia were driving her mad. "The overall feeling, not being able to get his attention," she said, "*night* after *night* after *night* after *night* with these girls. *Every single night.* It was something I just couldn't handle anymore." She devised a calculated and dangerous plan—a fake suicide attempt—to shock Elvis back into line, proof of the depth of her desperation. "I *wanted* him to think that I was going to [kill myself]. I wanted to be out. I wanted to be as close as I possibly could to that point. It was almost like that last ploy, to maybe make a change of mind here." Priscilla chose as her means an overdose of Placidyl, the drug that had accidentally sent her into a coma during her first Christmas visit to Graceland. She costumed herself glamorously in a long white satin gown and timed the event for just after 2:00 A.M., as Elvis was settling into his sultan routine. "I went down, like I would normally do, before I went to bed—eyelashes on!—because in my mind I'm thinking, 'Well, if he's going to find me, and if I go, at least I'll look halfway decent!' " Then she returned to the bedroom, arranged her hair, gown, and body alluringly on the bed, and took just enough Placidyl pills to frighten Elvis, but not necessarily to kill herself. "Although, you know, when you're so angry, so mad, and you're so desperate, at that point it doesn't matter. You just want out. I was conscious enough to know that this is a lot [of pills]. But knowing that he'd have to come in and catch me. He had to come in and find me at one point. So I was very clever in knowing how much I would take and what state I would be in when he would find me. So that's what cautions were taken. Did I really think I was gonna die? Well, there was one side that goes 'I don't care,' and there was that other side, 'I hope he *sees* me! I hope he finds me, you know, before it happens.' "

Elvis discovered Priscilla, as she had planned, before anything dire happened to her, but his reaction was not what she had written into the script. Rather than dissolving into tenderness and remorse, begging her forgiveness, "he was *very* angry at first. He asked me, 'Why would you do this?' Elvis usually got angry at first, before you could talk to him. You had to let him go nuts. And he went nuts: Why would I do this to myself? Why would I even consider such a thing?" Priscilla laughed at the memory. *"Guys!"* she exclaimed. At the time, she was as frustrated as he. "The girls were still out there. And I said, 'Why don't you go out the door and take a look?' Not that that was an excuse."

The obvious question was why would *Priscilla* stay in a relationship in which she was so plainly unhappy and to which she and Elvis were so unsuited? She had a difficult time answering that question thirty-some years later. "Because he did offer me other things," she said finally. "We did have a life." That may have been true, but the greater truth was that she was holding out for marriage. She had come this far in pursuit of her childhood plan, and Priscilla was not one to quit. There was also a question of pride, according to her later boyfriend Mike Stone. He said, "I know it became a point where she felt that if they did not marry she would really look like a laughingstock in some ways, that she had gone to live with him since the age of fourteen [sic] and grown up under him primarily—and then not have the marriage take place."

Whether due to Priscilla's staged suicide attempt or simply circumstances, things improved temporarily in her relationship with Elvis. They moved out of the house on Perugia Way and took another rental in Bel Air toward the end of 1965, this one on Rocca Place, and symbolically at least, Priscilla felt an emotional release. "I think that one of the problems was that he already had Perugia Way; there was already a standard set before I ever came into the picture." The new house on Rocca, set precipitously up in the hills, was more physically inaccessible, which cut down on the transient female population, pacifying Priscilla somewhat. Priscilla also attributed her improved relations with Elvis to the fact that they had purchased motorcycles (hers, to her dissatisfaction, was pink), so she and Elvis could take off alone, as he had done with Ann-Margret. "It was more [just the two of us] on a bike. . . . We could go out more." Elvis, being Elvis, bought not two but twelve motorcycles. "We were the original Hell's Angels," chuckled Priscilla. "Before Stallone and everybody else used them. We were doing it *way* before that."

This halcyon period was short-lived. Each time Elvis began a new movie, which was every few months, Priscilla was filled with fresh concern that he might be having an affair with his costar or someone else on the set; she occasionally found love notes in his closet, and she became paranoid when gossip columnists linked him to a costar. During the shooting of *Spinout,* just before Easter 1966, Priscilla decided to visit the set so she could meet Shelley Fabares, Elvis's leading lady. Elvis, so Priscilla would say, responded much as he had when she confronted him about Ann-Margret—by tearing her clothes off their hangers and threatening to send her to her parents.

The tempests in Priscilla's and Elvis's unusual relationship, and her insecurity about marriage, manifested themselves physically in the form of an ulcer when she was only twenty. She felt that Elvis was still spending too much time with Larry Geller, and he had ordered a special shelf constructed under his bed to keep the increasing number of spiritual tomes. The groupies were still underfoot as well. "It was *constant.* . . . What girl was being invited next? What girl was being passed off? The girls went from guy to guy to guy. It was not your normal home, that's for sure. By *any* means. I was always on edge. Always wondering, What now? What was the next move? What was the next adventure? Trying to go along, trying to accept it. I wasn't *married* to him."

There were also intervals of the sweetest pleasure. Priscilla had spoken, wistfully, of having her own horse, a carryover perhaps from her childhood fantasies of the Black Stallion, when she and Pam would steal off to a pasture near the base and pretend. In the fall of 1966, Elvis surprised her with a magnificent black quarter horse she called Domino, when he was about to start his latest movie romp, *Double Trouble.* Priscilla, according to Mike McGregor, Elvis's ranch hand, took to Domino as if she had been born to ride. "I didn't teach her anything," Mike said. "She seemed to know . . . and I don't know of any formal education she had in riding." The two together—Priscilla with her flowing black hair and Domino, jet black with one white stocking—were poetry to watch. "She was a real pretty lady, and she was riding a really good-looking horse, and it was a real striking thing." Priscilla's excitement infected Elvis, who bought himself a spectacular golden palomino named Rising Sun, which Priscilla taught him to ride. Elvis came to love Rising Sun, but he was no competition for Priscilla. "The lady didn't act like she had any fear of anything," recalled Mike McGregor. "She scared me a lot of times. I felt responsible for everybody who got on a horse, because the horses were my responsibility. And the lady would ride bareback." Mike was never sure why. "Why do you do anything? Maybe because she just wanted to see if she could do it, and she did it well." Priscilla had a fierce competitiveness; she challenged the Stanley brothers to foot races, which she invariably won, and she swam and dived in the pool at Graceland with a steely determination.

The strange saga of Priscilla and Elvis took another enigmatic turn at the end of that year, 1966, when he suddenly and inexplicably presented her with an engagement ring and told her they were to be married. Who or what precipitated this development would be a never-ending topic of debate in the Presley mythology. It was a mystery seemingly without resolution, perhaps not even known by Priscilla.

The catalyst for Priscilla's long-standing dream may have been, ironically, Currie Grant, the man who had made her original fantasy come true when he took her to meet Elvis in 1959. When Currie was in northern California on business in October or November of 1966, he called the Beaulieus, who were still stationed at Travis Air Force Base outside Sacramento. Paul and Ann invited him to dinner, he recalled, and Currie mentioned to Paul that he had heard Elvis "was about to dump Priscilla." The source of this rumor was Wes Bryan, the James Dean look-alike who occasionally stopped by Graceland at Elvis's invitation and who saw Currie from time to time. (Wes's information was substantiated indirectly in a book by aide Alan Fortas, who wrote that while Elvis "cared about Priscilla, he wasn't on fire about her the way he was in the early days and he wasn't sure he could ever settle down with one woman.") "I kinda felt sorry for Priscilla," Currie recalled, "because she had put in all that time waiting, and I didn't think that it was right for Elvis to get rid of her, and I ended up unloading on Paul Beaulieu, telling him what *really* went on up in Elvis's bedroom back in Germany." Priscilla's stepfather, Currie remembered, "turned ashen . . . the look on his face wasn't good. And the more I said, the worse his face got." Shortly afterward, Wes told Currie, Paul Beaulieu telephoned Graceland and "told Elvis he would put him *under* the damn jail if he didn't marry Priscilla."

Priscilla, already locked in battle with Currie in 1996 over how she was introduced to Elvis, angrily repudiated this account. "My dad would never— My father is not that kind of man. He'd never do that. That's embarrassing. He has too much pride."

Yet Currie's account did explain and reinforce the recollections of several in Elvis's inner circle, among them Marty Lacker, who remembered Elvis getting a phone call at Graceland from Major Beaulieu around Thanksgiving, reminding him that they had made a deal and that the time had come to fulfill his obligation to marry Priscilla. Both Marty and Lamar Fike told biographer Albert Goldman in 1980 that Priscilla was making anxious phone calls to her parents around this time, wondering whether Elvis was ever going to marry her. By her own admission she was consumed by doubts as to whether there would be a wedding. Mike Stone, Priscilla's lover while she was married to

Elvis, was also under the impression that Paul Beaulieu had put pressure on Elvis. Mike understood "that he really did not want to marry her, that she actually made a big fuss about it—that he had to." Elvis said as much later on to his backup singer Kathy Westmoreland, with whom he shared confidences. "He did not want to marry. All he said to me was 'I had to.'" Elvis Presley was a man, everyone agreed, who would honor a promise. His reluctance to marry seemed to arise more from his inability to remain faithful than from dissatisfaction with Priscilla. Elvis, according to everyone who knew him, did not feel he was suited to monogamy, although he respected the sanctity of marriage and believed a person should marry once and forever. He also had serious concerns about how being married would affect his image and his career.

The circumstances of the proposal were not what would traditionally be called romantic. Elvis knocked on Priscilla's bathroom–dressing room door one night in November or December carrying a box with a three-and-a-half carat diamond ring and announcing, "Sattnin [their special name for each other—one of Gladys's terms of endearment], we're going to be married. You're going to be his. I told you I'd know when the time was right. Well, the time's right."

It was not so much a proposal as a declaration of intent. Priscilla herself later seemed confused by the timing and unsure of what had prompted Elvis's sudden interest in a wedding. In her own autobiography, and in a 1984 interview with Barbara Walters, she attributed the proposal to Colonel Parker, Elvis's manager, as have many of the Elvis Presley biographies. The theory was that the Colonel was concerned about Elvis's image and felt he should legitimize his relationship with Priscilla. Yet nothing had occurred to provoke the Colonel's anxiety. Why would he suddenly press Elvis to marry Priscilla after five years of cohabitation—and would Elvis have acceded to his manager's demand on such a personal issue? Priscilla admitted, in the spring of 1996, that she included the story about Colonel Parker's involvement in the wedding in her memoir because she had read it in an earlier biography of Elvis. "I heard from some book that Colonel told Elvis, 'Well, it's time to get married,' and approached Elvis and said, 'Well, if you've been with Priscilla, you need to make a decision.'" Priscilla asked the Colonel about it a few years before his 1997 death. "I said, 'You know, Colonel, out of curiosity, [after] hearing different things and reading different books, it was said that you probably prompted Elvis's proposal to me.' He said, 'That *never* happened. *Ever.* I would never tell Elvis that. . . . That was none of my decision.'"

Priscilla's explanations for Elvis's sudden wedding plans in late 1966 are confusing and contradictory at best. She said, on the one hand, that she and Elvis wanted to start a family, yet she admitted, in the same conversation, that she hoped she *wouldn't* have children right away. "We were ready to get married," she said in one breath, then declared, "I was *afraid* of getting married." There *was* no catalyst, she also said. "It was just *time*. It was just the fact that we'd been together, and it was time to get married."

Jerry Schilling, who was a friend to both Elvis and Priscilla and had no ax to grind, subscribed to the theory that Major Beaulieu telephoned Elvis that late fall and pressured him to make good on his agreement to marry Priscilla. "I've heard that. And you know what? I can believe that. I do really, for a few reasons, I do think that happened. That's like—it's almost sure it happened." Jerry, who maintained a relationship with the Colonel through the years and witnessed his meddling in Elvis's personal life and those of others, was not *un*convinced that Colonel Parker might have played a part in the decision, possibly in combination with Paul Beaulieu. "There was pressure. I guarantee there was pressure on Elvis."

Priscilla's later confusion might have sprung from embarrassment that Elvis was pressured into marrying her, or she might not have *known* what transpired between her father, the Colonel, and Elvis, just as she might not have known the machinations behind her parents' arrangement with Elvis for her to move to Graceland when she was seventeen.

The details of the impending nuptials were as puzzling as the proposal. Elvis wanted, at first, to be married around Christmastime, Priscilla said, "because he was off at Christmas, and that seemed a good time to do it," though the holiday was just days away when he proposed. The only person who seemed to be informed about the upcoming wedding was Marty Lacker, whom Elvis had asked to be his best man, implying, Marty said, that he had been pushed into the decision. Jerry Schilling, too, found this silence odd. "I mean I never heard. You would think . . . If I had gotten engaged, I would have told all the guys. But I never heard him say that, and I don't think anybody else did." The mystery wedding was then postponed "because," said Priscilla, "we didn't want it to be in Memphis because then everybody would be in Memphis and it would have been a fanfare and we didn't want it to become a circus. So then we moved it to March."

Soon after the secret engagement, Elvis bought a ranch thirty minutes by car from Graceland. Ever since she had gotten Domino, Priscilla had dreamed of living with Elvis on a horse farm, a longing that was realized in February 1967, when they both fell in love with some ranch property on Horn Lake Road. The final selling point, for Elvis, was a fifty-foot white concrete cross that served as a marker for approaching airplanes, but which Elvis took, said Alan Fortas, "as a mystic sign."

Elvis adored being a gentleman farmer and leapt into ranch life with more than his usual freneticism and generosity, buying trucks and trailers for everyone in the entourage and setting them up on the property until it resembled a KOA trailer park, accumulating bills that sent his conservative father and Colonel Parker reeling. "I can still see him out there in the dirt," Priscilla said once, "in his jeans and heavy coat and cowboy hat, going around writing everybody's name on the stalls with a red marking pen, watering the horses, blanketing them. He looked so satisfied, so simple." Those first days on the ranch, which Elvis had named the Circle G—*G* for Graceland—were among the happiest of Priscilla's life with Elvis. They took up residence in a custom-built trailer. "It was just darling," remembered Joan Esposito, who stayed in the tiny ranch house with Joe. "It had been done by one of the big decorating stores in Memphis. Everything matched. They had done an absolutely perfect job; the kitchen was red, white, and blue and the pots red." Priscilla became as domestic as she would ever be. "She was able to cook breakfast for him," Joan recalled, "and have that intimacy."

As so often seemed the case with Elvis and Priscilla, there were storm clouds on the horizon. Elvis's spending escalated into a disturbing, almost manic spree, necessitating the Colonel to put him into another high-salary, low-art film, *Clambake*, to counter his losses. March arrived with no sign of a wedding. When Elvis received the script for *Clambake*, he became dangerously depressed and consoled himself by eating, bloating from 170 to 200 pounds within a few weeks. He had a tendency to carry weight, like his mother and her family, and favored the deep-fried, starchy southern foods that showed on his body immediately. Elvis's weight fluctuated as he let himself go between films and then turned to diet pills in order to shed pounds quickly before a shoot. This time the studio ordered him to go on a diet. Priscilla, meanwhile, had grown agitated by communal life on the ranch, which contrasted sharply with the cozy hideaway she had envisioned for herself and Elvis. More than one of the entourage found her prickly, irritable, and domineering as she and Elvis prepared to leave for California for the *Clambake* shoot.

The stage had been set for a crisis, and it arrived on March 10, the night before filming began on *Clambake*. Elvis, who was still depressed and taking both diet pills and sleeping pills, tripped in the middle of the night in the bathroom at the rented house on Rocca Place, reportedly on a telephone cord, and suffered a concussion. Colonel Parker used this opportunity to sweep into action, seizing control of Elvis's life. One of his first actions was to direct Larry Geller to "get rid of" his books. A doctor, arranged by the Colonel, confined Elvis to bed for two weeks. "Colonel never spent more than fifteen minutes with Elvis," said Larry. "Now for a week he went in every day. No one was allowed to see Elvis; he was heavily medicated. They were shooting him up with who knows what." At the end of two weeks "the Colonel calls a meeting," recalled Larry. "Elvis said, 'Larry, no matter what happens, I love you,' and I knew something was up. Colonel sat there, Elvis sat there, Priscilla sat there, we all sat there. I never saw Elvis like this. Elvis sat like a docile little kitten. He wouldn't look at me. The Colonel said, 'There's going to be some changes around here.' And everyone knew the whole meeting was directed at me. 'Anyone who thinks that Elvis is gonna put on robes and walk down the street to save people, they've got another think coming.' And he went on and on: 'This is a business. People are getting too personal here.' And it was all [directed at] me; everyone knew it. I knew what was happening. My heart was breaking. Elvis docile? Priscilla was there, backing the whole thing up, taking her position."

Larry left Elvis's employ shortly after that meeting, convinced that Priscilla and the Colonel had conspired to remove him and questioning Elvis's mysterious fall. "I think [Priscilla] thought Larry Geller was filling Elvis's mind with a lot of things that could never be answered," reasoned Joe. "Larry was trying to control Elvis to a certain point. To get Elvis to depend on Larry. And I feel that way myself, because he occupied so much of Elvis's time he lost his creativity. Instead of thinking about his career and doing something about that, it was all this mystery stuff—Eastern philosophies and stuff that took him away from what he was supposed to do: be an entertainer, perform. Priscilla wasn't too thrilled with Larry." Most of the entourage wasn't, for they had no understanding of Elvis's spiritual bent, and they felt that it distracted him from taking care of business—and them.

Elvis formed a new long-term agreement with Colonel Parker that was grossly advantageous to his manager, and within a month the Colonel was orchestrating Elvis and Priscilla's wedding. Larry saw this as further evidence that Priscilla and the Colonel were in complicity to remove him and that, in exchange, Priscilla would have her wedding. "'We'll get rid of the guru,'" was Larry's interpretation of the turn of events, "'and you're stepping in. You'll be the wife of Elvis Presley.' That's what happened. I know it."

There was no argument about the fact that, beginning that April, Colonel Parker took over every detail of Elvis and Priscilla's wedding. The new date was set for May 1, just a few weeks away, though Priscilla claimed she and Elvis had selected that day when the March plans fell through. Once Elvis's manager stepped into the scene, the twice-postponed, often discussed, but never realized nuptials surged ahead like a bullet train. Las Vegas—Colonel Parker's base of operations—was chosen as the location. "It was the Colonel who got the rings, the room, the judge," said Priscilla. "We didn't do any of that. It was all through his connections. We wanted it to be *fast*, effortless." Becky Yancey typed up a short guest list, the Colonel made arrangements for the newlyweds to fly out of Vegas on his friend Frank Sinatra's Learjet. The Colonel's wife even took Priscilla shopping for a wedding dress in Palm Springs, where the Parkers had a house.

The entire operation had all the poetry of a corporate takeover. It was also veiled in secrecy, more of the Colonel's doing, for he wanted to control and exploit the wedding for maximum publicity value, down to a prearranged press conference at the Aladdin in Vegas after the ceremony, during which he would surprise reporters with the news that Elvis Presley was married. Priscilla found herself in her familiar role as guardian of the secrets, even as she shopped for her own wedding gown. "I went with Colonel Parker's wife in total disguise. I went as Mrs. Hodge, and I had a blond wig on, trying to be very, very careful." She eventually found a dress at a bridal shop in Westwood, near UCLA, again posing as Charlie Hodge's future wife, accompanied this time by Charlie. "It was just a very, very simple long dress with beaded sleeves. I didn't have time to just stay there forever and look for dresses. I had one fitting for this dress and that was it, I was out of there." Alan Fortas wrote later that Elvis, meanwhile, "was desperately trying to find some way out."

Colonel Parker's carefully laid plans went forward with just one hitch: Gossip columnist Rona Barrett, who had a weekend house in Palm Springs a stone's throw from the cul-de-sac where Elvis had taken a rental that spring, noticed "signals" that "something was up." "The Memphis Mafia started to arrive in L.A.," she recalled, and sources at the Beverly Wilshire Hotel confirmed reservations. Rona reasoned that plans were afoot for Elvis and Priscilla's wedding, and concluded that "if he's going to do it, he's going to do it from Palm Springs." It was, she admitted, "intuition, pure intuition." Rona's finely honed gossip instincts were right on target, for the Colonel had made plans for Elvis and Priscilla to leave Palm Springs for Vegas by private plane at four-thirty in the morning on the day of the wedding, and return on Sinatra's Learjet to spend their first night as husband and wife at Elvis's Palm Springs house on Ladera Circle, literally and figuratively under Rona Barrett's nose. Within hours of Elvis and Priscilla's arrival in Las Vegas on May 1, before the ceremony had even begun, Rona was reporting their wedding. Priscilla, thirty years later, had no idea how she scooped the Colonel.

"I began calling all the florists," the columnist explained, "and I went down to Palm Springs and started looking around, and I knew there was something going on. . . . And then somebody gave me a tip about the kind of shirts that needed to be ordered that afternoon. . . . There was a sense of mystery surrounding all of this, and intrigue. I kept an eye on the house and the florist and checking the private airlines and the private jets. I was unaware that [the wedding] was going to take place in Las Vegas, but I knew something was going on at the house. Then I found out about the Colonel and the private plane, and that's how we got it confirmed."

The wedding itself took place at 9:41 that morning in the Aladdin Hotel suite of Milton Prell, a friend of Colonel Parker's who owned the hotel. Elvis and Priscilla were married by a judge named David Zenoff, another of the

Colonel's connections, in a traditional ceremony notable only for the absence of the word "obey" from Priscilla's vows, an apparent oversight that would prove prophetic. Fewer than twenty people attended the ceremony, a dictate of Colonel Parker's that caused bruised feelings among Elvis's entourage and friends forever after. Among the guests were Priscilla's parents, her sister Michelle (the maid of honor), the Colonel and his wife, Vernon and Dee, Joe Esposito and Marty Lacker (Elvis's two best men), Joan Esposito, and George Klein.

Priscilla's long-awaited wedding resembled nothing so much as a staged photo opportunity, which in fact it was. Elvis's manager hustled the groom and bride out of Milton Prell's suite directly into a press conference, where the new Mr. and Mrs. Elvis Presley spent their first moments of married life posing for publicity pictures and answering questions from a startled press corps. Elvis was dressed in a satin tuxedo that resembled something he might have worn on stage; both he and Priscilla wore manic, slightly dazed, expressions throughout the combination press conference and reception. Priscilla's hair and makeup fixation, combined with the Jean Shrimpton–Carnaby look of the sixties, reached its pinnacle that morning; her hair was nearly waist-length and coal black, teased into a bouffant style, framing her Dresden-doll face, which was made up to perfection with dewy pink lip gloss, six pairs of false eyelashes, and heavy eyeliner. Though they would later be mocked for going to extremes, Elvis and Priscilla looked more than beautiful that morning of their wedding; they were *mesmerizing,* two perfect-looking creatures who seemed to belong to another world than mere mortals.

Despite its lack of sentiment or genuine emotion, Priscilla's wedding day was, for her, the consummate moment of personal triumph, for she had at last achieved her goal. No longer would she have to endure descriptions such as "the freak child-lover of Elvis Presley, Hollywood's best-kept secret" (on the *Today* show), or "the girl Elvis is rumored to have hidden at Graceland" (in *Movie Mirror*). No longer was she seen as Elvis Presley's Lolita. Becoming Mrs. Elvis Presley was, she acknowledged three decades later, *"very"* satisfying.

Getting married, ironically, doomed Elvis and Priscilla's already strained relationship. Some of the reasons were plain to anyone who understood her psyche or had observed the dynamics between them. Other reasons, deeply imbedded in Elvis Presley's complicated subconscious, were soon to reveal themselves.

As dramatic as were the elements of seeming predestination that had drawn them together, Elvis Presley and Priscilla Beaulieu's marriage was a tragic misalliance of two strikingly incompatible people. They wed because they were both bound by dreams they had outgrown—he to an obligation undertaken on impulse four years earlier, she to the fantasies of a ten-year-old girl.

24

A MARRIAGE OF
INCONVENIENCE

Elvis and Priscilla never had a honeymoon to speak of.

Their hastily put together wedding was not even scheduled to occur *after* Elvis completed the calamitous *Clambake*. He and Priscilla spent their first few nights of marriage at the weekend house in Palm Springs so he could return to L.A. for reshoots. Rona Barrett's report and the Colonel's press conference alerted the public that the King had finally tied the knot, and a gaggle of Elvis fans clustered about the Ladera Circle house to congratulate him. Priscilla had the surreal experience of being observed by strangers as her new husband carried her over the threshold singing "The Hawaiian Wedding Song." As she said later, "With Elvis, it was always sort of strange."

In her book and in other public forums, Priscilla, perpetuating the myth, would say that her first night of marriage in the upstairs master bedroom of the Palm Springs house was the moment when she lost her virginity—conveniently overlooking her previous sexual relationships with Currie Grant, Tommy Stewart, Peter Von Wechmar, Jamie Lindberg, and possibly Ron Tapp, not to mention Currie's claim that she confessed to having had intercourse with Elvis during their first few months in Germany. Priscilla's tale of being a virgin bride until her wedding night, after having lived with Elvis for over four years, was given a patina of credibility by the birth of Lisa Marie, uncannily, nine months later. "I *had* to have conceived somewhere around then, because she was born nine months to the *day*" after the wedding, she later proclaimed.

Elvis and Priscilla talked idly of honeymooning in Europe, a plan that was blocked, rumor had it, by the Colonel, who reportedly kept Elvis from touring outside the United States because the promoter had disguised his status as a Dutch citizen and had no passport. Colonel Parker had nothing to do with this decision, according to Priscilla: "Elvis didn't really *want* to go to Europe." Discussions of a trip to Hawaii likewise evanesced. Priscilla and Elvis, possibly the most glamorous couple in the world, spent most of their honeymoon in a trailer. The setting was the Circle G. "He finished the movie, and then we decided to stay there, and we didn't really *do* anything," admitted Priscilla, who had resigned herself to the limitations of life with a superstar. "It would not have been a honeymoon anyway. It would have been fanfare. It would have been like always. Everywhere we went—if it was Hawaii, they would find out, and they would be all around the gate—so we decided just go to Memphis and just stay there and, you know, have it quiet. We always had to choose things that we thought would work. It was more like convenience than how it would be for us emotionally."

Priscilla did not even have her new husband to herself. Elvis, who thrived in the companionship of his male buddies, kept them around during his honeymoon. "He had his guys and she had her girlfriends," noted Dee, "but that's the way it was. There was no honeymoon or nothin'. *Everybody* was on the honeymoon." To make peace with the entourage and their overlooked friends, Elvis and Priscilla held a second reception at Graceland in tuxedo and gown.

A few months after the wedding, Priscilla took off her diamond engagement ring to go riding with Elvis at the ranch. She put the end of a bandanna through the ring and tied the scarf around her head. "She was pregnant with Lisa at the time," recalled Charlie Hodge, who was there that day, "riding bareback. She fell off the horse, she got up, got back on the horse and went, 'Oh, my gosh, I've lost my ring.' And we looked around, but we figured somewhere between the hill and the barn it came off." Around the same time, according to Mike McGregor, who tended the horses, Elvis lost *his* wedding ring on the ranch. "We were out there on our hands and knees, there was like five or six of us, Elvis was in the bunch, and we're crawling around in the grass. He didn't even know really where he lost it." Neither Elvis nor Priscilla ever found his or her ring; it was, perhaps, an augury.

Even her wedding night conception did not bring Priscilla immediate joy. She wanted to take birth control pills but Elvis was against it, she said, because he thought they might be harmful; she used no other form of contraception because "it was a hassle." Priscilla was dismayed that she became so quickly pregnant, for now that she had emerged from the shadows and acquired the so long-sought-after title of Mrs. Presley, she wanted the world to see her at her glamorous best. "Instead," she later wrote, "my debut as Elvis's bride was going to be spoiled by a fat stomach, puffy face, and swollen feet." Priscilla was also eager to travel the world with Elvis; a baby would tie her down. Elvis, by contrast, was "ecstatic," in Priscilla's word. Her own ambivalence about having a baby was so deep-seated that she contemplated having an abortion early that June as the entourage rode in Elvis's customized bus for him to start filming *Speedway* with Nancy Sinatra. She decided against it; Elvis, she said, gave her the freedom of choice.

"Priscilla was never a bride," Dee Presley reflected. "She was a child. She missed being the bride. She never got to be the wife, you know, and the bride that normally you go through."

Elvis as husband and father-to-be was his usual paradoxical self, fawning over Priscilla, whom he affectionately called Belly, spending more time with her than he ever had, while at the same time flirting with and dry-humping Nancy Sinatra on the set of *Speedway*, to Priscilla's anxiety. Nancy had a well-known crush on Elvis, and expressed disappointment, after his death, that she had *not* slept with him, her only hesitation being a personal code forbidding her from having sex with a married man. Rather fascinatingly, Elvis asked Nancy, who barely knew Priscilla, if she would give his wife a baby shower, presumably to reassure Priscilla that he and his costar were not having an affair, and Nancy and her mother, abetted by Joan Esposito, complied. Priscilla thus found her impending delivery celebrated by her rival as she opened baby gifts from people she scarcely knew. One of the guests was Patricia Crowley, the actress who starred in the television series *Please Don't Eat the Daisies*, who was then married to Ed Hookstratten, Elvis's lawyer. "It was such a peculiar thing," she said. "It was such a tiny little group. It was a very darling, simple, old-fashioned kind of shower."

Elvis reconnected with Ann-Margret, the girl he might have married, that June, backstage during one of her first performances in Vegas, where he confessed, Ann would write in her memoir, that his feelings for her had never changed. He also ran into Anita Wood, who had married former Cleveland Brown star Johnny Brewer. Elvis expressed regret, Anita said, over what might have been, an emotion that seemed to sweep over him at the time.

Priscilla contented herself with exerting her hard-earned authority as Elvis's wife. One of her first acts, said Joe, was to burn the religious books Larry Geller had given him. She then set about imposing some domestic order at Graceland, particularly where the entourage was concerned. "Now they knew that they had to contend with *me*—not that I threw my weight around, but it was a *home* now. And I wanted it to be a home. The guys were used to going into the kitchen, and the woman I hired was like a short-order cook! You know, 'I want a steak, I want ham, I want chicken, I want this. . . .' I *stopped* it. I said, 'There's no way it's going to be like this. This is what we're having for dinner. . . . If you would like to join us, you are welcome.' And I didn't do it in a nasty way. It was just 'This is the way it's going to be from now on.' So I gradually started making changes in the home. And actually, *he* liked it. *Someone* needed to take charge. *No* one was doing it; they had the run of the place. Total run of the place. And some of these guys weren't married, and they'd have girlfriends up there. It's like Graceland was a *breeding* ground or something. And then I started to feel that I *did* have some power, and he did give me that power." Priscilla's tastes, as Madame Presley, were modest; most of the furnishings she purchased, recalled Becky Yancey, came from Sears.

She *decreed* that she would not gain weight during her pregnancy. "I was just *not* going to use [pregnancy] as an excuse. I was *not* going to get fat, I was not going to be puffy, I was not going to have big breasts." Elvis had told her that those things happened to pregnant women, she said, and "I was just doing *everything* to prove him wrong, that not *all* women did this." Priscilla's vanity and iron will fueled her determination; she, in effect, starved herself during her pregnancy, eating only one meal a day, snacking on an apple or a hard-boiled egg, slathering her stomach with cocoa butter to avoid stretch marks. She lost ten pounds when she first conceived, and gained only nine back; when she gave birth, Priscilla weighed 109 pounds and never needed to wear a maternity dress. Elvis "couldn't believe it: Oh, I was amazing! I was Wonder Woman! I was unbelievable! 'She's still sexy,' he'd say."

Priscilla's delicate relationship with Elvis's fans, which grew more strained after she married him, reached its seriocomic nadir while they were in L.A., possibly during the *Speedway* shoot. Priscilla drove up to the Bel Air house on Rocca one night, followed by two sisters from Long Beach named Marian and Mary, die-hard Elvis fans and enemies of Priscilla who showed up regularly at the gate. They were accompanied in their car by a female friend named Susan. Priscilla and Susan would offer differing accounts of who provoked whom, but both versions ended in a fistfight between Priscilla and Marian, a sixteen-year-old who weighed over two hundred pounds. By everyone's version, Priscilla was annoyed at being followed and parked her car to block Marian, who was driving the fans' car, from leaving. Priscilla then got out of her car and confronted Marian, who was now standing on the street, demanding to know why she was being followed. By Priscilla's later account, "she called me a whore and jumped out at me." Susan's recollection was that names were exchanged before Marian called Priscilla a whore. All agreed on what happened next: Priscilla struck Marian with an uppercut to the face, knocking the teenage fan to the ground. A melee ensued near the Rocca driveway as Priscilla and Marian kicked, screamed, and pulled hair in a *Dynasty*-style catfight while Mary and Susan watched from inside their car. Priscilla, realizing she was out-weighed by a hundred pounds, rang the security buzzer for help, "and then Elvis came *raging* out," in her rendition. Marian ran to her car and locked the doors. "He busted the windows of her car," Priscilla recalled. "His fists were going into the windows trying to get to her, and the guys backed him off." Susan confirmed Elvis's white-hot anger, but was not certain whether it was directed at Marian, Priscilla, or all of them. Within several months, Mary, Marian, and Susan were back at the gates, and Elvis was talking to them as if nothing had happened.

The incident underscored Priscilla's lack of popularity among the Elvis faithful, who for the most part disapproved of her as the wrong woman for Elvis. Elvis's fans had an innate skepticism about Priscilla, and questioned whether she really loved him, a misgiving that appeared to go beyond petty jealousy and in fact had some basis in truth.

Priscilla cited the famous fistfight with Marian as the catalyst for her purchase, with Elvis, of a new house that year. "That's when we decided to move," she said, "and I started searching for another home," ostensibly because of the design of the Rocca Place driveway. But in truth, Priscilla, now that she was married to Elvis, wanted a house that would be *theirs,* not his. "I was now thinking, 'We're having a baby, and now we're really settling down, and where was I going to have her? Was it going to be in Memphis or was it gonna be L.A.?' I was more consumed with those thoughts than really having a lot of time with him." They decided on Los Angeles, Priscilla's choice, and she began house-hunting in earnest that summer.

The story would later surface, from more than one source, that Elvis collapsed into melancholy immediately after his marriage to Priscilla, bemoaning the fact that he had made a mistake. This bit of folklore was given credence by a strange contretemps between him and Priscilla sometime in the fall, as Elvis was choosing songs for a new album. He came to Priscilla one day—she was then nearly seven months pregnant—and told her he wanted to separate. "I had just come back from a trip," Priscilla said years later, "and he had found out that you could have a *trial* separation, that you didn't really have to have a divorce. . . . He told me, 'It's not a divorce. I just want to make it plain, there's not gonna be a divorce, and we'll just be separated.'" Priscilla was "devastated" and started crying. "I said, 'How . . . *why?*'" Elvis's doubts and misgivings came tumbling out in a conversation in their bedroom. "He got scared," Priscilla later reported. "He became *so* insecure. I was seven months pregnant, he was going to be a father, there was nothing else going *on*. He just had this commitment to do an album. He hadn't really sorted out how the fans would adjust to the fact that he was going to be a father, not just a husband. What was going to happen? He had to put this new album out. He was under pressure. Was that going to be it? Now the fans were going to see him as a family man; they were going to desert him. I think pressure was building in his head. He approached me [and said], 'Maybe we should have a trial separation. Then I can *think* better. I'll be able to know what I'm doing and where I'm going, and where all this is leading to, and who I *am*, and am I going to be . . . is this gonna be the end for me and my career? Am I going to provide for you and the baby?'"

Elvis was then immediately filled with remorse. "It was almost like after he said it, he then made up to me!" Priscilla recalled. "He was adoring. He brought me a *gift*! He went to the jeweler's and bought me a ring. He felt bad."

Priscilla spent an anxious few days wondering what the separation would mean, "because . . . he was very unpredictable. I didn't know what he was going to do."

The "separation" was evidently all in Elvis's mind, or perhaps he was moved by Priscilla's tears, for "he never discussed it again." Elvis left for Arizona to begin a western, *Stay Away, Joe,* with no further talk of separating. "It was unspoken," declared Priscilla. "I mean, I knew him well enough that he sometimes would say things on the spur of the moment and never mean them. How I survived that one, I justified it: 'He's just saying something he feels *at* the *moment,'* which he was known to do all the time. He was just like a little kid sometimes, he really was. He would just blurt out something. He was like this little boy, and he didn't know what to do with his feelings, and he would just come out with them, and then he'd feel really bad after it, and then he would do *everything* to make up for it. I mean, you had a love-hate relationship with him. It's unbelievable. He could be as charming and little-boyish, and then he could be—you'd be speaking with the devil." Elvis's pattern of fighting with Priscilla and making up later with gifts continued throughout their relationship. "I have a safe full of stuff I don't even know what I'm gonna do with! He was very generous. Very generous with me. Beautiful, beautiful jewelry."

Elvis was clearly wrestling with his decision to stay with Priscilla, though after he dropped his request for a separation, they settled into a happy domestic interlude awaiting the birth of their baby. "I even went to Sedona, Arizona, when he was doing *Stay Away, Joe,*" remembered Priscilla. "He was bragging about me and showing me off and patting my tummy." Priscilla spent her time on location scouting real estate ads in the trade papers, and found a French Regency mansion for $425,000 on Hillcrest Road in Beverly Hills as their marital home. At Christmastime, with her due date approaching, she and Elvis discussed baby names. They decided on John Baron for a boy, because Priscilla, with her fascination for machismo, wanted a "strong" name; Lisa Marie was selected for a girl. The speculation, later, was that this was in honor of the Colonel's wife, Marie, which Priscilla denied. She told the *Ladies' Home Journal,* after Elvis's death, that she and Elvis liked the name "because it was feminine." What Priscilla did not know was that Elvis had actually chosen the name Lisa Marie when he and Anita Wood were discussing marriage, because Anita's middle name was Marie and Elvis wanted to name a daughter after her. "He picked that name out," recalled Anita. Elvis wanted two children with Anita—"a girl and a boy, of course"; the boy was to be named Elvis Aaron Jr. When Priscilla gave birth to a girl and she was called Lisa Marie, Anita "thought it was a little unusual," since the name had been chosen to honor her.

Priscilla carried on throughout her pregnancy as if she were not carrying a child at all—to keep Elvis from "complaining that pregnancy stopped me," she later explained, though it seemed more willful than that, almost destructive, just as her disregard of her obstetrician's warnings about fasting suggested an almost subconscious desire to self-abort. Elvis's grandmother, according to the family cook, Mary Jenkins, and one of the maids, Nancy Rooks, became upset with Priscilla for riding Domino while she was pregnant, and Elvis was also concerned about her daredevil antics. Priscilla would later remark that "he was really a doting father-to-be, always making sure I was doing the things— I mean, *I* was the wild one. I was riding horses until it was almost time to deliver!" Priscilla fell off Domino riding bareback in her ninth month of pregnancy. "Luckily," Joe said, underplaying the scene, "she fell on her side and didn't fall on her stomach [and] everything was fine." Sheila Ryan Caan, who dated Elvis after the divorce, said he was still bitter that Priscilla had endangered their child by riding bareback. In Sheila's opinion, based on what Elvis had told her, "It was a vindictive thing."

Priscilla nonetheless gave birth without incident on February 1, 1968, though she almost didn't make it to the hospital. Graceland cook Mary Jenkins recalled Elvis being so nervous when Priscilla's water broke early that morning that he nearly drove off without her. Once she was in the car, Jerry Schilling, the designated driver, headed for the wrong hospital, confusing a plan Elvis and the guys had set up to send a decoy car to a different hospital to distract the media. Lisa Marie Presley made her debut at Baptist Memorial in Memphis at 5:01 P.M. to an ebullient superstar father passing out cigars to press from around the world and calling himself the "happy pappy." Lisa Marie's mother was in a standard-issue hospital gown, and two pairs of false eyelashes, by special arrangement with the hospital, which had assigned a police guard to protect the room. "I think Elvis wanted to buy [Lisa] a mink coat the day she was born," a Mafia member would later note wryly. It would set the pattern for Lisa Presley's surreal life to come.

For a brief, shining moment in their often turbulent history, Elvis and Priscilla actually lived the fantasy marriage they projected to an adoring world. Elvis reveled in being a father, and so missed Priscilla and Lisa when he started *Live a Little, Love a Little* in mid-March that he sent for them after three days. With President Kennedy's death five years earlier, Elvis and Priscilla seemed to replace, in the public consciousness, Jack and Jackie as the fairy-tale couple of the sixties. Like Jacqueline Kennedy, Priscilla was beautiful, glamorous, mysterious, and aloof. Both women wore dark hair in a bouffant style, and had romantic French surnames that began with *B*—Beaulieu and Bouvier. They were often photographed on horseback, spoke in airy, exaggeratedly feminine voices, and were interested in fashion and the decorative arts. And both women, of course, had married legends as famous for their philandering as their brilliance.

Priscilla's Camelot was no less flawed than Jackie's. The specter of sex which had so long haunted her relationship with Elvis now threatened to destroy it completely with the gradual unveiling of the star's second sexual secret. Elvis, contrary to the claims of his biographers, continued to have sex with Priscilla during her pregnancy *as* he preferred it—through foreplay, video-enhanced masturbation, role-playing, and, less often, intercourse. "He didn't do anything differently," Priscilla recollected. "I mean, it was still the same. We'd play games, and we just had a different kind of relationship that was not bad at *all*. And that continued." With the birth of Lisa, however, Priscilla began to notice that Elvis exhibited no sexual interest in her whatsoever. In her diary for April 5, 1968, she noted with despair, "It's been two months and he still hasn't touched me." Elvis and Priscilla's sex life came to a dead halt that spring.

Priscilla, whose self-image, for her own Freudian reasons, was almost pathologically intertwined with her physical and sexual desirability, was tormented by the now famous sexual pathology that led to Elvis's withdrawal from her: "He told me he was . . . He told me that it was *difficult* because you are a *mother*. These aren't *his* words, but me trying to put it all together for my *own* self. It turned the relationship into something else. It changed the dynamics. Not that I wasn't sexy to him, not that he didn't desire it—because, believe me, that wasn't the case at all—but as far as actual intercourse, it changed the dynamics."

Elvis, she said, never explained to her why he was uncomfortable having sex with a woman who had given birth. The friends of Elvis later offered theories based on their conversations with him. Alan Fortas claimed Elvis was repulsed by childbirth. Joyce Bova, who would become one of Elvis's girlfriends later in his marriage to Priscilla, said Elvis told her that having a child was God's way of telling a woman that she was not a little girl anymore, that it was time to be respected; she shouldn't "be trying to be sexy and attracting men." God, he believed, did not intend sex with a woman who was a mother to be exciting; a woman who had a child, Elvis told Joyce, was "not attractive in that way." Priscilla perceived Elvis's attitude, once she was older, as a variation on the madonna-whore syndrome. It did not, Gladys's great friend Willie Jane maintained, derive from anything Elvis's mother had instilled in him, nor had there been anything more than the deep southern tie of filial affection between Elvis and his mama. "He did not have a strange relationship with his mother," emphasized Priscilla, who viewed with rightful and righteous contempt as "off-the-wall and sensationalism" any suggestion to the contrary. Elvis's idiosyncrasy was, to be redundant, uniquely Elvis, and was likely idiopathic in origin, a by-product of his rural southern mores and individualistic religious beliefs.

The fourteen-year-old Priscilla had been Elvis Presley's sexual-romantic paragon. If only she could have remained frozen in time . . . As she grew up and into more adult sex, however, Elvis's preference for making out and playing games—a result of his anxiety about satisfying superhuman expectations—left her frustrated. Once Priscilla had a baby, the ultimate sexual taboo for Elvis, he no longer desired her at all in a physical way. It was a Catch-22. Though she later said otherwise, Priscilla wrote in her memoir that Elvis told her about his phobia before they were married, which cast the situation in a somewhat different light. If Priscilla married Elvis and had his child, *knowing* of his aversion to intercourse with a mother, she had either underestimated her own sex drive or was unwilling, once she had achieved her goal of marriage, to compromise her sexuality in order to sustain the relationship with Elvis. "I was certainly not prepared," Priscilla reflected, "emotionally or physically. Because, you know, having a child is an incredible experience that you have *with* the father. And you nurture and you love and you bond with your child. I mean, there can't be anything more stimulating, and so . . . from a woman's point of view, not to have that same feeling shared, you know, is somewhat a mystery for me too."

Elvis and Priscilla's intimacy began withering on the vine; she stopped going to Palm Springs on weekends, annoyed by the cast of female and male regulars, and uninterested, still, in joining Elvis in his spiritual pursuits, which continued despite Larry's expulsion from the entourage; the Circle G, which had been a fleeting source of joy, was sold as an extravagance. Priscilla spoke wistfully to a magazine, years later, of the nights when Elvis would go into Lisa's bedroom (he called her Yeesa) and read her nursery rhymes. Her happiest moments, she said—though they were few—were "when he dropped that wall, when he became the person he might have been without all the pressures."

The chasm between Elvis and Priscilla, exacerbated by his attitude toward sex with someone who had given birth, became a gulf. Priscilla's frustration revealed itself in snide, embittered comments. She told Memphis secretary Becky Yancey that it was more fun to be the girlfriend than the wife, and she mentioned to Willie Jane, more ominously, that she wanted no more children. Nancy Rooks, one of the Graceland maids, used to hear Elvis talk about how he wanted twenty children because he was an only child; Nancy asked Priscilla, after Lisa was born, if she was going to have another baby. "And she said, 'No more with him.' I told her, 'But he wants twenty kids.' She said, 'Not with me. I'm not having any more with him.' " It was impossible to know whether Priscilla's attitude was caused by Elvis's physical rejection of her, by her admitted concern about her figure, or by incompatibility with her mate. Presumably it was all three.

With Elvis on a separate path, Priscilla spent more time with the entourage wives and became especially close to Joan Esposito. She saw herself as—and probably was—the originator of fashion trends, the leader, the "female Elvis" of the distaff set. "All the girls would wear their hair like I did, dress like I did. They emulated [me]; basically what I came back with from California they tried to be and do." There was, not surprisingly, a certain resentment among the guys' wives toward Priscilla, who was gorgeous and glamorous and who was married to the king of their kingdom. Priscilla's critics referred to Joan Esposito, who was an open, friendly, accommodating sort, as Priscilla's coolie, a yes-person who did the boss's wife's bidding. "Some of them didn't like Priscilla," Joe Esposito said after the fact. "Patsy Lacker. And recently I found out Jo Smith didn't care for her, which I found really surprising. Billy Smith's wife really put her down in one of the books." The Memphis Mafia wives and girlfriends regarded Priscilla as a queen bee. "We all knew that she got special treatment," Joe said matter-of-factly, "because of who she was. She got resented for that."

By the end of April 1968, not even a year after her "fairy-tale" wedding to Elvis, Priscilla's diary telegraphed the eventual demise of the marriage; she was questioning her own sexuality, she wrote, and her physical and emotional needs were not being met. Priscilla began, quite literally, to transform herself. She started with little dance steps, enrolling in a modern jazz class, one of Elvis's approved activities for her. Then she enrolled in an acting class. Patricia Crowley took dance lessons with Priscilla that year and remembered her as extremely conscientious, "working all day long on her lessons. I think she really wanted a career." Patricia, an actress herself, got the impression that Priscilla's chosen career would be acting, though she was still shy about speaking in public. Her drama coach remembered Priscilla hanging on the sidelines, insecure. "Once in a while she'd get over there on the stage, but generally she was a looker. [Performing] was good for her."

Elvis was absorbed in his own private drama, an effort to revitalize his image as a rocker, which had suffered during his years of making predominantly disappointing B films. His five-year contract with MGM was ending, and he hoped to make a comeback in a television special for NBC, a prospect that both excited and terrified him, for he hadn't performed in concert in years. It was to this end that he was dedicating his considerable energies, nervous and creative, during the greater part of 1968, as his bride immersed herself in dance and drama.

Priscilla and Elvis flew to Hawaii in May for an unofficial second honeymoon—with an entourage—to disastrous results. Joe and Joan Esposito, who occupied a neighboring cabaña at the Ilikai Hotel with a common wall between the bedrooms, found themselves accidental eavesdroppers to a pathetic exchange between Elvis and Priscilla. "We were going to bed," recalled Joe, "and she was trying to have sex with him that night, and he didn't want to. Joanie and I both heard it; we were headboard to headboard in these little bungalows. I'll never forget that. Priscilla was screaming, 'You don't love me anymore since the baby!' and 'We never make love anymore!' and 'You never take your pajamas off anymore with me. We're always in the dark!'"

The trip was significant for another reason. Elvis, who had become interested in karate while he was in the army, took Priscilla and the rest of the group to watch an international tournament orchestrated by Ed Parker, a giant in the karate world who had become a personal friend of Elvis's. There, less than twelve months after their marriage, Priscilla spotted the future lover for whom she would eventually leave Elvis Presley. Mike Stone, a twenty-four-year-old half-Hawaiian onetime army enlistee, was karate's undisputed bad boy, a world champion for whom competition was a blood sport. The very sort of dark and dangerous rebel Priscilla had been attracted to ever since she was in elementary school. There was some question later about who was fawning over Mike that day, Elvis or Priscilla. Priscilla's version: "Everyone kept pointing this Mike Stone out. Elvis would point him out and, you know, I kept thinking, 'Jeez! *Okay!* He *is* good!'" Ed Parker and Mike later claimed that Priscilla went on and on about Mike to Elvis, who admired Mike as a great fighter but found him "cocky." Mike would later say that Priscilla told him, when the two of them were together several years later, that she decided, the day of the 1968 tournament, that she was going to have him one day—a characteristic Priscilla maneuver, similar to the way she had pursued and attained Elvis. Priscilla confirmed that Mike Stone caught her eye, though they did not meet that day, and she admitted there was an attraction. "A *little* bit, a *little* bit. I remember, just a *little*, because he was like a *cat*. But not in a sexual way, or not in a way that I was looking. There *was* a little something, *noticing* that he *was* a little different. I had no plans of having any kind of a relationship or any kind of a lover at that time, because we were still . . . so I guess, in my memory, it kind of stayed there." With Priscilla, that was tantamount to a tattoo.

Priscilla sublimated herself in dance, intensifying her schedule in L.A. that spring to include three demanding classes in addition to her continuing scene work, using a pseudonym, C. P. Persimmons, to disguise her identity—more secrets. Steve Peck, an exacting, tough-guy former New York stage dancer who owned the studio on Robertson and taught all the classes, dance and acting, coaxed Priscilla onto the stage. "She wasn't good [as an actress]," he observed, "but she worked very hard. She really got into it." Priscilla was excellent at dance, into which she threw herself body and soul, filling the voids in her life. Steve pegged Priscilla as a woman with needs, like many of the wives and ex-wives in his Beverly Hills dance classes. His advice to all of them was the same: "Stop talking about it and sweat. Forget about it or get out." He said later of Priscilla, "Something starts over with a need. With Priscilla, I think it was a building of desire. The life wasn't what she wanted. Elvis had evidently thought he had her, but she needed something." Dance began to open Priscilla, so long hidden inside the artificial persona she had created for Elvis; in Peck's creative environment, she unfolded like a flower. "I think this was the start of her emoting herself," he assessed. "She would enjoy it and she would laugh and have fun. No one bothered her. A lot of people there didn't even know who she was."

Rumors began circulating through Elvis's entourage that Priscilla was having an affair with Steve Peck. "I couldn't believe it," said Joe. "I just kept thinking about this little girl I knew would never do this." The prim, "good-girl" side of Priscilla's split personality had deceived even Joe, who had known her since she was fourteen, for Priscilla admitted in her memoir, which came out in 1985, that she had a sexual liaison with someone from her dance class, identified pseudonymously as "Mark." She later denied that it was her instructor, Steve Peck, saying only that her lover was a dancer. Steve Peck also disavowed the affair, though he acknowledged Priscilla was needy. "She had no romance with me. I was very, very close to her. A close creative— She used to come there, and I knew—I knew there was a problem . . . because it was obvious. If you really are in love, you don't go dedicate yourself to something, or if you do, you take him with you. We never [saw Elvis]. She introduced me to him twice."

"I was told it was Steve," countered Joe Esposito. The instructor was without question Priscilla's type: tall, dark, and Sicilian. Priscilla herself compared Steve admiringly to Anthony Quinn and was nervous, years later, about what he might have revealed about the "personal" side of their relationship. Patty Perry was certain the affair was with Steve. "I *saw* Priscilla with Steve Peck in the market. He was a very attractive guy. I would never tell Elvis." Someone did, apparently a member of the entourage. "We knew about it," said Charlie Hodge, who also believed Priscilla's lover was Steve Peck. "In fact, we were talking about it in a group with Elvis, and one of the guys said, 'We could get a detective to follow her.'" Elvis, according to Charlie and the rest of the Mafia, forbade them to use a private investigator to tail Priscilla and would not allow anyone to say a disparaging or unkind word about her in his presence. "Elvis said, 'Anybody does that, they're fired. There's a whole big world out there that little girl doesn't know anything about, and if she gets hurt a little bit, it'll make a better wife out of her.'"

Charlie, like Joe Esposito, "didn't think Priscilla would ever do anything like that," so successfully had she suppressed her true nature around Elvis and his friends. The affair was reminiscent of the Priscilla of old, back in Germany, when she maintained a double life with a series of boyfriends while Elvis was thousands of miles away in the United States, believing her to be faithful. She had seemingly remained true to Elvis throughout her four years sequestered at Graceland (except for lusting in her heart after Mylon LeFevre), perhaps because she was a virtual prisoner, and also because she and Elvis were not yet married. Priscilla was still clinging to the fallacy that she had never been with another man, and she was more than likely apprehensive about being caught in an affair, thereby jeopardizing her chances of ever marrying Elvis. Now that she had accomplished her goal, she could take that risk and fulfill her desires—which had never been wholly satisfied by Elvis—just as she had in Wiesbaden.

Priscilla wasted little time in doing so. During the first nine months of her marriage to Elvis she was pregnant; within weeks after having Lisa, she had taken a lover. She attributed the affair with the pseudonymous "Mark," years later, to "the intensity of the dance," saying the "drive" and her emotional state "peaked at that time. It helped me, certainly, get through—I hate putting myself in that lower level of existence, but it helped me get through and it helped me get my attention away from *me*. You know, it was exciting, it was something different. Not that I'm promoting it, nor am I using that as an excuse. I don't think it's right, but to survive I guess I needed . . . to be able to do what I needed to do as a woman. I needed to get *away* from Elvis. I needed to get away from his life and his lifestyle."

The mutual hypocrisy of Elvis and Priscilla's marriage became clear at the taping of his NBC special in June. Elvis, recalled his director, did not want Priscilla around during rehearsals, ostensibly because "there were too many other guys around," but actually because he was having an affair with Susan Henning, a pretty blond dancer in the special who openly stayed with Elvis on the set throughout preproduction. When Priscilla arrived for the taping, the first time she had seen Elvis perform live, she brought Steve Peck, along with several of the other dancers from her class, one of whom, remembered Steve, was a male hairdresser with an enormous crush on Priscilla—or "C. P. Persimmons," her false identity. It wasn't until Elvis introduced Priscilla to the audience during filming of the special that her classmate discovered he'd been pining after Elvis Presley's wife. Steve expected Priscilla's secret admirer to be crushed to find out she was married; instead, Steve chuckled, "the first thing he said was, 'I want to cut his hair!' Just like a real Hollywood situation."

Elvis's affair with Susan Henning lasted most of the rest of the year, as Priscilla carried on with her dancer-lover. They were leading separate lives, although their marriage was still in the post-honeymoon stage and their daughter was less than six months old. Priscilla had effectively made their new house on Hillcrest in Truesdale Estates, an exclusive section of Beverly Hills, a home for herself and Lisa, eschewing Memphis for L.A., which she had always preferred. Though the world envisioned theirs as a storybook marriage, in truth Priscilla and Elvis were married in name only. Being married gave Priscilla the confidence to be herself again, no longer needing to project a facade to induce Elvis to wed her. She later told *Redbook* magazine, "Inside, I was becoming my own person. I wanted to be more me." She said she had looked at some of her earlier photographs, with the beehive and black eyeliner and concluded that she "didn't look real in them." In a way, she wasn't; Priscilla had created a persona as artificial as the double set of false eyelashes she put on faithfully every morning, whether she was spending the day in the barn or going to a Tom Jones concert.

There was also strain between Priscilla and the Memphis Mafia, who resented her newfound power as Elvis's wife. She fired several members of the household staff in L.A., and Elvis sent for Mary Jenkins, the Graceland cook, to smooth things over. Willie Jane laid the blame for Elvis and Priscilla's eventual divorce on his male entourage. "They were against his marriage. I don't care what beautiful things they say now. They had no understanding for her at all. She had more for them than they did for her. They made Elvis do things. And they *worked* on her, to a certain extent. They were always introducing girls to him and trying to get him interested in girls. And naturally, that would hurt her." Priscilla's barely buried resentment came out years later, after Elvis died and she assumed control of the estate, when she would refer to certain members of the entourage as "has-beens and leeches," or worse. In truth, though, the guys hung around largely because Elvis *wanted* them around, for he romanticized the idea of having an entourage, and depended upon them for emotional support, possibly because he had been an only child, perhaps because he walked in his sleep and needed someone to spend nights with him, in part due to his intrinsically lonely nature, and he needed a human fortress between himself and the frightening force of fame.

At the end of that year, 1968, after ten months without sex of any kind with Elvis—not even "games," as Priscilla called Elvis's preference for foreplay, masturbation, home sex videos, and role-playing—she finally confronted him. "I told him that we couldn't survive that way. I could the *other* way [with the games as opposed to intercourse], because I mean, we had *that*. But it was like—I felt that it was *me*." Elvis, she recalled, "tried to make love to me. I mean, he *tried*. And I knew he was a little uncomfortable with it." (Elvis *did* have sex, on occasion, with other women who had children, but the fact that Priscilla's child was his own evidently reinforced his phobia.) The reality of her fantasy marriage had become untenable for Priscilla; the dream she had spun at ten, thrust upon her by her parents when she was seventeen, was becoming her personal nightmare. She was still in a masquerade, keeping secrets, pretending to be the radiant bride of the most famous sex symbol in the world, when she had not made love to him since the birth of their daughter and was carrying on a not-so-secret affair with a male dancer. Priscilla, as a child, had fallen in love with the image of Elvis Presley, not with the man she met in Bad Nauheim; Elvis was in love with the persona Priscilla had assumed in her effort to acquire him; now they were two strangers who shared the same last name. "To be a soul mate you've got to have a connection—lust," Mike Edwards analyzed. "You've got to be connected everywhere—philosophically, emotionally, mentally—on every level there is. And they didn't have it. They didn't have this great sex life. They *didn't*. You can't be a soul mate with someone if you don't have that. That's the true connection: when you get together and you can't *breathe*, and you're looking in someone's eyes and pressed so close you just want to get inside of each other. Elvis and Priscilla—that was a fantasy world."

Elvis's NBC special, which aired at the end of 1968, offered both the silver lining and the cloud in the Presleys' married life. Elvis had been fortuitously matched for the special with an innovative young director named Steve Binder, who challenged him to revive the rock-and-roll spirit that had originally defined him. Binder suggested a simple setting: Elvis seated on a chair, in the round, with his guitar, before an intimate studio audience, performing live on tape in addition to several production numbers—a concert that would bring him back to the purity of his rock roots. Bill Belew designed a pair of tight black leather pants and a black leather jacket for the special, an outfit Elvis feared might make him look foolish. The night the television show aired, December 3, 1968, the singer was a mass of raw nerves, Priscilla would recall, fearful that people would find his music, and his costume, ridiculous. But that concert electrified Elvis's career and would be referred to ever after as the "comeback special." Elvis Presley had never looked trimmer or handsomer; the tight black leather against his black hair projected a smoldering, Brando-like sexuality that recalled Elvis's early live performances, and his simple, classic rock arrangements helped obscure the inferior movies that had come between. He told Steve Binder, who had helped to mastermind it, "that the show had influenced him to never do another lousy movie or record another lousy song." Binder, nonetheless, had an ominous feeling, and told Elvis so. "I said, 'I hear you, but I'm not sure you're strong enough to back it up.' I didn't feel Elvis was all that strong to fight the elements and people and entourages and so forth."

Elvis followed the special with two critically and commercially successful singles, "In the Ghetto" and "Suspicious Minds," and the comeback briefly revived his dormant sexual relationship with Priscilla, though it was still a "different kind of relationship," in her words, meaning there was little intercourse. The heat from the comeback special and his two hit singles in early 1969 generated for Elvis a stunning new contract, negotiated by the Colonel, to perform live at the Las Vegas International Hotel twice a year, in August and January. Elvis filmed the last movie under his MGM contract, another tepid picture called *A Change of Habit*, in which he played a doctor opposite Mary Tyler Moore, who portrayed a nun.

It was the beginning of a new era in the lives of Elvis and Priscilla. For the next several years their routine revolved around his performing schedule, which consisted of his two concert dates in Vegas with six months of touring in between. Elvis eventually instituted a no-wives-on-the-road policy, which telegraphed the dismal state of his sexual and marital relations with Priscilla. She and the other wives were invited to Vegas for opening and closing nights only; the three weeks of shows in between were off-limits. She and Elvis, Priscilla said, usually had sex on the nights he opened and closed in Vegas each January and August, a ritual that resembled the mating habits of some exotic species, since they were seldom intimate on other occasions. After one of Elvis's 1970 openings or closings in Vegas, Priscilla missed her period for two months and thought she was pregnant. She told Elvis, and he was "elated. . . . He was calling me every single day to see if in fact I was. And then when I told him that I wasn't, it was a disappointment." Priscilla later claimed that she wanted another child, too, though this seems unlikely in light of the recollections of Willie Jane and others to the contrary—and Priscilla's own comment to the Memphis paper in 1969 that she didn't want to be "inconvenienced."

She was not happy in her lifestyle with Elvis; this was plain to all who knew Priscilla and from everything she said after their divorce. One of her primary complaints was that she and Elvis did not spend enough time together, but by show business standards, theirs was a relatively standard marriage in terms of family time as a couple: From 1967 to 1970 they took regular holidays in Hawaii, skiied once in Aspen, vacationed in the Bahamas, and spent Christmas at Graceland each year. Charlie Hodge remembered those years, after Priscilla and Elvis married, as "the happiest time, it seemed like, because we were more a family then. In the evenings we'd sit down and have dinner. In Memphis it would be Patsy and GeeGee [Elvis's cousin and her husband] and Elvis and Priscilla and me and the baby. And that was the family. And then when we were on the West Coast we'd have dinner every evening and sit together, and Joe and Joanie would come up some evenings; some evenings Colonel Parker and Tom Diskin, his associate, would come up. And it was just a wonderful time, wonderful dinners, a lot of laughs. All of my memories were so pleasant of that time."

Myrna Smith, who in 1969 joined the Sweet Inspirations, Elvis's Vegas backup group, and who eventually married Jerry Schilling, regarded Elvis and Priscilla as "two gorgeous people who looked very much in love." Becky Yancey, the Graceland secretary, remembered Elvis buying Priscilla diamond rings, watches, charm bracelets—expensive jewelry for which Becky saw the bills.

This would have been some women's Cinderella story, but the glass slipper did not fit Priscilla. She was restless, sexually unfulfilled, dissatisfied, and bored—as she had been, in truth, from her first days at Graceland, if not her first nights with Elvis in Germany. The difference now was that she had realized her goal—to marry Elvis Presley—and she could move on. Nancy Rooks, the longtime Graceland maid, always felt, interestingly, that Priscilla "was not as much in love with Elvis as he was with her." Elvis told Kathy Westmoreland, his friend and backup singer after 1970, that Priscilla never loved him, that "she only wanted a career for herself."

Their incompatibility was due in part to the fact that Elvis was nocturnal, by choice and by profession. "They were just not together," Pat Crowley observed. "He was up all night, and she was working all day on her career." Priscilla remarked, only half jokingly, in 1996, that she and Elvis might still be married "if I'd had my own room. We were on such different schedules. He was up all night, and I needed my sleep. We had different interests." They were, and had always been, mismatched on a practical level, whatever callings of the soul brought them together.

Elvis was gradually becoming a prisoner of his fame, remaining inside his dwellings in California and Tennessee or his hotel suite in Vegas, and Priscilla was feeling trapped by association, in conflict with her essentially adventurous spirit. She extended herself into the world in every way imaginable within the confines that Elvis had constructed for her. Joan Esposito recalled that Priscilla took "calligraphy at UCLA, cooking classes at the extension school, art classes. We took ice-skating lessons, we took French, she took Spanish." Joan was in the same circumstance as Priscilla. "We were trying to find ways to amuse ourselves. Joe was gone over nine tax-deductible months in one year. [He and Elvis] would show up two to three days here and go back for two weeks and come back."

Priscilla tried, at times, to include Elvis in joint pursuits, and originally took up French, she said, because one of their favorite albums was by French balladeer Charles Aznavour, called, appropriately, *Where Has Love Gone?* "That particular album was something that Elvis loved. There were a lot of wonderful songs on that album, produced by Barry Devorsian, and we both loved it and it really conveyed a lot of feelings that we had for each other. And it's just a beautiful language. As they say, 'the language of love.' "

Sadly, Elvis and Priscilla could not connect on a more temporal level, for their interests, schedules, and basic natures were light-years apart, to his soul's devastation and her more quotidian dissatisfaction. In 1969, Elvis met a pretty twenty-four-year-old government employee from Washington, D.C., through a backstage introduction in Las Vegas. Joyce Bova became Elvis's steady girlfriend that year and part of the next and had tender feelings for him, believing him to be, as he was, unsatisfied in his marriage. Priscilla was not the only one who felt incomplete in the relationship; Elvis told Joyce, a demonstrative Italian, that he found Priscilla "cold." This was something he told others as well, saying that he married her because he "felt pressure" and had an "obligation" to her. One of the things that struck Elvis, about Joyce, was that she was an identical twin, a circumstance that fascinated him and tapped into his own deep longing for the brother he never knew. He told Joyce he had come to believe that because he was the twin who lived (the letters in "Elvis" also spelled "lives"), he must have some higher purpose on earth, and he derived meaning from the fact that Joyce had a twin sister, "like we were meant to be or something, because of that common denominator." Elvis was still searching for answers to the spiritual questions that both haunted and compelled him, issues that did not intrigue Priscilla or most of his male companions, whose interests were more shallow.

The other thing that drew Elvis was Joyce Bova's resemblance to Priscilla, or to the look that Priscilla and Elvis had invented, for Joyce was petite with long, shiny black hair and dark, dramatic eye makeup. "He encouraged me to dress in a certain fashion," she said, "overdone clothes, overdone makeup, and overdone hair, and of course I did. Almost from the beginning, people were mistaking me for Priscilla. I would ask him if I looked like Priscilla, because that did bother me, and he would say that we were not similar at all. I hate to put Priscilla down or anything, but he said that I was a much warmer person inside, and she was not at all [warm] or friendly." Joyce felt that Elvis was possibly attempting to reproduce Priscilla, but it was not Priscilla he was yearning for, really; rather it was the fantasy of Priscilla he had been carrying in his heart, coupled with a regret for what might have been. The "Priscilla look," moreover, was actually Elvis's re-creation of Debra Paget, his first, lost love, who never left his mind.

Both Elvis and Priscilla had emotionally and physically abandoned the marriage by 1969. Elvis's new policy forbidding wives on the road afforded him the opportunity, and his empty shell of a marriage provided the motive, to seek other female companions. His entourage proved more than willing to procure young candidates, generally while they were in Vegas or on tour. Elvis's one-night stands acquired the nickname, within the entourage, of "Queens for a Day." Whenever Priscilla arrived for the closing night at the International, Elvis assigned Ricky Stanley the task of rearranging her clothes in the hotel closet where she had hung them before his latest girlfriend visited the room, so she would not know he had been with someone else.

This was not the life Priscilla had fantasized about when she was twelve years old and imagined herself married to Elvis Presley. Nor, presumably, was it the destiny Elvis envisioned for himself and his soul mate.

25

THE END OF CAMELOT

Elvis and Priscilla began the seventies on an optimistic note, purchasing a new mansion in Beverly Hills on Monovale Road, which Priscilla planned to decorate, creating her vision of their dream house.

Elvis kept the house on Hillcrest to live in during the Monovale makeover, which was a wise plan, for Priscilla's redecorating project took nearly a year, during which she kept Elvis from setting foot in the new house so that she could surprise him with the finished product. Ed Hookstratten, Elvis's lawyer, recommended a Beverly Hills interior designer named Phylliss Mann, who had decorated Sammy Davis Jr.'s residence and redone the Ambassador Hotel and the Coconut Grove.

Priscilla was a complete naif when it came to decorating. "I was really retained because I was the taste expert," declared Phylliss, who found Priscilla "a very willing pupil" who "learned in a hurry what she liked." During the summer and fall of 1970, Phylliss took Priscilla to wallpaper shops, art galleries, and antique stores. The redecorating of Monovale became a rite of passage for Priscilla, the beginning of her education in the home decorating habits of the rich and cultivated. According to Phylliss, who observed the process, Priscilla "wanted to express herself and . . . to find herself. And she wanted to please Elvis." Priscilla's preferences ran to the "romantic soft look" and "old things." Her bath and dressing room were yellow and "very feminine," in Phylliss's words. "His dressing room was very Elvis, early Elvis. Black patent leather ceiling, antique barber chair. All of his clothes and costumes could be seen; it was really quite interesting, it was an octagonal room."

The years 1970 and 1971 were a time of personal growth for Priscilla. In addition to putting her individual stamp on the new house, she was still dancing, which gave her greater confidence and independence. "I think it was the most honest time of her life, that moment, that time, that two or three years," said Steve Peck. Priscilla grew her hair past her waist and began lightening it to a golden brown rather than the silky black Elvis favored. She also took to dressing in a sexually provocative manner, particularly at Elvis's Vegas openings and closings. Myrna Smith of the Sweet Inspirations remembered Priscilla coming to the shows with her "belly out and the little hip-huggers. She dressed the way I always wanted to dress!" Priscilla's objective, presumably, was to arouse Elvis, to startle him into noticing her. "She knew that kind of thing would get his attention," said Myrna.

Priscilla had discovered a young designer named Olivia Bis (née Echeverria), who had a boutique on Doheny in Beverly Hills, when she drove by one day and noticed some cunning mother-daughter outfits in the store window. Olivia, strangely, had been expecting Priscilla Presley to come by her shop, purely by an intuition; when she finally did, the designer had no idea who she was. "There was this beautiful girl with two big boxer dogs at my door. She came in, she was trying on things, and she was wearing a beautiful diamond, and she was very young. And no one knew what Priscilla looked like at that time. Everybody, as I did, thought of her with the black hair and the eyelashes." Priscilla and Olivia were instant friends, with similar taste in clothes. "We would start to collaborate on designs; if she saw something that she liked, she'd buy it from me, but then if there was something she liked that she saw, I would make it for her." Priscilla favored "the bare midriffs, and she had a beautiful figure. . . . She used to love to wear long, bare midriff, hip-hugger skirts and flowing things, and then hot pants came out and we did hot pants. Everything that was coming in, everything that was different. And the thing that she loved about the shop was that everything she had was unique, designed just for her." Priscilla, as she had at thirteen, still obsessed about her hair, something Olivia noticed. "She had this thing with the brush and the hair. She had beautiful hair and she used to bend over and brush it. I used to tell her, 'If I ever want to drive you nuts, I'm going to take that brush away from you, because you will end up in a mental ward.' "

Priscilla's and Elvis's separate houses in Beverly Hills were a symbol of their divided lives. Priscilla had taken up photography, another time-filler, and sent pictures of Lisa to Elvis while he was on the road to keep him up-to-date on her development. "The only thing that really kept us together, of course, was the baby," she said once in a documentary, "and I was struggling to keep him involved. . . . Our link, you know, was her." Lisa, Priscilla said later, showed an early interest in music. "At three years old, or two, she was playing records like 'Sweet Caroline' and 'Leaving on a Jet Plane.' She had her own little music box, and she'd play, three years old—I have pictures of her doing this. So she always loved music, she has an ear for music." Jerry Schilling, who would later manage Lisa, said, "it's been in her soul since she was a baby." As a baby, Lisa led a somewhat lonely life, despite the carnival that often surrounded her. Priscilla was dancing, ice-skating, studying calligraphy, French, Spanish, or acting, and Elvis was performing, while Lisa crawled in her crib, often alone, according to Geraldine Kyle, Dee's best friend in Memphis, who felt sorry for the child. Priscilla herself wrote of being concerned, when Lisa was two or three, that she was becoming too attached to her nanny. One girlfriend of Elvis's enduring memory of Lisa, at the Hilton in Vegas with Elvis, was of a little girl of three clutching a doll that had a head but no body, "combing the hair and singing to her dad."

In May of 1970, Priscilla turned twenty-five and Elvis threw her a surprise birthday party. "In the home movies we have," recalled Charlie Hodge, "she was crying, just so shy." Elvis's decision to give her a surprise party and Priscilla's emotional reaction showed there were still feelings between them, but not enough to overcome the fact that they had nothing in common except their daughter.

Elvis entered into another liaison in the fall of 1970, with a sexy brunette he stole from legendary Hollywood womanizer Jim Aubrey, who made the mistake of flaunting actress Barbara Leigh in front of Elvis in Vegas. Barbara was a realist who understood the ways of the show business world and did not delude herself into thinking she would ever be anything beyond Elvis Presley's mistress. "When I was his girlfriend, I didn't tell anybody, I kept it private, and I didn't have my picture taken with him. I was a known actress in those days and it would have been too public; it wouldn't have been good for him. I respected his privacy, and I respected Priscilla's privacy and protected them." Barbara felt there was nothing immoral about her relationship with Elvis. *He* had pursued her, and he was not fulfilled in his marriage to Priscilla. Barbara also perceived Elvis as someone who had attained mythic status and for whom the rules no longer applied. "I didn't see it as cheating on Priscilla. I didn't look at it that way. Maybe good Christians out there would hate my guts. The world that we lived in, in Hollywood, was a very different world, and I never felt any guilt at all about it. . . . He wasn't just a man. He wasn't just a husband or a father. He was bigger than life. I think he belonged to the world, to anybody that wanted him or loved him. I think he belonged to everybody."

Joyce Bova, who started dating Elvis not too long before he met Barbara Leigh, naively believed their relationship *was* exclusive and entertained the thought that she and Elvis might even marry someday. Kathy Westmoreland, a pretty blond from Abilene, Texas, who became his backup singer in 1970, had a similarly bittersweet romance, beginning roughly around the same time. "Actually, Kathy had a very, very serious time with Elvis," said Myrna Smith of the Sweet Inspirations, "because he was the first man she slept with, so she went through a difficult time. Because she actually believed that when Elvis told her he loved her he meant 'I love you'—as in a relationship. Elvis loved *all* of us."

Elvis told Barbara Leigh that the spiritual dimension was missing from his relationship with Priscilla. Kathy Westmoreland was a kindred spirit. "I knew nothing about him," Kathy said of her first days as Elvis's backup singer in the summer of 1970. "I had no idea he was such a special person. I was so surprised by that, and how talented he was, until I saw him live and saw he had a thousand times the charisma that the majority of stars that I worked with before had. He had this gift—even though he was an untrained singer—he had this glorious gift of interpreting songs, and style. I had put him in this niche of rockabilly, and I had no idea that he was interested in such a variety of music." Kathy, like Priscilla, had a childhood connection to Mario Lanza, Elvis's musical idol. "One of the first conversations we had was about Mario Lanza," Kathy recalled. "My father had sung in some movies with him, and [Elvis] knew the movies—scene by scene what had happened. That surprised me too."

Kathy understood what Priscilla seemed to disdain: Elvis's great attraction to the spiritual realm. "We carried around a lot of the same books," she said. "Our relationship began with the metaphysical and spiritual aspects in life. We both were concerned with truth, you might call it. To me it wasn't strange at all; it was very healthy. He was surrounded by a lot of people who had no understanding of that. That's what drew me to him." Kathy related to Elvis's quest to understand why he had been given this great power over people. "He had questions and went to great lengths to study and find out what the truth was, and [he] came back to the thought that 'This is nothing I am ever going to find the answer to,' and [so he would] just rely on faith. Maybe that's why he had such a great love and empathy for people, for any living thing or creature. And his love of God. He was a Christian, but he had an extended awareness and thought out those answers. He continued to think out those answers."

Cecile Rhee, then the young wife of Elvis's Memphis karate master, Khang Rhee, felt, as Barbara Leigh did, that anyone privileged to cross paths with Elvis Presley "was one of the chosen ones. That man had saintly qualities, and there was no doubt about it. I think he was a prophet. A lot of people think that belief is a little far-fetched, but I don't."

Kathy Westmoreland found herself confused and torn when her spiritually based friendship with Elvis evolved into a physical relationship later in 1970. Elvis told her that he and Priscilla were "not committed" to each other. "He said that it was an open marriage, and obviously from his end of the deal it was. I didn't really believe that on her end it was. I just didn't realize that situations like that existed. And he did have other girlfriends. I didn't really know what was going on. It was all odd." Priscilla vigorously denied, later, that she and Elvis had an open marriage in the early 1970s. "Doesn't that sound like a guy?" she commented wryly. "If he even said that." Kathy's impression was that Elvis was bored with Priscilla, realized they were incompatible, and regretted his obligation to marry her. "He kept on saying, 'I wish she would divorce me so I wouldn't have to divorce her.'"

Elvis carried on at his series of Palm Springs weekend houses as if he *were* a single man. "Palm Springs was his getaway place," offered Sandi Miller, one of the women who frequented Elvis's desert parties. The scene was reminiscent of one of his low-brow pictures. Elvis and his guys relaxed around the pool or watched old movies on television, surrounded by a coterie of young women in bikinis, who, by Sandi's description, "kept their mouths shut and didn't cause problems." One weekend in the early 1970s, Priscilla and Billy Smith's wife, Jo, drove down to the Springs, where Priscilla found a now-infamous love note to Elvis in the mailbox, signed by "Lizard Tongue." Some attributed the eventual end of the Presleys' marriage to this note, but it was merely the straw that broke the camel's back, if that. Priscilla had long since disappeared from the relationship in all but name.

"First of all," she said later, still evincing bitterness, "when you're with someone, you want to be *with* them, okay? Elvis was a part of *my* life, but he had *other* things as part of *his* life: he had his music, he had his shows, he had Vegas, he had movies, he had *his* friends. Nothing really changed for *me*. You know, I was not fulfilled. I had my daughter. He didn't want me to work; he didn't want me to be in the business. I could dance–I danced. But now I started to create my own life. While he was gone, I was creating friends, I was creating my own life–never having had that before. Really. It had all been *him*, centered around *him*."

Priscilla, groomed from babyhood to be the center of attention, had grown tired of standing in someone else's shadow. Her resentment flared at Graceland that Christmas of 1970. Billy Stanley would later write that she criticized virtually everything Elvis did. The tension in the house erupted into an argument between Elvis, Vernon, and Priscilla concerning the entourage. It was so heated that Elvis, who had not ventured out alone for years, stormed out of Graceland and disappeared for several days. He surfaced in Washington, D.C., for his legendary face-to-face meeting at the White House with President Richard Nixon. The singer, who had left Graceland with no money, telephoned Jerry Schilling, who was in L.A., and asked Jerry to fly to D.C. with him, using assumed names. Elvis, who had a great respect for law enforcement and antipathy for substance abuse, wanted to meet with the president to discuss how he could help keep teenagers off drugs. He wrote a letter to Nixon on the plane to that effect and showed up unannounced at the White House on December 21. Elvis wore his traveling costume, a black jumpsuit and a theatrical black cape, to the Oval Office, and accepted a stunned Richard Nixon's official Narcotics Bureau badge while high on the prescription medication to which he was becoming increasingly dependent. While he was in Washington on his lost weekend, he stayed in a hotel with Joyce Bova, who was also with him in Memphis the following March, when he feared he was going blind and underwent eye surgery for glaucoma.

Elvis invited Joyce to spend New Year's Eve with him at Graceland, and though she did not, his request to have someone other than Priscilla with him to see in the year 1971 foretold the turbulence that was to come. Priscilla was by Elvis's side at Graceland in early January, as he personally wrote a short acceptance speech for an award that held great meaning to him: He was named one of Ten Outstanding Young Americans by the Tennessee Jaycees. Priscilla attended the ceremony with Elvis in Memphis on January 9, at the height of her Natalie Wood–style glamour. She wore dangling hoop earrings, long, sweeping chestnut hair, a romantic choker, a ring on nearly every finger, and a low-cut white minidress. Several sets of false lashes had been removed from her makeup routine, leaving Priscilla with a more natural, though still dramatic, dark beauty; her frosted lips were pursed, in a picture taken at the event, in a sexy moue. At nearly twenty-six, she had never looked more exquisite. Elvis had adapted to 1970s fashion equally wholeheartedly; he now wore oversize tinted aviator glasses and longish hair, and he favored the more wretched excesses of the decade, such as fur-trimmed bell-bottoms, his outfit of choice for Sonny West's wedding a few months before.

Early in 1971, Priscilla and Elvis discussed the prospect of Priscilla taking private karate lessons from Elvis's great friend Ed Parker. Elvis saw karate as a diversion for Priscilla, one that would also give her a way to protect herself; Priscilla viewed karate, in Ed's recollection and her own, as a means of maintaining some connection to Elvis, for all they really had at this point was Lisa. "It was Elvis's idea," recalled Joe, of the suggestion that would topple Elvis and Priscilla's marriage. "Because he was so into karate and thought this would keep her occupied while he was out of town. That's how it all started. Very innocently."

Priscilla saw Ed Parker three times a week for private lessons in Los Angeles that January and February. "It gave us something to talk about," Priscilla recalled. "It gave us something to *do*. It gave us a *bond*." It was a tenuous link at most. Priscilla and Elvis were essentially living in separate houses by March, as she put the finishing touches on the Monovale mansion and Elvis stayed at Hillcrest, a few blocks away, when he was not in Vegas or on the road touring. That spring, following his eye surgery, he told Joyce that he and Priscilla were separated, "that their marriage was over. That they were going to get a divorce and he wanted me to think about moving to Graceland." It was much the same story he had told Kathy Westmoreland. Who knew whether Elvis was sincere or if it was a convenient line to offer a mistress? Yet Elvis's romance with Joyce, like his relationship with Kathy, had more to do with companionship than sex. When he was with Joyce, he often showed more interest in his metaphysical books than in making love. "At the beginning it was romantic— [but then] it wears off," Barbara Leigh agreed. "And then you become kindred spirits together, and the thing we had was our spiritualism. That's what we shared."

Jamie Lindberg, the boy Priscilla Beaulieu loved and left for Elvis Presley that fateful spring she was seventeen, wondered, more than once, what might have been.

He went to college after Priscilla left Germany and then to Vietnam where, like Priscilla's real father, Jimmy, Jamie became a pilot. He married in the spring of 1971 and honeymooned in Las Vegas. On his honeymoon night, Jamie took his bride to Caesar's Palace to watch Tom Jones perform. Sitting directly behind him were Priscilla and Elvis Presley. "And I about died. I was really in love with the gal that I'd married, I was just back from Vietnam, so screwed up you wouldn't believe it, and I thought, isn't that ironic?" Jamie tried to make contact with Priscilla that night, "but the little guards wouldn't let me back, and I thought, So who needs that humiliation, anyway?" His bride, he recalled, was also "hyperjealous."

Priscilla was still intent, that spring, on learning karate and had proved as dedicated and athletic at the sport as she was at dance, or whatever her focus in life was. She enrolled in Khang Rhee's Tae Kwon Do classes in Memphis in June, so she could keep up her training whenever she and Elvis were at Grace-land. Her nickname, at Rhee's karate studio, was Tigress. (Elvis was Master Tiger.) When Elvis performed at the Sahara Tahoe that July, Priscilla and Lisa flew back to L.A., where Priscilla resumed her private lessons with Ed.

That summer Priscilla and Joan and a karate instructor named Bob Wall drove to Orange County, south of L.A., to watch a martial arts tournament. Part of Priscilla's homework in karate was to study other practitioners' techniques; she combined the exercise with her photography hobby, taking pictures of the better fighters so that Elvis could study their moves. By what appeared to be happenstance, Mike Stone, the aggressively macho karate expert who had captured her fancy at the Hawaiian tournament three years earlier, was in the audience, seated near Priscilla and her group. Mike had since grown his dark hair into an Afro; with his swarthy Hawaiian complexion, he appeared almost black. His wild, unkempt look held Priscilla in thrall. She spotted him instantly and, according to Mike, began devising a plan to entrap him. Chuck Norris, then in his pre–movie star days as a karate legend, introduced Priscilla to Mike in passing. When two of the fighters lunged in their direction during the tournament, Priscilla leaned back in her chair, hoping Mike would catch her. Instead, he stepped out of the way, and she fell flat on the ground. His coolness merely stoked Priscilla's interest. "Mike wasn't the kind of guy who would come up to you and just goo-goo ga-ga. He stayed indifferent, he kept his distance, almost to the point where you had to go to *him*. He wouldn't come to me. . . . Most guys were all over me, and he [wasn't]. He was very reserved and very noncommittal even in talking to me. He'd look, and then he'd look away, and it was almost like, 'This is interesting. I'm gonna talk to this guy.' "

Soon afterward, Ed Parker left town for summer vacation in Hawaii, and sent Priscilla to study with Tom Kelly, who managed the Parker karate school in Santa Monica. A few weeks later, the first of August, she returned to watch another karate tournament, the Long Beach International, this time in the company of Lamar Fike's wife, Nora, and Jerry Schilling. Priscilla would later claim her attendance at the tournament was part of her continuing karate instruction, or that she was there to photograph the match for Elvis, but her presence appeared to be a continuation of her familiar, calculated modus operandi, once she had focused on a goal—which in this case seemed to be Mike Stone. Mike was there as a spectator, and Chuck Norris again introduced him to Priscilla, then sat between them to watch the tournament. Priscilla flirted over Chuck's shoulder with Mike, who was still standoffish, thus intensifying her pursuit. After the tournament she saw Mike in conversation with a mutual friend, singer Dick Dale, and seized the opportunity to talk to him. By the end of the conversation, Priscilla had learned that Mike ran a karate school in Westminster, near Huntington Beach, and she suggested she stop by to watch the classes. "I said it was way too far from Huntington Beach to Beverly Hills," recalled Mike.

Within forty-eight hours, Priscilla, who had never driven on a freeway before and was terrified, recruited Nora Fike to drive her the hour or so to Mike's studio. "It didn't take much time to understand that she was interested," said Mike. "Because . . . it's a helluva drive. Normally nobody drives that kind of distance to watch somebody teach a class. And she wasn't that anxious to leave. We went next door to get a pizza. She still wasn't that anxious to leave. And then she came down several more times. And she wasn't that anxious to leave." Mike, who was married with a four-year-old daughter and a second baby due that month, seemed perplexed by Priscilla's aggressive attention and invited her to his house after one of the classes to meet his wife, Fran. Priscilla accepted and spent the evening chatting with Fran Stone—calculating, it was said later, how to lure her husband. Priscilla and Mike's friendship quickly shifted into dating, with Priscilla the seductress, according to Mike. "Things just kind of naturally take a course. For example, if she comes down and you say, 'Well, what do you want to do afterward?' That becomes a date. And then other things would come up—martial arts events. And then one thing just leads to another. And when these other things came up, I guess they were considered dating."

Priscilla would later describe Mike Stone as "just the right person at the right time. I mean, it wasn't like I was out looking for anyone." Bob Wall, a black belt who was close to Mike, Chuck Norris, and the others in their karate circle, considered Mike one of the few men who would have dared to have an affair with Elvis Presley's wife. Wall described Mike as "a masculine, manly kind of guy. Funny, good-looking, somebody that– How many people wouldn't be afraid of Elvis? Afraid of his image, afraid of his money, his ability to have them knocked off or something. A lot of things the average guy wouldn't be interested in taking on."

That was precisely the quality that attracted Priscilla, and had since she first laid eyes on him, for Mike Stone fulfilled the sexual power that Elvis only symbolized. "He was like an *animal* to me," she later explained, giggling. "I mean he was– I don't know. He was different. There was something about him that was very powerful. I mean he had a lot of strength; he was so good at karate, it was unbelievable." She was sexually excited by the fact that "he was the best at what he did; everyone raved about Mike Stone."

"I think it was partly the sexual part," Mike analyzed several years later. "That Elvis was maybe too busy with other things and didn't spend enough time with her, taking care of business. And a whole lot of other things that accumulated over the years. She was always very strongly wanting to be her own person, and that was a very driving thing for her at that time. To get out and experience things."

Mike's wife, Fran, gave birth to their second daughter, Lori, on August 4, as Priscilla and Mike were inching closer to consummating their new flirtation. Fran Stone would later write a magazine article called "How Priscilla Presley Stole My Husband," though Priscilla denied that she was a factor in the Stones' eventual divorce. "I didn't break up their marriage. He had already told me that there [were] problems in their marriage."

Mike would later say that his marriage to Fran was "on the rocks" when he met Priscilla, but Bob Wall, who was close to both the Stones and Priscilla, admitted that "it was a big shock to Fran, because she loved Mike deeply. She'd honor that he was vulnerable to another woman, and I think there was a lot of Mike being caught up in, 'This is Elvis's wife. This is Priscilla Presley; she's been with the King.' I think there was a lot of that in him initially." Priscilla, who could seem so demure, had–lest one forget–another side. Bob Wall described her as a "fireball" at karate, "very competitive." By 1996, more than twenty years and two divorces later, Fran would not discuss the triangle composed of herself, Priscilla, and Mike, saying she didn't want to "dredge up dirt."

Priscilla, beginning that summer, conducted her life in secrecy, a recurring pattern for her. Elvis, who was excited by the fight photos she took for him, invited Mike Stone and Chuck Norris up to the house in Beverly Hills a few times to talk about karate, unaware that he was entertaining his wife's paramour. He also invited Mike and Chuck to Las Vegas to watch him perform. Chuck took his wife Diane, and Mike went alone. Priscilla, who was in Vegas that night, wandered backstage, recalled Myrna Smith, and told the Sweet Inspirations about the "fine" and "foxy" guy in the audience, "so we were all kind of looking from the stage."

"I was in the Sweet Inspirations' dressing room," said Kathy Westmoreland. "Priscilla had come to see the show and brought Mike Stone with her. One of the girls mentioned how good-looking he was and Priscilla turned around and said, 'Hands off! That's mine!' I was shocked and we were all, 'Uh-oh! Something is going on.' "

Elvis had no idea that "something" was in progress. During the show, he introduced Chuck Norris and Mike Stone to the audience, praising their karate skills and describing Mike as one of his best friends. "If Elvis had had a drinking buddy," offered Myrna Smith, "that is how warmly he introduced him." Myrna and Kathy and the rest of the backup singers, who understood exactly what signals Priscilla had been sending to them concerning Mike Stone, could not believe what they were hearing.

The evening grew more curious after the show, when Elvis invited Chuck Norris and Mike Stone to join him and Priscilla and the Presley entourage in his dressing room. Elvis, his aides would recall, suggested to Priscilla that she study karate with Mike, since he was the best. Priscilla would later attribute her drives to Westminster to see Mike to Elvis's recommendation.

She was, in fact, on a dangerous, albeit carefully plotted, course. Tom Kelly, the ex-marine who was teaching her karate in place of Ed Parker, maintained a strict policy forbidding anyone but black belts to wear a black uniform to class, a rule Priscilla understood and had abided by. At the end of August, however, after she had been training with Tom for a month and a half, "she came in one morning wearing a black uniform," he remembered. "I told her it was our policy that the only people who wore black were the instructors. She said she wasn't going to wear white, and I said I was sorry, that was the rule." Priscilla, Tom recalled, "said, 'I can get any teacher,' and she quit." Ed Parker's belief, once Priscilla's affair with Mike Stone became known, was that she deliberately flouted the school's policy so she would be thrown out, giving her an excuse to switch to Chuck Norris's karate school, which she did that September. Chuck's studio was in Sherman Oaks, a quick ten minutes from Priscilla's house in Beverly Hills; Mike Stone often stopped by the school to train or to go out for pizza after class with Chuck and his partner, Bob Wall.

Once she had enrolled in Chuck's classes, Priscilla's secret dalliance with Mike Stone quickly grew more heated. They enlisted the aid of both Chuck

Norris and Joan Esposito, who was having her own marital difficulties with Joe, to go on a "double date" with them to a tropical restaurant called the Islander. "At that point in time," said Joan, "Chuck was married, I was married, Mike was married, Priscilla was married, and we would go places together before the tourneys and like that . . . like kids date together." Priscilla slipped out easily when Elvis was out of town; when he was in L.A., she pretended to go to a dance class, or said she was training at Chuck's karate school. "We never asked and were never told," explained Bob Wall of his part in the deception. "From observation, Elvis didn't spend a lot of time with her. And she was, like, lonely. She had the big house, the cars, the planes, the fame, but . . ."

Mike and Priscilla played their cat-and-mouse games for several months before the relationship turned seriously sexual. Priscilla, who was paranoid about being recognized, planned an outing to Catalina Island for their first encounter, hoping she would be anonymous there. She and Mike arranged to meet at the port in San Pedro, between Beverly Hills and Westminster, to catch the ferry for the island. "And she had to make that drive down there by herself," said Mike. "It was the first trip she ever made by herself on the freeway, and she was just absolutely horrified." Her effort illustrated the ferocity of Priscilla's sex drive. She boarded the boat shrouded in scarves and sunglasses and took a seat a few rows apart from Mike, only to have a few karate fans recognize *him* rather than her, to her obvious disappointment. Priscilla and Mike made out on the beach in Catalina during the day and rented a motel room that night back in Bel Air, where they had sex for the first time. Mike, who was briefly insecure about making love to Elvis Presley's wife, was shocked to learn, once they were in bed, that Priscilla had not had intercourse with Elvis in a year.

Priscilla's affair with Mike over the coming months was reminiscent of her high school romance with Tommy Stewart, for it was intense, sexual, and carried out in secrecy. The distinction, with Mike, was that *Elvis* was the father figure from whom Priscilla was disguising her romance. She and Mike carried on like teenage lovers, meeting to make love on the beach, in cars, at drive-ins. The karate wives—Diane Norris and Bob Wall's spouse—who knew about the affair and were friends of Fran Stone's, resented Priscilla and regarded her as a "home wrecker." "They were pretty sore at Priscilla," said Bob, "for her breaking up [Mike's] marriage."

Priscilla saw herself as a survivor, a theme that had, and would continue to, run through her life. Elvis's lifestyle, to her, "was not reality; it was not the real world. It was kind of—you get stuck in an aberration." She wanted out, to be what she considered normal again, and she demonstrated a certain ruthlessness—another trait that would define Priscilla—to attain that goal. Late in 1971, Priscilla and Mike took a small beach apartment in Belmont Shores, a seaside community near his karate studio, Golden West. Neither of their spouses knew of Priscilla and Mike's love nest, as it would come to be called. With Elvis in Vegas or touring, Priscilla had nothing but time, and she passed it with Mike, decorating their hideaway as she perceived her new boyfriend—in "somewhat primitive Hawaiian," by his description. She was entranced by his native customs and called him Mickey, short for Mikiala, Mike's given Hawaiian name. Priscilla, Mike recalled, was thrilled by the simplest pleasures—going to a drive-in movie or taking her shoes off, Hawaiian style, before entering their apartment. "She was just tickled to death. To her it was a big growing situation [an opportunity for personal growth], to get out and do these things." Priscilla was like an eighteen-year-old who had just left her parents' home and gotten her first apartment, her first adult boyfriend, and her first whiff of freedom—which, in truth, she had. The person she really was, so long veiled beneath the submissive personality she had affected in her effort to marry Elvis, began to reemerge. "I found Priscilla," she later said. She had her own life again. "I'm getting out and realizing that I've been missing a little bit here. I've lived in a bubble, I've been sheltered, I've been protected, and to a fault. I never really exerted any of my own talents or personalities. [Now] I was creating a life for myself. And [Elvis's] world now became more bizarre to me, because he only lived within his world. You did what he wanted to do. No one else had a life. You lived and breathed him."

Priscilla had also rediscovered her dormant sexuality. The key to her relationship with Mike—the key to Priscilla, really—was, in a word, sex. As Rona Barrett, who had heard through the Hollywood grapevine about Elvis's aversion to sex with a mother, remarked, "That was the frustration, I believe, with Priscilla, and that's how she ended up with Mike Stone. She was a young woman in search of her own sexual need and identity, and she was with the man considered the sexiest man alive, the biggest star in the world, and he couldn't perform." Priscilla once told a reporter that she and Elvis made love less than fifty times in their marriage. That estimate was probably high. A different sort of woman, with a less powerful sex drive and a shared understanding of Elvis's spiritual odyssey, might have been contented as his wife, but that woman was not Priscilla Presley. Priscilla was, and always had been, about *sex*. That was what had drawn her to the Elvis Presley persona in the first place. Her sexuality had shaped her self-image as a child beauty contestant, as the sixth-grade carnival queen, and as the fourteen-year-old girlfriend of a movie star/rock star. She could not survive without sex; and survival was at the core of Priscilla's being.

Priscilla and Mike began plotting how they could be together permanently, and—more trickily—how to broach the subject with Elvis-slash-Dad, for the parallels to a daughter leaving home were inescapable. "Even during the earliest stages that we were seeing each other regularly, there [were] always discussions between us—what was our next step?" recalled Mike. "And I believe at one point that we were both seriously in love with each other . . . we often talked about the consequences of approaching Elvis with this situation, knowing his temper and his mentality about something like this."

As they had during Priscilla's affair with the dancer several years earlier, the entourage surrounding Elvis became suspicious of her relationship with Mike Stone by the latter part of 1971. One of the first to question it was Judy West, Sonny West's new wife. Elvis and Priscilla had moved into the completed Monovale house, and the Wests, in true Elvis communal style, had their own upstairs bedroom. "Apparently Mike picked Priscilla up one time at the house, and Judy West could see the driveway from where they were living, and [she saw] Mike picking Priscilla up really late at night," said Joe Esposito, whose family was by then living in a house nearby that was a gift from Elvis. "So she was telling Sonny, 'There's something going on.' So [Sonny] and Red would talk." Sonny saw the affair for himself, according to a female martial artist who had acquired the nickname "Karate Pat" from Elvis. Elvis, recalled Pat, forgot his spiritual books during one of his engagements in Las Vegas and sent Sonny back for them. "And Sonny showed up there at the house, 122 Monovale, and Priscilla and Mike were coming out of the house. At the time, Elvis had an Excalibur, and they were getting in the car just as Sonny was pulling up in the driveway." Priscilla, according to Pat, said, " 'Sonny, don't tell Elvis,' and he was like, 'Oh, man, why do you put me in this position?' and he said to Mike, 'Man, if Elvis knew you were driving this car, he'd have you shot.' " Joe Esposito—whose wife, Joan, was going on double dates with Priscilla and Mike Stone—was so convinced that the Priscilla he thought he knew would never have an affair, he bet Red West a hundred dollars that Sonny was wrong about Mike Stone—despite his awareness of Priscilla's dancer-lover back in 1968. "I said, 'No, Priscilla would never do that. Impossible.' "

There were rumors that Lisa told one of the maids she saw Mommy kissing Mickey and that the maid then circulated the story. Columnist Rona Barrett claimed that Hollywood insiders knew about Priscilla's affair with Mike Stone before Elvis did: "We knew something was going on. Everybody knew how unhappy she was." Mike later admitted that he and Priscilla became "more careless about being seen in public," arriving separately at karate tournaments but then sitting together. "[The affair] became common knowledge in the martial arts world."

Ed Hookstratten, Elvis's Los Angeles lawyer, took it upon himself, sometime around that late fall, to use his private investigator, John O'Grady, to confirm or put to rest the rumors about Priscilla and Mike. Elvis's friends, he said, "had gotten rather rambunctious, and I wanted to find out who the instigators were ... and we came up with a lot of interesting things." The only one Hookstratten would name, later, was Priscilla's affair with Mike Stone. Elvis was not in L.A. when Ed confirmed Priscilla's infidelity, so he called Joe, who was with the singer, to break the news. "I wanted Joe to get him alone and be with him. So someone was with him when he was told this, rather than for me to cold-call him."

Joe was aghast. "I couldn't believe it. I was completely in shock that this little girl I'd known all these years— I was devastated." It was, perhaps, a lesson in Priscilla's ability to deceive, despite her aura of innocence; her secret affair with Mike also demonstrated the strength of her will and her sexuality—factors that lent credence to Currie's claims in his dispute with Priscilla over whether or not they had intercourse before he took her to meet Elvis. Despite proof positive that Priscilla had had sex with Mike Stone, Joe remained incredulous. "I warned Elvis, but I wanted to deny it," he said. Elvis, according to Joe, "couldn't believe it ... that that was going on. Completely wanted to deny it."

There followed the Christmas of Elvis and Priscilla Presley's discontent. If Elvis had any doubt as to Priscilla's dissatisfaction with her life, her behavior that December at Graceland clarified it. Two of the Stanley brothers remembered her being as "cold as ice." Elvis's Christmas gift to her was a car. Priscilla refused to accept it, recalled David and Billy Stanley, so Elvis threw ten one-thousand-dollar bills at her instead. On New Year's Eve, she brazenly handed Becky Yancey a manila envelope, told her it contained a picture of herself for Mike Stone, asked Becky to mail it, and told her how "manly" Mike was and how *he* had time for her. The envelope was addressed to "Mike Young" from "Beau," short for "Beaulieu," Mike Stone's nickname for Priscilla. Elvis celebrated the New Year dressed, portentously, all in black; Priscilla wore white boots and made a toast to herself, hailing 1972 as "the year little Priscilla finally came out!" This was, figuratively, true, for Priscilla—the *real* Priscilla—had been submerged since 1959.

A declaration signed by Elvis in his later divorce papers attested that he knew about Mike Stone by December and that Priscilla informed him, that Christmas holiday, that she wanted her freedom; Becky Yancey confirmed this in a book she wrote in 1977. The divorce declaration also stated that Priscilla effectively left Elvis a few days after her New Year's "coming-out" toast, just before his thirty-seventh birthday on January 8, when she took Lisa and flew out of Memphis. Willie Jane Nichols, who was in Memphis and around Elvis at the time, was of the same opinion. "She got mad and took that big dog and Lisa and left—before his birthday came around. I won't say what Elvis said when she left. He couldn't find her and Lisa for months. We heard it from Grandma [Presley]." Willie, who knew both Elvis and Priscilla well and was fairly objective where both were concerned, had mixed feelings about Priscilla's actions. On the one hand, she respected Priscilla for having "had the nerve to leave him—the guts. It boggles the average girl's mind." She also felt Priscilla was in some ways justified in walking out on Elvis, for Willie believed "she was mistreated. The guys were cruel to her. I don't know how she survived. I almost admired her when she left." On the other hand, reflected Gladys's friend, "she made her own bed. To come over all this way to live with him." Willie, who had spent many hours talking with Priscilla through the years, perceived that she had no choice. "I wasn't amazed at her taking off. Really I wasn't. I wondered how long she could take it, even though her love was deep for Elvis. It wasn't she didn't love Elvis. . . . She was in a nervous breakdown."

Elvis spent his birthday, January 8, at Graceland with Joyce Bova, while Priscilla rejoined Mike Stone at their tiny apartment in Belmont Shores. Fran Stone would name February 17 as the date of her official separation from her husband. Ed Parker later wrote of a conversation he had with Elvis around this time, when Elvis told him Priscilla was leaving him: "He poured out his soul that night, and I saw him cry for the first time."

Priscilla, Mike would later recount, decided in February that she wanted a divorce and determined to tell Elvis about her affair. "When you are in love you're not afraid to do things," Mike said, "because you think love conquers everything. So you just do what your heart tells you. And we decided we wanted to spend some time together and not hide anymore. . . . She had wanted—and I give her credit for how she thought about this situation—she wanted to tell Elvis personally what she was doing and didn't want it to come from other people. So she just decided to confront him with it herself at this stage." If this was true, she was several months too late, for Elvis had already suffered the embarrassment of hearing about her affair from Joe via Ed Hookstratten, and it was common knowledge in show business and karate circles.

There is still some confusion surrounding what exactly transpired during Priscilla's infamous divorce confrontation with Elvis, which took place when she flew to Las Vegas for his closing night on February 23. Mike's impression, and Joan Esposito's, was that Priscilla planned beforehand to tell Elvis during this trip that she was in love with Mike. Yet it was *Elvis* who summoned Priscilla, as she was having dinner in the Hilton, to come up to his dressing room between shows. When she arrived, *she* said, Elvis forced himself on her sexually, saying, "This is how a real man makes love to his woman." Priscilla claimed later it was *then* that she made the decision to leave Elvis and that she waited until the next day, as she was preparing to return to Los Angeles, to tell him, never mentioning Mike Stone. Elvis, according to her description, was surprised and anguished.

Elvis told a different story in his divorce declaration several months later.

He said that it was he who confronted Priscilla about Mike Stone that night in Vegas and that she was surprised he knew about the affair. This was very plausible, for Elvis had already heard about Mike from Joe, and Priscilla had told Elvis at Christmastime that she wanted out of the marriage. Priscilla's claim that Elvis was "surprised" to hear that she was leaving him just did not make sense. Jerry Schilling, who later worked on the miniseries based on Priscilla's autobiography, which included the rape scene in Elvis's dressing room, admitted that it "didn't sound like Elvis" to force himself on Priscilla sexually. Nor did Priscilla tell Joan, who was her best friend and who flew back to L.A. with her the next day, that Elvis had raped her. It would have been illogical for Elvis, without any discussion of Mike or divorce, and without provocation, to call Priscilla to his dressing room and force her to make love to him. "I can see," offered Joan, "that a man and his ego might think, 'Okay, I'll get her back one way or another,' that it will all turn around"—*if,* as Elvis depicted it, he confronted Priscilla about Mike. Moreover, Joan recalled Priscilla telling her that she had mentioned Mike's name to Elvis, and Myrna Smith of the Sweet Inspirations remembered that Elvis was extremely agitated before his second show. Ed Parker, who was at the Hilton the night after Priscilla checked out, said Elvis told him she had left him for another man. This was all consistent with the recollections of the entourage, who recalled Elvis gathering them about, after his second show, and announcing that Priscilla was seeing someone else. Kathy Westmoreland also spoke to Elvis shortly after Priscilla flew back to L.A. Elvis told Kathy he had confronted Priscilla about Mike Stone and that Priscilla had told him she wanted a divorce.

Elvis, according to Joe's characterization, was not heartbroken that night, as Priscilla portrayed him. "He was pissed off that someone would do something like this to him. He was really mad. Very upset." Everyone recalled that Elvis was depressed, but more than anything else, he felt betrayed—not just by Priscilla but also by Mike Stone, whom he had considered a friend and who excelled at the sport with which Elvis was obsessed. "I am a cocky fighter," Mike said later. "I'm extremely confident. I humiliate my opponents. Nobody's gonna beat me. And I think Elvis resented the flamboyant way I fought. I think he liked it. That somebody could do karate the way he sang on stage." That Priscilla would leave him for a karate champion was, in Mike's phrase, "another little twist of the knife, so to speak." Ed Parker, Elvis's friend and karate master, claimed that Elvis's ego was shattered by the fact that his wife would leave him—Elvis Presley—for another man. What, he wondered, would the public think of him, the most famous sex symbol in the world? Sheila Ryan Caan, who discussed the situation with Elvis more than once when they dated several years later, said he still felt betrayed by Priscilla *and* Mike, "because Mike was his friend and he thought that was a big disappoint-

The famous photo of Priscilla waving good-bye to Elvis as he left Germany on
March 2, 1960.

Photograph by Horst Schlesiger. Courtesy of Lilo Schlesiger.

Photograph from the German magazine *Film Journal.* Currie is shown taking Elvis and Priscilla to the base on Elvis's last day in Germany, clearly disputing Priscilla's claim that Currie was not with them because Elvis had barred him. *Photograph by Horst Schlesiger. Courtesy of Lilo Schlesiger.*

Peter Von Wechmar, the German aristocrat and Elvis impersonator, whom Priscilla dated when Elvis left Germany. *Photograph copyright © 1997 by Currie Grant. Used by permission.*

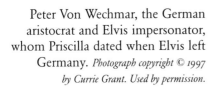

The picture of Priscilla, her mother, Ann, and Priscilla's half-siblings Jeff and Michelle Beaulieu, taken by Gene Wagner for Priscilla's grandmother when he was in Germany, Easter 1960. *Collection of Currie Grant. Photograph courtesy of Gene Wagner.*

Sophomore Priscilla at the Wiesbaden senior prom with boyfriend Ron Tapp. *Photograph courtesy of Ron and Starr Tapp.*

Currie's assistant sets up a shot of Priscilla outside her German military housing for the April 1961 photo shoot Elvis requested a year after they met. *Photograph copyright © 1997 by Currie Grant. Used by permission.*

Priscilla posing for Currie Grant outside her house in Wiesbaden, 1961. *Photograph copyright © 1997 by Currie Grant. Used by permission.*

A smiling Priscilla with Currie at the photo shoot in Germany in April 1961, the year after she claims he was banished by her parents and Elvis because he tried to rape her.

Photograph copyright © 1997 by Currie Grant. Used by permission.

Mother and daughter, Ann and Priscilla Beaulieu, beam at Currie for pictures to be given to Elvis, Wiesbaden, 1961.

Photograph copyright © 1997 by Currie Grant. Used by permission.

One of the shots Currie took for Elvis. Priscilla gave a copy to her football star boyfriend, Ron Tapp, along with pictures of herself in baby doll pajamas.

Photograph copyright © 1997 by Currie Grant. Used by permission.

A pensive Priscilla at
fifteen, posing for Elvis.
*Photograph copyright © 1997 by
Currie Grant. Used by permission.*

Priscilla at a senior dance
with Jamie Lindberg,
the boy she didn't want
to leave in Germany.
Photograph courtesy of Jamie Lindberg.

Senior Year: Priscilla in the 1963 H.H. Arnold yearbook. The caption refers to her boyfriend, Jamie Lindberg, whom her parents pushed her to reject in favor of Elvis. *Photograph courtesy of Rick Bresnan.*

"Dear John, err, aaa, Jamie. . . . . . ."

Dee Stanley Presley, with sons Billy, Ricky, and David, at the orphanage before taking them to Graceland, their new home, in 1960. Priscilla and Elvis would become Rick's surrogate sister and brother.

Photograph courtesy of Rick Stanley.

SENIOR SUPERLATIVES

Priscilla as "Best Looking Senior" in the class she left behind to live with Elvis.
Photograph courtesy of H. H. Arnold High School.

Elvis and his lost love Debra Paget on the set of *Love Me Tender* in 1956.
Priscilla would later re-create this image of Paget when she met Elvis.

Photograph by Twentieth Century Fox. Photograph courtesy of Debra Paget.

ment. And I think that was what was most hurtful. And it was going on behind his back for a time before he found out about it. That's just humiliating. And unnecessary."

There was an epic, tragic quality to the unraveling of the Presley marriage, which may explain why it fascinates, still. The Elvis-Priscilla-Mike triangle was, in reality, a variation on the legend of Camelot. Elvis, who was known as the King, was a modern King Arthur; Priscilla was his Guinevere. Mike Stone was the martial arts equivalent of Sir Lancelot, the premier knight at the Round Table. Elvis admired Mike Stone, even as King Arthur respected Lancelot; Elvis urged Priscilla to study karate with Mike, much as Arthur pressured Guinevere to befriend Lancelot. Once together, Priscilla and Mike, like Lancelot and Guinevere, became sexually addicted to each other in a way that Elvis and Priscilla, like King Arthur and Guinevere, were not. The result was the betrayal of the two kings' and the undoing of both mythic kingdoms.

Priscilla later called her decision to leave Elvis the most difficult of her life, but "it was a decision that I had to make. I *had* to take Lisa, and leave, unless he was going to change." Sheila Ryan Caan would later disagree: "I don't think it was a hard thing to *leave* him. I think it was a hard thing to *stay* with him." Sheila's would be the majority opinion, for Priscilla would be perceived, forever after, as the woman who had abandoned Elvis Presley, despite the comments of such as Willie Jane, who stated, after the fact, that Priscilla tried "desperately" to make the marriage work. Priscilla, the consummate achiever of goals, felt she had done everything. "Believe me. I gave it every shot possible. I just wouldn't walk off. [Marriage] has to be good for both of you; it can't be good for one and not the other. You both have to be happy and you both have to work on it. That's a relationship." By her own definition, Priscilla and Elvis had not had a real relationship in years, if ever.

Yet to the outside world, comparing Elvis Presley—one of the most famous, charismatic, gifted, and wealthy men in the world—to Mike Stone, a crudely masculine karate teacher who earned under $25,000 a year, Priscilla's decision seemed incomprehensible. Even Mike was mystified. "I would ask Priscilla, 'Aren't you giving up a *lot?*'" Elvis's fans, and to some degree Mike, had only seen the myth; they were unaware of Priscilla's reality, as a person repressed first by her childhood and then by her life with Elvis, a life that was imposed upon her by her parents and by her own stubborn adherence to a faded dream. Priscilla was declaring her independence, both from her parents' edict and her surrogate parent, Elvis. Leaving Elvis Presley's mansion and moving into a cramped beachfront apartment with a karate teacher was comparable to the willful daughter of a rich and controlling father running off with a poor poet. Priscilla was not thinking about money, only her freedom, something she had not had since she was fourteen years old. She had a phenomenal-some would see it as cold—ability to just walk away, another vestige of her military past, where every three years the Beaulieus would pack up and move to another state, a new neighborhood, another set of friends, without a backward glance.

Priscilla, by leaving Elvis, had, in effect, grown up and left home, for Elvis Presley had been, from the first, her replacement for Jimmy Wagner, the fantasy father she had recently discovered and had never known, her protector and guardian and savior from an unhappy girlhood. She revealed as much in an interview with *McCall's* magazine in 1979: "He was not only a lover but a father to me, and as long as I stayed with him I could never be anything but his little girl."

Mike Stone, when asked if he believed Priscilla was ever in love with Elvis, responded in an illuminating way: "Well, I can't speak for her, but I think any girl at fourteen may not necessarily know her mind that well. And being the man that he was, as far as the image, I can understand that she was infatuated with that. I'm not saying she wasn't in love with him; I'm sure at some stage of the relationship she was. And probably still is, as far as certain things about him."

That was the mystery of Elvis and Priscilla's enduring love, for it was just that—love, not a love *affair*. Theirs was the timeless love of a father and daughter, not that of a husband and wife.

26

THE EX-MRS. PRESLEY

The perfect home Priscilla had spent a year decorating for herself, Lisa, and Elvis scarcely saw the three of them in it at the same time.

Priscilla, with Lisa beside her, drove up to the apartment she and Mike rented in Belmont Shores within a few days of her final confrontation with Elvis, behind the wheel of a station wagon loaded with a few belongings. She and Mike found a slightly larger two-bedroom shortly afterward in Marina del Rey, an apartment-dominated community in west Los Angeles. She put her maiden name, Priscilla Beaulieu, on the front door and streaked her hair blond, evidence of what Mike called her rebirth.

Elvis, once past his initial anger over Priscilla's betrayal, slipped into a frightening decline. The maids at Graceland noticed that he lay around much of the time, exhibiting "a lot of depressed feelings and loneliness," as Nancy Rooks stated it. "There was a lot of talk about his mother. On Mother's Day he would cry. He wanted her picture by his bed." The catalyst was Priscilla's departure: "He thought they should always be together." Elvis and Red West wrote, and Elvis recorded, the song "Separate Ways" that year, a transparently autobiographical account of his breakup with Priscilla. Ricky Stanley, who was a teenager by then and traveled with Elvis as a personal valet, witnessed the devastation firsthand. "I was with him every moment of that divorce. I mean, I slept [on] a cot in the bedroom." The breakup "wiped him out," said Ricky. "Mainly at first, he was hurt by it all. And then you kinda go through different phases. He went through phases of anger, betrayal, anger, and then 'Hey, it's me.' "

For all his womanizing, Elvis cherished the institution of marriage and the *illusion*, at least, of a family. Barbara Leigh had ended her affair with him just the previous fall, because, ironically, she believed "he never would have left Priscilla." Elvis, who had such a complicated moral and spiritual code, was no less complex with respect to his marriage. "He really did say to me, 'I don't think I was the marrying kind,' " averred Kathy Westmoreland. "He felt that he shouldn't have ever married." Elvis married Priscilla, almost certainly, to honor the promise he had made to her parents when she was seventeen; once wed, he believed it was until "death do us part." The divorce left him torn. "He was worried about what was going to happen to Lisa," said Kathy. "He worried about the baby. He vacillated between 'he wants a divorce, the whole thing is a nightmare' and 'it was against the way that he was brought up—once you are married, it's forever' and knowing he felt like a failure." A common feeling, among people who knew him, was that Elvis belonged to the world, not to any one woman, which may have been the heaviest burden of his supernatural fame—and the source of his epic loneliness.

A great many of those close to Elvis regarded Priscilla's affair with Mike Stone and her decision to divorce Elvis as the trigger for the physical deterioration that led to his death at age forty-two in 1977, five years later. "She left Elvis and left him on this terrible spin that I think was the beginning of the end with him," declared Barbara Leigh, who maintained contact with Elvis. The star's loyal fans, who were not fond of Priscilla anyway, did not desert him or think less of him after she rejected him for another man, as Elvis feared they might; rather, the breakup calcified their disdain for Priscilla, for they held her personally responsible for their idol's physical and emotional deterioration. A number of Elvis's girlfriends, even those who had experienced his double standard and idiosyncrasies, shared the public's opinion that Priscilla had let Elvis down, abandoned him, failed to fulfill her end of their marriage contract. "She couldn't deal with it," Barbara Leigh said flatly. "She cheated on him. He cheated on her. Listen, when you are married to the King, come on, expect him to be faithful? I mean, she knew what he was when she married him." Even Willie Jane, who was sympathetic to Priscilla, allowed that Priscilla was aware she would never have a normal life with Elvis: "that was impossible and should have been *understood* by her." Priscilla had dated Elvis for seven years before she married him, and she had lived with him for four of those years. There were no surprises after the wedding; Elvis remained quintessentially Elvis. She should not have married him if she wasn't willing to honor that commitment, particularly since she and her parents had forced his hand. So the fans' argument went. "I don't think I would have divorced him like Priscilla did," Anita Wood confided, "because I knew him well enough to know that he wasn't going to change. And there were girls everywhere all the time. Why should that change just because he got married? I think he would have always come back to her and loved her, if she had hung in there. But I guess you do what you have to do." Barbara Leigh had little sympathy for the story Priscilla would later tell of her hellish life with Elvis: "I think she tries to paint herself as this saint, as the good one in the picture, when I know, in truth, that she broke his heart forever."

Ed Hookstratten, who handled the divorce, held Priscilla responsible as well. "After that, Elvis . . . started to slide," he said. "And after that, he slid and slid, until he finally died. [The divorce] was the turning point, and I was close to that situation. . . . I saw it with my own eyes." Sheila Ryan Caan didn't believe that Elvis lost the great love of his life so much as "he wanted to present an image to the world, and being left by his wife wasn't one of the things that he really wanted to present as his image. And I think that's what *really* killed him. I mean, obviously you don't love a woman if you sleep with every woman in your path. That's not love." Strangely, Linda Thompson, another of Elvis's girlfriends, would remember Elvis telling her how his mama had warned him to "beware of the blue-eyed woman," and both Linda and Barbara said that Elvis's mother advised him to marry a girl with brown eyes. Many of Elvis's fans saw Priscilla as the blue-eyed woman of Gladys Presley's apocalyptic prophecy. Yet Barbara Leigh would admit that Elvis "led a hard life. Living with those guys, eating that kind of food. After a while the glamour wears off and the real man comes out. Which is wonderful. I loved him, to the end, still do. But the glamour of the life wears off. And it's hard. It's a really hard life."

When Elvis and Priscilla were around Lisa, they both pretended that nothing had changed. That wasn't difficult to do, Priscilla said later, for Elvis was so often gone. Lisa, who was four when they separated, was not aware that her parents were getting a divorce. Priscilla and Elvis did have vastly different parenting styles. Priscilla was determined to teach Lisa the value of a dollar, to impose some form of discipline so she would not become spoiled; Elvis furnished her room at Graceland with a round canopy bed covered with faux fur and bought her diamond rings. Lisa, at Graceland, was akin to Eloise at the Plaza. "She would just tell us what she wanted," recalled Elvis's cook, Mary Jenkins. "One time she said, 'I want a different cake every day of the week, but don't tell Mama–she'll put me on a diet.' " Priscilla had Elvis return the jewels and furs he had bought for Lisa. "Priscilla was the stabilizing factor," said Rick Stanley. "You can count on her. She was predictable. You knew what she was gonna do. And that child needed that."

Even after Priscilla left Elvis, there was still a bond between them. Priscilla, at least, considered that "it worked out actually better, because then [Lisa and I] could pick our times to be with him. It was actually a better relationship." She told *Life,* years after he died, that to Elvis she was "like this kid he had raised." Like a father, Elvis had mixed feelings about the child he had brought up leaving home. "When I first spoke to him, he was resigned to the fact [that the divorce] was inevitable," said Kathy Westmoreland. "And then he vacillated between 'She has to have her own life and be happy' and being jealous and angry at the way that it happened."

Elvis did not view Priscilla as his romantic one and only, for George Klein, by that spring, was arranging for him to meet Cybill Shepherd, whom George knew from years earlier, when she won the Miss Teen-Age Memphis pageant. Cybill, in 1972, was twenty-three, at the height of her movie-star glamour, several years after *The Last Picture Show* and just before the release of *The Heartbreak Kid*. "She was in town," said George. "I mentioned it to Elvis, I mentioned it to Cybill, she said of course she'd like to meet him. She'd just broken up with Peter Bogdanovich, so I took her to Elvis. It was no big romance. Elvis really enjoyed her personality. She's . . . quick." She was also, according to Ricky Stanley, extremely adventurous and aggressive, sexually and otherwise. Ricky remembered Elvis's slightly startled reaction after he left Cybill's place at the Saint James on Sunset Boulevard in West Hollywood. "Let's put it this way," she said once. "I think that before I met him, he was sexually conservative, trapped in a stupid macho thing." The romance was torrid but brief. Cybill returned to Bogdanovich, and Elvis again embraced his old-fashioned southern sexual mores. "I couldn't handle the whole thing with the pills," said Cybill. "Pills to go to sleep. Pills to wake up. I think that lifestyle limits you." Elvis reconnected with Ann-Margret after one of her performances in Vegas that year. He called her late that night while she was in bed with her husband, Roger Smith, hinting that he wanted her to come to his room. Ann declined.

Priscilla and Mike further solidified their love relationship late in March when Fran Stone filed for divorce and Mike moved in with Priscilla and Lisa at their Marina del Rey apartment. By June, Fran had been awarded custody of the Stones' two small daughters, and Mike was a free man. A few weeks later Elvis was introduced to a tall, long-legged former Tennessee beauty queen named Linda Thompson—another George Klein fix-up—who would become his permanent live-in girlfriend. She was not the great beauty Priscilla was— Linda had the requisite long brown hair, but had a coarser, flashier appeal— though she was a virgin and, some believed, the most compatible of all Elvis's inamoratas. "She was really good for him," said Kathy, who spent a great deal of time around Elvis and Linda. "He laughed a lot with her. She was an intellectual and she was a poetess and enjoyed music to an extent. She had an understanding about the artistic side, and was very into metaphysical stuff. They had a good friendship." Ricky stressed that "Elvis's thing was not a sexual encounter. Elvis's thing was *companionship*, he wanted somebody around." Linda comprehended and accepted this, and put in her time.

It was Elvis who filed for divorce from Priscilla on August 18, 1972, six months after their final encounter in Las Vegas, though the instigator was clearly Priscilla. "He did not want the divorce," asserted Ed Hookstratten, who filed the petition for Elvis. "But then he agreed to it, apparently from the discussions they were having, and he agreed to do it with taste and style." Priscilla had been pressing for the divorce since February, and was about to go to Hawaii with Mike. She wanted the divorce from Elvis handled quickly–like their wedding, it could be said. Her subsequent attorney, Arthur Toll, said Elvis wanted to initiate the proceedings "to save his persona." Priscilla acquiesced to this request blindly, as she acquiesced blindly to virtually anything and everything that was presented or suggested to her in connection with the divorce, for she was naive, ignorant, and she desperately wanted out of her marriage to Elvis Presley.

She and Elvis discussed the settlement at what was to have been their dream house, on Monovale, in July, in a textbook example of the blind leading the blind. Elvis, who had no concept of money and even less interest in it, tossed out the ludicrous figure of $100,000 to Priscilla, who kept insisting she "wanted nothing." What happened next is a point of dispute between Priscilla and Ed Hookstratten, Elvis's lawyer. Hookstratten's version: "What basically happened was very simple. She had a boyfriend and she wanted a divorce, so she and Elvis worked out what they thought was fair. I was called to the house and said it was not fair, you are going to have to do more for her. And so they went back to work and the next day sent me a sheet of paper [showing their settlement figures], in which this was fair. All right?" Priscilla later claimed that Elvis told her $100,000 was "more than some people could make in a lifetime. . . . I thought I was going to be taken care of." Bob Wall, who became close to Priscilla during her romance with Mike, observed that, "To her, $100,000 was a billion. She had no concept [of money]."

Elvis and Ed Hookstratten asked Priscilla, after the original offer was extended, to calculate her monthly expenses so they could arrive at a settlement figure that would cover her financial needs. At the time, she had never even opened a checkbook, much less looked at a balance statement. Priscilla went to her friend Joan, who remembered that "she would say to me, 'You pay the bills. How much does it cost you to live?' She was trying to figure out a budget. She had no idea. . . . She couldn't have known how much it cost for groceries; she never bought them. . . . [There were] always twelve to fifteen people at meals. It was open house. And I had a three-bedroom house over in Beverlywood, nothing ostentatious; a maid came once a week, but it was very middle class. And so I showed her my books and took out the little ledger: 'This is what it costs me. The gas, the insurance. Yours is going to have to be more. Lisa's probably going to have private school . . .' She had no concept. She couldn't have. And I tried to help her in that way."

The revised settlement amount, arrived at and mutually agreed to a few days later, on July 19, included the original $100,000, to be paid to Priscilla in cash, tax-free; $50,000 up front; and $50,000 within a year, in addition to her new 1971 Mercedes, a 1969 El Dorado, and a 1971 Harley. Elvis also agreed to furnish Priscilla's apartment and to cover her monthly living expenses for the next five years, which she had budgeted at $1,000 a month. Lisa was to receive $500 a month in child support plus tuition, health care, and health and life insurance, along with Elvis's pledge that he would always take care of them.

Ed Hookstratten prepared the marital termination agreement and had it ready for Priscilla to sign on August 15, as she requested, just before her scheduled trip to Hawaii with Mike Stone. On that date he sent the settlement agreement and Priscilla to another attorney in his building, Robert Brock, for a quick meeting before she signed it, so it would be clear that she understood what she was doing. The "consultation" with Brock was cursory at best, for he barely had time to glance over the document, nor did he discuss it at any length with Priscilla. Priscilla, however, had repeatedly made it clear that she did not want anything from Elvis. Mike Stone occasionally would ask her about the houses, the cars, the clothes . . . all the riches she was giving up by divorcing Elvis Presley, "and she said, 'At no point in our relationship did I ever feel that any of the things were mine. They were always *his* things. I never felt like I shared in any of his life anyway.' She said, 'I could walk away from this right now with what I have—and what I have is mine, and what is back there is his.' "

"I did not go in there looking for something that was extraordinary," Priscilla confirmed later. "I didn't go in there to sink him. I didn't go in there to rip him off. I wanted to do this amicably." She wanted *out* at any cost.

Rona Barrett, who had broken the news of Elvis and Priscilla's wedding before it even happened, now announced their impending divorce on her television broadcast on July 13, a month before Elvis actually filed the petition. A week earlier, gossip Joyce Haber had reported the breakup in her column as a blind item, hinting that the wife of a superstar singer had more than a "casual interest" in her karate instructor. The coming months, in some ways the happiest of Priscilla's life according to Mike, were also, by her own description, "her struggle." Priscilla telephoned Elvis from Hawaii during her holiday with Mike, according to a later affidavit filed in the divorce, telling him they'd had a fight and that she might want to come back. The argument with Mike blew over, but it signaled Priscilla's confused emotional state.

When the movers drove up to her new little apartment with some of her belongings, Priscilla stood in the living room, "watching them set down the cartons, thinking, My God! Can I *do* this alone?" She was having an anxiety attack. Since July, when the Joyce Haber column had hit newspapers with a reference to her affair with Mike Stone, Priscilla had become the pariah of the Elvis world. "I had no idea the bigness of what I had encountered. The world loved this man. The world *loves* this man. And I was looked at, at that time, as the traitor. And no one really looked at it from [my] point of view." She saw herself as a victim of circumstance. "'She's this,' 'She's that'—and knowing you are not that way. So you realize you have to move on in life. The moving on that I did was to survive." Priscilla eventually stopped taking Lisa to the supermarket, for the divorce was the cover story of every tabloid. "The media blew everything so out of proportion. I felt like a little pea in this big world [that was] condemning me. . . . All I wanted was my life. I had no idea the impact [the divorce] was going to make." Priscilla eventually started taping her phone calls, because she got some threats. "I had no idea that it would be that ominous. Getting death threats from fans all over the world, that I had broken his heart. And I got threats for *marrying* him! No matter what I did, I was condemned. It was a no-win situation."

Priscilla did not feel responsible for Elvis's subsequent deterioration. "If there was any way of making things work out, it would have been great. But unfortunately, it didn't. It was a different time. Not that I grieve about it, you know. I mean Elvis was his own worst enemy. Elvis had a lot of demons that he carried with him. And when you are living with a person who is like that . . . Listen, his own *father* couldn't get through to him. He had a lot of baggage that he brought into our marriage." Priscilla, by leaving Elvis, was looking out for *Priscilla*, a survival skill she would advocate, two decades later, for other wives in similar situations. "I don't want to be portrayed as a victim. I'm not a victim. And I think that's the worst thing one can do. I want women to know the worst thing you can do is be a victim. Because then you've submitted. Then you've given [up] hope. You have got to be strong, know there is a way out, know there is a solution. But once you become a victim, that's it. You are no good to anybody. Your children, your husband, your future. And I'm sorry, I can't take the victim route. There is a way out; it may take a while, but there is a light at the end, but you have to have the right attitude, too, and know that there is."

She was not nearly so triumphant in the autumn of 1972, when her divorce was finalized. Phylliss Mann, who had helped Priscilla decorate the Monovale house in Bel Air the year before, was stunned to see the ex-wife of Elvis Presley living in a modest two-bedroom apartment in a singles complex in west L.A., and even more aghast when she learned the decorating budget her client allotted. "All of her furniture she got from Levitz," recalled Olivia Bis, the young fashion designer who owned Priscilla's favorite Beverly Hills boutique. "Which really astounded me." To say that Priscilla was caught by surprise at her financial struggles as a single mother and divorcée was "an understatement," declared Phylliss.

She began casting about for something to do with her time and energy, now that she was not constrained by Elvis's dictates, and she approached Olivia about taking on a partner in her clothing store. "At the time," said Olivia, "I was going through a lot of financial problems. I was more an artist; I was not a businessperson, and I had something happen with the IRS in which they had closed me up." Priscilla offered to buy into Olivia's boutique, thereby keeping Olivia from going out of business and providing Priscilla with an identity. Olivia needed $7,000 to keep the IRS at bay and to bring Priscilla in as a full partner. "And so she looked at me and said, 'You know what? I'm going to get the money from my lawyer, and I'm not going to tell him anything. I'm just going to tell him I want to open a business.'" The lawyer in question was Elvis's attorney, Ed Hookstratten, whom Priscilla asked for start-up money for her boutique.

She was also occupied with choosing the right preschool for Lisa, and turned to Ed's actress wife, Patricia Crowley, for advice. Pat recommended the John Dye School, an exclusive academy hidden in the hills of Bel Air. "We had friends who had a daughter there," Pat remembered, "and they . . . helped get her in." Lisa, at age four, was becoming a petty tyrant, ordering people about like the princess of rock she was. If she saw someone sitting on the fence at Graceland, she would command the person to get off, "and if they said, 'How come you can tell me that?'" one of the maids recalled, "she'd say, 'I *own* all this!'" Rick Stanley said simply, "She knew who she was. She knew who her daddy was."

Priscilla had embarked on a radically different lifestyle as the girlfriend of Mike Stone than she experienced as the cloistered wife of a celebrity demigod. "It was a whole new life for her," said Bob Wall. "Mike was very physical. I mean, my God, Mike did everything. He became a seven-handicap golfer in like a year and a half. A brilliant athlete. They'd come over to our place and we'd play Ping-Pong and pool, we'd swim, we'd play basketball, we'd go running. We'd do everything, and Priscilla would participate. Volleyball. We were all just a physical group. . . . Chuck [Norris] had a raceboat at his beck and call, so we'd go out on the boat all the time. I think that period of time opened Priscilla up to what life was like." Bob believed Priscilla and Mike to be "deeply in love," and Olivia assumed they would marry, from what Priscilla told her. "She wanted a normal life," Olivia said. "She wanted to try to have a normal life for Lisa."

Priscilla had emerged from a sheltered subculture into the real world with the sudden brutality of an infant delivered from the womb and slapped into a new reality. Bob Wall, who had a successful real estate business in addition to his karate classes, was struck by her utter naïveté with respect to money. "Elvis didn't give anybody much money. Apparently [his attitude toward] money was 'Whatever you want, put it on a credit card. What do you need money for?' So she didn't even really understand money. I remember being amused at her not knowing the value of things. She didn't know ten dollars from ten thousand dollars; it just had no meaning to her."

Priscilla asked Elvis for more money to decorate her apartment and to buy additional furnishings for her younger sister, seventeen-year-old Michelle, who was moving in with Priscilla and Lisa. Elvis flourished in the role of father-provider, doling out funds for furniture and giving Priscilla a new Jaguar for Christmas that year. In January 1973, Ed Hookstratten drew up plans for Priscilla's new 50-50 partnership with Olivia. Priscilla came up with a name for the new boutique—Bis & Beau, a combination of Olivia's last name and Mike's nickname for Priscilla. Neither Priscilla nor Olivia had the slightest notion how to operate a business. They were like girls playing Barbie. Priscilla was astonished at the price of fabric the first time she visited the garment center. Their ignorance was almost comical. "We were true babes in the woods," admitted Olivia. "It was really a shame that we didn't know anything at the time. We didn't [even] know about licensing. What we could have done then with the exposure that the shop was getting and Priscilla was getting, and we had just so much at our fingertips."

Elvis's physical decline began during his first Las Vegas appearance after the divorce, in January or February, 1973. He canceled three shows because of illness. Priscilla took Lisa to the Hilton, Elvis's new venue in Vegas, on February 1, Lisa's fifth birthday, to watch her daddy perform, an event that would become an annual ritual. Linda Thompson, Elvis's new girlfriend, sat at the same table but was reportedly ignored by Priscilla. "I know Priscilla and Linda really had a dislike for each other," said Sheila Ryan Caan, who came into Elvis's life a few years later, while he was still with Linda. Sheila's impression was that Elvis's new girlfriend and his former wife were jealous of each other, even though Priscilla had left Elvis. "She was finished with him, but you know wives—they like to exert control." Part of the rivalry, in Sheila's estimation, was "because they were similar in nature, as far as possessiveness and jealousy and envy and all of that." Sheila saw both Linda and Priscilla as "catty," an observation that was borne out by their public and private comments about each other. Priscilla would later describe Linda's redecoration of Graceland, while she was Elvis's girlfriend, as "a Mae West type of look." Linda, who was a friendly, demonstrative man's woman, naturally gravitated toward the brassy Vegas style that Elvis preferred. She had redone the first floor of his Memphis mansion in red, though "it wasn't just red," Priscilla once told a reporter, shuddering. "It had *feathers,* it had teardrop lighting, it had leopard-skin pillows, it had fake fur throw rugs." Linda, for her part, had ceased talking about Priscilla by 1996, saying she "didn't know her that well, and what I did know was fairly negative. . . . I don't know a lot of nice things that I could say." The evident tension between the two women was almost certainly heightened by Lisa's obvious affection for Linda, whom she "idolized," according to Dee Presley. "They were really, really close," seconded

Dee's son Ricky, who agreed that there "may have been a little bit of envy" on Priscilla's part for that reason.

Elvis's confusion, anguish, and regret about the end of his marriage revealed itself in long, rambling phone calls to Priscilla, during which he would occasionally express hope that they might get back together. Priscilla later cited this as evidence that Elvis was still in love with her: "Even though he was dating Linda, he was still on the phone with *me.* I don't know . . . how *she* did it, you know, because I never left his *life,* and that's hard for another woman to have to *cope* with." Linda and others felt that Priscilla exaggerated—or misinterpreted—Elvis's communications with her, and they denied that he was still in love with her. "I only heard negative [things]," said Linda. "[Of course,] I was there when he was going through his divorce with her."

Linda, by many accounts, including that of Cecile Rhee, who spent much time around Linda and Elvis in Memphis, was possessed to marry Elvis, at least in the early stages of their relationship. "Linda put a lot of pressure on him, I think, because she wanted to marry him so bad. Finally she just got to where she didn't talk about marriage so much because I guess she finally figured out Elvis just wasn't gonna get married again." Cecile asked Elvis, in the mid-seventies, if he and Linda were going to get married. "He goes, '*No,* honey! I'll never marry again.' He just looked at me [and] said, 'I've just realized that marriage isn't for me, Cecile.' He said, 'Well, experience is the best teacher.' " Ed Hookstratten, who later managed Linda Thompson, felt "she was climbing a mountain because of Priscilla, and I think that Elvis was horribly embarrassed."

The truth of that statement was made terribly, pathetically evident early in 1973, when Elvis again gathered his Mafia about him and told them, in apparent seriousness, that he wanted them to find and hire a hit man to kill Mike Stone. Ed Parker attributed this sad turn of events to an attempt on Mike Stone's part to restrict Elvis's access to Lisa, ostensibly out of concern over his increasing prescription drug use. Whatever the catalyst, exacting revenge on Mike Stone became Elvis's obsession. He called Priscilla at her apartment in Marina del Rey and threatened to come over and terrorize Mike himself. Mike overheard Priscilla's end of one conversation, when he saw her crying on the phone, "very nervous and scared." When Priscilla hung up, she repeated to Mike Elvis's threats—that he was going to bring some of the guys from Vegas on his private plane and "make your boyfriend get on his knees and beg." "And I said to her, 'Well, he can come over. I'm here all the time.' " Mike later claimed to have been unafraid. "My mentality might be a little different than most people's in certain respects. I accepted death; it's inevitable. And at that stage, [Elvis's reaction] was something we had talked about many times, and we had come to the conclusion—at least I had—that something might happen. So it didn't surprise me when the shit hit the fan, so to speak. And I just accepted it. If he wanted to come and take a shot at me, I wasn't gonna hide." Sheila Ryan Caan, who was around Elvis and his entourage constantly in the mid-seventies, scoffed at the idea. "He'd talk real big, but nobody was ever gonna really do anything. The Memphis Mafia was better tagged 'the gang that couldn't shoot straight.' They were just a bunch of southern boys! There wasn't nobody killin' anybody!" A few of the guys later claimed that Red or Sonny West had found a hit man to kill Mike for $10,000 and that Elvis's request was at one point just a phone call away from execution. Whether this was true or not, Priscilla was genuinely terrified. "Once Elvis got on something—and especially someone dealing with *me*, I think—he went berserk, he went nuts. It scared Mike too. I got horrible phone calls in the morning, telling me that he was going to do it in front of my eyes.... And Red and Sonny both thought that he was going to do it."

Elvis's ego had been destroyed by Priscilla, by the tormenting fact that she would leave him for another man—someone he considered his friend. It was this humiliation, coupled with the death of a cherished dream, that fueled his desire to eliminate Mike and reconcile with Priscilla—more so, it seemed, than any genuine romantic feelings for her. The love Elvis still felt for Priscilla was similar to a father's love for a daughter, and that love did not die with their divorce. As Cecile Rhee said, "Oh, he *always* loved her! When he said her name, he always had a look in his eye that . . . I don't know. It's like he had two little girls, instead of just one little girl." Cecile, who was herself a young girl married to an older man, understood. "I remember asking him did he think he would ever get back with Priscilla. He said, 'No, Cile. We won't get back together. We'll always be together in another way, though.' He said, 'She'll always be my little girl.' "

Elvis seemed to come to terms with that after a time. Priscilla's role in his life was a subject he often discussed with Larry Geller, who rejoined the entourage as Elvis's hairdresser and spiritual mentor after the divorce. Elvis told Larry he had finally figured out that Priscilla was like a little sister to him: "She grew up, and the person that grew up and I are just apart. We're not in love with each other." The pain of that realization was almost more than Elvis could bear.

Priscilla seemed not to harbor any such illusions or regret for what might have been. Mike asked her from time to time if she would ever consider going back to Elvis, "and she said she would not, that it was another part of her life and it was over and she would never go back. I think she found complete freedom for herself and what she wanted to do with herself." Mike likened Priscilla's life with Elvis to a form of near-imprisonment. With Mike, Priscilla seemed more relaxed, less standoffish. "At the time that we were involved, we were in love, so it's a different situation than her with Elvis. So my experiences were very joyous, and it was a happy time."

Priscilla carried on in her delayed adolescence, learning for the first time how to balance a checkbook, moving into a larger apartment in the marina, shopping for furniture with Phylliss Mann. She had to go through Ed Hookstratten for the money Elvis had promised her to redecorate, and she had difficulty, she would later complain, collecting it. Vernon, she said later, finally sent a check. Priscilla was discovering the financial realities of life outside the rarefied world of a superstar, and it was a harsh awakening. The $50,000 in cash, which she had thought would be her future security, was quickly dissipating to meet her weekly expenses and to start up her boutique. "Trying to make ends meet was very difficult. It was the first time I'd tried to deal with it. Sending my daughter to school, having braces, it was all piling up, it was all a reality—My God, this is a life! This is what people struggle with every day. And I was putting things on layaway and I was thinking, My God! Where is [the money] going to come from? I was allotted so much—gas, rent, everything was piling up." She was also, Mike observed, beginning to miss the luxuries of being a superstar's wife, perquisites Priscilla had taken for granted when she was Mrs. Elvis Presley. "She'd lived a particular lifestyle since she was fourteen, and she couldn't keep it up on what she got," said Mike.

Roughly a year after she left Elvis, with the newness of her independence and the excitement of her sexual adventure with Mike wearing off, Priscilla tired of apartment life in the marina and decided she wanted to buy a house in Beverly Hills. "So I went back . . . to Ed Hookstratten, and I said, 'I'm going to need more money. . . . I've decided to stay in L.A., and I need to get a house; I need to give my daughter a place to live. . . . This is not the place for me.' " Elvis's lawyer's response triggered something in Priscilla. "He goes, 'Oh, well, the next thing you are going to want is a house in Bel Air.' When he said that, it was like—my God, the light went on. My God, I'd asked for nothing! I'm barely making ends meet, my daughter now needed to wear braces, and saying 'the next thing I'd want was a house in Bel Air'? And I'm thinking, 'Yeah, you are darn right I want a house in Bel Air!' "

Priscilla, for whom the point of leaving Elvis was to emancipate herself, felt chained to him still. Like a teenager seeking her allowance, she had to go to Elvis or—more annoying still—Ed Hookstratten, his attorney, to ask for money. She eventually complained to Phylliss Mann, her interior decorator, about her lack of funds. "I thought, 'I'm desperate. I know no one.' And he had all these attorneys and I had no one." "She told me that she had a settlement," recalled Phylliss. "She told me the amount, and I said, 'You are kidding!' " Phylliss was astounded that the wife of the most popular entertainer in the world had received only $100,000 in her divorce settlement. Ed Hookstratten, she said later, "in effect was giving Priscilla the shaft. Priscilla was naive." Phylliss was not. She promptly recommended that Priscilla hire a good divorce attorney.

"And she said she didn't know any attorneys, and I said that I knew a lot of at-torneys. So I gave her several names." One of them was Phylliss's lawyer, Arthur Toll, who listened to Priscilla's story and agreed to challenge the settle-ment, which Toll considered "unfair." Ed Hookstratten took umbrage, then and later, at Priscilla's lawsuit, blaming Phylliss, whom he described as a "pushy, pushy individual. She began to run [Priscilla's] life. Started giving her all kinds of advice and brought in her lawyer." Olivia Bis denied that Phylliss was an unsavory influence. Priscilla, Olivia said, never had many close friends and had a hard time trusting people. "She really needed somebody to advise her, and Phylliss . . . really helped her." Phylliss's husband's succinct charac-terization was that "She saved [Priscilla's] ass."

Priscilla, defending her decision to sue Elvis, claimed years later that she heard from the "inner circle" that Elvis's strategy in giving her $100,000 was that "I'd run out of money and have to crawl back to him," a charge Jerry Schilling denied. Jerry attributed the small settlement to "very bad advice" and said Elvis did not knowingly shortchange Priscilla. "Elvis was not a stingy per-son, especially when it came to Priscilla, especially the mother of his child, whom [Lisa] was going to be living with." Priscilla later admitted that Elvis never refused her anything, even after their divorce, and ultimately gave her $10,000, a ridiculously high sum in those days, to decorate her tiny apartment. "He'd send a thousand dollars just because—for nothing. Or mink coats, this and that." However generous Elvis was, Priscilla was not happy, for this arrangement defeated her purpose in leaving, which was to resume control of her own life. "I didn't want to keep going to Elvis for money every month. That's bad control. . . . So no, I couldn't do that. Then I would not have my life."

Arthur Toll, Priscilla's newly retained divorce attorney, did not dispute that Elvis would have continued to provide for Priscilla; his perspective was that she needed legal protection to *ensure* that he would. "Who knows what could happen to him?" There followed what Priscilla later described as a "tense pe-riod," as her lawyer and Elvis's representatives renegotiated her divorce settle-ment. Elvis's side balked, finding it "insulting," Toll hypothesized, "to think that he wouldn't take care of her. His father's stance was generally 'Elvis would take care of everything, don't hassle him, leave him alone.' And [Elvis] was very fond of Priscilla, and . . . he didn't want to hurt anything; he just wanted everything left alone. . . . I just couldn't see that it was to her best interests."

Toll decided to press ahead with a lawsuit to set aside the original divorce settlement, and Priscilla agreed, claiming extrinsic fraud on the part of Elvis and his lawyer. To support her claim, she filed an affidavit explaining in detail that she had moved in with Elvis at sixteen [*sic*], that she knew nothing about his finances, and that she had in effect been manipulated into signing what she was told and believed was a fair settlement. It also alleged that Elvis's true net worth had been concealed from her. Ed Hookstratten was still incensed more than twenty years later. "They phonied up an affidavit. She filed a scathing affidavit against me, [saying] that I used duress and all that baloney, and it was a joke. I didn't use duress at all. [Elvis and Priscilla] were the ones who came to an agreement, in the master bedroom in their house in Holmby Hills. [The alleged duress] was not true. [Priscilla] got led down a path by an attorney and an interior designer. It was a disgrace." Arthur Toll dismissed Hookstratten's grousing and Priscilla's affidavit, as "the dynamics of litigation. . . . Ed Hookstratten had already advised Elvis and Priscilla that this was fair, and he didn't want to come along [later] and say it wasn't."

The divorce and Priscilla's adultery had been enough to immobilize Elvis; now her affidavit lifted the veil on her hidden years at Graceland as his teenage concubine, in addition to suggesting that he tried to defraud her out of her fair share of his marital property. This caused a fresh scandal that made its way to movie magazines, resulting in headlines such as "Priscilla Charges Elvis Tricked Her! Intimate Secrets Spilled in Sizzling Courtroom Battle!" Despite the bad press and Priscilla's decision to sue Elvis for fraud, recalled Harry Fain, the divorce lawyer Elvis hired to defend him and Ed Hookstratten, "I honestly must say that I don't think . . . I ever heard a single word of criticism [from Elvis] with respect to Priscilla." Ed Hookstratten was less charitable. "I did not have a lot of respect for her after she filed that affidavit. Because she knew exactly what she'd said and done and what she wanted. And what she was up to." Arthur Toll, Priscilla's lawyer, said, "I'm sure Ed did tell her [what she was entitled to], but he didn't make it very clear. I think it was a pro forma operation. She clearly didn't understand what her rights were, not only technically but what was involved financially; she didn't know. She had no concept of what was reasonable under the circumstances. She didn't know what the law was and community property. She knows it meant split something, but she didn't know exactly what." Harry Fain, who took Priscilla's deposition, perpetuated the legal Ping-Pong game years later. "There was no doubt that Priscilla was the very person who asked for and received what she wanted." There was no fraud involved, he insisted. In Fain's opinion, the agreement was not as lopsided as it appeared, since Elvis and Priscilla were married only five years, and much of his wealth derived from music royalties dating from before the wedding, making them his separate property. Priscilla's financial ignorance was evident in her deposition, where she referred to the value of the Hillcrest house—$350,000—as "thirty-five hundred thousand," a figure that does not exist.

That spring, as her lawyer continued discovery, Priscilla and Olivia celebrated the grand opening of their new boutique, Bis & Beau, with a champagne party. Phylliss Mann, who had decorated the store in a Victorian style, described the fashions, some of which Priscilla helped conceive, as "elegant rags," long, flowing, romantic dresses and bare-midriffed hip-hugger pants, heavily fringed. The attention the store received—it was packed with the curious, eager to see the schoolgirl Elvis Presley had kept secreted at Graceland all those years—taught Priscilla an invaluable lesson about the commercial potential of the surname she had just relinquished. She later told *Working Woman,* "I realized that it wasn't the clothes people wanted to see—it was me. They would come in the store and ask for Priscilla. They wanted to see what Elvis saw in me. That left a big impact on me. I saw then that there was a lot of interest in him." That lesson, and the folly of her blind compliance in the original divorce settlement, burned themselves into Priscilla's brain.

Not all of the publicity the ex–Mrs. Presley received was positive, of course, particularly among Elvis loyalists. The *Memphis Commercial Appeal* ran a photo story of Priscilla modeling bathing suits from her boutique that May, describing her as "neither an actress nor a model," and noting, critically, that one would think being Elvis's wife would be enough.

Priscilla was coloring her long hair a light henna now, abandoning her blond streaks, and she purchased a white Excalibur to complement her new image. Taking a cue from the response to the grand opening, she and Olivia decided to grant an interview with Priscilla to the *Ladies' Home Journal,* her first public profile, hoping to boost sales in Bis & Beau, for the two partners still had little money and even less practical business knowledge. Olivia recalled the two of them taking Priscilla's Excalibur downtown to the garment center to buy fabric, "so we buy all this fabric, but where are we going to put it? It doesn't fit [into the car]. So I had to drive back and pick up my station wagon and go back. And then when I did, I forgot to bring my I.D." She said, "We realized at one point that we weren't making any money, [and] . . . *Ladies' Home Journal* wanted to do a story on her. . . . She didn't want to do that, but she decided that she would do it as long as it advertised the store." Priscilla made the decision to begin calling herself Priscilla Beaulieu *Presley,* keenly aware now of the commercial value of Elvis's name. "We needed the exposure," admitted Olivia. "And that's basically why she did it."

For Priscilla, who was trained to keep secrets, and struggling as well to protect Elvis's privacy, the interview with *Ladies' Home Journal* was nerve-racking. The piece, published in August 1973, was Priscilla's coming-out. The magazine described her, appropriately, as Hollywood's "best-kept secret," the "mystery woman" in Elvis's life. She followed it with appearances on *The Merv Griffin Show* and *Donahue,* anything to promote her business, even though it was a form of personal torture for Priscilla, who was still mortified at speaking in public. "It was the first time she'd ever been on TV, being interviewed," recalled

Olivia, who watched from backstage, "and . . . Merv Griffin couldn't get a word out of her. He would ask her questions, and she would answer yes or no, and the producer was sitting back with us and she was like, 'Come on, Priscilla, say something!' " When Priscilla and Olivia appeared on *Donahue,* promoting their fashions—the first of several appearances—Priscilla was accused by a heckler of using Elvis's name to promote herself. "She didn't know she was going to be interviewed by the audience," said Olivia, "and they were really mean. Really mean. She was very poised. She wasn't defensive or anything. She handled it very well." Priscilla and Olivia's media campaign paid off in sales: The boutique, which was now located on Robertson Boulevard in Beverly Hills, soon began attracting a celebrity clientele that included Michelle Phillips, Suzanne Pleshette, Natalie Wood, Diana Ross, Jill Ireland, Carol Burnett, Mary Tyler Moore, Dyan Cannon, and Victoria Principal.

After all her years of frustration and boredom with Elvis's spiritual search, Priscilla began, ironically, "looking for a church" for herself and Lisa. "After the divorce, I really felt that Lisa needed something, I needed something." As a child, she had never related to Catholicism, Paul Beaulieu's religion. Priscilla wanted something *tangible,* when the essence of religion is faith. "I hated Catechism because there was [*sic*] never any answers. It was always 'Trust me.' It just didn't make sense. Is there a God? 'Just believe there is a God.' So it didn't work. . . . The service was in Latin, and you don't [*sic*] even understand what they are saying. And . . . you keep going to confession. It wasn't answering—it wasn't giving me [what] I needed as an individual." She "dabbled," by her description, in Elvis's philosophies, but "I just didn't really get involved with any of them." The only religion Elvis studied that interested Priscilla, even slightly, was Buddhism, for its "strong ethic and moral value," though she "found something missing." She considered Buddhism "very much for self—not that I minded." Priscilla was looking for something "realistic," she said at the time, and she began "toying with the idea" of Science of the Mind. The impetus, according to Olivia, was Michelle Beaulieu, who was living with Priscilla by then. "Her sister was involved with a guru, and so, through her sister, she was curious and had been interested in that. She was involved in the Eastern religions." During this phase, Priscilla also became a vegetarian.

In her interviews to promote Bis & Beau, Priscilla continued the ruse she had begun at thirteen, identifying Paul Beaulieu as her father, concealing James Wagner, her real father. She also began publicizing *her* account of her original meeting with Elvis, telling Mike Douglas and others how Currie Grant, a complete stranger, had approached *her* for an introduction to Elvis Presley in Germany—the raw beginnings of what would become the Priscilla-and-Elvis myth. Mike Stone would later hint at an inner torment he observed in Priscilla. Despite his descriptions of their relationship as joyful and happy, there was always something dark, he perceived, lurking just below the surface with Priscilla. He remembered taking her to a karate tournament once, where they encountered a female friend of Mike's who picked up feelings and insights and whom Mike considered psychic. She took Priscilla's hand and later told Mike, "That girl will never be happy." Mike later said, "I've thought of it many times, and I think that's somewhat true. I've known Priscilla in a lot of ways that other people don't know her. There is a lot of anxiety there. And I don't know what different things are there that are twisting at her. But she's lived a very unique life."

Elvis's demons were more visible. Barbara Leigh, who had not seen the star since their breakup in the fall of 1971, shortly before Priscilla left him, was shocked by the changes when she visited him at the Hilton in Las Vegas in the summer of 1973, less than two years later. Elvis was alarmingly bloated and dependent upon his prescription pills to fall asleep, to wake up, and to stay alert once he was awake. "He didn't do drugs when I knew him," said Barbara, speaking of 1970 and 1971. "He just did his downers." Although Linda Thompson was out of town, Elvis did not take advantage of her absence to take Barbara to bed. "I don't think he was interested in [sex]," she said. "He was lonesome and just wanted to talk and catch up and see me. We just did our normal spiritual stuff."

Elvis was still tortured to the point of being deranged over losing Priscilla to Mike Stone. He was apprehensive about others thinking "he wasn't man enough to keep his woman," as Barbara put it. He continued to make threatening calls to Priscilla occasionally. "He called me at my shop, at Bis & Beau, and told me—just heavy breathing," Priscilla recalled. "It was an *obsession*, almost, you know? 'You've done this to me, you broke my family up. [Mike Stone will be] dead, he's gone, in front of your eyes.' And then [he would] make the same call early in the morning, while I was sleeping. He'd wake me up with a phone call: 'Just remember, he's going to be dead.' I mean, he was talking insane." Priscilla later said she lived in fear. "*Living* it and watching every move that one makes, especially if you believe [the death threat], and you know that there is anger, and anger promotes whatever: I knew he had an obsession with guns, I knew that he was very unpredictable, depending on what state of mind he was in. . . ."

On the other hand, remembered Olivia, Elvis would send flowers to Priscilla at the boutique. "And the next day he would call. He would have given her anything she wanted. He had a real rough time with it. He was very hurt." Priscilla did not discuss the death threats with Olivia, nor did she mention anything to Lisa. "Never," she stressed later. "Never. I never put anything on her, *never*." Barbara attributed Elvis's erratic behavior and increasing dependence on prescription drugs, quite simply, to Priscilla; she believed that he was slowly dying of a broken heart. "She killed Elvis. That was the beginning. I believe that and I always will."

During that same summer of 1973, Arthur Toll's discovery in Priscilla's fraud case escalated, and he began to subpoena documents related to the profits from Elvis's records. He then subpoenaed Elvis himself, setting a date for the singer's deposition, which was postponed and rescheduled several times that fall. As Elvis's final deposition date of October 1 drew near, Harry Fain, his divorce lawyer, began talking settlement, though he was not convinced, years later, that Priscilla would have prevailed in demonstrating that either Elvis or Ed Hookstratten had defrauded her into signing the original property agreement. She had known, basically, how much money Elvis made and that she was entitled to half of it. Nothing was concealed from her. "It was only later that people told her she gave up too easily, [that] she should have asked for more," asserted Fain. Vernon Presley nonetheless made a counteroffer to Arthur Toll's suggested figure in October, based upon Harry Fain's recommendation, at Elvis's insistence that they avoid any confrontation or litigation. The revised settlement, for Priscilla, provided her with $725,000 cash, up front, in addition to her original $100,000, plus $720,000 in monthly payments of $6,000, to be paid in full by August 1982. She also received half of the profits from the sale of the Monovale mansion in Bel Air, 5 percent of Elvis's music stock in Whitehaven, as well as spousal support of $4,200 a month for a year and child support in the amount of $4,000 a month until Lisa turned eighteen. "I remember very vividly that when we had to finalize the settlement, Arthur arranged for an appointment at the home of Elvis at six P.M.," said Harry Fain, "and I think Elvis was coming down for his breakfast. He was very affable, never hesitated for a moment. We explained the terms, and he said, 'You have it.'" Even Arthur Toll, who was representing Priscilla, later said that Elvis wanted to be fair, "'and if she doesn't think it's fair, we'll change it.'" Harry Fain found Elvis consistently a gentleman, no matter the circumstances, ever asking, "Is there anything I can get you, Mr. Fain?" "He was very, very solicitous, very warm. Trying to obtain a warm feeling of connection with you, on the basis of trying to resolve any antagonism." The lawyer came away from his encounters with Elvis impressed by his natural grace and his heart, convinced that it was more than his talent, but "a warmth and a spirit" that contributed to his exceptional fame; feeling, finally, that Elvis Presley had been given a burden, in the form of that oppressive fame, that no mortal could carry. "Elvis reached a level that very few people in our lifetime have achieved. The vast majority of people, especially women, *worshiped* him. And I mean that."

The lawyers, the presiding judge—anyone and everyone who came into contact with Elvis and Priscilla during the litigation over their divorce settlement—

left the situation amazed. For all its potential for acrimony, noted Harry Fain, the fraud case was settled in four months, "and I believe that he was still in love with Priscilla, or at least wanted to develop a continuing relationship for the benefit of his daughter." Arthur Toll agreed: "You could feel that he still felt the same way about her and Lisa. To him, the divorce wasn't something necessary and shouldn't be done, but if that is what she wanted, what could he do? That's what I felt."

The final divorce hearing, on October 9, was both touching and tragic. The rock-and-roll sensation whom Priscilla had idolized at eleven was puffy and bloated, his eyes droopy and dull from prescription pills. Elvis appeared in court wearing his trademark tinted aviator glasses and a skier's warm-up suit, with a long, heavy gold chain around his neck and a small U.S.-flag pin on his jacket, over his heart. Priscilla, who had not seen Elvis in several months, was shocked at his rapid decline. When they sat down inside the judge's chambers, Elvis took Priscilla's hand and held it as the judge, Lawrence Rittenband, led them through the pro forma hearing that would forever sever the legal ties that bound them. Elvis's fingers, Priscilla could feel, were moist with sweat.

A few minutes later, the once legendary lovers strolled out of the court-house from their divorce hearing, walking arm in arm before a disbelieving corps of photographers. Elvis appeared sad and defeated; Priscilla looked like a walking advertisement for her boutique, dressed in tight white trousers, a white mock turtleneck, and a colorful long patchwork coat. She no longer wore the famous black beehive; her hair was now shoulder-length and brown again, as it had been when she was eight; her eyes bereft of false lashes, her brows plucked spare. As they parted, Elvis kissed Priscilla and whispered tenderly into her ear, "For always and ever." When Priscilla got to her Mercedes, she turned and waved a final farewell to the man she had devoted half of her life to possessing; Elvis Presley gave her a crooked half-smile and winked. Elvis and Priscilla, so extraordinary in their courtship, were equally unique in their divorce. Harry Fain later described their behavior as "just a beautiful quality to achieve."

"I sat in the courtroom and cried," Priscilla said later, "because his hands ... were swollen from God only knows what he had taken. But I was ... holding his hands and baby-talking him. And the judge couldn't believe it." Priscilla knew the divorce "was breaking" Elvis. "God only knows what was going to happen, but being so condemned for it, it was very difficult for me to break free. Very difficult to survive ... The love that I had for him was truly a love for him. I didn't leave him because I hated him; I left him because I loved him. I wasn't about to see him go, in front of me. He had to help himself. He didn't choose to do that."

The love between Elvis and Priscilla, so like that of a father and daughter, transcended even their divorce. Said George Klein, who had observed the dynamics between them from the day of Priscilla's arrival at Graceland when she was seventeen: "They were growing apart, and she was maturing. He knew that. He was nice enough a guy not to hold her back. He wanted the best for her."

There was no love, Priscilla would say to George's wife, Barbara, like the Presley love.

IV

REQUIEM: A LIFE RECLAIMED

27

THE KING IS DEAD, LONG LIVE THE QUEEN

Priscilla celebrated her second divorce from Elvis by investing a fraction of her new riches in Bis & Beau. With the cash influx, she and Olivia purchased a more fashionable space in Beverly Hills. She also bought a Mediterranean-style house for herself and Lisa, located on Summit Drive in Benedict Canyon, above the Beverly Hills Hotel, acquiring a maid, a pool, and a tennis court. Her social status, overnight, had risen dramatically. Phylliss Mann, whose advice and introduction to Arthur Toll had increased Priscilla's fortune tenfold, from just over a hundred thousand to well over a million, went unacknowledged by Priscilla. "I didn't get a thank-you," said Phylliss, later. "I'll tell you, she was so unschooled in the social graces that maybe she didn't know she had to do that." "I could have asked for more," was Priscilla's comment in 1996.

Elvis's response to the divorce was a near-breakdown that landed him in Baptist Memorial Hospital in Memphis with pneumonia and depression. His emotional and physical condition were sufficiently grave that Lisa, who was not quite six, looked up at him one day, and said, plaintively, "Daddy, I don't want you to die." She had seen him firing guns at the television, setting off firecrackers, and taking handfuls of pills, and even as a small child, she "picked up on something." Elvis, said Rick Stanley, who was with him nearly twenty-four hours a day, adored Lisa. "He would ask me to go to her room at night sometimes and take her out of bed and carry her down to the couch, just so he could watch her sleep."

Lisa drifted between the sane and the surreal, living with Mike Stone and Priscilla, whom Mike praised as a "good mom," staying, at intervals, with Elvis, who alternated between benign neglect and heartfelt overindulgence. When he wasn't sleeping or overmedicated, he would enchant Lisa with magical trips on his private jet, the *Lisa Marie,* just so she could see snow, or he would surprise her with real jewels. "She was pretty much his life," said Sheila Ryan Caan. "He wanted her to be perfect. He loved her, he just cherished her, and he could not have been more nurturing. I'm sure it was confusing for her, because he would sleep a lot, and sometimes be 'not feeling well,' as we would put it. But, to his capacity, he was as good as he could be toward her. And he loved her more than he ever loved anything or anybody in his life." "The two of them were crazy about each other," said Dana Rosenfeld, who met Lisa in 1975 and became her closest childhood friend. "She just loved him with all her heart. [To him she was] the little girl who could do no wrong and the most beautiful in the whole world and the most talented. The quintessential apple of her father's eye." Elvis, observed Dana, "never said no."

Lisa, bewildered by the dichotomy of her existence, was a willful, sometimes demanding, child. Sheila Ryan Caan, who saw Elvis's little girl with Elvis, treated like a princess, would watch Lisa's face transform when she asserted her authority. "I call it the sugar look. . . . When children think they're the boss, they have a fog over their eyes until somebody takes them, jerks them by the neck, and says, 'By the way, I'm the boss and you're the mud.' And Lisa spent a lotta, lotta time with that film over her eyes because she *was* the boss, and kids aren't supposed to be the boss. . . . She seemed kind of confused by her ability to control."

Ricky Stanley saw her as a normal, spirited kid. She appointed herself treasurer of the Sweet Inspirations Club, and collected the singers' quarters each week faithfully. "She was a tiny little thing," Myrna Smith recalled. She "used to walk around on tiptoe, and she hung out in our dressing room." Elvis and Priscilla bought her a golf cart for her sixth Christmas, and one of Lisa's favorite memories was of zooming about the grounds and driveway at Graceland. Both Rick and Sheila remarked on Lisa's "good heart," even as a little girl. "I don't think Lisa has a mean bone in her body," said Sheila. "I just think that she's a victim. Of circumstances: a father and her mother."

Jerry Schilling and Sam Thompson, Linda's brother, were two of the select few whom Elvis allowed to transport Lisa back and forth between Las Vegas and Los Angeles or between L.A. and Graceland. When she was with Elvis, "the only people he trusted to take her around for the day were Kathy Westmoreland and the Sweet Inspirations," said Myrna. "I don't think he let many people take her out of the house." Jerry and Joe and Paul Beaulieu took Lisa to a Michael Jackson concert that year while Elvis and the Jackson Five were appearing in Lake Tahoe. Lisa was six and Michael Jackson sixteen. "We went backstage and said hello and that was it," said Joe.

When Priscilla took over the parenting, Lisa adhered to a different set of rules. She found it confusing, according to Dana Rosenfeld, whose family lived next door on Summit Drive and who was in Lisa's first-grade class at the John Dye School. Priscilla was the disciplinarian, attempting to establish boundaries; Elvis "was always showering Lisa with love and presents." She had *respect* for her mother, according to Dana's account, and *happiness* with her father. Dana recalled once when Elvis took the two of them to Schwab's drug-store in Beverly Hills, closed the store, "and we got everything that our arms could hold . . . huge pieces of saltwater taffy." Dana's mother admonished Elvis, saying the girls would never understand the word "no." "And he was like a little boy. He said, 'I just love them and want to make them happy.' " Lisa took Dana with her occasionally to the Monovale house when Elvis was in L.A., "and we would sit and sing Christmas songs with him—not his songs, just songs—and rounds, like 'Row, Row, Row Your Boat.' "

Elvis, who had come to terms with his anger and anguish and had forgiven both Priscilla and Mike Stone, was bothered by the fact that Priscilla was liv-ing with a man, that his daughter was exposed to a situation he considered im-moral. Though she was officially divorced from Elvis, Priscilla made no move to marry Mike. She was also telling reporters for women's magazines she would not have another child, that it wouldn't be fair to Lisa or the baby for them to have different fathers—a carryover from her own strange upbringing and Ann Beaulieu's distinction between full-blood siblings and adopted or half siblings. Priscilla was becoming, Olivia Bis noticed, increasingly savvy about interviews, appearing on her second magazine cover—another *Ladies' Home Journal* profile—in June of 1974. Priscilla engaged Phylliss Mann to deco-rate her new house in Benedict Canyon, and she began to pick Phylliss's brain. "She was always interested in what I was doing," the decorator remembered, "because I moved in art circles and that was a world that she was not well known in. [She was] curious, because she thought that I was very cultured, and she wanted to learn."

Priscilla's emerging upper-crust lifestyle and Mike Stone were an incompat-ible blend. The karate teacher felt out of place in Priscilla's new milieu and could not afford the luxury travel she foresaw for the two of them. She was also becoming disenchanted with Mike, "with his lack of goals, and his lack of drive," Bob Wall surmised. "And Mike is pretty self-centered; the world rises and sets around Mike." Priscilla also began to resent what Olivia called Mike's "macho Hawaiian thing," a lifestyle "where the women stay at home and the men are with the men, and that's what he was doing with her. And he was try-ing to launch a business in Hawaii, so he had to spend a lot of time in Hawaii, and there she was, alone again." It was Elvis "all over again." Mike moved out of the house on Summit and into a small apartment nearby, as Priscilla eased him out of the relationship. By 1975 he was a footnote in her autobiography. Mike, according to Al Coombes, a reporter to whom he told his tale in the early 1980s, was embittered, for he felt he had left his wife for Priscilla "and she dumped him." Bob Wall described the relationship from Priscilla's perspec-tive: "He was a great guy as a transition for her from young girl . . . to mature woman."

Priscilla was also tiring of Bis & Beau and was showing up at the boutique less and less often, though she reveled in the publicity. She appeared on the cover of *Parade,* standing in front of the boutique, and she modeled for Bis & Beau brochures, posing seductively in the sexy leather costumes she and Olivia created. Someone in the business, seeing her in the layouts, suggested that she act in commercials, and Priscilla stored the information in the back of her brain, where it firmly remained.

She met the British photographer Terry O'Neill, who would later marry Faye Dunaway, when he came into Bis & Beau one day, and there was an instant attraction. Terry, a sophisticated European, was so embarrassed by Priscilla's "terrible" taste in clothes that he chose obscure restaurants when they went to dinner together to avoid being seen with her in public. "To be honest," he said once, "she was a bit of a fashion disaster at the time. I hated those big hats she was wearing and the ridiculously flared trousers." He was enchanted, however, by Priscilla's ultra-feminine sexuality, commenting later on how exquisitely she prepared before making love, describing her romantic master bedroom, which he said featured a four-poster bed, special dimmed lighting, and a mirrored ceiling.

Elvis's love life was effectively nonexistent by 1975. Linda Thompson had assumed more the role of caretaker than girlfriend, a relationship Shirley Dieu, who was dating the divorced Joe Esposito, characterized as "mother-son," dominated by baby talk. Joe introduced Elvis to Sheila Ryan, a petite, cherubic blond who was all of nineteen, and in the mid-seventies, she became Linda's alternate, though both had met Elvis too late to enjoy him as a genuine mate. "I don't believe that Priscilla's experience with Elvis was anything close to what mine and Linda's was," Sheila stated. "We were more or less keepin' him alive." Their duties were more medical than sexual. "We pulled food out of his mouth when he would fall asleep with a hamburger or whatever, because he took a lot of pills to sleep." Sheila never had an orgasm when she was with Elvis; he made out with her as if they were teenagers. There was, she felt, a sweetness to it. "I was just like a little angel to him. That was all. He liked . . . pretty lace underwear and that was it."

Terry O'Neill dropped Priscilla after two months to return to England—one of the few men who ever rejected *her*—and she was not pleased. "That was not a great experience for her," Olivia understated. Casting about for a replacement, she settled for Robert Kardashian, the Los Angeles lawyer who would later be made infamous as O.J. Simpson's best friend. To Priscilla, at the time, he was a convenient boyfriend, for his brother Tom had recently married Joan Esposito and the two couples could travel and do things together. "I think she was just going out with him because she had no one to go out with," expressed Joan Quinn, Robert's cousin. Elvis continued to call Priscilla, in spite of his girlfriends and her boyfriends, testing the waters about getting back together. For a time, recalled Terry O'Neill, Mike Stone was pressing her to return as well. "Elvis would come here at night," she said in 1996, sitting in the house on Summit Drive. "I would be with someone—I was in a relationship—and he would just show up. He didn't care whether I was with someone or not. . . . He'd show up at two in the morning, three in the morning . . . or he'd call me. So he dominated my life even after our breakup, because when you have someone who doesn't care, and has been the center of attention, and is no longer the center of attention, there's a loss. And Elvis was used to having his cake and eating it too. And there is no way that he was going to have that. And he still wanted to know that he was cared for, or that he could be cared for."

Lance Robbins, a friend of Kardashian's, remembered Robert telling him that Priscilla received long, incoherent phone calls from Elvis while she and Robert were in bed, "and she would put the receiver on the pillow between them and let him listen." Priscilla viewed the calls and Elvis's midnight drop-in visits as proof of his undying desire for her. In truth, Elvis Presley "was a dying man," said Kathy Westmoreland, who sang backup for him and slept beside him during his last months and years. "I knew he was dying," Sheila agreed, "and I wasn't in denial over it. You know, you just know things. He didn't really want to live. He'd done everything, and nothing seemed to work out. People were a disappointment to him time after time. I think mostly Priscilla disappointed him."

Elvis told Sheila and Kathy, separately, that he was going to die at the age of forty-two. "He knew he was gonna die," said Sheila. He also told Nancy Rooks, one of the maids at Graceland, that he would die at forty-two because his mama was that age when she died. "We talked a lot about life after death," said Nancy. "He said him and God was friends and if he died he would come back, because the strong come back and the weak don't." After one of his last concerts, remembered Kathy, he grew concerned that he would die without leaving an enduring legacy. "One of my last conversations with him, he was saying, 'What is this all about? How are people going to remember me? They aren't going to remember me.' He said, 'I've never done anything lasting. I've never done a classic film. What could I do before I go?' " He told Kathy he was going to write his autobiography, which he planned to call *Through My Eyes,* so that he could leave behind something he considered meaningful. It seems bizarre, years later, that Elvis Presley worried about whether he would be remembered.

Sheila had left Elvis by 1976, for she had fallen in love with James Caan, whom she would marry, and she could no longer bear to watch the man whom most women worshiped as a romantic god die in front of her, incontinent from prescription drugs, sleeping in a diaper. "It wasn't a dream," said

Sheila. "It was a nightmare." Elvis's lifestyle had become disturbingly similar to that of Howard Hughes, whom Elvis admired and wanted to meet. Strangely, Hughes had a high regard for Elvis Presley. The parallels between the two men were almost eerie. They were both Capricorns, only children, nicknamed Sonny, coddled by overprotective mothers who died early. Both were innately shy. Each became rich, and was a genius in his chosen field. Elvis accumulated a cadre of aides known as the Memphis Mafia; Hughes employed aides called the Mormon Mafia. Both Elvis and Howard Hughes were considered great lovers and ladies' men, yet they used intermediaries to procure beautiful women, then seldom touched them. Each instructed his aides not to talk to the women whom they sequestered. Elvis and Hughes both married abruptly, after a bizarre crisis in their lives, then rarely had sex with their wives. They both preferred to live in hotel suites behind blackout curtains, eating a certain food for months on end, watching the same movie over and over. Both men lived in and had a strong attachment to Las Vegas; both of them admired Richard Nixon and sent him secret communiqués; both believed they would die young because their mothers had. Hughes and Elvis deliberately shrouded their private lives in mystery. They were obsessed with cleanliness in those around them, yet they neglected their own personal hygiene. Both men wanted to create a foundation to fund charities, but their plans were thwarted, in part by their own inattention. Each man, greatly admired in youth, became a caricature of his former self in his final years; Elvis growing hugely bloated, Hughes becoming anorexic-thin. They spent their last years in near seclusion, addicted to prescription medication, surrounded by sycophants who watched them self-destruct. Each man, finally, left an estate mired in controversy that would make more money for him dead than alive. Howard Hughes died in April of 1976, just before the meeting with Elvis Presley could be arranged.

That same month, Priscilla sold her interest in Bis & Beau to travel the world, a dream of hers since her first years with Elvis, when, instead, she found herself entwined with a man in a lifestyle more insular than her years as a schoolgirl in Germany. She saw "something missing" from her life as a boutique owner, she told *TV Guide* several years later. "Her head just wasn't there," Olivia said. "After having gone through the major divorce, there was a lot of media attention on her, and people were starting to recognize her . . . [and] she decided to pursue other things. I think she thought maybe this wasn't her niche and that there were a lot of possibilities out there for her." In truth, she wanted to model and act, her twin fascinations since Immaculate Conception.

Priscilla began the year 1977 in a blaze of ambition. She had ended her six-month romance of convenience with Robert Kardashian, whom those who knew her considered too weak for Priscilla. Since her childhood, listening to

Mario Lanza's powerful voice on the stereo, Priscilla had been magnetized to forceful men—her soul's calling, perhaps, to the father she never knew about but whose loss she seemed to intuit. "I . . . would become the dominant one, and that almost keeps *me* in place," she tried to explain. "I know this is very old-fashioned thinking, but to have a relationship, you have to have a balance. I've dated submissive, nonaggressive men, and I found it very boring. And I realized then that I could never date a guy who was noncommittal, someone who sat back and [said], 'Whatever you want to do, hon.' I need much more of a challenge than that. I need someone to keep me on my toes. I need someone [to] look good for. I would never let myself go. Someone who . . . I don't know. That's just the type of person I am. It's a challenge for me. . . . I'll never become less than I am. So a challenge is good."

Without a boyfriend for the first time perhaps since she was six, Priscilla focused on the career she had suppressed during the Elvis years. The suggestion that she do commercials resurfaced in her psyche, and Priscilla set about to achieve that goal. Pursuing a career in show business, she would say, was the second biggest decision of her life. "I had to go to work for my own sense of self-esteem. I had to shake the image of just being Elvis Presley's wife and get people to accept me as *me*, a person with my own talent." Priscilla, the military brat who thrived on change and new experiences, was determined not to get stuck in a time warp. She was also eager to reinstate her childhood and adolescent standing, too long dormant, as the queen of her domain. Norman Brokaw, the powerful William Morris agent, approached her about getting into acting, and Priscilla, whose wings had been clipped by Elvis, sought, at long last, to fly. She enrolled in an acting workshop that focused on commercials, taught by Holly Hire. "I brought her in for a couple of commercials, and they thought that she was really lovely, but I don't think that she could cut it or something," said Hire. Maybelline, one of the companies that considered Priscilla for an endorsement, passed when they discovered that the smoky eyes she was so famous for from her wedding portrait with Elvis had actually been enhanced by several pairs of false eyelashes. Nina Blanchard, the modeling agent, rejected her as "too short."

Elvis continued his physical decline, which worsened when his relationship with Linda Thompson ended late in 1976. His entourage would say Elvis dismissed Linda, who was having an affair with a musician named David Briggs; Linda's account was that she moved out voluntarily, tired of Elvis's "vampire" life. Quite probably it was a combination. "I think that Linda was growing tired of it all," said Shirley Dieu, who was living with Joe Esposito. "If you were with Elvis, you had to stay in a locked room with foil on the windows. It had to be hard for anybody. I think she got fed up, and she heard that David was worth a million dollars and she latched right on to him. Everybody felt that Elvis knew it but didn't want to be embarrassed by it, and he got rid of her to make it look like he was getting rid of her before she left."

George Klein, ever the faithful procurer of women, found Elvis a replacement before Linda's bags were even packed. On November 19, George ferried to Graceland a trio of southern sisters, the Aldens, the older two of whom were beauty queens. George's intent was that Elvis would take to Terry, the reigning Miss Tennessee, but his eyes were riveted to her younger sister, nineteen-year-old Ginger, who had merely gone along to keep Terry and Rosemary Alden company. "His first words to me were, 'Ginger, you're burning a hole through me,' " she recalled. In a scene reminiscent of his first, electric meeting with Priscilla, Elvis had an immediate, almost out-of-body experience upon seeing Ginger Alden. "Elvis seemed to single me out that evening," as she put it, in understatement. Some would see Elvis's fascination with Ginger as an attempt to reproduce Priscilla, for like Priscilla in her prime Elvis years, Ginger had long, dark hair, a sweetly beautiful face, and darkly made-up eyes. Elvis told Ginger she resembled his mother, and in truth she did, particularly around the eyes, which, like those of Elvis's mother, were brown, deep-set, expressive, and soulful. "When I see Ginger, I feel like I'm falling into my mother's eyes," Elvis told Larry Geller.

Elvis became instantly obsessed with Ginger. Though the two had barely become acquainted, he telephoned her parents the next weekend, recalled Ginger, and invited her to join him on his tour. By December, less than three weeks later, while Elvis was appearing in Vegas, he was picturing them married. "Elvis told me when he closed his eyes he kept having visions of me in a white gown." He called Jo Alden, Ginger's mother, during the Vegas engagement and said, "Mrs. Alden, I'm in love with your daughter and I want to marry her," according to Ginger. "I was speechless and shocked, as I know she was." On January 26, back at Graceland, he proposed to an incredulous Ginger. The setting, as it had been with Priscilla, was a bathroom. "I noticed a lot of commotion at Graceland," Ginger recalled. "People coming in and out and phone calls being made often. He called me into his bathroom, where I sat in a chair as he knelt down in front of me. He said many beautiful things to me and then presented a gorgeous diamond ring, asking me to marry him. I was so surprised as I said yes." Jo Alden, an outgoing sort whose critics labeled her a social climber, admitted that "it took [Ginger] a while to get used to him. But he'd say, 'I need you for inspiration to go with me on my trips.' " Elvis showered the bewildered Ginger with gifts. "He gave her three or four rings at a time," said Jo Alden. "She told him one time, 'Elvis, I would be just as happy for a box of candy or flowers.' " Elvis responded, "Well, you're going to have to get used to it." Ginger recalled that "Elvis said he would love to have a son and he wanted me to be the mother. We had started a list of names." The entire courtship had an air of almost tragic desperation.

Most of the entourage, after Elvis's death, seemed to bear a grudge against Ginger and would later dismiss as fanciful her claim that Elvis planned to marry her. George Klein felt she was "misunderstood" by the guys, because, in Jo Alden's words, she "didn't pal around" with them, as had Linda, who was their undisputed favorite. Rick Stanley attributed this resentment to Elvis envy, a common affliction within the entourage, the same syndrome Priscilla had both suffered from and been guilty of. "These guys were so competitive and jealous," said Rick. "Anybody gets anything, any bit of attention—even a woman—they get weird." "Elvis was a perceptive person," declared Ginger's mother. "He could see right through someone, and he wouldn't have had [Ginger] around him up until his death if she were the kind of person they try to make her out to be." Elvis's signals concerning Ginger, were, in truth, conflicted, as were his emotions in general. Rick Stanley was around on January 6, when Elvis awakened his jeweler, Harry Levitch, in the middle of the night to order a custom-made 11-carat diamond engagement ring—the same size as the stone in his signature TCB ("Taking Care of Business") ring—to be created by the following morning so he could surprise Ginger. He ultimately removed the diamond from his own ring for Ginger's engagement band to meet the deadline. Ricky was present when Elvis called together the guys at Graceland on January 26 to announce that Ginger had accepted his marriage proposal. "He cared about Ginger, he really did," Ricky recalled. "He told me he was gonna marry her. Showed me the ring, the whole thing."

Conversely, Elvis told Myrna Smith, who had no reason to resent Ginger, "that he *wasn't* [going to marry Ginger]. Even though he told *her* different things. I don't know why he did that. Because he told people one thing and obviously got her a ring." Elvis, recalled Myrna, "came into our dressing room and took me in the back and told me that he wasn't going to. I won't tell you how he told me, but I knew that he wasn't going to marry her." The concern, for Elvis, was Ginger's fidelity. Myrna Smith and Joe's girlfriend, Shirley, both confirmed that Ginger had another boyfriend and "she wouldn't break up with him," said Shirley. Elvis enlisted the aid of Nancy Rooks, his Graceland maid, to spy on Ginger, calling her house to see if she was home when she was supposed to be. "Then we caught her!" whooped Nancy. "Elvis gave her a ring, okay? A $60,000 fur coat—I saw it all. Then he said, 'I spent all that goddamn money on her and I'm not gonna marry her!'"

Kathy Westmoreland, who was still keeping company with Elvis, occasionally sleeping beside him, believed that Elvis had changed, that he was maturing, that he genuinely wanted to be in a monogamous relationship with Ginger, but it was too late. "He was really in love with her. I felt that she was beautiful and sweet, but just too young to really understand him and cope with his needs at that particular point. And there were a lot of problems in his life too. He was a dying man. She was just so young to go through all that." Elvis, whose dreams had been broken—his hopes for a serious film career and a perfect union with his true soul mate—saw Ginger as his potential salvation, a means of resurrecting the shattered fantasy of finding his twin soul; and she, too, fit the visual pattern of his attempts to re-create the lost love of his youth, Debra Paget.

Larry Geller, who knew the inner depths of Elvis Presley's soul as well as anyone, understood this. Elvis had even asked Larry, who was a licensed minister, to perform his marriage ceremony to Ginger, though Larry did not think, ultimately, that Elvis would go through with it. "It was so new. He was infatuated with her. He went gaga, he went nuts for her. Overboard. He was getting ready to die. Something in him knew it. . . . He wanted a son. . . . He was waking up to the fact that he was becoming a redundancy. He was highly desirous to be known as an actor. He said, 'It's my only regret!' " Marrying Ginger, to Elvis, was the magic pill—like waving a wand and erasing the regrets of his past. He had long since given up sex—for a year and a half, according to Larry—although Kathy Westmoreland claimed she had intercourse with Elvis shortly before his death. "I know for a fact he didn't," refuted Larry. "For absolute fact. I was with Elvis every night when he went to bed. He told me everything. Everything. He couldn't even get a hard-on the last year of his life. He never even consummated his relationship with Ginger. He couldn't. And he didn't want to in a certain way, also."

Elvis and Larry had many deep conversations those last days, occasionally drifting to the subject of Priscilla. He had changed his mind, he told Larry, in thinking they were soul mates. He still believed there was a "karmic link" between them, but it had taken on a different meaning in Elvis's mind. "It took me a long time to realize she's not my soul mate," he told Larry during his last few months. "Priscilla came into my life for two major reasons: one, so we could have Lisa . . . and number two, so I could teach her. Priscilla came to learn a lot of lessons about life. I raised her, Larry." Larry recalled Elvis saying, "I had to push her out of the nest so she could fly with her own wings, and I'm only sorry I didn't push her out of the bird's nest when I should have." Elvis himself realized, at the end, the paternal—as opposed to carnal or erotic—connection he had with Priscilla.

Priscilla was herself confronting the psychological aspects of her intense relationship with Elvis that spring, in the person of Kirk Kerkorian. Kerkorian, the rich, much older, immensely powerful, secretive, and married owner of airlines, casinos, movie studios, and the International Hotel, where Elvis first performed in Vegas, had noticed Priscilla during Elvis's premier engagement at his hotel, but had waited for their estrangement to make his move. He and Priscilla began a clandestine affair in 1977, spending time on Kerkorian's yacht in Saint-Tropez, traveling to Europe on his private plane, until Priscilla began to panic. "It scared me, that relationship," she admitted. "It could have been a nice relationship. It was just too soon. Elvis was still alive at the time. And it was too close to what I just got out of."

Priscilla cooled the relationship with Kirk Kerkorian, which was conducted in such secrecy that Joe Esposito knew nothing about it at the time and would later express doubt that it ever happened; he was certain that Priscilla could not have been involved with Kerkorian without his knowing it. Maureen Donaldson, a photographer who was dating Cary Grant at the time, remembered flying to London with Cary, Kirk, and Priscilla on Kerkorian's private plane that June. She and Priscilla, Maureen would say, stayed up all night, drinking Château Lafitte and "comparing notes" on life in the shadows of a superstar, as Kerkorian and Grant slept. Priscilla, who had never been to London before, took the opportunity to quiz Maureen thoroughly on where to shop. Maureen regarded Priscilla as "fragile" at the thought of becoming involved romantically with another high-powered man. Priscilla instead opted for a friendship with Kerkorian, which she took advantage of by questioning him about his business dealings, soaking up the information like a sponge. That summer she signed with the William Morris talent agency.

She was clearly anxious to be in another relationship, having been essentially solo for several months, as proven by her romance, that spring, with her hairdresser, Elie Ezerzer. Elie, a shaggy-haired blond French Moroccan from Israel who ran a trendy salon, was closer to the smooth Warren Beatty character in *Shampoo* than to the stereotypical male hairdresser. He had in fact patterned himself after Vidal Sassoon and was "very sophisticated and masculine," according to the discerning Phylliss Mann. Joan Quinn, a Beverly Hills attorney's wife who ran in those circles, considered Elie "very macho" and remembered him doing Elvis Presley impersonations at parties, down to the black leather costume, before he met Priscilla. It was Joan's impression, however, that Elie "was just this absolute, total user of her. He wanted to be Elvis Presley, he wanted to sing. Everybody always said the only reason he was interested in her was that he always had this preoccupation with Elvis." The connection was doubly ironic, for Elie fit the pattern of nearly every male Priscilla had pursued since she was eight—only now *she* had become the object of identification for those who were interested in *Elvis*. Priscilla found Elie appealingly "flamboyant."

What drew her to him, she said, was that he was French. "I was attracted to Elie because he was unique, too. I just found Elie fascinating. He was a very emotional person, very French. Captivating, different." Priscilla had embarked upon her European period, and Elie was her bridge to the Old World, a live-in tutor in matters of taste and style, her latest self-improvement project. Phylliss Mann, who considered Priscilla and her mother completely bereft of breeding, credited Elie with instilling in Priscilla whatever sophistication she had acquired by the age of thirty-two, when they parted. As part of her French phase, Priscilla decided to transfer Lisa from the John Dye School the next fall to the Lycée Français, a prestigious academy in west L.A., where classes were taught in French. She asked Elvis if she and Elie could borrow his private plane to fly to Europe that summer, a request that annoyed him, according to Ginger.

One of Priscilla's last visits with Elvis at Graceland occurred in April, when he was just home from his latest hospital stay, and she stopped by to fetch Lisa. Marion Cocke, Elvis's favorite nurse from Baptist Memorial, was at the mansion and remembered Priscilla sweeping in, dressed like one of the characters from *Doctor Zhivago,* "looking like a star." Marion could sense the connection between her and Elvis. "You could tell by the way that they treated and looked at each other, it was a life experience."

Elvis and Rick Stanley watched their last movie together that month, a television movie about the life of Howard Hughes, starring Tommy Lee Jones, dramatizing the billionaire's fall from grace. As Jones, playing Hughes, descended further into paranoia and delusion, secreted inside darkened hotel suites, "I'd look over at Elvis," recalled Ricky, "and he'd look over at me, like, 'This is familiar . . .' and he kind of laughed." The movie, and Hughes's tragic demise, "had an effect on him," said Ricky. Elvis worried that his life might end as Hughes's had. "It made him start thinking, examining. Sometimes when you're used to a lifestyle like Elvis has, you're confronted with truths. Sometimes it's hard to act on them because there's so much stuff you have to get rid of."

David Stanley, Rick's brother, would later tell the story about driving Elvis to Priscilla's house on Summit that final summer, declaring that Elvis disappeared into a room with Priscilla and emerged a short while later, saying, "Everything's all right now," as if he had made some final farewell. Mike Edwards, who would soon become Priscilla's next boyfriend, recalled Priscilla telling him about the same visit. "She told me the last time she really saw Elvis he came by her house on Summit, and he was sort of asking her if they couldn't maybe see each other again. And she had moved on. She had someone else up in her bedroom. I think it was Elie. And Elie didn't come down, and she said, 'No, Elvis, I can't.' And I think maybe Elvis was coming by to be romantic or something. It was early in the morning. He'd been recording all night long. She said his hair was all greasy and he had on this jumpsuit. And she looked at him, and I think at that point, that was when she decided it was definitely over."

"This is the thing that upset me more than anything about Priscilla," responded Shirley Dieu, Joe Esposito's girlfriend, who was among the group with Elvis that night. "It may seem small, but to me it was heartfelt. That's not how it happened at all. What happened was that Elvis had bought a Ferrari and he wanted to take it by to show Lisa. So we were in the car, and I can't remember who was in what car, but I remember we pulled up to the Summit house and Lisa was in bed or something. And as I recall, Priscilla got out of her bed. We had just been to Vail and we had been snowmobiling, and Elvis had taken a liking to these overalls that zipped up the front to keep you warm. And it was cold and he was wearing a snowmobile suit. Not an Elvis onstage suit. He was talking and being very gentlemanly, and she kept turning her head, laughing at him and making fun of what he was wearing. I was tolerant of her, but I found it very offensive. He was seriously talking, and she was turning her head, laughing, mocking him. And it just irked me. That she was laughing behind his back. She would turn to the side where he couldn't see her laugh and make fun of him. I felt so sorry and embarrassed for him."

Elvis's spirit continued to flag during the rest of that summer. He and Larry Geller stood outside on his balcony at the Hilton late one night, gazing at the lights of Vegas, and Elvis pondered aloud whether he would ever know if any woman really loved him for himself, that he might die without being in a true love relationship. Larry answered him by saying that he already had that with his fans. They loved him unconditionally. "And he thought about it," recalled Larry, "and then said, 'Yeah, man, you're right. That's my destiny.' "

By August he was deeply despondent over the imminent publication of an exposé of his unusual lifestyle, written by three aides whom he had let go the previous year: Red and Sonny West, and Dave Hebler. Larry Geller likened the book to a crucifixion. Patty Perry said simply, "It broke his heart."

Priscilla, meanwhile, was busy making plans to go on safari in New Guinea with Elie, and sent Lisa off to spend a few days with Elvis at Graceland while she went to La Costa to lose five pounds. Elvis spent his last few days with the daughter he loved, renting Libertyland Amusement Park in Memphis, trying to obtain a copy of *Star Wars,* which had not yet been released. He died the day Lisa was due to fly home, August 16, the date of his mother's funeral twenty years earlier. He had ingested a pharmacy of prescription medications. The official cause of death was stated to be heart disease—later contested as a drug overdose—but in truth, Elvis perished of a broken heart. He was, as he had predicted, forty-two years old. Ginger Alden discovered Elvis's sadly bloated body in the bathroom, on or near a chair, holding a still-opened book about Jesus, which Larry Geller had given to him just a few hours before.

Priscilla had returned from La Costa and was at the hairdresser in Beverly Hills when Elvis died. Her sister, Michelle, picked her up around noon, saying that Joe had called from Memphis with an urgent message for her. Once she arrived home, Joe Esposito delivered the news of Elvis's death to her over the phone. "She was just dumbfounded at first," he said. "Nothing but silence. She put the phone down and I could hear her crying in the background saying, 'Oh, no, I can't believe it.'" The first person Lisa telephoned from Graceland, it was said, was Linda Thompson, not Priscilla, though Ginger maintained that it was not Lisa who called Linda but Linda's brother, Sam, who put Lisa on the phone. There would later be almost a competition within the Elvis ranks as to which of the women in his life responded with the sincerest expression of grief. The winner, in the opinion of Shirley Dieu, Joe's girlfriend, who called all but Priscilla with the news, was Ann-Margret. Shirley telephoned Ann at the Las Vegas Hilton, where she was staying, to inform her of Elvis's death before it made the news. Ann's husband, Roger Smith, answered the phone. Before Shirley said anything, "I heard her gasp. And she knew, exactly! It was weird. And she grabbed the phone, and then Roger grabbed the phone, and I said, 'How did she know?' and he said, 'She just felt it.'"

Joe sent Elvis's private plane, the *Lisa Marie,* from Memphis to L.A. to pick up Priscilla, her parents, Jerry Schilling, Ed Parker, Linda Thompson, and a few others that day. They were notified by phone via Shirley as to when to expect the jet to transport them to Memphis. While the plane was en route to California, Priscilla telephoned Joe to instruct Shirley to call everyone back, except the Beaulieus, and tell them they would have to take a commercial flight. Priscilla later told Linda that Elvis's jet was "for wives, not girlfriends." Shirley Dieu was convinced that Priscilla assumed control that day in the mistaken belief that Elvis had left the plane and everything else to her in his will. Shirley knew otherwise, for she had just delivered a copy of a new will to Elvis the previous March, unbeknownst to Priscilla. Elvis reportedly had revised his earlier will at Vernon's urging, to disinherit Priscilla, whom Elvis had planned to remove as a beneficiary since 1973, when they divorced. The revised will was cloaked in controversy, due to the fact that it was dated March 3, 1976, instead of 1977, when it was signed, and because Elvis had not initialed every page, the custom with legal documents. Shirley and others were of the opinion that Elvis never read the will before he signed it, for it effectively left everything to Lisa, and he had long said that he would include the entourage.

Shirley, who flew to L.A. on the *Lisa Marie* that day, claimed that Priscilla asserted her authority from the moment she stepped on board, though Carol Boutilier, the stewardess, did not observe it. "When she got on the plane," recalled Shirley, "she said, 'I guess I have the say-so around here; it's my plane now.' I was upset anyway, because Elvis had died. Priscilla acted like nothing had happened." Her chief concern, according to Shirley, was that she be awakened an hour before the plane landed so she could freshen her makeup, in case there were photographers waiting. "And I thought, 'You're thinking about your makeup?' That's when I started to dislike her."

The anti-Priscilla sentiment began to mount with Elvis's funeral, which occurred on August 18–the same day as his divorce from Priscilla–and would continue thenceforth. Priscilla said later that she and Lisa cried together in Elvis's bedroom that day, each choosing a memento of his to take with her. Those who attended the funeral never witnessed Priscilla shed a tear. One of the guests confided that he saw and heard her afterward with her sister, Michelle, upstairs at Graceland, giggling. "She was wearing sunglasses and she said, 'Everybody thinks that I'm crying behind these sunglasses. They don't know that I'm really laughing!' " Shirley Dieu compared her, that day, to a queen bee.

With Elvis Presley's death, Priscilla had at last resumed her childhood position as the center of attention.

28

DRAGON LADY

Priscilla and Lisa spent the first several months after Elvis's death, the late summer and early fall of 1977, in a form of exile, avoiding the reality of the carnival that would be their existence forever more, as the surviving links to Elvis Presley, the greatest rock legend of the twentieth century.

Priscilla's first act after the funeral was to sequester Lisa from the tabloids in a summer horseback riding camp near Santa Barbara, where the Espositos' two daughters, Cindy and Debbie, were enrolled. "I remember getting a phone call from my mom at camp," Debbie said years later. The next thing she knew, Lisa was in the next cabin, using the name Lisa Beaulieu. "The staff was informed who she was, but none of the other kids knew." Lisa coped alone with the loss of her father during those first days, something Priscilla would later admit might have seemed "insensitive" on her part.

Priscilla decided, that August, to put her quest for an acting or modeling career on hold for a year. The death of Elvis, the idol she had pursued from the age of ten, the man who had formed her identity since the age of fourteen, the one who had dominated her life for the past eighteen years, was suddenly gone. "I didn't know what I was, who I was, what I was going to do." Even though his passing emancipated her—"it was the happiest day of her life," Larry Geller said sardonically—Priscilla suffered a temporary identity crisis, as did her daughter. When Lisa, who was "a very young nine," in Priscilla's description, came home from camp at the end of August, the reality set in: She finally understood that she would never see her daddy again, that she would not be able to pick up the telephone and talk to him. She looked up at Priscilla with great bewildered eyes and asked, "Mommy, what's going to happen to us?"

Priscilla's response was to flee the country with her daughter and embark on a grand tour of Europe, which had been her own fantasy since adolescence. In November, Ann-Margret hosted a radio special called *Memories of Elvis,* a tribute to the late superstar. The madness had begun. Priscilla avoided it from Paris and London, then took Lisa to Hawaii in December. They spent Christmas at Graceland, for the first time without the man whose presence domi-nated, still *inhabited,* its rooms.

Priscilla returned to Beverly Hills with Lisa early in 1978. Her survival skills were showing, for she leapt into the new year with a passion. Her life in the shadows had officially ended; Priscilla determined to develop her *own* talent, her own personality, her own persona. She kept no photographs of Elvis in her house, and hadn't since she left him, a natural response for an ex-wife, though an underlying hostility toward Elvis had filtered through Priscilla's behavior from the time she exited his realm in 1972. The focus now was on *Priscilla.*

Priscilla had kept Lisa out of school that fall, and was now playing with the notion of sending her to a European boarding school, an extension of her cur-rent infatuation with all things French. The previous year, Lisa was in the third grade at the John Dye School in Bel Air, a struggling student with no interest in schoolwork, recalled her friend, neighbor, and classmate Dana Rosenfeld. Her schoolmates were the daughters of Dean Martin, Sydney Pollack, Carol Burnett—a celebrity student body that was "the *National Enquirer*'s dream," said one student—and Lisa, who was accustomed to the *Beverly Hillbillies* na-ture of Graceland and the fantasia of Vegas, felt out of place. Priscilla com-promised her dream of a European boarding school by enrolling Lisa in the Lycée Français, the stylish, academically rigid French school in west Los An-geles she had considered for her the prior summer, before Elvis's death. It was a decision Priscilla later admitted was "stupid" on her part. "I was a young mother. I probably would have been much better off leaving her at John Dye. She was having some problems. She needed to be tutored, and I felt maybe she wasn't quite getting it. So what did I do? Put her in a school that was much more stringent. I wanted her to speak French. You know, you have this ideal—your child is going to speak French. And the uniforms—it was my ideal scene for her. And I never should have done that. I should have kept her in school with her friends. It was a mistake."

Priscilla's obsession with her appearance sent her to a fitness class taught by Kim Lee on the outskirts of Beverly Hills. She filed a claim against Elvis's es-tate in February to collect the remainder of her unpaid monthly divorce set-tlement, proving she was no longer an innocent in money matters. "That was when he was alive," assessed Ed Hookstratten, Elvis's original divorce lawyer. "Once he died, then that all changed." Joe Moscheo, a family friend who was advising Priscilla at the time, said she took an interest in Elvis's estate, even though she was not a beneficiary in his will, "but there was always friction with the family," primarily from Vernon, who had been named executor. Lisa was the sole heir, Priscilla was her guardian, and "Priscilla had her settlement agree-ment; that kept her involved."

Contrary to her later claim that she was reluctant to capitalize on her link to Elvis, by that first spring Priscilla was already seeking in earnest to exploit her connection to the King—an enterprise that was fast becoming a cottage industry. "I never had the idea that she wanted to distance herself," proclaimed Joe Moscheo, who met with Priscilla that May to discuss Elvis-related money-making possibilities. Priscilla put out antennae in every direction in the spring of 1978. She engaged John O'Grady, the private investigator who had once gathered evidence of her affair with Mike Stone, to look for "any way in which she could capitalize on the fact that she had been married to the world-renowned singer, Elvis Presley." She promised O'Grady a finder's fee for any introductions he made that led to a contract.

She and Joe Moscheo, a former member of the Imperials who played piano for Elvis and became a friend of Priscilla's, ensconced themselves in her house on Summit for two weeks that May and brainstormed how she could profit from the phenomenal interest Elvis had been receiving since his death. "I was just kind of bird-doggin'," Moscheo recalled. "Everybody was coming at her with things, and I was just a set of ears and eyes that was looking out for her. I kind of weeded through some of it, listened to the good stuff, and passed it on to her." Moscheo and Priscilla emerged from their two-week confab with a seven-year contract for Joe "to exploit some of her memoirs. . . . I wouldn't say I was her agent, but I was acting as a negotiator on a couple of deals that we had." Joe sketched out a handwritten business plan for Priscilla that included a two-part network television interview to air as a special, based on her "Cinderella story" with Elvis. It was to be conducted by a "name interviewer," possibly Barbara Walters, Phil Donahue, or Tom Snyder, in a "strictly first-class" production, possibly using "never before seen and exclusive" home movies, photographs, and mementos. "Priscilla must be able to maintain her mystique and reputation and never compromise her integrity," Moscheo wrote in his notes from their sessions. "After all, she *is* the *only* woman E.P. ever really loved, and she alone knows who, what, where, when, how, and how much!" Joe Moscheo hoped to put together a package deal, tying the TV special in with a book, foreign rights, and a television movie. Priscilla had learned well from her divorce debacle with Ed Hookstratten and her conversations with financier Kirk Kerkorian. "She said, 'Hey, if you come up with something, I want to be in control, and legally,' " recalled Moscheo. "We used her lawyers, and they drew up the original contract."

Priscilla had connected with a financial mentor shortly before this, a flamboyant, showboating Texan named Morgan Maxfield, who ingratiated himself with the billionaire Hunts of Dallas and moved to Kansas City to join financial forces with Lamar Hunt. Maxfield had an eye and a taste for beautiful women, famous names, and potential moneymaking opportunities, all of which happily coexisted in Priscilla Presley. They were introduced by Bob

Wall, who had become an interim adviser to Priscilla during the second phase of her divorce from Elvis. "I kept saying to her, 'Priscilla, you've got to know these things yourself. You've really got to study it. You are going to have a lot of income in your life, and you are going to have a lot of people trying to take it away from you, and you've got to know enough so that people don't bull-shit you.'" Priscilla, said Bob, "got fascinated" by Morgan's daring and his flashy rise from H. L. Hunt's parking attendant to his financial adviser, and she began reading the economic pamphlets and other financial books that Bob passed on to her. She "was a sponge. Anything you gave her, she read it . . . and came back with questions." Priscilla, he observed, "asks smart questions. And she's not afraid to ask a dumb question, which is the sign of a smart person." Priscilla and Morgan Maxfield, by 1978, were eager to meet and became instant financial soul mates. Morgan was the Wall Street equivalent of Colonel Tom Parker, a high-rolling showman who had his own private jet and thought nothing of flying to NASA in Florida to watch a lift-off in the morning and then hopping up to Mount Rushmore for dinner that night. Priscilla, so long starved for adventure and eager to make money, was captivated. Maxfield was awed by Priscilla's fame and face, and immediately insinuated himself into the negotiations in her attempt to profit from her association with Elvis Presley. "I think there was a little jockeying for position there," said Joe Moscheo, her original adviser. "And [Maxfield] said, 'Well, I can help you do things, I work for ABC, I can make some deals for you,' whatever. So she was loyal to him at that point, saying, 'If anything happens through your efforts you can be involved.'"

Elie Ezerzer, meanwhile, had exited stage left, recalled Samira Goldman, who worked at Elie's salon. He was too busy with his hairdressing career to accompany her on her travels and to serve as her escort to the constant round of parties Priscilla was beginning to attend. She came close to a romantic involvement with Morgan Maxfield, according to her later boyfriend Mike Edwards. Priscilla was still exploring Eastern religions for herself and Lisa—she was a believer in karma and life after death—when she had a conversation with John Travolta, a high-profile Scientologist. Lisa had a schoolgirl crush on Travolta, the fantasy of every teenage girl that year because of *Grease,* and Priscilla arranged for her to spend time with him for her tenth birthday in February 1978. (She and Dana Rosenfeld also visited him on the set of *Welcome Back Kotter,* courtesy of Priscilla.) Priscilla was already drawn to the *name* "Scientology," for it reminded her of Science of the Mind, her earlier interest through her sister, Michelle. Both were founded in reality, where Priscilla felt more comfortable, as opposed to faith. Travolta told her a little about Scientology, which he called a "second cousin to Buddhism," an appealing comparison to Priscilla, and followed up their conversation by sending Priscilla an article to read. They met again for lunch, and John "had someone from the church come and talk to me," remembered Priscilla. She and John Travolta became friends that spring, "and I liked how John was. I mean, I liked how he thought. I liked, when we had conversations, where he was coming from. He seemed so clean, so concerned about not just himself but the planet. He told me about what Scientology does and what it gives you and how you are audited, and how there's a strong ethical bond with the universe. It was stuff I was just coming out of in the Eastern philosophy, and I thought, 'I'm going to try this. I can understand this a little bit better.' The other religions . . . go off the deep end a little bit." Significantly, Priscilla also admired John Travolta's *career.*

"So I joined," she said later. "I joined blindly, because there was a connection there that I felt for it." Priscilla's pull to Scientology was understandable in view of her preference for rational thinking and data, for Scientology, as it was conceived, was a philosophy, not a religion. Its founder, L. Ron Hubbard, a science-fiction writer, had written a best-seller in 1950 called *Dianetics,* which he defined as a "new mental science" that could conceivably cure every ailment through the power of the mind. The basis of Hubbard's theory was that human beings possess a "reactive mind," which contains "engrams," or reminders of painful events from our past. These engrams, he believed, caused illnesses and could be purged through the process of "dianetics" to "clear" the mind. A year later Hubbard developed the concept of Scientology, using the practices of dianetics to "clear" individuals of physical, mental, and emotional ailments, caused by their negative engrams, which he believed could be intentionally inflicted upon others via "implants." The structure of the Scientology organization held all the intrigue of a Hubbard science-fiction story. Hubbard invented a device called an E-meter, short for electropsychometer, somewhat similar to a lie detector, which he claimed measured the level of anxiety, registered as a "charge," in the person being tested, in order to uncover problem areas in one's life. The fundamental of Scientology is auditing, a process similar to psychotherapy, where an auditor—Scientology's equivalent of a therapist—listens to a member discuss his or her problems, then makes a record based upon an E-meter reading. Scientologists pay varying sums for auditing sessions, just as one would to see a therapist. Scientology condemns psychiatry as, in effect, drug pushing, but critics of the church suggest that this is to keep its members paying for auditing sessions rather than therapy.

Courses are also offered, for a range of fees. The objective, to a Scientologist, is to progress through the religion along what is known as the Bridge, on which available courses and auditing sessions are charted in a hierarchy. Once a certain number of courses have been taken and auditing sessions completed, a Scientologist achieves the level of "clear," meaning that person has cleared himself or herself of negative engrams, or painful memories, which Scientologists believe have accumulated from past lifetimes as well. Priscilla achieved the status of "clear" in 1982. To complete the Scientology courses and auditing sessions would cost an estimated $400,000 and take a lifetime, one of the primary complaints lodged against Scientology, since it calls itself a religion—a classification that enables Scientology to maintain a tax-free status. The fact that Scientology charges its members for its services bothered Priscilla at one point, "but then," she said recently, "I resolved it. They have to make their money somehow. The word has to be spread somehow. I certainly get a lot for what I'm paying. And I look at it from that viewpoint. I don't mind being charged for a book or a course or a class or for auditing. How else are they going to make money? How else are they going to be as big, and go from city to city to city to get established, if we all don't chip in? You can go to any other church and you can make a donation here and there, but where is that church? They are all faltering. Scientology is working; it is making a difference. Once you get it, you are not disappointed at all. And you can start out with one small course. You don't have to get the auditing, so it won't be as expensive." Other members, less famous than Priscilla, have complained about receiving incessant phone calls, however, or being followed around by Scientology recruiters who pressure them to sign up for more courses.

Elvis's most profound wish, throughout his relationship with Priscilla, was that she accompany him on his spiritual journey. How ironic that when he died, she should embark on a quest for a church. More ironic still was the fact that she would choose Scientology, for it was one of the few religions Elvis criticized. One of the entourage remembered driving Elvis to a Scientology center in L.A. in the late sixties or early seventies and waiting in the car while he went in to learn more about the philosophy. Elvis came out over an hour later, shaking his head and complaining, "All they did was try to sell me their books. They're just after my money and my name." He told Charlie Hodge about it later. "Elvis said, 'I looked at a bunch of books. A young man who was one of their people in the bookstore was showing everything and he showed me the price of all that stuff, and I knew it was because I was Elvis Presley.' He said, 'Probably when the bosses found out that Elvis was in there and that he didn't just give me all those books to try to get me hooked, they probably almost fired the guy.' And he said, 'These people want to control your mind, I think, so I'd never be interested in anything like that.'" Larry Geller had a similar experience with Elvis in the seventies, when they visited the Hollywood Celebrity Centre, a separate Scientology building catering exclusively to celebrities. "Elvis came out of there saying, 'No way, man,'" recalled Larry. "They're not interested in your soul or your heart. They're after your *mind*. Get me outta here." That was precisely the attraction for Priscilla, who wanted something that appealed to her logic, not her soul.

Priscilla's greatest draw to Scientology, according to Marco Garibaldi, who would become her lover in the mid-eighties, was that it gave her a sense of belonging. For Priscilla, who had felt as a child that she was not in the right family, that her parents were not really her parents, who had spent a nomadic youth moving from base to base, without a sense of permanence or roots, that was a powerful pull. Scientology was also, interestingly, an organization founded upon *secrets*. A secret society, with its own vocabulary—souls are called "thetans," and so on—a coded form of behavior, and a "hidden" answer to the riddle of life, provided to Scientologists only after they complete the final $6,000 course, called, appropriately, Truth Revealed.

Above and beyond all this, Scientology provided Priscilla Presley with a form of insulation from the prying eyes of the public. "I think," said artist Brett Livingstone Strong, a longtime friend, "that it was some sort of balance in the hull of the ship, weights to make sure the ship didn't flip over because it had such a high, high mast. And I think that basically Priscilla didn't feel that these people were after her because of her association with Elvis and [perhaps they] could generally help her achieve balance in her life. And that if people were knocking on her door, she could feel that [Scientology] was a form of protection . . . so I think she felt at home." Becoming a Scientologist and enrolling Lisa would become one of her more controversial decisions.

In June of 1978, Priscilla marked the end of her several-year relationship with Elie by giving a "coming-out" party, with a 1950s theme, at her house on Summit Drive. One of the guests that night brought a friend, a soft-spoken, devastatingly handsome male model named Michael Edwards, who had set his sights on Priscilla, much as she had set hers on Elvis years before. Priscilla lusted for Mike at first glance and with one dance, thinking he was from Europe, where he had spent time. She was thrilled to learn he was a model. At the end of the evening, Mike, who was high on cocaine, took Priscilla to a friend's apartment on Peck Drive. Each harbored a hidden agenda. "It must have been two or three in the morning," recalled Mike. "I'm sitting there, doing a line." Priscilla, unfazed, pressed ahead with her objective. "And I'm going 'sniff-sniff,' doin' coke. 'Well what do you wanna do, baby?' You know? . . . She says, 'I've never told anyone this. I want to be a model.' I'm going, 'Wait! You're Priscilla *Presley*!' " Priscilla's ears had perked when she heard Mike mention, earlier that night, that his agent was Nina Blanchard, who had rejected her the year before. Mike, she figured, might be able to help her with her career.

Mike Edwards had designs of his own on Priscilla. When they returned to her house on Summit in the middle of the night, he pretended to misplace his car keys so he would have to spend the night. This was the beginning of an elaborate plan—reminiscent of some of Priscilla's maneuvers—to seduce her.

After that night the game proceeded according to Mike's careful strategy, which included the purchase of an enormous black Jeep to replace his sports car—the better to appeal to Priscilla's preference for powerful men—and calculated late arrivals at her house, presenting himself as a challenge, to keep her interested. He also accepted $25,000 from Joe Levin, who was later famously murdered by Joe Hunt of the "Billionaire Boys Club," as payment for an introduction to Priscilla. Levin and Mike Edwards were friends, and Levin had hoped to interest Priscilla in one of his investment schemes. She had been, Priscilla said later, set up. "And I don't know why. Why would Mike set me up? Why?" Priscilla had bad vibrations about Levin, "and I told Mike that I didn't want him here. Then I came home one day and they were both in my pool! Unannounced. You don't do that. He crossed the line with me. And I told Mike I never wanted to see him again. I should have kept to it . . . [but later] I made the mistake of letting him come to my house."

Priscilla and Mike Edwards had an erotic pull to each other that they both found dangerously seductive. Priscilla promptly canceled her trip to New Guinea in order to pursue her new infatuation. Mike, the quintessential bad boy—drugs and sex without the rock and roll—appealed to the bad girl part of Priscilla's split personality. E. J. Preston, then the head of BMI, who would become a friend of both Mike and Priscilla, "used to call her Dragon Lady," Mike laughed. "He'd call me and say, 'Who *is* she today? A dragon or a lady? Is she breathing fire or is she all cozy?' He'd say, 'Well, you know, Michael, she's a Gemini. You gotta watch that!'" For Priscilla, Mike was her high school sweetheart Tommy Stewart of the Spartans, revisited. "There's an edge there, and there's a side of me that is a bit attracted to that edge," she admitted. "And I know that's a part that I was attracted to. He was very adventurous. . . . Being a model, there's this part of him that's very— There's a rawness there. And I was really attracted to that." Mike noticed immediately, he would say later, that there were "two Priscillas."

There were also, in a manner of speaking, two Michaels. Part of Mike Edwards was attracted to Priscilla because she had been married to Elvis Presley. Not so that he could possess the King's wife, as Mike Stone's ego had propelled him to do, but rather because, on some level, Mike Edwards was in love not with Priscilla but with *Elvis*. He admitted to having felt a deep fascination with Elvis Presley from boyhood, and he had always felt that Elvis, not Priscilla, might one day be part of his life. "I sensed that something with *him* first of all. First of all it was him." Mike was struck by the fact that Elvis had once played a character named Mike Edwards in a movie, and he felt they were kindred spirits. He sensed the presence of Elvis hovering about his relationship with Priscilla, he would later write, like some sort of spirit guide. Barbara Leigh had done a commercial with Mike Edwards, "and we knew each other very well," she said. "And when Priscilla started dating him, I knew that Michael was an interesting guy. He was bisexual. I don't know about him today—my son is gay, so that doesn't bother me at all—but he was very sensitive when I first met him. . . . I think that he might have been in love with everything that came along with that whole package."

Both Priscilla and Mike, by his description, tended to be repressed until they'd had a drink; then they would lose some of their inhibitions. He took a photograph of Priscilla, shortly after they met, during a sensual, wine-filled weekend at a little house on Fire Island. Mike considered this Priscilla the "true *her*," with her barriers down, wrinkles and all. "She was kind of sitting, sort of looking into the camera. I think she was topless." Mike took a series of nude photos of Priscilla that weekend. He was beginning to perceive for himself how inhibited Priscilla had been throughout her life, "repressed by her childhood, and then with Elvis," where she had played a role and was suffering a form of post-traumatic stress syndrome from the strain. To Mike, this role was "the Mask," and he would devote much of his energy in their relationship to "pushing" Priscilla to "tear it off." He was disturbed when he saw her strain to keep from smiling, as Elvis had instructed her to do, so she wouldn't create wrinkles in her face, and when he watched her spend an hour in the bathroom before presenting herself to make love. "I remember every time we'd go to bed, when we first met, she always smelled like Doublemint chewing gum, 'cause Elvis didn't like smells. She'd always take a little piece and chew it. And then the makeup and everything was perfect. I was going '*Wow!*'" She had been, as Priscilla herself described it, "programmed to please." Mike's self-appointed mission was to deprogram her.

Mike learned, fairly early on, the secret of Priscilla's real father, and he understood that it was "a taboo subject" in the Beaulieu family, whom he considered almost pathologically closed—another source of Priscilla's severe repression. "They just didn't confront the issues. Priscilla's whole drive was to try to get *out* of that [repressed atmosphere] because she was raised that way, being suppressed." Priscilla concurred with this statement. "Everything was kept quiet," she said. "Your life was very private. My parents are very private, just like my grandparents. No one shared secrets, or pasts. Everything was on a superficial level. There was never anything deep." Her dysfunctional family, according to Mike, was the reason "she got into Scientology," which was founded on the concept of confrontation: confronting the past, confronting one's problems. Mike, who was "*way* out there, trying to get away from that sort of repressed thing myself in *my* family," became a Scientologist too. For Priscilla, however, confronting her past was a losing battle. "I guess I'm the same way now," she said in 1996. "I don't share things with certain people." There was still that imaginary line she had drawn at age four to keep the real Priscilla in reserve, preserving her secrets, protecting and enshrining the myth that she, her parents, and Elvis had created.

Priscilla's mask included makeup. She was rarely seen, even in private, without the disguise of cosmetics, carefully painting her lips to define her famous cupid's-bow, as if her life would suddenly crumble if she should ever look less than flawless. Her vanity—or rather her *insecurity*—was so extreme that when she was nauseated, Mike noticed, she would even try to prevent herself from vomiting, which would not be ladylike. It was, he said, "painful" to witness. On the right occasion, "if she drinks enough," he observed, Priscilla could let loose. Mike saw that happen only rarely. "We did some drinkin' and she would just get . . . wonderful. She didn't care how she looked or if her face was perfect. The true her no one has ever seen." He said that once, on a trip to Africa together, he and Priscilla went out and had "a *little* too much to drink. She got up on the bed and she was doing a striptease, and I was going, '*God!* That's the woman I fell in love with! Right there.'" According to Mike, Priscilla's wild side sometimes frightened the prudish and proper Priscilla. "She's *afraid* of it because the other half of the Gemini goes, 'Oh, no, no, no, no, you can't do that.' " This internal conflict between the two Priscillas was illustrated in the myth of the virgin bride versus the true Priscilla, who had sex with Currie Grant so she could meet Elvis Presley, then slept with other boys, and later men, to compensate for Elvis's lack of interest.

With Mike, Priscilla fulfilled her lifetime longing to travel around the world and explore her adventurous side. "He introduced me to life, really. Eating from coconut shells in Samoa, going to the ocean and catching your own fish, cleaning it, making soup, and eating it out of coconut bowls, and having the natives make your spoons from the trees. He introduced me to a very primitive type of life that was adventurous. Going to the Australian Outback in a jeep. Bathing in rivers. We went to Japan, Australia, Samoa, Saint Bart's, all the islands in the Caribbean. He introduced me to nature. That was what I was attracted to. I'd never been with anyone so adventurous, who introduced me to such an adventurous lifestyle. And [we did] not stay in fine places. We lived in little tents with mosquito nets. And it was great. And I have that in me. So that's what I really loved about him. Going into waterfalls and staying on boats for days at a time. It was a bit wild, and he was unlike anyone I had ever met."

Priscilla's adventures with Mike were viewed by her detractors—and by some of her friends, who were concerned about Lisa—as hedonistic overindulgence, an extended period of self-gratification. Cindy Esposito—who, along with Dana Rosenfeld, was one of Lisa's few friends—would receive calls from Lisa, beseeching her to come over, for she was often alone. "We spent four to six days a week together," she remembered. Priscilla, Cindy noted disapprovingly, "was never around when Lisa was little, always pawning her off on the housekeeper or her sister or whoever." Priscilla, by her own admission, was completely absorbed in herself and Mike. "I went out every night at the beginning. . . . Lisa began saying, 'I thought you and I were going to be together, Mom!' "

Priscilla, with Mike, had lunged into a fast life of sex and drugs and airplanes and alcohol and nonstop partying. She even tried cocaine. Mike at the time was a heavy user, but he was quick to point out that Priscilla "barely dabbled. She was never into drugs. She wasn't like that. She was into loving her man." Drugs would never be a temptation for Priscilla, for to get high she would have to lose control, and control was the linchpin of her carefully calibrated existence. She and Mike lived the sexually dangerous lifestyle she had only imagined with Elvis. Priscilla made prank sex calls on the telephone when she was with Mike, calling complete strangers and using sexually suggestive or explicit language.

Priscilla would later contend that she went into her relationships with "the two Mikes," as she laughingly referred to them, "for the wrong reason"—the reason, she conceded, was sex. Priscilla was also still discovering for herself what falling in love really meant, for she had been sidetracked since fourteen in a father-daughter relationship masquerading as romantic love. "There was a conflict in my mind about the meaning of love," she remarked later. "I'd had a father figure and a protector, but I also wanted freedom, and very few men will allow that." Her relationship with Mike Stone had ended in part because of that conflict. She was also drawn to men who were younger, and she deliberately chose partners who were not famous, taking care not to re-create the situation from which she had just escaped. Myrna Smith, who had married Jerry Schilling and spent time with Priscilla and Mike Edwards, said she "always liked Mike. He's a nice guy, and they seemed . . . he knew every move to make a woman happy. He did all that stuff and that's what she needed." Priscilla had spent too long, in Myrna's estimation, gratifying Elvis Presley's ego. It was, she determined, *her* turn to be the star, the center of the universe, the one to whom others bowed. She now had the power, the glory—and the control.

Mike Edwards remembered that Mike Stone came by the house on Summit Drive sometime during that first year of their relationship. He had a movie script he wanted Priscilla to read. "She wouldn't let him in the house," Mike Edwards said. "She just walked out to the gate and talked to him out there for a moment." As he observed the scene, Mike Edwards had a fleeting premonition. "I remember sitting there thinking, God! Is this where I'm gonna be? I'm just gonna be knocking on the gate one day, out by the trash?"

29

A STAR IS REBORN

Priscilla's other fascination with Michael Edwards, beyond the sexual, was his status and expertise in the modeling profession, the goal to which Priscilla had rededicated herself, once she was past the chaos and confusion surrounding Elvis's death. She had a new focus, equally as strong as her earlier determination to marry Elvis Presley. "Priscilla is very goal-oriented," Bob Wall pointed out. "She's very achievement-oriented and had a deep need . . . to prove she was more than just a trinket on Elvis's arms and she was more than just Elvis Presley's wife."

She began, as she had in her quest to become Mrs. Elvis Presley, by inventing a new persona. This time it was Priscilla Presley the actress/model. "And that is who she created," said Mike Edwards. "A lot of stars . . . create this persona, and that's not who they are. And Priscilla did the same thing. She created *'Priscilla Presley.'* " Mike traced this change in her to the moment in his apartment when he was snorting coke, hoping to have sex, and Priscilla was describing her secret ambition to model. "The persona began at that point. . . . I said, 'I'll call Nina Blanchard tomorrow and take you down there.' And that's when the persona really took off. I . . . could open those doors for her. I was the catalyst . . . because she couldn't do it on her own. She's gotta have a man."

Nina saw Priscilla the next day, with Mike, and told her she had "perfect features" but was too short to model. Her future, advised Nina, was in commercials. Mike arranged for a photographer friend of his to take Priscilla's first commercial photos. Before the photo session, Mike had a serious conversation with her. "Do you really *want* this?" he asked Priscilla. "You're a sweet little girl now. You lived with Elvis, but somehow you still maintained that sweetness about you. You don't know what [fame is] like. It's gonna *get* you, Priscilla. It'll grab you and you *will* change. . . . And she said, 'No, I won't. How can you tell me this, Michael? I've been around Elvis all my life.' " Mike continued. "No. That spotlight was never on you. Once that light's on you, and you start doing things, you'll change. And I knew what I was saying because I've been in it and seen what it did to *me*."

Mike's friend took shots of Priscilla that day, and they were gorgeous. When she looked at them, Mike perceived, Priscilla felt she was bringing to fruition the promise of the baby beauty contestant, the carnival queen, the prettiest girl in school. "I could kind of see this woman, this dynamo who had been sitting in there from childhood. I think our fate begins when we have our first sense of awareness of something that we have. It's like her, with her eyes and her lips and cute little figure. I think that begins way back when you're three years old, five, seven, ten, or whatever, when you first look in the mirror and you see that. And I think she sensed that it began back there." Priscilla Ann, named by her mother after herself and actress Priscilla Lane, was fulfilling her next destiny.

Priscilla made the decision, with those first publicity stills, to use the professional name Priscilla Beaulieu *Presley,* more cognizant than ever, after Elvis's death, of the value of his name. "When I establish myself in the business, I'll drop that," she told Michael.

The Elvis mania that began on August 16, 1977, reached a crescendo in 1978, as the first anniversary of his death arrived. Priscilla agreed to do a short radio interview, as Priscilla Beaulieu Presley, for an ABC broadcast entitled *Elvis Memories,* heavily publicized as her "first time ever" to talk about Elvis. Joe Moscheo was still scouting for a syndicate to broadcast their proposed special featuring Priscilla in a two-part interview discussing her life with Elvis, and she was "starting to put a team together" to represent her. John O'Grady arranged an introduction to Burt Sugarman, a well-known talent agent, to conceptualize how to market Priscilla's new persona.

Priscilla's companion goal, established during her European phase with Elie and reinforced by her relationship with Michael Edwards, was to acquire sophistication and the patina of class. "The most change was with Michael," commented Myrna, who, she said, "groomed" Priscilla. "She stopped wearing all of those tassels and things." Priscilla met Joan Quinn, the social and socially connected wife of a Beverly Hills attorney, then the West Coast editor of Andy Warhol's hip *Interview* magazine, at Kim Lee's gym, a meeting place for the Beverly Hills ladies-who-lunch, and she and Mike began spending time with Joan and her husband. Joan had the same dismal perception of Priscilla's sense of style upon meeting her as Terry O'Neill, and attributed it largely to Priscilla's family background. Priscilla looked to Joan as her social mentor and followed her about like Eve Harrington did Margo Channing in *All About Eve,* studying her every gesture and replicating Joan's style and sensibilities, hoping to become a Beverly Hills socialite. Like Eve Harrington, she was the classic arriviste. "She'd never been anywhere," said Joan. "She knew nothing." Joan saw Priscilla's aura of innocence, the seemingly angelic naïveté that fooled so many, as a pose. "I don't think she was demure. I think she was intimidated by

anybody who was socially adequate. She was socially *in*adequate to the point
of pain, of just shutting up. But she's a very smart girl—street-smart. She could
sit with you and be afraid to say anything, but . . . she'll ask you where you got
the shoes, she'll ask you where you got the pen. . . ."

Priscilla's mystique—that sphinxlike aura of mystery and innocence she
conveyed—was, to Joan, another pose, a cover-up, in her opinion, for silent
calculation. "And that can then give you an attitude of being aloof—very, very
private. No matter how immature, how unstable—she's private. She won't tell
you anything. She's always sponging from you. She took [your advice and ex-
ample] and used it to better herself." Priscilla's "act," as Joan called it, was also
a disguise for a vapid personality, a "style of presenting herself as just a way of
covering that she was nothing. I don't think she was educated, that she could
read or spell."

Joan met Ann Beaulieu through Priscilla and saw her intermittently at the
manicurist's. Joan considered Ann an even greater poseur than Priscilla, "in
her own mind, the grand dame. She was always [acting] like she was better
than anybody there. Spoke to me but never to anyone else." Ann, like
Priscilla, "would never go out without makeup. Her mother never went to the
manicurist without being totally made-up. She would always wear a blazer and
slacks and tinted glasses. And her hands were just like Priscilla's, these long
hands and fingernails. She would look around and she smoked a lot." Ann
Beaulieu, the former riveter, was now discussing couturiers with Joan, but "she
didn't have any idea what labels were—Jimmy Galanos, Zandra Rhodes was
just coming in." Priscilla bought her parents a house in Brentwood, at 666
Waltham—paid for with part of her divorce settlement, Phylliss Mann understood—and hired Phylliss to help decorate it. Phylliss, like Joan, perceived Ann
Beaulieu as an uneducated woman who "put on airs." "Terrible airs," said
Joan. "And grand airs." They all derived, noted Joan, from Priscilla. "[Ann]
had a daughter who married Elvis. Or she *pushed* a daughter to marry Elvis."

Lisa was the unintentional victim of Priscilla's sybaritic lifestyle with Mike
Edwards. She was a lonely girl, at ten and eleven. Her only friends, Cindy Esposito and Dana Rosenfeld, were aspiring gymnasts, and the three girls created
dance programs in the backyard. "We played together . . . and had sleep overs
all the time. We were pretty inseparable for a long time," said Dana. "But it
was difficult. There were no kids in Beverly Hills, no small kids, and the only
other neighbor we played with was Sammy Davis Jr., and he was really good
to us. He would invite us over, and his wife, Altavise, was just the sweetest
woman."

Dana's traditional parents disapproved of Priscilla's lifestyle, "because she
had a series of lovers who lived with her, about fifteen feet down the hall from
Lisa's room. But it was never done irresponsibly, or without concern, without

making sure that Lisa really knew the person before they became a part of her life for a couple of years. There were problems and things that people could look down their noses at—how Priscilla lived her life and her own experimentation—but she was so young." Priscilla later admitted that she wasn't certain how to handle dating, or men spending the night, around Lisa.

Lisa had other problems, most of them centering on her identity as Elvis Presley's only child. Cindy Esposito remembered her as a rather morose girl who seldom smiled. She used the name Lisa Beaulieu, and "wasn't real happy because she didn't know whether her friends were her friends because of her or for who she was." In the assessment of Bob Wall, Lisa "was a great, closed-in child, probably because she had so much experience with her dad. She knew she was a princess. When she was around Priscilla, she wasn't. When she was around us, she wasn't. I've needled her her whole life because she was very closed in. It was like needle, needle, needle, needle. I teased the shit out of her. She used to get real angry. But that was the only way to let her know, 'I don't need you, you are just a friend!'" Mike Edwards remembered Lisa, at ten or eleven, as often in her room alone, behind blackout curtains, listening to Pat Benatar records, aloof with her mother, disenchanted with Beverly Hills.

Lisa's self-image as the princess of rock, spoiled utterly by a superstar father, with a staff at Graceland at her command at the age of six, continued even after Elvis died. She was imperious even with Dana, the one close friend she had. "It was always very clear that whatever Lisa wanted to do, or whatever game she wanted to play, that you'd say, 'Okay, we'll play this game,' or there would be a fight. . . . She had to have her way." In later years, Dana attributed this trait to Lisa's unexpressed anger over losing her father. "And even though Priscilla was a very attentive mother, there is no replacing a father who is your knight in shining armor." Priscilla, according to Mike, did her mothering as she did most other things in her life—by control. "She was in control of Lisa. Priscilla is in total control. She's got to be. Otherwise she would fall apart." Lisa, he observed, had a hard time simply being Lisa.

Dana Rosenfeld, in retrospect, regarded Priscilla as a good mother. She remembered sitting with Lisa once while Priscilla, who was being interviewed on television, was asked whether she would ever spank Lisa. When Priscilla responded that she would if Lisa misbehaved, Lisa became upset, embarrassed that her mother would say that on television, and she confronted Priscilla about it when she returned home. "And Priscilla said, 'You are no different from Dana, and don't you ever forget that you are a normal little girl. When you get out of line and need to be spanked, I will do it.' She wasn't Mommy Dearest or anything, but she was a really strong mother who tried to instill the absolute best values, and [Lisa] wouldn't get away with anything." Dana's recollection of Priscilla, as her childhood friend's mother, was of someone tender and kind. "She really was a woman who loved to love. I remember I used to skin my knees all the time, and they had this bumpy cobblestone driveway, and I slipped and ripped my knee open. And Lisa was like, 'Omigod! Omigod!' and Priscilla came out with Bactine and a cotton ball, and I looked at Priscilla and I thought she was going to cry. And I said, 'I'm like a Timex watch–I take a licking and keep on ticking.' And she started to laugh. I have only the fondest, sweetest memories of her being the best mother she could be. And being so kind to me and always making sure that if I wasn't staying the night at her house, that she or her sister would walk me to my house, even though it was just down the hill. She just exuded . . . charisma. There was something inner about her, that would come out and . . . just kind of wrap you up. She just tucked in the corners of . . . I can't describe it. You felt good when you were around her. And we wanted to come up with little projects to show her. [Priscilla] loved to love–I can't say it any differently–and she loved to have fun and be silly and giggle. She had this shining, beaming smile, and it always made you feel good."

Priscilla had a sweet, nurturing side, the same quality she had exhibited as a child, rescuing stray animals and bringing them home to nurse them back to health. When her house on Summit went through a massive remodeling, in 1996, she saved a pack of fourteen feral cats that had turned up around the property, naming each one. "I trapped them all, I got them spayed, I brought them back. And now they trust me. I call and they'll come to me. It's great, because you feel so at one with them and with nature."

Lisa, in 1979, had an even more arduous time at the Lycée Français, academically, than she'd had at the John Dye School. Priscilla was forced to transfer her to classes that were taught in English, for she could not keep pace, dashing Priscilla's dream that her daughter would speak French. She "always had a tutor," according to Mike, though Dana insisted that Lisa was "not dumb. You'd explain something to her and she would understand, but she was preoccupied a lot of the time, and she fought things all the time. If it wasn't something she wanted to do, she wouldn't be able to understand it. She chose what she gave her attention to." Lisa also felt overwhelmed by the Scientology courses her mother enrolled her in, at nine, which Priscilla admitted later "was a little too young for her." Lisa "rebelled against it" at first, said Priscilla. "There's a lot of studying that you have to do, and of course the auditing, for nine-year-olds, is a bit boring; they don't quite understand it. They don't know what they are doing." Cindy Esposito noticed that Lisa was up and down in her feelings about Scientology as a child, depending upon her mood, though "it doesn't matter," said Cindy. "Priscilla forced her into it."

Dana Rosenfeld, who was a musical prodigy at nine, took lessons from the same piano teacher as Lisa, Helena Lewin, "and there was no question who had the gift," Dana said charitably. Lisa's interests were gymnastics and dancing. "And we would constantly come up with another dance routine for 'Heart of Glass.'" Lisa's favorite singers were Blondie and Olivia Newton-John. "'Grease' was our song when it first came out, and 'Xanadu.' We saw *Grease* when it first came out; we knew all the words." Lisa's voice, at the time, seemed unremarkable to Dana, and she never mentioned anything about wanting to sing when she grew up.

Priscilla had enough ambition for both of them. She became annoyed when casting directors, auditioning her for a commercial, wondered why she bothered, or suggested, as one did, that she "take up needlepoint." Even Joe Moscheo, who was negotiating to sell Priscilla's memoir and set up her proposed two-part television interview, was surprised, at first, that Priscilla exerted herself working, until he understood her motivation. "She wanted *Priscilla* to be the name, not Elvis. I think she hid behind Elvis all those years, and now it was time for her to come out of the closet or whatever."

Priscilla flew to New York, around Christmas of 1978, and nearly froze pounding the pavement with one of Norman Brokaw's junior agents at William Morris, going from ad agency to ad agency, attempting to sell herself as a pitchwoman. She was nothing if not determined, refusing to allow herself to become just another celebrity divorcée, a forgotten, faded image, once known in the reflected glory of someone else. "I started looking at women who had really survived a relationship—the wealth, the celebrity. What 'wife of' had come through with anything? It's usually the humiliation, the embarrassment—get drunk, go to another guy, go to another guy. What wife made it? Without being another 'wife of'?" Priscilla's ego was too enormous for that result. "I just could not be the 'ex-wife of.' It's . . . like you are nothing. It's like you meant nothing: being the 'ex-wife of'—and you are stuck with that. That's what you carry around the rest of your life."

Priscilla began pursuing her modeling and acting career as ferociously as she had pursued Elvis at fourteen. "I did not want to fail. I just couldn't be a laughingstock." She hired Joel Stevens to manage her on the recommendation of one of her Scientology auditors, because she wanted a Scientologist to represent her and, perhaps more importantly, because "he was tough," said Mike Edwards. "If I wanted a personal manager, I'd certainly want someone like Joel. . . . People hate him in the industry—hate him. But they sure pick up the phone when he calls."

Things began to happen once Priscilla assembled her entourage, made up of William Morris agents, a personal manager, and the independent scouts she had prowling the industry to find her a contract, make her a star. Hollywood executives, interested in the curiosity value of Priscilla Presley, came forth with offers, badgered by Joel Stevens. Kate Jackson had just left *Charlie's Angels,* and

Priscilla was asked to replace her, or at least read for the part. She turned down the offer, saying later, "*Charlie's Angels* just didn't appeal to me. I was afraid of getting typed, just like most of the girls did. Once you do a *Charlie's Angels*, you are a *Charlie's Angels* girl. And you are just pretty. I wanted to do more." Priscilla posed for a *Playboy* layout and approved the cover shot but then backed out, a perfect illustration of the good girl–bad girl split that conflicted her. "I reneged on it. I guess they offered quite a bit of money to do it. . . . I couldn't live with myself. I've always been a bit shy in that area, and I always thought, It will come back to haunt me. I always think of that. And thank God, because look at all the girls it's come back to haunt."

The *Charlie's Angels* producers and Hugh Hefner saw Priscilla Presley as a name that would elicit attention and interest from the public. She got her first major contract shortly afterward as a spokesmodel for Wella Balsam, for essentially the same reason. "Because it was '*Priscilla Presley* represents Wella Balsam,'" recalled Mike Edwards, who had listened to Priscilla earlier announce that she would drop the Presley name when she got her first job and be known thereafter as Priscilla Beaulieu. Reality–*financial* reality–intervened, however. Mike said, "She's smart enough to know, 'Wow, I should probably . . . keep this [name], because it's a moneymaker.'" Priscilla was replacing Jaclyn Smith and Farrah Fawcett–two of the original Charlie's Angels, ironically–as the face of Wella Balsam, but she regarded the Wella contract as being "less cheesecake" than the TV series.

She and Mike and Lisa were featured in a *People* magazine cover story in December 1978. Priscilla taped a Tony Orlando special–he was a friend of hers–that same month, though her part would be cut before the show aired. In January 1979, Burt Sugarman issued a press release stating that Priscilla Presley was "about to happen," announcing that she would be starring that year in a national television commercial, a TV series, and a television movie. Only one of Sugarman's claims (the commercial) was true, though the hype signaled the building momentum of her career and the zeal with which her representatives strived to make it happen.

Mike, Priscilla's cheerleader, helped her create a new image, with lightened hair and a more sophisticated wardrobe. At the same time, she was becoming discouraged about her ability to act, and she froze at an audition, unable to perform. Priscilla, Mike observed from coaching her, could not drop the veil with which she protected herself, nor could she transcend her preoccupation with her appearance long enough to lose herself in a character. She was stiff and, at times, too shy to emote in public–the legacy of the child who was taught to keep secrets.

30
THE "WIDOW" PRESLEY

On June 26, 1979, Vernon Elvis Presley died and a new Priscilla was born.

This transformation occurred due to a clause in Elvis Presley's will. Elvis had appointed his daddy executor of his estate and had directed that Vernon appoint whomever he chose to succeed him upon his death. Vernon elected to empower his two coexecutors—the National Bank of Commerce of Memphis and his accountant, Joseph Hanks—to continue in their respective positions. Then he pondered, long and hard, whom he would choose to succeed himself as executor of his son's estate, which was primarily held in trust for Lisa until she reached the age of twenty-five.

Vernon Presley's decision, reached when he was in ill health and knew he was dying, would forever alter the course of Elvis Presley's estate, image, and likeness, and be one of the more controversial actions of his lifetime. His choice, upon great reflection, was Priscilla, the once shy teenager who had come to him for handouts to go to the movies. Why Priscilla? According to Joe Moscheo, Dee Presley, and others, there was no love lost between Vernon and his former daughter-in-law, nor had Priscilla demonstrated, to Vernon, any financial savvy. One of Vernon's last experiences with Priscilla was the divorce debacle, when she blindly agreed to accept $100,000 from Elvis. Priscilla was not even *married* to Elvis when he died. She was an ex-wife, not a widow—not even a beneficiary in Elvis's will. Elvis, in fact, had rewritten his will before he died specifically to *remove* Priscilla. "He was really upset," said Shirley Dieu, who hand-delivered Elvis's revised will to him in 1977, "and he'd gotten to a point where he'd just had it with Priscilla. He told his dad, 'Daddy, I want Priscilla taken out of the will. . . . Everything goes to Lisa.' So what Vernon did was have *everyone* taken out of the will, including the guys. When Elvis signed the will, he didn't even read it. And so Elvis didn't know the guys were taken out. All he knew was that Priscilla was taken out, and that was his main concern."

The key to Vernon Presley's otherwise inexplicable choice was Lisa. His only grandchild would become, upon Grandma Presley's death, the sole heir to Elvis's estate. Vernon wanted to ensure that whoever was named coexecutor to replace him had Lisa's best interests at heart. Whom could he trust more than her mother? "I think that my dad didn't have any other choice," commented Rick Stanley, Vernon's stepson. "He couldn't hand it to Lisa, and who else could protect her interest? You see, my daddy adored Lisa. In my dad's way of thinking, Priscilla was blood contact." Said Dee Presley, "Lisa Marie was the only reason [Vernon] would tolerate Priscilla. And Priscilla didn't care for Vernon, either. In the end, she really didn't care for Elvis. I'm not sure if she ever did." Vernon and Dee had divorced shortly before Elvis died, and Vernon had married his nurse, Sandy Miller (a different person than Sandi Miller, the Elvis fan who spent time at his Palm Springs residences). The last Mrs. Vernon Presley agreed with the second Mrs. Vernon Presley. "I think," she said, "he felt that Elvis's intention was to leave a legacy for his daughter. And of all the people in the world, Priscilla had more knowledge and more understanding of that. And she provided a balance with the other two people who were named, in order to provide her with the expertise." Beecher Smith–the Memphis attorney who drew up Elvis's will, represented the estate, and discussed with Vernon whom to appoint as his successor–later acknowledged that Priscilla was "a stranger to the estate," as he put it in legal jargon. "And Lisa's best interest became the paramount question after Vernon Presley knew that his health was declining. If Vernon had done nothing, there would have been a bank involved. And the bank would have been well and good . . . but he wanted to have a couple of individuals he knew and trusted to make things work and make an orderly transition." Vernon, said Beecher Smith, "knew that Priscilla could get competent assistance where she needed it. And he trusted her to do what she needed to do as a mother."

Priscilla would later maintain that her appointment as coexecutrix of Elvis's estate was a curse to her at first, for it replanted her squarely in the spotlight of Elvis's world–the world she had fought so feverishly to escape. Mike Edwards, in fact, perceived her as taking on an obligation, something it was necessary for her to do for Lisa's benefit.

Other evidence suggests that Priscilla embraced her new power from the outset. At Vernon's funeral, she was already seeking releases from the Stanley brothers for the right to market home movies in which they appeared, and she seemed willing to go to extraordinary lengths to obtain them. She told the Stanleys, at Vernon's funeral service, that she wanted to sell the home footage for a TV special, and she apparently promised them they would be paid if they signed and the movies were sold. After Vernon was buried, Priscilla–who had been, by Billy's description, "cold" to the Stanleys at Elvis's funeral two years before, their last contact–invited David, Ricky, and Billy to a Mexican restaurant in Memphis, where she swapped Elvis stories and ordered an extra bottle of wine for them to keep. The seduction of the Stanleys continued through-out the night. Priscilla took the three brothers bar-hopping, and between stops, Billy would later recount, he stumbled upon Priscilla making out in the backseat with David. According to all three brothers, she suggested they stop at Graceland for a quick skinny-dip before she left for Los Angeles. Rick had to catch a plane for Florida, but David, Billy, and Priscilla's sister, Michelle, ac-cepted the invitation. Both David and Billy would later say that Priscilla be-came suddenly shy once they got to the pool and stripped instead to her bra and panties. After the swim, Billy would later write, Priscilla stood–completely naked–in an open doorway in front of him and David and asked for something of theirs to wear. "Oh, yeah," chuckled Rick. "I heard all about it." By the time she caught her plane for L.A., Priscilla had her signed release. David and Billy never heard from her again. She sold the home movies soon afterward for a large sum of money, but she never compensated the Stanleys. All but Ricky–who remained friends with Priscilla and did not consider the footage was his to sell anyway–felt misled and deceived. "But see," he ex-plained, "that's a part of a prevailing mentality. It was like sharks in a frenzy after Elvis died. Nobody is gonna do anything unless it is for money. Which is really weird. Where is the compassion and understanding?"

Nancy Rooks, the Graceland maid with whom Elvis shared his vision of the afterlife, noticed an immediate change in Priscilla after Vernon's funeral. "She became the boss after Vernon died," she said simply. "She took over."

Priscilla, in one of her first actions as an executrix, met in Memphis with Joe Hanks, the Presley family accountant and a coexecutor since Elvis's death, to discuss the state of the estate. She was shocked, she would say later, to discover that Lisa's fortune–the value of Elvis Presley's estate–had dwindled to less than $8 million and that it could diminish to zero if she did not take drastic action. Elvis, it seemed, had not died as rich a man as one would have be-lieved. "Elvis had a very high lifestyle," said his probate lawyer, Beecher Smith. "Elvis would spend his money as he went along. He enjoyed life. He had a lot of people who were depending on him for their livelihood." The es-tate, Smith noted, did not have many liquid assets. One of its chief assets, Graceland, was in fact a cash drain, for it required an outlay of nearly half a million dollars a year to keep it open.

Vernon's death was the catalyst for change in the management of the estate, for reasons that are still being debated. A new regime, symbolized by Priscilla, had taken control. The other coexecutors–the Memphis bank and Joe Hanks–according to Beecher Smith, needed to find a way to turn the situation around, now that Vernon had passed on. "Vernon Presley had been in bad health, and it had been hard to get things done," was Smith's explanation, "and when he died, we had people who were basically healthy and were trying to move things along. Basically, they were playing catch-up ball." The original coexecutors and Smith brought Priscilla up to speed that summer. "She had to have an overview," said Beecher Smith, "because she had not been involved at all, and here she comes in as an executrix, and we had to come up with a business plan for where we needed to go." According to Smith, the idea of opening Graceland as a tourist center—to offset the cost of its upkeep—was discussed "pretty early on."

Priscilla, in those early months, admittedly leaned on Joe Hanks, the Presley accountant and her coexecutor, for she was more interested at that time in establishing herself as an actress or model. She engaged Arthur Toll, her former divorce lawyer, to represent her and brought in Arthur's attorney-son Roger to assist in overseeing Elvis's estate and Lisa's inheritance. Arthur Toll found Priscilla an eager student from the first. "She wanted to accept the challenge of being involved," as he put it, and she "thought she could learn to do that." Priscilla's lawyer was surprised at "how little money there really was" in Elvis's estate. *He* felt the problem was its existing lawyers in Memphis, who had been advising Vernon and who, in his opinion, "were not being very aggressive about the estate." Priscilla, he said, "wanted to make sure that it was maximized to Lisa's benefit."

Joe Moscheo, who had been discussing Elvis-related commercial ventures with Priscilla since the singer's death in 1977, two years earlier, dived in, with Priscilla, to explore the opportunities her new role as executrix presented her. "It was time to—I hate to use the word—cash in on him," said Moscheo, "but it was time to do this in a businesslike way and form some real strong business relationships, or this whole thing was just going to go by the wayside." Moscheo intensified his "bird-dogging" for Priscilla. By September he had sent her a letter outlining his progress. He had spoken to representatives of the state of Tennessee about opening Graceland as a state park; he'd met with RCA to discuss repackaging and reissuing Elvis's records; he had examined the possibility of recouping some of Elvis's lost royalties; and he had entertained the thought of the estate joining forces with the Country Music Foundation to create a permanent exhibit at Graceland. Priscilla, in those early months, was "real, real confused," allowed Moscheo. She "didn't know what to do," particularly about Graceland, knowing it was a sensitive issue and that Elvis's fans would erupt at any decision they felt was contrary to the wishes of the King. The experience was both bewildering and intimidating. "Lo and behold, she's an executrix of this extremely complicated estate," said John Robert Soden, or Jack, as he was called, a junior associate of Morgan Maxfield's in Kansas City, later director of Graceland, "and now the pressure's really on her, because they keep dragging her into rooms filled with bankers and lawyers, and she's supposed to hold her own."

Priscilla approached her new position as executrix of Elvis Presley's estate with a vengeance, as she did everything else she had chosen to pursue—from marrying Elvis to becoming a socialite to establishing an acting career—by total immersion in her subject, asking questions, making lists, meeting the right people. "I don't want to fail," she said. "I do my research. I do what I have to do. I'll talk to anybody I have to talk to before I make a decision, [people who] know their field and are leaders in their field." Priscilla began subscribing to the *Wall Street Journal,* to *Barron's.* "She read everything," said Bob Wall. Morgan Maxfield, her would-be suitor and financial wunderkind, spent hours with Priscilla, dreaming up financial schemes for her and for the estate. Priscilla—unlike Elvis, who was an artist, first and only—found the business world, and the prospect of making money through investments, to be sexy, exciting. Jack Soden remembered taking a call from Priscilla at the office one day while Morgan was out. "She was calling from a pay phone in an airport, and she had read an article in the business section of the *New York Times,* and it was about gold," he recalled. "Gold had gone bananas." Priscilla "had scribbled down about four questions as a result of this article. So I ended up having this discussion with her." As her interest in high finance piqued, she utilized her formerly romantic relationship with Kirk Kerkorian, and developed friendships with other rich and powerful men, then ferreted out their business secrets, just as she had earlier studied Joan Quinn in order to become the perfect Beverly Hills social mannequin. "You pick their brains," Priscilla explained, "and you find out what they do. I love it when I'm around people like Kirk Kerkorian and Morgan and Bill Holland and Lee Iacocca, and people who have made their mark. Steve Winn. Kenny Winn, his brother. Colonel Parker. I love sitting for hours talking to them, thinking, They are brains." Priscilla had, by the strangest fate, stumbled onto her calling.

Shirley Dieu, Joe Esposito's girlfriend at the time, remembered Priscilla calling Joe around this period, to ask if he wanted to contest Elvis's will. Priscilla employed tactics similar to those she had used to obtain the Stanleys' signatures on the release of home movies. "She invited us out to dinner," said Shirley. "And I was, like, Why is she inviting us out to dinner? We haven't talked to her in a year. And as we were eating dinner, she said, 'Joe, Elvis wanted you to have something. He wasn't coherent when he signed that will. And if you want to contest it, I'll back you all the way.'" Joe, who had never seen through Priscilla's maneuvering, accepted the offer at face value. Shirley, disenchanted with Priscilla over how she had mocked Elvis at her house on Summit Drive and by her behavior prior to and during his funeral, suspected that her offer to help Joe was a ruse. "After we left, I said, 'Joe, are you nuts? The reason she wants you to contest the will is so that everything will go back to her.'" Shirley's point was that if Elvis's March 1977 revised will was thrown out, his earlier will—in which Priscilla was the primary beneficiary—would prevail, and Priscilla, not Lisa, would be Elvis's chief heir. "I don't think [Joe] really comprehended that," Shirley would say, long after their breakup. "But once we talked about it, he decided, 'No, I'm not going to do that.' Joe is not a money-hungry person, an evil person."

Priscilla Presley made her debut as a spokesmodel, the role she had worked so assiduously to attain, just as she began to assume her duties as Elvis's executrix in the fall of 1979. Her first appearance, appropriately, was in Memphis, where she represented Wella Balsam at a trade show. It was, she would say later, "probably the hardest thing I've ever done." Priscilla's crippling insecurity around crowds came back to haunt her, as did her fear of speaking in public. "I had to speak in front of so many people," she said of the Wella conference. "To be able to speak to a group of women and to answer their questions forced me to come out a little bit." She requested that she be called Miss Presley during her Wella appearance, and she discouraged questions about Elvis, the beginning of her public efforts to separate herself from her former husband, to keep the spotlight on *Priscilla*.

She and Mike decided to participate in a Scientology program that fall called the Purification. The Purif, as it was known to Scientologists, was a treatment of variable duration that cost several thousand dollars and consisted of eight-hour days spent in a quasi-sauna following a special diet, designed to rid the body of toxins, chiefly from drugs. Scientology doctrine forbids the use of drugs, and Mike had resolved to quit using cocaine, a decision that he credited with saving his relationship with Priscilla, who disapproved of his drinking and drugging. "I don't think we would have stayed together as long as we did if it wasn't for Scientology. But I know we would have stayed together longer if I had gotten into AA. Because there are some philosophies that Scientology just doesn't realize—that you've got to cut out alcohol till you take care of your life, confront yourself." Priscilla further strengthened her commitment to Scientology that fall, transferring Lisa from the Lycée Français, where they had threatened to hold her back a year, to the Scientology-run Apple School in west Los Angeles. It was Lisa's third school in eight years.

Mike and Priscilla flew to New York in October. Joan Quinn had been pushing her colleagues at *Interview* to do a piece on Priscilla, and when Henry Kissinger dropped out of a cover story, Andy Warhol brought in Priscilla as a last-minute replacement. Warhol, the quintessential gossip and people-watcher, had long been an enormous Elvis fan and harbored a fascination for Priscilla, the "widow Elvis," as his right-hand man, editor Bob Colacello, dubbed her. Colacello saw Elvis, like Marilyn Monroe, Elizabeth Taylor, and John F. Kennedy, as one of "the saints of our secular culture. People seeing Elvis in parking lots—that's straight out of seeing the Virgin Mary at Lourdes."

The fixation on Priscilla, in Colacello's analysis, was that "she's the link. She's the widow [sic] of a saint." The equivalent of Jackie Kennedy, he believed. "And it is intimidating to be the widow of a saint. The Elvis myth was so overwhelming, and people are so curious about it."

Andy Warhol's only comment about Priscilla, later, apart from remarking on her beauty, was his catty speculation that she must have had a nose job. Colacello found her closed to the point of paranoia, "very unforthcoming, very nervous and uncomfortable, frightened, and tense about the whole situation. She seemed really worried about saying the wrong things." This was apparently another vestige of Priscilla's lifelong practice of secret-keeping, the fear of revealing something that she had been instructed, or that she preferred, not to disclose. One of her few comments to Andy Warhol that day—and it said more about Priscilla than she realized—was "Sex is everything." Apart from that, according to Bob Colacello, Mike Edwards dominated the conversation to a degree that Colacello found slightly discomfiting, though he liked Edwards immensely. "She seemed to be almost controlled by him," Colacello remembered. "She did not answer a question without looking at him first. . . . She was kind of weird, very much under his spell, almost. There was a slight . . . Svengali aspect to it." According to Mike, Priscilla was too shut down, too insecure, to speak for herself.

Bob Colacello had sensed that Priscilla and Mike were very much in love; but there were problems beneath the surface appearance of two gorgeous people leading glamorous lives. Priscilla's career was advancing just as Mike's was on the wane, and his ego could not tolerate the disparity in their fortunes, or Priscilla's offers to fund their lifestyle. "The timing wasn't right," he said. "The way I was raised, I couldn't live under that. I like to be the breadwinner." Mike still had a problem with alcohol, "and I think when he would get drunk he would be embarrassing," said Myrna Smith. He tried to discuss their difficulties with Priscilla, but he could not get past the mask. "I'd say, 'Priscilla, you and me, we are a problem.' And she said, 'No, I've *dealt* with it.' And I'm saying, 'No! You can't say *I've* dealt with it. It takes a *we*. And that's what her philosophy is: 'I've dealt with it. It's taken care of and it's in the past and it's out of my head.' And it still continues. She still puts the veil up and makes up her face, does the little thing with her lipstick: 'I'm not gonna see the world.'" Joan Quinn noticed this same denial, as if Priscilla was protecting some forbidden secret—Currie, maybe? The truth, not the myth, of her relationship with Elvis? Her real identity? Her unhappy childhood? Her stepfather's possible abuse? "Even with Mike," noted Joan, "she wouldn't unlock the door. She wouldn't tell you everything; there was always something that was locked. I wondered if Scientology unlocked her door."

Priscilla became pregnant by Mike in the midst of their difficulties and decided, after Mike's silence on the issue, to have an abortion. "When she asked, I didn't say, 'Yes, let's [have the baby], I was just going, 'God!' I can't say it was the biggest mistake, but it's a real— I wasn't ready. I was still running wild, and I was thinking, 'I don't want to be living under this roof that much longer.' That would be unfair, just to [have a child] to be connected to the Presley name. . . . We'd toss and turn until all hours of the night, talking about it. And by not saying no and by not saying yes, I think she just kind of realized, Well, he doesn't really want [a child]." Priscilla later said emphatically that she would never have married Mike Edwards, a contention Mike disputed and that she contradicted herself in a contemporaneous interview in the *Los Angeles Times.* "She wanted to get married," said Mike. "She would have changed her name. It was a lot of responsibility for me, though, and I just wasn't ready to make that commitment. . . . It didn't happen."

The abortion symbolized the end of Priscilla and Mike's love affair, though it would continue in gasps for another couple of years. Priscilla's concentration, moreover, was on her career and on making money. Mike Stone sold a tell-all about their love affair to the tabloids in 1980, and Priscilla talked to the reporter, Al Coombes, for nearly a month about collaborating on her autobiography. According to Coombes, she was looking for a way to make money, and she wanted $250,000, which was more than he could offer, for the book. Her plans to market her memoir or a TV interview special through Joe Moscheo "lost steam," Moscheo said. Mike Edwards was asked to pose for a *Cosmopolitan* piece called "Love in the Afternoon" in February and persuaded the editors to hire Priscilla to model with him, her first legitimate commercial work apart from the Wella endorsement. She was, suddenly, attracting attention. "They were like all *over* her," Mike said of the *Cosmo* editors, "and she was kind of nervous, because she'd never really done that. And the pictures came out and she was *gorgeous.* So so beautiful."

Priscilla made her first career breakthrough that spring, when Merrill Grant, who produced the popular *That's Incredible!* television series, asked her to audition for the part of cohost for a new television series called *Those Amazing Animals.* The three producers of the show—Grant, Alan Landsburg, and Woody Frasier—were putting together a trio of hosts for an animal variety show similar to *That's Incredible!* and hoped to appeal to a wide range of viewers. They had selected country-western singer Jim Stafford for folksiness and Burgess Meredith as the authority, and they wanted a female cohost who was a "Cathy Lee Crosby type," as Frasier phrased it. "Pretty but straight-ahead." Their first choice was Bo Derek, flush from her success in *10,* but "she wanted too much money," recalled Frasier. "She was pretty hot then." Someone—Alan Landsburg had "no memory of who" it was—suggested Priscilla Presley, whom several of the staff had seen on *The Mike Douglas Show* and *Donahue* when she was promoting her boutique, and the producers "jumped right on it," said Frasier. They sold Priscilla to the network "based on the Presley name," per Frasier, something that irked her, recalled Mike. "Her thing was that she wanted to get out from the shadow. She'd say, 'Everywhere I go, every casting I go on, whether it's *Charlie's Angels* or Wella Balsam or whatever, it's all leading into Elvis.' And this is Priscilla *Presley*. And *that* is who she *created*."

The producers and the network had their own concerns. They were not particularly worried about Priscilla's lack of experience—the format "could cover for an amateur," as Landsburg put it. As a cohost, Priscilla merely had to introduce clips of interesting animal stories and recite a few scripted live spots in front of a studio audience, supported by Meredith and Stafford. Their anxiety, Frasier recounted, "was could she read? Would she have the energy level?" Priscilla, commented Landsburg, did not have a "magnetic" personality. "In the beginning, we had our problems," Frasier admitted, of Priscilla's performance. "We had to go through many takes. The network was very nervous after the first taping. I remember we got lots of notes back." But Priscilla, true to form, proved "a very determined woman," according to Frasier. She persevered. The show debuted on August 24, 1980, in the 8:00 P.M. Sunday slot and received good ratings, which assuaged the networks. Priscilla, they discovered, had a "curiosity factor" that motivated people to tune in, eager, as Priscilla had discovered with Bis & Beau, to gawk at Elvis Presley's child bride. *Daily Variety* found Priscilla "rigid," but it made little difference, for as Kay Hoffman, Alan Landsburg's head of production, who reviewed the video after each taping, discovered as she was freeze-framing to edit, "she did not have a bad camera angle. Her face was *perfect*."

Priscilla marketed herself as the commodity she was becoming, doing a *TV Guide* cover, meeting the local press in various cities to promote the show. The reporter who interviewed her for the *Washington Star* found her, as Bob Colacello had, exceedingly nervous and quick to defer to her "handlers." Priscilla embarrassed herself a few times, once referring to calves as "veal" in a discussion of animals, but no lasting damage was done. Alan Landsburg assessed her, quite astutely, as a woman with a sensible attitude who "knew her own limits." Priscilla, he perceived, would not be auditioning for Lady Macbeth.

She was, however, trolling for a "dramatic" role, now that *Animals* had, in her view, provided her with a comfort level in front of a camera. She commissioned her ambitious manager, Joel Stevens, to comb the possibilities, for *Animals* was a formatted variety show, and Priscilla wanted to act. Priscilla Presley had become a bona fide Hollywood personality, flitting from audition to audition, leaving Lisa in the primary care of Mike Edwards, who had become a househusband of sorts. Lisa, Dee Presley said critically, "didn't have the mother she needed. She needed her mother when her mother was out pursuing a career." The task of ferrying Lisa back and forth from her Scientology school, and of entertaining her, fell to Mike, who was, said Dana Rosenfeld, "an absolute doll. We had so much fun with him, he was great. He was the ultimate friend, a very positive spirit to be around all the time." Unbeknownst to Lisa or Priscilla, Mike found himself increasingly attracted to Lisa, then a preadolescent, though she considered herself, he would later say, "funny-looking." This marked the beginning of a mother-daughter competition that would carry through Lisa and Priscilla's relationship. It was difficult for Lisa, as Mike observed, to be the daughter of Elvis Presley, a popular icon, and a mother who was "always a picture of perfection." While Lisa as a child was cute, she did not begin to possess the rare beauty of Priscilla, who had already captivated a rock star by the time she was fourteen through the sheer power of her face. Lisa went through a phase of copying Priscilla, recalled Mike. "She was always like, 'Oh, you're so beautiful, Mommy.' They had their quiet, wonderful moments in Priscilla's bathroom. They just kind of sat there and talked and shared a lot of things." Lisa, remembered Dana Rosenfeld, "would sit on the floor when her mom would get ready to go out, and just look at her mommy and sit and talk with her while she was putting her makeup on, setting her hair. She knew her mommy was beautiful. She would look at her and say, 'My mommy's so pretty.' " Lisa went to Dana's house one day carrying a hairbrush of Priscilla's, saying, "My mommy paid twenty-five dollars for this hairbrush because her hair is so beautiful."

Priscilla enrolled with Mike in an acting class taught by Milton Katselis, a respected L.A. drama teacher who was also a Scientologist. Although she tried determinedly to perform the exercises in class, Priscilla could not break free from her inhibitions, to Mike's continuing frustration. "I directed her in a scene in class," he said, "and I remember the scene. I said, 'Just rip that apart. Don't be afraid to let your face slide off.' " Priscilla could not do it. She and Mike attended a costume ball at one of the L.A. art museums that year, where they met a genial young British artist named Brett Livingstone Strong, and they became close friends with Brett and his wife. The setting was appropriate for Priscilla, for as Brett recalled, they were all wearing masks.

Brett Strong was a great connector of people and had a number of friends in the music industry. He introduced Priscilla and Mike to Russell Hitchcock of the rock group Air Supply. Priscilla became close to both Russell and his wife, Paula. Through Brett, Priscilla also met and befriended Graham Russell, another member of Air Supply. "I'm the one who introduced everybody to everybody!" Brett would later joke.

Priscilla's acting career and social life were put on hold that December, when the Presley estate became embroiled in a headline-making controversy over Colonel Parker's commission arrangement with the executors. Earlier that year the probate judge presiding over the Presley estate, Joseph Evans, appointed a young, feisty Memphis lawyer named Blanchard Tual as Lisa's guardian ad litem, a standard procedure in a case involving a minor. Tual, representing Lisa's interests as sole heir, took it upon himself to conduct an exhaustive investigation of Elvis's estate and was appalled to discover an earlier agreement between the Colonel and Elvis that gave Elvis's manager a 50 percent commission on everything the singer earned—in an industry where 10 percent was the standard agent's fee. Tual was even more disturbed to find that Vernon Presley had carried the Colonel's arrangement over to the estate, contracting to pay Parker 50 percent of any earnings Elvis generated after his death. Shortly after Tual was appointed, in May of 1980, the coexecutors—Joseph Hanks, the Bank of Commerce, and Priscilla—along with the attorney for the estate, Beecher Smith, submitted a management plan to the court for approval. In it they requested that Judge Evans approve the continuation of the Colonel's 50 percent split.

A scandal erupted in December when Blanchard Tual presented, in open court, a report he had compiled outlining what he considered the near-extortion Colonel Parker had committed upon Elvis and, by extension, his estate. The hearing erupted into a near brawl, with Tual accusing Beecher Smith and the executors—with the exception of Priscilla, whom he considered not personally involved with the management of the estate—of "sandbagging" him, declaring them "incompetent" and "yes-men" for the Colonel because they had ratified his exorbitant fee arrangement. Beecher Smith still smarted over the incident, and Tual's criticism of his decision to approve the Colonel's contract with the estate, sixteen years later. "I felt like I had somebody looking over my shoulder and prejudging the work that was done before me and by me. And there was a time when I took umbrage at it." Judge Evans, however, agreed with Tual's assessment of the Colonel's arrangement, which he said later "seemed a little strange to me. I figured it was too much, too much, excessive. . . . I was saying he'd received too darn much all those years. No telling how much more he received that there's no record of."

Tual had opened a Pandora's box. After the explosive hearing, which even made its way into the pages of *People* magazine, where the Colonel's "exploitation" of Elvis was reported, everyone's eyes were on the Presley executors. Priscilla, who had been somewhat lackadaisical about the estate, turned her attention to the fee arrangement with Colonel Parker and to her two coexecutors' decision to approve it. The following weeks, as the executors, in accordance with Judge Evans's order, began to renegotiate with the Colonel, were awkward for Priscilla, who found herself at odds not only with Colonel Parker, the intimidating figure whom she had met as a little girl and to whom even Elvis deferred, but potentially with her fellow executors as well. Bob Wall recalled her being "in a lot of agony over it," continually outvoted two-to-one by the other executors. "I know it was an aggravating, upsetting period for her." Priscilla's legal adviser, Arthur Toll, decried the Colonel's fifty-fifty arrangement with the estate as excessive and "felt something should be done about that agreement. I remember that we had a meeting in the Colonel's office on Sunset trying to resolve things. And I think we went a long way toward getting an agreement with the Colonel at that time."

Colonel Parker and the executors of Elvis's estate eventually made a private settlement, which Jerry Schilling, who had remained close to the Colonel after Elvis's death, stated to be $2 million but which Judge Evans recalled as $50,000. Jerry, who was sympathetic to the Colonel, said Parker had no choice but to settle, since "he was up against the wall—no communication with Priscilla or anybody, no contact." The fee conflict ruptured Priscilla's relationship with the Colonel, whom Arthur Toll perceived to be "very disappointed in her." "It created more, believe it or not, *hurt* on the Colonel's part," said Jerry, who eventually reconciled the two to a polite friendship. (Though when Parker died in January of 1997, neither Priscilla nor Lisa attended his funeral.) "He's lucky he got what I approved," reflected Judge Evans.

No sooner had the smoke begun to clear from the exposé of the Colonel than Priscilla was thrust into another scandal of sorts. The instigator was her old nemesis, Currie Grant. He had been researching a book about her and Elvis for several years and, in the spring of 1978, had stumbled upon Priscilla's lost grandmother in Pennsylvania. Currie already knew that Paul Beaulieu was not Priscilla's blood father, for she had told him during their intimate encounters in Germany, before he took her to meet Elvis. Kathryn Wagner had revealed to Currie the Wagner family's heartbreak over Ann's 1949 disappearance with Priscilla, Jimmy Wagner's only child. Currie developed a strong attachment to Mrs. Wagner, and she to him, in the course of their conversations and meetings. Moved to tears by her grief at losing contact with Priscilla, he determined to do what he could to reunite her with the granddaughter she had not seen since Priscilla was three. Kathryn Wagner had long since intuited, correctly, that Paul Beaulieu was at the root of Ann's estrangement from them and her decision not to respond to Mrs. Wagner's long letter to Germany in 1960—if Paul Beaulieu had ever given it to her. What Mrs. Wagner never understood was *why*.

Currie had not spoken to Priscilla since their strained conversation in 1964, when he had telephoned Graceland hoping to find out, for the piece in *Photoplay*, whether she had married Elvis. His only contact with her since then had been the day Elvis died, when he went to her mansion on Summit and stood by the gate to pay his respects—and she drove past him as if he did not exist. Currie decided to take drastic action to induce Priscilla to contact her grandmother Wagner, for he believed she would not respond if he merely telephoned her with the suggestion. On January 8, 1981, what would have been Elvis's forty-sixth birthday, Currie placed an ad in the Hollywood trade papers, *Daily Variety,* and the *Hollywood Reporter:*

PRISCILLA ANN WAGNER BEAULIEU PRESLEY

Call your grandmother Wagner. A wonderful, sweet little lady of 80. For no apparent reason, you were cut off com-pletely from your grandparents at 3 years of age when your mother remarried. You are her only grandchild. Please Priscilla, she has suffered 32 years of heartaches over you. Your grandmother knows nothing of this plea. For her number call Carol or Karon

The ad ended with a phone number for Priscilla to call. Currie's intention was to embarrass or shame Priscilla into action, and his plan worked. Ruth Batchelor, the Hollywood correspondent for *Good Morning America,* saw the ad in *Variety* and ran a segment on Priscilla Presley's abandoned grandmother on *GMA* a week later, on January 15. Batchelor concluded her television piece by saying, "When I contacted Madame Presley's agent, I got a curt 'No comment.' So will the star of *Those Amazing Animals* reunite with her alleged grandmother? Stay tuned for further reports." By the next day, Priscilla was on a private plane en route to Titusville to see the grandmother whose exis-tence had been kept from her for thirty-two years.

Mike Edwards, who at that time was with Priscilla in New York, where she was doing a promotion for Wella Balsam, remembered her as "furious" over Currie's ad in the trades. "She wouldn't deal with it," he said. Mike himself was horrified to discover that Priscilla had a grandmother the Beaulieus had hidden from her since she was three. "I always thought that was a *horrendous* thing to do. . . . There were little things like that along the way that happened, and I thought, 'You can't *do* that.' " Priscilla flew through a snowstorm to Erie, and took a limousine from there to Titusville to see her grandmother. Mrs. Wagner, at Priscilla's request, had not told a soul Priscilla was coming when she received a phone call from a Presley representative the day before to schedule Priscilla's visit. She was not aware that Currie had placed an ad in the trades, for he wanted to surprise her with a visit from Priscilla. When the call came, Kathryn Wagner "almost burst," she said later. "The night before, I didn't ever close my eyes!" She welcomed Priscilla into her house shortly after noon on January 16, 1981, as if no time had passed since the last time Priscilla was there, on her third birthday in 1948. "I just feel," she said later, "that I have been with her all my life."

Kathryn Wagner and her now famous granddaughter drank coffee, looked at family pictures, including photos of the years that had been "missing" from Priscilla's childhood, and they went through mementos in an old trunk. Those were the happiest two hours of Mrs. Wagner's last thirty years. She and Priscilla talked, Kathryn Wagner would say, "mostly about Jimmy. She wanted to know everything I could remember about her father." Priscilla asked for copies of several photographs of Jimmy, including one where he was in his navy uniform, smiling his famous smile, a replica of Priscilla's. Before Priscilla left, her grandmother gave her keepsakes that had belonged to her dead father: James Wagner's wings, a gold ring, and some trinkets he had picked up in Scotland while stationed aboard the USS *Beaver* and exchanging love letters with Anna Iversen. The father Priscilla had imagined since she was a child began to take human form. "My grandmother told me things about my father," she said later. "She has a trunk for me, in fact, filled with things. And she has letters for me that were his. I think he wrote her so many letter–letters and letters. He was talking about me in many of them. She has all that for me too." Priscilla expressed regret, later, at what her grandmother had gone through during all those years of wondering where Priscilla was, whether she might be dead, before Mrs. Wagner finally discovered that she had been deliberately cast aside. "It *is* sad," Priscilla acknowledged. "It saddens me, because she was a very sweet lady."

One of the first persons Kathryn Wagner spoke to after Priscilla left was Currie Grant, her knight in shining armor. "I'm on cloud nine!" she said breathlessly. "You won't believe it. Priscilla was here yesterday! Oh! It was *wonderful.* Currie, I have you to thank to my dying day. It couldn't have been nicer. It was just perfect . . . it was–I can't describe it! My feet aren't touching the ground. I am just the most happiest woman in this whole wide world. And oh! I thank you. You're the one that has brought this all about. You've made my whole *life* over." Currie was so pleased that Priscilla had mended her grandmother's broken heart by visiting her that he placed a second ad in *Daily Variety,* on January 21, thanking her:

PRISCILLA PRESLEY
BORN PRISCILLA ANN WAGNER
A Public Thank-You
On Jan. 8, 1981, I ran an ad in the Hollywood trade papers asking you to call your grandmother Wagner. (You were cut off completely at age 3 from your grandparents when your mother remarried.) A few days later, in freezing weather and after not seeing each other in 32 years, you arrived at the home where you played as a child and had a wonderful, joyful and tearful reunion. In 1959, I brought you and Elvis to-

gether. In 1981, I am extremely pleased that I was able to make your grandmother "the most happiest woman in this whole, wide world." Her words, not mine.

—*CURRIE GRANT, AUTHOR OF FORTHCOMING BOOK,*
ELVIS AND PRISCILLA

Priscilla was decidedly *not* the "most happiest woman in the whole wide world" that January. She was angry with Currie for humiliating her, for exposing a family secret in a public newspaper. He had, she would say later, "bad intentions." Mike was with Priscilla just before she left for Titusville and as soon as she got back. "And I said, 'So how was it?' " With Priscilla, he observed, "sometimes this stuff has to be shaken up." Mike "wondered why she didn't connect [with her grandmother more meaningfully] or stay [longer]. But I recall her saying, 'Oh, it was a *wonderful* talk,' and 'Oh, it was *so* nice, and we *hugged* and everything like that." Priscilla seemed, to Mike, touched by the reunion. "At the moment. But as soon as it's gone, then it's back to fantasyland, being 'Priscilla Presley.' "

Mike could see, from Priscilla's reaction to finding her grandmother, that she was still dominated by fear—"fear of opening up, of being honest." It was the family affliction. Currie's ad in the trade papers, Priscilla said later, was the first time her brothers found out she had a different father. The subject would never be spoken of in the Beaulieu family. "Even to this day," Priscilla said in 1996, "it's not talked about. It is *not talked* about. My brothers have *never* mentioned any of this to me." Priscilla herself would never intimate to Paul Beaulieu that she knew he was not her father. "And that's why I find it so ironical that she is so connected to Scientology," Mike commented later. "That's what it's all about. Confronting." This was quite possibly the same form of denial that led to Priscilla's refusal, in 1996, to acknowledge her 1959 affair with Currie, for it too would have revealed a secret she preferred to remain undisclosed, for it would shatter the powerful myth of the virgin bride.

Priscilla told her grandmother, as she was leaving her house in Titusville, that the next time she came to see her, she would "try to get her mother to come with her." Kathryn Wagner died nearly fifteen years later, on October 19, 1995, at the age of ninety-four. Ann Beaulieu never wrote her, never telephoned, never visited. (Priscilla kept up the relationship with her grandmother, mostly by phone and flowers, though she never took Lisa or her second child, Navarone, to meet Mrs. Wagner. Nor did Priscilla attend her grandmother's funeral in the fall of 1995. Kathryn Wagner remained, to the end, free of any bitterness toward Ann and grateful beyond words for the restored contact with her sole grandchild.)

Priscilla's life, at the time of her reunion with her long-lost grandmother, was in turbulence. She and Mike were both having affairs. Priscilla later claimed she was "trying to figure out how to get out of the relationship." One of her concerns, said Priscilla, was Mike's bisexuality. "I did ask him [about it], and he did tell me that he did have some encounters." It bothered Priscilla, she said later, "*very* much." But, she added, "it was very difficult getting out of that relationship." She distracted herself, in the summer of 1981, with a dalliance with Julio Iglesias, whom she met while attending a music festival in Viña del Mar, Chile, at Iglesias's invitation. Julio, like many of Priscilla's suitors, had been enthralled with Elvis Presley and viewed a romance with Priscilla as his chance to be sprinkled with "Elvis dust," as Priscilla would sometimes refer to it. When she left Chile for Japan, "I started getting flowers from Julio every day. He was sending me I-love-you notes—I love you this, I love you that." Priscilla soon reconnected with Julio at his mansion in Florida, where she contemplated the possibility of dating him, until he took her to a recording session. "I just went back to a certain period in my life and I thought, This is not what I want." She panicked when they went to his bedroom that night, insisting they sleep in separate rooms. The déjà vu was horrifying. "I woke up about four in the morning and knocked on his door and said, 'Can we get me a driver?' "

The ghost of Elvis was ever around her, in the management of his estate, which was tottering precariously. With the money from the Colonel's buyout agreement, the Presley estate was reappraised at $22.5 million, up from $4.5 million. The difference would have to be covered by estate taxes. Priscilla wrestled, throughout 1981, with the dilemma of whether or not to sell Graceland, a decision facing the executors, who were confronted with a diminishing estate. Gary Hovey, who was dating Priscilla's sister, Michelle, and later married her, remembered Priscilla as "torn about this decision. She would come over and talk to us about it at night. . . . There were advisers saying, 'You should sell everything.' "

When *Those Amazing Animals* was canceled in the spring of 1981 (the last episode aired on August 23), Priscilla had more time to devote to the Presley estate, and she swung into high gear, assisted, at first, by the Tolls. "She talked to other people and talked to us," said Arthur Toll. "We felt that there should be people operating the estate who were maximizing the potential. And we looked around and found some people." Priscilla had been in serious conversation with Morgan Maxfield, her "business mentor," as Mike called him, about how to resolve the Graceland conundrum when she received word by phone, one night, that he had been killed. His private plane had exploded as he was taking off from the Kansas City airport for Mount Rushmore, a few days before he was scheduled to meet with Priscilla for further discussion of the fate of Graceland. Morgan, according to Bob Wall and others, had suggested to Priscilla that she open the house to the public. Mike, who was with her when she got the call that Morgan had been killed, was slightly disturbed by her reaction, which he considered very revealing. "I was sitting on the bed, *sobbing* over Morgan, whom I didn't know as well as she did—and I didn't see any tears. And those are the little things that I *require* in a relationship with someone else. To know that, hey, you're vulnerable, you're real, you're not so totally strong. I didn't see that. I saw too much strength, too much *un*emotion, too much coldness." In the seven years he and Priscilla were together off and on, Mike had seen Priscilla cry, "but it was more of just maybe a tear."

Priscilla flew to Kansas City for the funeral with Bob Wall, who had introduced her to Morgan. Paramount in her thoughts was Graceland. "Flying to Kansas City, that's what we talked about," said Bob. " 'God, who's gonna run Graceland?' Morgan *was* going to run it."

The solution appeared, as if on cue, at the funeral, for Maxfield's junior colleague, Jack Soden, had been waiting for just such an opportunity for years. Jack, who would often be described, in later articles about the estate, as a wizened, wizardly investment adviser when he connected with Priscilla, was in fact a disgruntled young former stockbroker with modest business experience who had majored in English and dreamed of doing something "exciting" rather than "cold-calling doctors." He had a sense of manifest destiny, "a great sense of wanting to build something, to make something happen." Like Priscilla, once he had his goal in mind, Jack made a thorough study of how to achieve it, by asking questions and meeting key people. "For about a year I asked people: I'd say, 'I am just fascinated with your job. How did you get from an accounting firm to this job?' " The common denominator, he concluded—the "lesson"—was to place himself in a position where he could meet people he envied and "let them know that I'm looking." His "short-term solution" was Morgan Maxfield, whom he knew only slightly, socially from a Kansas City bachelor club. Jack Soden quit the brokerage business to accept a position as a glorified assistant to Morgan, planning to stay for a year or two, with the unabashed ambition of meeting and mingling with the rich and fascinating, with whom Morgan surrounded himself, hoping serendipity would strike. Later, when he had achieved his own success, Soden would distance himself from Morgan, whose reputation had been sullied when he ran for the U.S. House of Representatives and it was revealed that he was married with children, after having achieved notoriety as Bachelor of the Year in Kansas City society. Other allegations surfaced that he had misled the public about his financial status and educational background. Maxfield's estate ultimately ended in controversy and near poverty, belying his admirers' contention that he was a financial genius.

Following Morgan's funeral, Jack Soden, Priscilla Presley, and Bob Wall spent the afternoon in his old office, repeating Morgan anecdotes. Priscilla was concerned about her outstanding investments with Morgan's company and felt an immediate camaraderie with Jack, who was soft-spoken, polite—and deferential to her. By the end of the day, they had confirmed plans for Priscilla to meet again with Jack during a Wella promotional trip to Missouri at the end of the week so they could talk seriously about Graceland. Jack Soden's strategy for finding his dream job had worked brilliantly. He had discovered his key person in Priscilla Presley. The two met for breakfast in a coffee shop at the Alameda Plaza Hotel, where Jack scribbled out his thoughts for Graceland on a place mat. "All I remember about that place mat was writing down these things: 'Graceland' and Memphis,'" he said later. Priscilla, recalled Jack, had been subjected to intense pressure by legal advisers to sell the estate, pay off the taxes, invest the remaining money, and turn the profits over to Lisa. That was, he admitted, the conservative route, but "her instincts were just screaming at her, 'Don't sell it.'" Jack compared Elvis Presley's death to Kennedy's, selling Priscilla on the notion that Elvis's name was a marketable commodity, like a brand name, with brand-name recognition. He would take credit for suggesting to Priscilla that day the idea of opening Graceland as a permanent museum, claiming Morgan's plan had been to open the house for six to eight months as a "one-shot deal" and then to create a foundation. "It's so self-serving to say [that Morgan] didn't 'get it' and I did and that's made all the difference, you know what I mean?" commented Soden, doing just that.

Whatever the genesis of the plan, by the end of breakfast Priscilla had targeted her man and made her decision to open Elvis's estate to the public. Jack Soden, henceforth, would become the very image of Graceland. Never mind that he was not, and never had been, a fan of Elvis Presley. Critics of both Priscilla and Jack Soden would later assert that this indifference, if not aversion, to Elvis was the tie that bound them.

Elvis's fans, already devastated by the lacerating biography of Elvis that had recently been written by Albert Goldman, now heard the rumors that his house was to become a tourist site and began writing letters of protest. Priscilla once again received hate calls and threats. "She got over a hundred death threats," said Bob Wall. "A horrible way to live. There are a lot of pluses in Priscilla's lifestyle, but there's lots of negatives."

Priscilla took a wild gamble in deciding to transform Graceland into a museum and in following her instinct about Jack Soden. Both decisions would profit her immensely in the years to come. In the beginning, the plans for Graceland appeared more like a high-wire act, for the money needed to convert the house to a tourist attraction—roughly $500,000—would almost deplete the liquid assets of the estate, though Elvis's royalties would continue to accrue. She and Jack had definite, and similar, ideas for the museum. They flew, that fall, to the Biltmore estate, to the Hearst castle at San Simeon, to Mount Vernon, and to other estates they admired, to glean ideas to incorporate into the Graceland Museum. Priscilla had been following this same pattern since she was fourteen: immersion in a subject, copying an accepted role model, studying the options, talking to experts, meeting the right people. The very model Jack Soden had used to place himself in proximity of Priscilla. Graceland, the museum, Jack later admitted, "was honestly a composite of all the successful pieces we'd found at other famous homes and museums. There wasn't one little experimental piece in the whole machinery. . . . There isn't one original idea working up here. Every single piece was taken from someplace else that had worked out all the kinks. We reaped the benefit on opening day of tens of thousands of hours of experience and money." Jack Soden had mastered the Priscilla technique.

Jack Soden and Priscilla Presley's vision opened to the public less than a year after he scribbled the words "Graceland" and "Memphis" on a coffee-shop place mat. Within a month the house had earned back its original $560,000 investment, and the profits would grow exponentially in the years to come. Jack claimed, a number of years later, that he never doubted Graceland's ability to recoup the investment, though Priscilla's instinct not to sell, he said, was admirable. "It was easy to do the safe, conservative thing, and [her decision] took a little more courage—it took a lot more courage, honestly—at that time. Now, in retrospect, it looks like a no-brainer. But believe me, it wasn't a no-brainer in 1981."

Priscilla had made up her mind, said Steve Binder, the producer of Elvis's spectacular 1968 Comeback Concert and, later, the producer of a Graceland special, that the museum be a class act. "I'm convinced without a shadow of a doubt that without Priscilla, Graceland would have been a circus," Binder said. "She went in and literally undressed it so it would at least have some quality aside from its normal tackiness. I'm sure she brought some quality to the project." George Klein, remembering Priscilla at seventeen when he had met her, and then through the Elvis years, "wouldn't in my wildest imagination have seen her doing this." She had advanced light-years, from the twenty-nine-year-old divorcée who didn't know the difference between ten dollars and ten thousand dollars.

As her reputation for transforming Elvis's estate swelled into hyperbole, skeptics often questioned her intelligence. Variations on a theme would recur. Mike Stone, for one, referred to Priscilla's acumen as "practical" knowledge. Phylliss Mann likened it "more to curiosity" than to intelligence. Jack Soden, who was in the best position to assess, "thought that in a way she was trying to compensate for the fact that she was not formally educated; she really wasn't focused on school, and she came out of that experience with not a good deal of education. And a tremendous desire to be educated. And kind of soak it up. She's kind of like a street student." Arthur Toll, who met Priscilla at her financial nadir, during the divorce from Elvis, described her in 1996 as a "bright girl who really didn't have an opportunity to get into those things." He said, "There are two Priscillas. The one then and now. And it's the same woman. She had all of the abilities that she didn't use before and that she's using now."

Now that she was entering a new phase of her life, as the "widow" Presley and First Lady of Graceland, Priscilla set about, in her usual way, creating a persona. Her role model, according to Steve Binder, who witnessed the transformation in the early eighties, was Jacqueline Kennedy Onassis. "I see that every time I see her being interviewed. And I think it's, truthfully, very calculated. This is the face she's going to wear in her public persona." Steve also noticed the two faces of Priscilla. There was "the public image, which is very conservative and ladylike. And then the *other* Priscilla—a fun-loving woman who really enjoys life."

That was the secret to the contradictions that would forever follow her, and it was the key, concluded Mike Edwards, to Priscilla's mystique.

31
DÉJÀ VU

Priscilla, ever since Elvis's death in 1977, had been browsing for someone to publish her memoir. In 1982, with the publication of Albert Goldman's deeply unflattering biography of the father of her only child, she had fresh incentive.

The motivation, for Priscilla, was more personal than redemptive of Elvis. She told Mike Edwards, with whom she shared her thoughts in bed during "sleepless nights," that she wanted to set herself free, to "get out from the shadow" of Elvis. To become something *else*. To restore herself to the Priscilla she was before she assumed the persona necessary to marry a legend. The book, Priscilla kept insisting, would tell the *truth*. Finally. She met with writers throughout that winter, conducting interviews over high tea at the Westwood Marquis Hotel, finally settling on Sandra Harmon, who had once been married to the actor who played Bozo the Clown. They connected, Sandra would later say, for they were "both girls from a low-middle-class background who moved into glamour worlds," both "ambitious women who were attracted to men in that world." Priscilla would devote three years to the book project, meeting with Sandra between acting assignments. Mike described the process as "grueling" for Priscilla, who he believed was reencountering the demons from her past—all the secrets and fears—so she could confront them and triumph over them. Sandra Harmon described her interviews with Priscilla as "difficult," saying that "it took her a year to trust me. It took a year for us to get close."

Lisa Marie Presley turned fourteen that same year on February 1, a dangerous age for the women in Priscilla's family, for it was at just past fourteen that Anna Iversen met and fell in love with Jimmy Wagner, to her parents' horror, and at fourteen Priscilla realized her fantasy of dating Elvis Presley.

Lisa did not break from family tradition.

Priscilla was away much of the time auditioning or tending to the estate, so Mike and Lisa continued to spend great expanses of time alone together, growing increasingly close. One day, Mike said later, he realized that his love for Lisa had shifted from that of a father figure to something more erotic. "I fell in love with her," he said. Mike Edwards's "love" for Lisa was a complicated psychological conundrum, much as Elvis Presley's and Priscilla Beaulieu's relationship, in 1959. There were no deviant Lolita undertones, asserted Mike, no older man sexually obsessed with nubile teenager. "It wasn't like Humbert Humbert. It wasn't like that. I just loved her." Part of the love was a form of sympathetic identification, for Mike could perceive, in Lisa, the sensory deprivation from her mother he himself was experiencing with Priscilla. "I guess sometimes love can stem from different things. Can come from different areas. But I just felt so sorry for her, 'cause her mom would do this kind of nonhug hug. I never saw the little girl with someone who'd just give her a wonderful, wonderful hug."

The other fascination for Mike, more compelling, was intricately entangled with his own childhood obsession with Elvis Presley, for he saw Elvis in Lisa, who so resembled her dead father, just as Priscilla resembled hers. Just as he had tried connect to Elvis through Priscilla, Mike now attempted to merge somehow with the King via his daughter. "She was the epitome of her father, and as a little boy, he *saved* me with his music. I'd go to the movies, and . . . he was a person who [stood up] against authority. And when I met Lisa she was the same way. She was this wonderful little kid who would go into her room and listen to her music after school every day and was like the antithesis of her mom. She'd give you a hug and you knew you'd been hugged. She's got a heart of gold. She's a lovely, lovely little lady." It was also not lost on Mike—deeply embroiled in a love relationship with Priscilla—that Lisa was the same age, fourteen, as her mother had been when Elvis fell in love with her. The Freudian implications were dizzying.

Mike did not physically consummate with Lisa the relationship he had in his mind, though he would, once or twice, stand beside her bed, as she was sleeping, and pull the sheets back and stare. Lisa awakened during one of these vigils, and it so unnerved both her and her mother that Priscilla ordered Mike out of the house, one of several separations during their tempestuous seven-year relationship. He eventually returned, and Priscilla said later she had no idea he was actually in love with her fourteen-year-old daughter. "I thought it was a flirtation on *her* part. You know, she'd flirt around and he'd chase her around and things like that. But when it's not a part of your thoughts, it's very difficult to see. I never in my wildest dreams thought that there was anything there. Never. He played hide-and-seek with her. But Michael was a very different type of being, as far as I was concerned. He was sexual anyway . . . so he would show signs, not just to Lisa, but to all these women. He didn't do anything, really, but . . . there would be little flirtations here and there: 'Mmmm, she looks cute,' or 'Don't you look cute today, Lisa?' But it's like 'Okay, so it's a guy saying she looks cute.' So I had nothing, nothing, nothing, nothing there." Priscilla, in fact, regarded

Mike's demonstrativeness—the fact that he hugged tightly and wished to be hugged back—as aberrant, the very thing he cited as evidence of Priscilla's repression. "He would say, '*Feel!* You are used to having your feelings guarded. You are used to suppressing your feelings. Just let go. Just let go and hold me.' "

Priscilla visited her grandmother Wagner the day after Easter and told her she was thinking of sending Lisa to Switzerland to school, though Lisa did not want to go. More evidence, Cindy Esposito would later point out, of Priscilla's "pawning off" Lisa. "See," she said cynically. "Priscilla tried to send Lisa away again." Priscilla also expressed to her grandmother her disenchantment with Beverly Hills, saying that she did not know one neighbor, and that she would prefer to live somewhere else.

When she returned to L.A., Priscilla stopped by her publicist's office at Rogers & Cowan. Another client, director Hall Bartlett, who was casting a new movie, took one look at Priscilla and was, said one member of his crew, "enthralled." He determined, on sight, to cast Priscilla in his next film, *Comeback,* a true adventure story starring Michael Landon. It mattered little to Bartlett whether or not Priscilla Presley could act. "She went up and read for it a couple of times," said Mike, "and Hall then called Joel Stevens, who was her manager at the time, and said, 'She's not the greatest actress, but I think I can get out of her what I need to for the part.' " What Hall Bartlett needed—or, more importantly, *wanted*—was simply beauty. Michael Landon's other female lead, hand-selected by Hall, was Moira Chen, an exotic black actress from Holland who had appeared in a black version of *Emmanuelle.* Said Mike Vendrell, who worked on the picture: "I kept asking, 'What are we doing with a black soft-core porn actress from *Emmanuelle?*" The answer was Bartlett. "Hall was into the old kind of filmmaker style," explained his then assistant, Celia Vendrell. "Glamour and beauty were important to him." Those qualities Priscilla Presley possessed in abundance, leading to her departure, in May, for Bangkok, to start shooting *Comeback.*

Hall had cast her in the part of a diver who assists a photojournalist, played by Michael Landon, in his efforts to rescue his Laotian fiancée. Priscilla, in her inimitable way, had prepared for several months, overcoming a terror of diving by working, first with a UCLA diving coach, then with Mike Edwards, whose diving skills helped temporarily resuscitate their faltering relationship. The shoot, which took place in various locations in Thailand, Florida, and the Bahamas, was so fraught with intrigue—love affairs, feuds, pregnancies, takeovers—that one crew member, a ten-year veteran of filmmaking, described it as a movie within a movie. "You could write, seriously, a book—a comedy—about it." The prevailing drama was a vicious power struggle between Michael Landon and Hall Bartlett, the larger-than-life, old-style Hollywood director who was a Harvard graduate, a Rhodes scholar, and a professional tennis player. "He was a huge guy," described a stuntman who worked on the film. "Maybe six-three, 310 pounds. Used to wear those buccaneer shirts that lace up the front [with] big collars and puffy sleeves. . . . I went to his house for dinner, and he had his name [embossed] on the toilet paper. A big 'HB' on his toilet paper. He was Old Hollywood." Michael Landon, by contrast, was high-tech television. The two mixed dangerously, with Landon attempting to overthrow Bartlett and take over the direction of the film in an almost unheard of cinematic coup that left the cast and crew alternately astonished and amused. Priscilla, by her bad fortune, got caught in the crossfire.

Michael Landon, in his frustration, singled Priscilla out for persecution. "Not really persecution," said Edward Woodward, another of the stars. "He found it difficult to hold his feelings, and his feelings were that she was an amateur, and just because she has a famous name why do I have to put up with this?" Landon would make sarcastic comments whenever Priscilla brushed her hair, which was often, saying, "It's *Charlie's Angels* time." Worse yet, he "ignored her completely" most of the time, according to Woodward. Priscilla eventually summoned Mike Edwards to Thailand for moral support, and he arrived to find her terrorized. "I remember sitting on the set in Bangkok with Hall Bartlett . . . and she didn't know what to do. She was saying, 'Oh, my God! Oh, my God!' "

Priscilla, Woodward remembered, demonstrated extraordinary pluck and determination. Principal photography took place on the Thai side of the Mekong, a few miles from the river Kwai, the same site used to represent Vietnam in *The Deer Hunter*. Priscilla's diving sequences were shot later on, in the Bahamas. Woodward said, "I'll never forget, when we actually got to Nassau, she had to go in the water with sharks. Now, if somebody said to me, 'We have this wonderful role for you, Edward, marvelous role. You are going to get six or seven million for it. There's just one difficult thing: You've got to go into the water with sharks. . .' It would be lovely having the seven million, and it would be great doing the role, but you can stick it up your armpit. I think she, at one point, said, 'Do I really have to go into the water with the sharks?' And they said, 'Of course you do.' So they had this wonderful British underwater team, and they were thrilled with her. They were bowled over. There she was, swimming around with these lemon sharks, under the water, out of sight, and the guys, with all of the equipment, were ready to go speeding in, should she need help."

Priscilla's determination, as usual, was boundless. She had once again proved she was willing to do whatever it took to achieve her goal—in this case, stardom. She and Edward Woodward and his girlfriend, now his wife, would have long conversations over dinner about acting. Edward, a gifted Shakespearean actor from Great Britain, thought stardom was what Priscilla aspired to—not necessarily to be an *actress*. "I'm being cynical here, actually. If you are born and bred in and around Hollywood, and born and bred to that kind of stardom, there's nothing wrong with that. That's what I think she was going for . . . but on the way, she began to realize you've got to put some time in to learn the trade." Her greatest weakness, he felt, was that she did not *listen* to whomever she was acting opposite in a scene. "Because she hadn't done it. The mind wanders." Edward, who got to know Priscilla quite well over the course of the shoot, for they had dinner together nearly every night, found her to be "the most on-guard person I ever met . . . and she couldn't really drop it." His analysis was that she was "split down the middle about what she wanted to be and do." Primarily, he felt, she wanted to prove that Priscilla Presley was a name "to be reckoned with on her own."

The irony of that desire became dramatically, albeit humorously, evident during the shoot. On each night that Edward Woodward and his girlfriend accompanied Priscilla to dinner, at any given restaurant in Thailand, she would be recognized. "And every single time, even when there were only Thai musicians, there would be this astonishing rendition of 'Hound Dog' or some other Elvis number. And if you could hear 'Hound Dog' on Thai instruments! Quite bizarre." Priscilla, he said, "would nod. She looked a bit like the Queen Mum."

Priscilla's film debut was notable for another reason: It brought Lisa into contact with her first real boyfriend, a nephew of Hall Bartlett's named Scott Rollins, a nineteen-year-old production assistant. Lisa was instantly smitten by Scott, a charming, smooth-talking film student whom Priscilla would later compare, unflatteringly, to Eddie Haskell. Lisa, who was a pudgy, inexperienced fourteen, fell hard for Scott, whom Priscilla, at first, considered adorable.

Lisa and Priscilla's relationship was already strained, according to Cindy Esposito and Edward Woodward, who was around mother-and-daughter when Lisa visited the Bahamian set. Lisa had graduated from the Apple School, which went through eighth grade. Priscilla enrolled her in another Scientology school, called Happy Valley, this one a boarding school located in Ojai, just south of Santa Barbara. She chose it to remove Lisa from the influence of drugs. Priscilla would later describe this period, when Lisa turned fourteen, as her "karma" for creating such tumult herself at fourteen over dating Elvis. Lisa, as she put it, began to "test life a bit. And it was very troubling. She started to dabble a bit into drugs."

Priscilla described the next several years with Lisa as "hell," much of which she blamed on Scott Rollins, Lisa's older infatuation. Priscilla's original affection for Scott began to diminish when Lisa began bordering on anorexia to keep him interested. She also cut classes at Happy Valley to spend time with him. "I kept warning Lisa about him. I just didn't trust him. I felt that he was a con artist and was a liar. Which he was. He knew all the right things to say—

just too perfect. And he was a bit flirtatious with *me*. And that didn't set well with me. That was already a red flag—something is wrong here. And, you know, Lisa was a kid. She was in love. She felt he was God's greatest gift to woman. . . . I was not in favor of him at all, and I tried to tell her that, but of course . . . Then she started dressing entirely different, you know, very sexy—bare midriff, low-cut tops. I mean, this just wasn't Lisa. This was not my daughter. Believe me, she was not like this. So I could already see some changes in her. And then drugs started entering the picture. [Scott] started introducing her to the drug scene." Lisa saw herself as replicating her mother at fourteen, going out with an older man, leading a fast-paced life. She was rebelling.

Priscilla's schedule was cluttered with career. She shot a *Fall Guy* episode with Lee Majors, nervous about her first on-screen kiss, but relieved, afterward, to experience normalcy on a set after the *Comeback* debacle. Both came out in the first part of 1983, though *Comeback* had been downgraded from a theatrical film to an ABC movie, retitled *Love Is Forever.* She met Richard Gere while table-hopping at Morton's restaurant in West Hollywood one night with her manager, and woke up in bed with him the next morning at the home of legendary Hollywood womanizer Robert Evans. It was possibly Priscilla's only experience as a one-night stand, for Gere never phoned her and did not respond to the indignant note she sent him a few days later. They were, said the cuckolded Mike, "two people who had too much to drink. They wouldn't remember anything. I thought that was intriguing because I always liked him."

Priscilla's big break occurred that spring when her aggressive manager launched an all-out campaign to win her the role of Jenna Wade, Bobby Ewing's first, and long-suffering, love, in *Dallas.* The role became available just as Mike was named the new Kent man, the image of the cigarette. Joel Stevens sent Priscilla's relatively paltry reel to the producers, and then hounded them, relentlessly, until Phil Capice capitulated, casting Priscilla as Jenna—for her beauty and her last name. "I had not been known as an actress," she said defensively. "I really hadn't done anything. And then *The Fall Guy* came along—thank God that came along when it did. So Joel said, 'Okay, we'll put a clip together of *The Fall Guy* and *Comeback* and send it right over to *Dallas.*' And they liked it."

On Priscilla's first day in her first series, Patrick Duffy and Steve Kanaly, who portrayed Ray Krebbs, Jenna Wade's eventual husband on *Dallas*, initiated her into the cast with what they considered a practical joke. Jenna's character was being reintroduced, at a country-western club called Billy Bob's, where the cast was doing location work. After the morning's shoot, during a scorching 110-degree July day in Fort Worth, recalled Kanaly, "Lunch is coming up, and we're all bored with catered food, and there is a place [nearby], and I said, 'Hey, let's run. I have my car here and let's jump in the car.' So we go over. . . . We get into a two-seat Mercedes, three of us–Priscilla and Patrick and me. And it's really tight and it really is 110. It's like a sauna, and I can't get this air-conditioning to do anything. And it's only four or five blocks, but by the time we get to [the restaurant] we are drenched. . . . We had lunch and a couple of margaritas. And Patrick and I got Priscilla off on the right foot, in a kind of a loose, fun way." They returned to the set late, soaked with sweat, and pleasantly buzzed.

This was one of the rare moments when Priscilla let down her guard. Suzy Kalter, a journalist who spent twelve months on the set with the cast and crew, researching a book called *The Complete Book of Dallas*, remembered Priscilla as "truly scared of everyone. She would not talk in front of a journalist." Her inhibitions carried over into her work, where she was still, Mike noticed, "so locked in. I'd just pray that some director would come along and see what was locked inside of her and open that up, and then people would go, 'My God! That's who she is! She's a red-blooded, hot, fiery woman inside there.' " Shortly after she started on *Dallas*, Priscilla began working with Elizabeth Sabine, a voice coach. "The director said, 'Speak up! We can't hear you,' " recalled Elizabeth. "She must have heard from someone that I was a voice strengthening specialist." The lessons improved Priscilla's delivery, said the instructor. "She listened very intently to everything I did, [and she] liked the exercises."

She was remembered fondly by cast members, who found her to be extremely professional and cooperative–the same adjectives that had followed her through school. Priscilla, however, remained an enigma, even to them. She was asked to return after her one-year contract expired, and she played the continuing role of Jenna for five years. "I don't believe she was terribly close to any of the other actors," said Kanaly. As she had at Immaculate Conception, "she came to work," he said, "and went home."

Lisa had become a serious concern by her sixteenth birthday, in 1984. Her drug use had escalated to cocaine. Priscilla had tried grounding her, enforcing 10:00 P.M. curfews with Scott, but nothing worked. She dropped out of the Happy Valley School, where she had never been happy, and Priscilla enrolled her in yet another new school affiliated with Scientology. This one was located in the Los Feliz section of Los Angeles and was also an Apple School. Lisa's personal crisis was the discovery, in the summer, that Scott, the boyfriend she blindly adored, had–she and Priscilla said–sold photographs of Lisa and him in the park to the *Globe* for $10,000. Scott, in 1996, denied any involvement, blaming Priscilla for meddling in his relationship with Lisa, and ultimately "blocking" it. As for Priscilla, he commented, "I don't even want to open that can of worms. She has a lot of power and a lot of strength." He had "nothing nice to say about her." The feeling was decidedly mutual, though Lisa, for a time, "still didn't want to believe" he'd sold the photos, said Priscilla, until Priscilla's assistant persuaded the police to search Scott's house, where they found the negatives.

Lisa plummeted before, during, and after Scott's betrayal. She dropped out of the second Apple School in the eleventh grade and never went back, though she and Priscilla would give the impression, in interviews conducted then, that she was still enrolled in high school and contemplating where to go to college. "I knew," said Lisa, "I was either going to stay there and die or I was going to have to get out." Her downward slide climaxed after she had been awake for three straight days. "I was high on cocaine," she said later, "and I had some more. It was either do it or go to sleep. I looked at it and I decided, 'That's it. I don't want this anymore.' And I flushed it down the toilet." Priscilla put Lisa through the Purif, Scientology's antidrug regime, then cloistered her in the Scientology Celebrity Centre Hotel, the Manor House, which is in an elegant old-world building resembling a castle, located in the Hollywood foothills. She was, by her admission, not pleased at Lisa's decision to drop out of school, and it created a major conflict between them. "My daughter is very strong-willed, and she didn't want to go back to school. That's when I put her in the Purif and the Scientology Celebrity Centre Hotel, to get herself straightened out."

It was then that tabloids began to report that Lisa was in the clutches of an "evil cult" to which she intended to leave her fortune. What Scientology provided, to Lisa and Priscilla, according to their friend Brett Livingstone Strong, "was a form of protection." The veiled activities of Scientologists—an attractive and familiar existence to Priscilla—buffered the Presley women, kept tabloid journalists at bay, offered them a "celebrity center" where they could feel insulated, pampered, taken care of, "where they could meet other celebrities," said Brett. "I think Lisa liked it because she felt kind of special," said Mike, a fellow Scientologist back then. "You know, they treated her special. . . . They understood her."

Priscilla, for the most part, disregarded the more unusual, and at times seemingly sinister, aspects of the organization. She admitted to having "concerns" about reported heavy-handed tactics by church officials, from wiretapping to breaking and entering. "There have been changes," she asserted, attributing policies to an earlier regime. "But it's not any different from any other church . . . that goes through changes, that goes through growth. It goes through different managements. They've made some major changes in the last few years, and it seems to have all gotten better. So I'm happily satisfied, at this point, because they have changed, and the new management has taken over."

Priscilla admitted to being "somewhat" disturbed by Scientologists' adulation of L. Ron Hubbard, the organization's founder, whom they call LRH, though she considered his status as a godlike figure no "different from [that of] Buddha, [or] Christ [or] Jimmy Swaggart. I mean, they are all leaders in their religious field. [Scientologists] have L. Ron Hubbard, who gave all the materials to them. They are giving their 'exchange' back to him. And I don't get caught up in that. . . . Maybe management is over-PR-ing him. But all I know is that the literature is there, and I am for the literature."

She had little comment on the report that the "secret" of the universe, disclosed in the final reportedly $6,000 Scientology course called Truth Revealed, is that the world was started by an intergalactic ruler named Xenu who captured beings and froze them, then deposited them near ten volcanoes, which were hydrogen-bombed. This course allegedly teaches that Xenu captured the "thetans," or souls, of these beings and "implanted" them with various perversions, which then attached themselves to humans as "body thetans." He is said to have done this in order to create confusion and conflict. The course supposedly teaches Scientologists to find the "pressure points" on their bodies so that they can make telepathic contact with these thetans and be reminded of Xenu; at that point, the body thetans are released. "I don't question it," Priscilla remarked. "I'm not there yet, I'm not there to criticize, I'm not there to question it. All I know, what I've gotten out of it, [is that] it's been very, very beneficial to me. So I'm not going to criticize what I don't understand. When I get there, maybe it will make more sense to me. So why should I criticize or doubt it? So far, what I have applied, I have gotten everything from. Whatever course I've taken, whatever auditing I've done, has not disappointed me. Nothing surprises me anymore."

Priscilla and Lisa, suggested Myrna Smith, a friend of them both, "take the aspects of Scientology that they can put in their lives and deal with, and some of it I don't think they are concerned about. Realistically, they are using the organization, and the organization is using them." Scientology has benefited from the public endorsement of high-profile celebrities like Priscilla and Lisa—from their name value as much as from any financial contributions. Both Priscilla and Lisa have denied making extravagant contributions to Scientology; Priscilla, both critics *and* supporters would suggest, would not part with her money.

Both Lisa and Priscilla later attributed Lisa's withdrawal from drugs to Scientology. "It got her off drugs," Priscilla said simply, in 1996. "And it helped her tremendously. God only knows where she would be right now. So I do attribute that to Scientology. And she does, too." Priscilla sent Lisa off for a summer in Spain, under an assumed name, when she checked out of the Celebrity Centre Hotel, easing her out of what she would later refer to as an "identity crisis." When Lisa returned, she thought of singing, something she and Scott batted about from time to time. Priscilla dissuaded her. "I never knew Lisa could sing, to be honest with you," she said later. "She never took any lessons." Priscilla placed Lisa's notion of singing, at seventeen, in the same category as her failed piano lessons, at nine, or the $2,000 drum set she desperately wanted, which "she played a week and that was it. So when she said she wanted to sing, I discouraged it, only because it looked like she'd dabble in it and that was it. So I discouraged her singing. In my mind, I thought, My God, she's got some feet to follow here. She cannot be a dilettante. If she's going to do something, she has to be extraordinary. She never wanted to take singing lessons. . . . [She just said,] 'I want to be a singer.' So I discouraged it . . . because she had proved that she didn't commit to anything. So I figured, Gosh, I'm not going to put her out there in the world." Instead, Lisa took an office job as a gofer for Jerry Schilling, who was doing some freelance work for Elvis's estate.

Priscilla closed out the difficult year of 1984 on the cover of *TV Guide* as one of television's "Ten Most Beautiful Women." At thirty-nine, she could easily have passed for twenty-something–the result of extraordinary natural beauty and, it was rumored, cosmetic surgery. Kathy Westmoreland discussed with Elvis, on more than one occasion, both his and Priscilla's plastic surgeries up to 1977. "He thought it was wonderful," she said. Priscilla's work, "from what I understood, was nose, chin, cheekbones. He was telling me what she had done." Joan Quinn claimed Priscilla "was doing a lot" in terms of cosmetic work in the late seventies, "always going to spas, but always in private situations." Joan recalled Priscilla having liposuction, and Shirley Dieu learned about her plastic surgery through Myrna Smith–Joe Esposito, Shirley's boyfriend, had kept Priscilla's secret. "It is such a guarded secret. She had her nose and her breasts done in Palm Springs. And she's also had two face peels." Priscilla, recalled her voice teacher, Elizabeth Sabine, was extremely interested in Elizabeth's skin and questioned her at length about skin peels.

Mike, Priscilla, and Lisa flew to Mike's hometown of Pensacola for what would be their last Christmas together. Mike had noticed tremendous changes in Priscilla from when they first met, more than six years before–the consequences of fame he had forewarned her about. "I saw it sucking her up, and the name *Priscilla Presley* was getting bigger and bigger. I shake a little when I think about it, because I go back to that original conversation I had with her, 'Do you really want this?' "

Priscilla really wanted it. She and Mike effectively ended their relationship after Christmas, when she was named, as a result of *Dallas,* the most popular television star in Germany, where she had been a schoolgirl twenty-five years before.

She had also encountered the man she would come to consider the true love of her life, via an introduction through Kathy Monderine, a costumer on *Dallas* with whom she was friendly. Kathy's Brazilian husband, Roberto, mentioned to Priscilla that he had a friend who was a screenwriter who had a "couple of scripts that might be good for her," as Kathy Monderine put it. "I was looking for a script to do right after *Dallas*," said Priscilla. "We had time off; it was during hiatus. And I was talking to Roberto, and I said I'd like to do a movie-of-the-week, and he goes, 'Do you have anybody yet?' and I said, 'No, not really. I'm looking. I'm going to put the word out through my agent.' And he said, 'You know, before you do that, I have a very talented guy that I know. . . . He's a wonderful writer.' Well, I usually don't do things like this, but I know Roberto, so I told him, 'Gosh, I don't know. Do I have to meet him?' And he said, 'I'll have him come to the set.' So I then told Roberto it was okay." Roberto's friend was a tall, well-built Brazilian of Italian descent named Marco Garibaldi. He had already met with Linda Gray and Victoria Principal, two of Priscilla's costars on *Dallas*, to discuss "hiatus ideas" with them. Roberto Monderine was, quite evidently, using his costumer wife's access to the cast of *Dallas*–the attractive *female* cast–to help his handsome Brazilian friend shop a screenplay, or himself, in the classic Hollywood tradition. Linda Gray and Victoria Principal weren't interested in Marco or his script.

On the day of the appointed meeting, "I got cold feet," recounted Priscilla. "So I called Marco and said, 'I can't meet with you.' And Marco says, 'Well, I just canceled two or three appointments, and I was really planning on doing this.' And I felt so bad." Marco told Jerry Schilling about it later. "She canceled on him," said Jerry, "and he called her up and told her he thought his time was valuable and how could she do this?" Whichever version was correct, Priscilla was impressed by Marco's boldness and rescheduled their meeting. Marco, accompanied by Kathy Monderine, went to Priscilla's dressing room on the set of *Dallas*, where the three of them spent about an hour, according to Kathy, mostly laughing. The third time was the charm for Marco. Linda Gray and Victoria Principal had passed on what he had to offer; Priscilla responded instantly. Neither Marco nor Kathy–nor Priscilla–ever mentioned his proposed screenplay during their hour-long conversation in Priscilla's dressing room, though he had several scripts with him, Priscilla said later. "It was so relaxed," said Kathy. "It was friends getting together, and that's how it started off. There was no, 'Oh, my God, I'm meeting a star!' He's not a starstruck person. We had fun, and that impressed her. Here was a guy who could laugh and have a good time." Though she denied there was a romance, Kathy admitted later that "sparks flew" between Marco and Priscilla. Roberto Monderine had, quite inadvertently, tapped into everything Priscilla looked for in a man, on the conscious and subconscious level. Garibaldi was the very essence of the strong, dark, powerful male Priscilla had been seeking, in one form or another, since she was a child listening to Mario Lanza. Jerry Schilling, who would spend time with Priscilla and Marco as a couple, would later "kid" her, saying she had finally found her tall, dark Latin lover. "There is a certain strength I feel with dark men," Priscilla once told *Vanity Fair.* "They're very virile." Sex was fundamental to Priscilla.

Priscilla talked to Kathy about Marco afterward, saying what a "cute guy" he was, that she liked him, how "sweet" he was. "And she is very private about her thoughts, too." Marco said later it was not "love at first sight" for him, with Priscilla, "though she is obviously a beautiful woman." The exact progression of the relationship was confusing, by the various parties' accounts. Kathy remembered Priscilla and Marco getting together for several "lunch meetings," and "from there I guess time went on and they realized how much they liked each other." Priscilla said, "We met a few more times. I really liked him. We'd meet for lunch, or he'd come to the set." She described the meetings as "working" conversations, stressing that she and Marco had a "business relationship" for about three months before they became lovers; for the first time, she said, sex did not come first. The irony was interesting, for, in Marco, Priscilla had finally found romantic fulfillment. "It was the first relationship that I had that we were friends first. The sex didn't get in the way. . . . And it really meant a lot to me, because we really liked being with each other. We got to know each other really well. It had nothing to do with sex. It was just strictly business. And having a good time. And it evolved to us going out and dating." The screenplay, which had ostensibly brought them together, fell by the wayside. "We didn't do the script," said Priscilla. Neither the Monderines nor Priscilla nor Marco would later recall what the screenplay was even about.

Marco would say, later, that he and Priscilla were just friends for "six or seven months" before the relationship turned romantic, as opposed to Priscilla's estimate of three months. Both timetables indicated that Priscilla was involved with Marco while she was still seeing Mike Edwards. Priscilla and Mike split over Christmas of 1984, after they returned from Pensacola. Less than a month later, sometime in January of 1985, when Priscilla returned to L.A. after filming *Night of 100 Stars* in New York, Mike stopped by her house on a Saturday night in the hope of reconciling, as he and Priscilla had done so often before. When he learned Priscilla was out of town for the weekend, he telephoned, on an intuition, Two Bunch Palms, a couples spa in Palm Springs they had once spoken of trying. Posing as Priscilla's manager, he learned that she was staying at the spa with Marco, indicating that the friendship had already crossed the line from business into romance. Mike, hoping to "pull her back with sex," drove to Priscilla's house on Sunday night, knowing she would have to return to the *Dallas* set the next morning. He sat in his car and waited. He soon had the answer he was seeking. "She came back alone, dressed all in red. In tight, tight pants. She didn't wear tight pants. She hates them, because they hurt. I knew then that there was another man in her life."

As he sat in his car and watched Priscilla go into her house, Mike Edwards realized he was living the premonition he'd had six years before, when *he* watched Mike Stone stand on the driveway with a script, talking to Priscilla through the gate. Priscilla, he knew, would coldly excommunicate him. That, he had observed, was her pattern when someone no longer served a purpose in her life. She simply discarded that person. Mike had seen her do it with everyone from acting teachers to friends. "It was like you no longer existed. You were gone. Suddenly—*wham!*—the big gate came down. And they were on the outside of the gate. They no longer exist. And the same thing happened to me."

Joan Quinn, Priscilla's society role model during her long relationship with Mike Edwards, had witnessed, and to some extent experienced herself, the metaphor of the closing of the gate. "[Priscilla] started distancing herself from all of us," she said, "and becoming more and more private. She was too good to sit at the beauty shop with us anymore. She had already done the gym, worked off of Michael. She learned a lot from Michael, learned a lot from us. Why would she want to be friends with someone like me, who told her what restaurants to go to, what to wear, what to eat, what to read, what we were doing and what movies to see?" Priscilla—Eve Carrington—the seemingly meek, submissive, demure child-woman, had quietly observed, absorbed, and eventually surpassed those she had once held up as ideals and sought to emulate, or in a way, to *become*. It was, to a degree, the same thing she had done with Elvis Presley. Her admirers considered this proof that Priscilla was the consummate survivor; her critics perceived it as raw opportunism.

32

GHOSTS FROM THE PAST

By April, Priscilla and Marco Garibaldi were in Rio de Janeiro, being photographed by tabloid reporters locked in a kiss in their bathing suits on the beach. They had flown to Brazil together, during Priscilla's hiatus from *Dallas,* so she could meet Marco's parents, appearing very much like a couple headed toward a serious commitment. Brazilian newspapers reported that Marco had been introducing Priscilla Presley as his fiancée.

Kathy Monderine, who had introduced them, said they "just seemed to belong together" despite the difference in their ages—Priscilla was thirty-nine; Marco was twenty-eight. Marco was dubbed, in both legitimate magazines and tabloids, the "mystery man" in Priscilla Presley's life—a title he seemed rather to enjoy. It was also appropriate. Marco's past, even his occupation, were clouded in confusion. The Monderines had described him to Priscilla as a screenwriter and director. He called himself a producer, though he had never produced or published anything. Jerry Schilling remembered Marco telling him that he had met Priscilla while he was interviewing her, possibly for a documentary. Marco said later that he wrote a screenplay called *Warlords,* which was "almost but not quite made" and that he had once directed MTV music videos. Mike Edwards had heard, through Brett Strong, that Marco was "selling posters in the back of his car" when he met Priscilla.

Marco told fanciful tales of a cloak-and-dagger past, of being recruited, as a teenager in Brazil, for an intelligence organization, where he learned to fly a helicopter and acquired arcane knowledge of "voice imprinting" and digital voice analysis—his "spy stuff," as Bob Wall would refer to it, laughing good-naturedly. Whether it was true or not was almost impossible to prove, but it was fitting that Priscilla would find herself in love with a man who had as many secrets as she. Marco told her about an early marriage to an American named Carolyn.

Sometime before summer, Marco moved into Priscilla's hilltop house on Summit Drive, behind the fabled gate. He opened an office in west Los

Angeles, which he called Destiny Productions. Marco was a great believer in destiny. When he was a boy of eleven or so, in Brazil, he was stopped by a derelict as he was on his way to go swimming. "A star will shine on you in a place far, far away," she said to him cryptically, "and you will be protected." He often wondered, once he had begun his love affair with Priscilla Presley and entered the rarefied world she inhabited, if that was what the old woman meant.

The September after Marco moved in with Priscilla, *Elvis and Me*, her fever-ishly anticipated autobiography, was released, coinciding with the celebration of what would have been Elvis Presley's fiftieth year. The book Priscilla had anguished over for three years, that she had told Mike Edwards would be her great unveiling—the truth, finally, about her life, her past—instead set in stone all the myths she had been hiding behind for years: that Currie had ap-proached her, out of the blue, to meet Elvis Presley; that she was never an Elvis fan; her strict parents; Elvis's enraged response to her near-rape by Cur-rie; waiting by the phone in Germany for Elvis to call; that Elvis was her one and only love; that the Beaulieus disapproved of Elvis; that she tearfully pleaded to move to Memphis; that she was a virgin bride.

She had, by Mike Edwards's characterization, created an artificial reality. This was something Priscilla had talked about when they were together. He said, "Priscilla once told me, 'Michael, you gotta learn PR.' And I said, 'Well, how do *you* know it?' And she said, 'Because I learned from the best.' And that was Elvis and Colonel Parker. Colonel Parker was a wiz with PR—how to fabricate some-thing great. And he taught that to Elvis, and Priscilla learned it from Elvis. You *create* stuff. You create an *un*-reality, which works better for you."

Priscilla had become locked into her pattern of denial back in Germany, posing as a virgin for Elvis, who demanded that the woman he married be chaste. Concealing her serious boyfriends in Wiesbaden, leading Elvis to be-lieve she had been faithful to him. This image of Priscilla as the demure inno-cent was perpetuated by Elvis and ingrained in the public perception of Elvis and Priscilla. Priscilla had unwittingly become a mythic symbol, like Jackie Kennedy. How could she reveal to millions of Elvis fans, faithful to the myth, that she had never really loved Elvis in the way they believed, that she was not his mama's virginal reincarnation, that in fact she hadn't wanted to move to Memphis at all, that she was in love with someone else? "She was trying to keep this image up that Elvis had created for her," said Mike, "and then she had to keep up the image for Lisa. And then she felt . . . that she had to carry on that image." The lie had become too big.

Sandra Harmon, who wrote the book for Priscilla, later acknowledged that her only source was Priscilla. She did not attempt to verify anything she was told. *Elvis and Me* was strictly *Priscilla's* account of her life. Priscilla was now committed, irrevocably, to the Priscilla Myth. "And then," as Mike pointed out, "you've got to continually–I don't want to say *lie*, but you've got to continually hold on to that story, which may not be the whole truth. And I think that makes you very– You just live a life of dishonesty." That was the reason Priscilla challenged Currie Grant's story with a vehemence that bordered on mania, for Currie's truth, about their intercourse and her eagerness to meet Elvis, was like a loose thread on a hand-woven sweater: one tug, and her intricate fabric of lies would unravel.

Mike's wish that Priscilla would emancipate herself, in her memoir–from the secrets, the suppression, the myths–went unrealized. "That's what she wanted to do," he lamented. "She wanted to be set free. She wanted to do that book and set herself free–and she didn't do it." Telling the truth about her life, he believed, was the only way Priscilla could escape what she considered the tyranny of being forever linked to Elvis. "You want to get out from the shadow, get out! Become something *else*. I don't have anger; I have just *empathy* and *pain* for that. I think you get so entrenched in something that, like a drug addict, you can't let it go and take that step. The book, *Elvis and Me,* was supposed to be the step to get out from the shadow."

Elvis and Me did make Priscilla an even greater fortune than she had already accumulated, for it was a phenomenon in the publishing industry, on best-seller lists for months and months. What it did reveal about Priscilla–as did the subsequent miniseries based on the book, also called *Elvis and Me*–was her thinly disguised hostility toward Elvis Presley, her deep resentment at having sublimated herself to *his* superstardom, *his* ego, for so many years of her life. Her memoir was proof of a lasting regret on Priscilla's part for the child-woman she once was, the little girl who suppressed her own identity, assumed a false persona, to become the child bride her parents wanted her to be. Larry Geller, Elvis's close friend in spiritual matters, called the book, and the miniseries, *Me and Me,* and saw them as a testament to Priscilla's ego, proof of her desire to be the one in the spotlight, as an opportunity to "vent her anger" toward Elvis. "I thought the movie was an abomination. That was not Elvis, in any way, shape, or form." Shirley Dieu, who was offended by Priscilla's behavior the last time Elvis and Priscilla saw each other, when she mocked him behind his back about his snowmobile suit, was outraged by the miniseries. In the last scene, the actor playing Elvis appeared at Priscilla's door in an over-the-top Las Vegas stage–style "zoot suit," as Shirley described it, begging Priscilla to take him back. "And in the movie, she said, 'Oh, Elvis, you don't have to wear that suit. People will like you for who you are!' and I thought, 'You lying little bitch. He wasn't even wearing that, he was wearing a snowmobile outfit, and you were laughing your butt off at him, and [in the miniseries] you are sitting there acting like a prima donna.' "

Robert Lovenheim, who produced *Elvis and Me,* admitted, later, that even he had questions about the credibility of Priscilla's account. "There are two sides to the story," he said. "And I don't know which is right and which is wrong. I mean, we went with the book. How close it is to reality, I don't know. One story is Priscilla's story, which is [that] she fell in love, Elvis was in love with her, her parents were very much against it, but slowly they conceded to her wishes and let her move into Graceland. The other version is that the parents were starstruck; they loved the idea that their daughter was going out with Elvis Presley, and they made no attempt to really restrict it in any way." Lovenheim included the scene where Priscilla claimed Currie had tried to rape her. "After the film was made, or when it was in postproduction, somebody who worked for me on the crew met Currie." Currie mentioned, to Lovenheim's crew member, that it was *Priscilla* who pursued him, and that she had consensual sex with him so she could meet Elvis. "It made a lot of sense, I'll tell ya," Lovenheim admitted. "That's what rock and roll is about." By then the film had wrapped, and Currie's version of events "didn't suit the story we were telling," said Lovenheim, who was contracted to dramatize Priscilla's book—*her* life as *she* told it. "There is the Priscilla myth," as he put it, "and then there is the truth."

Lovenheim and his director, Larry Peerce, could see for themselves the protective armor Priscilla wore to shield herself. They knew how "covered" she was. They originally planned to open and close the miniseries with on-camera interviews with the real Priscilla and the real Lisa. Peerce asked Priscilla and Lisa questions, off-camera, about their lives and about Elvis, and they responded improvisationally. Priscilla was so rigid that her comments were unusable. "If you look at her in this interview, she is so stiff," commented Lovenheim. "And she's so incapable of even *thinking* of what [really] went on. All she can do is recite the party line. . . . We tried for hours with her. We could not get her to crack." Peerce, the director, had the same observation. "It was quite interesting," he recalled. "You'd ask Lisa, and she'd just answer—*boom.* But you ask Priscilla, she'd count one, two, three. Then she'd answer. You could see her selectively editing." Calculating her responses, perhaps, to make certain she stayed within the myth she had created. Both Robert Lovenheim and Larry Peerce had great affection for Lisa, whom they considered a "terrific kid," enveloped by the continuing Elvis world, "and our feeling was, 'God, please break away and become your own person,' " said Lovenheim. "Which unfortunately didn't happen."

Priscilla's personal life, with Marco, reached a new level of happiness as her memoir came out. She discovered she was pregnant, and made plans to marry Marco, his brother Antonio told a newspaper, and which Priscilla would later repeat to columnist Marilyn Beck and to *People.* The *Dallas* producers wrote her pregnancy into the story line, so that Jenna Wade would give birth just as

Priscilla did. Much was made, in the media, of Priscilla's pregnancy, for she turned forty that year, making older motherhood suddenly chic. She was named one of *Harper's Bazaar*'s Ten Most Beautiful Women of 1985. Priscilla, so long lampooned for the "Elvira" hair and makeup she had worn when she was with Elvis, was now being extolled for her "natural look." She seemed to change her hair color and cut with the seasons—a "Madonna with class," one celebrity photographer called her. All of this was possibly a backlash to having been frozen in the Cleopatra image during her twenties, but it was also a reflection of Priscilla's quest for variety, for new experiences, new adventures.

Sometime near the end of 1985, as she was solidifying her commitment to Marco, making plans for the birth of their child, his mysterious past surfaced in the form of a warning call, to him, from a tabloid. A reporter for the *Star* had uncovered information about a second ex-wife named Joann Nilsen, who had divorced him on the grounds of fraud. The reporter also told Marco that they had learned his name was originally Garcia, not Garibaldi. Marco denied both accusations, saying he had never heard the names Joann Nilsen or Marco Garcia, and he directed a lawyer to write to the *Star* threatening legal action if they published the information. Marco's lawyer stated it was "gross misinformation" to suggest that Marco had had a previous marriage dissolved on the basis of fraud.

In truth, there *was* a Joann Nilsen to whom Marco had been married in 1980, a striking blond from South Africa who lived in L.A. Just before Christmas, Joann received a telephone call from a frantic, distraught Priscilla Presley, who asked if she had ever been married to Marco Garibaldi. "She found out from the tabloids," said Joann. "She wanted to know, was it true or was it tabloid junk? There wasn't too much I could say to comfort her, except that I hadn't been in on the story, but that it was basically true." Priscilla told Joann she had asked Marco about her. "And he denied having known me," recalled Joann, who related that she'd had an "ugly experience" with Marco. Priscilla, understandably, was devastated. "She was getting married to someone . . . and she's a very well known woman. All of a sudden this tabloid thing came out and he was denying it."

Joann Nilsen referred to her marriage to Marco as "a bad dream, a nightmare." Marco approached her, she said, as she was leaving a private club in L.A. called Bar One in the spring of 1980. He had spotted her in the club and followed her to her car to offer her a single rose, and "within one month, he pretty much swept me off my feet." They married in May of 1980. Marco, at the time, was a computer programmer at Hollywood Community Hospital, trying to get into the import-export business with his brother, "always dabbling in all these things, trying to do something," stated Joann. "I laugh when people say he's a producer, writer, all this." When he met Joann, Marco had written a "very rough sketch" for a novel called *City of Angels* and was, she believed, hoping to capitalize on her connections to get it published. "I'm sure it never went anywhere. He had approached a friend of mine, a publisher in New York, to try to publish his novel, and of course it went nowhere." The sketch, according to Joann, was written in broken English—"it would be like if I went to Brazil and tried to speak Portuguese. The publishers laughed." At first, Joann was enthralled with Marco. "He's very smooth. Obviously I fell for something." A year and a half into the marriage, she came to consider Marco an opportunist. "It was . . . hurtful. He had no money. I was young, and I had a certain amount of money. I sold everything I had to help him do what he wanted to do. I was very badly hurt." The coup de grâce occurred in the spring of 1982, when Joann discovered that Marco was still married to his first wife, Carolyn, and when Marco began to perceive that Joann's "connections were running dry." They both wanted out of the marriage. Joann felt that she "was monetarily being used"; Marco "wanted out because he wanted bigger and better things." Joann filed a petition to have the marriage annulled on the basis of fraud, since Marco was committing bigamy. He tried to persuade her not to mention the fraud, Joann recalled, "because he was going to be rich and famous one day," and he did not want that to come back to haunt him.

Joann believed Marco's "whole intention" was to attach himself to a wealthy woman. "I drove a nice car, I lived in Beverly Hills, and I think that was his whole thing with me. And that was his whole goal in life." When they met, his name was Marco Garcia. He legally changed it to Marco Garibalddi (then spelled with two *d*s) while they were married, said Joann, for he felt Garcia sounded "too Mexican" and would not create a sophisticated enough image for a producer. "Garibalddi" was Marco's mother's maiden name; on his legal application for a name change, he described it as "an ancestral name." He preferred, remembered Joann, to be regarded as Italian, his mother's descent, rather than Brazilian, though he was born and reared in Curitiba, Brazil.

Priscilla, Joann recalled, asked her to relate her experience with Marco. "I told her [the relationship] was very hurtful and very painful to me, and he was not the type of person I wished to be around." When Joann repeated what happened to her, "she was really distressed. I guess Marco had not told her what had gone on. She and Marco were about to get married, [though] they hadn't had the child yet." Priscilla told Joann "that she was going to get some kind of injunction . . . against Marco ever doing anything."

Priscilla, who had just come out of the Mike Edwards relationship, doubtless felt she had once again been set up. To discover, on the eve of her wedding, that her fiancé, the father of the child she was carrying, had deceived her, that he had concealed a wife who considered him "cruel," clearly traumatized Priscilla. "She obviously was," remarked Joann, "because she didn't go through with the marriage. And never has." The Christmas wedding of Priscilla and Marco that had been mentioned in various media reports did not take place.

It was ironic that Priscilla had fallen in love with a man whose past, like hers, was scattered with secrets. "His life," stated Joann, "was quite a bit of a lie." Rumors abounded that, prior to meeting Priscilla, Marco was the escort-boyfriend of a sixtyish Beverly Hills socialite. "He's very beautiful," said a Hollywood wife he pursued at the same time, "and it's paid well."

On the other side of the coin, Marco Garibaldi (he dropped the second "d" sometime after the annulment), from the description of the Monderines and the majority of those who met him through Priscilla, was a charming, person-able, thoroughly likable guy, "a genuine gentleman," said Brett Strong, who remained friends with both Priscilla and Mike Edwards after their split, and who regularly went to the movies with Marco. He was intelligent, well read, and knowledgeable on a variety of subjects. In fact, remarked one of the women he earlier pursued, "I always thought he wasted his talents, in a way."

Marco's explanation of his marital history was that he married his first wife, Carolyn, to obtain his American citizenship, so it was not a "real" marriage and he was not committing bigamy with Joann Nilsen. His marriage to Joann, he would argue, was never a marriage, legally, since it was annulled. Carolyn Garcia, however, did seem to consider her relationship with Marco a bona fide marriage. They lived in Chicago after the wedding, attending Southern Illinois University, and she had only glowing things to say about her former husband, who was then known as Marco Garcia. "He's a nice guy and Priscilla lucked out," Carolyn said. "And he lucked out because she's a nice lady. And I wish them lots of happiness." Joann Nilsen, his second wife, was not surprised when Priscilla decided to stay with Marco after she evidently canceled the wedding. "He does have that way about him," Joann remarked. "Then of course, from what I understand of the way Elvis treated her, I would probably say she could be suckered in. . . . There was definitely a multitype personality with Marco."

Priscilla evidently resolved her internal conflicts about Marco, though it must have bothered her on some level. Still, her second pregnancy brought her perhaps the greatest joy of her life. She and Marco learned, that fall, through amniocentesis that they were having a boy, and they chose the name Navarone Anthony—Navarone, explained Marco, from the film *The Guns of Navarone*, the "river that brought two different sides of people together." Anthony, he said, "because all Italians are [named] Anthony," and if the child ever wanted a more conventional name, he could call himself Anthony. Navarone Garibaldi was born on March 1, 1987. He was, from birth, Priscilla's love child, the center of her universe, in a way Lisa had never been. This time around, Priscilla reveled in her pregnancy, had classical music playing in the delivery room, and a man who fully shared the childbirth experience. Marco was by her side, placing the baby in warm water as soon as he was born. If anything, the birth of Navarone bound her more tightly to Marco, in stark contrast to her traumatizing experience with Elvis. Priscilla happily attended Mommy and Me classes, took Navarone to bed with her and Marco, and turned down any location work that would separate her from her son.

The pregnancy also drew her closer to Lisa. This was ironic, for Priscilla had brooded about the effect on her daughter of having a half sibling—one of the strange legacies of her own upbringing. Vestiges of the Beaulieu-Iversen pathology were still in evidence. Priscilla did not display any photographs of Elvis in her home, for, she explained in 1996, "I would never do that to Marco and Navarone." Journalists had puzzled over this oddity for years, but it made perfect sense, in light of Priscilla's past. She had absorbed, by osmosis, the family paranoia about acknowledging a dead first love. Just as her mother was pressured to destroy all evidence of *her* first love, Jimmy, to assuage Paul Beaulieu's ego and to avoid creating conflict between siblings from different fathers, so too Priscilla had obliterated Elvis from her personal life.

Lisa, in fact, took such great delight in Navarone that she determined to become pregnant herself, another case of daughter emulating mother. She had been dating an aspiring young musician named Danny Keough, whose family was deeply entrenched in Scientology. Suddenly, in October 1988, several months pregnant, Lisa married him. Priscilla, by all accounts, including her own, was not pleased, for she now believed it was a mistake for a woman to marry or have children before she was thirty, that she should experience life first. This, no doubt, was the voice of her own bittersweet experience as a reluctant child bride and a neglected young mother. Obviously she had also fully assimilated her years of financial homework, studying *Barron's*, managing Elvis's estate, and picking the brains of millionaire moguls, for Lisa, at Priscilla's insistence, had Danny Keough sign a prenuptial agreement, according to their friend Brett Strong. "She wanted some protection for Lisa's inheritance."

The wedding, in the Presley family tradition, was veiled in secrecy, abetted by the Church of Scientology. Lisa and Danny were married at the Hollywood Celebrity Centre by a Scientologist minister in front of the immediate family. So carefully protected had Lisa's life been, both by Priscilla and by the cloak of Scientology, that it was reported in the Suzy's society column, two days earlier, that she was dating Prince Albert of Monaco. Lisa and Danny honeymooned, as well, under the auspices of Scientology, on a yacht owned by the church, where higher-level members were allowed to take special courses. Priscilla, a few years later, would admit to a certain relief over Lisa's marriage and pregnancy, for it diminished the relentless media speculation "about what she was going to do with her life. It was always, 'Is she going to follow in her mom's footsteps? Or is she going to follow in her dad's footsteps?' And she'd go, 'Mom, what am I going to do?' "

One area in which Lisa had clearly exhibited little interest was the Presley estate, to which she was the sole heir. She began to attend occasional estate meetings in February of 1986, her eighteenth birthday, but she did not share her mother's passion for corporations or the finer points of making money. Lisa, in fact, had remarkably little concept of what others had obsessed over for years—her inheritance from Elvis Presley. Her friend Dana Rosenfeld remembered sitting at the dinner table with Priscilla, Lisa, Michelle, and a few friends once when she and Lisa were preteens. "And one of the kids said to Lisa, 'So is it true that you are going to get $50 million when you turn eighteen?' And Michelle said, without a beat, 'We do not discuss that. Ever. And don't ever bring that up again.' And that was that." Lisa's ignorance about her legacy was reminiscent of Priscilla's as a new divorcée. She told a Memphis newspaper, on the occasion of her eighteenth birthday, that she had only recently understood what her inheritance comprised. "I thought I was getting cash," she said, "not an estate."

Priscilla, by way of contrast, embraced her accidental position as executrix as she had once embraced karate, Chinese cooking classes, Beverly Hills society, French culture, and false eyelashes. She and Jack Soden, her hand-selected executive in matters involving Elvis's estate, shared an outward demeanor of gentle affability that belied the business instincts of a shark. The positive consequences of this characteristic, with respect to Elvis Presley Enterprises, the corporate spin-off of Lisa's inheritance, was a dramatic financial turnaround that increased the value of Elvis's estate from $4.6 million to $50 million by 1988, a figure that would double by 1996. Under Soden's direction and Priscilla's stewardship, the estate had reacquired the rights to Elvis's record royalties, which the Colonel had sold to RCA, transformed Graceland into a cash cow, and turned Elvis Presley Enterprises into a cottage industry. The key to the takeover, and similarly to Priscilla, was *control*.

Soden had ingeniously acquired the land across the street from Graceland, which had been a huckster's carnival of Elvis exploitation, selling Elvis sweat and worse. His strategy was to purchase the property for the estate through a coalition of anonymous Kansas City investors who were front men for Elvis Presley Enterprises. With that land acquisition, Soden and Priscilla cleaned up the image of both Graceland and Elvis, removed the competition of other vendors, and set the stage for Soden's vision of a Graceland Hotel, convention center, movie theater, and rock-and-roll museum—four more venues from which the estate could profit. He and Priscilla, through attorneys for Elvis Presley Enterprises, successfully lobbied for a Tennessee statute to extend the commercial rights to a celebrity's name *past his death,* thereby ensuring that any profits arising through the sale of anything related to the image or likeness of Elvis Presley would belong to the estate. Elvis Presley was making more money dead than he ever did while he was alive, and the instigator was Priscilla.

She told *Us* magazine in 1988 that she had "done better with the estate than anyone," and she commented to a reporter, only half jokingly, that Elvis should have hired *her* as his agent. *Vanity Fair* published a profile of Priscilla, in 1991, calling her "The New Colonel Parker." *Working Woman* featured her as its cover girl in September of 1993, praising Priscilla as a businesswoman extraordinaire who projected a "cool, tough quality" in an article entitled, in an unintentional double entendre, "Making Elvis Pay." *Prime Time Live* devoted a segment to Priscilla Presley, multimillionaire, portraying her as a control freak made rich by her ex-husband's estate.

How much, really, did Priscilla have to do with the estate's dramatic success story? Less, probably, than the hype would suggest but more than her critics would give her credit for. "If you've ever read *The Prince* by Machiavelli," suggested Beecher Smith, counsel for the estate, "he says there are three types of intelligence. There's the first, which is both intelligent and learned; the second, which is intelligent but not learned; and the third, which is neither intelligent nor learned. I would say she is— Let's face it: We are all ignorant about something. I don't know how sophisticated Priscilla is from the education standpoint, but she seems to have shown very good judgment in picking the people to help her with her management and in putting together a management team. And of course they all keep her advised. You can't argue with results. The results have turned out to be excellent. I've seen what she's done and how she's done it. And it's interesting to watch her go from being a divorcée and a young lady who was just kind of finding her way in the world a couple of years before Elvis died, to where she is today. Very impressive. I think it comes from getting good advice." Smith likened Priscilla, as chair of Elvis Presley Enterprises, to a politician perusing reports from advisers who have distilled the complexities to the bottom line for her review. "Priscilla can read a financial statement as well as anybody else. Read and look at where things are going and know who is getting things there. And that's how she makes her decisions. She monitors the progress of various people at different levels. She comes in and spends as much time as needs to be spent in Memphis or L.A., reviewing operations, and then she and the board of directors at Elvis Presley Enterprises make decisions."

The dark side of this corporate aggressiveness on the part of Elvis Presley Enterprises began to manifest itself by 1987. One of the first to suffer the cold brutality of Priscilla's and Jack Soden's business decisions was Joe Esposito. "I wanted to do a video," said Joe. He had taken home movies of Elvis over the years and had begun piecing the footage together into a video of "Elvis, not on stage performing, just being himself. Great videos." He discussed the project with Priscilla and the administrators of the estate. "They kept fighting me," he recalled. Elvis Presley Enterprises had decided that, since Elvis allegedly asked Joe to shoot the home movies, they belonged to the estate, not to Joe. "I was going to make a deal with them." In the midst of the discussions, Joe accepted an invitation to speak at an Elvis convention in New Jersey. While he was at the convention, he was served with a subpoena. "I went to talk about my friend Elvis Presley, and I got sued by the estate. Which really got me upset. And I realized Priscilla is suing me. *Priscilla* and Lisa are suing me! I'd known Elvis Presley since 1959. Is that thirty-eight years I'd known him? And that's how I get paid back." The Presley estate went forward with the litigation, eventually reaching an out-of-court settlement with Joe. "Cost me a fortune," he said. The experience forever altered Joe Esposito's perception of Priscilla, who, he had believed at first, was simply being misadvised. In truth, he decided, Priscilla hid behind that explanation, for the final decision was hers. "She uses people. She's Miss Innocent, but she's the one in charge. She's a tough person. She's got a lot tougher in later years."

Joe had the sympathy of a battery of female supporters, including Barbara Leigh and Sheila Ryan Caan, who deemed Priscilla's actions betrayal and greed of the highest order. "They were Joe's movies," insisted Sheila, who considered Joe "one of the kindest, softest, best human beings you'll ever meet. Priscilla said, 'Well, the lawyers told me, the lawyers told me . . .' The lawyers *told* her? She's not an idiot. She could have helped him out. And that I find *inexcusable.*" Cindy Esposito, Lisa's childhood friend, could not believe that Priscilla was suing her dad. "I mean, how much money do you need?" she wondered.

Priscilla, during this period, began accumulating enemies and a reputation for ruthlessness. The estate became embroiled in a lawsuit against Ginger Alden, who claimed Elvis had promised to buy her a house, and Priscilla began soliciting witnesses to testify against Ginger. Elvis Presley Enterprises evicted Linda Thompson's elderly parents from a modest home Elvis had purchased for them. The Thompsons had a letter from Elvis stating that the house was theirs. Linda, who had not protested when Priscilla kept her off the plane en route to Elvis's funeral, could not constrain her fury. "I wonder how Priscilla would like it if I filed a palimony suit? It's just like with the plane scene," she told Lamar Fike. "She expected me to say, 'Mama and Daddy, get out of the house,' because I didn't try to make her let me get on the plane.' " Linda and several of the entourage toyed with the idea of distributing the pictures Elvis had taken of Priscilla with one of her female lovers "in a compromising position" to retaliate. "Why would a multimillion-dollar estate care about $250 a month [for my parents' house payments]?" she queried. "I wonder what Priscilla ever did for Elvis except take him for two million dollars." Ginger Alden found it offensive that Priscilla "acts more like a widow than an ex-wife. She was out of the picture for quite a while, and I certainly don't think Elvis would be happy that she has been in charge of the estate."

Ginger's comment was the prevailing opinion among the members of Elvis's entourage. They were like a dysfunctional family brawling over Daddy's will, which had come under the control of the wicked stepmother. Jack Soden, Priscilla's estate alter ego, characterized Elvis's aides as "people who seem to blame the world because Elvis died and forced them to confront their lives and get jobs." Priscilla described three of them as "total has-beens and leeches of another mentality that I don't quite understand," stuck in a "time warp." Rick Stanley, who overcame a severe drug problem and became a minister after Elvis's death, agreed with Priscilla that some members of the entourage, who had taken the low road with exploitive books, were "greedy gutless wonders." On the other hand, Rick himself felt displaced, almost orphaned, after Elvis Presley died, for the entourage had become a family of sorts. "Everybody scattered around. You know, that really wounded me, 'cause I was there with these guys when their children were being born. And I was really torn up. [Elvis] was my life—big brother, best friend, everything." Priscilla, as executrix, was a divisive rather than a unifying force. She created resentment over her control of the money, and she made Elvis's entourage feel left out. Red West, by 1996, had no real interest in talking about her. "We're not too close," he explained, "on her part, I guess. We have no animosity toward her, but she's my son's godmother, and he hasn't heard from her since the christening—and he's twenty-four years old."

The great disappointment, for the entourage—a heartache, really—seemed to be the realization that Priscilla was *not* Elvis and never would be, even though she had assumed that parental and fiduciary role. "Elvis," said Joe, "was the type of person, if you had a friend, should always be a friend. And she doesn't even talk to them anymore. It's more like business, making a dollar, making herself a big star. I think she's got really wrapped up in all that. He wasn't really wrapped up in being a big star as much as she is." The difference, distilled to a single concept, was that Elvis came from the heart, whereas Priscilla reacted with her mind. That, in essence, was why Elvis's religious quest had led him to ponder, endlessly, the deepest spiritual questions and Priscilla's took her first to Science of the Mind, finally to Scientology.

It was "totally unfair," argued Priscilla's brother-in-law, Gary Hovey, a member of the estate management team, to paint Priscilla as "this bad person." He perceived her as a businesswoman doing her job. "She was in a tough situation with people she's known a long time, who felt that they should get some-thing—jobs or whatever—and that wasn't easy for her. This is a business and look what it's turned into." Priscilla herself seemed wounded by the sugges-tion that she would be so "petty" as to exact revenge on Ginger or Linda, and denied she had anything to do with the estate's decision to sue for possession of their parents' homes.

It was not just Elvis's ex-girlfriends and aides who criticized the Presley es-tate's aggressive tactics. Elvis Presley Enterprises (known as EPE) began to ac-quire a barracudalike image to go along with its reputation as a well-run, profitable machine. In 1989, EPE threatened to sue the producers of *Designing Women* for an episode in which the characters visited Graceland. Filmmakers hoping to make a movie about Elvis or his music dared not go forward without the approval, and the control, of the estate, without risking costly litigation. Vendors could no longer sell merchandise depicting Elvis in any shape or form without paying a fee to the estate. Lawsuits initiated by EPE proliferated throughout the early 1990s, occasionally extending to the ridiculous. While ar-guments were advanced that Priscilla and Jack Soden were protecting Elvis's im-age—and in the majority of cases, they probably were—critics found this obsessive control and profit-mongering in stark contrast to the very spirit of Elvis that his fans worshiped. The idea persisted that Elvis Presley belonged to the world, not to the estate or even to Lisa—and certainly not to Priscilla.

A fresh controversy sprang up in the early 1990s, when two events occurred. Lisa—who turned twenty-five on February 1, 1993, the age at which Elvis's es-tate was to be distributed to her under the terms of his will—decided to keep her mother's management team, and the estate, in place indefinitely. Priscilla Presley, Elvis's ex-wife, and Jack Soden, a self-admitted non-Presley fan, thus became the permanent symbols of Elvis, in control of his estate, image, and likeness, in conceivably lifetime positions. The reason for Lisa's decision was obvious. She had no interest in the inner workings of the estate; her mother and Soden were making more money than anyone had ever dreamed of; and Lisa had the power to dismantle the operation if she so chose. Soden ex-plained that "there's a new trust that will stay in place as long as she wants it to. When she wants to change it, she can, and she should." After her twenty-fifth birthday, Lisa would appear, obligatorily, at an occasional meeting of the estate management team, "clearly bored to death" at times, said Soden. "She looks like a kid in Latin class. There are parts where she dives in, because it's something she likes, and it's something she's interested in . . . like a company that has proposed an idea for a television show."

The second hot-button development, in early 1990, was Priscilla's decision to restructure the management of the estate, resulting in a power struggle. The architect of the change was Jack Soden. He described himself as a "peacemaker," but others characterized him as a despot who manipulated Priscilla into creating an even greater power base for him at EPE. "Anybody with knowledge and foresight," complained one insider, "he will start a campaign to get rid of." Soden persuaded Priscilla to "streamline" the management of the estate. As part of the purge, Priscilla and Jack removed Joseph Hanks, the Presley accountant and a coexecutor; Fletcher Haaga, who represented the Memphis bank; Joe Roskoff, a New York music attorney; and Jerry Schilling. In the process, Jack Soden became CEO of Elvis Presley Enterprises, with Priscilla as president.

Jerry Schilling, who had become almost as close a friend to Priscilla as he had been to Elvis, had worked with Priscilla on her miniseries and had been running the music division of EPE. It was he, said Jerry, who negotiated with RCA to release the royalties to Elvis's records, a source of enormous profit to the estate. Priscilla replaced Jerry with her sister Michelle's husband, Gary Hovey, who worked in his family's car business. This decision, Jerry said, "almost destroyed" him. The explanations were as varied as the participants. Jack Soden said he wanted EPE staffed by individuals for whom the job was a fulltime occupation, and that Jerry was freelance. Joe Esposito likened Priscilla's brother-in-law to a male Eve Carrington, or to Priscilla, when she spent time with Fran Stone, studying her relationship with Mike so she could replace her. "Gary was a car salesman. And he kept wanting something to do in the music business. So Jerry had him hang around with him, to learn a lot of it. And little by little, he eased Jerry out of the position. And that's how they got rid of Jerry—backstabbing by somebody who [was] supposed to be helping [him] out." Gary would not comment on being hired by the estate. "I don't really want to talk about it," he said. "That was a decision people above me made and that was their decision." Priscilla said that the decision to restructure management was made "for the greater good" of the estate. "It wasn't even that people had to be let go. There are people that just, in some cases, weren't doing their job up to par of what we were looking for. And there isn't a bad feeling there. It's just that we have to move on and we have to make decisions for the greatest good. And that's how we base our decisions." Rick Stanley later said that Jerry was told he could stay if he became a Scientologist.

Priscilla had become, to Elvis's estate, what Elvis had been in life: the center of a financial fiefdom, the person upon whom the entourage, and others who were vicariously connected to Elvis Presley, depended for their livelihood, since she made the decisions regarding the use of his name, image, likeness, and music. With that power, she exercised a tremendous amount of control. The Elvis aides now deferred to her. Anyone with any business connection to the estate dared not speak freely about her without fear of repercussions. Even George Klein, who had been a close friend of Elvis's since high school, was reticent to comment on the Presleys without seeking Priscilla's permission. He explained, "She is real picky about what is printed on her, so I'm in a very precarious position, because I work for the estate on a freelance basis. . . . I try to be real guarded about what I say."

Priscilla, acknowledged Jack Soden, had the final authority on any decision made at Elvis Presley Enterprises, an irony many found difficult to bear. "The fact that she ends up running this institute . . . has always pissed me off. It always will," commented Barbara Leigh, who still held Priscilla responsible for destroying Elvis—emotionally and physically—by betraying and divorcing him. "It's not fair that she became famous and rich on Elvis's death, when Elvis is the one who put her there, and then she killed Elvis and she gained from it." Ed Hookstratten, who as a Hollywood lawyer and manager had seen nearly all there was to see, found it an "unbelievable story" that Priscilla should assume control of Elvis's estate not "because of anything Elvis decreed [but just because] she's the guardian of [his] daughter." Even Jack Soden conceded that "it's an odd thing." Priscilla, he noticed, had become the subject of more than one comedian's monologue, a running joke. "It's a lot of guys' nightmares that their ex-wife would come back to be an executor of their estate." What bothered Jerry Schilling most about Priscilla's authority was that she "didn't have a clue about music."

Exactly how much Priscilla Presley earned as coexecutrix of the estate and president of Elvis Presley Enterprises was, like so much of her life since birth, a closely guarded secret. She and Jack Soden deliberately structured EPE as a privately held business so they would not be required to divulge the numbers. Not even the profits of Elvis Presley Enterprises were known with certainty. "We never talk about that," stated Soden. "Never. We just don't."

The entire enterprise had an air of mystery. The estate offices on Sunset Boulevard had an unlisted phone number and an unmarked door. The parking attendants downstairs would claim that no such company existed in the building. And Priscilla's office, as president of Elvis Presley Enterprises, had no photographs and not one memento of Elvis Presley.

33

LIKE MOTHER, LIKE DAUGHTER

Mogul" would be the word used to describe Priscilla Presley as she entered her late forties. Elvis Presley Enterprises, she would say, was a "nice family business." Her sister, Michelle, was employed as Priscilla's personal assistant. Michelle's husband ran the music division of the estate. Lisa was the beneficiary.

Priscilla had emerged as a conglomerate. Her exposure on *Dallas* had led, in the late eighties, to a phone call from Larry Pesin of Colonia, a subsidiary of a German perfumery, inquiring if Priscilla would be interested in endorsing a perfume. She agreed, on certain conditions: She wanted something other than Priscilla as the name of the perfume, and she wanted to select the fragrance, design the bottle, and plan the ad campaign. In short, she wanted total control—and she got it. In her now familiar pattern, she visited six perfume houses over a two-year period, tested two hundred scents, and launched Moments. The television ads, featuring Priscilla and an actor portraying Elvis capturing the legendary "moment" when they met—"We were just two people, not a myth"—were savaged by *AdWeek,* which mocked Priscilla's "Brooklyn accent," but the perfume was a modest success in America and a triumph in Europe. Another perfume, called Experiences, followed several years later and became the top-selling European scent. Indian Summer, Priscilla's third perfume, debuted in 1996, with Priscilla, an eternally youthful fifty-one, seen in the television commercial driving a sports car through farm country on an Indian summer afternoon to meet a handsome young man.

More endorsements accumulated, Kathie Lee Gifford–style, throughout the nineties: Priscilla in an advertisement for L.A. Gear; Priscilla drinking Crystal Light; Priscilla creating and designing a line of children's clothes called Gioco, Italian for "playful"; Priscilla and Lisa in a mother-daughter Oldsmobile commercial; Priscilla promoting hair extensions on the Home Shopping Channel. Elvis, she told a newspaper reporter, might not like the woman she had become. Mike Edwards was not so certain *he* did, either, though he did not condemn Priscilla. "I understand what the business can do to you," he said, "and it took her like it did most everyone else." Priscilla was, it seemed, in perpetual overdrive, pedaling furiously to make up for those lost years when she was subjugated to an idol.

The once scandalous Lolita of the rock world and Most Hated Woman in America had metamorphosed into a role model who received letters from mothers asking her advice on rearing children, on surviving as a single parent. Priscilla, beyond anything else, was the consummate survivor. She had endured the torment of her confused identity in childhood; the discovery of the secret in her mother's trunk; the trauma of her sexual experience with Currie Grant; her indoctrination, at fourteen, into sex, drugs, and rock and roll; her parents' dictate separating her from the boy she loved and forcing her to move to Memphis to live with a complex rock star she no longer desired; the scandal and embarrassment of her years in sequestration at Graceland, hidden away like Mr. Rochester's lunatic wife in *Jane Eyre;* the hard-earned achievement of her childhood goal to marry Elvis; her years of sexual rejection by her husband; and betrayal by three lovers in succession, one of whom lusted after her daughter. The single greatest challenge of her life, Priscilla would say in 1996, was "coming out of the past," emerging as *Priscilla,* not as an appendage to Elvis. "To survive the bigness and [yet] still be attached to [the Elvis phenomenon] in so many ways. And yet I've moved on. I think I've proven myself to the world so far, I think I have. I certainly wasn't what they thought."

She added another title to her list of credits when she served as executive producer of a television series, *Elvis: The Early Years,* in 1990, an estate project. She retained "absolute power," as she put it, over every script. The absence of dominion over her own life during her childhood and the thirteen years she was with Elvis had given Priscilla a near obsession with control.

Her self-containment, the reserve that everyone who met her remarked upon, led her, ironically, to the role that would force her to let loose and forever change the public's perception of the actress/model persona she had created, with Mike Edwards, back in 1977. Once more, Elvis was responsible for the opportunity. David and Jerry Zucker, the creative team behind *Airplane,* had conceived a zany police comedy called *The Naked Gun* and were casting about for an actress to play their leading lady, opposite Leslie Nielsen and O. J. Simpson. Two things led them to Priscilla: her wooden persona, and her association with Elvis. The Zucker brothers' gimmick, in the picture, was to hire actors known for their stiffness and place them in outrageous situations. Priscilla fit this criterion like a glove. The Zuckers were also rabid Elvis Presley fans. "These guys have such a good time doing what they do," said the casting director, Pamela Basker. "Somebody might have mentioned that they would get to meet Elvis's wife [if they cast her], and they have such a good outlook on life, they have such a slant on it, they just go for the totally bizarre and weird. They wanted to cast O.J., which isn't something you'd think of, but O.J. was so perfect for the role, and yet O.J. is not really a competent actor. But they made it work." Their first choice for the female lead, by a coincidence, had been Bo Derek, whose rejection of *Those Amazing Animals* had given Priscilla her first acting break in 1980.

Priscilla was floored by the request. "I guess she was flattered someone would think of her for comedy," recalled Pamela. The other attraction, according to the casting director, was the "stigma" attached to Priscilla, a sense of the "supernatural" by her association with Elvis. "We were thinking of something that would catch people's eye, and yet is funny when you just say the name." David Zucker, one of the rare directors to cast people after a conversation with the actor, rather than a reading, sensed that Priscilla "was kind of puzzled as to why we wanted her."

She was terrified. Priscilla told *USA Today* she feared, as she started filming, that her career might be over. At the first rehearsal, recalled David Zucker, "she thought she had to be funny, because I think she played the first line kind of quirky, and I said, 'You know, you really don't have to do that at all,' and I think she was very relieved." Priscilla had missed the point of her casting. "All she had to do was what she was experienced at doing," explained the director. "With our kind of comedy we don't need the Jerry Lewises or the Jim Carreys. We only need actors to do what they've done before. It was similar to Peter Graves's reaction the first time we met with him about *Airplane:* 'It's a funny script, but why me?' And we said, 'Peter, trust us, you are going to be funny,' and it's precisely *because* these people had never been in a comedy and didn't have a comedy reputation that they were more valuable to us."

The continuing surprise with Priscilla was her courage to take on situations that frightened her, to challenge herself, and to do what people would never expect of her. So it was with *The Naked Gun*. The fear of the unknown, of doing a comedy, was possibly, speculated Leslie Nielsen, why Bo Derek passed. Priscilla plunged forward, however, and no one on the set had any idea how panic-stricken she was, for her greatest acting accomplishment, always, was to hide what was really inside her. "I remember when we first met. We were sitting across the soundstage from each other," said Nielsen. "I glanced over and happened to catch her eye, and made a face and crossed my eyes. And she did it promptly right back to me." That camaraderie would mark the atmosphere on the set for all three *Naked Gun* movies over the next several years.

Priscilla's acting gamble was a delirious success. *The Naked Gun* opened at the top of the box office and earned Priscilla a People's Choice nomination as Favorite Comedy Motion Picture actress, along with Bette Midler and Jamie Lee Curtis. Priscilla didn't win the award, but she gained the respect of the Hollywood film community. Edward Woodward, who had witnessed her painful struggle through the disastrous *Comeback* with Michael Landon a decade earlier, was happily surprised. By the third *Naked Gun,* he judged her "absolutely superb" with "amazing comedy timing." Most ex-wives who aspired to acting careers, he observed, were viewed as "a little bit silly, pretentious, possibly. She aimed for something that was ridiculous to aim for, and she . . . got it. She did it against all odds." That could be said to be the theme of Priscilla Beaulieu Presley's life, starting with her childhood game of "Imagine If . . . I were Mrs. Elvis Presley."

Priscilla was cast in another film spoof, *Ford Fairlane,* opposite Andrew Dice Clay, amid the *Naked Gun* series and longed, she said, to be considered for the roles Kathleen Turner took. The naughty half of Priscilla expressed a desire to star in another *sex, lies, and videotape* or *Blue Velvet*—something "shocking" and sensational; the demure Priscilla recanted in 1996, saying she would never appear nude. "I have a son to answer to. I couldn't embarrass him. I don't care what the role is . . . I don't want my son seeing me nude. I don't know how these mothers do it. I don't know how Demi Moore does it. I'm sorry—she's got three kids. I don't know how Cybill Shepherd does it. I don't know, it's just not in me. It just isn't in me. I've got an aunt and my grandchildren. I don't want to embarrass them."

Lisa still had not separated herself fully from Priscilla after she married Danny Keough. Her baby, a daughter named Danielle, was the very image of both Priscilla and Lisa as toddlers. A paparazzi's exclusive baby photograph of Danielle, Elvis Presley's first grandchild, fetched $450,000 from *People* magazine and the *Star.* According to Myrna Smith, who had been close to Lisa since she was a child, "Lisa had problems with Danny all along. She's doing to her men what her dad did to his women, which is isolating them and not letting them go out and get a job." When he married Lisa, Danny Keough was a young twenty-one, a good-looking musician wanna-be who played in the occasional gig with a few other Scientologists and was known to flirt with the ladies. Brett Strong, the artist and family friend, noticed a conflict between Danny and Lisa that was similar to the one that had existed between Priscilla and Elvis: a competition between spouses as to who would be famous and who would stay at home. "It was frustrating to Danny that Lisa was the one who had all of the fame and glory [even though] she hadn't accomplished anything; she just happened to be born that way, where I think Danny wanted to be this famous musician. And I know for sure that detracted from their relationship, because Lisa was looking for love and attention." When Danny was on the road performing, Lisa and the baby stayed at the Summit house with Priscilla and Marco and Navarone. Lisa, recalled a close friend, was "leery" of Marco at first, and her relationship with Priscilla was, as it had been for some time, "strained."

Sometime in 1991, after she had been married three years, Lisa, then twenty-three, telephoned Brett Strong. It was not the first time Lisa had turned to Brett to commiserate about her life. "She used to call me now and then when the relationship with Danny wasn't working out to the effect that she wanted, love-wise." Prior to Danny, Lisa had dated Roberto Domine, the son of a restaurateur, and Kevin Jeffcoat, both of whom she had met through the Scientology Celebrity Centre, her social meeting ground. Brett's impression was that she was "passionately in love" with one of her earlier boyfriends, but when Priscilla became pregnant with Navarone, Lisa desperately wanted to be married and have a child, like her mother. "Danny was the one who wanted children, and she got into that."

In 1991, Lisa was restless and unfulfilled. "She wanted to do more with her life than just have her life go by," Brett said. She and Danny were arguing mildly about his career versus hers, "and now he was going off snowboarding and taking trips all of the time, probably trying to resolve his life." Lisa was clearly in a struggle to find her identity, which was not surprising considering the surreal nature of her existence. Her life—indeed the entire American culture—was inundated with images, retrospectives, movies, books, and bizarre theories about her dead father. The U.S. Postal Service issued the Elvis Presley stamp that year, after a national vote on whether to use an image of the young Elvis or the older, Vegas Elvis, creating a media blitzkrieg and the largest sale of stamps in U.S. history. Bill Bixby hosted a serious television special that summer called *Is Elvis Alive?*

Lisa Marie, as her father called her, had become a celebrity and a multimillionaire simply by virtue of her birth, and the unrelenting media glare was overwhelming. The year before, she had telephoned a young producer's office by mistake, thinking she was dialing Marco's production company, and according to the producer's girlfriend, she opened her soul to a perfect stranger. Lisa apparently confided in the producer her marital woes, discussed the possibility of aborting another child by Danny, and talked about writing a book about her life, as if she had dialed a crisis hot line. The astonished producer would not comment on the bizarre experience later, except to say, "Even to this day I'm sort of at a loss at what exactly happened, so I think it's best to just let it go. It's really, you know, a mystery to me, the whole thing. . . . I'm sure Lisa's totally got her life together at this stage."

She was, by all appearances, deeply troubled. Lisa still had a desire to be in show business, to be famous in her own right, and she turned, that year, to Jerry Schilling for guidance. Having decided to become an actress, she enlisted Jerry as her manager. She wanted, he recalled, to be a star. Jerry went along with it, not so secretly hoping she would switch to singing, which she had flirted with during her Scott Rollins romance and had then abandoned, in

Priscilla's opinion, as a passing phase. "I managed her as an actress," said Jerry, "but I kept saying, 'Lisa, you are going to sing.' And she said, 'I don't want to hear about it.' " Lisa's acting career fizzled, going no further than a false press report, in May of 1991, that she would costar with Vanilla Ice in his next movie. She took a few acting lessons and became bored and discouraged because she was not an instant success.

During the summer or early fall of 1992, Jerry Schilling received the green light from Lisa he had been hoping for since she was a child. "She called me from the car phone one day and said, 'I can sing!' And I knew what that meant." Lisa Marie Presley had suddenly decided, for whatever reason, that her voice could be compared to her famous father's and she was ready to withstand the media scrutiny and aim full-tilt for a recording career. She was, recalled Jerry, "scared and happy, and I liked that." Jerry Schilling again became Lisa Presley's manager. "Jerry would tell me," recalled Brett, "when he was married to Myrna, 'If only [Lisa] would practice, she would be as good as her father.' Jerry always wanted to be the manager, I saw that."

Jerry thought Lisa had a "great" voice, "a cross between Aretha and Bonnie Raitt." Once Lisa's decision was made, Jerry took her through "the normal process." She engaged her husband, Danny, as her producer and began writing songs with him, recalled both Jerry and Brett. Lisa was excited. "We went to the studios and got the musicians," said Jerry. "When we got there, Aretha was the first thing she did on demo." Jerry, who had sat in with Elvis on countless recording sessions and regarded him as "the most underrated producer in the world," considered Lisa to have the same gift. "She'd say, 'Listen to this; it doesn't sound right.' She knew, musically, what was right for her." Lisa, aware of all the pressure on her, was inhibited, remembered Jerry. The only person she would allow inside the studio—the only one who could get *her* into the studio—was Danny. "Danny started working with her and did a great job. A lot of it was confidence and pulling her along."

Myrna Smith, who had sung with Lisa when Lisa was a child, spending time with the Sweet Inspirations, sang backup and witnessed Lisa's nervousness. "She had never sung with a microphone in front of anybody, so . . . I wasn't sure how she would sound." Myrna also assessed Lisa's voice as great, "more R&B. Her voice is husky and she can hit high notes, too, and has her own style."

Jerry sent Lisa's demo tapes to a large record company "and didn't tell them who it was. She got three major deals." Lisa played her demo recording that fall for Priscilla, who was not aware she had been working with Jerry and Danny, "and it's unbelievable!" recalled Priscilla, still shocked in 1996. "It's beautiful. Sounds like Aretha Franklin. I was blown away. She's talented."

Lisa became pregnant in the process of recording her demos and gave birth to a son named Benjamin in October of 1992, putting a temporary halt to her plans to record. She was also, recalled Myrna, concerned about her lack of experience but too self-conscious to acquire the necessary practice in front of an audience. "I tried to get her to sing at a karaoke bar out of town, where everybody is singing out of tune." It was too "scary" for Lisa, said Myrna.

Jerry was, by his recollection, finalizing plans to close a record deal for Lisa with Epic when things suddenly shifted course. Unbeknownst to Jerry, Lisa was impatient with the conservative, traditional route he was taking as her manager, representing her as an "upcoming new young talent," taking the steps he would have followed for any other beginning artist. She phoned Brett Strong "every now and then" throughout the summer of 1992, expressing her dissatisfaction. "That didn't [set well] with Lisa," as Brett put it. "She was, 'Hey, hang on a second! I'm *Elvis Presley's* daughter! . . . Separate me from any other young and upcoming singer.' But she obviously didn't say that to Jerry."

Lisa's phone calls gave rise to an inspiration on Brett's part. He had become a successful artist, famous for a million-dollar portrait he had painted of Michael Jackson, who had become his personal friend. Brett, the great connector, considered introducing Lisa to Michael. "She had the talent as well as the beauty and the name, so I thought Wow! The sky is the limit. What an image! I had known Michael Jackson for six years or more, and I thought maybe I could introduce Lisa to Michael Jackson. I thought, Hey, the person to get is Michael Jackson, because he's an artist, instead of dealing with businessmen who would just categorize her and work her way up." Michael had a new record label, Brett knew, and was looking for exciting, undiscovered talent. Who better than Lisa Marie Presley? "I didn't discuss this with anyone," said Brett. "I just thought about it and went about my business and thought that sometime in the future Lisa would like to have a conversation with Michael. What I could see, Lisa was disenchanted with Jerry's representation because she didn't like what the head guy at Sony in New York had told her and what Jerry was telling her about where she had to begin and what she had to do—that she had to crawl before she walked." Lisa Presley wanted to emerge a full-blown star, and Michael Jackson, Brett believed, could help her.

Several months after the idea occurred to him, Brett telephoned Lisa, who was taking courses at the Scientology center in Clearwater, Florida. He said, "Lisa, if you're really serious about your career, why don't I put you in touch with Michael Jackson? . . . I think you should meet him and play your music and sing for him, and I think he could really encourage and inspire you on a direction you could take." Brett told her that Michael had his own company, Nation Records, sponsored by Sony, and that he could "really launch her big time." Lisa was intrigued.

Brett's next step was to telephone Michael Jackson. "I said, 'Michael, what would you say if I found talent for you that had the potential to be number one in the world in the recording industry–beautiful girl, great voice, and also a reputation that would be a public relations dream come true?' and he said, 'Who . . . are you talking about?' So I said, 'Lisa Presley.' And he said, 'What? She can't sing!' and I said, 'She can.' And then I asked, 'Have you ever met Lisa?' and he said no." The conversation, recalled Brett, was brief, followed by "lots of other conversations about it." Michael "was amazed at first, and then said, 'Well, get her to send me a tape.' "

At the time, neither Michael nor Lisa recalled their fleeting introduction, backstage, at the Sahara Tahoe when Lisa was six and Michael was sixteen. Myrna Smith, who was with Jerry and Joe Esposito when they took Lisa to that long-ago concert, confirmed this. "Lisa didn't even remember meeting Michael as a child," Myrna said. "She asked me, 'Did I ever meet Michael Jackson?' and I said, 'Don't you remember? We took you to see the Jacksons.' "

When Brett told Lisa about his conversation with Michael, she was offended that she should have to send a demo. She told Brett, "Forget it. I'll play [the tape] for him in person." Lisa called Brett "constantly" afterward, inquiring about the meeting with Michael. She told Myrna excitedly that Brett had arranged to have Michael and her get together at his house in Pacific Palisades and for Lisa to play her demo tape. Lisa took her husband, Danny, along to that meeting, and the group gathered in Brett's living room. "Michael . . . was blown away by her music," according to Brett. "She played the tape and was really excited that Michael Jackson was here, and at that point she looked like a fan of his. And he was really tickled to see that she had a lot of potential, but he didn't think too much more than 'Wow, Brett is onto something here.' " There was, according to Brett, not even the slightest suggestion of anything romantic between Michael and Lisa at that meeting. "Her husband was here."

Michael carried on with his own career interests after that meeting, but Lisa, recalled Brett, "kept calling me after that. Constantly calling me. And she wanted to get together with Michael more." Lisa met with Brett a few times to talk about it, remarking that she had "a few things in common with the Jacksons and maybe she should pursue a friendship with Michael." Brett, still their intermediary, offered to represent Lisa in a business contract with Michael for a recording deal, even though he had an art partnership with Michael and had been his friend for years. Brett worked up some figures and talked to Michael, who arranged for Brett to take Lisa to meet Michael Greenberg, the head of Jackson's company, Nation Records, in Santa Monica. Lisa brought Danny and her attorney, John Coale. "I didn't know anything about that business," said Brett, "but I wanted to make sure that Lisa made a deal at the top level . . . by saying, 'Hey, Elvis is the King and she's the Princess. She's got the talent. All she needs is Michael to help record at the highest possible level and help her choose the songs and teach her some presence on stage. l was trying to get Michael to . . . make a deal with Lisa at the top—the deal that the other recording companies were making with Madonna and Barbra Streisand. And he was like 'Are you crazy? They have proven themselves.' And I said, 'No, make the same deal; a deal over a period of time . . . based on performance as the records sell. And not only will you make the deal with Lisa, you'll promote the company.' And I knew that is what Lisa would love, if she was put on a pedestal."

Lisa was torn. Part of her was in "turmoil," recalled Brett, for "on her mind was 'I have my kids,' and she was in turmoil with her husband and what should she do? If she wanted to be a star, she had to really want to live and breathe that." Michael Jackson also advised Lisa similarly: If she wanted to pursue a singing career, she would have to dedicate herself to it. During the coming weeks, Brett found himself the hapless man in the middle, caught between a balking and busy Michael, and an ambivalent yet driven Lisa. Brett made arrangements for Lisa to visit Michael in Japan while he was on tour for *Dangerous,* and tried to facilitate other plans, some of which occurred while others dissipated. Lisa, "in relentless pursuit of Michael Jackson," began phoning Brett constantly to find out whether the deal would occur. Michael, in Brett's characterization, was obviously intrigued by the thought of signing Lisa Presley, "but there was more desire on Lisa's part for something to happen." Lisa, recalled Brett, finally said to him, "It doesn't seem like I can make that deal with him, and I don't want to push him too much." Brett, who was still hoping to bring them together for a record deal, finally arranged for a representative from Michael's office to send a formal letter to Lisa stating that Michael was still interested in "keeping things going." At the same time, Prince also began pursuing Lisa to sign a recording contract.

Lisa celebrated her twenty-fifth birthday with a huge party, planned by Priscilla, at Six Flags Magic Mountain. Prince was among the guests, along with a sprinkling of celebrity Scientologists such as Kirstie Alley, Nicole Kidman, and Juliette Lewis, as well as the Espositos. Lisa invited Michael Jackson as her special guest, "and he would have loved to have gone," said Brett, "but he had other things." Brett suggested to Michael he should at least send Lisa a birthday gift, "so he told me, 'Well, you get it!' " Brett selected, as Michael Jackson's gift to Lisa, an art book on Michelangelo and a silver picture frame, in which he placed a photograph of Michael and Lisa's original meeting in his living room. Brett, attempting to be gallant in Michael's behalf, wrote sweet birthday inscriptions in the art book and on the birthday card, making them appear to be from Michael. "I was just trying to be a good friend for him," said Brett. "I went to the party with my son Jason, and when I got there, Lisa was like 'Oh! Where's Michael? I hope it's all right that Prince is here.' I said, '[Michael] just couldn't make it, but here is a gift from him.' And I didn't say anything

[else]." Lisa, recalled Brett, latched on to the gifts excitedly and immediately opened them to "check them out."

He later figured out, said Brett, that he had inadvertently played match-maker to Michael and Lisa by buying the birthday gifts, for Lisa, seeing the card and the inscription in the art book, both of which she believed to have been written by Michael, misinterpreted Brett's affectionate words as an indication that *Michael Jackson* had feelings for her. "I wasn't trying to bring two people to-gether to get married. I look back on it now as a sign that [she was thinking], Wow! He really cares about me. And she secretly wanted a relationship with him, because I always talked about him as a passionate man [who was] ex-tremely loving . . . and that attracted Lisa, that loving part, and loving chil-dren." Lisa never knew Brett wrote the birthday card and signed her book. "I can't recall what I wrote exactly in the book or card," said Brett, "but that might have been something she read over and over again and thought, Jeez!" After-ward "Lisa kept calling me, and eventually, after the many calls and pursuits and my little bit of fairy dust that I sprinkled around the place, hey, those guys [got] together, and I thought, 'Maybe they'll record something.' And I remem-ber Lisa saying, 'Brett, what do you want out of this?' and Michael Jackson asked me the same thing, and I thought, 'Boy, there must be something hap-pening here.' I told Lisa, 'You can give me whatever you think is fair,' and I told Michael the same thing. I thought up the idea and executed it, and I stayed on top of it. And any other businessperson would be claiming something, but since I am an artist, I told them, 'If you do record something, give me a job at art direction instead of hiring somebody else.' So we didn't think anything else or more about that other than that it was going to happen."

In late February, a few weeks after her twenty-fifth birthday, Jerry Schilling re-ceived a mysterious phone call from Lisa. "Something is going on," she told Jerry, "but I can't tell you what. And it has nothing to do with you, but I'm not going to continue with this record contract right now." Lisa told him, said Jerry, that she was busy with her new baby and wanted to put the Epic deal on hold. Jerry, who had no idea Lisa had even met Michael Jackson, simply said fine and puzzled over what might be happening in Lisa's life.

Mike Edwards, who had also remained close to Brett after the breakup with Priscilla, began getting phone calls from an amazed Brett about this time. "He's saying, 'Gosh, Lisa's calling me, and Lisa's really interested in *Michael*!'" Brett's impression, said Mike Edwards, was that Michael was absorbed in his work, but that Lisa was really interested in him. "And I said, 'Come on! What do you mean?' [Brett] said, 'You haven't met him, but he's very charismatic.' And I said, 'Yeah, but I can't believe it. He said, 'Yeah, she's kind of pursuing him.' And I went, 'My God! What's gonna happen?'"

"I could see that Lisa fell in love with him," confirmed Brett. What attracted her in part, he felt, was that Michael was not after her money. "I think she didn't know him very well, though. She didn't know his quirks and eccentric lifestyle, and she thought, This guy is going to be great. A stepfather for my kids."

Lisa, according to Brett, was the one who was in pursuit. "I think it was the passion of a woman who fell in love. And [Michael] wouldn't have been interested at all. And he is a gentleman and wouldn't have wanted to pull her away from her marriage to Danny. And she pursued him." Family friend Bob Wall, who heard about it after the fact, confirmed this. "I know Lisa is the one who pursued the relationship." She did it, Bob felt, to create an identity separate from the Presley name, to be known as something other than "the daughter of," the same anxiety that Priscilla had experienced during and after the Elvis years. "Lisa really wants to be credible," said Bob. "You've got her father, who's a genius. Her mother's done incredibly well. And all she's got is a lot of money. So maybe that's important to her, to create her own identity. Maybe it's necessary for her sanity."

Brett, seeing the progression of the friendship, suggested that Michael take Lisa to the Oscar ceremony that March, just as he had escorted Madonna the year before, but Michael balked, since Lisa was a married woman. The relationship intensified on Michael's part that fall, however, after thirteen-year-old Jordan Chandler charged him with child molestation, causing a scandal to erupt worldwide. In November Michael quietly escorted Lisa to the Jackson Family Honors.

Lisa was spending time with Myrna, who by then was divorced from Jerry Schilling. Lisa told Myrna about her secret romance with Michael Jackson. Myrna perceived that Lisa felt sorry for Michael because of the sexual molestation charges and the devastating effect the scandal had had on his career and his image. Myrna also believed Lisa had sincere feelings for Michael. "Yes, she did, according to what she told me. She did. She's like her father: They like the underdog. . . . She did it for her own reasons, but she didn't do it [because] Michael coerced her. She genuinely cared about him and thought he cared for her." Myrna, who knew and knew of Michael through music circles, tried to warn Lisa about the relationship, which she considered both dangerous and absurd. "I can only guess what his motives were, and I could only tell her what I thought, what a smart businessman he was, and that he was only pursuing her for what she could do for him, and that he wasn't interested in women. And she told me that he was." Lisa did not tell Myrna whether she and Michael had sex, though Brett believed they did. "Yeah, sure, I think, because of what happened. I didn't want to ask any questions. I could have asked Lisa the nitty-gritty."

By Christmas 1993, Lisa was discussing with Myrna the possibility of marrying Michael Jackson. "He told her," said Myrna, "that she was the only woman he could see himself marrying. And I was like, 'You got to be kidding.' " Myrna recalled that Lisa responded, "Myrna, you don't understand." Myrna reminded Lisa that she was married and tried to convince her that Michael's motives were not, in her opinion, pure. "When she was telling me what was going on, I was thinking, This is a plan. He's got this calculated plan, and [he has] thought this all through: 'This is the girl who is going to make me . . . Elvis is the King of Rock and Roll, and I'm going to be bigger than that.' And that was his whole purpose. And she didn't want to believe it." Lisa asked Myrna not to tell Jerry or her mother about her romance with Michael. Priscilla did not have a clue that her only daughter was being courted by Michael Jackson.

In February 1994, Lisa and Michael stayed at Mar-a-Lago in Palm Springs with Donald Trump and Marla Maples. Then they moved into one of the millionaire's luxury condominiums at Trump Tower in New York while Michael cut a new album. There were a few Michael-and-Lisa sightings in the press that early spring, but no one thought much about it, for no journalist would have imagined there was a romance. The next step in the strange progression of the relationship was Lisa's public announcement, in April, that she was ending her marriage to Danny Keough, just as the second sequel to *The Naked Gun* was released. Priscilla, in an interview to promote the movie that May, expressed regret that her daughter's marriage was "headed for divorce court," but commented, she had no idea how sagely, "I don't have much to say in Lisa's decision-making now."

What she did not realize, at the time, was that Lisa was already preparing to marry Michael Jackson, in the same high-espionage fashion in which Priscilla had earlier married Elvis Presley. That April, Michael's Beverly Hills attorney, Robert Kaufman, reportedly placed a call to a judge in the Dominican Republic, inquiring about the procedure for his client to be married on the island. Divorce papers for Lisa and Danny were quietly filed, and finalized, in Santo Domingo in early May. On May 24, Lisa and Michael flew on Sony's private jet to La Romana in the Dominican Republic and checked into the Casa de Campo resort, accompanied by Danny's brother and sister-in-law, Thomas and Eva Keough, both Scientologists, like Danny. Lisa and Michael checked into separate suites. That day, Michael's lawyer telephoned Francisco Alvarez Perez, the same judge he had spoken to earlier, to confirm plans for the wedding, which would take place at Perez's house on May 26. His client, Kaufman told the judge, had requested that the ceremony be "short and fast," like Elvis and Priscilla's. Lisa's marriage to Michael took place in La Vega, as her mother's had been in Las Vegas, in a ceremony performed, as Priscilla's had been, by a judge arranged through a third party. Again like Elvis and

Priscilla, Michael and Lisa flew secretly by private jet from their small wedding ceremony back home to L.A.

By mid-July rumors were flying wildly in the press about a suspected wedding between Michael Jackson and Lisa Marie Presley, who were reported to be—and were—ensconced in the Trump Tower in New York. Priscilla, who knew nothing of her daughter's marriage, questioned Brett Strong about the newspaper accounts, for she knew he and Michael were friends. "And I told Priscilla that Michael had told me once when I was at his home, years ago, that he always wanted a son and a daughter, and didn't know how he was going to get it, 'cause who was he going to marry? But he always wanted that, and had a room full of dolls and other toys. . . . He had a train set rigged up so that you thought he already had a kid somewhere." Priscilla, Brett recalled, laughed nervously and said, "Oh, my God! He's going to get his son and daughter by marrying my daughter!" Priscilla seemed embarrassed, said Brett, and "didn't want to let on to anybody that she didn't know anything."

Lisa informed her mother she was married to Michael two weeks before she announced it publicly, just as Priscilla's costar in the *Naked Gun* pictures, O. J. Simpson, was arrested for the brutal murder of his ex-wife, Nicole Brown. Priscilla, by everyone's account, was appalled at the news of her daughter's marriage. Marco Garibaldi would later compare Lisa's marriage to Michael, and his and Priscilla's feelings about it, to "a mole on the end of someone's nose. Everybody knows it's there, and nobody's happy about it, but you just don't say anything about it." Priscilla, who had shocked the world as Elvis Presley's child bride, had now become, extraordinarily, Michael Jackson's mother-in-law.

In the ever unusual world of Elvis and Priscilla—and now Lisa—there were some bizarre parallels between Lisa's marriage to Michael and her mother's marriage to Elvis. In addition to their similarly secretive weddings in Las Vegas and La Vega, Lisa had married a man she would discover had little interest in taking her to his bed, just as Elvis rarely had intercourse with Priscilla. Lisa had wed, by an obvious Freudian motive, the nineties equivalent of her staggeringly successful superstar father. Elvis was the King of Rock; Michael was the King of Pop. Both singers, oddly, had pet chimpanzees at one time; both shared an interest in UFOs. Elvis lived in semiseclusion at an estate called Graceland. Michael lived a reclusive life at Neverland. Elvis often rented amusement parks, one of his favorite forms of entertainment; Michael had re-created Disneyland on the grounds of his estate and took Lisa, incognito, to the California theme park on their honeymoon. Both men had married to avoid scandal in their careers: Elvis to erase the stigma of his live-in relationship with a seventeen-year-old girl, or to avoid the Beaulieus' revelation of their illicit arrangement for Priscilla; Michael to rehabilitate his shattered image following the molestation charges. Michael and Elvis entertained small groups of fourteen-year-olds in their bedrooms for slumber parties. The two music legends were notorious eccentrics trapped in an arrested adolescence, existing on unorthodox diets.

Lisa, some of her friends surmised, had married Michael—on a subconscious level at least—to "save" the father she had loved and lost. By restoring Michael to his former position of glory, by elevating him from the ruin of his molestation scandal, she might, in her mind, redeem and perhaps resurrect her father. Choosing Michael also reinforced Lisa's lifetime obsession with her mother, for by marrying the pop superstar, she had, in effect, become Priscilla's equivalent in celebrity. The proof of that theory was evident after the wedding, when Lisa, who had spent most of her teens and twenties in grunge fashions, underwent an extensive cosmetic makeover. She emerged as Mrs. Michael Jackson that summer, the epitome of couture chic, with a different facial bone structure, a newly slender body, and customized glamour by makeup stylist Kevin Aucoin. She looked, suddenly, like *Priscilla*.

The Espositos, who had lost touch with Priscilla and Lisa through the years—an estrangement they attributed to the Presleys' conversion to Scientology, which encourages its disciples to socialize together—construed Lisa's marriage to Michael as an act of rebellion against her mother. Lisa, they concurred, had never *looked* happier. "She's got a smile on her face," Joe said. "Before, she never, ever smiled. Never, ever."

Priscilla declined, after Lisa's marriage to Michael ended, to comment on the relationship. "It's her situation, it's her life. As a mother, I have to honor that. I don't want to come out and say anything bad about Michael, or bad about her, or bad about the relationship. It certainly surprised me, I will say that." She told Rick Stanley, shortly before the divorce, that she followed Scientology doctrine vis-à-vis Michael, and considered him a "granted being," meaning, she said, "I grant people the right to be what they are." That, according to Mike Edwards, was Priscilla's modus operandi with any problem: "She'll block it out of her existence, and she'll let Scientology deal with it for her."

Scientology's protective cloak certainly enveloped Lisa throughout the secret wedding to Michael and afterward. As Lisa and Michael Jackson prepared to do their much-publicized, hugely anticipated and watched July 14 interview with Diane Sawyer on *Prime Time Live*, answering questions about their bizarre marriage, Lisa was seen coming out of the president's office at the Celebrity Centre in the Hollywood Hills the afternoon before, where she was being advised on how to handle the questions and answers. Her childhood friend Dana Rosenfeld, who watched the show along with most of the rest of America, was stunned by her former friend's aggressive, almost hostile stance during the interview and analyzed it as a delayed reaction to unresolved emotional issues concerning Elvis's death and her strained relationship with

Priscilla. "Just Lisa's whole body language. She was so angry. That element of her personality when she was a child, when she was angry, was still there." After seeing the videotape of the wedding, with Lisa chewing gum and giggling, Dana said, "My only take on that is that for so long she was hidden from everybody and nobody knew anything, and what better way to just catapult yourself to the center of the media's attention than to marry someone like that?"

Brett Livingstone Strong's response to Lisa and Michael's *Prime Time Live* interview was, quite simply, anger, for both created the illusion—the lie—that they had been friends for years, ever since their initial meeting at a Jackson Five concert when they were children. Michael and Lisa did not even name the correct city where the concert was held: They said Las Vegas when in fact it was Lake Tahoe. Michael and Lisa told the world, on television, that Michael had lusted after Lisa since she was six, that they had been in frequent contact over the years, and that it was always in his mind that he would marry Lisa one day. Brett, who knew the truth—that he had orchestrated the meeting not two years before, for the express purpose of getting Lisa a record contract with Michael's company—was deeply offended, particularly since Scientology is founded on truth. The interview was, he realized, classic media manipulation. "Michael thought that was the way he should present it, as if it had always been in the background, whereas . . . the truth [was] that I did it as a business thing. . . . He was trying to defend his life [after going] through this traumatic period of being an accused child molester, and now [he's] married to Lisa Presley—and is that a beard, or what? So he says, 'Well, I've known her all my life,' when the truth of the matter is that they had briefly met one another, but Lisa had never [considered it a real] meeting, and Michael exaggerated it out of all proportions."

Mike Edwards, to whom Brett expressed his indignation, understood Lisa's strategy in lying to the media about her private life, for he had witnessed it, for seven years, with Priscilla, who learned it from Elvis. "A friend of mine once said, 'The apple doesn't fall far from the tree.'"

Lisa's ill-founded marriage to Michael came tumbling down within six months of the Diane Sawyer interview, when Lisa filed for divorce in January of 1995. The inside word was that, before the marriage, Michael had promised Lisa a recording contract with his company and had later reneged. "That's what he might have been promising her," commented Myrna, who had disapproved of the marriage from the outset, "but that might not have been his intention." Lisa, she revealed, was devastated by the experience. Both Myrna and Brett believed Michael did not want the competition from his wife. "He's very much top of the pile in his world, and that's probably one reason Lisa filed for divorce," said Brett. "And the things that she asked for from Michael he wasn't willing to do." Priscilla's response when she heard that Lisa had filed for divorce, said Rick Stanley, who happened to be staying at her house at the time, was, "Praise the Lord!" Marco said simply, "The mole has been removed."

Lisa had discovered the reality of her sham marriage to Michael even as she was being interviewed by Diane Sawyer in May of 1995. That July she was at a housewarming party in Los Feliz for her ex-husband, Danny, eyeing him possessively as he danced with other women. Lisa and Danny continued to vacation together in Hawaii throughout her marriage to Michael and afterward, patterning their relationship, said Priscilla, on "my relationship with her dad. They are very good friends. [Danny's] around a lot. He's always around the children, which is great." Myrna felt that Lisa would eventually reconcile with Danny, possibly even remarry him.

Lisa followed her mother's example as a new divorcée, springing from marriage into a concentrated effort to launch a show business career. She signed with Priscilla's longtime agent, Norman Brokaw of William Morris, and toyed with modeling, as her mother had, appearing on the cover of *Vogue* in April 1996 and becoming the image of Versace, just as Priscilla had once endorsed Wella Balsam.

There was, Rick Stanley would observe, a keen and ever-so-delicate competition between mother and daughter, exacerbated by Priscilla's milestone birthday on May 24, 1995. Priscilla, the perpetual child-woman, had a psychologically difficult time turning fifty. That "really did a number," said Rick. "And she's in a part of the country where the physical is *it.* She's going through a really, really tough time. She's in a tough spot." It was Priscilla's jealousy of Lisa, in Rick's analysis, that caused her to discourage Lisa's singing and acting career, for Priscilla wanted, as she had with Elvis, to be the center of attention herself. "There is a rift between her and her daughter. I mean, it's *there.* There's a jockeying for position between those two."

Priscilla continued her self-promotion and marketing frenzy into her fifties, with Indian Summer perfume and a new line of skin-care products she began developing, in her customary methodical way. A new woman's clothing line was discussed for the Home Shopping Network. There was talk of developing a situation comedy. She accepted a limited recurring role on *Melrose Place* as a glamorous Nurse Ratchit, because, she admitted, "I was informed that it was one of the hottest shows on television. A cult show. It seemed to be something everyone was watching. I figured it was something to do that was a top show." As Alan Landsburg, the producer of *Those Amazing Animals,* had observed of her sixteen years before, Priscilla was a woman who recognized her limitations—and exploited herself to the maximum within them. She had come to accept, by 1996, that she would not be offered and probably could not execute the sort of artistically interesting, demanding roles other actresses she admired—Isabella Rossellini, Kathleen Turner, Bette Midler—chose and excelled at. She was, as Mike Edwards had perceived during their long romance, trapped behind a mask of inhibitions. "Being crazy, letting go—I can't do that," Priscilla recently admitted. "I know my limitations. I'm too restrained to do this. But I admire people who can do that. They can make a fool out of themselves. I am too aware, I can't." Acting roles, for her, would be vehicles designed to launch her next commercial venture. Something that "keeps me out there, and from that something else becomes of it. I got a fragrance because of *Dallas*. You know, it's the benefits I get from acting, actually."

Priscilla made an effort to stretch as an actress in the spring of 1997 on "Touched by an Angel." It was a role she considered the most dramatic of her career—a doctor forced by circumstance to deliver her husband's mistress's baby. She also continued to maximize her position as the Presley executrix, signing on as executive producer in *The Road to Graceland*, a feature film about a man who fantasizes himself to be Elvis Presley. She announced late in 1995, semiprivately, her intention to eventually dedicate herself to the cause of child abuse. True to her nature, she first planned to research the subject matter. "I have to wait until I have some credibility and learn my stuff so people won't question my involvement."

Priscilla had seemingly found, in Marco, her ideal mate, although she still expressed reservations, in private. By 1996, Marco had mostly abandoned his long-frustrated attempts to establish a career as a director, producer, or writer and had started a computer company, working out of Priscilla's house on Summit Drive. Priscilla, according to Myrna, in an opinion shared by others, preferred that Marco remain low-profile and devote his time and attention to her. "I think that's why [the relationship] works." According to Shirley Dieu's analysis, Priscilla retained control that way, and that was her comfort zone.

The life of a wealthy woman's lover suited Marco Garibaldi. He amused himself with his computer business, formulating plans for his own vintage of wine, tinkering with inventions, reading books on all manner of subjects. It bothered him not at all, in Brett Strong's assessment, that Priscilla possessed the wealth and the fame. "I think that is the magic that he's got. He feels that Priscilla has the money and [he's] got the time, so he helps her and she helps him, and they do their thing."

The shadow of Elvis, which had lurked about Priscilla's relationship with Mike Edwards, was nowhere present with Marco. His ego seemed unfazed by living with the ex-wife of the King, whom he described as "this person in a black cape." As Brett said, "Marco decided that he is every bit the man that Elvis was and he could be a better husband. . . . He's a charming fellow. Personally I think that she is happy to have him." Myrna agreed that Marco had "done the best for her of anyone," perhaps because of his "strength. He knows just how far to take his strength where she won't turn away. She can't run over him. She treats him with respect."

Priscilla had finally found her idealized companion: a dark, genuinely virile man with the outward machismo of Elvis Presley whose focus was, solely and exclusively, on her.

Priscilla and Marco, by the observation of Jerry, who spent time socializing with them separately and together, had "a great life. They're *incredible* parents. They both *love* that little boy." If Marco was not the ultimate love of Priscilla's life, her son, Navarone, was. The only potential dilemma in the Priscilla-Marco relationship, and it was a large one, centered on Scientology, for Marco was not a Scientologist and would never become one, he said staunchly. "I don't go for organizations," he stated. "And they know I know too much about them." When Priscilla's Scientology friends came by the house on Summit and asked Marco to sit with them, he would "politely decline" and leave the room, though, stated Priscilla, "he doesn't mind me being in Scientology. He supports me very much and doesn't have any qualms whatsoever, so that doesn't conflict." Priscilla, deferring to Marco, did not enroll Navarone in Scientology courses as a child, as she did Lisa. "We teach him morals, we teach him ethics, we teach him values. We don't feel that we have to send him to a church. He gets that from Marco and me." When he turned fifteen, said Priscilla, Navarone would be able to choose for himself. "But I decided when Navarone gets around fifteen, it would probably be a good time to put him in Scientology, once I introduce him to certain theories." Marco told a friend, in private conversation, that "he would take Navarone out of the country if that happened."

Priscilla, in her early fifties, had come close to reclaiming her lost life. She had submerged, sublimated, and suppressed the person inside her and played the role necessary to realize the obsessive dream she fantasized for herself as a child: to marry Elvis Presley. Yet a part of her identity remained in subjugation to someone else, for she was still Priscilla *Presley.*

This issue would dangle continuously throughout her three serious post-Elvis relationships—with Mike Stone, Mike Edwards, and Marco Garibaldi—as she contemplated whether to marry each man. The question became acute with Marco, for she had his child, a son she adored, and Priscilla was not the sort of woman, by nature, to choose living with a man over marriage. She justified her single status with various rationalizations: that marriage implied ownership, that she did not want Marco to take her for granted or vice versa simply because they were married, that after her experience with Elvis, she did not want another man to "control" her. There was some validity to these rationales, but they did not tell the complete story.

Priscilla and Marco, alone and with friends, referred to each other as "husband" and "wife." Marco described his relationship with Priscilla as his "first marriage." Marco said, facilely, that marriage was unimportant to him, that it was a technicality simply for "the state," but friends such as Jerry and Brett belied that, acknowledging that Marco wanted to marry Priscilla.

What really held Priscilla back, most who knew her agreed, was, simply, the Presley name, for it was magic, and it was money, and Priscilla feared she could never duplicate either one on her own. Until she did, in Mike Edwards's opinion, she could never truly be set free, as she claimed so long to desire. "*Marry* the guy!" Mike urged. "Come on. Give the fucking name *up*! You've got Marco's child. Take on his name."

It was ironic, finally, that Priscilla should be at this point of her life with the same identity complex with which she had begun it, mired in confusion over her last name. In a way, Priscilla's true identity, her real name, had been taken from her by her mother and stepfather when she was three. Priscilla Ann Wagner had disappeared, replaced by a fiction that was Priscilla Beaulieu.

Acknowledgments

This book could not have been written with the same depth or breadth without the invaluable assistance of many. I am deeply grateful to everyone with whom I came in contact while researching this biography, nearly all of whom demonstrated a remarkable generosity of spirit.

Among those who graciously gave of their time, energy, or insight: Paul Abascal, Ginger Alden, Jo Alden, Rosemary Alden, Carol Ann Heine Allen, Melinda Allen, Martha Anderson, Nancy Anderson, Evangeline Segura Anguiano, Cindy Esposito Bahr, Mary Ann Williamson Barks, Rona Barrett, George Barris, Shirley Barris, Antje Bartsch, Pamela Basker, Dixie Jayne Beck, Helen Deshevy Beebe, Judy Comstock Bell, George Bennett, Phil Berdoll, Lillian Bicknell, Steve Binder, Olivia Bis, Ruth Blake, Nina Blanchard, Elsie Boaz, Denny Bond, Lorene Fielding Booker, Carol Boutilier, Joyce Bova, Barbara Klein Bower, Jane Breighner-Blackman, Rick Bresnan, Anita Wood Brewer, Hazel Brock, James D. Browe, Paul Büngener, Chuck Burns, Sheila Ryan Caan, Sue Cameron, Mauro Caputo, Stuart Cardy, Gerta Gleaves Carter, Marion Cocke, Bob Colacello, Joe Condrill, Al Coombes, Albert H. Corey, Yvonne Craig, Rosemarie Barrasso Cross, Richard Davis, Spencer Davis, Irena Deaderick, Helen Delahunt, Joe Delahunt, Donna Pollen DeSando, Diane Dinsmore, Sylvia Dinsmore, Mike Dodd, Maureen Donaldson, Peggy Dotson, Ann K. Dunham, Michael Edwards, Jack Edwinson, Jo Haynes Eldred, Joyce Eliason, Robert Ellis, Debbie Esposito, Joe Esposito, LaNelle Fadal, Harry Fain, Lamar Fike, Lynn Baskett Fort, Steve Fox, Patricia Crowley Friendly, Pam Rutherford Gaines, Joan Gansky, Paul Gansky, Marco Garibaldi, Bill Geddie, Larry Geller, Ann George, Ray Geunther, Cliff Gleaves, Albert Goldman estate, Samira Goldman, Dana Rosenfeld Gordon, Carol Grant, Currie Grant, Dave Grant, Karon Grant, Michael Gray, Arthur Gridé, Elizabeth Sauersopf Haderer, Theresa Giannini Harrison, Jack Harwood, Patricia Heins, Donna Hennen, Jere Herzenberg, Richard Hirata, Holly Hire, Ysobel Hirsch, Charlie Hodge, Mike Hodnett, Kay Hoffman, Christine Laws Holcombe, Karen Hollander, Mary Ann Holstrom, Ed Hookstratten, Geraldine Hopper, Gary Hovey, Elisabeth Howard, Albert Iversen, Margaret Iversen, Wendy Iversen, Millie Iwomoto, Mary Jenkins, Darrell Johnson, Robbie Jones, Suzy Kalter, Steve Kanaly, "Karate" Pat, Joan Esposito Kardashian, Kimberley Kates, Taylor Keen, William Keen, Janet Strebel Kelly, Tom Kelly, Mike Kimball, George Klein, Debbie Ross Klinger, Gerald Knoepfel, David Krieff, Margie Prater Kugler, Debra Paget Kung, Geraldine Kyle, Alan Landsburg, Harry Langdon, Patricia La Pointe, Barbara Sobelman Larkin, Peggy Lebel, Wendy Lebel, Joey Ledford, Mylon LeFevre, Barbara Leigh, Harry Levitch, Gary Lewis, Leonard Lewis, Jamie Lindberg, John Linkletter, Eric Linterman, Gloria Linterman, Beatrice Locarno, John Love, Robert Lovenheim, Diana Magrann, Phylliss Mann, Elisabeth Mansfield, Rex Mansfield, Sister Mary Adrien, Sister Mary Gabriella, Patrick Mayo, Eddie McCann, Jo Lynn McCleary, Mike McGregor, Sandra Purkey McWilliams, Linda Williams Merrill, Mindy Miller, Sandi Miller, Jackie Graves Momberg, Kathy Monderine, Ricardo Montalban, Joe Moscheo, Stephie McCann Muhlhausen, Tom Muldoon, Ann Dickey Murrah, Leslie Murray, Willie Jane Nichols, Leslie Nielsen, Joann Nilsen, Mavis Nilsen, Virginia Overholt, Ed Parker, Sue Patterson, Katherine Patton, Steve Peck, Larry Peerce, Patty Perry, Doris

Pieracinni, Larry Powell, Shirley Dieu Powell, Dee Presley, Joan Quinn, Beryl C. Quinton, Margaret Ramis, Fay Heim Rankin, Ron Redd, John Reddington, Suni Ernst Reskin, Carolyn Garcia Reynolds, Cecile Rhee, Khang Rhee, Frances Rhodes, Dr. Dale Rhoney, Kay Rhoney, Katie Neece Ricks, Sherry Riggins, Lance Robbins, Scott Rollins, Nancy Rooks, Elizabeth Sabine, Dee Dee Saunders, Mike Saunders, Jerry Schilling, Lilo Schlesinger, Bernard Seibel, Melanie Sherwood, Sandy Silverberg, Nancy Sinatra, Mike Sinclair, Donna Wells Sklute, Hank Smith, Lois Smith, Myrna Smith, Paula Smith, Vernon Smith, Mark Snider, Tom Snyder, Jack Soden, Reed Sparling, Charlotte Spurlock, Billy Stanley, Rick Stanley, Jess Stearn, Diane Edenbo Stevens, Steven Stogel, Fran Stone, Mike Stone, Renate Strauss, Brett Livingstone Strong, Virginia Norwood Strong, Doug Sweetland, Ronald Aaron Tapp, Starr Tapp, Paul G. Taylor, Bob Thomas, Linda Thompson, Sam Thompson, Joseph Tobin, Arthur Toll, Roger Toll, Dora Keen Townsend, Donald Trull, Dr. P. A. Turman, Vandy Vandever, Mrs. Billie Vaughan, Celia Low Vendrell, Mike Vendrell, Baroness Vera Von Cronthall, Güdrun Von Heister, Michele Von Wechmar, Victor Von Wechmar, Gene Wagner, Kathryn Wagner, Bob Wall, Barbara Walters, Phyllis Wapner, Sonny Washington, Dorothy Fellows Weems, Red West, Kathy Westmoreland, Mrs. Sherman B. Wetmore, Sandy Brunke Whalen, Deborah Whalley, Calvert White, Dr. Peter Whitmar, Jackie Wiegand, Sue Wiegert, Barney Williams, Janie Williams, Ronnie Garland Williams, Edward Woodward, Michelle Woodward, Becky Yancey, and David Zucker. My gratitude, as well, to the reference librarians at the Academy of Motion Picture Arts and Sciences, the Museum of Radio and Television in Beverly Hills, and the Beverly Hills, Memphis, New London, and Titusville libraries, as well as to the staffs at the Memphis probate court, the Los Angeles County archives, the National Personnel and Records Center, and the office of Congressman Richard Gephardt. My sincere thanks, also, to the superbly organized Wiesbaden Alumni Association, especially Margie Kugler.

Several people deserve special mention. Joel Gotler and Alan Nevins. My editor, Shaye Areheart, for her continuing enthusiasm and support. And the Harmony/Crown team, with special thanks to Dina Siciliano. Diana Dahlen, who appeared as if an angel to tirelessly search for names, people, and places, and to provide aid in countless other ways. My underpaid and overqualified transcriber/researchers: Marlene Noble, Cheryl Chan, and the heroic Melissa Blazek. Currie Grant, who generously gave of his research materials, asking nothing in return. Dixie Jayne Beck, who surpassed friendship to become an aide-de-camp. My parents, Lesley and Bruce, for their time and insight. Kimberley Kates, Wendy Lebel, and Karen Hollander, for a window into Priscilla and Scientology. Rick Stanley, Joe Esposito, Jerry Schilling, Michael Edwards, Jere Herzenberg, and Patty Perry, for help or insight beyond the ordinary.

My wish for Priscilla Presley is that she may, one day, free herself from the past—her true past and the imaginary past she created to perpetuate a myth that no longer needs to exist.

Sources

The following are some of the research sources I consulted or reviewed in the prep-aration of this biography. In the relatively infrequent instances where I have quoted directly from a secondary source, such as another book or magazine, the source is generally cited in the text. Otherwise, all quotes contained in the book come from personal interviews with the named subject.

References, Psychological Background

Abadie, M. J. *Child Signs.* Stamford, Conn.: Longmeadow Press, 1994.

Bachrach, Judy, "When a Man Molds a Woman," *Allure,* January 1996.

Bradshaw, Dr. John. *Family Secrets: What You Don't Know Can Hurt You.* Audio from the PBS television series. Houston: Bradshaw cassettes, 1995.

Dobb, Edwin, "The Brutality of Beauty," *Vogue,* February 1995.

Farley, Walter. *The Black Stallion.* New York: Random House, 1941.

Forward, Dr. Susan (with Craig Buck). *Toxic Parents: Overcoming Their Hurtful Legacy and Reclaiming Your Life.* New York: Bantam, 1989.

Gandee, Charles, "Beauty's Legacy," *Vogue,* February 1995.

McNamara, Mary, "Looking Truth in the Face," *Los Angeles Times Book Review,* May 26, 1996.

Wertsch, Mary Edwards. *Military Brats: Legacies of Childhood Inside the Fortress.* New York: Harmony, 1991.

Official Documents

Applications of Marco Antonio Garcia and Joan Mavis Garcia (petition for name change). Los Angeles County. Case #346816. 1980.

Bangor, Maine, School Department. Priscilla Ann Wagner's school records, 1945.

Elvis Aaron Presley v. Priscilla Ann Presley (divorce). Los Angeles County. Case #WED20795. 1973.

Estate of Elvis Aaron Presley. Shelby County, Tenn. Case #A-655. 1977.

Francine Carroll v. Ronald M. Carroll (divorce). Orange County, Calif. Case #D-215353. 1983.

Francine M. Stone v. Michael M. Stone (divorce). Orange County, California. Case #D-57002. 1972.

In re Lisa Marie Presley, a minor. Los Angeles County. Case #637551. 1978.

Irwin Fuchs v. Marco Garibaldi and Priscilla Presley. Los Angeles County. Case #106429. 1986.

Joann Nilsen Garibalddi v. Marco Antonio Garibalddi (annulment). Los Angeles County. Case #WED 41101. 1982.

National Archives at College Park, Md. Official deck logs, USS *Beaver,* 1946.

National Personnel Records Center, St. Louis, Mo. Military records, Joseph Paul Beaulieu Jr. and James Frederick Wagner.

Office Memorandum, Director of FBI. Official report on Laurenz Johannes Griessel-Landau. 1959–60.

Priscilla Presley v. Bob Anderson. Los Angeles County. Case #43922. 1983.

Priscilla Presley v. Brazan Randi Brooks. Los Angeles County. Case #121187. 1988.

Priscilla Presley v. Joe Esposito. Los Angeles County. Case #126761. 1988.

Priscilla Presley v. John Doland, Charlotte Doland, and Lalo Gijon. Los Angeles County. Case #C304226. 1979.

Priscilla Presley v. John O'Grady. Los Angeles County. Case #320259. 1980.

Saint Paul's United Church of Christ. Baptismal record, Priscilla Ann Wagner, August 19, 1945.

PERIODICALS

Andrews, Suzanna, "Making Elvis Pay," *Working Woman,* September 1993.

"Ann Iversen Becomes Bride at Pensacola," *New London (Conn.) Evening Day,* August 18, 1944.

"Ann L. Wagner, J. P. Beaulieu Jr., Exchange Vows," *New London (Conn.) Evening Day,* September 16, 1948.

Armstrong, Lois, "A Mom Again," *People,* February 15, 1988.

Armstrong, Lois, "A Mother's Plea: 'When Will It All End?'," *People,* September 9, 1986.

Armstrong, Lois, "Priscilla Presley Finds a Vocation," *People,* November 8, 1982.

Armstrong, Lois, and Robin Michel, "The Presleys' Newest Star," *People,* June 19, 1989.

Arthur, Allene, "Elvis in Palm Springs," *Palm Springs Life,* August 1995.

Ashley, Barbara, "I'm Afraid of Losing Him!," *Movie Mirror,* June 1970.

"Auf Wiedersehen, Elvis!," *Film Journal,* Germany, March 1960.

Baker, Jackson, "The Keeper of the Kingdom," *Memphis,* August 1992.

Bangay, Joe, "Priscilla Presley: How Elvis Made Me Prisoner of Love," *Star,* September 7, 1982.

Battelle, Phyllis, "Priscilla Presley: Her Struggle to Raise Elvis' Daughter," *Ladies' Home Journal,* January 1984.

"Beauty Secrets," *Harper's Bazaar,* September 1986.

Beck, Marilyn, *Los Angeles Daily News,* May 14, 1987.

Behar, Richard, "The Thriving Cult of Greed and Power," *Time,* May 6, 1991.

Benet, Lorenzo, "Harmon, Presley: The Kinship of Collaboration," *Los Angeles Daily News,* November 3, 1985.

Blake, Carolyn, "The Girl Elvis Has Loved for Seven Years!," *TV & Movie Screen,* November 1966.

Boston Herald, March 15, 1985; December 24, 1986.

Brinton, Larry, *The Associated Press,* August 17, 1977.

Brisbane, Arthur S., "KC Man's Keeper of Elvis' Keys," *Kansas City Times,* April 21, 1982.

Buck, Jerry, "Susan Walters Stars as Priscilla Presley in 'Elvis and Me,'" *The Associated Press,* February 4, 1988.

Byron, Ellen, "Priscilla Presley Just Gets More Gorgeous," *Redbook,* January 1987.

Calistro, Paddy, "Priscilla and the Jungle," *Los Angeles Times,* February 20, 1981.

Calistro, Paddy, "The Ten Most Beautiful Women in Los Angeles," *Los Angeles,* January 1986.

Caulfield, Deborah, *Los Angeles Times,* May 27, 1988.

"Celebrity Interview of the Month: Priscilla Presley," *Celebrity,* Minor Issue 253.

Chicago Tribune, February 8, 1988.

Daily Mail, May 14, 1994.

Daily Variety (London), January 8, 1981; January 21, 1981; October 25, 1984; September 8, 1992.

Dan, Judith, "A Hot Time in the Old Gown Tonight," *Los Angeles,* December 1980.

Dangaard, Colin, "Priscilla Looks Back on Life with Elvis," *Memphis Commercial Appeal Mid-South Magazine,* November 24, 1974.

Darrach, Brad, Lois Armstrong, Eleanor Hoover, Karen G. Jackovich, and Jacqueline Savaiano, "Wedding Belle," *People,* October 24, 1988.

Davidson, Bill, "It Was Michael Landon Against the Director," *TV Guide,* March 19, 1983.

Davidson, Bill, "Priscilla Presley: Her Life Since Elvis," *McCall's,* March 1987.

Davidson, Bill, "The Second Time Around," *McCall's,* April 1988.

Dawson, William, "Lawyer Backs Court Action on Elvis Pact," *Memphis Commercial Appeal,* October 5, 1980.

Deeb, Gary, "ABC Is Planning to Launch 'Elvis' Series," *North America Syndicate,* February 26, 1989.

DeVries, Hilary, "The New Priscilla Presley," *McCall's,* January 1992.

Diamond, Sara, "Unhappy Together, Unable to Stay Apart," *Movie Mirror,* June 1971.

Dunn, Ed, "Wella Corp. Hires Priscilla Presley," *Memphis Press-Scimitar,* August 30, 1979.

Easton, Nina J., "Naked Truth Behind 'Naked Gun,' " *Los Angeles Times,* December 2, 1988.

Eldorado, Dea, "Fall's Big Picture," *Los Angeles,* September 1984.

"Elvis Off for Home and His Date—with Relatives Here—Is Left Behind," *New London (Conn.) Evening Day,* March 2, 1960.

"Elvis Presley's Black Cook Tells," *Jet,* October 20, 1986.

"Elvis: The Last Days," *Us,* August 24, 1987.

Evans, Bill, " 'She's Too Much,' Says Elvis," *Memphis Press-Scimitar,* February 5, 1968.

Fair, Elizabeth, "Ms. Presley Launches New Career," *Memphis Commercial Appeal,* September 10, 1979.

"Farewell to Priscilla—Hello to U.S.A.," *Life,* March 14, 1960.

Fidler, Jimmie, "Priscilla Lane Wed Secretly and Divorced," *Los Angeles Times,* May 29, 1940.

Field, Michelle, "State of Grace," *Chicago Tribune,* August 4, 1991.

"The Fifty Most Beautiful People in the World 1992," *People,* May 4, 1992.

Fink, Mitchell, "The Insider: Mrs. Jackson's Scar," *People,* September 12, 1994.

Finke, Nikki, "Naked Truth Behind 'Naked Gun': Priscilla Presley Shows Off Her Laugh Lines," *Los Angeles Times,* December 2, 1988.

Firstman, Richard C., "Elvis Frenzy: Baby Pix Signal Open Checkbook Time in Tab Valley," *Newsday,* October 15, 1989.

Fit, swimsuit pictorial: Priscilla Presley, June 1982.

Flander, Judy, "Mum's the Word on Elvis," *Washington Herald-Examiner,* October 11, 1980.

Fleming, Charles, "The Predator," *Vanity Fair,* February 1996.

Gannett News Service, taken from *USA Today,* November 6, 1990.

Glasgow Herald, October 13, 1994.

Globe. 1967–97. [Numerous articles]

Gordon, Meryl, "Priscilla Presley Today," *McCall's,* October 1994.

Grant, Currie, "Elvis Secretly Engaged to 18-Year-Old," *Photoplay,* January 1964.

Grant, James, "Elvis' Baby: All Grown Up," *Life,* December 1988.

Grant, James, "Priscilla Presley: Never Better than Now," *McCall's,* July 1989.

Green, Tom, "Elvis Rocks Tonight on Prime Time," *USA Today,* February 6, 1990.

Green, Tom, "Priscilla Presley," *Los Angeles,* June 1990.

Guttman, Monika, "Presley Meets the Pressure," *USA Weekend,* March 27, 1994.

Hall, Jane, "The Gloves Are Off," *Los Angeles Times,* June 11, 1995.

Hannah, Marilyn, "Elvis: Victim of a Strange Triangle," *TV Picture Life,* March 1964.

Harmetz, Aljean, " 'Elvis' Defies Convention," *New York Times,* May 18, 1989.

Harper's Bazaar, May 1984.

Hart, Bob, "Elvis' Teen-Age Sweetheart," *Movie Mirror,* August 1963.

Hassell, Greg, "Rough Going at the Velvet Elvis," *Houston Chronicle,* May 29, 1996.

Henry, Don, "Hectic Week Topped by Gals' Pajama Party, Gabfest at Boys' Dorm," *The Overseas Family,* Frankfurt, Germany, April 1, 1960.

Hilburn, Robert, "Eternal Revenue," *Los Angeles Times,* June 11, 1989.

Hockaday, Laura Rollins, "He Opened Graceland Mansion's Gates," *Kansas City Star,* September 7, 1982.

Holland, Jan, "Priscilla Presley," *Venice,* March 1994.

Hopkirk, Peter, "Army Stops Presley Goodbye Kiss—Priscilla Is Hustled Away from Plane," *London Daily Express,* March 3, 1960.

Hopper, Hedda, "New Comedy in Works," *Memphis Press-Scimitar,* August 8, 1963.

Horowitz, Craig, "The Presley Inheritance," *People,* March 1, 1993.

Iley, Chrissy, "Why Men Go to Priscilla's Head," *You,* August 22, 1993.

"Is Elvis' Priscilla Area Woman's Kin?," *Titusville (Penn.) Herald,* March 16, 1960.

Italie, Hillel, "Is She Really That Clumsy?," *The Associated Press,* December 19, 1988.

Jacobs, Jody, "A Bacchanal for Johann Sebastian," *Los Angeles Times,* February 17, 1983.

Jerome, Jim, "My Daughter, Myself," *Ladies' Home Journal,* August 1996.

"Jimmy Wagner, Navy Pilot, Dies in Plane Crash," *Titusville (Penn.) Herald,* November 5, 1945.

Johnson, Paul, "In Death, Elvis Is Bigger than Life," *Gannett News Service,* December 7, 1989.

Johnson, Robert E., "Michael Jackson and Lisa Marie Presley," *Jet,* August 22, 1994.

Jones, Jack, "Elvis Presley Ends Marriage with a Kiss and $1.5 Million," *Los Angeles Times,* October 10, 1973.

Kaye, Elizabeth, "Life After Elvis," *TV Guide,* September 20, 1980.

Kelly, Katy, "Lisa Marie's Kingdom," *USA Today,* February 4, 1993.

Kennedy, Caroline, "Graceland," *Rolling Stone,* September 22, 1977.

Kershaw, Alex, "The King's Ransom," *The Independent,* November 17, 1991.

Kessler, Judy, cover profile of Priscilla Presley, *People,* December 14, 1978.

"Ladies Who Launch," *Harper's Bazaar,* May 1990.

Langley, Leonora, "Priscilla Presley: How to Live with a Legend," *Woman's Day*, November 27, 1990.

Ledford, Joey, *United Press International*, December 10, 1980.

Lee, Luaine, "Priscilla Presley Tells How She Outgrew Shadow of 'The King,' " *Scripps Howard News Service*, March 21, 1994.

Leiby, Richard, "Harmonic Conversion? Ex-Scientologists Speculate on Why Michael and Lisa Wed," *The Washington Post*, August 4, 1994.

Lippert, Barbara, "Priscilla Sells an Elvis Souvenir Disguised as Perfume," *Adweek*, July 2, 1990.

"Lisa Marie Presley," *Us*, February 13, 1984.

Littwin, Susan, "Will This Actor Capture the Dark Side of Elvis Too?," *TV Guide*, January 30, 1988.

"Love in the Afternoon," *Cosmopolitan*, August 1980.

Lurie, Rod, "Now They're Playing Dirty," *Los Angeles*, February 1992.

Lurie, Rod, "Priscilla Presley and Leslie Nielsen," *Los Angeles*, July 1991.

Mann, May, "Priscilla Presley Talks About Her Life," *Movieland*.

Marlowe, Lisa. "The Wedding Was a Farce," *Daily Mirror (London)*, August 25, 1994.

McAllister, Bill, "Unglued Over Elvis," *Washington Post*, January 8, 1993.

McDonald, Peter, "I'm So Sorry My Lisa Wed Jackson," *Evening Standard (London)*, September 21, 1994.

Meisler, Andy, "The 10 Most Beautiful Women on Television," *TV Guide*, December 15, 1984.

"Milestones," *Time*, May 9, 1994.

Millar, John, "Granny Presley," *Scottish Daily Record (Glasgow)*, May 17, 1994.

Montefiore, Simon Sebag. "A Cloistered Life," *Psychology Today*, November/December 1993.

"Morgan Maxfield Dies in Plane Crash," *The Kansas City Times*, September 5, 1981.

"Mrs. Presley's Boutique," *Parade*, July 7, 1974.

Murphy, Mary, "Cybill Shepherd: A Passion for Pillow Talk," *TV Guide*, April 20, 1996.

Murphy, Ryan, "Cybill Shepherd: The *US* Interview," *Us*, June 1995.

National Enquirer. 1967–97. [Numerous articles.]

"Navy Flier En Route Here to Visit Wife, Child Killed in Crash," *New London (Conn.) Evening Day*, November 5, 1945.

Newcomb, Peter, "The New Aristocracy," *Forbes*, October 3, 1988.

Newsday, April 16, 1991.

New York Daily News, March 25–26, 1984; "Is She the Devil in Disguise?," November 19, 1986.

New York Post, October 22, 1980; October 5, 1985.

New York Times, February 10, 1991.

O'Hallaren, Bill, "The Ticklish Plight of Being Priscilla Presley," *TV Guide*, March 17, 1984.

Orth, Maureen, "The Jackson Jive," *Vanity Fair*, September 1995.

O'Sullivan, Kevin, "Wedded Blitz," *Scottish Daily Record (Glasgow)*, December 4, 1994.

Pacha, Terry, "Elvis, Priscilla and Del Valle," *The Red Wing,* Del Valle High School, March 1978.

Pawlosky, Mark, "Morgan Maxfield's Estate Sued," *The Kansas City Times,* February 4, 1982.

"People," *USA Today,* September 16, 1983.

Petrucelli, Alan W., "Priscilla Presley: I Have to Shatter the Myths," *For Women First,* April 18, 1994.

Presley, Priscilla, "Bringing Up Elvis' Daughter," *Ladies' Home Journal,* June 1974.

Presley, Priscilla, "He Saved Me for So Long," *People,* September 16, 1985.

Presley, Priscilla, "We Have Plenty of Time, Little One," *People,* September 9, 1985.

Presley, Priscilla, "What My Life Is Like Without Elvis," *Modern People,* 1979.

Presley, Priscilla Beaulieu, "Elvis and Me," *Ladies' Home Journal,* October 1985.

Presley, Priscilla Beaulieu, "I Don't Think He Really Wanted to Live Beyond 40," *TV Guide,* January 30, 1988.

Presley, Vernon (as told to Nancy Anderson), "Elvis: By His Father," *Good Housekeeping,* January 1978.

"Presley's Wife Dates Karate Champ," *The National Tattler,* September 3, 1972.

"Presley's Wife Visits Relative in Titusville," *The Titusville (Penn.) Herald,* January 17, 1981.

"Priscilla Arrives in Her Bright, New Red Auto," *Memphis Press-Scimitar,* April 2, 1963.

"Priscilla Presley Presents . . .," *Memphis Commercial Appeal Mid-South Magazine,* May 27, 1973.

"Priscilla Presley Visits Titusville Grandmother," *Franklin (Penn.) News Herald,* January 17, 1981.

Pugh, Clifford, "Elvis U.," *Houston Chronicle,* August 9, 1995.

Pugh, Clifford, "Eternally Elvis," Houston Chronicle, *Texas Magazine,* September 17, 1995.

Rader, Dotson, "There Had to Be Something More Out There," *Parade,* February 9, 1997.

Radovsky, Vicki Jo, "A Nice Visit to 'Place,' " *Entertainment Weekly,* May 1, 1996.

Rayl, Salley, "Did Colonel Parker Take the King for a Ride?," *People,* December 1, 1980.

The Red Wing, Del Valle Junior-Senior High School, February 1959.

Reed, J. D., "The Mansion Music Made," *Time,* December 19, 1988.

Richardson, John H., "Catch a Rising Star: Scientology," *Premiere,* September 1993.

Rickerd, Stacy, *London Sunday Mirror.* November 1, 1990.

Rosenberg, Howard, " 'Interview of the Century'? Now That's a 'Scream,' " *Los Angeles Times,* June 16, 1995.

Ross, Shelley, "From Elvis to 'Dallas,' " *McCall's,* February 1984.

Royal, Susan, "An Interview with Priscilla Presley," *American Premiere,* June/July 1990.

Santow, Dan, and Peter Mikelbank, "Hungarian Rhapsody," *People,* August 22, 1994.

Sappell, Joel, and Robert W. Welkos, "The Scientology Story: A Special Report," *Los Angeles Times,* June 1990.

Schaefer, Stephen, "Sequel Star Reveals the 'Naked' Truth," *Boston Herald,* March 14, 1994.

Schiffler, C. J., "Vegan–'I Didn't Steal Elvis Presley's Wife,' " *The Valley Times (Las Vegas, Nev.),* 1977.

Schlinkman, Mark, "Entrepreneur Inspired Admiration, Dislike," *Kansas City Times*, September 5, 1981.

Scott, Vernon, "Elvis' Daughter Denies Rift with Mom," *United Press International*, August 11, 1986.

Scott, Vernon, "A Frank Talk with Priscilla Presley," *Good Housekeeping*, November 1994.

Scott, Vernon, "Presley Name Doesn't Get Jobs," *United Press International*, December 1, 1988.

Scott, Vernon, *United Press International*, June 12, 1991.

Sessums, Kevin, "Viva Priscilla!," *Vanity Fair*, July 1991.

Sharp, Amanda, "Presley Home Televised," *United Press International*, January 3, 1985.

Shevey, Sandra, "My Life With and Without Elvis Presley," *Ladies' Home Journal*, August 1973.

Shevey, Sandra, "Priscilla Reflects on Life with Elvis," *Memphis Commercial Appeal*, February 12, 1978.

Silver, Susan M., cover profile, *Us*, Priscilla Presley, December 12, 1988.

Smith, Ron, "Princess Presley: Elvis' Little Girl Grows Up," *Ladies' Home Journal*, February 1989.

Sobran, M. J. Jr., "Heirs of Elvis," *National Review*, October 14, 1977.

Sokol, Marlene, Kitty Bennett, and Wendy Lemus, "Elvis' Second Grandchild Makes His Local Debut," *Times Publishing Company*, October 24, 1992.

Star. [Complete Presley collection, reviewed at the *Star* offices in Tarrytown, New York.]

Stern, J. David, "The King Is Back." *TV Guide*, February 17, 1990.

Stone, Mike, as told to Al Coombes, "My Secret Love Affair with Priscilla Presley—By the Man Who Stole Her from Elvis," *Star* three-part series, June 1980.

Sunday Telegraph, November 13, 1986.

Tannenbaum, Rob, "The Meaning of Elvis," *GQ*, January 1995.

Terry, Polly, "We Say Elvis Is Married!," *Photoplay*, February 1964.

Thomas, Bob, "TV Talk: Priscilla Presley in Debut on 'Dallas,' " *Associated Press*, November 11, 1983.

Thomas, Cynthia, "The Long Arm of Elvis," *Houston Chronicle*, September 15, 1995.

Tompkins, Stephen G., "Heir Says She Won't Put Graceland on the Market," *Memphis Commercial Appeal*, February 7 1988.

Trenwick, Van, "Elvis' Wife Dates Karate Champ," *The National Insider*, August 20, 1972.

Wallace, Amy, "Scholarly Study of Elvis," *Los Angeles Times*, September 2, 1995.

Wallace, Carol, "Elvis," *People*, January 14, 1985.

Warhol, Andy, "Priscilla Presley," *Interview*.

Weller, Sheila, "Priscilla Presley: Surviving Elvis," *McCall's*, May 1979.

Werner, Laurie, "Elvis Has Left the Résumé," *Los Angeles Times*, March 24, 1994.

Wilson, Earl, "Lover Boy," *Photoplay*, 1958.

Woods, Chuck, "Priscilla Charges Elvis Tricked Her," *TV Picture Life*, September 1973.

Woods, Vicki, "Daddy's Girl," *Vogue*, April 1996.

"Young Officer Laid To Rest In Woodlawn," *Titusville (Penn.) Herald,* November 10, 1945.

Zekas, Rita, "Priscilla Presley: Naked Truth III," *Toronto Star,* March 16, 1994.

TELEVISION BROADCASTS

American Journal, May 2, 1995.

Astrology with Signe Quinn Taff, Century Cable, Los Angeles, August 4, 1996.

Barbara Walters Special #33, "Priscilla Presley," ABC-TV, September 13, 1985.

CBS 48 Hours, "Crazy About Elvis: No Place Like Home," CBS-TV, August 12, 1992.

CBS This Morning, Priscilla Presley interviews, CBS-TV, July 2, 1991; April 24, 1992; June 4, 1992; March 1, 1996.

A Current Affair, December 13, 1995.

Dateline NBC, "The King and Us," NBC-TV, May 23, 1995.

Donahue, interview with cast of "Naked Gun," March 4, 1994.

Elvis and Me, ABC-TV, February, 1988.

Elvis: The Movie, Dick Clark Productions, ABC-TV.

Entertainment Tonight, May 23, 1995; March 1, 1996.

Extra, May 2, 1995.

First Person with Maria Shriver, Priscilla Presley interview, NBC-TV, June 29, 1991.

Geraldo Rivera Show, Nancy Sinatra interview, April 17, 1995.

Good Morning America, Priscilla Presley interview, ABC-TV, June 27, 1991.

Hard Copy, "I, Elvis," © Paramount Pictures, Inc.

Hard Copy, November 6, 1996.

Larry King Live, interview with Earl Greenwood, CNN-TV, August 12, 1991.

Live with Regis & Kathie Lee, Priscilla Presley interview, September 19, 1996.

Melrose Place, guest star Priscilla Presley, Fox-TV, Spring 1996.

The Oprah Winfrey Show, "Priscilla Presley," November 28, 1988.

Primetime Live, Michael Jackson and Lisa Marie Presley interview, ABC-TV, June 14, 1995.

Primetime Live, "The King's Ransom," ABC-TV, March 3, 1994.

Showbiz Today, CNN-TV, August 3, 1994.

Tales from the Crypt, guest star Priscilla Presley, HBO, January 1995.

Today Show, Priscilla Presley interview, NBC-TV, March 25, 1994; October 7, 1994.

Touched by an Angel, guest star Priscilla Presley, CBS-TV, March 9, 1997.

DOCUMENTARIES

Biography, "Elvis Presley," Arts and Entertainment.

A Current Affair, April 27, 1992.

"Elvis," NBC-TV, December 3, 1968.

Elvis: His Life and Times.

Elvis Memories, ABC Contemporary Radio, August 13, 1978.

Elvis on Tour, 1972.

Elvis Presley's Graceland, Showtime, January 1985.

Elvis Presley: That's the Way It Is, 1970.

Elvis: The Great Performances, CBS-TV, April 2, 1992.

Gore Vidal's Gore Vidal, Arts and Entertainment, October 1995.

This Is Elvis!, 1981.

FILMS

The complete Academy of Motion Picture Arts and Sciences research materials on *The Adventures of Ford Fairlane, Blue Hawaii, A Change of Habit, Charro, Clambake, Comeback, Double Trouble, Easy Come, Easy Go, Flaming Star, Follow That Dream, Frankie and Johnny, Fun in Acapulco, G.I. Blues, Girl Happy, Girls! Girls! Girls!, Harum Scarum, It Happened at the World's Fair, Kid Galahad, King Creole, Kissin' Cousins, Live a Little, Love a Little, Love Me Tender,* the *Naked Gun* series, *No Way Out, Paradise Hawaiian Style, Speedway, Spinout, Stay Away Joe, Tickle Me, The Trouble with Girls, A View to a Kill, Viva Las Vegas,* and *Wild in the Country,* as well as biographical files on Priscilla Lane, Mario Lanza, Debra Paget, Elvis Presley, Priscilla Presley, Ann Sheridan, and Nancy Sinatra.

PLAYS

Shakespeare, William. *As You Like It.* Jacques's Speech, Act 2, Scene 7.

SONGS

Blackwell, Otis, and Winfield Scott, *Return to Sender,* 1962.
Turk, Roy, and Lou Handman, *Are You Lonesome Tonight?,* 1926.

BOOKS

Adler, David, and Ernest Andrew. *Elvis My Dad.* New York: St. Martin's Press, 1990.
Ann-Margret. *Ann-Margret.* New York: G. P. Putnam's Sons, 1994.
Bartel, Pauline. *Reel Elvis!* Dallas: Taylor Publishing Company, 1994.
Bova, Joyce (with William Conrad Nowels). *My Love Affair with Elvis.* New York: Kensington Books, 1994.
Burk, Bill E. *Elvis: A 30-Year Chronicle.* Tempe, Ariz.: Osborne Enterprises, 1985.
Buskin, Richard. *Elvis: Memories and Memorabilia.* London: Salamander Books, 1995.
Church of Scientology staff. *What Is Scientology?* Los Angeles: Bridge Publications, Inc., 1993.
Clayton, Rose, and Dick Heard, eds. *Elvis Up Close: In the Words of Those Who Knew Him Best.* Atlanta: Turner Publishing, Inc., 1992.
Cocke, Marion J. *I Called Him Babe: Elvis Presley's Nurse Remembers.* Memphis, Tenn.: Memphis State University Press, 1979.
Colacello, Robert. *The Warhol Diaries.* New York: Warner Books, 1991.
Curtin, Jim. *Unseen Elvis.* Boston: Little, Brown, 1992.
DeBarbin, Lucy, and Dary Matera. *Are You Lonesome Tonight?* New York: Villard, 1987.
Donaldson, Maureen, *An Affair to Remember.* New York: G. P. Putnam's Sons, 1989.
Dundy, Elaine. *Elvis and Gladys: The First Revealing Look at How the King's Mother Shaped His Life.* New York: Macmillan, 1985.
Edwards, Michael. *Priscilla, Elvis and Me: In the Shadow of the King.* New York: St. Martin's Press, 1989.
Esposito, Joe, and Elena Oumano. *Good Rockin' Tonight: Twenty Years on the Road and on the Town with Elvis.* New York: Simon and Schuster, 1994.

Fortas, Alan. *Elvis: From Memphis to Hollywood, Memories from My Twelve Years with Elvis Presley.* Ann Arbor, Mich.: Popular Culture, Inc., 1992.

Geller, Larry, and Joel Spector, with Patricia Romanowski. *If I Can Dream.* New York: Avon Books, 1990.

Gibson, Robert (with Sid Shaw). *Elvis: A King Forever.* New York: McGraw Hill, 1987.

Giuliano, Geoffrey. *The Illustrated Elvis Presley.* Edison, N.J.: Chartwell Books, 1994.

Goldman, Albert. *Elvis.* New York: McGraw-Hill, 1981.

Goldman, Albert. *Elvis: The Last 24 Hours.* New York: St. Martin's Press, 1991.

Gray, Michael, and Roger Osborne. *The Elvis Atlas—A Journey Through Elvis Presley's America.* New York: Henry Holt, 1996.

Greenwood, Earl, and Kathleen Tracy. *The Boy Who Would Be King: An Intimate Portrait of Elvis Presley by His Cousin.* New York: Penguin Books, 1990.

Gregory, Neal and Janice. *When Elvis Died.* New York: Communications Press, Inc., 1980.

Guralnick, Peter. *Last Train to Memphis: The Rise of Elvis Presley.* Boston: Back Bay Books, Little, Brown and Company, 1994.

Hammontree, Patsy Guy. *Elvis Presley: A Bio-Bibliography.* Westport, Conn.: Greenwood Press, 1985.

Hanna, David. *Elvis: Lonely Star at the Top.* New York: Nordon Publications, Inc., 1977.

Hodge, Charlie (with Charles Goodman). *Me 'n Elvis.* Memphis, Tenn.: Castle Books, 1988.

Hopkins, Jerry. *Elvis.* New York: Simon and Schuster, 1971.

Iglesias, Julio. *Entre el Cielo y el Infierno.* Barcelona: Editorial Planeta, 1981.

James, Antony. *Presley: Entertainer of the Century.* New York: Tower Publications, Inc., 1977.

Jenkins, Mary. *Elvis: Memories Beyond Graceland Gates.* West Coast Publishers, 1989.

Kalter, Suzy. *The Complete Book of Dallas.* New York: Abrams, 1986.

Kirkland, K. D. *Elvis.* Lincoln, Neb.: Bison Books, 1988.

Lacker, Marty, Patsy Lacker, and Leslie S. Smith. *Elvis: Portrait of a Friend.* New York: Bantam, 1980.

Latham, Caroline. *Priscilla and Elvis.* New York: Signet, New American Library, 1985.

Lichter, Paul. *The Boy Who Dared to Rock: The Definitive Elvis.* New York: Doubleday Dolphin, 1978.

Lichter, Paul. *Elvis in Hollywood.* New York: Simon and Schuster, 1975.

Mann, May. *Elvis and the Colonel.* New York: Pocket Books, 1976.

Mansfield, Rex and Elisabeth. *Elvis the Soldier.* Bamberg, West Germany: Collectors Service, 1983.

Nash, Alanna (with Billy Smith, Marty Lacker and Lamar Fike). *Elvis Aaron Presley: Revelations from the Memphis Mafia.* New York: HarperCollins Publishers, 1995.

Parish, James Robert. *The Elvis Presley Scrapbook.* New York: Ballantine, 1972.

Parker, Ed. *Inside Elvis.* Orange, Calif.: Rampart House Ltd., 1978.

Pierce, Patricia Jobe. *The Ultimate Elvis: Elvis Presley Day by Day.* New York: Simon and Schuster, 1994.

Presley, Dee, et al. *Elvis, We Love You Tender.* New York: Delacorte, 1979.

Presley, Priscilla Beaulieu (with Sandra Harmon). *Elvis and Me.* New York: G. P. Putnam's Sons, 1985.

Pritchett, Rev. Nash Lorene Presley. *One Flower While I Love.* Tennessee: Shelby House, 1987.

Ridge, Millie. *The Elvis Album.* Gallery Books, 1991.

Shaver, Sean, and Hal Noland. *The Life of Elvis Presley.* Timur Publishing Inc., 1985.

Stanley, Billy (with George Erikson). *Elvis, My Brother.* New York: St. Martin's Press, 1989.

Stanley, David. *Life with Elvis.* Old Tappan, N.J.: Fleming H. Revell Company, 1986.

Stanley, David (with Frank Coffey). *The Elvis Encyclopedia.* New York: General Publishing Group, 1994.

Torgoff, Martin, ed. *The Complete Elvis.* New York: G. P. Putnam's Sons, 1982.

Vellenga, Dirk (with Mick Farren). *Elvis and the Colonel.* New York: Delacorte Press, 1988.

West, Red, Sonny West and Dave Hebler, as told to Steve Dunleavy. *Elvis: What Happened?* New York: Ballantine Books, 1977.

Westmoreland, Kathy (with William G. Quinn). *Elvis and Kathy.* Glendale, Calif.: Glendale House Publishing, 1987.

Wiegert, Sue. *Elvis: For the Good Times.* Los Angeles: Century City Instant Printing, 1978.

Worth, Fred L., and Steve D. Tamerius. *Elvis: His Life from A to Z.* Chicago: Contemporary Books, 1988.

Yancey, Becky, and Cliff Linedecker. *My Life with Elvis: The Fond Memories of a Fan Who Became Elvis' Private Secretary.* New York: St. Martin's Press, 1977.

INDEX

ABOUT THE AUTHOR

SUZANNE FINSTAD received her law degree from the University of Houston. Her experience as an estate litigator on the Howard Hughes estate case led to her first book, *Heir Not Apparent*, for which she was awarded the Frank Wardlaw Prize for a first work of literary excellence. She also received an American Jurisprudence Award from Bancroft-Whitney. Her other books include *Ulterior Motives* and *Sleeping with the Devil*, a national best-seller that she coproduced as a television movie for CBS. She has appeared on *Larry King Live, CBS Late Night*, and *Unsolved Mysteries* as well as on countless other TV and radio shows. She lives in West Hollywood.